Everyone and Everything in George Eliot

George Eliot at age 46
(etching from Frederic Burton's portrait)

EVERYONE AND EVERYTHING IN GEORGE ELIOT

Volume II

The Complete Nonfiction
The Taxonomy and
The Topicon

Compiled and Edited by

GEORGE NEWLIN

Routledge
Taylor & Francis Group
LONDON AND NEW YORK

First published 2006 by M.E. Sharpe

Published 2015 by Routledge
2 Park Square, Milton Park, Abingdon, Oxon OX14 4RN
711 Third Avenue, New York, NY 10017, USA

Routledge is an imprint of the Taylor & Francis Group, an informa business

Library of Congress Cataloging-in-Publication Data

Everyone and everything in George Eliot / edited by George Newlin.
p. cm.
Includes bibliographical references and indexes.
Contents: v. 1. The complete fiction : prose and poetry—v. 2. The complete nonfiction, the taxonomy, and the topicon.
ISBN 0-7656-1589-4 (alk. paper)
1. Eliot, George, 1819–1880—Handbooks, manuals, etc. 2. Eliot, George, 1819–1880—Stories, plots, etc. 3. Eliot, George, 1819–1880—Characters. 4. Eliot, George, 1819–1880—Settings. I. Newlin, George. II. Eliot, George, 1819–1880.

PR4688.E94 2006
823'.8—dc22 2005057489

ISBN 13: 9780765615893 (Set)
ISBN 13: 9781032316338 (Volume 2)

IN MEMORY OF PHILIP WELLINGTON CLARK (1930-1999),
OUR DEAR FRIEND FROM EARLY GRAMMAR SCHOOL,
AND IN GRATITUDE TO LOUISE KINSEY CLARK,
HIS WIDOW, FORTUNATELY STILL WITH US

Contents

Illustrations

Preface

One of the pleasures I find in being a direct descendant of George Henry Lewes, famous to all the literary world as the consort of George Eliot and a distinguished figure in letters and science in his own right, is the opportunity to keep up to date on the evolution of George Eliot scholarship. When my grandmother Elinor Southwood Ouvry (*née* Lewes) died in 1974, she left me by her Will the copyright in all unpublished writings of George Eliot, since when I have filled several bulging files with correspondence from all over the world (but principally from the United States).

The continuing prominence of this great woman has given rise to much diligent work by highly respected scholars and enthusiastic readers—a process which seems to grow and accelerate with each passing year. As the President of the George Eliot Fellowship, I have the pleasure of meeting many such scholars and readers. The ability to use email in recent years has greatly facilitated contact with correspondents.

It is a particular pleasure to me to be in on the rediscovery of forgotten Eliot material, such as the two essays George Newlin recently came upon at Princeton University. They had been first noticed and published in 1980 and then immediately disappeared, but these volumes should ensure that this cannot happen again.

Newlin's work, which, in addition to its other achievements, canvasses all Eliot's nonfiction with unprecedented thoroughness, adds another cubit to the structure of appreciation and knowledge which has been rising ever since Eliot died on the 22nd December 1880, just 125 years ago as I write. These volumes, which cover everything Eliot wrote—fiction and nonfiction, prose and poetry—are a fine new commemorative and will be consulted for many years to come.

—Jonathan Ouvry
Blackheath, London
United Kingdom
December 22, 2005

Introduction

by Janice Carlisle

To see George Eliot's work through the lens offered by George Newlin's compendium is to be struck by the magnitude of her achievement as a novelist, as an essayist, and even as a poet. Although the editor in his introduction describes the value of these volumes to "the general reader" and "the young scholar," this compilation provides a salutary lesson for any Victorianist, amateur or professional, by setting George Eliot's fiction in the context of her nonfiction prose and her efforts in poetry, many of both of which are reproduced here in full. Comprehensiveness characterizes each section of *Everyone and Everything in George Eliot* from its accounts of her early fictional sketches in the Coventry *Herald and Observer* and its Taxonomy, which lists, among other things, Eliot's characters and place names, to the extensive Topicon, which extracts passages from her works on a wide array of themes. The main goal of this work is to offer its readers information, and generous transcriptions of Eliot's words are carefully selected and placed in contexts that reveal their connections to other passages and other works. At times, however, the interpretive aims of this collection come to the fore, and the editor shares his views on the achievements of this "great lady," as he calls Eliot in his characteristically courtly fashion. Readers of all kinds will profit from the rich resources of both information and interpretation with which this collection provides them.

Anyone looking for an account of one of George Eliot's novels, tales, essays, or poems will find it here, along with either the text of the piece if it is relatively brief or numerous quotations from it if transcription in full is impractical. In the treatments of her fiction, lengthy extracts describe the characters and their reactions to plot developments. Then categories are created for the materials relevant to a specific text according to what the editor finds remarkable about it: "foreshadowings" merit an entry for *The Mill on the Floss*, "significant bachelors" appear among the headings for *Middlemarch*, and twelve "other clerical figures" are listed for "The Sad Fortunes of Amos

Barton." One of the most revealing categories recurs in each account of a fictional work: after "minor figures" come those "also mentioned." These genuinely insignificant characters often never appear directly in a narrative, but they are important because references to their existence create a sense of the densely populated towns and villages of Eliot's imagination. Moreover, the "also mentioned" reveal the ways in which her characters live within complicated networks of people, about some of whom they may have only heard, but whose experiences necessarily impinge on their own. There are thirty such figures in "The Sad Fortunes," and the numbers increase as George Eliot's novels become more elaborate, with more than eighty in *Felix Holt* and over one hundred in *Middlemarch*.

The first volume of this collection, which treats both Eliot's fiction and her poetry, contains in its summaries and excerpts some genuine revelations: by offering the narrative portions of Eliot's earliest essays from the Coventry *Herald and Observer* and of her last work, *Impressions of Theophrastus Such*, George Newlin makes a case for the continuities of her career: her earliest works may seem awkwardly jejune, even though she was in her twenties when she wrote them, but they also address concerns that will be central to "The Lifted Veil" and *Middlemarch*, just as the political conservatism of *Theophrastus Such* looks back to the Tory sympathies of *Adam Bede*. Noteworthy as well are two items in the section on Eliot's poetry: a fragment that posits a revealing equation—sense plus image equals thought—and a short poem on London, a powerful evocation of the city as a fog-bound prison that recalls both Blake and Dickens (I: 726-27). A compilation of the poetic epigraphs that Eliot wrote for her fiction starting with *Felix Holt* makes it clear why one of her nineteenth-century fans, a young man named Alexander Main, was moved to publish his *Wise, Witty, and Tender Sayings in Prose and Verse: Selected from the Works of George Eliot* (1872): in her epigraphs as well as in her narrative commentary, she seems self-consciously to have promoted herself as a writer of wisdom literature.

Most remarkable of the items offered in the sections dealing with each of George Eliot's works, however, are the two once-published and then forgotten essays that George Newlin came upon in the rare-books collection at Princeton University. The second, here titled "A Note on Truth in Art," recalls the famous argument of the seventeenth chapter of *Adam Bede*, though it casts its call for "severely veracious likenesses," not in terms of genre painting, as the narrator of *Adam Bede* does, but in terms of portraiture, praising Rembrandt, Bellini, Holbein, and Titian as artists who eschew the creation of "ideal portraits" (II: 228). The first of these essays, called "Thoughts on Anthropology," invites speculation about its relation to *Middlemarch*. It recalls the descriptions of social processes in that novel—"constantly increasing complexity or interaction of various conditions"—but more important is its concern with theories of cultural origins. Eliot argues that the natural "limits" on the forms of human life—the range of sounds that the voice can make, the structure of the body "as our four limbs & trunk" (II: 227, 226)—ensure that the qualities of different cultures, no matter how distant in time or space from each other, will be similar in certain basic ways. After applying this idea to practices that are often used to distinguish one culture from another— language, costume—Eliot uses these examples to denounce "that irrational exclusiveness of theory which insists on interpreting the resemblances between the mythologies & legends of different people as a result of tradition or identity of descent" (II: 227). Here we enter the realm of Casaubon and his unfinished "Key to All Mythologies": without naming him here, Eliot has gone through a careful process of thought to prove him wrong, as Will Ladislaw does in *Middlemarch* by pointing out his fatal lack of German. Remarkably in this instance, however, Eliot mounts a case against Casaubon's bad scholarship, not by citing the early nineteenth-century thinkers who discounted the theory that many mythologies could be traced to one origin, but by referring to the new conceptions of culture that were developing in the 1860s and 1870s. This essay sheds light, I think, on George Eliot's greatest novel by revealing how careful she was to provide in it explanations consonant with its earlier historical setting even when—especially when—the impetus for a particular depiction may have come from much later sources contemporaneous with her writing of the novel.

In more general ways, the section on George Eliot's nonfiction prose encourages a new sense of the extent and importance of her work as a journalist. Serving as a reviewer for the *Leader*, *Fraser's Magazine*, the *Saturday Review*, and the *Pall Mall Gazette*, as well as the *Westminster Review*, she was a thorough professional who frequently dealt with a staggering range of topics and literatures. Simply looking at the table of contents for the second volume of this compilation makes that point. It is supported even more effectively by the material summarized in George Newlin's account of just one essay on *"Belles Lettres"* for the *Westminster Review*: in the article for January 1856, George Eliot commented on Browning's *Men and Women*; poetry by Augustine Daganne, Longfellow, Mrs. D. Ogilvy, and N. L. Frothingham; translations of *Agamemnon* and Greek romances, as well as an edition of Cicero; a tale from the Italian; an autobiographical sketch by Beatrice Reynolds; novels by Holme Lee, Currer Bell, Edmund About, G. F. Pardon, Friedrich Gerstäcker, Ludwig Bechstein, Theodor König; an instructive narrative for "young servant girls" by Margaret Maria Brewster; Brougham's essays; a study of da Vinci; an account of a French art exhibition; and Thoreau's *Walden*.

Such a list, amplified by Newlin's copious extracts from the text of the review, is a testament to George Eliot's enormous erudition and the difficulties she must have faced in dealing with this mass of diverse works—I had almost said "mess." This account also reveals how out of touch with the variety and prodigality of Victorian literary culture we have become. Most impressive about George Eliot's journalism was her ability to pick out of the torrent of texts that she encountered those that would stand the test of time: Thoreau's *Walden* she finds notable for both its "sturdy sense" and "unworldliness" (II: 171); Arnold's poetry appears "prosaic" (II: 150), but Tennyson's will last "as long as the English language is spoken" (II: 160); and Charlotte Brontë's *Villette* is more worth reading "for the third time than most new novels for the first" (II: 170). These views, like Tennyson's poetry, have tended to last.

Those who fancy lists will find much pleasure in the various entries in the Taxonomy in the second volume here. Characters are presented by given name and surname; occupations are catalogued; relationships are enumerated; and characteristics defined and tallied, as are localities, pets, and historical figures. Much of this information reflects the values and practices of the Victorian world in which George Eliot wrote her fiction—the occupation most frequently held by women in her fiction is, as it was in her society, that of domestic servant—but it also attests to the relative gentility of the fictional world that she created. The three traditional professions of medicine, church, and law dominate the occupations pursued by her male figures. Even the names she chose for characters reflect their social status: there is only one Dorothea, but there are three Selina's. Index XI, which treats the literary, biblical, musical and mythological allusions in George Eliot's works, offers an impressive insight into her mental world: although references to her contemporaries occur with some frequency, and Wordsworth appears fairly often, writers of the eighteenth century are cited more than one would have expected. Goldsmith, Gray, and Johnson are all important reference points for Eliot, but Milton is even more so; and citations of Shakespeare predictably outnumber them all—except, of course, for references to the Bible, which George Newlin traces in the second part of this section of the Taxonomy, helpfully offering the actual words cited as well as the relevant chapter and verse. The section on "Words and Thoughts" provides an anthology of sayings of both the narrators and the characters in Eliot's works, so that if one wants to find out, for instance, where one of her narrators says that "the happiest women, like the happiest nations, have no history," one can do so easily (II: 411). (The answer is the third chapter of the sixth book of *The Mill on the Floss*.)

Although there are points in the first volume of *Everyone and Everything in George Eliot* when George Newlin offers an opinion on a particular work—he makes a good case for taking *The Spanish Gypsy* more seriously than most Eliot scholars do—he allows his interpretive skills freer range in the second volume. Included there are three "essays," one on Eliot's re-use of character types and plot devices, another treating her "ineptitude" in dealing with legal matters (II: 297), and a third on the possibility that Gwendolen Harleth of *Daniel Deronda* suffers the after effects of having been sexually abused by her step-father. George Newlin has good evidence for his claims in all three—his account of the numerous instances of failed fathers and foster fathers and missing mothers makes his point about the extent to which Eliot "revisited" her earlier fictions throughout her career (II: 278-79)—but the last of these essays is the most controversial. Citing the narrator's oddly extreme choice of words to describe Gwendolen's childhood before her step-father's death and childhood in general—"evils" and "foulness," respectively—and her thoughts of her step-father when she sees her husband die (II: 318, 320, 322), Newlin offers an incitement for more discussion on this topic.

That effect is also the outcome of reading other, more apparently neutral presentations of information in the second volume. Like the Taxonomy, the Topicon is a selection; and since any selection is an act of interpretation, the choices that have been made here often provide implicit critical assessments. The section on "social classes," for instance, offers a passage from *Felix Holt*: "the sense of ranks and degrees has its repulsions corresponding to the repulsions dependent on difference of race and colour" (II: 545)—a reminder to American readers in particular not to underestimate the power of class in Victorian culture to make damaging and sometimes even violent discriminations. The passage also emphasizes the economic issues, the bases for "ranks and degrees," that form so crucial a part of the love story in *Felix Holt* and in virtually every other piece of fiction that George Eliot wrote. At points in the Topicon, as in his three essays, George Newlin boldly presents his views. Under the entry for "duty" appears transcribed the entire fortieth chapter of *Romola*, the scene in which the heroine listens as Savonarola encourages her to embrace renunciation. According to Newlin's note, "George Eliot chose to write *Romola* so she could write this scene . . . . [resulting in] the greatest achievement of her life" (II: 485). That judgment has two bracing effects, asking readers to reconsider, first, whether *Romola* is a much better novel than it is usually taken to be and, second, whether one ought to take more seriously, as Eliot clearly did, the emotional appeal of the religion that she otherwise so bravely rejected. Such moments in *Everyone and Everything in George Eliot* simply epitomize what will be its effect on anyone who reads its entries with care or even browses through the wealth offered in its pages: its enormously comprehensive as well as judiciously selected compilations will send its readers back to George Eliot's texts with a fresh appreciation of the scope of her achievements in matters both small and great.

Yale University
New Haven CT
January 30, 2006

Editor's Introduction

This work is the editor's third "CIA"—Concordance, Index, Anthology—of great mid-Victorian authors. Charles Dickens appeared this way in 1995 (three volumes from Greenwood Press) and 1996, and Anthony Trollope (four volumes—M.E. Sharpe) arrived in 2004. The gestation of each was about seven years. George Eliot, with a much smaller *oeuvre,* has come quicker—not much more than two years—and, if anything, with even more joy.

Our essential goal with each of these works is (1) to identify and assemble the *complete* work of the author in question and (2) make it accessible to the general reader and particularly to the young scholar, by an organizational scheme which in effect spares the student a great deal of "scut work" and encourages the development of new ideas and explorations with the data ready at hand to build upon.

The satisfaction accruing to me is enormous, arising from the nature of the assignment I gave myself: to read or reread *everything* by the author within a close time-frame and organize it while the works are fresh in my mind. Instead of picking a single novel, or a couple, from the production of a great author, I must read them all—and by so doing I see immediately relationships between the various books which could otherwise easily escape notice.

One of the results, in the case of George Eliot, is an overview which exposes the degree to which she re-used plot ideas and character configurations—not necessarily in a manner to heighten our admiration. (See "Parallels and Echoes: Eliot Revisits Eliot" at II: 275.) But often this kind of insight adds to our pleasure, perhaps by showing how an idea gained maturity on re-use, or sparkles freshly in a different context, and thus enhances our appreciation of the author's ability to achieve variety even while renewing her acquaintance with old devices.

Another aspect of my gratification is the ability I have now, and expect to expand on in the future, to take an overview of each author and make comparisons between them. I can say, if anyone were to ask, defensively on Eliot's behalf, whether *all* authors didn't do that, "Well, no: at least not Dickens, who waited to start a new novel until a totally fresh idea or 'gimmick' had occurred to him"; or Trollope, who somehow miraculously over 47 novels never really repeats himself even while writing about people of almost exclusively the same social class. But Eliot, despite working in only eight different major works of fiction, seems to turn to the same idea (the missing mother, the defective or unsuccessful father, the lost and foundling heiress, the exotic maiden's rescue) with almost perfunctory frequency.

But make no mistake about it, I agree with John Blackwood's famous and frequent dictum, "What a *wonderful* woman!"

To live for years inside the mind of George Eliot is a privilege I am proud to have been able to create for myself. I will never forget the many moments of wonder and delight, admiration, and spiritual inspiration she has given me. To leaf through and browse in the *Topicon,* for example (II: 418ff), is to enjoy an unimaginably provocative richness. There is wit in abundance; humour, tolerance, humanity, spirituality, scientific knowledge, beautiful writing, variety, vividness— every virtue we can hope for from a great writer. Reading her usually lapidary essays on an immense variety of subjects with her fictional achievements bubbling in the back of my mind induces a sense of prayerful awe, almost of incredulity.

And then, to look at the Taxonomy and to see, for example, the proofs of her enormous erudition (the historical figures of Index X, the literary and biblical references of Index XI), is to get a sense of why many today consider George Eliot not only the most brilliant woman of her time, but the brightest, most thoroughly educated (except in the law) and insightful *person* of her age.

There is another aspect of my mode of working which I feel bound to share with the reader. The discipline of reading *everything* in the case of Eliot produced a thorough understanding and appreciation of her knottiest challenge: *Impressions of Theophrastus Such.* The number of citations to and quotations from this work in the *Topicon* is out of all proportion to its length.

Even beyond this unexpected treasure-house, there were the immense rewards I obtained from slogging through all those columns of *Belles Lettres* in the *Westminster Review.* When I saw that Eliot had been the first British reviewer to look at and quote something called *Leaves of Grass* (no author mentioned), I tingled from face to feet. I was looking at an epochal instance of literary history not made—a great opportunity missed. That feeling was worth all my thirty months of labour by itself. Her unseeing glance at Whitman seems to have gone unremarked by Eliot scholars, though not, I gather, by Whitman specialists (II: 190).

And, finally, there was the thrill of excitement, disbelief, and elation when a staffer at Princeton's Firestone Library handed me the bound manuscript with "Three Essays" on the spine, and I suspected that I had found something which not only had been lost but that no scholar, biographer, or even husband had ever *known* had been lost: two essays by George Eliot as erudite, as polished, as thought-provoking as anything in the *oeuvre.* (They begin at II: 225.) This must have been the feeling Thomas Pinney had when he found and gave back to us "Notes on Form in Art" (II: 232). My later discovery that these essays had indeed been found and published (in 1980) was a dasher, but I take heart from the fact that, as now rediscovered, they can never be lost again (that is, unless *my* work is also lost).

To think I'm getting paid for this!

Acknowledgments

My long-time friend David Parker, Curator Emeritus of the Dickens House Museum in London, Fellow of Kingston College, London, and distinguished author, offered aid of a kind no editor has a right to expect of another. He went physically to the Colindale repository of the British Library, hunted out the Coventry *Herald and Observer* for the requisite dates, transcribed into his laptop computer, and transmitted to me by the modern electronic miracle of the internet, two articles I needed and had not known I needed when I last visited David and his wife Elinor for a blissful weekend of rambles in Devon. His effort allows me a reasonable hope that I have provided the reader with every published piece of Eliot's nonfiction. Words cannot express my gratitude to David, a colleague and friend beyond price.

I am very grateful to Jonathan Ouvry, the present generation's lineal descendant of George Henry Lewes, for permission to publish four essays by George Eliot, including the two I rediscovered at Princeton described below, and for writing the Preface to this work. Jonathan retired seven years ago from a family law practice in the third generation of serving private clients. His great-great uncle Frederic Ouvry was, of all things, solicitor to Charles Dickens.

Janice Carlisle, Professor of English at Yale University, was my colleague in younger days at the Dickens Universe in Santa Cruz, California, and I reencountered her when my brother Carl audited her course at Yale in the Victorians last year. I am especially gratified that she was able to budget the time to write the Introduction to this work, and grateful to her for her extraordinary investment of effort and insight, and for her kind words.

I lived in Princeton, New Jersey, for two years while I completed my work on Anthony Trollope (*Everyone and Everything in Trollope,* M.E. Sharpe, Inc., 2004), in the course of which I came to know well many of the staff at the Department of Rare Books and Manuscript Collections at Firestone Library. When I went on to George Eliot, still in place there, I asked if they had anything, and they made available a bound volume of manuscripts, from which I transcribed, with amazement and delight, eight pages of holograph containing the two essays given the reader at pages 225-8 of Volume II. I am grateful to Princeton's library staff for their support and the photocopies they provided at nominal cost, and especially grateful to the unknown library representative who had the wit to bid for and obtain these theretofore unknown works at Parke-Bernet in 1955.

The later discovery that the essays had been noticed and published in 1980 (thereafter apparently quite forgotten) only mildly mitigated my satisfaction, and I salute Professor K. K. Collins for her scholarship in resurrecting these pieces in a special issue of *Nineteenth Century Fiction* (Vol. 35, No. 3; Dec. 1980) and for her fine commentary upon them. The issue's title is "Special Issue: George Eliot, 1880-1980," and to it I enthusiastically refer the reader (and, with an admonitory nod, the editors of the *Oxford Reader's Companion to George Eliot*, published in 2000, which makes no mention of it).

From Princeton to Yale (I took degrees from both sometime last century): the staff at the Beinecke Library, in particular Jill Haines, were cordial and efficient in promptly connecting me with the manuscript of Eliot's "Versification" (Volume II, page 229), which I happily transcribed on the premises (having no intimation that Antonie van den Broek had recently done the same thing), and for furnishing me with Yale's examples of the Blackwood Stereotyped edition of some of the Eliot novels.

My dear friend and fellow Quaker at Princeton Monthly Meeting, Michael Dawson, generously and trustingly let me borrow and burrow into a valuable and now very rare edition of Eliot's complete works: the twelve-volume set published in 1894 by Thomas Crowell under the supervision of Eliot's widower, John Cross. Without the aid of this edition I could not have provided most of the more or less contemporaneous illustrations which appear in these volumes, nor could I have organized the poetry as I did, the van den Broek edition of the shorter poetry (see *Bibliography*, page xxiiff) being still on the wrong side of the horizon at the time.

Beryl Gray, editor of the *George Eliot Review,* put me in touch with Eliot's literary executor, Jonathan Ouvry, an indispensable assistance.

I am blessed to continue to have to help me the staunch and resourceful editors at M.E. Sharpe, particularly Lynn Taylor, and my indefatigable production editors, Jane Lerner and Ana Erlic, all of whom have always been ready with counsel and corrective.

Abbreviations and Dates

3M	"Three Months in Weimar"	*Fraser's Magazine*	June 1855
3N	Reviews of three novels	*Westminster Review*	Oct 1856
AA	"The Art of the Ancients" (review)	*Leader*	March 17 1855
AAG	"The Art and Artists of Greece"	*Saturday Review*	May 31, 1856
AB	**Adam Bede**	Blackwood (3 vols)	Feb 1 1859
AG	*Agatha*	*Atlantic Monthly*	August 1869
AM	"The Antigone and Its Moral"	*Leader*	March 29 1856
AN	*Arion*		1874
AR	*Armgart*	*Macmillan's, Atlantic Mo*	*wr* July 1871
ATS	"A Tragic Story"	*Leader*	July 19, 1856
BJ	*Brother Jacob* (written summer 1860)	*Cornhill Magazine*	July 1864
BL	*Belles Lettres*	*Westminster Review*	sundry dates
BL 1	*Belles Lettres* (reviews Kingsley's *Westward Ho!*; a novel by Jewsbury)		July 1955
BL 2	*Belles Lettres* (reviews Tennysons *Maud*; a study of Milton)		Oct 1855
BL 3	*Belles Lettres* (reviews Browning's *Men and Women*; and *Hiawatha*)		Jan 1856
BL 4	*Art and Belles Lettres* (reviews Ruskin's *Modern Painters*, vol. 3)		April 1856
BL 5	*Belles Lettres and Art* (reviews several books of poetry, others on art)		July 1856
BL 6	*Belles Lettres* (reviews Stowe's *Dred*, poetical works, a Charles Reade novel)		Oct 1856
BL 7	*Belles Lettres* (reviews E. B. Browning's *Aurora Leigh*, miscellaneous works)		Jan 1857
BS	*Brother and Sister* (sonnet sequence)		*wr* July 1869 pub 1874
CA	"Memoirs of the Court of Austria" (review)	*Westminster Review*	April 1855
CA2	"The Court of Austria"	*Leader*	April 12, 1856
CB	*A College Breakfast-Party* (extended poem)	*Macmillan's*	July 1878
CC	"The Creed of Christendom" (Greg; review)	*Leader*	Sept 20 1851
CH	*Constance Herbert* (Jewsbury; review)	*Westminster Review*	July 1855
CH19	"Church History of the Nineteenth Century"	*Leader*	April 5 1856
CHE	*The Comic History of England* (review)	Cov'try *Herald, Observer*	Nov. 13 1846
DD	**Daniel Deronda**	*Blackwood's Magazine*	Feb- Sept 1876
DM	*The Death of Moses*	Blackwood	1878
E	*Erinna*		1874-5?
EH	Essays in Holograph (two unpublished works)	*Nineteenth Century Fiction*	Dec 1980
EOL	*Ex Oriente Lux*		1865
ET	Evangelical Teaching: Dr Cumming	*Westminster Review*	Oct 1855
F	Farewell (Knowing that shortly I must . . .)	*Christian Observer*	Jan 1840
FC	"Ferny Combes" (review)	*Leader*	Aug 16 1856
FF	"Futile Falsehoods"	*Pall Mall Gazette*	April 3 1865
FGP	"The Future of German Philosophy" (review)	*Leader*	July 28 1855
FH	**Felix Holt, the Radical**	Blackwood (3 vols)	June 14, 1866
FO	"Felice Orsini"	*Leader*	Aug 30 1856
GL	**Mr Gilfil's Love-Story** (SCL 2)	*Blackwood's Magazine*	Apr-July 1857
GML	"German Mythology and Legend" (review)	*Leader*	Sept 22 1855
GO	"The Grammar of Ornament"	*Fortnightly Review*	May 15 1865
HB	"History, Biography, Voyages and Travels"	*Westminster Review*	Jan 1857
HBS	"Heine's Book of Songs"	*Saturday Review*	April 26 1856
HGP	"History of German Protestantism" (review)	*Leader*	Feb 9 1856
HH	"German Wit: Heinrich Heine"	*Westminster Review*	Jan 1856
HL	*How Lisa Loved the King*	*Blackwood's Magazine*	May 1869
HP	"Heine's Poems" (review)	*Leader*	Sept 1 1855

IG	"Introduction to Genesis"	*Leader*	Jan 12 1856
IR	"The Influence of Rationalism"	*Fortnightly Review*	May 15 1865
JR	**Janet's Repentance** (SCL 3)	*Blackwood's Magazine*	Aug-Nov 1857
JS	*The Life of John Sterling* (Carlyle; review)	*Westminster Review*	Jan 1852
LB	"Lord Brougham's Litereature" (review)	*Leader*	July 7 1855
LD	"Love in the Drama" (review)	*Leader*	August 25 1855
LFN	"Pictures of Life in French Novels"	*Saturday Review*	May 17, 1856
LJ	*The Legend of Jubal*	*Macmillan's, Atlantic Mo.*	May 1870
LL1	*Letters on the Laws of Man's Nature* (review)	*Leader* (first of two)	March 1, 1851
LL2	*Letters on the Laws of Man's Nature* (review)	*Leader* (second of two)	March 8, 1851
LNB	"Leaves from a Note-book"	not published	1884
LOM	"Life and Opinions of Milton"	*Leader*	August 4 1955
LS	"The Lover's Seat" (review)	*Leader*	August 2 1856
LV	*The Lifted Veil*	*Blackwood's Magazine*	July 1859
LW	"Liszt, Wagner and Weimar"	*Fraser's Magazine*	July 1855
LWG	*Life and Works of Goethe* (Lewes; review)	*Leader*	Nov 3 1855
MF	**The Mill on the Floss**	Blackwood (3 vols)	April 4 1860
MFI	"Margaret Fuller's Letters from Italy"	*Leader*	May 17, 1856
MFW	"Margaret Fuller and Mary Wollstonecraft"	*Leader*	Oct 13 1855
MGC	"Menander and the Greek Comedy"	*Leader*	June 16, 1855
MH	"Modern Housekeeping"	*Pall Mall Gazette*	May 13 1865
MM	**Middlemarch**	*Blackwood's* (8 pts)	Dec 1871-Dec '72
MP	*A Minor Prophet*	Blackwood	1874
MR	"Michelet on the Reformation" (review)	*Leader*	Sept 15 1865
MW	"The Morality of *Wilhelm Meister*"	*Leader*	July 21 1855
NE	"From the Notebook of an Eccentric"	Coventry *Herald and Observer*	Dec 4 1846-Feb 19, 1847
NF	"Froude's *The Nemesis of Faith*" (review)	Coventry *Herald and*	March 16 1849
NFA	"Notes on Form in Art (1868)	Thomas Pinney	1963
NH	"The Natural History of German Life: Riehl"	*Westminster Review*	July 1856
OM	*"O May I Join the Choir Invisible"*		1867
PI	*The Progress of the Intellect* (review)	*Westminster Review*	Jan 1851
PPA	"The Poets and Poetry of America" (review)	*Leader*	March 1 1856
PY	"Worldliness and Other-Worldliness: the Poet Young"	*Westminster Rev.*	Jan 1857
QM	"Quinet and Michelet" (review)	Cov'try *Herald, Observer*	Oct 30 1846
R	**Romola**	*Cornhill Magazine*	July 1862-Aug '63
RG	"Rachel Gray" (review)	*Leader*	Jan 5 1856
RH	"Recollections of Heine"	*Leader*	August 23 1856
RMP	*Modern Painters* (Ruskin vol 3; review)	*Westminster Review*	April 1856
RSM	"The Romantic School of Music"	*Leader*	Oct 28 1854
S	*Stradivarius*	Blackwood	1874
SAL	*Self and Life*	Blackwood	1878
SBB	"Story of a Blue-Bottle"	*Leader*	April 26, 1856
SCL	**Scenes of Clerical Life**	*Blackwood's Magazine*	Jan-Nov 1857
SE	*"Sweet Evenings Come and Go, Love"*	Blackwood	1878
SF	**The Sad Fortunes of the Rev. Amos Barton** (SCL 1)	*Blackwood's*	Jan-Feb 1857
SG	*The Spanish Gypsy*	Blackwood	1859
SGT	"Sight-seeing in Germany and the Tyrol"	*Saturday Review*	Sept 6 1856
SL	"Servants' Logic"	*Pall Mall Gazette*	March 17 1865
SM	**Silas Marner**	Wm Blackwood & Sons	April 2 1861
SN	"Silly Novels by Lady Novelists"	*Westminster Review*	Oct 1856
SS	"The Shaving of Shagpat" (review)	*Leader*	Jan. 5 1856
TC	"Thomas Carlyle" (review)	*Leader*	Oct 27 1855
TL	*Two Lovers*		1866
TS	**Impressions of Theophrastus Such**	Wm Blackwood & Sons	May 19 1879
TT	"Translations and Translators"	*Leader*	Oct 20 1855
V	"Versification"	unpublished	1867
WF	"Woman in France: Madame de Sablé" (rev)	*Westminster Review*	Oct 1854
WG	"A Word for the Germans"	*Pall Mall Gazette*	March 7 1865
WH	"Westward Ho!" (Kingsley; review)	*Leader*	May 19 1855
WM	"Address to Working Men, by Felix Holt"	*Blackwood's Magazine*	Jan 1868
WN?	"Who Wrote the Waverley Novels?"	*Leader*	April 19 1856

Alphabetic Locator

Chronology
Life and Works

The brief summary below is provided as a convenience. The Oxford *Reader's Companion to George Eliot* has an excellent time chart (page 495), and some of the biographies include carefully crafted versions, not extending to the outside world as completely as does Oxford. I have expanded the data usually supplied to include more of the nonfiction.

	Events	Works
1819	Birth at South Farm, Arbury Nov. 22 Christened Mary Anne Evans	
1820	The family moves to Griff House	
1824	First schooling commences	
1828	Begins boarding school at Nuneaton	
1832	School in Coventry with the Misses Franklin	
1836	Her mother dies	
1837	Her sister Chrissey marries She takes over the household at Griff	
1839	Begins to study Italian	Farewell (poem) Sonnet
1840	Begins to study German	Question and Answer (poem)
1841	Leaves Griff for Coventry with her father	
1842	First break with her father over church attendance	"Mind the rich store of nature's gifts"
1844	Begins work on the translation of *Das Leben Jesu*	
1846		*Das Leben Jesu* (anonymous) "Quinet and Michelet" *Poetry and Prose from the Notebook of an Eccentric*
1849	Spinoza translation started Her father dies; she goes abroad Lodgings in Geneva	
1850	Returns to England Begins with the *Westminster Review*	
1851	Editing at the *Review*	Mackay's *The Progress of the Intellect*

		"The Creed of Christendom"
1853	Relationship with Lewes begins	
1854	Leaves for Germany with Lewes	Feuerbach's "The Essence of Christianity" translation published under her name
1855	Back in England, living with Lewes	essays and reviews proliferate Eliot's first *Belles Lettres* for the *Westminster Review* (July) "Memoirs of the Court of Austria" "Three Months in Weimar" "Menander and the Greek Comedy" "The Morality of Wilhelm Meister" "The Future of German Philosophy" "Heine's Poems" "Evangelical Teaching: Dr Cumming"
1856	Spinoza's *Ethics* completed (not published)	"The Natural History of German Life" "German Wit: Heinrich Heine" "The Antigone and its Moral" "The Art and Artists of Greece" —many other essays and reviews *The Sad Fortunes of Amos Barton* submitted as by George Eliot
1857	Brother Isaac breaks with her over her liaison with Lewes	*The Sad Fortunes* published *Mr Gilfil's Love-Story* *Janet's Repentance* "Worldliness and Other-worldliness: The Poet Young"
1858	Meets John Blackwood and reveals her identity to him Second visit to Germany	***Scenes of Clerical Life***
1859	Chrissey dies	***Adam Bede*** *The Lifted Veil*
1860	Holiday in Italy	***The Mill on the Floss***
1861	Second trip to Italy (research)	***Silas Marner***
1862	Receives £7,000 advance for *Romola*	***Romola*** serialization begins
1863	Buys her first house, the Priory	***Romola*** in volume form
1864	Work on *The Spanish Gypsy*	*Brother Jacob* "The Influence of Rationalism: Lecky's History"
1865	Depression forces suspension of her work on *The Spanish Gypsy*	Other articles for the *Pall Mall Gazette*, the *Fortnightly Review* A Minor Prophet (poem) Two Lovers (poem) In a London Drawing-Room (poem)
1866	Accepts £5,000 for *Felix Holt*	***Felix Holt, the Radical*** Arms! To Arms! (poem) Ex Oriente Lux (poem)
1867	Tours of France and Spain	"O May I Join the Choir Invisible" In the South (poem)
1868	Holiday in Switzerland, the Schwarzwald Darwin visits	"Address to Working Men" ***The Spanish Gypsy***
1869	Lewes's son Thornton dies Henry James visits	The Legend of Jubal (poem) Agatha (poem) How Lisa Loved the King (poem) Brother and Sister (sonnet cycle)
1870	Lionized in Berlin and Vienna Work on *Middlemarch*	

1871	Turgenev visits; meets Tennyson	Armgart (poem)
1872	Travels in Germany	***Middlemarch*** (Dec. 1871-Dec. 1872)
1873	Studying Judaism	Stradivarius (poem) Arion (poem)
1874	First kidney attack	A College Breakfast-Party (poem) "I Grant You Ample Leave" (poem) *The Legend of Jubal and Other Poems*
1875	Lewes's son Bertie dies	
1876	Health problems mount	***Daniel Deronda***
1877	Cabinet edition of works agreed on	
1878	George Henry Lewes dies in November	Self and Life (poem) "Sweet Evenings Come and Go" (poem) The Death of Moses (poem) *The Legend of Jubal and Other Poems, Old and New*
1879	John Blackwood dies	***Impressions of Theophrastus Such***
1880	Marriage to John Cross (four proposals) Health deteriorates; death December 22	

Bibliography

As Jonathan Ouvry's remarks in his Preface to this work suggest, scholarship and discovery in the field of George Eliot is a burgeoning and dynamic field. It is at times fraught with peril and surprise to a laborer in that vineyard with a project lasting years, who is continually at risk of superseding developments. The following lists cannot be definitive, only illustrative, and of perhaps modest value as a convenience to other laborers. As to perils and surprises, see the Supplementary Comment below.

Certain of the works listed have been mentioned frequently enough in this work to warrant abbreviation in reference, as indicated in **bold**.

Volumes

Allen, Walter. *George Eliot.* Macmillan, 1964 (Masters of World Literature Series, Louis Kronenberger, ed.)

Ashton, Rosemary. *George Eliot: A Life.* Hamish Hamilton, 1996; Penguin Books, 1997 ("**Ashton**")

—*George Eliot: Selected Critical Writings.* Oxford, 1992

—*The Mill on the Floss: A Natural History.* Twayne Publishers, 1990

Baker, Wm., and John C. Ross, eds. *George Eliot: A Bibliographical History.* Oak Knoll Press/British Library, 2002

Bennett, Joan. *George Eliot: Her Mind and Her Art.* Cambridge University Press, 1948

Blind, Mathilde. *George Eliot.* University Press of the Pacific, 2003; reprint of 1883

Bodenheimer, Rosemarie. *The Real Life of Mary Ann Evans: George Eliot; Her Letters and Fiction.* Cornell University Press, 1996

Bullett, Gerald William. *George Eliot: Her Life and Books.* Greenwood Press, 1971

Byatt, A. S., and Nicholas Warren, eds. *George Eliot: Selected Essays, Poems and Other Writings.* Penguin Books, 1990

Correa, Delia da Sousa. *George Eliot, Music and Victorian Culture.* Palgrave, 2003

Dodd, Valerie A. *George Eliot: An Intellectual Life.* St. Martin's Press, 1990

Ermarth, Elizabeth Deeds. *George Eliot.* Twayne Publishers, 1985

Feuerbach, Ludwig. *The Essence of Christianity.* George Eliot, transl. Harper, 1957

Gardner, Charles. *The Inner Life of George Eliot.* Sir Isaac Pitman & Sons, 1912

Gray, Beryl. *George Eliot and Music.* Macmillan, 1989

Haight, Gordon S. *George Eliot, a Biography.* Oxford University Press, 1968; reprint Viking Penguin, 1993 ("**Haight**")

—ed. *The George Eliot Letters.* Yale University Press and Oxford University Press, 1954-78; 9 vols.

Hands, Timothy. *George Eliot Chronology.* Macmillan, 1988

Hartnoll, Phyllis. *Who's Who in George Eliot.* Taplinger Publishing, 1977

Hornback, Bert G. *Middlemarch: A Novel of Reform.* Twayne Publishers, 1988

Hughes, Kathryn. *George Eliot: The Last Victorian.* Farrar Straus & Giroux, 1989

Jankins, Lucien, ed. *George Eliot: Collected Poems.* Skoob Books, 1989

Karl, Frederick. *George Eliot: Voice of a Century.* Macmillan, 1995

Kaufmann, David. *George Eliot and Judaism: An Attempt to Appreciate 'Daniel Deronda.'* Transl. J. W. Ferrier; first published 1888; facsimile Haskell House, 1970

Kenyon, F. W. *The Consuming Flame: The Story of George Eliot.* Dodd Mead, 1970

Laski, Margherita. *George Eliot.* Thames and Husdon, 1987

MacKenzie, K. A. *Edith Simcox and George Eliot.* Greenwood Press, 1978

McSweeney, Kerry. *George Eliot (Mary Ann Evans): A Literary Life.* St. Martin's Press, 1991

Main, Alexander, ed. *Wise, Witty, and Tender Sayings in Prose and Verse, Selected from the Works of George Eliot.* William Blackwood and Sons, 1871-1896

Mudge, Isadore Gilbert. *George Eliot: Dictionary.* MSO House, 1972

Paris, Bernard J. *Experiments in Life: George Eliot's Quest for Value.* Wayne State University Press, 1965

Pinion, F. B., ed. *A George Eliot Miscellany: A Supplement to her Novels.* Barnes & Noble, 1982

Pinney, Thomas, ed. *Essays of George Eliot.* Routledge and Kegan Paul, 1963 ("**Pinney**")

Rignall, John, ed. *Oxford Reader's Companion to George Eliot.* Oxford University Press, 2000 ("**ORC**")

Sheppard, Nathan. *The Essays of George Eliot.* Funk and Wagnalls, 1883

Smith, Anne, ed. George Eliot: *Centenary Essays and an Unpubished Fragment.* Vision Press, London, 1980

Taylor, Ina. *George Eliot; Woman of Contradictions,* n.p. 1989

Uglow, Jenny. *George Eliot.* Knopf, 1987

van den Broek, Antonie, ed., and William Baker, consult. ed. *The Complete Shorter Poetry of George Eliot.* Pickering Chatto, 2005; 2 vols. ("**CSP**")

Viont, Elfrida. *Towards a High Attic: The Early Life of George Eliot.* Holt, Rinehart & Winston, 1970

Wiesenfarth, Joseph, ed. *George Eliot, A Writer's Notebook 1854-1879, and Uncollected Writings.* University Press of Virginia, 1981

Articles

Collins, K. K. "Questions of Method: Some Unpublished Late Essays," *Nineteenth Century Fiction,* Vol. 35, No.3, Special Issue: George Eliot, 1880-1980 (Dec., 1980), 385-405

Higdon, David L. "George Eliot and the Art of the Epigraph," *Nineteenth Century Fiction,* 25 (1970), 127-51

Hudd, Louise. "The Politics of a Feminist Poetics: 'Armgart' and George Eliot's Critical Response to *Aurora Leigh,*" in Kate Flint, ed. *Poetry and Politics,* D. S. Brewer, 1996, 62-83

La Porte, Charles. "George Eliot, the Poetics as Prophet," *Victorian Literature and Culture* (2003), 159-79

Paris, Bernard J. "George Eliot's Unpublished Poetry," *Studies in Philology* 56 (July 1959), 539-58

Works of George Eliot

Folio Society of London, 1999 (general editor not identified):

Scenes of Clerical Life, introduction by Jill Payton Walsh; following the cheap edition published in one volume by William Blackwood and Sons, 1863

Adam Bede, introduction by Jane Gardam; following the cheap edition published in one volume by Blackwood, 1862

The Mill on the Floss, introduction by Bel Mooney; following the cheap edition published in one volume by Blackwood, 1862

Silas Marner, the Weaver of Raveloe, introduction by Jill Paton Walsh, following the Cabinet edition published by Blackwood, 1878

Romola, introduction by Gillian Beer; following the cabinet edition published in two volumes by Blackwood, 1877 and 1878

Felix Holt, the Radical, introduction by Kathryn Hughes; following the first edition published by Blackwood, 1866

Middlemarch, a Study of Provincial Life, introduction by Penelope Fitzgerald; following the single-volume edition published by Blackwood, 1874

Daniel Deronda, introduction by A. S. Byatt; following the Cabinet edition published by Blackwood, 1878

Henry, Nancy, ed. *Impressions of Theophrastus Such.* University of Iowa Press, 1994

Lewes, Charles Lee, ed. *The Complete Works of George Eliot.* Thomas W. Crowell, 1884; 12 vols.

Shuttleworth, Sally, ed. *The Lifted Veil* and *Brother Jacob.* Penguin Classics, 2001

Supplementary Comment

Cynthia Ann Secor's unpublished doctoral dissertation on George Eliot's poetry (Cornell University, 1969) may be one of the most useful works of scholarship never to have found its way to the public under a publisher's rubric. It is generously acknowledged in Antonie Gerard van den Broek's *The Complete Shorter Poetry of George Eliot,* which appeared just after we had submitted this work to the publisher for processing. We saw CSP advertised in the *George Eliot Review,* gulped at the price and paid it. We are glad we did, as it buttressed and confirmed our work (based primarily on the 1884 edition of Eliot's complete works edited by Charles Lewes) and added valuable insights, historical background and careful textual analysis in its introductory comments to each of the poetical works covered and in its elaborate notes on variants in Eliot's holographs.

We salute Mr van den Broek for an achievement of high importance to all who are fascinated by the full range of George Eliot's *oeuvre.* We differ only in that we do not include the poem "On Being Called a Saint," which may have been schoolgirl Mary Ann Evans's work or, on the other hand, may have been written by one of her school friends, as Mr van den Broek carefully notes. Mentioned and partially quoted in Haight (but attributed only tentatively), it contains seven complete quatrains but ends in a fragment and can be found at pages 5-6 of the first volume of CSP.

Mr van den Broek's admirable Introduction to his work contains in its notes much bibliographical citation which will be of use to scholars wishing to explore the subject of the Poetry. And the book is more nearly complete than this one in that it quotes *all* of the shorter poems in their entirety, though without the *précis* we provide.

So, that was a surprise. The peril narrowly averted arose from the undeserved obscurity of K. K. Collins's discovery and astute analysis of two unpublished essays of Eliot—essays we had long thought we were the first to unearth. But we learned in time that she had been ahead of us—a quarter of a century ahead of us—and we are thankful we avoided a modest embarrassment. (*See* II: 225)

One further note: it took a good deal of tracking to locate Alexander Main's *Wise, Witty, and Tender Sayings in Prose and Verse, Selected from the Works of George Eliot,* published by Blackwood over a period exceeding a quarter of a century (see above); and once having found it, we thought we had the perfect source for our section on Words and Phrases. But Mr Main created his enormous achievement in a time when scholarship did not provide citations. It would have taken years to wrestle his final product into a useful form for today, and we can do no more than cite it to the eager and persistent reader. Princeton University's Firestone Library has a copy. 1871-1896

Guide to the Use of These Volumes

Each principal segment of this work begins with a summary table showing what is to follow. You are encouraged to take a little time at first to look around and get acquainted with the organization scheme.

The table of Abbreviations and Dates covering all the works of George Eliot is an essential reference point. The abbreviations which are omnipresent in the Taxonomy and the *Topicon* are here explained. Each volume has an alphabetic locator covering the works in that volume, with page references. There follows a Chronology of Eliot's life events, with her works presented in parallel.

As will have been apparent from a persual of the Table of Contents, Volume I is organized primarily on a chronological philosophy, with first the Prose Fiction and then the Poetry presented. The two short stories follow the novelistic works, and in their placement chronology is disregarded.

The works of nonfiction in Volume II are divided into the two principal segments of Essays and Reports, and then Reviews and Notes, each again presented in chronological sequence. Then there follow the elements of the Taxonomy, with three editor's essays interspersed, succeeded by the *Topicon,* or topical concordance. There is a Glossary and a summary of Words and Phrases which will be of interest.

If you know a character's name but do not remember the work, refer to the Indexes at the back of Volume I. There are Indexes as well at the back of Volume II, covering all figures mentioned in the nonfiction, as well as the Notable Individuals highlighted in the *Topicon.*

Citations to the prose fiction are by chapter. Quotations of poetry are usually by line.

Where the symbol ¶ appears, it indicates that we have broken Eliot's paragraphing, which is often far less frequent than modern usage would favor, to improve readability and page appearance.

The Nonfiction

Essays and Reports

Seven of the Essays discussed and extracted below were assembled by Charles Lee Lewes, the son of GE's greatly beloved partner in life, George Henry Lewes, for a posthumous edition of GE's complete works. They were published in New York (hence, with American orthography) in 1884 by Thomas W. Crowell & Co., and these are the versions we use in this work. Charles Lewes' Preface, dated at Highgate, December 1883, reads in part as follows

> "Wishes have often been expressed that the articles known to have been written by George Eliot in the 'Westminster Review' before she had become famous under that pseudonym, should be republished. Those wishes are now gratified—so far, at any rate, as it is possible to gratify them. For it was not George Eliot's desire that the whole of those articles should be rescued from oblivion. And in order that there might be no doubt on the subject, she made some time before her death a collection of such of her fugitive writings as she considered deserving of a permanent form; carefully revised them for the press; and left them, in the order in which they here appear, with written injunctions that no other pieces written by her, of date prior to 1857, should be republished.
>
> "It will thus be seen that the present collection of Essays has the weight of her sanction, and has had, moreover, the advantage of such corrections and alterations as a revision long subsequent to the period of writing may have suggested to her."

These works are highlighted in the following list with ** . They include two which began as Reviews ("The Progress of the Intellect" and "The Influence of Rationalism") but deserve Lewes' classification as Essays. We are comfortable publishing *all* Eliot's nonfiction pieces, despite Mr Lewes' report that she did not wish this, as this inhibition has long been disregarded (if they knew of it) by scholars. Mr Lewes himself disregarded it by publishing materials from Eliot's notebooks which had never been published before. (*See* pages 237-46.) Admittedly, there are some items here the loss of which would not mitigate our appreciation of and respect for George Eliot, but even the weakest has something from which to glean a mote of understanding of the great lady.

Essays and Reports

Coventry *Herald and Observer* **NE 2, 3, 5**
January 15-February 19, 1847

Poetry and Prose, From the Notebook of an Eccentric
(nonfiction elements)

Despite the title, there is no proper verse in these pieces, but there is deep and extraordinary poetry in passages on Purpose in Life and other philosophical matters. George Eliot, at the age of 27, eloquently displays insight and depth. Though most editors consider this material under the heading of Essays, there is noteworthy fiction here—Eliot's first published fiction. See I: 1-3, for the fictional elements.

NE 2

How to Avoid Disappointment (January 15, 1847)

The narrator visits the studio of an artist friend.

"I soon acquire an almost passionate interest in the progress of a noble picture. I love to think how the perfect whole exists in the imagination of the artist before his pencil has marked the canvas—to observe how every minute stroke, every dismal-looking layer of colour conduces to the ultimate effect, and how completely the creative genius which has conceived the result can calculate the necessary means. I love to watch the artist's eye, so wrapt and unworldly in its glance, scrupulously attentive to the details of his actual labour, yet keeping ever in view the idea which that labour is to fulfil. I say to myself—this is an image of what our life should be—a series of efforts directed to the production of a contemplated whole, just as every stroke of the artist's pencil has a purpose bearing on the conception which he retains in his mind's eye. We should all be painting our picture, whether it be a home scene after **Wilkie**, a **Paul** preaching at Athens, or a **Brutus** passing sentence on his son. We should all have a purpose in life as perfectly recognized and definite as the painter's idea of his subject."

purpose in life: "It is to live, not for our friends, not for those hostages to fortune, wives and children; not for any individual, any specific form; but for something which, while it dwells in these, has an existence beyond them. It is to live for the good, the true, the beautiful, which outlive every generation and are all-pervading as the light which vibrates from the remotest nebula to our own sun. The spirit which has ascertained its true relation to these can never be an orphan: it has its home in the eternal mind, from which neither things present nor to come can separate it. You may infallibly discern the man who lives thus. His eye has not that restless, irresolute glance which tells of no purpose beyond the present hour: it looks as you might imagine the eye of **Numa** to have looked after an interview with **Egeria**; the earnest attention and veneration with which it gazed on the divine instructress still lingering in its expression."

"Who would not have some purpose in life as independent in its value as art is to the artist?"

NE 3

The Wisdom of the Child (February 5, 1847)

"It may not be an original idea, but never mind, if it be a true one, that the proper result of intellectual cultivation is to restore the mind to that state of wonder and interest with which it looks on everything in childhood. Thus **Jean Jacques Rousseau**, couched on the grass by the side of a plant that he might examine its structure and appearance at his ease, would have seemed to a little child so like itself in taste and feeling that it would have lain down by him, in full confidence of entire sympathy between them in spite of his wizard-like, Armenian attire."

" . . . the wonder of a child at the material world is the effect of novelty, its simplicity and purity of ignorance; while the wonder of the wise man is the result of knowledge disclosing mystery, the simplicity and purity of his moral principles, the result of wide experience and hardly-attained self-conflict."

"The true philosopher . . . gathers his rule of conduct, not from the suggestions of appetite, not from the dictates of expediency, but from the indications of man's highest destiny, to be found in those faculties of his nature which may be justly said to be more than human, since they might belong to conditions of being far less limited than those of man. Self-renunciation, submission to law, trust, benignity, ingenuousness, rectitude—these are the qualities we delight most to witness in the child, and these are the qualities which most dignify the man."

"The true philosopher, then, constructs his moral code with a view to preserve these sentiments in that state of unsullied purity and freedom of exercise which he loves to see in a child. If he were to admit that all things were lawful to him, he would add, 'I will not be thought under the power of any; I will not circumscribe or bring into bondage the action of any one of my highest endowments.' He feels that in submitting to the restraint of a self-imposed law, he would be presenting humanity in its grandest aspect. But it is *only* the highest human state at which he aims—not anything superhuman. He seeks exercise for all the minor feelings—nay, he holds that these are the only nest in which the ever-aspiring eagle, Nature, can be properly fledged and winged; but he baptizes and hallows them all with the chrism of the diviner soul within him, and regulates their indulgence by his consciousness of the degree in which they encourage or repress the impulses of his moral sentiments. He would be neither an angel, an anchorite, nor a saint; but a man in the most complete and lofty meaning of the name—a man to whom the 'child is father,' perhaps in more senses than the poet thought, and who is no degenerate offspring, but a development of all the features impressed on that heaven-born parent."

NE 5

Hints on Snubbing (February 19, 1847)

There is a numbered summary of types of snubbing: the richer of the rich; the wittier diner-out of the humbler; country newspaper editors of those of wrong opinion, by the use of epithet; those elevated in society of those left behind; ladies at balls, of the plain and ill-dressed; the feminine religious snubber.

"**Hobbes** defined laughter to be the product of a triumphant feeling of superiority: substitute snubbing for laughter and you have a more just definition. The idea of snubbing presupposes inferiority in the snubbed. You can no more snub your betters than you can patronize them; on the contrary, toadyism towards superiors is the invariable attendant on a large endowment of the snubbing faculty. Toadyism, in fact, is the beautiful concavity which corresponds to the snubbing convexity: the angular posture of **Baillie MacWheeble**'s body is a perfect illustration."

Rev. Anylatus Stultus. "All ladies of decidedly orthodox sentiments and serious habits, who, in short, form the public for whom young clergymen print volumes of sermons which may be compared to that popular specific, treacle and brimstone—all such ladies, we say, may snub any man not marriageable, and any woman not an heiress . . . if he or she be suspected of diverging in opinion from that standard of truth which is lodged in the brain of the Rev. Amylatus Stultus, who keeps the key of these same ladies' consciences."

And there is the snub domestic by a husband of his wife; ladies of their governesses; servants of shoe-blacks and vendors of hareskins; shoe-blacks of dogs and cats.

" . . . and doubtless the beautiful chain, if we could trace it, descends to the lowest grades of existence. We have no warrant, however, to suppose that a faculty for snubbing is given to any other races than the terrestrial, since we have express authority for the fact that the archangel **Michael**, on a very remarkable occasion, abstained from snubbing the devil."

"Vice and Sausages"

As noted on page xix, we are indebted to David Parker, who made the below transcription. The item is given complete, as the earliest instance known of a facetious essay by Eliot.

"We should think ourselves culpable if we did not direct attention to the "awful disclosures" of the Police contained in our last week's paper. Inspector VICE saw a cart, containing a dead body, or a beast, he says, deliver its burden at a butcher's shop in this TOWN; the animal, of whatever kind, was dressed and hung in the back of the shop, *with a cloth before it.* Vice being suspicious, watched, and behold! in the outskirts of the town—at a back entrance to a cheap sausage shop, a cart again deposited its burden, containing, as he avers, part of the dead beast in question.

¶"Now a veil of mystery hangs about this horrible tale, which the sausage eating public have a right to demand should be withdrawn. In the first place, what was the beast? Was it an anti-temperance man? does any jovial circle mourn a boon companion? or what kind of beast was it? We have heard of a man who committed suicide by rashly converting himself into sausages in his own 'patent-never-leaving-off sausage engine,' and he, it is affirmed, did not spoil the sausages; but then he was a living man, and not a dead beast.

¶"Again, who was the butcher and who the vicious sausage man, so well known to VICE, in the outskirts of the town? for we agree with MAYOR, 'that the odium of buying unwholesome meat ought not be thrown unjustly upon the respectable shop-keepers in the Town.' In the name, therefore, of every *virtuous* sausage maker—in the name of common justice—of England—of Great Britain at large, we say Name! Name! Now, we know no reason why Inspector VICE should not do this; the Police themselves may be lovers of sausages, and ought to feel a pleasure in protecting the respectable manufacturers of that savoury article. The poet [**Pope**] justly observes—

'Vice is a monster of so frightful mien,
That to be hated needs but to be seen;
But seen too oft, familiar with his face,
We first endure, then pity, then embrace.'

"Now, however familiar the cheap sausage may thus become with VICE, and to whatever embraces the Inspector may be subjected in consequence from the fair sausage makers, yet we trust he will not become equally friendly with them, but at least let us know 'when cats is in,' that is, when they are considered to be in season in the outskirts of the Town; for there may be those among the lovers of this savoury meat who may not consider that the virtue lies *all* in the seasoning, and that the meat is nothing, and that whether the animal died in the natural way, by being killed, or from the neglect of sanitary regulations, is equally of no consequence. We agree with Mr. WELLER that every kind of animal, mice, rats, kittens, puppy dogs, up to a dead beast or a body, may all be made, by judicious seasoning, to taste like pork sausages; but there may be people with over-nice appetites, who object to them notwithstanding, and we think for their sake that the Police ought to give the fullest information as to where real pork (*killed* pigs) is used."

The Progress of the Intellect
(pp 353-68)

The Progress of the Intellect, as Exemplified in the Religious Development of the Greeks and Hebrews, by Robert William Mackay (pp 353-68)

Any student of George Eliot who omits to consider carefully this review, and in particular the extracts which she uses and comments upon with fervent admiration, will miss her essence: in her ethics, her morality, her religion, her spirituality, her world-view. Written when she was in her early thirties, it astounds by its competence, its insight, and its catholic objectivity. One wonders how this anonymous, magisterial judgment of a seminal work on the philosophy of religion made an impact, if it did, and whether inquiry was made as to its authorship. Sad to say, the sex of the author probably had to be concealed in order not to undermine the seriousness with which it was read in intellectual and religious circles.

"Holding, with **Auguste Comte**, that theological and metaphysical speculation have reached their limit, and that the only hope of extending man's sources of knowledge and happiness is to be found in positive science, and in the universal application of its principles; [critics] urge that the thinkers who are in the van of human progress should devote their energies to the actual rather than to the retrospective.

"There is, undeniably, truth in this view. It is better to discover and apply improved methods of draining our own towns, than to be able to quote **Aristophanes** in proof that the streets of Athens were in a state of unmacadamized muddiness—better to reason justly on some point of immediate concern, than to know the fallacies of the ancient sophists—better to look with 'awful eye' at the starry heavens, and, under the teaching of **Newton** and **Herschel**, feel the immensity, the order, the sublimity of the universe, and of the forces by which it subsists, than to pore over the grotesque symbols, whereby the Assyrian or Egyptian shadowed forth his own more vague impression of the same great facts.

"But it would be a very serious mistake to suppose that the study of the past and the labours of criticism have no important practical bearing on the present. Our civilization, and, yet more, our religion, are an anomalous blending of lifeless barbarisms, which have descended to us like so many petrifactions from distant ages, with living ideas, the offspring of a true process of development. We are in bondage to terms and conceptions which, having had their root in conditions of thought no longer existing, have ceased to possess any vitality, and are for us as spells which have lost their virtue.

"The endeavour to spread enlightened ideas is perpetually counteracted by these *idola theatri*, which have allied themselves, on the one hand with men's better sentiments, and on the other with institutions in whose defence are arrayed the passions and the interests of dominant classes.

"Now, though the teaching of positive truth is the grand means of expelling error, the process will be very much quickened if the negative argument serve as its pioneer; if, by a survey of the past, it can be shown how each age and each race has had a faith and a symbolism suited to its need and its stage of development, and that for succeeding ages to dream of retaining the spirit along with the forms of the past, is as futile as the embalming of the dead body in the hope that it may one day be resumed by the living soul." ¶353-4

—adaptation: "It may be doubted, whether a mind which has no susceptibility to the pleasure of changing its point of view, of mastering a remote form of thought, of perceiving identity of nature under variety of manifestation—a perception which resembles an expansion of one's own being, a pre-existence in the past—can possess the flexibility, the ready sympathy, or the tolerance, which characterizes a truly philosophic culture." 354

—the author: "Now and then . . . we meet with a nature which combines the faculty for amassing minute erudition with the largeness of view necessary to give it a practical bearing; a high appreciation of the genius of antiquity, with a profound belief in the progressive character of human development—in the eternal freshness of the founts of inspiration, a wonderful intuition of the mental conditions of past ages with an ardent participation in the most advanced ideas and most hopeful efforts of the present; a nature like some mighty river, which, in its long windings through unfrequented regions, gathers mineral and earthy treasures only more effectually to enrich and fertilize the cultivated valleys and busy cities which form the habitation of man.

"Of such a mature, with valuable qualities thus 'antithetically mixt,' we have evidence in the work before us." 354

—England and Germany: "England has been slow to use or to emulate the immense labours of Germany in the departments of mythology and biblical criticism; but when once she does so, the greater solidity and directness of the English mind ensure a superiority of treatment." 354-5

—introduction: " . . . this preliminary chapter is a sort of lofty, airy vestibule, in which we gather breath and courage to descend with the author into the crypts of citation and conjecture, into which he is about to introduce us." 355

—premise: "It is Mr Mackay's faith that divine revelation is not contained exclusively or pre-eminently in the facts and inspirations of any one age or nation, but is co-extensive with the history of human development, and is perpetually unfolding itself to our widened experience and investigation, as firmament upon firmament becomes visible to us in proportion to the power and range of our exploring instruments." 355

—the key: "The master key to this revelation, is the recognition of the presence of undeviating law in the material and moral world—of that invariability of sequence which is acknowledged to be the basis of physical science, but which is still perversely ignored in our social organization, our ethics and our religion. It is this invariability of sequence which can alone give value to experience and render education in the true sense possible."

—evolution: " . . . every past phase of human development is part of that education of the race in which we are sharing; every mistake, every absurdity into which poor human nature has fallen, may be looked on as an experiment of which we may reap the benefit . . . . In this view, religion and philosophy are not merely conciliated, they are identical; or rather, religion is the crown and consummation of philosophy—the delicate corolla, which can only spread out its petals in all their symmetry and brilliance to the sun, when root and branch exhibit the conditions of a healthy and vigorous life." 355-6

—subject-matter: " . . . Mr Mackay commences his survey and delineation of religious development, selecting that of the Hebrews and Greeks as the most typical and complete, and tracing it up to the period when the combination of the two modes of thought in the Alexandrian theosophy formed that web of metaphysical and religious dogma, which constitutes speculative Christianity. While the Hebrew and Greek religions are his main subject, he has not neglected the copious illustration to be drawn from the Persian, the Hindoo and the Northern mythologies, by indicating instances of analogy and of possible derivation, and thus the 'Progress of the Intellect,' is, perhaps, the nearest approach in our language to a satisfactory natural history of religion." 359

—Biblical myth: "The fact, that the history of all other nations has a mythical period, urges a strong presumption, that the Hebrew records will not present an exception in this respect, and an unprejudiced examination confirms this presumption. We find there not only a generic similarity to the gentile myths, in a degrading conception of the divine attributes, with a corresponding crudeness and obliquity of moral views, in an ignorant interpretation of physical phenomena, a love of prodigy, and lavish supposition of gratuitous miracle, but also a specific resemblance in symbolism.

"This is visible on a cursory glance, but a nearer investigation discloses overwhelming proof, that the Hebrew writings, far from meriting an exceptional confidence, require, from the evidence they exhibit that the Hebrew mind was peculiarly deficient in a true historical sense, special canons of caution in their interpretation.

"On applying the test of a critical analysis, the books of the Pentateuch resolve themselves into a compilation of distinct documents, differing in date and frequently in spirit and purpose, as may be seen from the variations and contradictions in their accounts of the same event; and the more ancient of these documents presents internal evidence, that it was not in existence earlier than the time of **Samuel,** about 400 years after **Moses**. The same artificial coherence, the same arbitrariness of classification and of titles, together with palpable inaccuracies and indications of partisanship, characterize large portions, not only of the remaining historical works, but also of the prophetic.

"Since these conclusions are denied by no competent critic uncommitted to the maintenance of certain tenets, it would be wise in our theological teachers, instead of struggling to retain a footing for themselves and their doctrine on the crumbling structure of dogmatic interpretation, to cherish those more liberal views of biblical criticism, which, admitting of a development of the Christian system corresponding to the wants and the culture of the age, would enable it to strike a firm root in man's moral nature, and to entwine itself with the growth of those new forms of social life to which we are tending.

"The spirit which doubts the ultimately beneficial tendency of inquiry, which thinks that morality and religion will not bear the broadest daylight our intellect can throw on them, though it may clothe itself in robes of sanctity and use pious phrases, is the worst form of atheism; while he who believes, whatever else he may deny, that the true and the good are synonymous, bears in his soul the essential element of religion." ¶364-5

—*summary:* "Mr Mackay holds that the original God of the Israelites was no other than the Nature-God, **El** or **Ilus**, worshipped in Arabia, Palestine, and Phoenicia, with licentious and sanguinary rites, under the double aspect of **Baal** and **Moloch**; and that the purer worship of **Jehovah**, inculcated by the prophets, and established by **Josiah**, was a religious reformation among the Hebrews, generated by the growth in civilization consequent on an enlarged commercial intercourse with foreign nations, and contemporaneous with a movement of religious reform which took place throughout Asia, about 700 B.C., connected in India with the name of **Buddha**, in Persia (or Media), with that of **Zoroaster**, and a century later extending itself by **Xenophanes** and **Heraclitus** into Greece." 356

—*Passover:* "In Mr Mackay's opinion, the account of the Passover, as it now stands, is the veil which the purer conceptions of later Hebrews cast over the ancient custom of sacrificing first-born children to the bloodthirsty **El**; the massacre of three thousand Israelites, represented in Exodus as retributive, was probably sacrificial—a huge offering to the same demon, the rather that **Aaron**, the leader in the calf-worship, was not involved in the same destruction; the command by which God is said to have tempted **Abraham**, the vow of **Jephthah**, the slaughter of the seven descendants of **Saul**, whereby **David** sought to propitiate his God and avert a famine, are indications that human sacrifices were familiar to the Hebrews . . . . " 366

The Creed of Christendom

The Creed of Christendom: Its Foundations and Superstructure, by William Rathbone Greg (John Chapman was publisher)

Mr Greg speaks very much to Eliot's heart. Long extracts from his work are included by her in a way which makes it clear that she approves heartily of his views in most respects.

"English Protestantism, effete as it seems in its ecclesiastical and sectarian forms, is manifesting the vitality of its roots in the vigorous and rapid growth of free religious inquiry among earnest men. The writers who are heading the present movement against dogmatic theology, are not mere speculators enamoured of theory, and careless of its practical results. Still less are they anti-religious zealots, who identify all faith with superstition. They are men at once devout and practical, who have been driven into antagonism with the dominant belief by the force of their moral, no less than of their intellectual nature, and who have been led to the avowal of that antagonism, not simply by the impulse of candour, but by an interest in the spiritual well-being of society. They know that to call dogmatic Christianity the popular creed is a misnomer; that the doctrines taught in our pulpits neither have, nor can have, any hold on the masses; and that if our population is to be Christianized, religious teaching must be conducted in a new spirit and on new principles. They protest against the current faith, because they would substitute for it one purer and more influential; they lay the axe to the old, only that there may be freer play for the energies which are ever tending to the development of the new and more perfect.

"Among these pioneers of the New Reformation, Mr Greg is likely to be one of the most effective. Without any pretension to striking originality or extensive learning, his work perhaps all the more exhibits that sound, practical judgment which discerns at once the *hinge* of a question, and it bears throughout the impress of an honesty, geniality, and refinement which imply a moral nature of a very high order. The absence of any very profound critical erudition, far from disqualifying Mr Greg for the task he has undertaken, is essential to the aim of his book—namely, to show at what conclusions concerning the Bible and Christianity a sensible, educated layman is likely to arrive, with such an amount of critical attainment as is compatible with the work that lies before him in daily life. If such conclusions must necessarily be unsound because they are formed in ignorance of the last new edition of every

Biblical critic, orthodox or heterodox, the right of private judgment is a nullity, and the unclerical mind must either dismiss the subject altogether, or surrender itself to a more consistent spiritual despotism than that of Protestant divines. *The Creed of Christendom* claims the attention of the theologian, not that it may teach him Biblical criticism, but that it may render him more familiar with the impression made by the vexed questions of his science on an earnest, cultivated mind, cut off by no barrier of caste or prejudice from full sympathy and acquaintance with the spirit and wants of the age. Another class of readers to whom it is adapted, are those struggling towards free religious thought amidst the impediments of critical ignorance and early artificial associations. To such, Mr Greg's book will be valuable, both as an introductory manual of Biblical criticism and as a help in the consideration of certain moral questions."

"Mr Greg sets out by examining the dogma of Scriptural inspiration, which he justly regards as the keystone of Protestant orthodoxy. After considering separately each of the grounds on which it rests, he concludes that there is no valid foundation for believing the Hebrew and Christian canonical writings to be inspired, in the ordinary acceptation of the word—that is, dictated or suggested by God; that hence we must regard them *'as records, not revelations;* as histories, to be investigated like other histories; documents, of which the date, the authorship, the genuineness, the accuracy of the text, are to be ascertained by the same principles as we apply to other documents.' Having thus cleared away the dazzling haze with which the inspiration dogma invests the Biblical writings, he proceeds to investigate the genuineness and authenticity of the Old Testament canon, and traces briefly but forcibly the chief results of modern criticism in relation to this subject; indicating such of the reasons on which they are founded as are readily appreciable by the general reader. According to these results, no longer held debatable by critics of high standing, the Pentateuch, instead of being, as is popularly supposed, the production of Moses, is a compilation from separate documents, the earliest of which must have been written as late as the time of Saul; while the whole book of Deuteronomy, and many parts of the preceding books, are irrefragably proved by the subsequent history of the Hebrews to have had no existence prior to the reign of Josiah. Mr Greg instances some of the straits to which English divines have been driven, in the effort to maintain the authority of the Old Testament in the face of scientific discovery; and dwells on the advantage which would accrue, not only to the truthfulness of divines, but to the real instructiveness of the Hebrew writings, if the latter were regarded as merely human narratives, traditions, and speculations . . . . In his opinion—

> 'The Hebrew prophets were wise, gifted, earnest men, deeply conversant with the Past—looking far into the Future—shocked with the unrighteousness around them—sagacious to see impending evil—bold to denounce wickedness in high places—imbued, above all, with an unfailing faith, peculiarly strong among their people, that national delinquency and national virtue would alike meet with a temporal and inevitable retribution—and gifted "with the glorious faculty of poetic hope, exerted on human prospects, and presenting its results with the vividness of prophecy"—but prophets in no stricter sense than this.'

"The Theism of the Hebrews, Mr Greg maintains, was impure and progressive; they arrived at their monotheism by the same stages that characterize the development of the human race in general, the Old Testament exhibiting strong evidence that the Hebrew deity was originally a family god, elevated by Moses to the dignity of a national god, and ultimately, owing to the influence of prophets and sages, and yet more to the contact of the Hebrews with other Oriental nations, expanded into the God of the Universe.

"The claims of the New Testament on our credence are next considered. The chapters on the Origin of the Gospels and the Fidelity of the Gospel History contain no fresh contributions to Biblical criticism, nor anything new to persons conversant with this class of subjects; but they are a well arranged summary of salient facts and arguments, gathered chiefly from **Strauss**, **Hug**, **Schleiermacher**, and **Hennell**. The conclusions to which the writer is led are, that we have no certitude as to the Gospels conveying the testimony of eyewitnesses, while, on the other hand, there is the strongest evidence of their containing a large admixture of legend, and that we can trust them no further than as giving an outline of Christ's life and teaching. Hence Mr Greg holds that dogmas founded on sayings attributed to Jesus, but discordant with the impression of his character conveyed by the general tenor of the Gospels, must be rejected; for example, the dogmas of the necessity of belief to salvation, the proper Deity of Christ, and the Atonement. We quote some of his reflections on these results:—

> ' . . . The uncertainty thrown is not over the main points of Christ's history, which . . . still stands out an intelligible, though a skeleton account—nor over the grand features, the pervading tone of his doctrines or his character, which still present to us a clear, consistent, and splendid delineation; but over those individual statements, passages, and discourses which mar this delineation—which break its unity—which destroy its consistency—which cloud its clearness—which tarnish its beauty. The gain to us seems immense.
>
> "It is true we have no longer *absolute* certainty with regard to any one especial text or scene; such is neither necessary nor attainable; it is true that, instead of passively accepting the whole heterogeneous and indigestible mass, we must, by the careful and conscientious exercise of those faculties with which we are endowed, by ratiocination and moral tact, separate what Christ did, from what he did not teach, as best we may. But the task will be difficult to those only who look in the Gospels for a minute, dogmatic, and sententious creed; not to those who seek only to learn Christ's spirit that they may imbibe it, and to comprehend his views of virtue and of God, that they may draw strength and consolation from those fountains of living water.'

" . . . In the chapter on Miracles, he treats the subject chiefly on a priori grounds, and only cursorily touches on the question whether the miraculous narratives in the Gospels bear the marks of credibility. He argues for the position, long ago strenuously maintained by Locke, and admitted by many even of our orthodox divines, that a miracle can never authenticate a doctrine . . . . The crowning miracle of the Resurrection he considers separately, giving a condensed analysis of the evidence on which it rests. The conclusion that this evidence is insufficient is, he thinks, rendered needlessly painful by the undue doctrinal value assigned by theologians to the Resurrection of Christ, whether as a sanction of his doctrines, or as a type and pledge of our own resurrection; for, viewed in the one light it is superfluous, while in the other, it utterly fails of the supposed end, since a bodily resurrection after three days' interment, can bear no resemblance to anything that awaits ourselves.

" . . . Mr Greg 'finds no adequate reason for believing Jesus to be the son of God, nor his doctrines to be a direct and special revelation.' The following is his conception of Jesus:—

' . . . We hold that God has so arranged matters in this beautiful and well-ordered but mysteriously governed universe, that one great mind after another will arise from time to time, as such are needed, to discover and flash forth before the eyes of men the truths that are wanted, and the amount of truth that can be borne. We conceive that this is effected . . . by having arranged that nature and the course of events shall send them into the world endowed with that superior mental and moral organization, in which grand truths, sublime gleams of spiritual light, will spontaneously and inevitably arise.

¶'Such a one we believe was **Jesus of Nazareth**—the most exalted genius whom God ever sent upon earth; in himself an embodied revelation; humanity in its divinest phase—"God manifest in the flesh," according to Eastern hyperbole; an exemplar vouchsafed, in an early age of the world, of what man may and should become, in the course of ages, in his progress towards the realization of his destiny; an individual gifted with a glorious intellect, a noble soul, a fine organization, and a perfectly balanced moral being; and who, by virtue of these endowments, saw further than all other men . . . . He was, as **Parker** beautifully expresses it, "the possibility of the rare made real." He was a sublime poet, prophet, hero, and philosopher; and had the usual fate of such—misrepresented by his enemies, misconstrued by his friends; unhappy in this, that his nearest intimates and followers were not of a calibre to understand him; happy in this, that his words contained such undying seeds of truth as could survive even the media through which they passed. Like the wheat found in the Egyptian catacombs, they retain the power of germinating undiminished, whenever their appropriate soil is found. They have been preserved almost pure, notwithstanding the Judaic narrowness of **Peter**, the orthodox passions of **John**, and the metaphysical subtleties of **Paul**.

¶'Everything seems to us to confirm the conclusion that we have in the Christianity of Scripture a code of beautiful, simple, sublime, profound, *but not perfect* truth, obscured by having come down to us by the intervention of minds far inferior to that of its Author; narrowed by their uncultivation; marred by their misapprehensions; and tarnished by their foreign admixtures. It is a collection of grand truths transmitted to us by men who only half comprehended their grandeur, and imperfectly grasped their truth.'

"If Christianity be no longer regarded as a revelation, but as the conception of a fallible though transcendantly gifted mind, it follows that only so much of it is to be accepted as harmonizes with the reason and conscience: Christianity becomes 'Christian Eclecticism.' Mr Greg unhesitatingly receives many of Christ's precepts as unsurpassable and unimprovable: for example, those which inculcate the worthlessness of ceremonial observance and the necessity of active virtue, purity of heart as the security for purity of life, universal philanthopy, forgiveness of injuries, self-sacrifice in the cause of duty, humility, and genuine sincerity. He regards as next to perfection the views which Christianity unfolds of God as a Father.

'In the two great points essential to our practical life, viz., our feelings towards God and our conduct towards man, the Gospels contain little about which men can differ—little from which they can dissent. He is our Father, we are all brethren. This much lies open to the most ignorant and busy, as fully as to the most leisurely and learned. This needs no priest to teach it, no authority to endorse it. The rest is speculation; intensely interesting, indeed, but of no practical necessity.'

"Other tenets taught in the Christian Scriptures, however, Mr Greg thinks open to grave objections. He urges, for example, that the New Testament assigns an efficacy to prayer incompatible with any elevated conception of Deity; that it inculcates resignation, not as the result of a self-reasoning faith in the wisdom and justice of the supreme will, but on the narrow ground that sufferings are especially ordained for the benefit of the individual; and that it appeals to the selfish motives—the desire for recompense, rather than to the highest—the love of the good for its own sake. He holds that the conception of the pardon of sin, or repentance and conversion, tends to contravene the system on which man is trained and disciplined, and the entire scheme of God's government—the conviction that every breach of the Divine law is attended with inexorable consequences, being essential to a healthy condition of the conscience and a just theory of Providence:—

'Let any one look back upon his past career, look inward on his daily life, and then say what effect would be produced upon him, were the conviction once fixedly embedded in his soul, that everything done is done irrevocably, that even the omnipotence of God cannot *uncommit* a deed, cannot make that undone which has been done . . . .

'Perhaps you have led a youth of dissipation and excess which has undermined and enfeebled your constitution, and you have transmitted this injured and enfeebled constitution to your children. They suffer, in consequence, through life; suffering is entailed upon them; your repentance, were it in sackcloth and ashes cannot help you or them. Your punishment is tremendous, but it is legitimate and inevitable. You have broken Nature's laws, or you have ignored them, and no one violates or neglects them with impunity. What a lesson for timely reflection and obedience is here! . . .

'But in all this, let it be understood, in no degree militates against the value or the necessity of repentance. Repentance, contrition of soul, bears, like every other act, its own fruit—the fruit of purifying the heart, of amending the future; not as man has hitherto conceived—of effacing the past. The commission of sin is an irrevocable act, but it does not incapacitate the soul for virtue. Its consequences cannot be expunged, but the course need not be pursued. Sin, though it is ineffaceable, calls for no despair, but for efforts more energetic than before. Repentance is still as valid as ever; but it is valid to secure the future, not to obliterate the past. . . .'

"Mr Greg also shows that Christianity teaches an ascetic and depreciating view of life, incompatible with that energetic devotion to the improvement of our races, and with that delight in the innocent adornment of our existence in this world, which are essential to a noble and well-balanced soul . . . .

"We have endeavoured to give our readers a faithful idea of Mr Greg's work. Though far from setting our seal to all his opinions, we think that the *Creed of Christendom* sets forth very powerfully much truth of which society is in urgent need, while it opens to us an acquaintance with an individual mind possessing a strong moral and intellectual charm."

Eliot adds at this point a reflection on **Hennell**'s *Inquiry concerning the Origin of Christianity,* published twelve years before. She considers that the *Inquiry* was the production "of a mind which has brought to the independent study of the New Testament the rare combination of analytic acumen with breadth of conception." She feels the book had an important influence to promote unprejudiced and dispassionate study of the Scriptures; nevertheless, when it first appeared it received contemptuous treatment in some quarters. She is delighted with the change since then:

"In this *annus mirabilis* of 1851, however, our reviewers have attained a higher standard of courage and fairness than could be ascribed to them in 1838, or even in 1845. *'La terre tourne,'* says **Pascal**, *'malgré qu'on le nie; et vous aussi, mes révérends pères, vous tournez avec elle*—The earth turns in spite of all denials; and you also, my reverend fathers, turn with it.' "

Woman in France: Madame de Sablé
(pp 448-73)

1. *Madame de Sablé: Etudes sur les Femme illustres et la Société du XVII siècle Par* M. Victor Cousin. Paris: Didier.
2. *Portraits de Femmes. Par* C. A. Saint-Beuve. Paris: Didier
3. *Les Femmes de la Révolution. Par* J. Michelet

GE begins with a general exploration of the literary talents of French women and offers her theories to account for them, ranging from the phrenological to the sociological. She then turns to the Cousin book and describes the attributes and friendships (as well as her hypochondria and dietary niceness) of Mme de Sablé, in her day a much-admired doyenne of French society and beloved for her intercessions for her friends, for her equable temper, and for her forbearance and charities over a very long life. We are given insights into the works and lives of Pascal and La Rochefoucauld and are told something of the great religious controversy, the Fronde. We do not see a word about Saint-Beuve or Michelet's works.

Extracts are in the *Topicon* at LM:Marriage—*effective,* LM:The Sexes—*in literature* and LM:Woman—*in France,* and in LC:Communications—*telegraph,* LC:Notable individuals —*Blaise Pascal* and *La Rochefoucauld*, and LC:Press—*journalism.*

"With a few remarkable exceptions, our own feminine literature is made up of books which could have been better written by men; books, which have the same relation to literature in general, as academic prize poems have to poetry: when not a feeble imitation, they are usually an absurd exaggeration of the masculine style, like the swaggering gait of a bad actress in male attire. Few English women have written so much like a woman as **Richardson**'s Lady G." 448-9

"And those delightful women of France, who, from the beginning of the seventeenth to the close of the eighteenth century, formed some of the brightest threads in the web of political and literary history, wrote under circumstances which left the feminine character of their minds uncramped by timidity, and unstrained by mistaken effort . . . . One may say, at least with regard to the women of the seventeenth century, that their writings were but a charming accident of their more charming lives, like the petals which the wind shakes from the rose in its bloom. And it is but a twin fact with this, that in France alone woman has had a vital influence on the development of literature; in France alone the mind of woman has passed like an electric current through the language, making crisp and definite what is elsewhere heavy and blurred; in France alone, if the writings of women were swept away, a serious gap would be made in the national history." 449

"And to this day, **Madame de Sévigné** remains the single instance of a woman who is supreme in a class of literature which has engaged the ambition of men; **Madame Dacier** still reigns the queen of blue-stockings, though women have long studied Greek without shame; **Madame de Staël**'s name still rises first to the lips when we are asked to mention a woman of great intellectual power; **Madame Roland** is still the unrivalled type of the sagacious and sternly heroic, yet lovable woman; **George Sand** is the unapproached artist who, to **Jean Jaques**' eloquence and deep sense of external nature, unites the clear delineation of character and the tragic depth of passion." 450

Marquise de Rambouillet. "The presiding genius of this *salon* [1630-1648] . . . was the very model of the woman who can act as an amalgam to the most incongruous elements: beautiful, but not preoccupied by coquetry or passion; an enthusiastic admirer of talent, but with no pretensions to talent on her own part; exquisitely refined in language and manners, but warm and generous withal; not given to entertain her guests with her own compositions, or to paralyze them by her universal knowledge . . . . In her mild, agreeable presence was accomplished that blending of the high-toned chivalry of Spain with the caustic wit and refined irony of Italy, which issued in the creation of a new standard of taste—the combination of the utmost exaltation in sentiment with the utmost simplicity of language." 452-3

Madame de Sablé. "M. Cousin justly appreciates her character as 'un heureux mélange de raison, d'esprit, d'agrément, et de bonté;' and perhaps there are few better specimens of the woman who is extreme in nothing, but sympathetic in all things; who affects us by no special quality, but by her entire being; whose nature has no *tons criards,* but is like those textures which, from their harmonious blending of all colours, give repose to the eye, and do not weary us though we see them every day." 456

"**Madeline de Souvré**, daughter of the **Marquis of Courtenvaux**, a nobleman distinguished enough to be chosen as governor of **Louis XIII**, was born in 1599 . . . when in 1635 her more celebrated friend, **Mademoiselle de Bourbon**, afterwards the **Duchess de Longueville**, made her appearance at the Hôtel de Rambouillet, Madame de Sablé had nearly crossed that table-land of maturity which precedes a woman's descent towards old age. She had been married, in 1614, to **Philippe Emanuel de Laval-Montmorency, Seigneur de Bois-Dauphin,** and **Marquis de Sablé**, of whom nothing further is known than that he died in 1640, leaving her the richer by four children, but with a fortune considerably embarrassed." 456-7

" . . . this is the place to mention what was the subject of endless raillery from her friends—her elaborate precaution about her health, and her dread of infection, even from diseases the least communicable. Perhaps this anxiety was founded as much on aesthetic as on physical grounds, on disgust at the details of illness as much as on dread of suffering: with a cold in the head or a bilious complaints, the exquisite *précieuse* must have been considerably less conscious of being 'the ornament of the world,' and 'made to be adored.' " 460.

"A religious retirement, which did not exclude the reception of literary friends, or the care for personal comforts, made the most becoming frame for age and diminished fortune. Jansenism was then to ordinary Catholicism what Puseyism is to ordinary Church of Englandism in these days—it was a *recherché* form of piety unshared by the vulgar; and one sees at once that it must have special attractions for the *précieuse.* Madame de Sablé, then, probably about 1655 or 6, determined to retire to Port Royal, not because she was already devout, but because she hoped to become so . . . " 464

"She was much more than [a *précieuse*]: she was the valuable, trusted friend of noble women and distinguished men; she was the animating spirit of a society whence issued a new form of French literature: she was the woman of large capacity and large heart, whom **Pascal** sought to please, to whom **Arnauld** submitted the Discourse prefixed to his Logic . . . . The papers preserved by her secretary, Valant, show that she maintained an extensive correspondence with persons of various rank and character; that her pen was untiring in the interest of others; that men made her the depositary of their thoughts, women of their sorrows; that her friends were as impatient, when she secluded herself, as if they had been rival lovers and she a youthful beauty." 465

"Was not the woman, who could unite the ease and grace indicated by this [quoted] letter, with an intellect that men thought worth consulting on matters of reasoning and philosophy, with warm affections, untiring activity for others, no ambition as an authoress, and in sight into *confitures* and *ragoûts,* a rare combination?" 466

"Whether or not Madame de Sablé's influence served to enrich the *Pensées* of Pascal, it is clear that but for her influence the 'Maxims' of La Rochefoucauld would never have existed." 467

"It is worth while to notice, that with Madame de Sablé, as with some other remarkable Frenchwomen, the part of her life which is richest in interest and results, is that which is looked forward to by most of her sex with melancholy as the period of decline. When between fifty and sixty, she had philosophers, wits, beauties, and saints clustering around her; and one naturally cares to know what was the elixir which gave her this enduring and general attraction. We think it was, in a great degree, that well-balanced development of mental powers which gave her a comprehension of varied intellectual processes, and a tolerance for varied forms of character, which is still rare in women than in men." 471

Guy de Laval. "In the midst of [her] pecuniary troubles came a more terrible trial—the loss of her favourite son, the brave and handsome Guy de Laval, who, after a brilliant career in the campaigns of **Condé**, was killed at the siege of Dunkirk, in 1646, when scarcely four-and-twenty. The fine qualities of this young man had endeared him to the whole army, and especially to Condé, had won him the hand of the **Chancellor Séguire**'s daughter, and had thus opened to him the prospect of the highest honours. His loss seems to have been the most real sorrow of Madame de Sablé's life." 463-4

Also mentioned

[in addition to more prominent figures listed in Index X]

The Romantic School of Music

Liszt on Meyerbeer—Wagner

Weimar, Oct. 1

In the canon as laid down by Pinney, except for CC this is the earliest of GE's contributions to the *Leader.* But the piece's opening words seem clearly enough to contradict this. We have searched prior issues for further thoughts on the subject-matter, without success. Pinney, furthermore, describes the article as a "triple collaboration" of Eliot, Lewes and Liszt and states that it is "a translation by George Eliot" of an article Liszt wrote for the *Neue Zeitschrift* on Meyerbeer's opera *Robert le diable,* and that Lewes "added his own comment to the translation and the result was published as a letter to the *Leader* from Weimar." But that is not what we found in the *Leader.* Rather, we have GE's own views, and her approving paraphrase of Liszt's views, on the history of opera (published in the *Zeitschrift* June 16, 1854), and no visible contribution by anyone else.

"It has been my duty and my pleasure several times in this journal to raise my voice against [**Giacomo**] **Meyerbeer** and his school; which may have something to do with the selection of the subject for the third letter [clearly enough indicating that there have been two prior pieces]. I am glad to have **Liszt** fighting in the same ranks, although he fights under another standard. My opinion has always been that Meyerbeer's unmistakable ability and knowledge of theatrical effect have given his works a popularity which for a time may cast in the shade the music of far deeper and more enduring character, just as the popularity of a **Dumas** may for a time eclipse **Racine**: but whatever we may think of Meyerbeer's theatrical talent, his *musical genius* is of quite a secondary order. Instead of Music he has striven for Situation; instead of Poetry, Effect. To bring stage pomp, splendour, dance, and the clang of tumultuous orchestras, as a substitution for passionate and melodic expression, was an innovation indeed, but no real reform. The primary aim of the musical Art was given up in favour of a secondary and accessory aim of *stage effect.*

"Such, briefly, was the point of view taken. In [**Franz**] **Liszt**'s criticism I find perfect agreement with these ideas, except that he regards Meyerbeer's innovation as a real reform, a transition from a worn-out form of Art to a newer and grander form. [**Gioachino**] **Rossini**—*il maestro di color che sonno*—the greatest dramatic genius, as I conceive, who ever used Music as a form of expression, Liszt regards as the culmination of that style which aimed at *Feeling* above all things, careless of dramatic propriety, careless of character, truth, or *couleur locale*. Meyerbeer, on the other hand, is regardless of the mere melodic delight, and thinks mainly of *Effect*. Let us see how Liszt establishes this by an historical survey of the development of modern Opera.

"He very properly brings into its deserved prominence the part which the libretto plays in Opera. Thus, he says, among all the libretto-writers of the last century, the one who won a lasting celebrity was [**Pietro**] **Metastasio**. He was the poet *par excellence* of that Italian opera of which we may take [**Johann Adolf**] **Hasse** as the most typical representative. Though not so fertile as some other composers of his time, Hasse produced more than fifty operas, which will not appear surprising if we reflect that in that day every musical author held it quite natural to compose several operas to the same text, and *vice versa*. This fact is a significant proof of the then existing indifference to *effects* which are appropriate to specific situations; for these are not translatable, whereas the same feeling may be expressed in a hundred ways, and it is easy to adapt a new melody to words, or new words to a melody, if both the one and the other simply express joy, sorrow, or love in general, and if no great weight is laid on declamation and prosody, which are the sole indissoluble bond between words and musical expression.

¶"Thus, during the first epoch of the opera, the expression of *feeling* was the dominant tendency. In the beginning of the present century the society whose favourite poet was Metastasio, and whose favourite musician was Hasse, had disappeared. New social conditions demanded a new form of art. Already, in *Don Giovanni* and *Il Flauto Magico,* new elements are observable; tragic horror alternates with comedy, evidently for the sake of avoiding the uniformity of the sentimental fustian and bombast which were then inseparable from the *opera seria*. The signal once given, everything was sought that could introduce variety into the libretto, and the distinction between the *opera seria* and the *opera buffa* was obliterated in favour of the *opera mezzo carattiere*. Antiquity, the middle ages, romances, the poetical incidents of modern history, even anecdotes, were ransacked for themes that admitted of amplifications, variations, and accessories; and this was done without any system, as in the case of transitional works, which, while they depart from the old form, do not fully bear the stamp of the new. When [**Augustin Eugène**] **Scribe** wrote *Robert le Diable* it was evident that even in the lifetime of Rossini, the most illustrious master of the old school, a new period in the conceptions of opera-subjects had thoroughly set in.

¶"Rossini had more than parried the effect of [**Daniel-François-Esprit**] **Auber**'s *Masaniello* by producing *William Tell*, but when *Robert* appeared he left Paris, conscious that the school, of which he was the head, had received a blow which sooner or later must be fatal. The expression of feeling in arias, duettos, and finales, which called forth no pregnant dramatic crisis, ceased to be the basis of an opera. The demand was for *situations*. This element was not entirely novel; instinctively it had already been striven for. The inauguration of a new period in the opera through Scribe's *Robert* and Meyerbeer's musical conception of it, presented nothing unheard of, or unprecedented. In art, as in nature, no species stands in isolation—it is always united by intermediate links with species of a different or even opposite form. There had been the hell-flames in *Don Giovanni,* the explosion of the fleet in *Cortez,* the hammer and anvil chorus in *Aleidor,* the burning Vesuvius and the tumultuous scenes in *Masaniello,* the popular insurrection and the glowing Alps in *William Tell,* the terrors of the Wolf Ravine in *Der Freischütz.* But Scribe surpassed all, making that a main object which had previously been only an accessory. Splendour of decoration, profusion of scenic arrangement, marvellous *ballets,* supernatural machinery, in short, spectacular magnificence, ceased to be adjuncts and became an integral element, an organic part of every operatic work, since they were essential to the interest and artistic effect of the *situations.*

¶"Simultaneously arose the necessity for developing new resources in the orchestra and chorus, if they were not to be annihilated or reduced to the second rank by scenic splendour. From this time it was an absolute requisite in every opera that there should be some grand spectacle in the most thrilling moment, as a sort of climax to the situations. The dance of the phantoms in *Robert* was succeeded by the crowd of horses in *La Juive,* and this again by the fabulous wonders of the *Juif Errant* and *L'Enfant Prodigue,* till at last it seems as if the force of decoration can no further go. Scribe, like a man of talent as he is, did not use half measures; he laid hold on situations wherever he could find them, and being in no dread of absurdity, he won the game. His name will be inseparable from the *second* period of the opera, less fertile than the first, but more important from the intrinsic value of its productions. The school of which Metastasio was the chief poet, was adapted to a period and to courts in which effeminate, insipid refinement reigned; Scribe, on the contrary, belongs to an epoch in which exaggeration was the order of the day. Romanticism was then in full bloom, and French poetry was still under the influence of **Byron** and **Hoffmann**.

¶"The public, accustomed to horrors, could hardly be made to shudder by the most startling contrasts. **Victor Hugo** created chaste courtesans, devoted mothers, and artistic poisoners, in one and the same person: **Nodier** paraded with his *Jean Stogar:* beautiful countesses and duchesses were enamoured of the heroes in **Eugene Sue**'s *Salamander,* and gave their approval to *Dorial,* in Dumas' *Antony.* Extravagance was asked for at any price. Hatred and love, terrific dangers and ineffable bliss, the brightest light and the darkest shade were placed in juxtaposition. Scribe crowned all in his *Robert* by making Satan himself a tender father. It would be difficult now to bring forward such a sentimental devil, but at the time when *Robert* appeared it was precisely this extravagance which made its fortune. The different relation which the libretto bears to the music in the first and second periods of the opera is strongly indicated by the fact that though Rossini applied himself to the creation of nearly forty operas, no one cares to know the author on any one of his librettos, whereas the name of Scribe is indissolubly bound to that of Meyerbeer. In that form of the opera which they have jointly brought to its culminating point, they have made love merely an episode, if [*sic*] order to step out of the narrow circle of simple, individual feeling, and to multiply dramatic motives which may give rise to an abundance of striking situations.

¶"Simple melody is superseded by combinations of musical effect, the expression of feeling has given way to situation. These must be had at whatever cost, and it must be admitted that in pursuit of them the interest and the truthful presentation of character are often left unregarded, though not so entirely as critics are now wont to allege. It is true enough that the character of *Robert* has no sort of self-subsistence, that *Isabella* is but a voice, *Bertram* falsely drawn, and the *Prophet* erroneously conceived, *Bertha* a nullity, and *Fides* a failure; but on the other hand, *Alice*—the pure, pious country maiden, who rescues the son of her benefactress from hellish snares, not out of egotistic love, but out of divine compassion and child-like obedience—and *Marcel*, who presents the same kind of self-devotion in a severer form, are true characters and noble creations. And if Scribe is to be reproached for his love of situations, he knows how to select impressive ones, witness the fourth act of the *Huguenots*.

"It is undeniable that Scribe and Meyerbeer have made a great step towards the complete union of musical and poetical requirements on the stage, towards the conversion of the opera into a real *musical drama*. They have given a necessary prelude to the position maintained by the new operatic school, namely—that the moment is come in which the poetry of opera-texts should have more elements of the tragedy and recited drama than hitherto; that all the splendours of scenery can be applied to heighten the interest of situations without sacrificing the indispensable poetical features of the drama. The first period of the opera of which Rossini is the greatest representative, had for its aim the expression of feeling: the second period, represented by Meyerbeer, has striven after situations and musical effects; the third period inaugurated by the operas of [**Richard**] **Wagner**, seeks to ally situations with *character*. Wagner saw that in striving for situations the operatic author was in danger of neglecting tragical requisites and beauties; whereas the presentation of characters and their mutual relations necessarily evolved situations. He does not, like Scribe, combine situations as external events; he makes them spring out of the passions which heave in the bosom of man, out of the impulses which determine the nature of his joys and griefs.

¶"In the first scene of *Tannhäuser*, it is the will of man which, inasmuch as he breaks loose from one feeling and submits to the sway of another, suffices to call forth the marvellous situation. The school of Wagner is at present too young for any opinion to be pronounced on its future destiny, on the excellences which constitute its greatness, or the faults which will ultimately bring about its decline. For Art never stands still, but lives under successive forms as under so many tents, which are pitched and taken down again on the path to the Ideal. But even now, at the very rise of this school, there is ground for maintaining that it has become impossible any longer to create and carry out enduring works on the model of Scribe and Meyerbeer. The presentation of character, that first condition of perfection in tragedy, will henceforth be a necessity for the musical drama also. And this element makes the regeneration and creation of a declamatory style indispensable. Character manifests itself on the stage by words as well as actions; hence Wagner lays so much stress on the intrinsic beauty of the operative poem. [**Christoph Willibald**] **Glück** lent to dramatic music all the lustre, majesty, and weight of the declamatory style, while [**Niccolò**] **Piccini** held to the old faith, the main article of which was, that melodic expression sufficed for true rendering of feeling. Piccini appeared to have the advantage, and to carry general opinion with him, but Glück had planted the standard of a principle which was destined to be triumphant.

¶"In the mean time Rossini appeared like a meteor, and won all sympathies, especially those of the elegant world, to the old form of opera. Then, at a moment when the melodic and declamatory style stood in opposition, came Meyerbeer and combined the two; without rejecting melody, he gave declamation an important share in the merit of his works. Wagner has gone a step further, and so far from making melody an object, he rather rejoices when the melodic motives, which are treated by him in a declamatory and specially dramatic manner, are denied the name of melodies.

"This is Liszt's point of view, which, in the history scheme he sets forth, gives to Meyerbeer a far higher significance than I am disposed to grant. But for the present you may content yourself with Liszt's ingenious history, and the position which, according to him, Wagner is to fill in the history of art. In some future letter I may be able to say more of Wagner."

Westminster Review
April 1, 1855

Memoirs of the Court of Austria

(pp 303-35)

Geschichte des östreichischen Hofs and Adels unter der östreichischen Diplomatie, by Dr Eduard Vehse (11 vols., 1851-53)

Eliot comments on the censorship prevailing in Germany since 1848. It has the effect of increasing interest in the writings of less famous authors. She notes that "several of the German governments have had the *naiveté* to prohibit the volumes relating to their own court, and at the same time to admit the volumes relating to other courts —*Ognuno ama la gustizia nella casa d'altrui,* says the Italian proverb; in other words, 'We all think truth a good thing for our neighbours.' " Vehse is no hot democrat, but a moderate liberal, "and we must do him the justice to say that, so far as we are acquainted with his volumes, we trace in them no spirit of partisanship." 304
The article is intended to illustrate, "through the medium of such records, anecdotes, and sketches of character and manners, as Dr Vehse's work affords—the life and *personnel* of the Austrian court during the last three centuries." 305
The description of various ceremonies and festivals emphasizes the extravagance and poor taste of the emperors, and there are anecdotes of murders and other atrocities among the nobility. The murder of his gaming companion, **Count Hallweil**, to whom he had lost heavily, by the **Prince de Ligne** is given generous space.

" . . . readers who come to it with recollections of the piquancy of **St Simon** or **De Grammont**, the quaint interest of **Pepys**, the gossiping charm of **Walpole**, or the panoramic picturesqueness of **Macaulay**, will find but slight gratification from its pages. Dr Vehse pretends to no art in the presentation of his materials . . . [his] mosaic of extracts, combined as it is with lists of ministerial, diplomatic, and court officials, necessarily gives his volumes all the artistic disadvantages of mere compilations." 304-5

The Hapsburg Dynasty

" . . . perhaps there is no aristocracy whose antecedents present so much selfishness, venality, and unscrupulousness as that of Austria; no history which unfolds a more hideous course of misgovernment and persecution than that of the Imperial rule in Bohemia and Hungary. The dynastic interest of the House of Austria certainly served to knit together the forces of middle Europe so as to form a bulwark against Turkish invasion on the one hand and French domination on the other; but the details of its operation to this end are an almost unvaried tissue of the worst vices which belong to arbitrary government." 305

—*sea-change:* "The Peace of Westphalia, which terminated the Thirty Years' War, left the emperor in an entirely new relation to his aristocracy. Great numbers of the old hereditary nobles in Austria, Bohemia, and Hungary, had been proscribed on account of their Protestantism; and their places had been, to a great extent, taken by military adventurers and *parvenus*—Scotsmen, Spaniards, Walloons, and Italians—who had risen to prominence in the war. Many of the old nobility, indeed, did not hesitate to declare themselves converts to Catholicism for the sake of retaining their fortunes or winning advancement; but their position was thenceforth necessarily one of obligation to the court. Thus the chain of aristocratic families, which had once been able to defy the emperor, was broken. From this time, the list of Austrian nobility is variegated with Scotch, Spanish, Flemish, and Italian names—a means of amalgamation which is, probably, less objectionable in its result than in its origin.

"It is a striking fact in the history of Austria, that the German race has never furnished her most distinguished statesmen and generals. As diplomatists and statesmen, Sclavonians predominate; and among them are, perhaps, the two greatest—**Lobkowitz** and **Kaunitz**. Of her generals, **Tilly** was a Walloon, **Wallenstein** a Bohemian, **Eugene** and **Montecuculi** Italians, and **Loudon** of Scotch extraction." 312

Maximilian I

(1459-1519)

Holy Roman Emperor 1493-1519

"Max is one of the most bizarre figures in history. Mythical stories, which we may accept as a sort of loud reverberation of the truth, represent him as a **Hercules**, who could bend iron as if it were hemp; who went into the cage of a lion, wrenched open its mouth, and tore out its tongue; and who (rather gratuitously, as it seems) went to the summit of the minister at Ulm, and, standing on a thin iron bar, raised one leg into the air. He would play at letting off cannon against practised artillerymen; and was the best bowman, the best shot, the best huntsman of his time." 306

"He was full of wise saws and repartees, and many a *bon-mot* which old-fashioned jest-books attribute to the **Duke of Marlborough** or one of our own **Georges**, had Max for at least an earlier putative father. Some of these *mots* are epigrams on the nothingness of rank, yet no one had a stronger genealogical mania or adopted more sounding titles. He was determined, he said, to 'outbrag **Julius Cæsar**, and at all events to have **Charlemagne** for his ancestor.' " 307

Charles V
(1500-1558)
Holy Roman Emperor 1519-56

"To the gay eccentric Max, succeeded his grave, stern grandson, Charles V. Of all great potentates who, according to the Persian compliment, have had 'the sun for their hat,' Charles is to us the least attractive. A hero with a sallow complexion and no teeth, a melancholy debauchee, in whom the demon of gout takes turn with the demon of asthma; a non-masticating gourmand, who in his dyspeptic after-dinner hours amuses himself with dwarfs and court fools; and a bigot withal, plagued with religious terrors, always sinning and always trembling—[he] presents a most uncomfortable sample of Imperial majesty." 307

"Charles, however, had some of the elements of greatness—a deep penetration into men, an iron strength of will, and a proud directness, which made him despise flattery . . . . He had an eye for genius of all kinds; and not only, like every other great commander, chose his generals well, but could tell a nobleman to hold the ladder for **Titian**." 307

"He was a Spaniard by nature; and under him began that inoculation of German awkwardness with Spanish hauteur, which characterized the manners of the Austrian court during two centuries." 308

Vesalius. "One of [**Charles V**'s] physicians was the great Vesalius, the father of modern anatomy, the first who dissected a *human* body; and it is an interesting example of genius co-operating with genius, that **Titian** helped Vesalius in producing the illustrations to his great anatomi l work." 308

Ferdinand I
Holy Roman emperor 1558-64
(Charles V's brother; GE states he became Emperor in 1556)

" . . . Ferdinand was by compulsion tolerant, though he was a bigoted Catholic, and had a Jesuit for his confessor." 309

Maximilian II
Holy Roman Emperor 1564-76
(son of Ferdinand I)

"[He] was tolerant by choice. He was a liberal-minded, strong-hearted man, who had little of the Hapsburg in him besides the gout, which seems to have been so inevitable an attribute of Imperial majesty in those days, that courtiers could hardly have hit on a more delicate mode of flattery than swathing their limbs in flannel and hobbling. During Maximilian's short reign, Austria enjoyed the last good government it ever saw under the house of Hapsburg. His successors down to **Maria Theresa** were a compound in different proportions of the virtuoso and the bigot." 309

Rudolf II
Holy Roman Emperor 1576-1612

"In Rudolf II, the next emperor, the virtuoso predominated; and throughout his reign of thirty-six years he neglected all the business of government to shut himself up in his palace, the Hradshin at Prague, in company with his coins and pictures, his pet lions, leopards and eagles, his mechanics, alchemists, and magicians . . . he was acquainted with six languages, was versed in mathematical, mechanical, and physical science, and yet more in astrology, magic, and alchemy . . . he spent immense sums on antiquities of all kinds . . . . " 309

Marco Bragadino. "To Prague came also the 'Illustrissimus' Marco Bragadino, with his two bull-dogs, supposed to be familiar spirits. He was honoured as a second **Paracelsus,** especially as he seemed to esteem gold no more than brass or quicksilver, made great presents, and kept open table. The 'Illustrissimus,' however, died on the gallows." 310

John Dee "drove the black art with such success, that he could boast of always seeing his genius, when he left his desk, obligingly sit down in his place and carry on his studies; when he returned, he had only to tap his genius on the shoulder, and it stood up." 310

Edward Kelley "paid dearly for the honour which Rudolf bestowed on him in making him a Freiherr (Baron) of Bohemia; for, finding that he could not or would not make gold, Rudolf imprisoned him in a Bohemian castle, where he lay for six years. Queen Elizabeth applied for his release in vain; and at last, in an attempt to escape by a rope, the unfortunate alchemist broke his leg, and died in consequence of the fall."

Matthias

Holy Roman Emperor 1612-19

(in whose favour Rudolf was deposed)

"[He] was a lover of pleasures, and his court was gay with festivals and spectacles . . . . It is characteristic that in a contemporary description of a wedding, when 294 guests were invited and 141 assembled, [and] 'neither curses nor unseemly speech was heard from any one, nor was there any excessive drinking' . . . the floor fell in, and the gay ladies and gallant gentlemen had to be extricated from dust, beams, and mortar . . . . Before the reign of Matthias closed, the first scene in the terrible tragedy of the Thirty Years' War was acted. Two Catholic noblemen, the representatives of the emperor at Prague, were hurled out at window by the deputies of the exasperated Protestants, who had been forbidden to continue the building of their churches. This was the famous *Defenestratio Pragensis* of 1618. On the 20th of March in the next year, the insignificant Matthias died; an event which was regarded as a marvellous fulfilment of **Kepler**'s prophecy, with the seven M's for the year 1618:—Magnus Monarcha Mundi Medio Mense Martii Morietur: such is the tribute which great men must pay to the spirit of their age!" 311

Ferdinand II

Holy Roman Emperor 1619-37

—devout: " 'Better a wilderness than a land full of heretics,' was the favourite saying of Ferdinand II, who had early made a vow to our Lady of Loretto and the Pope, that he would restore the Catholic religion. The aspect of the court must have been anything but lively in his day, with an emperor at the head of it whose most important occupation was hearing masses, and assisting, with bare head and taper in hand, at religious pilgrimages." 311-2

Ferdinand III

Holy Roman Emperor 1637-58

—devout: "His son, Ferdinand III, inherited his spirit, and further distinguished himself by his zeal for the doctrine of the Immaculate Conception, though he had not, like us, had the edification of seeing it established on papal authority." 312

Leopold I

Holy Roman Emperor 1658-1705

(GE has him succeeding in 1657)

"[He] reigned nearly half a century, [and] had bigotry enough to merit the epithet 'Great' from the Jesuits; but this dark background was relieved by a gay embroidery of virtuosism, love of sports, and splendour." 312

"Twenty years later, this engaging youth had matured into a little man, still lax as to his mouth, of mumbling speech and weak legs, crushed beneath a huge perruque, and dressed, after the Spanish fashion, with red shoes and stockings. In devotion he was not behind even **Ferdinand II**; he heard three masses a day, and was persuaded that he was under a special supernatural guidance." 313

"This 'Leopoldus Magnus' limited his activity in state affairs to signing the papers presented to him by his ministers, writing confidential letters to his brothers and cousins on the thrones of Europe, and giving audiences." 313

"Leopold's great passion was music. He played on several instruments, and often conducted the orchestra from his box at the opera . . . . The world, however, is really indebted to the musical taste hereditary in the House of Hapsburg; the Imperial Kapelle at Vienna, always kept up on a high scale of magnificence, has been a nursery for the highest music, and has furnished a *point d'appui* for the genius of such men as **Caldara**, **Gluck**, **Moza**rt, and **Beethoven**. The **Ferdinand**s had only patronized church music, but Leopold was an enthusiastic admirer of the opera; and under him representations were got up in a lavish style." 314

Lobkowitz. "The most remarkable man among **Leopold**'s ministers was Lobkowitz, who held high posts for more than thirty years, and for a long time had almost unbounded influence over the Emperor. In many points Lobkowitz resembled his great successor, **Kaunitz**: he loved luxury and splendour, was full of caustic repartee, and had a strong liking for France and French fashions. He was inwardly opposed to the league with the maritime powers against France, which formed the policy of Leopold's reign; and this probably was the real cause of his fall.

"To the Jesuits, in spite of their formidable power, he was an open foe, and directed the arrows of his wit against them without fear or scruple. Leopold was completely in the grasp of the Jesuits, and could deny [them] nothing. Lobkowitz, however, obviated several of his foolish gifts; for example, on one occasion, when the Emperor had made the Society a grant of the important Grafschaft of Glatz, the determined minister tore up the document, and when the Jesuits came to him to receive the parchment, he showed them a crucifix, and pointing to the letters I. N. R. I., he interpreted them to mean, *Jam nihil reportabunt Jesuitæ.* 'This time the Jesuits will carry away nothing.'

"Even in his will he prepared a final sting for them. After an apparently decent preamble, at the bottom of a page he bequeathed to the Fathers of the Society of Jesus 82,000—here the leaf had to be turned over, and on the other side followed—'nails towards a new building.'

"To the bitter enemies whom Lobkowitz thus made for himself he had imprudently added a woman and an empress—**Claudia of Tyrol**, Leopold's second wife. Their united intrigues, together with his opposition to the French war, at length brought about his disgrace: he was suddenly deprived of all his employments, forbidden to ask the reason, and banished to his country house, where he gratified his sarcastic humour by having a room furnished half with princely splendour, and half as a miserable hut; in the one half he commemorated his former elevation, in the other, on the walls of which he wrote satires and epigrams on his enemies, he indicated his utter fall." ¶318

Montecuculi. "The ablest military commander in the earlier part of **Leopold**'s reign was Montecuculi, celebrated for his victories over the Turks and his 'Memoire della Guerra.' Like **Eugene**, who near the close of the same reign commenced a similar and yet more brilliant career as generalissimo of the Imperial army against the French and the Turks, Montecuculi was a statesman, a philosopher, and a man of letters, as well as a great general." 318

Conte Ruggiero, "whose full title was a mosaic of three languages—Don Dominico Manuel Caëtano, Comte de Ruggiero, Neapolitano, Kurbairischer Feldmarschall und Statsrath—had a salary of 15,000 gulden *en attendant* the preparation of a certain tincture which was to do the work of **Midas**'s fingers. But before the tincture was prepared, **Leopold** died." 316

John Sobiesky, "king of Poland, who had joined his forces to the Austrians under the **Duke of Lorraine**, and had posted himself on the neighbouring heights. The evening before, a note from **Starhemberg**, who commanded in Vienna, and a shower of rockets from the tower of St Stephen's, had given the signal that 'no time was to be lost;' and the answering rockets and cannon from John Sobiesky had thrown the Viennese into an ecstasy of joy. With the first rays of the sun the troops poured down from the heights, and the city which had so long been the outwork of Christendom was saved." 315

"No sooner had it been known that the Turks were approaching Vienna, than Leopold had fled in terror with his family. That he returned in peace and safety he owed to John Sobiesky; yet when he was about to meet the deliverer of his capitol, his grand preoccupation was, how he should compliment the King of Poland without compromising his Imperial dignity . . . Leopold behaved with the most repulsive coldness. Sobiesky, indignant, wrote to his wife: 'Any one would think now that we had the plague, and people were afraid to come near us; while before the battle my tents which, thank God, are tolerably roomy, could scarcely hold the multitude of comers. . . . Every one is disheartened, and wishes we had never helped the Emperor; so that this proud race might have been overthrown, never to rise again.' " 315-6

Count Sporck. "One of the next to [**Montecuculi**] in command was Count Sporck, who was a type of the tribe of military adventurers and *parvenus* fostered by the Thirty Years' War—a mixture of the rudeness and ignorance of the common soldier, the instincts of an able commander, and the astuteness of a man of the world who can push his way to fortune, make money, and keep it. In the battle of St Gothard, when Montecuculi commanded the last attack on the Turks, Sporck knelt down and prayed thus: 'Almighty Generalissimo above, if thou will not to-day help us, thy believing children, at least do not help the Turkish dogs, and it shall be the better for thee!' " 318-9

Joseph I

"Joseph I, who lived only six years after his accession, was not without sense and spirit. He had been brought up by men who were no friends to the Jesuits, and he was the first emperor, since the institution of the Order, who had not a Jesuit for his confessor. This was by no means satisfactory to the fathers of the Society; they accused the confessor to the Pope of being more devoted to the Emperor than to the Vatican, and he was cited to appear at Rome. Hereupon Joseph declared, that 'If his confessor must go to Rome, he should not go without plentiful companionship, for all the Jesuits in the Austrian dominions should go with him!' The Pope gave way to this energetic threat." 320-1

Charles VI

"Charles VI had spent eight years of his youth in Spain, and had come back with a double incrustation of Spanish hauteur overlaying his Austrian phlegm . . . . It seems indeed that he had the smallest possible liking for our country and ways, for notwithstanding the cordial reception given him by **Queen Anne**, and the rows of young ladies who stood like a grove of dahlias and hollyhocks lining the way to his apartment, he hurried away from Windsor the next day . . . . " 321

"In person and in taste Charles was very nearly a reproduction of his father, Leopold I; he inherited the thin legs, the hanging lip, the confused utterance, and the love for hunting and music. The bigotry in him was of rather a milder cast, owing perhaps to his travels and his intercourse with Englishmen and Hollanders; but all the hatred he economised on heretics he gave to the French." 321

Prince Eugene. "Far above all other men at **Charles**'s court, like an oak among brambles, was Prince Eugene, one of the seven generals whose genius **Napoleon** declared to be worth studying, a far-sighted and liberal-minded statesman, a student as well as a patron of art and science, and an ingenuous, unaffected, and warm-hearted man. The youngest of the five sons of **Olympia Mancini**, one of **Mazarin**'s celebrated nieces, he was brought up at the French court, but was looked on with little favour by **Louis Quatorze**, who made the great mistake of refusing him a military commission, which he had asked for as a substitute for ecclesiastical dignities. On his refusal, Eugene left France, declaring that he would not set foot there again but with sword in hand as an enemy, a threat which nine years later he fulfilled. Louis thus made the fatal blunder of unconsciously presenting his enemy Austria with the greatest general she ever possessed." 324-5

"**Charles**, however, never heartily liked his great general, and only endured the predominance which his achievements and character made inevitable. But unmindful of coldness and jealousies, happy in his own activity, in his correspondence with men of science, his collections, and his buildings, as well as his political projects, he remained, to the good old age of seventy-three . . . . For a quarter of a century he had scarcely ever failed, when in Vienna, to spend his evening at the **Duchess of Holstein**'s, where he met his beloved friend the **Countess Batthiany**, or at the Countess's own house. His well-known horses, with their rose-coloured harness, might be seen in the last years of his life, finding their way from his palace to the hôtel of the beautiful Countess, and standing still at the door, though for some time no one got down; for the aged servants were asleep outside the carriage, and their aged master asleep within." 325

Maria Theresa

"With **Charles VI**, the male line of the House of Hapsburg terminated, and his daughter Maria Theresa, by her marriage, introduced what is called the House of Lorraine. Under Maria Theresa the thick ice of Austrian etiquette began to thaw. Her proud and high spirit was tempered with a certain bourgeoise good nature; the troubles which surrounded her on her accession compelled her to court popularity, and the predilections of her husband, added to the alliance with France which was ultimately brought about by **Kaunitz**, helped to introduce French fashions and the French language." 325-6

"But her mother-wit and strength of character secured for her a personal influence which no mere acquirements can obtain; perhaps, also, she owed some of her ascendency to her beauty, which, as pictures and the less questionable testimony of eye-witnesses assure us, was imperial. It was a tall, luxuriant, Gothic beauty, with blue eyes, magnificent blond hair, and admirable hands and arms . . . . She was the most intrepid of horse-women, and won the enthusiastic affection of her troops by showing herself among them continually, bestowing marked distinction on military merit, and giving liberal largesses." 326

"Her most fatal weakness was bigotry. It led her into the wretched mistakes of pensioning converts to Catholicism, and forcing the children of Protestant parents into conventual education and Catholic marriages . . . . She was equally tyrannical in morals, and visited aberrations with a severity almost as inquisitorial as that of the English Puritans . . . . In spite of her active and temperate habits, she became so corpulent as she advanced in life, that all movement was difficult to her, and she was conveyed up and down stairs in a machine." 328

Francis, consort of the empress. "She would allow her husband no share in the direction of affairs, she even checked him in the presence of her council, for giving his opinion on business of which he knew nothing . . . his natural inclination to gallantry led him into flirtations with the fair ladies of the court. Francis was a handsome, fascinating, easy-tempered man, affectionate, temperate, free from bigotry, and a hater of constraint and etiquette. His education had been so neglected that he could barely read and write, but he had abundant sense, had travelled much in Germany, France, Italy, and England, and had a taste for art. His talent at calculation he turned to practical account, not only by conducting profitable speculations for himself, but by exposing many financial abuses in the state. Maria Theresa at once domineered over him and doated on him." 326-7

Gluck "was an especial favourite with [**Kaunitz**]; and the great composer often showed his broad, scarred, manly face in the minister's circle, where he must have looked very much like a rough shepherd's dog among the sleek pets of the drawing-room." 330

Kaunitz, "the soul and right hand of Maria Theresa's policy, was so highly valued by her that she tolerated the licence of his life, which he took no pains to conceal from her. He one day put a stop to an incipient lecture on this subject, by saying, 'Madam, I came here to speak on your affairs, not mine.' In his efforts towards an alliance with France he won her hearty co-operation . . . . Kaunitz had more difficulty in winning over the Empress to his second great scheme, the expulsion of the Jesuits . . . . At length the discovery that her confessions had been revealed by her Jesuit confessor, and other secrets of the Order which Kaunitz had become possessed of through an apostate, prevailed, and the edict for their expulsion was signed in 1772.

"These two wise measures of Kaunitz were more than counterbalanced by his co-operation in the partition of Poland, into which he was cajoled by the flattery of **Frederick the Great**. It is honourable to the judgment of Maria Theresa that she saw at once the impolicy and the moral turpitude of this measure." ¶329

"Indeed, this acute diplomatist, who was all his life occupied in piercing the minds of other men, had a colossal vanity and self-valuation that made him appear quite *naive*. 'Heaven,' he used to say, 'requires a hundred years in order to produce a mind great enough to restore a monarchy. Then it rests a hundred years; this makes me fear for the Austrian monarchy after my death.' The **Prince de Ligne** heard him say to a Russian, who was presented to him: I advise you, Sir, to buy my portrait, for your countrymen will be glad to become acquainted with the person of a man who for fifteen years governed this monarchy as its greatest minister; who knows everything, understands everything, and *sits better on horseback than any man of his time.*' " 329-30

"[He] thought himself entitled to exact no slight deference from artists, as well as from the rest of the world. When the **Archduke Leopold** was about to be married at Innspruck, Kaunitz went there before hand to see that all was in order for the festivities. The opera, above all things, was the object of his attention; and when **Gluck** assured him that everything was in perfect preparation, 'Good,' said Kaunitz, 'let the opera be at once performed.' 'How!' exclaimed Glück, 'without an audience?' 'Monsieur Gluck,' answered the minister, 'sachez que la qualité vaut bien la quantité; je suis moi seul une audience.' " 330

Joseph II

"When Joseph II was eight-and-twenty, **Frederick the Great** passed this significant judgment on him: 'He has grown up at a bigoted court, and has rejected superstition; he has been brought up in splendour, and has adopted simple habits; he has been nourished on incense, and is nevertheless modest.' An emperor filled with enthusiasm for the general well-being, a venerator of **Rousseau**, an asserter of right in opposition to privilege, was indeed a new apparition on the throne of the Hapsburgs." 332

"To the lavishness of **Maria Theresa**'s reign was substituted the utmost economy in every department. Joseph's personal habits were simple and laborious: he rose at five, and devoted his whole morning to work . . . so that his dinner, prepared for two o'clock, was often, to the anguish of cooks, kept waiting till four. His chief amusements were music,—for which he had considerable talent, writing a sonata, which **Mozart** told him, was 'good, though he who composed it was better'—the theatre, travelling *incognito,* and conversation." 333

"Joseph had a feverish impetuosity, a haste to set everything right, which was often self-defeating, and made **Frederick the Great** say of him, that 'he always took the second step before the first.' But, as if to justify this haste, death soon came to put an end to his noble efforts." 333

Leopold II

"The two years of [**Joseph**'s] feeble and dissolute brother Leopold's reign, from 1790 to 1792, were made memorable by the declaration of war against France . . . . " 334

Francis II

[**Leopold**'s two years] "were followed by the long reign of Francis II, who, in that notable shuffling of the cards known as the Congress of Vienna, dropped the venerable but long unmeaning title, 'Emperor of Germany,' and be me 'Emperor of Austria.' Francis's affectation of the Viennese dialect, his professed interest in the private affairs of his citizens, his ostentatious observance of trivial laws, and his will, in which he bequeathed his love to his people, and promised to 'pray for them at the throne of God,' prevailed on some of his credulous subjects to believe that the virtual gaoler of **Spielberg**, the man who imprisoned **Pellico** and **Gonfalonieri**, and who betrayed **Hofer**, was a kind soul—a people's emperor. Civil crimes, such as murder, theft, and swindling, he often pardoned, but towards political crimes he was implacable; and he said of himself, 'I am a bad Christian at pardoning—that is hard work for me; **Metternich** is much milder.' " 334

Metternich. "On the high priest of these wooden Dagons, Metternich, we have not space to dwell. Those who watched the earlier part of his career, saw no prognostics that he was to become, like **Kaunitz**, 'the coachman of Europe,' and keep the reins for nearly forty years." 334-5

Other Historical Figures Mentioned

[for literary, musical, and mythological figures, see Index XI]

Three Months in Weimar

[pp 153-68 in the 1894 Crowell ed.; citations are to pages]

A travelogue begins with a sleepy arrival by rail at Weimar, followed by disappointing first impressions of the town's dull sleepiness and an absence of any picturesqueness. Could **Goethe** have stood it here? We are given a tour of **Schiller**'s and Goethe's houses and of the **Herder** Platz. We hear of the confectioner **Rabenhorst**, a rogue who, we suggest, inspired **David Faux** in GE's short story "Brother Jacob," written five years later. GE expresses contentment over peaceful scenery and pleasant walking.

Weimar

—*nature:* "To any one who loves Nature in her gentle aspects, who delights in the checkered shade on a summer morning, and in a walk on the corn-clad upland at sunset, within sight of a little town nestled among the trees below, I say—come to Weimar." 154

—*populace:* "The inhabitants seemed to us to have more than the usual heaviness of *Germanity;* even their stare was slow, like that of herbivorous quadrupeds." 154

—*the Belvedere grounds:* "The inexhaustible charm of Belvedere, however, is the grounds, which are laid out with a taste worthy of a first-rate landscape-gardener. The tall and graceful limes, plane-trees, and weeping birches, the little basins of water here and there, with fountains playing in the middle of them, and with a fringe of broad-leaved plants, or other tasteful bordering round them, the gradual descent towards the river, and the hill clothed with firs and pines on the opposite side, forming a fine dark background for the various and light foliage of the trees that ornament the gardens—all this we went again and again to enjoy, from the time when everything was of a vivid green until the Virginian creepers which festooned the silver-stems of the birches were bright scarlet, and the touch of autumn had turned all the green to gold." 165-6

Goethe. "One's first feeling was, How could Goethe live here in this dull, lifeless village? The reproaches cast on him for his worldliness and attachment to Court splendor seemed ludicrous enough, and it was inconceivable that the stately Jupiter, in a frock-coat, so familiar to us all through **Rauch**'s statuette, could have habitually walked along these rude streets and among these slouching mortals." 154

Rabenhorst. "Our landlady's husband was called the '*süsser* Rabenhorst,' by way of distinguishing him from a brother of his who was the reverse of sweet. This Rabenhorst, who was not sweet, but who nevertheless dealt in sweets, for he was a confectioner, was so utter a rogue that any transaction with him was avoided almost as much as if he had been the Evil One himself, yet so clever a rogue that he always managed to keep on the windy side of the law. Nevertheless, he had so many dainties in the confectionery line—*so viel Süssigkeiten und Leckerbissen*—that people bent on giving a fine entertainment were at last constrained to say, 'After all, I must go to Rabenhorst', and so he got abundant custom, in spite of general detestation." 162

We may be the first to observe that GE's inspiration for the despicable David Faux in "Brother Jacob" is likely to have been Herr Rabenhorst.

Also mentioned

[relatively important historical or literary figures are in Index X or XI]

Amalia, Duchess; mother of Karl-August	166
Bettina, sculptor who designed a monumental statue of Goethe	156
Carl August, Grand Duke of Weimar	155
Dannecker, with a bust of Schiller	158
Jacobi, a German author denounced by Goethe for his "Voldemar"	167
Duke Karl-Friedrich, the late	166
Kestner, correspondent of Goethe's	163
Körner, correspondent of Schiller's	160
Loder, comparative anatomist from Jena	158
Prince Pückler Muskau	167
Rauch, sculptor of a famous statuette of Goethe	154
Schaller, sculptor of a statue of Herder	160
Schwanthaler, with a portrait of Goethe	159
Stieler, with a portrait of Goethe	159
Trippel, sculptor with a bust of Goethe	158
Frau von Stein, a correspondent of Goethe's	163
Winterberger, an actor who knew Goethe well	159

Menander and the Greek Comedy

Ménandre: Etude historique et littéraire sur la Comédie et la Société Grecques, by M. Guillaume Guizot

"Those are pleasant epochs in our lives when what has hitherto been a mere name for us becomes the centre for a group of pleasant and fertile ideas—when, for instance, our travels bring us to some southern village which we have only known before as a mark in our map, and from that day forth the glowing sun, a cluster of tall trees with tame goats browsing on the park of grass beneath them, and a large stone fountain where dark-complexioned women are filling their pitchers—or when Mr. A. B., whose name we have seen in the visiting-book of an hotel, becomes the definite image of a capital fellow, whose pleasant talk has beguiled a five hours' journey in a diligence, and who turns out to be a man very much like ourselves, with dubious theories, still more dubious hopes, and quite indubitable sorrows.

¶"And there is the same sort of pleasure in getting something like a new conception of an ancient author, whose name has all our life belonged to that inventory of unknown things which so much of our youth is taken up in learning. If we may suppose that to any of our readers Menander has hitherto thus remained a mere *nominis umbra,* let such readers to M. Guillaume Guizot's very agreeable volume, and they will learn, without the least trouble to themselves, all that scholarly research has hitherto been able to discover of Menander and his writings. It is true that all the preliminary hard work had been done by **Meineke**, for what hard work in the way of historical research and criticism has *not* been done by Germans? They are the purveyors of the raw material of learning for all Europe; but, as Mr T—— suggests, raw materials require to be cooked, and in this kind of cookery, as well as in the other, the French are supreme. To have the Latin words of a German writer *boiled down* to a portable bulk and served up in that precious crystal vessel, the French language, is a benefit that will be appreciated by those who are at all acquainted with the works of Germans, and still more by those who are *not* acquainted with Latin. This is the service rendered buy M. Guillaume Guizot, and the way in which he has performed it surely merits, as it has won, the prize of the French Academy. It is a double pleasure to welcome a young author when he is an exception to that melancholy generalization, that great fathers have insignificant sons; and we think this book on Menander gives some promise that we may one day have to speak familiarly of Guizot the Elder, lest our hearers should confound an illustrious father with an illustrious son.

"In the first chapter of this work, which is only an octavo of about 450 pages, we have the history of Menander's reputation and writings:—the abundant jealousy and the sparing justice awarded him by his contemporaries, his long reign as a 'dead but sceptred monarch' over the comic stage, first of Athens and then of Rome, the almost total destruction of his works, first through the bigotry of Byzantine priests and subsequently through the oblivion of Greek literature in the middle ages, and lastly the awakened interest about his works on the revival of learning, when scholars, amongst whom it is interesting to know that **Grotius** was one, began to collect the fragments—the *disjecti membra poëtae*. In the second chapter M. Guizot presents all the accessible details concerning Menander's life and character, details which may be summed up under his early but not unquestioned success as a dramatist, his friendship for **Epicurus** and **Theophrastus**, his addiction to pleasure in general, and to the pleasure of loving **Glycera** in particular . . . .

¶"The third chapter discusses the Subjects of the Drama in the three periods of Greek comedy: the ancient period, when its main object was political satire, a form of comedy peculiar to Greece, and made immortal by the genius of Aristophanes; the middle period, when its subjects ceased to be political and became purely social, but when the manners were chiefly caricature and the characters conventional types, corresponding in many respects to the early comedies of **Molière**; and the new period, when it became what the highest modern comedy is, a picture of real domestic life and manners. Of this last species of comedy, Menander was, by the common consent of critics subsequent to his own age, the greatest master Greece ever produced; and the simple statement of this fact is enough to indicate how great a loss is the destruction of his comedies to those who care about a knowledge of Greek life; for **Terence**, while appropriating the plots and characters and poetry of Menander, threw away all that was specifically Greek and substituted what was specifically Roman. The succeeding chapters on the plot, the characters, the sentiments, and the passions in the Greek drama of the three periods are really fascinating, from the skill with which M. Guizot weaves together his materials and the judgment with which he chooses his illustrative extracts. . . ."

GE discusses the status of women in 300 B.C., as reflected in the "fragments" of Menander still extant (it was better than at many subsequent times) and that of cooks, who had an excessively high opinion of their own importance but could deceive their employers with great cleverness on occasion. Guizot lists "no fewer than seven hundred and fifty-seven aphorisms, which are preserved to us in greater abundance than other fragments, because they were collected as 'beauties' by ancient scholars. Very grave and very melancholy some of these moral sentences are, but probably an equal number of sad and serious sayings might be culled from Molière."

"Among the fragments of Menander there are some passages of elegiac sadness; for example: 'O Parmeno, I call him a happy man, nay, the happiest of all men, who soon returns to the place whence he came, after having contemplated, without sorrow, the magnificence of this world, the sun that everywhere diffuses its beams, the stars, the ocean, the clouds and fire; whether he lives an age or only a few short years, this spectacle will always be the same: never will he see one more sublime. Think of life as a fair, where man arrives like a wayfarer: tumult, market, thieves, games of chance and amusements! If thou set out first for the place of halting and repose, thou wilt be the better provided for the end of the journey, and thou wilt go without having made enemies. But he who late in the day falls into poverty—a wretched old man, weary, disenchanted, and ruined—loses his way, and meets nothing but hatred and snares: a long life leads not to a gentle death.'

"But perhaps we are dwelling a little too long on this subject of Menander and Greek Comedy—we should rather say flitting about it a little too long. Let us hope, however, that we have dwelt enough on it to persuade the reader that he will find in M. Guizot's book a masterly treatment of a subject which has a really human and not merely a scholarly interest."

GE included a note on Guizot's book in BL 1.

Fraser's Magazine LII
July 1855 **LW**

Liszt, Wagner, and Weimar

(pp 48-62)

[This caption was not used in the reprinted version, which combined the June and July installments under "Three Months in Weimar."]

Franz Liszt

"Most London concert-goers, for whom Liszt has 'blazed the comet of a season,' think of him as certainly the archimagus of pianists, but as otherwise a man of no particular significance; as merely an erratic, flighty, artistic genius, who has swept through Europe, the Napoleon of the *salon,* carrying devastation into the hearts of countesses. A single morning's interview with him is enough to show the falsity of this conception. In him Nature has not sacrificed the man to the artist; rather, as the blossom of the acacia is a glorious ornament to the tree, but we see it fall without regret because the tree itself is grand and beautiful, so if Liszt the pianist were unknown to you, or even did not exist, Liszt the man would win your admiration and love. See him for a few hours and you will be charmed by the originality of his conversation and the brilliancy of his wit; know him for weeks or months, and you will discern in him a man of various thought, of serious purpose, and of a moral nature which, in its mingled strength and gentleness, has the benignest influence on those around him.

"The lovers of characteristic heads could hardly have a more interesting study than the head of Liszt. No wonder **Ary Scheffer** is fond of painting him, and that the type of Liszt's face seems to haunt this artist in so many of his compositions. I never saw features having at once so strong and clear an outline and so rich a gamut of expression; at one moment you think what a capital face he has for a witch in *Macbeth,* with knitted brow and preternatural grey light in his eyes; at another, with head thrown back and nostril dilated, he suggests a prophet in the moment of inspiration: and then again, seated placidly silent amidst a group of gay talkers, he is a perfect model of a **St John**. Scheffer has seized something of the second expression in a picture in which he expressly intended to introduce an idealization of Liszt. The picture represents the three Magi, two of whom are venerable bearded sages watching with a bent head the third—a young man in the likeness of Liszt—who is gazing in ecstasy at the guiding light above them. In Liszt, of course, there is baser metal mingled with the fine gold; and besides this natural alloy, there is the tarnish contracted in a life spent in the midst of adulation. Even an ordinary man has to pass through so many 'mud baths' before he reaches his fortieth year, and some of the mud will become ingrained in the process. But, take him all in all, he is a glorious creature—one of those men whom the ancients would have imagined the son of a god or goddess, from their superiority to the common clay of humanity." 48

Richard Wagner

" . . . I may say that, though unable to recognise Herr Wagner's compositions as the ideal of the opera, and though, with a few slight exceptions, not deeply affected by his music on a first hearing, it is difficult for me to understand how any one who finds deficiencies in the opera as it has existed hitherto, can give fair attention to Wagner's theory, and his exemplification of it in his operas, without admitting that he has pointed out the direction in which the lyric drama must develope itself, if it is to be developed at all. Moreover, the musician who writes librettos for himself, which can be read with interest as dramatic poems, must be a man of no ordinary mind and accomplishments, and such a man, even when he errs, errs with ingenuity, so that his mistakes are worth studying.

"Wagner would make the opera a perfect musical drama, in which feelings and situations spring out of *character,* as in the highest order of tragedy, and in which no dramatic probability or poetic beauty is sacrificed to musical effect. The drama must not be a mere pretext for the music; but music, drama, and spectacle must be blended, like the coloured rays in the sunbeam, so as to produce one undivided impression. The controversy between him and his critics is the old controversy between Gluck and Piccini, between the declamatory and melodic schools of music, with the same difference in comprehensiveness as between the disputes of **La Motte** and the **Dacier**s about the value of the classics, and the disputes of the classical and romantic schools of literature in our own day."

"If it were admissible for a person entirely without technical qualifications for judgment, to give an opinion on Wagner as a musician, I should say that his musical inspiration is not sufficiently predominant over his thinking and poetical power, for him to have the highest creative genius in music. So far as music is an art, one would think that the same rule applied to musicians as to other artists. Now, the greatest painters and sculptors have surely not been those who have been inspired through their intellect, who have first thought and then chosen a plastic symbol for their thought; rather, the symbol rushes in on their imagination before their slower reflection has seized any abstract idea embodied in it."

"Certainly Wagner has admirably fulfilled his own requisition of organic unity in the opera. In his operas there is a gradual unfolding and elaboration of that fundamental contrast of emotions, that collision of forces, which is the germ of the tragedy; just as the leaf of the plant is successively elaborated into branching stem and compact bud and radiant corolla. The artifice, however, of making certain contrasted strains of melody run like coloured threads through the woof of an opera, and also the other dramatic device of using a particular melody or musical phrase as a sort of Ahnung or prognostication of the approach or action of a particular character, are not altogether peculiar to Wagner, though he lays especial stress on them as his own."

GE hates *Lohengrin* but likes the Dutchman and *Tannhäuser*. She tells the story of each, with commentary.

"Of these three operas, we heard the *Fliegender Holländer* to the greatest advantage, from the fact that the principal man's part, being a baritone, was filled by an excellent artist—**Herr Milde**. His wife sang admirably, as the heroine in each of the operas; but *Tannhäuser* and *Lohengrin* absolutely demand a tenor with a voice, and the first tenor at Weimar had only 'intentions.' "

The Morality of Wilhelm Meister

(page 703)

"Perhaps Mr Lewes's *Life of Goethe,* which we now see advertised, may throw some new light on the structure and purpose of the much-debated novel—*Wilhelm Meister's Apprenticeship.* In the meantime, we are tempted by the appearance of a new translation to give the opinion which our present knowledge enables us to form on one or two aspects of this many-sided work.

"Ask nineteen out of twenty moderately educated persons what they think of *Wilhelm Meister,* and the answer will probably be—'I think it an immoral book; and besides, it is awfully dull: I was not able to read it' . . . .

"But is *Wilhelm Meister* an immoral book? We think not: on the contrary, we think that it appears immoral to some minds because its morality has a grander orbit than any which can be measured by the calculations of the pulpit and of ordinary literature. Goethe, it is sometimes said, seems in this book to be almost destitute of moral bias: he shows no hatred of bad actions, no warm sympathy with good ones; he writes like a passionless Mejnour,* to whom all human things are interesting only as objects of intellectual contemplation. But we question whether the direct exhibition of a moral bias in the writer will make a book really moral in its influence. Try this on the first child that asks you to tell it a story. As long as you keep to an apparently impartial narrative of facts you will have earnest eyes fixed on you in rapt attention, but no sooner do you begin to betray symptoms of an intention to moralise, or to turn the current of facts towards a personal application, than the interest of your hearer will slacken, his eyes will wander, and the moral dose will be doubly distasteful from the very sweet-meat in which you have attempted to insinuate it.

¶"One good reason of this is, that the child is aware you are talking *for it* instead of *from yourself,* so that instead of carrying it along in a stream of sympathy with your own interest in the story, you give it the impression of contriving coldly and talking artificially. Now, the moralising novelist produces the same effect on his mature readers; an effect often heightened by the perception that the moralising is rather intended to make his book eligible for family reading than prompted by any profound conviction or enthusiasm. Just as far from being really moral is the so-called moral *dénouement,* in which rewards and punishments are distributed according to those notions of justice on which the novel-writer would have recommended that the world should be governed if he had been consulted at the creation. The emotion of satisfaction which a reader feels when the villain of the book dies of some hideous disease, or is crushed by a railway train, is no more essentially moral than the satisfaction which used to be felt in whipping culprits at the cart-tail. So we dismiss the charge of immorality against *Wilhelm Meister* on these two counts—the absence of moral bias in the mode of narration, and the comfortable issues allowed to questionable actions and questionable characters.

"But there is another ground for the same accusation which involves deeper considerations. It is said that some of the scenes and incidents are such as the refined moral taste of these days will not admit to be proper subjects for art, that to depict irregular relations in all the charms they really have for human nature, and to associate lovely qualities with vices which society makes a brand of outlawry, implies a toleration which is at once a sign and a source of perverted moral sentiment. Wilhelm's relation to Mariana, and the charm which the reader is made to feel in the lawless Philina, many incidents that occur during Wilhelm's life with the players, and the stories of Lothario's loves in the present, preterite, and future, are shocking to the prevalent English. It is no answer to this objection to say—what is the fact—that Goethe's pictures are truthful, that the career of almost every young man brings him in contact with far more vitiating irregularities than any presented in the experience of Wilhelm Meister; for no one can maintain that *all* fact is a fit subject for art.

¶"The sphere of the artist has its limit somewhere, and the first question is, Has Goethe overstepped this limit, so that the mere fact of artistic representation is a mistake? The second: If his subjects are within the legitimate limits of art, is his mode of treatment such as to make his pictures pernicious? Surely the sphere of art extends wherever there is beauty either in form, or thought, or feeling. A ray of sunlight falling on the dreariest sand-bank will often serve the painter for a fine picture; the tragedian may take for his subject the most hideous passions if they serve as the background for some divine deed of tenderness or heroism, and so the novelist may place before us every aspect of human life where there is some trait of love, or endurance, or helplessness to call forth our best sympathies. **Balzac**, perhaps the most wonderful writer of fiction the world has ever seen, has in many of his novels overstepped this limit. He drags us by his magic force through scene after scene of unmitigated vice, till the effect of walking among this human carrion is a moral nausea. But no one can say that Goethe has sinned in this way.

"Everywhere he brings us into the presence of living, generous humanity—mixed and erring, and self-deluding, but saved from utter corruption by the salt of some noble impulse, some disinterested effort, some beam of good nature, even though grotesque or homely. And his mode of treatment seems to us precisely that which is really moral in its influence. It is without exaggeration; he is in no haste to alarm readers into virtue by melodramatic consequences; he quietly follows the stream of fact and of life; and waits patiently for the moral processes of nature as we all do for her material processes. The large tolerance of Goethe, which is markedly exhibited in *Wilhelm Meister,* is precisely that to which we point as the element of moral superiority.

¶"We all begin life by associating our passions with our moral prepossessions, by mistaking indignation for virtue, and many go through life without awaking from this illusion. These are the 'insupportables justes, qui du haut de leurs chaise d'or narguent les misères et les souffrances de l'humanité.' But a few are taught by their own falls and their own struggles, by their experience of sympathy, and help and goodness in the 'publicans and sinners' of these modern days, that the line between the virtuous and vicious, so far from being a necessary safeguard to morality, is itself an immoral fiction. Those who have been already taught this lesson will at once recognise the true morality of Goethe's works. Like *Wilhelm Meister,* they will be able to love the good in a Philina, and to reverence the far-seeing efforts of a Lothario."

*Mejnour is a character in Bulwer-Lytton's occult novel *Zanoni* (1842). He is a long-lived Rosicrucian sage who has abjured all human ties and sentiments. He is not evil, but inhumanly calm and dispassionate, and is a kind of personification of pure intellect.

The Future of German Philosophy

(pp 723-4)

Gegenwart und Zukunft der Philosophie in Deutschland, by Otto Friedrich Gruppe

"[Professor Gruppe] is a man of very various accomplishments, and throws his active intellect with equal fervour and facility into many channels—into poetry and politics as well as into classical literature and philosophy. This versatility in authorship is rare among erudite Germans, and is held rather in suspicion by them, in spite of the fact that some of their greatest men—**Lessing**, **Herder**, **Goethe**, and **Schiller**—were productive in several departments. Those who decry versatility—and there are many who do so in other countries besides Germany—seem to forget the immense service rendered by the *suggestiveness* of versatile men, who come to a subject with fresh, unstrained minds. You have perhaps been spending much time and ingenuity in planning a house or in spinning a theory which seems to you to account satisfactorily for many things: an intelligent neighbour comes in—and you show him your plan, or explain to him your theory. He is not an accomplished architect, but he sees at once that you have put a door and a chimney in incompatible positions; he is not, perhaps, a profound thinker, but he makes an observation on your theory which directly shows you that it will not 'hold water'. Such is the service which the versatile man will often render to the patient, exclusive inquirer . . . .

"The object towards which Herr Gruppe chiefly directs his consideration is the Reformation of Logic, or the rectification of the *method* of philosophical inquiry, which, as he justly insists, is the essential preliminary to all true progress. It is, he says, simply to a reform in method that we owe all the splendid achievements of modern natural science, and it is only by the extension of that reform to every department of philosophical inquiry that here also any of what **Bacon** calls 'fruit' can be obtained. In fact, the gist of his philosophical labours is partly to map out the road which **John Mill** (to whose work he seems to have given imperfect attention) has actually wrought out and made available. It is curious that while **Locke** is, on the one hand, accused of being the originator of the French Sensational Philosophy, he is, on the other hand, as in the present work, reproached for having formed a step towards the speculative systems of Germany, in admitting *ideas of reflection,* thus severing *ideas* from *things.* This, says Professor Gruppe, is the fundamental error of philosophy, and, from **Parmenides** downwards, has issued in nothing but the bewilderment of the human intellect. **Kant**'s classification of Infinity and Universality as ideas *a priori,* and on Space and Time as purely subjective forms of the intelligence, is a further elaboration of this fundamental error. These abstract terms on which speculation has built its huge fabrics are simply the *x* and *y* by which we mark the boundary of our knowledge; they have no value except in connexion with the concrete. The abstract is derived from the concrete: what, then, can we expect from a philosophy the essence of which is the derivation of the concrete from the abstract?

¶"The chief argument in favour of *à priori* ideas, as insisted on by **Leibnitz** and **Kant** is, that they can never be arrived at by induction; that induction may lead to the *general* but never to the *universal,* and that, nevertheless, this idea of universality is found in speech and in thought with the mark of necessity. But this argument will not bear a rigid examination. The language of all peoples soon attains to the expressions *all, universal, necessary,* but these expressions have their origin purely in the observations of the senses; they are simply a practical expedient, and are valued only under certain well-known and presupposed conditions. To isolate such expressions, to operate with them apart from experience, to exalt their relative value into an absolute value, to deduce knowledge from them alone, and to make them a standing point higher than all experience—this, which is what **Parmenides** and all speculative philosophers since him have done, is an attempt to poise the universe on one's head, and no wonder if dizziness and delusion are the consequence.

"These views are familiar enough to us in England, but to find them urged by a German professor is not so familiar."

GE goes on to summarize Gruppe's discussion of the distinction between the à priori (deduction) and à posteriori (induction) methods. Gruppe comes down hard for observation and the formation of judgments, which GE finds congenial and positive. Clearly, he has not come to terms thoroughly with Mill's *A System of Logic* (1843), and GE faults him in this.

"What then, asks Herr Gruppe in conclusion, is the future sphere of Philosophy? It must renounce metaphysics: it must renounce the ambitious attempt to form a theory of the universe, to know things in their causes and first principles. But in its function of determining logic or method, it is still the centre and heart of human knowledge, and it has to apply this method to the investigation of Psychology, with its subordinate department Æsthetics; to Ethics; and to the principles of Jurisprudence. A sufficient task!

" . . . we have at least been able to present one point of interest to our readers, in the fact that a German professor of philosophy renounces the attempt to climb to heaven by the rainbow bridge of 'the high *priori* road', and is content humbly to use his muscles in treading the uphill *à posteriori* path which will lead, not indeed to heaven, but to an eminence whence we may see very bright and blessed things on earth."

Love in the Drama

(pp 820-21)

Cours de Littérature Dramatique, ou l'Usage des Passions dans le Drame, by M. Saint-Marc Girardin (third volume)

"M. Saint-Marc Girardin is a writer who makes the public not only desire his volumes, but wait for them. The reason of this, in the case of the *Cours de Littérature Dramatique,* is that it consists of lectures given by him at the Sorbonne, so that the volumes can only appear after their contents have been delivered in 'winged words.' The first volume was published in 1843, the second in 1849, and it is only now, after the lapse of another six years, that we obtain the welcome third. Nothing can be more charmingly easy and conversational than the style of these volumes. We have all experienced that 'who writes about amusing books must himself be amusing,' is as far from being an axiom as **Johnson**'s immortal parody, 'Who drives fat oxen must himself be fat'; and that a work on the *belles lettres* may be as drowsy as one on weights and measures. But M. Saint-Marc Girardin is one of those writers who make a graceful subject still more graceful; he enhances the beauty of the flowers he gathers by the tasteful way in which he weaves them together. Qualities which make him delightful as a critic are his ready appreciation of beauty, even when the beauty is mingled with much quaintness and absurdity, and his lively sensibility to every trait of genuine feeling. He has at once chastity and largeness of thought—not a common conjunction anywhere, and perhaps especially uncommon in France; he is liberal without being lax, and pure without the least *soupçon* of prudery.

"In the latter part of his second volume he examined the three grand influences which have modified the character of Love, and made us differ widely from the ancients in our conception and presentation of that passion, namely, Christianity, chivalry, and the doctrine of Platonic Love. In the present volume he pursues the subject of Love, and traces its modifications in the sixteenth and seventeenth century, by analysing, or rather graphically sketching the three typical romances. The *Amadis,* which represents chivalrous love in its more softened and effeminate stage: the *Astrée,* which mingles Platonic with chivalrous love, under the name of pastoral love; and the *Clélia,* which is the code of *la galanterie honnête,* and marks the apogee of woman's preponderance in the world and in literature.

¶"We recommend readers who would like to be told, in the pleasantest way, something about those antediluvian romances, to turn to this volume of M. Saint-Marc Girardin's. He will show them matter for admiration, even in [**Honoré**] **D'Urfé** and Mlle. [**Madeleine de**] **Scudéry**, and it is always worth while to widen our circle of admiration. After thus surveying the general expression of Love under the varying conditions of society, from antiquity down to the seventeenth century, M. Girardin enters on an examination of the particular expression given to this passion in the drama, the romance, and the pastoral; and it is this part of his work which is most attractive. He opens for us one book after another, perhaps lying dusty on our shelves, points out beautiful passages and significant traits, makes **Theocritus** appear the most tempting author in the world, and pastorals in general seem readable—which we humbly concede we have rarely found them—shows a fine appreciation of **Shakspeare** and winds up by charming his reader's interest to **Madame Deshoulières**, and ought to be held in grateful recollection, if for nothing else, at least to having written those incisive lines—

Nul n'est content de sa fortune,
Ni mécontent de son esprit—

An epigram to which **La Rochefoucauld** has given a new dress in his *Maximes.*

"It is of course impossible for us to follow him through this lengthy survey, so, by way of selection, we turn to his observations on *Romeo and Juliet,* in which he compares Shakspeare's tragedy with the novel of *Luigi da Porto:* in the novel it is Juliet who makes the first advance to Romeo: at the first glance they exchange, the young maiden feels that her heart is no longer her own, and when the progress of the dance brings Romeo near to her, she says, 'Welcome to my side, Messer Romeo.' M. Girardin observes that this treatment of the subject is entirely in the spirit of ancient poetry, and he proceeds:—'Why, in ancient poetry and in the Italian novel which is here in entire unison with ancient poetry, why do the women love before being loved? Why do they feel the passion before inspiring it? and why, in modern poetry and romance, do we find the contrary? *Dido* loves *Eneas* whether she was ever loved. *Medea* loves *Jason* before being loved by him. Is it that the love-smitten heroines of antiquity had less modesty than the love-smitten heroines of modern times? or is it that the modern poets and romancers are more refined and reserved in the pictures they give of feminine sentiments?

¶"The manners of antiquity may explain why, in ancient poetry, woman wants that reserve in feeling, and yet more in words, which is the rule in modern times. Shut up in the gyneceum, and never mixing in the society of men, who themselves found objects of love elsewhere, women were compelled, when love took possession of their hearts, to proffer the avowal of their passion; they must themselves reveal their secret, or let it remain for ever unknown . . . . The less free woman is made by laws and conventionalities, the freer does she become through passion when she yields herself up to it. Thus, the women whose passion made them famous in antiquity were compelled to forget at once the first and last proprieties of their sex. In order to be loved, they were forced to say that they loved: and hence ancient poetry was accustomed to represent its heroines as making the first avowals of love.'

"M. Girardin then goes on to say that Shakspeare, 'who is altogether modern,' differs in his treatment from the Italian novelist, in assigning the first movement and expression of love to Romeo; as if he meant to imply that Shakspeare is an example of the antithesis he has just been stating between ancient and modern love, or rather love-making. He could hardly have made a more unfortunate selection of a case in points, for—inconvenient as the fact may be for those whose creed includes at once the doctrine of Shakspeare's infallibility and the doctrines of modern propriety—Shakspeare's women have no more decided characteristic than the frankness with which they avow their love, not only to themselves, but to the men they love. If Romeo opens the duet of love with a few notes *solo,* Juliet soon strikes in, and keeps it up in as impassioned a strain as he. Sweet *Desdemona*, 'a maiden never bold,' encourages *Othello*, not only by a 'world of sighs,' but by the broadest possible hint that he has won her heart. *Rosalind*, in her first interview with *Orlando*, tells him he has 'overthrown more than his enemies;' *Portia* is eloquent in assurances of her love before the casket is opened—

> One half of me is yours, the other half yours—
> Mine own, I would say; but if mine, then yours,
> And so all yours!

And this frankness towards the lover is generally followed up by the most impassioned soliloquies or confessions to confidants. Then there are the women who love without being loved in return, and some of whom even sue for love. *Helena* in *All's Well That Ends Well,* the *Helena* in the *Midsummer Night's Dream,* the shepherdess Sylvia, Viola, and Olivia, who wooes so prettily that the action justifies itself. Curious it is to contrast these Shakspearean heroines with some of **Walter Scott**'s painfully-discreet young ladies—the *Edith Bellendens, Alice Bridgworths,* and *Miss Wardours*! Whatever may be the respectability of these modern heroines, it is clear that little could be made of them dramatically; they are like trees trained in right lines by dint of wall and hammer. But we are wandering from the point we had undertaken to prove, namely, that Shakspeare cannot properly be contrasted with the ancients in the expression he gives to woman's love. If so—if this feminine frankness is not peculiar to the ancients, the cause of it in them must lie deeper than the restraints of the gyneceum, to which M. Girardin attributes it: it must be simply a natural manifestation which has only been gradually and partially repressed by the complex influences of modern civilisation.

"In his criticism of Shakspeare, M. Girardin sometimes reminds us of the Germans by his discovery of profound philosophical intentions where Shakspeare had probably nothing more than poetical and dramatic intentions. For example, *Caliban*, he tells us, is meant in the first instance to typify the inevitable brutality of human nature in the savage state, in opposition to the marvellous stories of voyagers in Shakspeare's days; and in the second instance, when he 'tastes of civilisation'—that is, of *Trinculo*'s wine—Caliban is meant as a caveat to the hasty panegyrists of civilised life. But, unlike the Germans, M. Girardin touches lightly on such subjects—just dips his wings in the *mare magnum* of philosophical interpretation, but generally floats along in the lighter medium of tasteful criticism and quotation. He promises us, at some future time, a fourth volume on the dramatic treatment of religious enthusiasm, a volume which will come to us recommended by the memory of much pleasure due to its predecessors."

The above is the complete text of this piece, not heretofore reprinted.

Heine's Poems

(pp 843-4)

Pictures of Travel, translated from the German of Henry [*sic*] *Heine* by Charles G. Leland

"Nature one day resolved to make a witty German. But as this supreme paradox was not to be achieved all at once, it happened that in the ardour of a great purpose she mistook Hebrew blood for German, and while she was busy adding the wit, allowed the best moral qualities of the German to slip out of her hands. So, instead of the witty Teuton she intended, she would have produced merely a Voltairian Jew, speaking the German language, if she had not, perceiving her mistake before it was too late, superadded, as some compensation for the want of *morale,* a passionate heart blending its emotions with the most delicate and imaginative sensibility to the beauties of earth and sky, and a supreme lyrical genius, which could weave the wit, and the passion, and the imagination into songs light and lovely as the rainbows on the spray of the summer torrent.

"Thus it came to pass that we have that wonderful human compound Heinrich Heine, a writer who is master of a German prose as light and subtle and needle-pointed as **Voltaire**'s French, and of a poetical style as crystalline, as graceful, and as musical as that of **Goethe**'s best lyrics; but a writer who is destitute of the distinct moral conviction which often inspired Voltaire, and still more utterly destitute of the profound wisdom and the depth of love and reverence which roll like a deep river under the sparkling, dimpling surface of Goethe's song. Indeed, we know nothing more likely to impress a reader with the grander elements of Goethe's mind than a comparison of his lyrics with Heine's, for the very reason that Heine quite equals Goethe in all the charms of *mere song,* and has one quality mingling itself with his lyrical power which Goethe had not—namely, wit, or rather, to express it more specifically, French *esprit.* For, alien as this quality might seem to passionate love-songs and thrilling legendary pictures, such as form the majority of Heine's poems, it is, nevertheless, almost everywhere present, giving your rising tears the accompaniment of a laugh, and, before you have lost the cold shudder at his spectral visions, appealing irresistibly to your sense of fun.

¶"We cannot agree with his very clever American translator that *Humour* is Heine's grand characteristic. He certainly has humour—perhaps even enough to set up an inferior genius as a humourist—but we think it will be found that his greatest effects in prose, and most of the contrasts that startle us in his poetry, arise from a Mephistophelean wit, a *vereinender Geist,* rather than from humour which affirms all that is genuinely human instead of denying it, and is, in fact, an exuberant sympathy acting in company with a sense of the ludicrous, while wit is the critical intellect acting in company with that same sense. Nevertheless, it must be admitted that there are many passages of **Sterne**-like humour in Heine, and herein he is least akin to the French, and most nearly allied to the broader and deeper German nature, which atones for the want of *esprit* by something which *esprit* will never supersede—loving earnestness.

"But it is time to turn from such rambling remarks to the object that suggested them—namely, the translation of Heine's *Reisebilder,* by a very gifted American. Of Heine, more even than the majority of poets, we must say that he is untranslatably felicitous. Many of his lyrics are mere gossamer webs—touch them, try to transfer them, and all their qualities disappear. Hence, when we praise Mr Leland's translation—and we do so very sincerely—we must not be understood to mean that it will give the English reader a true conception of Heine's genius. Mr Leland has that grand requisite of a translator, rigorous faithfulness; he has also poetical sensibility, command of language, and an evidently acute perception of wit: in short, he spoils Heine's poems perhaps as little as it is possible to spoil them in a translation. This may not seem to be high praise, but we firmly believe it is the very highest praise that can ever be given to a translation of Heine's poems, and we recommend the reader who is hopeless of knowing these poems in the original to make his acquaintance with them through Mr Leland's version. He, of course, succeeds best in the poems which are legendary and ballad-like rather than purely lyrical."

GE then sets forth three balladic poems in English translation from the book. The above is the first reprinting of this piece, as far as we are aware.

GE's proficiency in German and her love of poetry combined to make her England's principal advocate of the works of Heinrich Heine. She wrote four articles on the poet. See HH, HBS, and RH.

Westminster Review LXIV
October 1855 **ET**

Evangelical Teaching: Dr Cumming

[pp 79-106 in the 1894 Crowell ed.; citations are to pages]

If her readers ever doubted GE's aversion to the evangelical style of religion, the opening of this essay ("one of the most arresting in all periodical literature") would put their uncertainties to rest with a vengeance (*see Topicon* TP:Clergy—*evangelical*). To Ashton, the piece "has a claim to be her best" (p 144), and it seems to have opened George Lewes's eyes to her writing genius. GE disclaims any personal knowledge of John Cumming: neither his appearance, nor his habits, nor his charity (she does not tell us his date(s) or his Christian name). She only knows his writings, as taken from nine volumes of his sermons, and these she considers meretricious, dishonest, and damaging to society: "profoundly mistaken and pernicious."
She spends much space on Dr Cumming, more than would seem warranted by his intellectual attainments and churchly importance. There is castigation: "Imbecility that is not even meek, ceases to be pitiable, and becomes simply odious." There is in Cumming, she says, no truthfulness and no charity, and she notes the "perverted moral judgment that everywhere reigns in" his works. Cumming, she says, emphasizes the "Glory of God" as the only motive, the only justification for man's actions. Love, compassion, loyalty—all natural human sympathies— are irrelevant and count for nothing.
It is in a way surprising that there was no law of libel to inhibit the publication of such an explicit assault (anonymous, of course): it is carefully couched to be impersonal, but it hits very hard, and apparently the cleric in question was alive and (presumably) well at the time.

Rev. John Cumming

"He is at home in the external, the polemical, the historical, the circumstantial, and is only episodically devout and practical . . . . It is a favorite exercise with him to form conjectures of the process by which the earth is to be burned up, and to picture **Dr Chalmers** and **Mr Wilberforce** being caught up to meet **Christ** in the air, while Romanists, Puseyites, and infidels are given over to gnashing of teeth. But of really spiritual joys and sorrows, of the life and death of Christ as a manifestation of love that constrains the soul, of sympathy with that yearning over the lost and erring which made **Jesus** weep over Jerusalem, and prompted the sublime prayer, 'Father, forgive them,' of the gentler fruits of the Spirit, and the peace of God which passeth understanding—of all this, we find little trace in Dr Cumming's discourses." 82

—*style:* "His style is in perfect correspondence with this habit of mind. Though diffuse, as that of all preachers must be, it has rapidity of movement, perfect clearness, and some aptness of illustration. He has much of that literary talent which makes a good journalist—the power of beating out an idea over a large space, and of introducing far-fetched à propos. His writings have, indeed, no high merit: they have no originality or force of thought, no striking felicity of presentation, no depth of emotion." 82

—*overwrought:* "We feel ourselves in company with a voluble retail talker, whose language is exuberant but not exact, and to whom we should never think of referring for precise information, or for well-digested thought and experience. His argument continually slides into wholesale assertion and vague declamation, and in his love of ornament he frequently becomes tawdry . . . so prosaic an injunction to his hearers as that they should choose a residence within an easy distance of church, is magnificently draped by him as an exhortation to prefer a house 'that basks in the sunshine of the countenance of God.' " 82-3

—*no charity:* "Dr Cumming's religion may demand a tribute of love, but it gives a charter to hatred; it may enjoin charity but it fosters all uncharitableness." 97

—*concluding:* "We have no theory which requires us to attribute unworthy motives to Dr Cumming, no opinions, religious or irreligious, which can make it a gratification to us to detect him in delinquencies. On the contrary, the better we are able to think of him as a man, while we are obliged to disapprove him as a theologian, the stronger will be the evidence for our conviction, that the tendency towards good in human nature has a force which no creed can utterly counteract, and which insures the ultimate triumph of that tendency over all dogmatic perversions." 106

Also mentioned

[relatively distinguished historical or literary figures are in Index X or XI]

Margaret Fuller and Mary Wollstonecraft
(pp 988-9)

Woman in the Nineteenth Century, and Kindred Papers relating to the Sphere, Condition, and Duties of Woman, by Margaret Fuller Ossoli (1855)
A Vindication of the Rights of Woman, by Mary Wollstonecraft (1792)

"The dearth of new books just now gives us time to recur to less recent ones which we have hitherto noticed but slightly; and among these we choose the late edition of Margaret Fuller's *Woman in the Nineteenth Century,* because we think it has been unduly thrust into the background of less comprehensive and candid productions on the same subject. Notwithstanding certain defects of taste and a sort of vague spiritualism an grandiloquence which belong to all but the very best American writers, the book is a valuable one: it has the enthusiasm of a noble and sympathetic nature, with the moderation and breadth and large allowance of a vigorous and cultivated understanding. There is no exaggeration of woman's moral excellence or intellectual capabilities; no injudicious insistence on her fitness for this or that function hitherto engrossed by men; but a calm plea for the removal of unjust laws and artificial restrictions, so that the possibilities of her nature may have room for full development, a wisely stated demand to disencumber her of the

Parasitic forms
That seem to keep her up, but drag her down—
And leave her field to burgeon and to bloom
From all within her, make herself her own
To give or keep, to live and learn and be
All that not harms distinctive womanhood.*

"It is interesting to compare this essay of Margaret Fuller's published in its earliest form in 1843, with a work on the position of woman, written between sixty and seventy years ago—we mean Mary Wollstonecraft's *Rights of Woman.* The latter work was not continued beyond the first volume; but so far as this carries the subject, the comparison, at least in relation to strong sense and loftiness of moral tone, is not at all disadvantageous to the woman of the last century. There is in some quarters a vague prejudice against the *Rights of Woman* as in some way or other a reprehensible book, but readers who go to it with this impression will be surprised to find it eminently serious, severely moral, and withal rather heavy—the true reason, perhaps, that no edition has been published since 1796, and that it is now rather scarce.

¶"There are several points of resemblance, as well as of striking difference, between the two books. A strong understanding is present in both; but Margaret Fuller's mind was like some regions of her own American continent, where you are constantly stepping from the sunny 'clearings' into the mysterious twilight of the tangled forest—she often passes in one breath from forcible reasoning to dreamy vagueness; moreover, her unusually varied culture gives her great command of illustration. Mary Wollstonecraft, on the other hand, is nothing if not rational; she has no erudition, and her grave pages are lit up by no ray of fancy. In both writers we discern, under the brave bearing of a strong and truthful nature, the beating of a loving woman's heart, which teaches them not to undervalue the smallest offices of domestic care of kindliness.

¶"But Margaret Fuller, with all her passionate sensibility, is more of the literary woman, who would not have been satisfied without intellectual production; Mary Wollstonecraft, we imagine, wrote not at all for writing's sake, but from the pressure of other motives. So far as the difference of date allows, there is a striking coincidence in their trains of thought; indeed, every important idea in the *Rights of Woman,* except the combination of home education with a common day-school for boys and girls, reappears in Margaret Fuller's essay.

"One point on which they both write forcibly is the fact that, while men have a horror of such faculty or culture in the other sex as tends to place it on a level with their own, they are really in a state of subjection to ignorant and feeble- minded women . . . . "

GE here cites both writers on this subject, with extracts which, among other things, strikingly remind us of the unhappy Lydgates in *Middlemarch.*

"There is a notion commonly entertained among men that an instructed woman, capable of having opinions, is likely to prove an impracticable yoke-fellow, always pulling one way when her husband wants to go the other, oracular in tone, and prone to give curtain lectures on metaphysics. But surely, so far as obstinacy is concerned, your unreasoning animal is the most unmanageable of creatures, where you are not allowed to settle the question by a cudgel, a whip and bridle, or even a string to the leg. For our own parts, we see no consistent or commodious medium between the old plan of corporal discipline and that thorough education of women which will make them rational beings in the highest sense of the word. Wherever weakness is not harshly controlled it must *govern,* as you may see when a strong man holds a little child by the hand, how he is pulled hither and thither, and wearied in his walk by his submission to the whims and feeble movements of his companion.

¶"A really cultured woman, like a really cultured man, will be ready to yield in trifles. So far as we see, there is no indissoluble connexion between infirmity of logic and infirmity of will, and a woman quite innocent of an opinion in philosophy, is as likely as not to have an indomitable opinion about the kitchen. As to airs of superiority, no woman ever had them in consequence of true culture, but only because her culture was shallow or unreal, only as a result of what Mrs Malaprop well calls 'the ineffectual qualities in a woman'—mere acquisitions carried about, and not knowledge thoroughly assimilated so as to enter into the growth of the character.

"To return to Margaret Fuller, some of the best things she says are on the folly of absolute definitions of woman's nature and absolute demarcations of woman's mission. 'Nature,' she says, 'seems to delight in varying the arrangements, as if to show that she will be fettered by no rule; and we must admit the same varieties that she admits.' Again: 'If nature is never bound down, nor the voice of inspiration stifled, that is enough. We are pleased that women should write and speak, if they feel need of it, from having something to tell; but silence for ages would be no misfortune, if that silence be from divine command, and not from man's tradition."

At this point, GE provides an extended extract from each writer on the subject of potential occupations, ranging from sea-captain to physician.

"Men pay a heavy price for their reluctance to encourage self-help and independent resources in women. The precious meridian years of many a man of genius have to be spent in the toil of routine, that an 'establishment' may be kept up for a woman who can understand none of his secret yearnings, who is fit for nothing but to sit in her drawing-room like a doll-Madonna in her shrine. No matter. Anything is more endurable than to change our established formulæ about women, or to run the risk of looking up to our wives instead of looking down on them. *Sit divus, dummodo non sit vivus* (let him be a god, provided he be not living), said the Roman magnates of **Romulus**; and so men say of women, let them be idols, useless absorbents of precious things, provided we are not obliged to admit them to be strictly fellow-beings to be treated, one and all, with justice and sober reverence.

"On one side we hear that woman's position can never be improved until women themselves are better; and, on the other, that women can never become better until their position is improved—until the laws are made more just, and a wider field opened to feminine activity. But we constantly hear the same difficulty stated about the human race in general. There is a perpetual action and reaction between individuals and institutions; we must try and mend both by little and little—the only way in which human things can be mended. Unfortunately, many over-zealous champions of women assert their actual equality with men—nay, even their moral superiority to men—as a ground for their release from oppressive laws and restrictions. They lose strength immensely by this false position. If it were true, then there would be a case in which slavery and ignorance nourished virtue, and so far we should have an argument for the continuance of bondage. But we want freedom and culture for woman, because subjection and ignorance have debased her, and with her, Man: for—

> If she be small, slight-natured, miserable,
> How shall men grow?**

"Both Margaret Fuller and Mary Wollstonecraft have too much sagacity to fall into this sentimental exaggeration. Their ardent hopes of what women may become do not prevent them from seeing and painting women as they are. . . . " [with a Wollstonecraft extract on the sexes' relative moral excellence.]

*Tennyson, *The Princess,* VII, 253-8 ** *Ibid.* 249-50

Translations and Translators

(pp 1014-5)

Critique of Pure Reason, by Immanuel Kant translated by J.M.D. Meiklejohn (1855)

Specimens of the Choicest Lyrical Productions of the Most Celebrated German Poets, translated by Mary Anne Burt (2 vols. 1855)

"A clergyman (of the Charles Honeyman [in **Thackeray**'s *The Newcomes*] species) once told us that he never set about preparing his sermons till Saturday evening, for he 'trusted to Providence.' A similar kind of trust, we suppose, must be prevalent among translators, for many of them are evidently relying on some power which

Can teach all people to translate,
Though out of languages in which
They understand no part of speech—*

a *Nachklang* or resonance, perhaps, of the famous legend about those early translators, the Seventy who turned the Old Testament into Greek, which legend tells how **Ptolemy** shut them up in separate cells to do their work, and how, when they came to compare their renderings, there was perfect agreement! We are convinced, however, that the translators of the Septuagint had some understanding of their business to begin with, or this supernatural aid would not have been given, for in the matter of translation, at least, we have observed, that 'God helps them who help themselves'. A view of the case, which we commend to all young ladies and some middle-aged gentlemen, who consider a very imperfect acquaintance with their own language, and an anticipatory acquaintance with the foreign language, quite a sufficient equipment for the office of translator.

"It is perfectly true that, though geniuses have often undertaken translation, translation does not often demand genius. The power required in the translation varies with the power exhibited in the original work: very modest qualifications will suffice to enable a person to translate a book of ordinary travels, or a slight novel, while a work of reasoning or science can be adequately rendered only by means of what is at present exceptional faculty and exceptional knowledge. Among books of this latter kind, **Kant**'s *Critique of Pure Reason* is perhaps the very hardest nut—the peachstone—for a translator to crack so as to lay open the entire uninjured kernel of meaning, and we are glad at last to believe that a translator of adequate power has been employed upon it. For so far as we have examined the version placed at the head of our article, it appears to us very different indeed from the many renderings of German metaphysical works, in which the translator, having ventured into deep waters without learning to swim, clings to the dictionary, and commends himself to Providence. Mr Meiklejohn's translation—so far, we must again observe, as we have examined it—indicates a real mastery of his author, and, for the first time, makes Kant's *Kritik der reinen Vernunft* accessible to English readers.

"It may seem odd that we should associate with this mighty book—this terrible ninety-gun ship—such a little painted pleasure-boat as Miss (or Mrs) Burt's miscellaneous collection of translations from German lyric poets. But we are concerning ourselves here simply with translation—not at all with Kant's Philosophy or with German Lyrics considered in themselves, and these two volumes happen to be the specimens of translation most recently presented to our notice. With regard to prose, we may very generally use **Goldsmith**'s critical recipe, and say that the translation would have been better if the translator had taken more pains; but of poetical attempts we are often sure that no amount of pains would produce a satisfactory result. And so it is with Miss Burt's *Specimens of the German Poets.* She appears to have the knowledge and the industry which many translators want, but she has not the poetic power which makes poetical translations endurable to those acquainted with the originals. Amongst others, however, who have no such acquaintance, Miss Burt's translations seem to have been in some demand, since they have reached a second edition.

¶"She has been bold enough to attempt a version of **Goethe**'s exquisite *Zweignung* (Dedication), and here is a specimen of her rendering. Goethe sings with divine feeling and music:

Für andre wächst in mir das edle Gut,
Ich kann und will das Pfund nicht mehr vergraben,
Warum sucht' ich den Weg so sehnsuchtsvoll,
Wenn ich ihn nicht den Brüdern zeigen soll?

Miss Burt follows him much as a Jew's harp would follow a piano—

Entombed no longer shall my *talent* be,
That treasure I amass, shall other's share?
To find the road—oh, why such zeal display,
If I guide not my brethren on their way?

A version like this bears about the same relation to the original as the portraits in an illustrated newspaper bear to the living face of the distinguished gentleman they misrepresent; and considering how often we hear opinions delivered on foreign poets by people who only know those poets at second hand, it becomes the reviewer's duty to insist again and again on the inadequacy of poetic translations.

"The Germans render our poetry better than we render theirs, for their language, as slow and unwieldy as their own post-horses in prose, becomes in poetry graceful and strong and flexible as an Arabian war-horse. Besides, translation among them is more often undertaken by men of genius. We remember, for example, some translations of **Burns**, by [**Ferdinand**] **Freiligrath**, which would have arrested us by their beauty if we had seen the poems, for the first time, in this language. It is true the Germans think a little too highly of their translations, and especially are under the illusion, encouraged by some silly English people, that **Shakspeare** according to **Schlegel** is better than Shakspeare himself—not simply to a German as being easier for him to understand, but absolutely better as poetry. A very close and admirable rendering Schlegel's assuredly is, and it is a high pleasure to track it in its faithful adherence to the original, just as it is to examine a fine engraving of a favourite picture. Sometimes the German is as good as the English—the same music played on another but as good an instrument. But more frequently the German is a feeble echo, and here and there it breaks down in a supremely fine passage . . . ."

GE goes on to cite unfortunate translations by Schlegel from *The Merchant of Venice* and *Coriolanus,* and another, by **Tieck**, of a monologue in *Macbeth.*

"Such examples of translators' fallibility in men like Schlegel and **Tieck** might well make less accomplished persons more backward in undertaking the translation of great poems, and by showing the difficulty of the translator's task, might make it an object of ambition to real ability. Though a good translator is infinitely below the man who produces *good* original works, he is infinitely above the man who produces *feeble* original works. We had meant to say something of the moral qualities especially demanded in the translator —the patience, the rigid fidelity, and the sense of responsibility in interpreting another man's mind. But we have gossiped on this subject long enough."

*Samuel Butler, *Hudibras* I, i 660-2

Thomas Carlyle

(pp 1034-5)

Passages Selected from the Writings of Thomas Carlyle: With a Biographical Memoir, by Thomas Ballantyne

"It has been well said that the highest aim in education is analogous to the highest aim in mathematics, namely, to obtain not *results* but *powers,* not particular solutions, but the means by which endless solutions may be wrought. He is the most effective educator who aims less at perfecting specific acquirements than at producing that mental condition which renders acquirements easy, and leads to their useful application; who does not seek to make his pupils moral by enjoining particular courses of action, but by bringing into activity the feelings and sympathies that must issue in noble action.

¶"On the same ground it may be said that the most effective writer is not he who announces a particular discovery, who convinces men of a particular conclusion, who demonstrates that this measure is right and that measure wrong; but he who rouses in others the activities that must issue in discovery, who awakes men from their indifference to the right and the wrong, who nerves their energies to seek for the truth and live up to it at whatever cost. The influence of such a writer is dynamic. He does not teach men how to use sword and musket, but he inspired their souls with courage and sends a strong will into their muscles. He does not, perhaps, enrich your stock of data, but he clears away the film from your eyes that you search for data to some purpose. He does not, perhaps, convince you, but he strikes you, undeceives you, animates you. You are not directly fed by his books, but you are braced as by a walk up to an alpine summit, and yet subdued to calm and reverence as by the sublime things to be seen from that summit.

"Such a writer is Thomas Carlyle. It is an idle question to ask whether his books will be read a century hence: if they were all burnt as the grandest of Suttees on his funeral pile, it would be only like cutting down an oak after its acorns have sown a forest. For there is hardly a superior or active mind of this generation that has not been modified by Carlyle's writings; there has hardly been an English book written for the last ten or twelve years that would not have been different if Carlyle had not lived. The character of his influence is best seen in the fact that many of the men who have the least agreement with his opinions are those to whom the reading of *Sartor Resartus* was an epoch in the history of their minds.

¶"The extent of his influence may be best seen in the fact that ideas which were startling novelties when he first wrote them are now become common-places. And we think few men will be found to say that this influence on the whole has not been for good. There are plenty who question the justice of Carlyle's estimates of past men and past times, plenty who quarrel with the exaggeration of the *Latter-Day Pamphlets,* and who are as far as possible from looking for an amendment of things from a Carlylian theocracy with the 'greatest man', as a **Joshua** who is to smite the wicked (and the stupid) till the going down of the sun.

¶"But for any large nature, those points of difference are quite incidental. It is not as a theorist, but as a great and beautiful human nature, that Carlyle influences us. You may meet a man whose wisdom seems unimpeachable, since you find him entirely in agreement with yourself; but this oracular man of unexceptionable opinions has a green eye, a wiry hand, and altogether a *Wesen,* or demeanour, that makes the world look blank to you, and whose unexceptionable opinions become a bore; while another man who deals in what you cannot but think 'dangerous paradoxes', warms your heart by the pressure of his hand, and looks out on the world with so clear and loving an eye, that nature seems to reflect the light of his glance upon your own feeling.

¶"So it is with Carlyle. When he is saying the very opposite of what we think, he says it so finely, with so hearty conviction—he makes the object about which we differ stand out in such grand relief under the clear light of his strong and honest intellect—he appeals so constantly to our sense of the manly and the truthful—that we are obliged to say 'Hear! hear'! to the writer before we can give the decorous 'Oh! oh'! to his opinions.

"Much twaddling criticism has been spent on Carlyle's style. Unquestionably there are some genuine minds, not at all given to twaddle, to whom his style is antipathetic, who find it as unendurable as an English lady finds peppermint. Against antipathies there is no arguing; they are misfortunes. But instinctive repulsion apart, surely there is no one who can read and relish Carlyle without feeling that they could no more wish him to have written in another style than they could wish Gothic architecture not to be Gothic, or **Raffaelle** not to be Raffaellesque.

¶"It is the fashion to speak of Carlyle almost exclusively as a philosopher; but, to our thinking, he is yet more of an artist than a philosopher. He glances deep down into human nature, and shows the causes of human actions; he seizes grand generalisations, and traces them in the particular with wonderful acumen; and in all this he is a philosopher. But, perhaps, his greatest power lies in concrete presentation. No novelist has made his creations live for us more thoroughly than Carlyle has made **Mirabeau** and the men of the French Revolution, **Cromwell** and the Puritans. What humour in his pictures! Yet what depth of appreciation, what reverence for the great and god-like under every sort of earthly mummery!"

GE, after a brief transition, here turns to Carlyle proper, with three extracts from *On Heroes, Hero-Worship and the Heroic in History.*

German Wit: Heinrich Heine

(pp 1-13)

(pp 46-78 in the 1894 Crowell ed.; citations are to these pages)

GE begins with an exploration of Wit, Humor, and their differences. She notes the sad lack of a contribution from Germany to this aspect of literature and points to the great Heinrich Heine as the exception. She surveys his life briefly (mistaking the year of his birth), touching on his politics, his religion, his long sojourn in Paris, and his terminal illness. She discusses his works in general terms and concludes with a summary examination of his achievements as lyric poet, prose stylist, and humorist. GE quotes generously from the prose, in clear and entertaining English, and modestly from the poetry, which she largely refuses to translate. She concludes by excerpting two of Heine's most comical and witty satires: on **Victor Cousin** and **Louis Philippe**.

The *Topicon,* at LC:Wit and Humour, contains many extracts from this essay, and there are others in RW:Germany.

GE's proficiency in German made it possible for her to take the lead in introducing Heine to the English public. She wrote no fewer than four pieces on him, of which this is the most important. The others are *Heine's Poems,* at page 57 in this volume; *Heine's Book of Songs,* page 92; and *Recollections of Heine,* page 204.

Wit and Humor

—in general: "Humor is of earlier growth than Wit, and it is in accordance with this earlier growth that it has more affinity with the poetic tendencies, while Wit is more nearly allied to the ratiocinative intellect. Humor draws its materials from situations and characteristics; Wit seizes on unexpected and complex relations. Humor is chiefly representative and descriptive; it is diffuse, and flows along without any other law than its own fantastic will; or it flits about like a will-o'-the-wisp, amazing us by its whimsical transitions. Wit is brief and sudden, and sharply defined as a crystal: it does not make pictures, it is not fantastic; but it detects an unsuspected analogy, or suggests a startling or confounding inference." 46-7

—and intellect: "This affinity of Wit with ratiocination is the more obvious in proportion as the species of wit is higher and deals less with words and with superficialities than with the essential qualities of things. Some of **Johnson**'s most admirable witticisms consist in the suggestion of an analogy which immediately exposes the absurdity of an action or proposition; and it is only their ingenuity, condensation, and instantaneousness which lift them from reasoning into Wit—they are *reasoning raised to a higher power.* On the other hand, Humor, in its higher forms, and in proportion as it associates itself with the sympathetic emotions, continually passes into poetry: nearly all great modern humorists may be called prose poets." 47

—quick and slow: "Wit is an electric shock, which takes us by violence quite independently of our predominant mental disposition; but humor approaches us more deliberately and leaves us masters of ourselves. Hence it is that, while coarse and cruel humor has almost disappeared from contemporary literature, coarse and cruel wit abounds." 48

—together: "We rarely find wit untempered by humor, or humor without a spice of wit; and sometimes we find them both united in the highest degree in the same mind, as in **Shakespeare** and **Molière**. A happy conjunction this, for wit is apt to be cold, and thin-lipped, and Mephistophelean in men who have no relish for humor, whose lungs do never crow like Chanticleer at fun and drollery; and broad-faced rollicking humor needs the refining influence of wit." 48

—national considerations: "Perhaps the nearest approach Nature has given us to a complete analysis, in which wit is as thoroughly exhausted of humor as possible, and humor as bare as possible of wit, is in the typical Frenchman and the typical German. **Voltaire**, the intensest example of pure wit, fails in most of his fictions from his lack of humor . . . . The sense of the ludicrous [in *Candide*] is continually defeated by disgust, and the scenes, instead of presenting us with an amusing or agreeable picture, are only the frame for a witticism. On the other hand, German humor generally shows no sense of measure, no instinctive tact; it is either floundering and clumsy as the antics of a leviathan, or laborious and interminable as a Lapland day, in which one loses all hope that the stars and quiet will ever come. For this reason **Jean Paul [Richter]**, the greatest of German humorists, is unendurable to many readers, and frequently tiresome to all. Here, as elsewhere, the German shows the absence of that delicate perception, that sensibility to gradation, which is the essence of tact and taste, and the necessary concomitant of wit." 49

" . . . it is a remarkable fact that, among the five great races concerned in modern civilization, the German race is the only one which, up to the present century, had contributed nothing classic to the common stock of European wit and humor . . . . Italy was the birth-place of Pantomime and the immortal Pulcinello; Spain had produced Cervantes; France had produced Rabelais and Molière, and classic wits innumerable; England had yielded Shakespeare and a host of humorists. But Germany had borne no great comic dramatist, no great satirist, and she has not yet repaired the omission; she had not even produced any humorist of a high order." 50

Heinrich Heine [1797-1856]

"Perhaps there is already an earnest of that future crop [of wits and humorists] in the existence of Heinrich Heine, a German born with the present century, who, to Teutonic imagination, sensibility, and humor, adds an amount of *esprit* that would make him brilliant among the most brilliant of Frenchmen. True, this unique German wit is half a Hebrew; but he and his ancestors spent their youth in German air, and were reared on *Wurst* and *Sauerkraut*, so that he is as much a German as a pheasant is an English bird, or a potato an Irish vegetable." 51

—summarized: "But whatever else he may be, Heine is one of the most remarkable men of this age; no echo, but a real voice, and therefore, like all genuine things in this world, worth studying; a surpassing lyric poet, who has uttered our feelings for us in delicious song; a humorist, who touches leaden folly with the magic wand of his fancy, and transmutes it into the fine gold of art—who sheds his sunny smile on human tears, and makes them a beauteous rainbow on the cloudy background of life; a wit, who holds in his mighty hand the most scorching lightnings of satire; an artist in prose literature, who has shown even more completely than **Goethe** the possibilities of German prose; and . . . a lover of freedom, who has spoken wise and brave words on behalf of his fellowmen. He is, moreover, a suffering man, who, with all the highly wrought sensibility of genius, has to endure terrible physical ills; and as such he calls forth more than an intellectual interest.

—a negative: " . . . Heine's magnificent powers have often served only to give electric force to the expression of debased feeling, so that his works are no Phidian statue of gold, and ivory, and gems, but have not a little brass, and iron, and miry clay mingled with the precious metal. The audacity of his occasional coarseness and personality is unparalleled in contemporary literature, and has hardly been exceeded by the license of former days. Hence, before his volumes are put within the reach of immature minds, there is need of a friendly penknife to exercise a strict censorship." 52

—underrated at first: "Perhaps even the deep-sighted were far from detecting in that small, blond, pale young man, with quiet, gentle manners, the latent powers of ridicule and sarcasm—the terrible talons that were one day to be thrust out from the velvet paw of the young leopard." 57

—published, but let alone: "In those days, a small blond young man, with the brim of his hat drawn over his nose, his coat flying open, and his hands stuck in his trouser-pockets, might be seen stumbling along the streets of Hamburg, staring from side to side, and appearing to have small regard to the figure he made in the eyes of the good citizens." 59

—Paris, and illness: "For sixteen years—from 1831 to 1847—Heine lived that rapid concentrated life which is known only in Paris; but then, alas! stole on the 'days of darkness,' and they were to be many. In 1847 he felt the approach of the terrible spinal disease which has for seven years chained him to his bed in acute suffering . . . .

"Since 1848, then, this poet, whom the lovely objects of Nature have always 'haunted like a passion,' has not descended from the second story of a Parisian house; this man of hungry intellect has been shut out from all direct observation of life, all contact with society, except such as is derived from visitors to his sick-room. The terrible disease has affected his eyes; the sight of one is utterly gone, and he can only raise the lid of the other by lifting it with his finger. Opium alone is the beneficent genius that stills his pain." 67-8

—*religion:* "In the second volume of the 'Salon' and in the 'Romantische Schule,' written in 1834 and '35, the doctrine of Pantheism is dwelt on with a fervor and unmixed seriousness which show that Pantheism was then an animating faith to Heine, and he attacks what he considers the false spiritualism and asceticism of Christianity as the enemy of true beauty in Art, and of social well-being . . . . At length, in the epilogue to the 'Romanzero,' dated 1851, there appeared, amidst much mystifying banter, a declaration that he had embraced Theism and the belief in a future life . . . . " 69

—*offences:* "The real offences of Heine are his occasional coarseness and his unscrupulous personalities, which are reprehensible, not because they are directed against his fellow-countrymen, but because they are *personalities.* That these offences have their precedents in men whose memory the world delights to honor, does not remove their turpitude, but it is a fact which should modify our condemnation in a particular case . . . . " 71

—*defense:* "For the rest, why should we demand of Heine that he should be a hero, a patriot, a solemn prophet, any more than we should demand of a gazelle that it should draw well in harness? Nature has not made him of her sterner stuff—not of iron and adamant, but of pollen of flowers, the juice of the grape, and Puck's mischievous brain, plenteously mixing also the dews of kindly affection and the gold-dust of noble thoughts. It is, after all, a tribute which his enemies pay him when they utter their bitterest dictum—namely, that he is *'nur Dichter'*—only a poet." 72

Works

"In his 'Reisebilder,' Heine carries us with him to the Harz, to the isle of Norderney, to his native town Düsseldorf, to Italy, and to England, sketching scenery and character, now with the wildest, most fantastic humor, now with the finest idyllic sensibility—letting his thoughts wander from poetry to politics, from criticism to dreamy revery, and blending fun, imagination, reflection, and satire in a sort of exquisite, ever-varying shimmer, like the hues of the opal." 60

"Between 1833 and 1845 appeared the four volumes of the 'Salon,' 'Die Romantische Schule' (both written, in the first instance, in French); the book on **Börne**; 'Atta Troll,' a romantic poem; 'Deutschland,' an exquisitely humorous poem, describing his last visit to Germany, and containing some grand passages of serious writing; and the 'Neue Gedichte,' a collection of lyrical poems. Among the most interesting of his prose works are the second volume of the 'Salon,' which contains a survey of religion and philosophy in Germany, and the 'Romantische Schule,' a delightful introduction to that phase of German literature known as the Romantic School." 64

"The book on Börne, which appeared in 1840, two or three years after the death of that writer, excited great indignation in Germany, as a wreaking of vengeance on the dead, an insult to the memory of a man who had worked and suffered in the cause of freedom—a cause which was Heine's own. Börne . . . was a remarkable political writer of the ultra-liberal party in Germany, who resided in Paris at the same time as Heine—a man of stern uncompromising partisanship, and bitter humor. Without justifying Heine's production of this book, we see excuses for him which should temper the condemnation passed on it. There was a radical opposition of nature between him and Börne: to use his own distinction, Heine is a Hellene—sensuous, realistic, exquisitely alive to the beautiful; while Börne was a Nazarene— ascetic, spiritualistic, despising the pure artist as destitute of earnestness." 64-5

"Börne could not forgive what he regarded as Heine's epicurean indifference and artistic dalliance, and he at length gave vent to his antipathy in savage attacks on him through the press, accusing him of utterly lacking character and principle, and even of writing under the influence of venal motives. To these attacks Heine remained absolutely mute—from contempt, according to his own account; but the retort, which he resolutely refrained from making during Börne's life, comes in this volume published after his death with the concentrated force of long-gathering thunder . . . . Whatever else we may think of the book, it is impossible to deny its transcendent talent—the dramatic vigor with which Börne is made present to us, the critical acumen with which he is characterized, and the wonderful play of wit, pathos, and thought which runs through the whole." 65

—*as lyric poet:* "Heine is too impressible and mercurial for any sustained production: even in his short lyrics his tears sometimes pass into laughter, and his laughter into tears . . . . His song has a wide compass of notes: he can take us to the shores of the Northern Sea and thrill us by the sombre sublimity of his pictures and dreamy fancies; he can draw forth our tears by the voice he gives to our own sorrows . . . he can throw a cold shudder over us by a mysterious legend, a ghost-story, or a still more ghastly rendering of hard reality; he can charm us by a quiet idyl, shake us with laughter at his overflowing fun, or give us a piquant sensation of surprise by the ingenuity of his transitions from the lofty to the ludicrous . . . . Heine's great power as a poet lies in his simple pathos, in the ever varied but always natural expression he has given to the tender emotions." 73

—*and other greats:* " . . . we must say that there is no general resemblance between either **Wordsworth**, or **Tennyson**, and Heine. Their greatest qualities lie quite away from the light, delicate lucidity, the easy, rippling music, of Heine's style. The distinctive charm of his lyrics may best be seen by comparing them with **Goethe**'s. Both have the same masterly finished simplicity and rhythmic grace; but there is more thought mingled with Goethe's feeling—his lyrical genius is a vessel that draws more water than Heine's, and though it seems to glide along with equal ease, we have a sense of greater weight and force accompanying the grace of its movement.

"But, for this very reason, Heine touches our hearts more strongly; his songs are all music and feeling—they are like birds that not only enchant us with their delicious notes, but nestle against us with their soft breasts, and make us feel the agitated beating of their hearts. He indicates a whole sad history in a single quatrain: there is not an image in it, not a thought; but it is beautiful, simple, and perfect as a 'big round tear'—it is pure feeling breathed in pure music . . . .

"He excels equally in the more imaginative expression of feeling: he represents it by a brief image, like a finely cut cameo; he expands it into a mysterious dream, or dramatizes it in a little story, half ballad, half idyl; and in all these forms his art is so perfect, that we never have a sense of artificiality or of unsuccessful effort; but all seems to have developed itself by the same beautiful necessity that brings forth vine-leaves and grapes and the natural curls of childhood." ¶73-4

—*writing prose:* "But in Heine's hands German prose, usually so heavy, so clumsy, so dull, becomes, like clay in the hands of the chemist, compact, metallic, brilliant; it is German in an *allotropic* [variation of physical properties without change of substance; as, charcoal and diamond] condition . . . crystalline definiteness and clearness, fine and varied rhythm, and all that delicate precision, all those felicities of word and cadence, which belong to the highest order of prose. And Heine has proved . . . that it is possible to be witty in German; indeed, in reading him, you might imagine that German was pre-eminently the language of wit, so flexible, so subtle, so piquant does it become under his management.

"He is far more an artist in prose than **Goethe**. He has not the breadth and repose, and the calm development which belong to Goethe's style, for they are foreign to his mental character; but he excels Goethe in susceptibility to the manifold qualities of prose, and in mastery over its effects. Heine is full of variety, of light and shadow: he alternates between epigrammatic pith, imaginative grace, sly allusion, and daring piquancy; and athwart all these there runs a vein of sadness, tenderness, and grandeur which reveals the poet." 75-6

"The most poetic and specifically humorous of Heine's prose writings are the 'Reisebilder.' The comparison with **Sterne** is inevitable here; but Heine does not suffer from it, for if he falls below Sterne in raciness of humor, he is far above him in poetic sensibility, and in reach and variety of thought. Heine's humor is never persistent, it never flows on long in easy gayety and drollery; where it is not swelled by the tide of poetic feeling, it is continually dashing down the precipice of a witticism. It is not broad and unctuous; it is aerial and sprite-like, a momentary resting-place between his poetry and his wit." ¶76

Also mentioned

[relatively distinguished historical or literary figures are in Index X or XI]

Introduction to Genesis
(pp 41-2)

Introduction to the Book of Genesis, James Heywood editor—an abridged translation of *Die Genesis, historisch-kritisch erläutert* (1835) by Peter Von Bohlen

"What is the office of the Biblical critic in relation to the Old Testament? There are various answers to this question.

"Extreme orthodoxy says, that since there is irrefragable external evidence for the Divine origin and direct verbal inspiration of the Hebrew Scriptures, the critic has simply to interpret the meaning of the text: any record which is in contradiction with the text, if not reconcileable by hypothesis, is to be pronounced false; but if an undeniable fact turns out to be in contradiction with the text, the received interpretation is to be reconsidered and altered so as to agree with the undeniable fact. According to this theory the critic has not to examine the Hebrew writings in order to ascertain their origin, but having beforehand settled their origin, he has to explain everything so as to make it accord with this premiss. He is not an inquirer, but an advocate. He has not to weigh evidence in order to arrive at a conclusion, but having arrived at a conclusion, he has to make it the standard by which he accepts or rejects evidence.

¶"His criticism is a deductive process, which has for its axiom, the Hebrew writings are from beginning to end revealed truth. And it is only while orthodoxy strictly adheres to this point of view that it is on safe and consistent ground; for if we are to examine a book for proof—though it be only confirmatory proof—of its origin, we must have some criteria to judge it by, and we can only obtain such criteria by borrowing them from pure historical criticism, an ally that must be ultimately incompatible with rigid orthodoxy. As long as we rely implicitly on testimony as evidence of a man's health, we have no need to examine the indications of health in his person; but the moment we feel the testimony insufficient, we must have recourse to physiological criteria, which are common to every human organism.

"The first symptom that orthodoxy begins to feel the pressure of historical criticism is shown in an extension of the 'accommodation' theory. As the Deity, it is said, in speaking to human beings, must use human language, and consequently anthropomorphic expressions, such as the 'eye of God,' the 'arm of God,' the 'laughter and jealousy of God,' which we have no difficulty in understanding figuratively, so he must adapt the form of His revelations to the degree of culture, which belongs to men at the period in which His revelations are made. He teaches them as a father teaches his children, by adapting the information he gives to their narrow stock of ideas. It was in this way that the candid **Dr Pye Smith** explained the narratives of the Creation and the Deluge, to the great scandal of his Evangelical brethren.

¶"It is easy to see that this system of interpretation is very elastic, and that it may soon amount to little more than a theological formula for the history of human development. The relation between the theory of *accommodation* and that of *development* is analogous to the relation between the doctrine that the brain is the organ of mind, and the doctrine that mind is the function of the brain; in both cases the manifestation of mind is determined by the conditions of the body. And thus the 'accommodation' theory necessarily leads to what may be called a mitigated orthodoxy or a mild heterodoxy, which allows the presence of mythical and legendary elements in the Hebrew records, and renounces the idea that they are from beginning to end infallible, but still regards them as the medium of a special revelation, as the shell that held a kernel of peculiarly Divine truth, by which a monotheistic faith was preserved, and the way prepared for the Christian dispensation.

¶"They who hold this theory believe that the Hebrew nation was the grandest instrument of Providence—the Hebrew writings, the vehicle of superhuman truth; but they do not believe in talking serpents and talking asses, or in divine commands to butcher men wholesale; and they hold that, to identify a belief in such fables with the faith of a Christian, is as dangerous to reverence as it would be to fix an absurd popinjay on the divine symbol of the Cross. The laws of **Moses** are something more to them than the laws of **Menu***—a Hebrew prophet something more than a religious and patriotic poet; a chapter of Isaiah something more than the Hymn of **Cleanthes**.** They do not feel about the Hebrew temple and the Hebrew worship as they feel about a temple of Isis or the Eleusinian mysteries: the history of Israel is a sacred precinct to them—they take their shoes from off their feet, for it is holy ground. To them, therefore, the Old Testament is still an exceptional book; they only use historical criticism as a winnowing fan to carry away all demands on their belief, which are not strictly involved in their acceptance of Christianity as a special revelation.

"Extreme heterodoxy, on the contrary, holds no conviction that removes the Hebrew scriptures from the common category of early national records, which are a combination of myth and legend, gradually clarifying at their later stages into genuine history. It enters on the examination of the Old Testament with as perfect a freedom from pre-suppositions, as unreserved a submission to the guidance of historical criticism, as if it were examining the Vedas or the Zendavesta, or the fragments of Metho and Sanchoniathon.*** On thus looking at the Hebrew records by the 'light of common day,' without the lamp of faith, heterodoxy finds in them no evidence of anything exceptionally divine, but sees in them simply the history and literature of a barbarous tribe that gradually rose from fetichism to a ferocious polytheism, offering human sacrifices, and ultimately, through the guidance of their best men, and contact with more civilised nations, to Jehovistic monotheism. It finds in them, as in other early records, a mythical cosmogony, an impossible chronology, and extravagant marvels tending to flatter national vanity, or to aggrandise a priesthood; it finds discrepant conceptions of Deity in documents attributed to one and the same source; it finds legislative enactments, springing from an advanced period, stamped with the sanction of primeval names, or of mythical crises in the national history; in short, it not only finds in the Hebrew writings nothing which cannot be accounted for on grounds purely human, but it finds them of a character which it would be monstrous to attribute to any other than a human origin.

"These are results arrived at in the present day by very grave and competent scholars, and whatever opinion may be held concerning them, no educated person can dispense with some knowledge of the evidence on which they are based. There are few books, at least in English, better adapted to give such knowledge in a concise form than the *Introduction to Genesis* by Von Bohlen, named at the head of our article. Von Bohlen's was a thoroughly earnest and reverent mind, and orthodox believers need never be shocked by his manner, if they are inevitably pained by his matter. To this admirable qualification he added that of immense learning, especially in the department of Hindoo literature, his fame having been first won by a work on 'Ancient India.' We have only to regret that Mr Heywood did not heighten the value of his disinterested labour in editing the *Introduction to Genesis,* by publishing it in a cheaper and more portable form."

GE then gives details of the purview of each of the Heywood volumes and for quotation chooses a Hebrew myth on religious toleration.

*alternatively Manu, who in Hindu myth created mankind and the laws to govern him

**Stoic philosopher (c331-c232 BCE), successor to Zeno and author of the *Hymn to Zeus*

***the sacred texts of the Hindus and the Parsees, respectively

The Antigone and Its Moral

(page 306)

The Antigone of Sophocles: Text with Short English Notes for the Use of Schools (Oxford, 1855)

" 'Lo! here a little volume but great Book'—a volume small enough to slip into your breast pocket, but containing in fine print one of the finest tragedies of the single dramatic poet who can be said to stand on a level with **Shakspeare**. Sophocles is the crown and flower of the classic tragedy as Shakspeare is of the romantic: to borrow [**A.W.**] **Schlegel**'s comparison, which cannot be improved upon, they are related to each other as the Parthenon to Strasburg Cathedral [Pinney points out that the comparison was between the Pantheon and Westminster Abbey or St Stephen's in Vienna].

"The opinion which decried all enthusiasm for Greek literature as 'humbug,' was put to an excellent test some years ago by the production of the Antigone at Drury Lane. The translation then adopted was among the feeblest by which a great poet has ever been misrepresented; yet so completely did the poet triumph over the disadvantages of his medium and of a dramatic motive foreign to modern sympathies, that the Pit was electrified, and Sophocles, over a chasm of two thousand years, once more swayed the emotions of a popular audience. And no wonder. The Antigone has every quality of a fine tragedy, and fine tragedies can never become mere mummies for [**Johann Gottfried Jacob**] **Hermann**s and [**August**] **Böckh**s to dispute about: they must appeal to perennial human nature, and even the ingenious dulness of translators cannot exhaust them of their passion and their poetry.

E'en in their ashes live their wonted fires*

"We said that the dramatic motive of the Antigone was foreign to modern sympathies, but it is only superficially so. It is true we no longer believe that a brother, if left unburied, is condemned to wander a hundred years without repose on the banks of the Styx; we no longer believe that to neglect funeral rites is to violate the claims of the infernal deities. But these beliefs are the accidents and not the substance of the poet's conception. The turning point of the tragedy is not, as it is stated to be in the argument prefixed to this edition, 'reverence for the dead and the importance of the sacred rites of burial,' but the *conflict* between these and obedience to the State. Here lies the dramatic collision: the impulse of sisterly piety which allies itself with reverence for the Gods, clashes with the duties of citizenship; two principles, both having their validity, are at war with each. Let us glance for a moment at the plot.

"**Eteocles** and **Polynices**, the brothers of Antigone, have slain each other in battle before the gates of Thebes, the one defending his country, the other invading it in conjunction with foreign allies. Hence **Creon** becomes, by the death of these two sons of **Œdipus**, the legitimate ruler of Thebes, grants funeral honours to Eteocles, but denies them to Polynices, whose body is cast out to be the prey of beasts and birds, a decree being issued that death will be the penalty of an attempt to bury him. In the second scene of the play Creon expounds the motive of his decree to the Theban elders, insisting in weighty words on the duty of making all personal affection subordinate to the well-being of the State. The impulses of affection and religion which urge Antigone to disobey this proclamation are strengthened by the fact that in her last interview with her brother he had besought her not to leave his corpse unburied. She determines to brave the penalty, buries Polynices, is taken in the act and brought before Creon, to whom she does not attempt to deny that she knew of the proclamation, but declares that she deliberately disobeyed it, and is ready to accept death as its consequence. It was not Zeus, she tells him—it was not eternal Justice that issued that decree. The proclamation of Creon is not so authoritative as the unwritten law of the Gods, which is neither of to-day nor of yesterday, but lives eternally, and none knows its beginning . . .

"Creon, on his side, insists on the necessity to the welfare of the State that he should be obeyed as legitimate ruler, and becomes exasperated by the calm defiance of Antigone. She is condemned to death. **Hæmon**, the son of Creon, to whom Antigone is betrothed, remonstrates against this judgment in vain. **Teiresias** also, the blind old soothsayer, alarmed by unfavourable omens, comes to warn Creon against persistence in a course displeasing to the Gods. It is not until he has departed, leaving behind him the denunciation of coming woes, that Creon's confidence begins to falter, and at length, persuaded by the Theban elders, he reverses his decree, and proceeds with his followers to the rocky tomb in which Antigone has been buried alive, that he may deliver her. It is too late. Antigone is already dead; Hæmon commits suicide in the madness of despair, and the death of his mother **Eurydice** on hearing the fatal tidings, completes the ruin of Creon's house.

"It is a very superficial criticism which interprets the character of Creon as that of a hypocritical tyrant, and regards Antigone as a blameless victim. Coarse contrasts like this are not the materials handled by great dramatists. The exquisite art of Sophocles is shown in the touches by which he makes us feel that Creon, as well as Antigone, is contending for what he believes to be the right, while both are also conscious that, in following out one principle, they are laying themselves open to just blame for transgressing another; and it is this consciousness which secretly heightens the exasperation of Creon and the defiant hardness of Antigone. The best critics have agreed with Böckh in recognising this balance of principles, this antagonism between valid claims; they generally regard it, however, as dependent entirely on the Greek point of view, as springing simply from the polytheistic conception, according to which the requirements of the Gods often clashed with the duties of man to man.

"But, is it the fact that this antagonism of valid principles is peculiar to polytheism? Is it not rather that the struggle between Antigone and Creon represents that struggle between elemental tendencies and established laws by which the outer life of man is gradually and painfully being brought into harmony with his inward needs? Until this harmony is perfected, we shall never be able to attain a great right without also doing a wrong. Reformers, martyrs, revolutionists are never fighting against evil only; they are also placing themselves in opposition to a good—to a valid principle which cannot be infringed without harm. Resist the payment of ship-money, you bring on civil war; preach against false doctrines, you disturb feeble minds and send them adrift on a sea of doubt; make a new road, and you annihilate vested interests; cultivate a new region of the earth, and you exterminate a race of men. Wherever the strength of a man's intellect, or moral sense, or affection brings him into opposition with the rules which society has sanctioned, *there* is renewed the conflict between Antigone and Creon; such a man must not only dare to be right, he must also dare to be wrong—to shake faith, to wound friendship, perhaps, to hem in his own powers. Like Antigone, he may fall a victim to the struggle, and yet he can never earn the name of a blameless martyr any more than the society—the Creon he has defied, can be branded as a hypocritical tyrant.

"Perhaps the best moral we can draw is that to which the Chorus points—that our protest for the right should be seasoned with moderation and reverence, and that lofty words—*megaloi logoi*—are not becoming to mortals."

*A slight step from a line in Thomas Gray's *Elegy Written in a Country Churchyard*

Church History of the Nineteenth Century

(pp 331-2)

Kirchengeschichte der neusten Zeit, von 1814 bis auf die Gegenwart (History of the Church from 1814 to the Present Time), by Dr. Gieseler; edited by Dr. Redepenning

"The history of the Church, as of every other department of human affairs, is the history of revolutionary movements and of reactions: the tide of opinion and sentiment is never really stationary, though to the unobservant eye it seems to sleep lazily at ebb, and to sustain for a long while the force with which it rushes against the barriers at high water. The reaction towards positive religion and pietism, which followed the revolutionary movement of the eighteenth century, did not *begin* in 1814, but it reached that point at which its onward movement became palpable. The War of Liberation in Germany had exalted the religious and imaginative tendencies of the nation; enthusiasm was the order of the day: the 'Kaltes Verstand'—the cold understanding was shuddered at as an evil principle, and through the haze of fervid emotion, *Gott, König, and Vaterland* were blended together, and shone as a Trinity in Unity. This religious and political reaction was strengthened by its alliance with the Romantic movement in literature and art which began with the nineteenth century.

¶"The main feature of this movement was the exaltation of the Mediæval above the Classic, of art animated by Christian spiritualism above the art animated by Greek humanism. And as mediæval art was developed in the closest union with Catholicism the Romantic school naturally had little sympathy with the Reformation, which had gone on the principle, so highly lauded by **Andrew Fairservice**, of 'combing off' from the churches the productions of mediæval art, as unhealthy adjuncts to religious worship. Hence, some of the chief Romanticists, notably **Frederic Stolberg** and **Frederic Schlegel**, became converts to Rome, and of course these large fish were not netted without an accompanying haul of small fry. Here we see the religious reaction exhibiting itself in its more imaginative and poetic phase. Its intellectual or ratiocinative phase was seen in the increased fervour and more thorough investigation thrown into the controversy between Rationalism and Supernaturalism in the Protestant Churches, and in the various theories by which it was attempted to place Christianity on a philosophical basis, at the head of which, and in an opposition to each other, stand the systems of **Schleiermacher** and the **Hegel**ians. To these elements of interest have been added the fermentations within the Catholic Church, dating from the affair of the 'Holy Coat'—the struggle between Prussia and Rome on the question of mixed marriages, and the attempt at a Union of the Lutheran and Reformed Churches.

"France comes next to Germany in the interest of its Church History during the last half century; but here the drama turns not on the collision between Protestant interpretations or between Catholicism and Protestantism, but on the contest between Catholicism and Infidelity, and on the question of the external constitution of the Church. In the first act of the drama, we see Jesuit missionaries planting huge crosses decked with lilies and little hearts, or frightening untheological laymen on their deathbeds by questions about **Jansenius**, **Quesnel**, and the Bull *Unigenitus,* while Liberalism in the background vents its scorn in a loud 'aside.' Here are the elements of the main plot; the secondary plot is the struggle between Ultramontanism and Gallicanism, and we are still far from the catastrophe.

"The religious struggles of Germany and France are typical of those which have been going forward with greater or less vigour in every other country of Western Europe. Everywhere there is the same conflict between Reason and Faith; everywhere the question is—shall the Church govern itself, or shall it be governed by the State? And it is a splendid task to tell the history of this conflict as it has exhibited itself during the last fifty years.

"Something towards this task has been done by Dr Gieseler in the volume before us; but it is probable that he would have achieved much more if his labours had not been cut short by death. As it is, he has given us no more than a text-book of Church History since 1814; admirable for the ability with which he has digested facts, and the impartiality with which he has presented them, but affording scarcely more than an outline, and in most cases not extending beyond 1848. The volume has been formed from the materials left by him, to which he would, perhaps, have made large additions before publishing them himself. However, most persons who care about Church History, and all who make it a study, will find Dr Gieseler's volume an acceptable source of information and a valuable book of reference. The section on English affairs if very meager; but the sketch of religious history in the Papal States, in France, in Catholic Switzerland, and in Germany, is especially well done, and will make an excellent starting-point for further study of the subject.

"The battle between Rationalism and Supernaturalism in Germany is chiefly confined to the clerical and professorial class, and their polemics have little interest even for the educated portion of the people. But, about fifteen years ago, there commenced a movement amongst the Protestants (corresponding to that of the German Catholics under **Rouge** and **Czerski**) which has given the controversy a more popular aspect. This is the association of the *Lichtfreunde* or Friends of Light, springing from various centres—Magdeburg, Breslau, and Konigsberg, and brought together by the common desire to free Christianity from the fetters of ecclesiastical confessions and dogmas, that its essential principles may have free development in accordance with the wants of the present age. The movement was proximately caused by the indications of an increased tendency in the government, on the accession of the present King of Prussia, to favour the more rigid adherence to dogmatic formulæ; but **Uhlich**, the leader of the party in Magdeburg, seems, like **Wesley**, to have had in the first instance no desire that his associates should separate from the National Church, but that they should remain in it, in order gradually to effect a reform in spirit and doctrine.

¶"The Government, however, frowned on the *Lichtfreunde,* and the result has been the formation of numerous free churches, in which the bond of faith seems to be of the most elastic kind, being woven apparently out of a mixture of Rationalism and of that Pantheistic interpretation of Christianity which has been promulgated by the younger Hegelians. The following fundamental principles adopted by the Free Church of Nordhausen may be taken as an example:—I. God is the father of all, the living God, the eternal Spirit, the sole Lord of the world: His rule is eternally Truth and Love.' II. 'Jesus is the Christ, the Saviour of Man: his message of reconciliation is Truth and Love.' III. 'The Spirit is holy in his nature, he fills the Universe, and brings us forth from God at our birth, makes us live through God in our life, and return to God at our death: The blessing wherewith he blesses us is Truth and Love.'

"It was to be expected that the ideas and movements of the *Lichtfreunde* would be saluted by loud denunciations from the orthodox party in the Church. The rigid Lutherans have become more intense and intolerant in their assertion of doctrines since the Government has made the attempt to amalgamate them with the Reformed Church; and orthodox theologians in Germany differ from the same class in England rather in their greater theological culture than in the greater amiability of their spirit. Hence, it is not surprising that before the *Lichtfreunde* had separated from the national church, they were declared to have forsaken the true Light of the World, and to be no longer brethren in Christ, and that the *Evangelische Kirchenzeitung,* the organ of **Hengstenberg** and his party, proclaimed them to be much farther removed from the foundations of true Christianity than the Pope and the Jesuits.

"Such denunciations had their usual effect in heightening the centrifugal force in the dissidents, and the protest of the *Lichtfreunde,* like other protests, has ended in carrying the Protestants far beyond the limits they at first contemplated."

Who Wrote the Waverley Novels?

(pp 375-6)

Who Wrote the Waverley Novels? Being an Investigation into certain Mysteries and Circumstances attending their Production, and an Inquiry into the Literary Aid which Sir Walter Scott may have received from many Persons, by W. J. F.

"**Queen Elizabeth** once proposed to have the suspected author of an offensive pamphlet racked in order to extort confession from him. 'Nay, Madam,' said **Bacon**, 'never rack his person, but rack his style. Command him to write another pamphlet, and I will undertake to pronounce whether he be the author of this.' Some persons who are credited with more than their own, are obliging enough voluntarily to place themselves on the critical rack. For example, it was at one time reported that the novels of a very fertile living author were written by his wife; but circumstances at length induced the lady to publish a novel avowedly her own, and that example of her quality as an authoress set the report at rest for ever.

"Unfortunately, no such test is possible with regard to those for whom W.J.F., the author of the above-named pamphlet, claims the chief authorship of the *Waverley Novels.* We have no opportunity of racking their style, for their right hand has long forgotten its cunning, and they have left nothing behind them which will enable us to gauge their power. Their works belong to the same famous category with bachelors' wives and old maids' children.

"We know, indeed, of a brain and hand lying these four-and-twenty years under the sod at Melrose which have left behind them indisputable proof of a genius inspired with all the powers exhibited in the *Waverley Novels,* of a memory stored with all the knowledge required for writing them, of a nature characterised by all the tastes and idiosyncrasies betrayed in them. That this brain should have produced the *Waverley Novels* has hitherto seemed no more surprising to the majority of well-informed mankind than that the man who wrote *Hamlet* should have written *As you Like It,* than that the conqueror of Jena was the conqueror of Austerlitz, than that the vine which bears purple clusters one year should bear other purple clusters the next. A sufficient cause for the existence of the *Waverley Novels* seemed to be given in the genius of Scott.

"But now we are called on to revise this opinion. According to W.J.F., those novels—at least the best of them produced between 1814 and 1823, were not written by Walter Scott, who has unfairly monopolised the credit of them, but by his brother, **Thomas Scott**, and **Elizabeth MacCulloch**, the wife of the said Thomas; the husband contributing the humorous character and dialogue, and the military sketches, and the wife supplying the descriptions of scenery, the feminine characters, and the construction of the plot. The utmost Walter did, it appears, was to throw in some of his dead historical lore among the living scenes that were due to the joint genius of Thomas and Elizabeth, and to add a few limbs and flourishes of style.

¶"But the vital part of *The Antiquary, Guy Mannering,* and the rest was all begotten in Canada, by a man whose hand shook with drink, and a woman who 'may possibly' have written some feeble poems and articles signed 'Eliza,' in the corner of an American newspaper. It was not possible for Walter Scott, a practised writer, to have produced the best of the *Waverley Novels* in such rapid succession, but it *was* possible for Elizabeth MacCulloch and her husband. And what is yet more remarkable, the man and woman, who had genius enough to produce works which won not only a world of fame but a world of money, were contented to live an utterly obscure life, and to get nothing but a miserable gleaning of hundreds that you may count by units, while their brother pocketed his tens of thousands and carried away immortal fame as the fruit of *their* labours. Yet more: Thomas and Elizabeth Scott had several children, yet none of those children have, apparently, breathed a word in vindication of their parents' rights.

"Not a probable case, certainly, considering what we know of human nature. However, *le vrai n'est pas toujours le vraisemblable,* and we are prepared to bow to sufficient evidence. When W. J. F. has backed his case by adequate proof, we will unlearn half our piety towards Walter Scott, place him in a humble niche of our temple, and make room for W. J. F.'s 'strange gods' —Thomas and Elizabeth.

"At present, however, we are far from feeling coerced by his evidence, and we have taken up his pamphlet, not as a matter of any importance, but simply as a literary—or rather as an illiterate—curiosity. From an editorial note in the *Irish Quarterly* we gather that the initials W. J. F. represent 'a gentleman who has obtained a respectable literary status,' and having been amused ourselves, we propose to amuse our readers, with the indications afforded in this pamphlet as to the amount of logical ability and literary acquirement with which such a 'status' may be obtained.

"The chief points in W.J.F.'s argument are—1. That an anonymous letter, published in a Quebec newspaper in 1830, states that the writer saw the manuscript of the *Antiquary* in Thomas Scott's handwriting, and that Elizabeth Scott 'wrote the character of Flora Mac Ivor.' 2. That Thomas Scott is pronounced by all who knew him to have possessed great humour and story-telling faculty, and that his wife had a 'talent for writing' and was stored with Scotch traditions. 3. That the dates in *Lockhart's Life* are irreconcileable with the production of the novels by Walter Scott. 4. That among the letters *not suppressed* by Lockhart there is one written shortly after the appearance of *Waverley,* in which Walter urges his brother to try his hand and sent it him to dress up. 5. That certain scenes and characters in the novels are known to have been familiar to Elizabeth Scott from her childhood. 6. That Walter's denial of the authorship in the first instance nullifies his ultimate assertion of it.

"A skilful advocate might create an effect with such a brief as this. But W.J.F. so manages his arguments that they either prove too much, or else contradict each other. At one moment he tells us that Walter Scott could not possibly have had time to write the novels; at another, that it is not surprising if the manuscript of most of them is extant in Walter Scott's handwriting, *since he thought nothing of the trouble of copying*—at another, that 'an adaptation must take a longer period to accomplish than a story written *currente calamo.'* Again, he brings forward **Sophia Scott**'s declaration, that though the whole family had access to her father's papers, they had never seen a scrap of the manuscript of any of the novels, forgetting that, if, as he says on another page, Walter Scott acted the part of 'a skilful editor who fluently fills up and judiciously strikes out,' the difficulty of his daughter's statement is rather increased than lessened. His family would be much more likely to notice a strange manuscript on his desk, than to notice his own. But we do not undertake to dissect W.J.F.'s arguments, still less to disprove them. Our readers, we fancy, will thank us more for having given them a few specimens, which, to speak in the style of the able editors, 'need no comment.'

"Searching for cumulative evidence, W.J.F. procured an old *Army List,* in which he read the names, first, of the officers in the 70th regiment, of which Thomas Scott was Paymaster, and, subsequently, of the officers in other regiments, engaged in Canada, with which the 70th was brought into frequent intercourse. Hereupon, he tells us, he was struck with 'some remarkable coincidences;' and probably the reader with be equally 'struck' when he learns what some of these coincidences were."

GE at this point devotes several lines to citations of obviously lame and far-fetched naming coincidences. She allows these weak stretches and other jejune observations to speak for themselves. The publisher of this sad effusion, surprisingly, was the distinguished firm of Smith and Elder. What were they thinking?

Story of a Blue-Bottle
(pp 401-402)

La Folle du Logis, by M. Léon Gozlan

We set forth below in its entirety the most flagrant (we almost could say the only) example of Homer nodding in all the work of George Eliot. No more gratuitously charmless, clumsy, improbable, and unpleasant story was ever given the respect of a great author as worth retelling in a review which is otherwise without point. For her to call this story the "best" in the book she has in hand and bothers to spend her and her reader's time on is appalling, if true, and witless otherwise.

"Have you ever seen a huge blue-bottle buzzing in all the contentment that sunshine and the vicinity of a good larder can give, suddenly entangled in the web of an ill-conditioned spider, who is lurking in the corner ready to pounce on his victim, and nourish his venemous body on its innocent juices? It is an entomological tragi-comedy which 'as many parodies in human society—parodies which **Balzac**, of all artists, best loved to describe; witness his incomparable *Curé de Tours.* M. Léon Gozlan, apparently under the inspiration of Balzac, gives us, in the volume of tales which he rather whimsically calls *La Folle du Logis,* some new versions of the blue-bottle and spider drama, under the title of *Les Petits Machiavels.* Here is a sketch from the best of these stories, which will, perhaps, interest the admirers of the *Scènes de la Vie de Province*.

"M. Maes, a rich Belgian merchant, had become possessor, in May, 1837, of an enviable property on the banks of the Seine, not very far from Villeneuve, comprising, besides a charming villa and stables, a garden, a conservatory, pleasure-grounds, with statues and labyrinths—in short, everything a retired merchant could desire as his elysium after traversing the world from Antwerp to Java. To crown his happiness, he had excellent health and was a bachelor, proof against all the assaults of coquetry. With a constitution which had resisted yellow fever, and a sensibility which had resisted matrimony for two-and-forty years, he was sure at once of his heart and his stomach. You can conceive the sensations with which M. Maes took his first walk in his garden, with his hands under his coat-tails, in all the glories of proprietorship!

¶"The sun was shining with the splendour of commencing June on garden, corn-field, and meadow, and, above all, on the river—that river which promised endless fishing, the ruling passion of M. Maes. The close neighbourhood of the river had chiefly decided him to purchase Folie Margot at rather a bouncing price, and he had provided himself with all the apparatus dear to the piscatorial imagination. How happy M. Maes was going to be! He almost envied himself as he thought of the thrill with which he should perceive his line vibrating to the bite of a twenty-pound carp. Next to fishing, like a true Belgian, he loved flowers, and there was a whole army of them at his feet. He stooped to gather a tulip, and on rising saw, about two paces from him, a man as short and fat as himself, with little grey eyes sunk into his head, and a costume between a miller's and a mason's.

¶"The stranger bowed as low as the parabolic section of his body would permit, and smiled elaborately. 'You are the gardener, doubtless?' 'No, Monsieur Maes, I am Nicholas Merrain, your poor neighbour, the owner of that slip of ground, no bigger than a pocket-handkerchief, that lies between your property and the river. I come to bid you welcome, Monsieur Maes.' 'And what crop does your ground yield you, Monsieur Merrain?' 'Pebbles in summer, mud in winter. But I have an affection for it; my poor wife used to come and wash her linen there in her life-time.' 'Very good. You keep your bit of ground in memory of your wife. I esteem you for it, Monsieur Merrain. We shall be good neighbours, I see.' 'You do me an honour in thinking so, Monsieur, and if in anything you need my poor services——' 'What is your trade, my good friend?' 'I do a little of all sorts. I buy standing crops; I buy old buildings when they are not too dear, and sell the materials by lot.' As M. Maes, in haste to make the tour of his grounds, bade his neighbour good day, that worthy murmured to himself, 'I shall make a good job of it. This man must be fond of fishing.'

"You see at least one spider on the watch for our human blue-bottle. But he, happy in not knowing his coming unhappiness, smoked his cigar with a new relish as he sauntered in his garden the next morning. All at once he perceives that his domain, which has two gates towards the Villeneuve road, has no outlet at all towards the Seine. How, then, did the former owners of Folie Margot get down to the river? Pooh! The reason was simple. They could not have cared about fishing. M. Maes lost no time in sending for a mason, but no sooner was a breach made in the wall, than it disclosed the figure of that obliging neighbour Nicolas Merrain, who with his former unctuous politeness is charmed to think that M. Maes will enjoy having a door that opens on the river, because M. Maes is an excellent man, and he, Nicolas Merrain, who of all things dislikes the idea of being a bad neighbour, had been constrained to build up a similar door which had been made by the former proprietors of Folie Margot. 'This fellow built up a door like mine?' said M. Maes to himself. 'Then I can only go to the river by his indulgence. How is it my notary did not acquaint me with this?' But he prudently suppressed his annoyance, and, afraid to offend a man who could put a veto on his fishing, accepted his proposition to furnish him with a door and fit it up.

"The weeks rolled on, and M. Maes, in the enjoyment of uninterrupted fishing, forgot his momentary annoyance at his subjection to Nicolas Merrain. He avoided all advances towards acquaintance made by neighbouring proprietors, for what company can do more for you than a carp, which serves as your amusement one day, and your dinner the next? One morning, as he was angling opposite to a boat in which one of his neighbours came to fish with a regularity equal to his own, he became aware that he had hooked a tremendously heavy fish. At the same moment his *vis-à-vis* perceived his bait dragged with the same force. The prey was a carp weighing twenty pounds, and of corresponding voracity, for it had swallowed both baits at once. Now ensued a contest of politeness, each being quite sure that the fish belonged to his neighbour. At length the unknown rival consented to accept the fish on condition that M. Maes would come and partake of it at his table. The stranger, we see, had hooked two heavy fish at once.

"On returning home the vexation of having made an acquaintance in spite of himself, was not at all alleviated for M. Maes by his receiving a bill of three hundred francs from Nicolas Merrain, for putting up his new door. Three hundred francs for a door not worth ten! But Nicolas Merrain must not be offended, so M. Maes paid the three hundred francs, inwardly resolving that he would let his neighbour have nothing to do with the building of a new summer-house which he contemplates in the highest part of his pleasure-grounds. The next day our Belgian betakes himself, according to engagement, to the houſe of his new acquaintance, M. Cornillard (who is no less a personage than the receiver-general), on the opposite bank of the river. While the carp is going through the last stages of the culinary mysteries, the two proprietors walk amongst the flowers, discussing, like other well-bred persons whose acquaintance is only beginning, a variety of subjects of which they are mutually ignorant, until at last they arrive at the perfectly lucid question, 'I think we are neither of us married?' "Note well that this question was put by M. Cornillard. 'I am not married,' said M. Maes, 'because I love liberty, and hate children. If a child were to break one of my cups of Dresden china, I think I should break its head.' 'But suppose you were to take the precaution of having no Dresden china?' 'Give up china and have children! You are joking.' 'Then you should see if it would not be possible to marry and keep the china without having children. The thing is possible; the age of your wife might reconcile everything.'

¶"At this moment a formidable voice cried through a speaking-trumpet, 'The dinner is ready, uncle!' 'My niece calls us,' said M. Cornillard. 'You will see her—a charming person; not absolutely young, but with admirable qualities.' On entering the dining-room, M. Maes started to see a bony figure, six feet high, on the confines of five-and-forty, with a nose which would have made an excellent finger to a sun-dial. This divinity, whose name was Palmyre, wielded, as a symbolic scepter, a feather brush by way of duster. During dinner, Mademoiselle Palmyre, who had been hitherto silent, suddenly rose, and pounced, brush in hand, on M. Maes's coat-collar. The pacific Belgian thought she had descried a venemous insect. No! It was a grain of dust. 'Ah,' said Cornillard, 'Mimire has such a passion for cleanliness. She dusts the very trees. You, too, who are a Belgian, must love cleanliness.' On conducting his neighbour home in the evening, M. Cornillard observed, 'Now the acquaintance is made, I hope we shall see each other sometimes.' 'Very often,' replied M. Maes, meaning 'as seldom as possible.' You see there is another spider spreading his web for our unconscious blue-bottle.

"M. Maes, a little hastened by a spirit of vengeance towards Nicolas Merrain, proceeded forthwith to the construction of his summer-house. Nicolas saw everything, but seemed to see nothing, though every plank he had not furnished entered into his soul. The only change observable in him was that he redoubled his politeness, and that he avoided passing through M. Maes's ground to his own, choosing rather to make a long circuit, or to reach it by the river. One morning, as the Belgian, bent on fishing, had set his foot outside the door on Merrain' ground, he was meekly requested to observe that he was treading on cultivated soil—on land dedicated to carrots and turnips, and that he had no right to pass.

¶"M. Maes got angry. Nicolas remained honey-sweet, but firm, and in the end M. Maes did *not* proceed to the river, but went instead, fuming, to his notary, who was unable to deny that Nicolas was standing on a real right. An advocate is next consulted, who advises M. Maes to compromise the matter. After a struggle, the obese Belgian gives way, and Nicholas Merrain is asked what sum he will accept for his contemptible piece of ground. 'Ten thousand francs, without abatement.' The Belgian ire rises again, in spite of obesity, and M. Maes turns his back on Nicholas, observing, with anything but friendly significance, 'that they shall meet again.'

¶"The dispute had meanwhile become the talk of the neighbourhood. Wherever the unhappy M. Maes appeared, there was always some one at hand to say, 'That is M. Maes, who is at law with Nicolas Merrain.' Such was the cruel position of the man who had come to Folie Margot in the hope of peace and quietness and unlimited fishing! He unbosomed his sorrows to his neighbour Cornillard, who told him that Merrain would not have dared to behave so to a Frenchman. M. Maes, as a stranger, lacked the sympathies of the neighbourhood. 'If you were only a Frenchman, or married to a Frenchwoman——' 'He is talking about marriage again,' thought M. Maes; 'can he want me to marry his niece? Never, never!' he groaned, as he walked away with despair in his soul. For two months he confined himself within his own grounds, and it was all the while the most magnificent weather for fishing. The very carp seemed to taunt him as he watched them from his summer-house, while they bounded in the river.

"One morning he could endure it no longer. He seized his line, marched defiantly through Merrain's ground, jumped into his boat, and had an ecstatic day of fishing. On reaching home a summons was handed to him. A summons! Nicolas Merrain had seen all. M. Maes consulted another advocate, who discovered that the Commune had the power of reclaiming the fatal strip of ground on the payment of a slight indemnity to Merrain. But how was the Commune to be induced to take this step in which it had no real interest? A new mayor was to be elected in a week; M. Maes must be that mayor, and he could then obtain what he pleased of the Commune. 'But,' urged M. Maes, 'no one in the Commune knows me.' 'Yes; you have just told me that M. Cornillard, the receiver-general, knows you. He is omnipotent over the municipal council. Apply to him.' The advocate was ready to aid M. Maes in the matter, because he dreaded being elected mayor himself.

¶"Time pressed, so M. Maes hurried to the receiver-general. But one good turn deserves another. M. Cornillard has a niece, fit to constitute the happiness of any man. He will make a present of her to M. Maes, whom he will be delighted to have for a nephew. 'But I had sworn never to marry!' 'People always come to that in the end.' 'Nevertheless, you yourself——' 'I am a widower for the second time. Still, nothing obliges you to marry Palmyre.' 'But if I don't marry her I shall not be mayor, and if I am not mayor——O mon Dieu!' M. Maes asked three days for decision. To avoid marrying Palmyre he even brought himself to call on Nicolas Merrain and offer him the ten thousand francs. They were refused: it was clear to Nicolas that the slip of ground had risen in value. M. Maes, furious, wrote to M. Cornillard that he accepted Mlle. Palmyre with her feather brush.

"A few days later, M. Maes became mayor and the husband of Mlle Palmyre. Nicolas Merrain's ground was claimed by the municipality, and was converted by the mayor into a public washing-ground. Nicolas turned pale for an instant. But a short time afterwards it was stated in the newspapers that a terrible outrage had been committed on the property of M. Maes, a rich Belgian. Trees had been torn up by the roots, walls pulled down, the roof of the house taken completely off. M. Maes and his wife had only escaped by a miracle from the malefactors, who had hitherto succeeded in eluding the inquiries of justice. Six months after the catastrophe, Folie Margot was sold by auction, and had become the property of a certain speculator in purchases at forced sales, named Nicolas Merrain.

"M. Maes and his charming spouse had set out for Java. The blue-bottle had ceased even to struggle, and the spiders were triumphant."

Saturday Review of Politics, Literature, Science, and Art I
April 26, 1856 **HBS**

Heine's Book of Songs

Heinrich Heine's Book of Songs. A Translation by John E. Wallis

"Heine's *Book of Songs,* like Tennyson's *In Memoriam,* draws its inspiration from a single theme. But the English poet, while adhering to the same poetic form, and revolving round the same central emotion, takes a wide sweep of thought—the German poet, on the contrary, keeps within a narrow circle of ideas and feelings, but perpetually varies his poetic form. Unhappy love is the almost unvarying theme of the *Book of Songs;* but we have read them *seriatim,* again and again, without any disagreeable sense of monotony—so ever changing, ever charming, are the melodies of Heine's verse, so inexhaustibly diversified are the modes in which his imagination presents the same feeling. He gives it us in eerie dreams, in ballads, in idyls, in sonnets, and most of all in delicious little lyrics, which he seems to find as easy as sighing; and everywhere there is the same wonderful grace— everywhere there is that completeness of expression without effort, which reminds us of nothing so much as of the rapid revelations of feeling which may be read in a beautiful and expressive human face. There is no awkward inversion—no far-fetched combination of epithets—no betrayal of art. Song seems as natural to Heine as to the thrush and the nightingale, and, while you are reading him, it is prose that appears artificial.

"Here is the reason why his poems are so difficult to be translated—or rather, so utterly untranslatable by any one who is only a versifier and not a poet. Rhythm and rhyme are no fetters to Heine—they are rather the wings on the sandals of the God, that help him to float through ether with all the more buoyancy. To be simple, idiomatic, and poetic is with him the same thing; but with the generality of translators it is quite another affair. Instead of floating through ether, they toil heavily along the ground. They may make a meritorious effort to be faithful—to say just what Heine says; but there is much the same likeness between their verses and his as between the phrase 'I love you,' which no one can hear quite unmoved, and the phrase 'I feel a tender passion for you,' which probably would not greatly move any one; or as between the ever-to-be-quoted phrase lines—

I could not love thee, dear, so well,
Loved I not honour more;—

and the never-to-be-quoted paraphrase—

My love would be inferior, dear
Were honour not supreme.

"In translation, something might be done by patient labour towards compensating for the want of the original *afflatus;* but, unfortunately, translators have usually either too little patience or too low an ideal. They are too easily tired, or too easily satisfied, or they give their patience to the production of quantity rather than quality. A few of Heine's poems finely translated would make the English reader better acquainted with the poet than a feeble English version of the whole. But the American translator, Mr Leland, undertakes to translate all the poems as well as all the prose—so that, notwithstanding his ability, he necessarily achieves a much larger amount of failure than of success; and Mr Wallis now presents us with the whole *Book of Songs,* when we should probably have been able to thank him much more for a small selection. This might have been one of the cases in which a part is greater than the whole.

"Mr Wallis writes very modestly in his preface. He has not thrust his translations on the public hastily, but had long withheld them because they fell below his own requirements; and he was only encouraged to publish them at last by the fact that other translations of Heine, perhaps not superior to his own, have been favourably received. He is clearly a very competent German scholar, and his rendering is generally a close one. With some exceptions, he reproduces faithfully the meaning of the original; but, alas! he fails to reproduce their charm. The scent of the violet is gone; the living song has become mechanical verse; and very often the line-for-line rendering only makes the contrast more striking.

"Every reader of Heine remembers the little lyric—

Herz, mein Herz, sei nicht beklommen,
Und ertrage dein Geschick,
Neuer Frühling giebt zurück,
Was der Winter dir genommen,
Und wie viel ist dir geblieben!
Und wie schön ist noch die Welt!
Und, mein Herz, was dir gefällt,
Alles, Alles darfst du lieben!

"The English reader will understand the charm of this little lyric, when we tell him that it resembles that of **Burns**'s more pathetic songs. The following is Mr Wallis's version:—

Heart, my heart, oh, be not troubled!
  Bear thy lot, though hard it be;
Spring will give them back redoubled,
  All that winter took from thee.

Think how lovely is creation!
  Think what joys await thy call!
All things bring thee consolation,
  Thou art free to love them all!

This assuredly does not resemble Burns. 'Think how lovely is creation!' sounds very much like a quotation from a Unitarian Hymn-book. We are amazed that a mind so evidently accomplished as Mr Wallis's could allow such a miserable platitude to stand.

"In another lyric of the same class, he seems to have missed Heine's meaning entirely, and turns a bit of imaginative pathos into a flat prosaism—

They both of them loved, but neither
    The truth to the other would say;
They met so proudly and coldly,
    While both were pining away.

They parted at length, and in future
    Encounter's in dreams alone;
They died long since, and to neither
    The fate of the other was known.

"The two last lines in the original are—

Sie waren längst gestorben
Und wussten es selber kaum—

meaning that the state of separation from each other was so like death, that death was hardly a change.

"Again, Mr Wallis entirely loses the point of Sonnet III. He renders the concluding lines thus:—

For when fair Fortune's gifts are from us reft,
And broken by the hand of destiny;
And when the fragments at our feet are flung;
And when the heart within our breast is wrung,
Wrung, rent, and wounded irrecoverably,—
A bitter laugh is all that we have left.

In the original the last line is

Dann bleibt uns *doch* das schöne gelle Lachen.

This does not mean—nothing is left to us but laughter. It means—laughter is still left to us. And Heine valued that residuum considerably.

"We were bound to indicate the deficiencies in Mr Wallis's book, and to warn the reader that it will not in the least qualify him to pronounce on Heine's merits as a poet. But there is no need to dwell longer on those deficiencies, and we may now do what is more agreeable—give a specimen of Mr Wallis's more successful efforts as a translator. Here is a little poem which he has rendered at once closely and poetically:—

My love, we sat together,
    Alone in our fragile bark.
The night was still, and we floated
    Over the waters dark.

The spirit Isle, the lovely,
    Lay dim in moonlight trance;
Sweet sounded magic music,
    And waved the misty dance.

The music grew sweeter and sweeter
    The dance waved to and fro;
But we, on the wide, wide ocean,
    Floated in silent woe.

Pictures of Life in French Novels

Le Dernier Rendezvous, by Henri Murger
La Résurrection de Lazare, by Henri Murger

"Henry Murger is a very popular novel writer in France. He excels in the extravagantly humorous, and his *Vie de Bohème* is read by the admirers of the *style buffon* with explosions of laughter. In that novel he gives us abundance of that intentional absurdity which is the privilege of wit; but when he enters on a more serious vein, he sometimes gives us that peculiar kind of *un*-intentional absurdity which is the privilege of the sentimental French novelist. In *Le Dernier Rendezvous,* the first of two tales contained in the volume before us, the heroine is one of those ladies who cut off their hair on the slightest provocation, and startle a lover by suddenly placing in his hands *cette magnifique chevelure noire, without* the head it adorned—who never hear their lover's name without blushing, raising one hand to their forehead to hide their blushes and placing the other on their *poitrine agitée*—who quit their husband's home some fine morning, with no more than a *petit paquet* of clothing which never wants renewing—who sublimely ignore that base necessity, an income—and, in short, innocence excepted, live in all respects like the lilies of the field.

¶"They sow not, neither do they spin,' and you have the smallest possible confidence in their knowledge of the multiplication table. Any man a little fatigued with the commonplace qualities of a wife who bears in mind that 'black hair,' once lost, is not easily renewed—who finds a moderate allowance of pin-money indispensable—and who has been initiated into that department of arithmetic called 'bills of parcels,' will do well to read such tales as *Le Dernier Rendezvous.* He will return from them with new relish for 'human nature's daily food'—a woman who has some knowledge of common things, and some sense of common obligations.

"*La Résurrection de Lazare* is a different sort of story, written more in the epigrammatic than the sentimental style. It is called a *drame en lettres,* each of the *dramatis personae* contributing his quota to the drama in the shape of letters. The **Lazarus** in question is not the brother of **Martha** and **Mary**, nor is the resurrection one of the body from a literal tomb. As the reader may be curious, we will extract the drama from the letters and tell it in brief.

"The Lazarus of M. Murger is a genius—a poet of this nineteenth century, who is to initiate a great literary revolution. At the opening of the drama, however, this high destiny is not apparent, except to the prophetic eye of friendship; for during the last four years Lazarus has been wasting his patrimony and his time, and tarnishing his *beau nom,* by a life of mad Parisian dissipation—a conscious victim to the Mephistophelean temptations of two cynical rakes, the Vicomte Séraphin and the Comte Antony de Sylvers. At the age of eight-and-twenty he has so exhausted the possibilities of life and imagination that even the diabolical ingenuity of his two friends is unable to devise anything that can astonish him.

¶"Still there is one sacred spot in his memory, one window in his mind, through which heaven's daylight shines in on the fumes and the gaslight. He has once seen at the opera a woman whose calm loveliness (and *blond* complexion set off by blue ribbons) so impressed itself on his imagination that he has painted a miniature of her from memory. At last, sick of his Parisian life, he has entered on the second stage of his Byronic career, and retreated to a cottage at Verrières, where he spends his days in solitary roaming through the woods. In the background is a certain M. de B., a *grand poéte,* the self-elected providence or good genius of Lazarus, who opposes his protecting watchfulness to the machinations of the evil genii, Antony and Séraphin, and induces another poet (not great) named Theodore, to act as deputy providence in the shape of valet to Lazarus. Now opens the story.

"Late one evening, on returning from his rambles, Lazarus, as he is about to enter his house, sees a body of some sort precipitated with great force from his bedroom window. While he is gazing, with the unwonted sensation of astonishment, at the said body, which proves to be that of an elegantly-dressed woman (with blue ribbons!) a crowd collects in his gardens, the gensd'armes appear, and he is arrested as a murderer. At this point, there appears on the sport Madame Marie d'Alton—a lady possessed of all charms, and residing in great privacy at Verrières, who has risen from her bed on hearing that her mysterious neighbour, the mad poet, has assassinated a woman, and who from a benevolent impulse, has repaired to the scene of action.

¶"She finds a lovely woman lying pale and blood-besprinkled on the ground, and Lazarus standing with folded arms, looking on with calm contempt at the indignant crowd and the inquiring police. Marie d'Alton has the woman carried to her house, and laid in her own bed, and Lazarus is carried off to prison at Versailles, where he is disappointed to find that it is impossible to *poser* with effect as a martyr, owing to the delicate consideration exhibited towards criminals. He thinks of betaking himself to the classic amusement of taming spiders, but the elegant *salon* he occupies gives no promise of zoological specimens. He entreats his gaoler to furnish him with a spider, and that functionary presents him with a *carte des distractions,* in which a tame mouse is charged five francs, a tame spider four, and an untamed spider two and a half.

¶"We leave Lazarus lamenting the prosaism of modern prisons, and return to Verrières. The houri with the strongly gravitating body, on whom Marie d'Alton has taken compassion, is neither more nor less than a *danseuse* of the *Cirque,* who, being madly in love with Lazarus, had been easily prompted by Antony and Séraphin to attempt the conquest of his resolute indifference by a *tour de force.* She had spent all her money in buying splendid apparel for the occasion—had come from Paris, and gained admission into the house by means of her acquaintance, Theodore—had sprinkled a little blood over her clothes by way of brightening the effect, and on hearing the footsteps of Lazarus, had executed in perfect safety her terrible *saut périlleux en arrière* from the window.

¶"She had meant to take the heart of Lazarus by assault—and she had caused him to be sent to prison as her assassin¡ However, if he will not love her, she will make him feel her power by continuing to act the assassinated woman. She allows a doctor (a lover in disguise) to dress her unfractured skull, and accepts the devoted nursing of Marie d'Alton. And who is Marie herself? The beloved of Count Antony de Sylvers, for whose sake she has given up friends and fortune—being one of those astonishing women who, with the utmost intellectual and moral insight, are unable, on the most intimate acquaintance, to discern the difference between a shallow, vicious egotist and a man worthy of all devotion.

¶"In the meantime, Lazarus has written to his friend Séraphin, begging him to send him a small tortoise-shell box, which will be found at his lodgings. Séraphin finds the box, does *not* send it, but does open it, and discovers in it a miniature of Marie d'Alton—of course, the miniature painted from memory, by Lazarus, of his unknown *Hebe.* Séraphin, exulting in a discovery which promises annoyance to many people at once, writes to Louisa, the *danseuse,* taunting her with the failure of her stratagem, and crowning his taunts by announcing to her that Lazarus loves Marie d'Alton. This letter, having fallen into the hands of Marie, is communicated by her to Antony, who regards it as a proof that his false friend Séraphin is conspiring to rob him of Marie. A duel is the consequence, and Antony is killed.

¶"Before the catastrophe, Louisa has induced Theodore to escort her on a visit to Lazarus in prison, where she makes a last attempt on his obdurate heart, by telling him their relative position. He receives her story with contemptuous indignation, and in her jealous rage she reveals the fact that his unknown adored one is Marie d'Alton. Does the reader foresee the *dénouement?* Louisa reflects, and confesses the truth to a magistrate— Lazarus is set at liberty, and declares his love to Marie 'Alton, who discovers that she has been unconsciously giving him the precedence in her heart from the time he began to interest her at Verrières. And now Lazarus, a wiser but not a sadder man, enters on his great career, and is saluted by M. de B. in a dithyrambic letter as the poet who '*l'aurore de la poésie et de la religion renouvelée, viendra proclamer la divinité de la matière immortelle!*' Louisa marries Theodore, and is not happy ever after.

"Since this story is so very far from real, there is probably some moral to which its idealism points. For our own part, we choose to draw a moral of our own, after the fashion of Renzo in *promissi sposi,* and we deduce the following piece of advice, which we offer to our feminine readers:—When you wish to conquer a man's heart, do not begin by throwing yourself out of the window."

The Art and Artists of Greece

Torso. Kunst, Künstler und Kunstwerke der Alten, by Adolf Stahr (two volumes)

"Probably many readers will be glad to hear of a German work which tells the history of Greek Art neither in the bald fashion of an introductory manual nor with the elaborate pedantry of a German Dryasdust, but with that agreeable combination of philosophic insight, picturesque narration, and poetic enthusiasm, to be found only in minds that have prepared themselves for a special study by thorough general culture. Such a work is *Torso,* by Adolph Stahr, a writer whose *Jahr in Italien*—two volumes of Italian travel, exhibiting rare artistic feeling as well as knowledge—prepared its readers to welcome from him a book more exclusively dedicated to art. It is a book not written to settle vexed questions, or to present any new results of independent research, but simply to give such a view of Greek art as will enable ordinarily cultivated persons to understand its organic relation to human development, and to have an intelligent and appreciatory enjoyment of its remains.

¶"Critics of a more negative disposition, and possibly of greater technical acquirement than Professor Stahr, will assail him for his too admiring attitude towards ancient art; and a certain tendency towards the oracular in his manner of writing will probably provoke them to detect many errors of statement or of judgment. But the 'general reader'—by whom, we imagine, is usually meant a reader of no particular information—is likely to find *Torso* an acceptable book, which will conduct him through a pleasant region of knowledge without causing him the least weariness in the journey. German writers have too often the uneasy pace of the camel—they take us to many remote quarters which we could hardly reach without their aid, but they cause us much aching and grumbling in the process. Stahr, however, has a style as agreeable as the canter of a well-trained horse. If it ever divides our attention with his subject, it also divides our admiration.

"Was Greek art a purely indigenous growth, or only a transplantation from the East? This question of genealogy, of course, presents itself in the first place to the historian, and with especial urgency to the German historian, who, of all others, feels constrained to *commencer par le commencement.* **Winckelmann** pronounced against the supposition of an Oriental origin; and German critics, more coerced by his authority than by arguments from facts and analogy, went on maintaining the same opinion long after it has been renounced by the best foreign critics.

¶"When at length **Ludwig Ross** returned from his travels to the Levantine countries, and brought evidence for the affiliation of Oriental and Greek art, gathered from a careful investigation of art-remains, he was derided as a 'Tourist'—a superficial man who allowed his opinions to be modified by observation, instead of spinning them, as a philosophic spider should, from a theory-secreting sac provided for the purpose! However, since then, there have been plenty of German critics who have not only accepted the newer idea, but have been its most laborious and valuable illustrators. Stahr follows in their track, treating the question in a rapid and popular way. The reference of Greek art to an Oriental source brings it, he observes, under a generalization which is more and more confirmed by the discoveries of science and scholarship . . . .

"In the Æginetan sculptures we see Greek art beginning to emancipate itself from Oriental and Egyptian symbolism, and advancing towards naturalism. But still, though the artist gave a high degree of finish to the limbs, he was incompetent or indifferent to the rendering of expression of character in the face. Athene is like the Trojans, and the Trojans are like the Greeks. In this respect the Æginetan sculptures present an interesting point of contrast with the works of Giotto, which hold a corresponding position in the development of Italian painting. Giotto and his immediate successors, in opposition to the early Greek artists, threw all their power into the face, and seemed to regard the body as an insignificant appendage to it. This difference in the order of artistic progress corresponds with the fundamental difference between Greek and Christian conceptions. To the Greek, a fine body was the primary condition of a fine mind; but to the spiritualism of the fourteenth century the body was but the transient and unworthy dwelling of the immortal soul, which flourished in proportion as the body was emaciated. Its canon of art was—

Give us no more of body than shows soul.

"It seems a great leap to pass from the Æginetan sculptures to those of the Parthenon, in which we see art at its highest point of development as an essentially religious and political outgrowth. Yet we have no knowledge to fill up the chasm, and to show us how far the immense advance was due to the individual genius of Phidias, how far it was prepared by his predecessors. The age of Phidias, having the period of supreme interest in the history of Greek art, is naturally also the most delightful part of Professor Stahr's book. From inference, from historical details, and also from mythical anecdotes, which always have their historic significance, he forms as vivid a picture as can be obtained of **Phidias** in his position as an artist; he reconstructs the Parthenon, and enables us to imagine it as it stood in its glory; he tells the sad story of its destruction, and describes with very fine discrimination the fragments which remain to us—the only works we possess that come immediately and indisputably from the genius of Phidias. Among the sculptures which may with probability be regarded as copies from his originals, is one of the famous Colossi on the Monte Cavallo, and we single it out from the rest for the sake of giving a legend admirably characteristic of the mode in which the mediaeval mind explained the relic as of classic antiquity . . . . "

"The works of **Polykletos** and **Myron**, the great contemporaries of Phidias, with those of **Praxiteles** and **Scopas** in the succeeding age, are subjects wide enough to carry us nearly to the end of the first volume— leaving room, however, for a long chapter on the Social Position of the Artist in Greece, and a discussion of the colouring and nudity of Greek statues. Apropos of Scopas, who was the most fertile originator of grotesque ideal beings as attendants on the deities, Stahr observes that, when the Greeks conceived combinations of the human with the brute form, they made the upper part human and the lower part bestial, as in the centaurs, satyrs, mermaids &c., while we see the reverse in the symbolism of the Egyptians. Like many other ingenious distinctions, however, this will not bear a very rigid examination. The sphinx, at least, might have occurred to him as a sufficiently remarkable exception.

"**Lysippus**, whose history opens the second volume, was the first great master of portrait sculpture. But in all cases of origination or discovery, it is 'the hour and the man,' and not the man alone, that accomplishes the transition from the old to the new. Lysippus was the contemporary of **Alexander**, and with the Macedonian conquests began a new political relation for art. The glory of the individual was no longer checked by democratic jealousy—the days of royal patronage began, and art glorified royalty in return. An amusing indication of the change that had come over the spirit of art is the story told by **Plutarch** of the sculptor **Stasikrates**. This artist went to Alexander, and proposed to him to fashion Mount Athos into an imperishable statue of the conqueror of the world, which should touch the sea with its foot and the clouds with its head, holding in one hand a populous city, and with the other pouring a perpetual mountain torrent into the sea. Alexander was wise enough to beg him leave Mount Athos alone."

"The revival of Greek art under Roman patronage is treated very fully by Professor Stahr; but we have touched on points enough in his agreeable volumes. They are easily accessible, and readers of German will find it worth while to look into *Torso* for themselves."

An earlier review of the first volume of *Torso* is at page 144.

The Natural History of German Life: Riehl

(pp 51-79)

[pp 122-52 in the 1894 Crowell edition; citations are to these pages]

"[The] conception of European society as incarnate history, is the fundamental idea of Riehl's books." 142

This piece is "one of her finest articles for the *Westminster*" in Haight's view. "The article is one of the richest she ever wrote. In it we see her mind turning back to the memories of her childhood among the common people of Warwickshire with the vivid sympathy that was soon to flower in her fiction. *Any one who wishes to understand the origin of George Eliot's novels should read the essay on Riehl.*" (Haight, pp 201, 202; emphasis supplied). The article may be found in its entirety in Pinney, pp 266-99 and in Ashton, pp 260-95.

GE begins with a discourse on truthfulness in art and the degree to which English painters are prejudiced by the literature they have read and ill-informed as to peasant actualities. She alludes to the paintings of **Holman Hunt** and criticizes the writings of **Charles Dickens**. She then turns to Riehl's work in Germany and a discourse on the "uncultivated classes" (*see Topicon* H:Social class). She notes Riehl's advocacy of what today we would call an "organic" approach to social policy: paying attention to the particular rather than seeking truth in generalization. " . . . a wise social policy must be based not simply on abstract social science, but on the Natural History of social bodies." 144

We are given a detailed geography lesson on the three natural divisions of Germany, even to gradations in suicide rates. And there are details on the way villages, towns and cities have grown up, and religions and rank have made themselves felt. The three great social classes—the landed aristocracy, the commercial bourgeoisie, and the agricultural, laboring class—are the focus of an analysis noting the gradual development of a "fourth estate," with ominous portents. GE touches on the *Philister* (Philistine) and extends Riehl's characterization of the type. And she describes the dangers of the growing "intellectual proletariat," of titled offspring without provision.

Additional extracts from this essay are in the *Topicon* at H:Art and Artists, RW:Germany and the Germans, and FM: Censure and Judgment—*denigration*.

"Our readers will perhaps already have gathered . . . that Riehl is not a man who looks at objects through the spectacles either of the doctrinaire or the dreamer; and they will be ready to believe what he tells us on his Preface—namely, that years ago he began his wanderings over the hills and plains of Germany for the sake of obtaining, in immediate intercourse with the people, that completion of his historical, political, and economical studies which he was unable to find in books. He began his investigations with no party prepossessions, and his present views were evolved entirely from his own gradually amassed observations. He was, first of all, a pedestrian, and only in the second place a political author." 140

—the argument summarized: "What has grown up historically can only die out historically, by the gradual operation of necessary laws. The external conditions which society has inherited from the past are but the manifestation of inherited internal conditions in the human beings who compose it; the internal conditions and the external are related to each other as the organism and its medium, and development can take place only by the gradual consentaneous development of both. Take the familiar example of attempts to abolish titles, which have been about as effective as the process of cutting off poppy-heads in a corn-field . . . . As a necessary preliminary to a purely rational society, you must obtain purely rational men, free from the sweet and bitter prejudices of hereditary affection and antipathy; which is as easy as to get running streams without springs, or the leafy shade of the forest without the secular growth of trunk and branch." 141

—things as they are: "After the notable failure of revolutionary attempts conducted from the point of view of abstract democratic and socialistic theories, after the practical demonstration of the evils resulting from a bureaucratic system which governs by an undiscriminating, dead mechanism, Riehl wishes to urge on the consideration of his countrymen a social policy founded on the special study of the people as they are—on the natural history of the various social ranks. He thinks it wise to pause a little from theorizing, and see what is the material actually present for theory to work upon." 142-3

—where Socialist theory fails: "For, says Riehl, the more deeply we penetrate into the knowledge of society in its details, the more thoroughly we shall be convinced that *a universal social policy has no validity except on paper*, and can never be carried into successful practice. The conditions of German society are altogether different from those of French, of English, or of Italian society; and to apply the same social theory to these nations indiscriminately, is about as wise a procedure as **Triptolemus Yellowley**'s application of the agricultural directions in **Virgil**'s 'Georgics' to his farm in the Shetland Isles." 143

—the Sciences: "It has not been sufficiently insisted on, that in the various branches of Social Science there is an advance from the general to the special, from the simple to the complex, analogous with that which is found in the series of the sciences, from Mathematics to Biology. To the laws of quantity comprised in Mathematics and Physics are superadded, in Chemistry, laws of quality; to these again are added, in Biology, laws of life; and lastly, the conditions of life in general branch out into its special conditions, or

Natural History, on the one hand, and into its abnormal conditions, or Pathology, on the other." 143.

—*ominous development:* "In his view, the Fourth Estate is a stratum produced by the perpetual abrasion of the other great social groups; it is the sign and result of the decomposition which is commencing in the organic constitution of society. Its elements are derived alike from the aristocracy, the bourgeoisie, and the peasantry. It assembles under its banner the deserters of historical society, and forms them into a terrible army, which is only just awaking to the consciousness of its corporate power." 148

—*English painting:* "The notion that peasants are joyous, that the typical moment to represent a man in a smock-frock is when he is cracking a joke and showing a row of sound teeth, that cottage matrons are usually buxom, and village children necessarily rosy and merry, are prejudices difficult to dislodge from the artistic mind, which looks for its subjects into literature instead of life. The painter is still under the influence of the cultivated and town-bred, rather than the truth of rustic life. Idyllic ploughmen are jocund when they drive their team afield; idyllic shepherds make bashful love under hawthorn-bushes; idyllic villagers dance in the checkered shade and refresh themselves, not immoderately, with spicy nut-brown ale. But no one who has seen much of actual ploughmen thinks them jocund; no one who is well acquainted with the English peasantry can pronounce them merry." 123-4

—*conclusory:* " . . . Riehl's conservatism is not in the least tinged with the partisanship of a class, with a poetic fanaticism for the past, or with the prejudice of a mind incapable of discerning the grander evolution of things to which all social forms are but temporarily subservient. It is the conservatism of a clear-eyed, practical, but withal large-minded man—a little caustic, perhaps, now and then in his epigrams on democratic doctrinaires who have their nostrum for all political and social diseases, and on communistic theories which he regards as 'the despair of the individual in his own man-hood, reduced to a system,' but nevertheless able and willing to do justice to the elements of fact and reason in every shade of opinion and every form of effort.

"He is as far as possible from the folly of supposing that the sun will go backward on the dial, because we put the hands of our clock backward; he only contends against the opposite folly of decreeing that it shall be mid-day, while in fact the sun is only just touching the mountain-tops, and all along the valley men are stumbling in the twilight." ¶152

Also mentioned

[relatively distinguished historical or literary figures are in Index X or XI]

Hornung, a painter	125
Stone, Frank; pre-Raphaelite who painted "Cross-Purposes"	123
Triptolemus Yellowley, agricultural theorist	143

 TS

A Tragic Story

(page 691)

Schatzkostkia des Gerattersmanns ("The Godfather's Jewel-Casket"), by Berthold Auerbach

"Berthold Auerbach is so deservedly celebrated for his tales of peasant life, that we could not open a new volume of stories by him without some pleasant expectations. The principal defect of his fictions is a too predominant moralizing tendency which often leads him to sacrifice truthful representation to the desire of enforcing a lesson. This defect is particularly conspicuous in *The Godfather's Casket,* where he seems divided between the purpose of writing tales about the poor which shall convey a moral to the rich, and that of writing moral tales for the poor themselves. The result is a book that is not well suited to either class. Still he is too sincere and striving a student of popular manners and character to produce a volume of fiction which does not contain some striking and true sketches, and there are several such in *The Godfather's Casket.* We select one as a specimen, not because it is the very best or most agreeable in the book, but because the lesson which he intends to convey by it to wealthy German mothers might be successfully adopted by certain English mothers also. Here is the story.

"Christiane, a blooming young country-woman, rejoicing over her first-born, has been induced by destitution to accept the office of wet-nurse in the family of a rich merchant, and, as a necessary consequence, to place her own baby in the care of a *ziehfrau*—a woman who makes it her profession to bring up children orphaned in this way. A slight shudder betrayed the recollection of the mother when the foster-child was first placed in Christiane's arms, but instinct is even more easily transferred than sentiment, and by-and-by her tenderness for her nursling grew into a passion. Living vicariously, she became brighter and more blooming than ever, and was inexhaustible in her songs, caresses, and playful chat. The merchant's young wife thought she had found the best of nurses. Winter passed into spring, and Christiane, dressed in a new suit of her peasant costume (the wealthy townspeople in Germany delight in exhibiting a blooming country nurse), went to take her nursling, warmly nestled in furs and satin, to enjoy the sunshine on the Parade, and surprise the father by meeting him on his return from the Exchange. Decked out in this way, obliged to exhibit herself to the gaze of strangers, Christiane began to have an uneasy sense of something false and artificial in her position; and this vague feeling presently grew into a feverish anxiety to see her own child.

¶"At length the impulse was irresistible. She hastened from the Parade, and threaded the damp, narrow streets, to the house where she had left her child. She found it lying, thin and yellow, in its cradle, with a half-peeled potato on the coverlet. Casting a look almost of hatred on the little Hermann, her foster-child, she sank down by the cradle and sobbed aloud, the two babies crying with her. Presently she snatched up her own child, alternatively showering caresses on it, and quarrelling with the woman who had the care of it, till at last she seemed struck with the fact that she was expected at home, took up the little Hermann, and hastened away. She found her mistress in a state of consternation. The husband had returned from the Exchange without meeting the nurse and child. Christiane would not confess where she had been but pretended that she had lost her way. It was resolved that she should never go out with the child alone again, and there were thoughts of dismissing her; but the intercession of the medical man who had recommended her procured her pardon.

"A day or two after, Christiane seemed to have recovered her equanimity and cheerfulness, and the merchant and his wife, quite at ease about their nurse, went out in the evening to pay a visit. The house was perfectly quiet, and Christiane was chanting by the cradle one of her melancholy songs. Suddenly she hastened to the window and pushed it open. A housemaid at work in the next room asked her what she was doing, and told her to shut the window—the night air would come in. Christiane asked her if she had heard nothing; for it seemed to her as if some one in the street below was calling her by name. The housemaid said she heard nothing—it was all imagination. But Christiane could not rest; she went up and down the nursery like a wild beast in its cage. She stopped and listened—again she seemed to hear her own name. She slipped off her shoes and stole down stairs. The house-door was fastened, but she opened a window and was quickly in the street. No sooner did her feet touch the ground than she rushed like lightning through the streets; the watchmen were terrified at her noiseless speed.

¶"She arrived at the house where her child was: the door was open, for the woman had just gone for a moment into a neighbour's. Christiane found her child in its cradle; it neither cried nor moaned, and she could only see it indistinctly by the faint rays of the moon. Presently the woman entered with a candle, and Christiane shrieked as the light fell on the emaciated little form of her baby. She snatched it from the cradle and pressed it in her arms. Oh, bliss! it opened its eyes, put its lips to her bosom and its little hand to her mouth. After a while, she laid it carefully in its cradle, kissed the covering under which it slept, or at least closed its eyes, and rocked it, singing a cradle song. But she rocked a dead child. The next time she bent down to touch it, she found it cold and stiff, and she sank senseless over the cradle. On recovering her consciousness, she glided out of the house, rushed back along the streets as swiftly as she had come, stole gently up to the nursery, took the little Hermann from his cradle and caressed him, singing:—

'Sleep, my baby, sleep.
Thy father keeps the sheep,
Thy mother . . . . '

"While she was singing, the carriage entered the court-yard, and presently her mistress opened the door and said, 'How is my child?' '*Your* child!' cried Christiane, with madness in her voice, '*my* child . . . . Yes, your child. . . . Yes, it has murdered my child. Murder!' she shrieked, and dashed the baby to the ground.

"The medical man entered and found the child dead on the floor, the mother lying beside it in a swoon, and Christiane singing and running wildly about the room. The same night Christiane was taken to a lunatic asylum.

"Auerbach suggests, as the moral of this story, that the rich mother who consents to use the services of a poor one should remember that she incurs a responsibility beyond the mere payment of wages—should consider that in procuring a foster-mother for her own child, she has herself adopted, though in a somewhat different sense, the position of foster-mother to the child of another woman."

Sight-seeing in Germany and the Tyrol

Sight-seeing in Germany and the Tyrol in the Autumn of 1855, by Sir John Forbes
On Foot through Tyrol in the Summer of 1855, by Mr Walter White

"Two kinds of summer tourists find fit representatives in Sir John Forbes and Mr Walter White. The one travels along railroads and rivers, easily and leisurely, seeing whatever his guide-book points out to him, and jotting down all those obvious and common-place remarks which everybody makes in ordinary conversation. The other rushes from London to the mountains of Central Europe as fast and as cheaply as steam can take him, and then, with staff and knapsack, plunges into their defiles. It is good that elderly and well-to-do gentlemen should make tours in Germany, thus spending their money sensibly, and getting in exchange for it some new ideas; and it is good that young men should shake off the trammels of business, and gain health among fresh breezes and clear streams; but it is not good that those same persons should come home and publish books about the places through which they have passed, containing scarcely a single scrap of knowledge which was not long ago familiar to the instructed, and easily accessible to uninstructed, men.

¶"Neither of these authors appears now for the first time before the public. We are not acquainted with their former works; but if they at all resembled their present productions, the taste of the people who liked them must be strange indeed. In the volumes under review we find hardly anything to amuse, and little to interest. Yet such books are bought by the libraries, and read, and praised. For the benefit then, of those who have not the courage to wait till they 'blow over,' we proceed to give a short account of their contents. . . ."

Silly Novels by Lady Novelists
(pp 442-61)

This noted and several times reprinted essay is not as witty as it might be. GE's classifications seem laboured, and the silliness of the targets hit makes them seem hardly worth the trouble, since the results are not very funny.

—mind and millinery species: "Silly Novels by Lady Novelists are a genus with many species, determined by the particular quality of silliness that predominates in them—the frothy, the prosy, the pious, or the pedantic. But it is a mixture of all these—a composite order of feminine fatuity, that produces the largest class of such novels, which we shall distinguish as the *mind-and-millinery* species.

"The heroine is usually an heiress, probably a peeress in her own right, with perhaps a vicious baronet, an amiable duke, and an irresistible younger son of a marquis as lovers in the foreground, a clergyman and a poet sighing for her in the middle distance, and a crowd of undefined adorers dimly indicated beyond.

"Her eyes and her wit are both dazzling; her nose and her morals are alike free from any tendency to irregularity; she has a superb *contralto* and a superb intellect; she is perfectly well-dressed and perfectly religious; she dances like a sylph, and reads the Bible in the original tongues.

"Or it may be that the heroine is not an heiress—that rank and wealth are the only things in which she is deficient; but she infallibly gets into high society, she has the triumph of refusing many matches and securing the best, and she wears some family jewels or other as a sort of crown of righteousness at the end.

"Rakish men either bit their lips in impotent confusion at her repartees, or are touched to penitence by her reproofs, which, on appropriate occasions, rise to a lofty strain of rhetoric; indeed, there is a general propensity in her to make speeches, and to rhapsodize at some length when she retires to her bedroom.

"In her recorded conversations she is amazingly eloquent, and in her unrecorded conversations, amazingly witty. She is understood to have a depth of insight that looks through and through the shallow theories of philosophers, and her superior instincts are a sort of dial by which men have only to set their clocks and watches, and all will go well.

"The men play a very subordinate part by her side . . . . They see her at a ball, and are dazzled; at a flower-show, and they are fascinated; on a riding excursion, and they are witched by her noble horsemanship; at church, and they are awed by the sweet solemnity of her demeanour. She is the ideal woman in feelings, faculties, and flounces . . . .

"The vicious baronet is sure to be killed in a duel, and the tedious husband dies in his bed requesting his wife, as a particular favour to him, to marry the man she loves best, and having already dispatched a note to the lover informing him of the comfortable arrangement.

"Before matters arrive at this desirable issue our feelings are tried by seeing the noble, lovely, and gifted heroine pass through many *mauvais moments,* but we have the satisfaction of knowing that her sorrows are wept into embroidered pocket-handkerchiefs, that her fainting form reclines on the very best upholstery, and that whatever vicissitudes she may undergo, from being dashed out of her carriage to having her head shaved in a fever, she comes out of them all with a complexion more blooming and locks more redundant than ever." ¶442-3

—high society: "We may remark, by the way, that we have been relieved from a serious scruple by discovering that silly novels by lady novelists rarely introduce us into any other than very lofty and fashionable society. We had imagined that destitute women turned novelists, as they turned governesses, because they had no other 'lady-like' means of getting their bread. On this supposition, vacillating syntax and improbable incident had a certain pathos for us, like the extremely supererogatory pincushions and ill-devised nightcaps that are offered for sale by a blind man. We felt the commodity to be a nuisance, but we were glad to think that the money went to relieve the necessitous, and we pictured to ourselves lonely women struggling for a maintenance, or wives and daughters devoting themselves to the production of 'copy' out of pure heroism—perhaps to pay their husband's debts, or to purchase luxuries for a sick father. Under these impressions we shrank from criticising a lady's novel: her English might be faulty, but, we said to ourselves, her motives are irreproachable; her imagination may be uninventive, but her patience is untiring. Empty writing was excused by an empty stomach, and twaddle was consecrated by tears.

"But no! This theory of ours, like many other pretty theories, has had to give way before observation. Women's silly novels, we are now convinced, are written under totally different circumstances. The fair writers have evidently never talked to a tradesman except from a carriage window; they have no notion of the working-classes except as 'dependents'; they think five hundred a-year a miserable pittance; Belgravia and 'baronial halls' are their primary truths; and they have no idea of feeling interest in any man who is not at least a great landed proprietor, if not a prime minister. It is clear that they write in elegant boudoirs, with violet-coloured ink and a ruby pen; that they must be entirely indifferent to publishers' accounts, and inexperienced in every form of poverty except poverty of brains. It is true that we are constantly struck with the want of verisimilitude in their representations of the high society in which they were to live; but then they betray no closer acquaintance with any other form of life. If their peers and peeresses are improbable, their literary men, tradespeople, and cottagers are impossible; and their intellect seems to have the peculiar impartiality of reproducing both what they *have* seen and heard, and what they have *not* seen and heard, with equal unfaithfulness." ¶443-4

—*oracular:* "The most pitiable of all silly novels by lady novelists are what we may call the *oracular* species—novels intended to expound the writer's religious, philosophical, or moral theories . . . . You will rarely meet with a lady novelist of the oracular class who is diffident of her ability to decide on theological questions—who has any suspicion that she is not capable of discriminating with the nicest accuracy between the good and evil in all church parties—who does not see precisely how it is that men have gone wrong hitherto—and pity philosophers in general that they have not had the opportunity of consulting her." 449-50

—*white neck-cloth:* "A more numerous class of silly novels than the oracular, (which are generally inspired by some form of High Church, or transcendental Christianity) is what we may call the *white neck-cloth* species, which represent the tone of thought and feeling in the Evangelical party. This species is a kind of genteel tract on a large scale, intended as a sort of medicinal sweetmeat for Low Church young ladies; an Evangelical substitute for the fashionable novel, as the May Meetings are a substitute for the Opera. Even Quaker children, one would think, can hardly have been denied the indulgence of a doll; but it must be a doll dressed in a drab gown and a coal-scuttle bonnet—not a worldly doll, in gauze and spangles." 455-6

—*modern-antique:* "But, perhaps, the least readable of silly women's novels, are the *modern-antique* species, which unfold to us the domestic life of Jannes and Jambres, the private love affairs of Sennacherib, or the mental struggles and ultimate conversion of Demetrius the silversmith. From most silly novels we can at least extract a laugh; but those of the modern antique school have a ponderous, a leaden kind of fatuity, under which we groan." 458

—*flexible requirements:* "No educational restrictions can shut women out from the materials of fiction, and there is no species of art which is so free from rigid requirements. Like crystalline masses, it may take any form, and yet be beautiful; we have only to pour in the right elements—genuine observation, humour, and passion. But it is precisely this absence of rigid requirement which constitutes the fatal seduction of novel-writing to incompetent women. Ladies are not wont to be very grossly deceived as to their power of playing on the piano; here certain positive difficulties of execution have to be conquered, and incompetence inevitably breaks down. Every art which has its absolute *technique* is, to a certain extent, guarded from the intrusions of mere left-handed imbecility. But in novel-writing there are no barriers for incapacity to stumble against, no external criteria to prevent a writer from mistaking foolish facility for mastery. And so we have again and again the old story of **La Fontaine**'s ass, who puts his nose to the flute, and, finding that he elicits some sound, exclaims, 'Moi, aussi, je joue de la flute;'—a fable which we commend, at parting, to the consideration of any feminine reader who is in danger of adding to the number of 'silly novels by lady novelists.' " 461

GE deals with a number of novels, none with identified authors: *Compensation, Laura Gay, Rank and Beauty, The Enigma, The Old Gray Church,* and *Adonijah, a Tale of the Jewish Dispersion.* She mentions many characters.

Worldliness and Other-Worldliness: The Poet Young

(pp 1-41)

GE feels that Edward Young, the author of the once highly-regarded *Night Thoughts* written after the deaths of his wife, step-daughter and step-son-in-law, has been overpraised, overindulged, and under-examined. She seeks to redress the balance. She considers one of Young's most striking characteristics "his *radical insincerity as a poetic artist*" (her emphasis; 26). His adherence to abstractions she believes inherent in his *want of genuine emotion* (her emphasis; 30-31). She limns Young's lack of human sympathy and his bad taste, his selfishness and his egoism. She draws a telling comparison between his fustian and arrogance and **William Cowper**'s intimacy and warmth.

Rev. Edward Young (1683-1765). "About the year 1730 we have hauled up a remarkable individual of the species *divine*—a surprising name, considering the nature of the animal before us; but we are used to unsuitable names in natural history. Let us examine this individual at our leisure. He is on the verge of fifty, and has recently undergone his metamorphosis into the clerical form. Rather a paradoxical specimen, if you observe him narrowly: a sort of cross between a sycophant and a psalmist; a poet whose imagination is alternately fired by the 'Last Day' and by a creation of peers, who fluctuates between rhapsodic applause of **King George** and rhapsodic applause of Jehovah." 3

—*balance:* "And he personifies the nicest balance of temporalities and spiritualities. He is equally impressed with the momentousness of death and of burial fees; he languishes at once for immortal life and for 'livings;' he has a fervid attachment to patrons in general, but on the whole prefers the Almighty." 3

—*religion:* "His religion exhausts itself in ejaculations and rebukes, and knows no medium between the ecstatic and the sententious. If it were not for the prospect of immortality, he considers, it would be wise and agreeable to be indecent, or to murder one's father; and, heaven apart, it would be extremely irrational in any man not to be a knave." 4

—*a poet:* "With all this, our new-made divine is an unmistakable poet. To a clay compounded chiefly of the worldling and the rhetorician, there is added a real spark of Promethean fire. He will one day clothe his apostrophes and objurgations, his astronomical religion and his charnel-house morality, in lasting verse, which will stand, like a Juggernaut made of gold and jewels, at once magnificent and repulsive . . . . " 4

—*a parasite:* "But where the fully developed insect is parasitic, we believe the larva is usually parasitic also, and we shall probably not be far wrong in supposing that Young at Oxford, as elsewhere, spent a good deal of his time in hanging about possible and actual patrons, and accommodating himself to their habits with considerable flexibility of conscience and of tongue . . . . " 5

—*wild oats:* "He probably sowed his wild oats after the coarse fashion of his times, for he has left us sufficient evidence that his moral sense was not delicate; but his companions, who were occupied in sowing their own oats, perhaps took it as a matter of course that he should be a rake, and were only struck with the exceptional circumstance that he was a pious and moralizing rake." 6

—*inspirations:* "Among all the trivial efforts of conjectural criticism, there can hardly be one more futile than the attempt to discover the original of those pitiable lay-figures, the 'Lorenzos' and 'Altamonts' of Young's didactic prose and poetry. His muse never stood face to face with a genuine, living human being; she would have been as much startled by such an encounter as a stage necromancer whose incantations and blue fire had actually conjured up a demon." 13

His Poetry: A Critique

—*low and false:* "Young's biographers and critics have usually set out from the position that he was a great religious teacher, and that his poetry is morally sublime; and they have toned down his failings into harmony with their conception of the divine and the poet. For our own part, we set out from precisely the opposite conviction—namely, that the religious and moral spirit of Young's poetry is low and false; and we think it of some importance to show that the 'Night Thoughts' are the reflex of a mind in which the higher human sympathies were inactive.

"This judgment is entirely opposed to our youthful predilections and enthusiasm. The sweet garden-breath of early enjoyment lingers about many a page of the 'Night Thoughts,' and even of the 'Last Day,' giving an extrinsic charm to passages of stilted rhetoric and false sentiment; but the sober and repeated reading of maturer years has convinced us that it would hardly be possible to find a more typical instance than Young's poetry, of the mistake which substitutes interested obedience for sympathetic emotion, and baptizes egoism as religion." ¶21-22

—*narrow thought:* "Whether he writes prose or poetry, rhyme or blank verse, dramas, satires, odes, or meditations, we see everywhere the same Young—the same narrow circle of thoughts, the same love of abstractions, the same telescopic view of human things, the same appetency towards antithetic apothegm and rhapsodic climax." 22

—*adumbrations:* "The passages that arrest us in his tragedies are those in which he anticipates some fine passage in the 'Night Thoughts,' and where his characters are only transparent shadows through which we see the bewigged *embonpoint* of the didactic poet, excogitating epigrams or ecstatic soliloquies by the light of a candle fixed in a skull." 22

—*strengths:* "Young could never describe a real complex human being; but what he *could* do with eminent success, was to describe with neat and finished point obvious *types* of manners rather than of character—to write cold and clever epigrams on personified vices and absurdities. There is no more emotion in his satire than if he were turning witty verses on a waxen image of **Cupid**, or a lady's glove." 25

—*wit:* "Young's wit will be found in almost every instance to consist in that antithetic combination of ideas which, of all the forms of wit, is most within reach of clever effort. In his gravest arguments, as well as in his lightest satire, one might imagine that he had set himself to work out the problem, how much antithesis might be got out of a given subject. And there he completely succeeds." 25-6

—*his merits:* " . . . we ought, if a reviewer's space were elastic, to dwell also on his merits—on the startling vigor of his imagery—on the occasional grandeur of his thought—on the piquant force of that grave satire into which his meditations continually run." 29

—*abstractions:* "He sees Virtue sitting on a mount serene, far above the mists and storms of earth: he sees Religion coming down from the skies, with this world in her left hand and the other world in her right: but we never find him dwelling on virtue or religion as it really exists—in the emotions of a man dressed in an ordinary coat, and seated by his fireside of an evening, with his hand resting on the head of his little daughter; in courageous effort for unselfish ends, in the internal triumph of justice and pity over personal resentment, in all the sublime self-renunciation and sweet charities which are found in the details of ordinary life." 34

"Night Thoughts"

—*early books:* "The outburst of genius in the earlier books of the 'Night Thoughts' is the more remarkable, that in the interval between them and the Satires, he had produced nothing but his Pindaric odes, in which he fell far below the level of his previous works. Two sources of this sudden strength were the freedom of blank verse and the presence of a genuine emotion . . . in these earlier Nights there is enough genuine sublimity and genuine sadness to bribe us into too favorable a judgment of them as a whole." 28

—*subject-matter:* "Young had only a very few things to say or sing—such as that life is vain, that death is imminent, that man is immortal, that virtue is wisdom, that friendship is sweet, and that the source of virtue is the contemplation of death and immortality—and even in his two first Nights he had said almost all he had to say in his finest manner." 28

—*no human sympathy:* "If we except the passages in *Philander, Narcissa,* and *Lucia,* there is hardly a trace of human sympathy, of self-forgetfulness in the joy or sorrow of a fellow-being, throughout this long poem, which professes to treat the various phases of man's destiny." 34

—*the last judgment:* "But, for a reflection of Young's moral personality on a colossal scale, we must turn to those passages where his rhetoric is at its utmost stretch of inflation—where he addresses the Deity, discourses of the Divine operations, or describes the last judgment. As a compound of vulgar pomp, crawling adulation, and hard selfishness, presented under the guise of piety, there are few things in literature to surpass the ninth Night, entitled 'Consolation,' especially in the pages where he describes the last judgment—a subject to which, with naïve self-betrayal, he applies phraseology favored by the exuberant penny-a-liner." 38

—his religion: "Young has no conception of religion as anything else than egoism turned heavenward; and he does not merely imply this, he insists on it. Religion, he tells us . . . is 'ambition, pleasure, and the love of gain,' directed towards the joys of the future life instead of the present." 39

—monotony: "It is this pedagogic tendency, this sermonizing attitude of Young's mind, which produces the wearisome monotony of his pauses. After the first two or three Nights, he is rarely singing, rarely pouring forth any continuous melody inspired by the spontaneous flow of thought or feeling. He is rather occupied with argumentative insistence, with hammering in the proofs of his propositions by disconnected verses, which he puts down at intervals. The perpetual recurrence of the pause at the end of the line throughout long passages, makes them as fatiguing to the ear as a monotonous chant, which consists of the endless repetition of one short musical phrase." 41

—another poet: "Young applauds God as a monarch with an empire and a court quite superior to the English, or as an author who produces 'volumes for man's perusal.' **Cowper** sees his Father's love in all the gentle pleasures of the home fireside, in the charms even of the wintry landscape . . . .

"The sum of our comparison is this: In Young we have the type of that deficient human sympathy, that impiety towards the present and the visible, which flies for its motives, its sanctities, and its religion, to the remote, the vague, and the unknown; in Cowper we have the type of that genuine love which cherishes things in proportion to their nearness, and feels its reverence grow in proportion to the intimacy of its knowledge." 44-5 *See also Topicon* LC:Notable Individuals—*William Cowper*

Mrs Hallows, "understood to be a woman of discreet age, and the daughter (or widow) of a clergyman who was an old friend of **Young**'s, became housekeeper at Welwyn. Opinions about ladies are apt to differ. 'Mrs Hallows was a woman of piety, improved by reading,' says one witness. 'She was a very coarse woman,' said **Dr Johnson**; and we shall presently find some indirect evidence that her temper was perhaps not quite so much improved as her piety. Servants, it seems, were not fond of remaining long in the house with her; a satirical curate, named **Kidgell**, hints at 'drops of juniper' taken as a cordial (but perhaps he was spiteful, and a teetotaler); and Young's son is said to have told his father that 'an old man should not resign himself to the management of anybody.' The result was, that the son was banished from home for the rest of his father's lifetime . . . . " 16-17

Rev. John Jones. "Our latest glimpses of the aged poet are derived from certain letters of Mr Jones, his curate . . . . Mr Jones was a man of some literary activity and ambition—a collector of interesting documents . . . . On these and kindred subjects he corresponded with **Dr Birch**, occasionally troubling him with queries and manuscripts. We have a respect for Mr Jones. Unlike most persons who trouble others with queries or manuscripts, he mitigates the infliction by such gifts as 'a fat pullet,' wishing he 'had anything better to send; but this depauperizing vicarage (of Alconbury) too often checks the freedom and forwardness of my mind.' " 17

Lady Elizabeth Lee: in 1731 "when [Young] was just fifty, he married Lady Elizabeth Lee, a widow with two children, who seems to have been in favor with **Queen Caroline**, and who probably had an income—two attractions which doubtless enhanced the power of her other charms." 12

Duke of Wharton. "That brilliant profligate, the Duke of Wharton, to whom **Young** afterwards clung as his chief patron, was at this time [during Young's Oxford years] a mere boy; and, though it is probable that their intimacy had already begun, since the Duke's father and mother were friends of the old Dean [**Young**], that intimacy ought not to aggravate any unfavorable inference as to Young's Oxford life." 5

—ability: " . . . the known ability of the Duke, who, as **Pope** tells us, possessed

'Each gift of Nature and of Art,
And wanted nothing but an honest heart.' 8

Dean Young, "the poet's father, who was quadruply clerical, being at once rector, prebendary, court chaplain, and dean." 4

Also mentioned

[relatively distinguished historical or literary figures are in Index X or XI]

A Word for the Germans

(page 201)

"John Bull is open to instruction; slowly, by gentle degrees, he revises his opinions, his habits, and his laws. It is not to be expected that he will ever cease to regard himself as the supreme type of manhood, or to think that the most unmixed truth may always be known by the mark 'British,' which prevents imposture. But he does modify his opinions about other nations. It is no longer his belief that a Frenchman is invariably of the dancing-master type, demanding nothing from existence, but 'his girl, his fiddle, and his frisk', and that if he has a soul at all it is really of too light a quality to be worth saving. The Italian of John Bull's imagination is no longer exclusively that dangerous jesuitical personage, with dark hair and darker intentions, who avails himself of momentary privacy to feel the edge of his stiletto; a personage adorned now with a false title, but in his earlier years nothing better than a small vagrant, who went about exhibiting his white mice and white teeth for casual halfpence.

"Having shown himself thus ready to abandon those favourite old portable notions of Frenchmen and Italians, it is a pity he should obstinately retain certain worn-out phrases about the Germans, which hardly imply a more comprehensive estimate. In these days when the excellent Bull is ethnological, and feels himself at home with the widest-grinning 'natives'—nay, shows an eager anxiety as to the personal habits of the gorilla, it might be wished that he would conceive the typical German under some more average aspect than that of 'the cloudy metaphysician.' We venture to suggest that this phrase is quite insufficient to express the *differentia* of the German people. In the first place, only a small proportion of them are metaphysicians; quite as many are bakers, making excellent bread—not inferior, perhaps, to the British in any quality except heaviness.

¶"Secondly, the most eminent of German metaphysicians, **Kant**, is cloudy in no other sense than that in which a mathematician is cloudy to one ignorant of mathematics. What book more nebulous than *Euclid* to a reader acquainted neither with the subject-matter nor with the terminology? What more Laputan and unpractical than algebraic formulæ to one who has never studied algebra? Kant was a rigorous thinker, who, like all other rigorous thinkers, felt the need of terms undefaced by a long currency, free from confusing associations. The recipe for understanding Kant is first to get brains capable of following his argument, and next to master his terminology. Observing this recipe, the *Critique of Pure Reason* is not indeed easy reading, but it is not in the least cloudy. It is not fit for the club table. Some gentleman there, turning over the pages and seeing such terms as *synthetic judgments, antinomies,* and the like, would be conscious of superior clearness of head, and say: 'Bosh! what dreamers these Germans are!' But possibly, if that clear-headed clubman were imperatively called upon to declare the meaning of *co-efficient* and *hypothenuse* and assured that no smiling would be accepted as legal tender for knowledge, he would discover that these terms also are painfully cloudy. It is one of the interesting weaknesses common to us men to suppose that clearness ends where our own vision fails. The sound British thinker kicks a stone to prove that matter exists, and so confound the metaphysicians; concluding that their arguments are necessarily shallow because he can't see far into them.

"Thirdly, we object to 'cloudy metaphysician' as the accepted periphrasis for a German, because it has begotten another habit of speech which the most constant familiarity could not endear to us. Views are set aside by saying that 'they are German.' Doubtless there is a peculiarly German view of things as there is an English view, a French view, a Hindu view, and so on, down to a Patagonian view, perhaps the least metaphysical of all. The English view may be the soundest, and all but born Englishmen may be comparatively pitiable. But the human race has not been educated on a plan of uniformity, and it is precisely that partition of mankind into races and nations, resulting in various national points of enriching and rendering more and more complete man's knowledge of the inner and outer world. The Seventy who translated the Hebrew Scriptures into Greek are said to have been placed in separate confinement that each might produce his independent version, and their versions, when afterwards compared, were found to be identical. This agreement as to the meaning of a text was highly satisfactory, and some inconvenience might have been saved if subsequent interpretations had been equally harmonious. But it would have been a dreary issue for mankind, if the division into nations had ended in such an identity of mental products, even though the standard had been English. And no one who has an acquaintance worth mentioning with the productions of the German mind in any one department, is unaware that the peculiarities of that mind, its characteristic qualities, have been the source of pre-eminently important contributions to the sum of our mental wealth.

"The German mind possesses in a high degree two tendencies which are often represented as opposed to each other: namely, largeness of theoretic conception, and thoroughness in the investigation of facts. So undeniable is it that the typical German has these tendencies, that their excess is the very vice he is reproached with by those who know him and don't like him. Your German, it is said, can not write about the drama without going back to the Egyptian mysteries; he sees that everything is related to everything else, and is determined to exhaust you and the subject; his doctrine is all-embracing, and so is his detail. Quite true. No man is less disposed than our German to accept a too slight induction, to let pass an inaccuracy of statement, or to report a conclusion from imperfect observation or experiment; on the other hand, no man is more likely to be contemptuous towards desultory labours which are not *wissenschaftlich* (scientific)—*i.e.* not bound together by a rational doctrine, or conducted in the full sense of a need for such a doctrine. If he is an experimentor, he will be thorough in his experiments; if he is a scholar, he will be thorough in his researches. Accordingly no one in this day really studies any subject without having recourse to German books, or else wishing he knew their language that he might have recourse to them; and the footnotes of every good French or English book that appears, whether in scholarship, history, or natural science, are filled with references to German authors. Without them, historical criticism would have been simply nowhere; take away the Germans, with their patience, their thoroughness, their need for a doctrine which refers all transient and material manifestations to subtler and more permanent causes, and all that we most value in our appreciation of early history would have been wanting to us.

"It is true the German rarely writes well, rarely arranges his matter well, or manages it with economy, and therefore seldom produces a good book in the fullest sense of the word. From the necessity his mind is under of looking at a subject in every one of its facets, he is prone to pile one modifying consideration on another, and so perpetually to disappoint a reader who is in a hurry for a conclusion. The German is never in a hurry: for him, art is long, and life, expanded by the absence of adventitious needs, is not so short as for Englishmen making haste to be rich. His writing will sometimes seem to be all stairs and landing-places without any floors. Then the structure of his language lends itself to the formation of involved sentences, like coiled serpents, showing neither head nor tail.

¶"Nevertheless, the proportionate badness of German books is much exaggerated. The cumbrousness of the language apart, there is not perhaps a much larger proportion of poor books in German than in French or English; it would be nearer the truth to say that there are more books in German of which the matter is valuable, and the style bad, than in any other tongue. Our own literature does not positively swarm with good writers. The difference lies chiefly in this, that when a German author is a blockhead, he is, as **Heine** says, *kein oberflächlicher Narr*—no superficial blockhead: his sentences and his book do not come to an end so soon as if he were an Englishman or a Frenchman. He has a great deal more straw to chop, and he chops it slowly. Still, a blockhead is never exhilarating, though he may have learned to write in epigrams, and to give stupidity the most dapper air of neatness. His sentences may each have a paragraph to itself, and his book may be half white paper, but we decline it as resolutely as if it were covered with German print without a break from beginning to end. It is as short work *not* to read one book as another.

"In fact, if anyone in the present day can be called cultivated who dispenses with a knowledge of German, it is because the two other greatest literatures of the world are now impregnated with the results of German labour and German genius. Let those who know this have the piety to acknowledge it. Let those who do not know it abstain from portraying the typical German until they have made his acquaintance. We have no objection to caricatures; each nation should be content to lend itself to the humour of the world in this passive way. But a caricature to be good, must come from close observation."

Servants' Logic

(pp 310-11)

There is some little wit and an occasional pungent turn of phrase in this idle meditation on tribulations with domestic servants, but it is a mystery to this editor that GE bothered, and more of a mystery that it has been anthologized.

" . . . We might smile (bitterly) while platform orators held audiences spell-bound by the triumphant irrelevance of their statements, and console ourselves with the reflection that the life of collective mankind is slowly swayed by the force of truth and not of twaddle; our views may be hissed to-day, but in the next century they will be held too undeniable to be applauded. Unfortunately, our keenest experience of this sort has reference to our own domestic affairs: the fellow-mortals we most need to involve, and whose minds we find ourselves the most incapable of grasping, are our servants, and especially our cooks. We may look to the next century for the triumph of our ideas, but it is impossible to look there for our dinners. When the thing to be achieved by argument is a soup or a dish of vegetables that will not plunge you in the horrors of dyspepsia, the immediateness of the success is everything.

"In reasoning with servants we are likely to be thwarted by discovering that our axioms are not theirs. For example, they presuppose that an effect may exist without a cause, that like causes will constantly produce unlike effects, that *all* may mean only some, that there is no difference between little and none, that any two or more circumstances which can be mentioned will account for a given fact, and that nothing is impossible, except that they can have been in the wrong. Their standard measures, too, are of a private kind; a good lump, a handful, a tea-cup, a littleish basin, as much as will stick on your knife-end, a big spoon, and a good sup . . . .

"You, gentle madam, discover with some dismay that the scalloped oysters with which you would fain load a friend's plate have their beards on. The beard movement not having yet reached this point, you take an early opportunity of asking your cook whether she is not aware that cooked oysters ought to be bearded. 'Oh, yes, mum, for soup and sauce. I put the beards into that last little saucepan with the liquor, and strain 'em; but there's that little strainer, I must have a new one.' 'Yes, yes, but they must always be bearded, however you may cook them.' 'What, the natives, mum?' 'All oysters; the beards are tough, unfit to be eaten. 'Well, but what we have from that little fishmonger in Brick-street? I'm sure to pay the same price a dozen for 'em as for the last big ones, it's imposing on them that's got the money; and I did take the knife and just strip a beard or two off the biggest of all—we used to take 'em off at Mrs Tompkins's, but you've never had scalloped oysters before, and I said to Jane, "Jane, there'll be hardly time for these oysters to be done, and as for that clock, it's beyond everything for losing, it deceives *me,* nobody knows, and the clockmaker a whole hour at it only a week ago." ' &c. You depart with a sigh, feeling that to deposit rules in Sally's mind is very much like depositing your thimble in a dust-heap.

"You, sir, are perhaps a dyspeptic physiologist, with a weakness for spinach, and you wish to impress on your cook the importance of thoroughly squeezing green vegetables. You tell her the water in which they are boiled is as bad as poison. It follows that the next day they come up only a little less like a soft morass. 'This will not do, Sally; the greens must be squeezed perfectly dry.' 'La, sir, I squeezed 'em ever so long.' 'But you saw there was still water left in them.' 'Well, sir, I'm sure it was very little for any gentleman as can eat greens at all.' You are, perhaps, a little nettled, and you wish to be impressive; your mind goes in search of illustration. 'I tell you, there must be no water. Suppose it was arsenic, instead of poisonous water—should you think there was no difference between little and none?' Fatal ingenuity! Sally fires up; she has heard of cooks being hanged for putting arsenic in food; she feels herself unjustly accused . . . .

"Again, you desire soup, but desire it without fat. You are perhaps a genius; the world is in need of your new poem; or you are evolving a momentous theory, and the evolution of fatty acids within you is a serious impediment. Your mental activity is reduced to the consciousness that interesting facts in animal chemistry are going on within you; you begin to think you can serve mankind only by leaving your body for dissection. At length you ask your wife with hardly suppressed peevishness, and unusual emphasis on 'My dear,' to inquire into the making of the soup. Your wife, who is rather frightened at the cook, tells her that **Mr Queasy**, in spite of his orders, discerned fatty particles in the soup yesterday. 'It's a thing impossible there can be fat, mum—for skimming and everything—there's nothing neglected in *my* power.'

¶" 'Show me your cold stock.' Exit **Sally**, returning with a vessel in one hand and a spoon in the other. There is a white film of fat over the surface of the stock. 'See, now, Sally, there is fat!' 'La, mum,' says Sally, plunging her spoon in and turning up the jellied soup from beneath as a gardener turns the soil when he is digging for roots, the cold fat getting underneath in the process, 'that's nothing; besides, I take my soup from under, and I take the fat off with the spoon.' (The spoon itself is studded plenteously with fragments of cold fat.) 'But unless you wash your spoon each time you dip it, there will be fat, and, however little, Mr Queasy suffers from it. Besides'—(Mrs Q. here exerts all her courage)—'it belongs to a good cook to send up her soup free from fat.' Sally smiles bitterly . . . . Here, Sally sets down the vessel of stock emphatically, and tapping the outside of it with her finger-ends, looks hard out of the window. **Mrs Queasy** is nonplussed. If she says more Sally will give warning; she draws her dress round her crinoline, and rustles upstairs again.

"Servants are rich in intuitions. They have a vast number of certainties which are deep by reason of their groundlessness. The postman brings a letter for Maria: she was sure he would—she didn't know from whom it would come, and if you were to knock her down she couldn't tell you why; but this morning when she got out of bed, and drew up the blind and saw the wind blowing the leaves about, she seemed to see the postman coming with the letter in his hand. You make a great mistake if you suggest certain conditions which might have given rise to the expectation . . . .

"On the whole, servants are little disposed to think that the opinions of gentlefolks can have any practical value for them. Our remedies, our methods, our explanations, are like the drapery and tailoring we pay so much for; they correspond to the supposed scale of our income; but servants, for their part, get their stuffs and their views from other quarters. The cure for a gentleman's toothache is not likely to suit Sally's molar so well as the cure recommended by the grocer's boy on the authority of his first cousin, who went about with a blue handkerchief round his head for weeks and weeks. And for the probabilities concerning the dryness of the coming summer, or the guilt of the man last taken up for murder, the person to be consulted with the most deference is the laundress who serves very good families, and whose husband is in the carrying line.

"The moral of all this is, that wise masters and mistresses will not argue with their servants, will not give them reasons, will not consult them. A mild yet firm authority which rigorously demands that certain things be done, without urging motives or entering into explanations, is both preferred by the servants themselves, and is the best means of educating them into any improvement of their methods and habits. Authority and tradition are the chief, almost the only safe guides of the uninstructed—are the chief means of developing the crude mind, whether childish or adult. Reason about everything with your child, you make him a monster, without reverence, without affections. Reason about things with your servants, consult them, give them the suffrage, and you produce no other effect in them than a sense of anarchy in the house, a suspicion of irresoluteness in you, the most opposed to that spirit of order and promptitude which can alone enable them to fill their places well and make their lives respectable."

Futile Falsehoods

(pp 470-71)

GE's beloved companion, George Henry Lewes, was asked by the publisher George Smith late in 1864 to act as editorial adviser to the newly-established *Pall Mall Gazette*. It was a lucrative post, and GE contributed to her dear friend's early support with four pieces: WG, SL and two "letters to the editor" signed "Sac[c]harissa," of which "Futile Falsehoods" was the first. GE's tongue is firmly in her cheek, but lightness and real humour are missing. As "Servants' Logic" (page 119) shows, facetiousness is not her great strength. We set FF forth at length that there may be no doubt on the subject. We miss Mrs Poyser.

To the EDITOR *of the* PALL MALL GAZETTE.

"SIR—I have been so much edified by the letters of your correspondents that I venture with some diffidence to add myself to their number. I am disposed to regard you as a shadowy, powerful, and beneficent personage, like the *Spectator* of old; to whom somehow or other it will be of use to complain of oppressive social customs and even domestic grievances, since you can distil helpful wisdom through your pages, teaching us how to endure our griefs, or (what would be more satisfactory) teaching those who grieve us to be ashamed of themselves. I may as well confess at once that I am a woman, and have not the pen of a ready writer; I have often to think for a long while what I shall say next, and then to think whether it is worth saying, which I suppose never happens to those who have been taught composition. But I have read in the *Saturday Review,* which I hold to be the greatest authority on such matters, since it knows not only what people have done, but also what they will be able to do to the end of their lives, that women often succeed in writing letters even better than men. Indeed, anyone may see that there are some things which must needs be best done by small creatures, and there is nothing so clever at nibbling as a mouse.

"What I want to complain of, Mr Editor, is the provoking confidence people seem to have in each other's stupidity. I find them seeing through their neighbours' little attempts at deception with great ease. They never take an old man for a young one: his wadding does not pass with them for muscle, or his hair-dye for the vigour of youth, and however the pitiable old creature may twiddle his cane, they can see that his boots pinch him. They are not in the least disposed to take an elderly gentleman for a young one because he wishes it. Why, then, when they see so clearly through the small tricks, and shams, and affectations of others, and are so far from being swayed in their opinions by the wishes of others, do they nevertheless go on using small tricks, and shams, and affectations of their own, and imagine that these are believed in as something genuine? Cinderella, whom I am really rather fond of, for I admire her little feet very much, and she is kind when she sees me looking ill, indulges herself in giving me long confidences about her heart affairs and other feminine matters, such as the foibles of her acquaintances, which, by the air of exaggeration they carry on the very face of them, as well as by a comparison my memory enables me to make of her different versions, I am convinced cannot be more than half true. It is not to be supposed that she would go on telling me these things if she thought that she thereby made me believe in nothing more than the untrustworthiness of her narratives; yet I observe that Cinderella is rather sharp in detecting the petty mendacity of her acquaintances, and not unfrequently uses such phrases as 'He or she says so; but we are not bound to believe it.' If I had not noticed that she is quite as free and inventive in her talk to her other friends, I should have concluded that she relied on my exceptional dulness and simplicity, for I gather from many indications that I impress my fellow-creatures as not being particularly bright.

"Now, Mr Editor, I do not pretend to be witty—I suppose that would be a pretence more futile than hair-dye; I am not conscious of presenting in my own person any cheering prophetic glimpses of woman's great achievements in the future; but, Sir, I am not slow at accounts. I know my addition table and multiplication table well, and I argue in this way: Would any one who gave me credit for knowing my tables imagine that he could persuade me into anything he pleased, by going on the supposition that nine and six make twelve, and that three times eight are twenty? Yet I am constantly talked to more or less smilingly by various classes of people, with the evident expectation that I shall be swayed by suppositions hardly less monstrous. For some time I was disposed to be rebellious against Providence, which seemed to have made me look much sillier than I am, till I had satisfied myself that many persons who have an average air of common sense are subjected to precisely the same treatment as myself.

¶"To go no farther than the shopmen. One would not say that they are a class who hold that a generous spirit of self-sacrifice, a burning zeal for the good of man as man, was quite an ordinary motive to action, easily credible as the ruling impulse of any personage in a well-starched collar and wristbands. Yet I hardly ever enter even the most fashionable shops without hearing something which implies an expectation on the part of the speaker that I shall believe he loves me better than he loves himself He brings out a piece of stuff which I see is of a somewhat peculiar colour, and perhaps not highly saleable; he assures me that the firm have had a special order for this colour from the Roman Court; that it ought to be charged two shillings per yard more than the other pieces (which are of colours favoured by the public); but that, *since it is not yet marked,* he will let me have it—not for the same price as the others, which would already have been generous—but for a shilling a yard less! On hearing this I reflected that my crinoline was not large; that my dress did not sweep the ground; that altogether, to a draper, I must seem a pitiable object.

"But immediately there swept into the shop another lady, of the most commanding presence, who swept down a pole and two pieces of alpaca on her passage. I was all ear to observe whether she, too, would be expected to believe the draper's assertion rather than her own senses, and when she proved intractable on this point she was expected to change her wants in a moment at his suggestion. She said a certain mauve ribbon was of too red a tone. 'No, ma'am, we do not call this a red tone.' She persisted that it was too red to suit her purpose. 'The reddish mauves are all the fashion, ma'am; in fact, we have not provided ourselves with the bluer shades, because they are not being asked for.' Thus, in spite of her irreproachable costume, this lady was expected to believe that red was not red, and to be so sure that a salesman had no motive for saying this save the desire that she should make a purchase satisfactory to herself, that she would rather believe herself suddenly afflicted with colour-blindness than doubt his statement.

"I confess, Sir, when I have recovered from my angry humiliation at being talked to in this strain, the mental state of these fellow-creatures behind the drapers' counters is a source of melancholy to me. That this stupid mendacity, this palpable lying, this almost idiotic reliance on the nullity of the human understanding, should be an outgrowth of our civilization, affects me much more than any missionary accounts of the poor heathens who worship shapeless idols . . . . These salesmen have the advantage of knowing their arithmetical tables: could they not be made to understand, for example, that to love one's neighbour more than oneself transcends the spirit even of the law and the prophets, and is generally known not to be the spirit of the drapery trade? and that to urge such preposterous pretences on their customers is nearly equivalent to telling them that five and four make ten?

"I know there is a great deal of successful falsehood in the world, but then it is clever falsehood, and must be sustained by rare natural gifts. I leave that deep evil to deep thinkers. The nuisance I complain of is the futile falsity which reduces a great deal of one's intercourse with one's fellows to a simpering acquiescence that covers an inward disbelief, and runs through society like this nipping north-east wind, chilling our kindly feelings, checking our respect, and encouraging a self-defensive, resistent [*sic*] attitude toward neighbours who are in the main estimable. Why will Placidia, who, I know, has many virtues, try to persuade me before she asks a favour, that the interval of a year which has elapsed since her last visit to me has been a subject of much regret to her, and has been entirely due to the distance between her residence and mine—a distance which has been so easily surmounted on the present occasion? I am quite willing to do her a service without believing that my society has great charms for her; and even if I were not, it is really unfair to my small understanding for her to suppose that if I had been offended by her absence I should be propitiated by so transparent an excuse. And why will the handsome Autumna, whom I would rather look at than at many more youthful beauties, use little parenthetic devices to persuade me that she is no more than forty, when a little reflection might convince her that I am in possession of probabilities which must outweigh her testimony on this personal matter?

" . . . Surely energy could hardly be more utterly wasted than on falsehoods which deceive nobody . . . . I remain, Sir, your humble and admiring reader,

SACHARISSA [*sic*]"

Modern Housekeeping

(page 880)

This time we have little laboured humour, and more a sadly brave, straightforward account of the difficulty Saccharissa encounters in making ends meet. Her cross, evidently, is crinoline. The piece closes with evidently sincere and touching eloquence, bemoaning the loss of simplicity, replaced by expensive, dirt-attracting luxury. But we don't know why Eliot bothered.

"*To the* EDITOR *of the* PALL MALL GAZETTE.

SIR—It is perhaps well that I am not a woman of much leisure, for since you were so obliging as to print my former letter, I have thought of so many grievances which I should like to complain of, that if there had not been some still stronger check on my pen than my slowness in composition, you might have begun to find me troublesome . . . .

"You already know my grievance, Mr Editor. It is the difficulty of making both ends meet, with every payment increasing except the payment one is receiving as income. I do not mind telling you that we have only £800 a year, that we have four children (two boys to be educated, and two girls to be dressed), and that, as my husband's spare time is entirely occupied in writing books for private circulation, with the motto 'Fit audience, though few,' enclosed in an elegant cipher on the title-page, it is not likely that we shall ever have more money at our command than at present. Now, Sir, I am proud of my husband. It is true he sometimes irritates me by calling me loquacious, when the only reason he can show is that all women are so by nature, which seems to me no proof at all that I am loquacious, who sit with my mouth buttoned up for hours together while he is talking to his learned friends. Of course talk gathers inside one a little in those long silences, and, when a change of speaking comes, the words hurry out all the faster, especially as there is no knowing when another chance may come; but I call this reason, and not loquacity.

" . . . I know there are the gold-fields, and the spread of commerce, and the demand for labour, and the increase of the national wealth, and that everything is explained in the books on Political Economy; and really, Sir, to hear some people talk, one would think that explanation was as good as a dinner, and I dare say it may be to some gentlemen of very hungry minds, whose clothes do not cost much. But if they like explaining, I wish they would explain to me how people with fixed incomes are to go on living respectably when the prices are always rising, and the fashions for ever changing and getting more foolish and expensive. Will there always be fixed incomes? or is the discovery of gutta-percha a ground for hoping that everything will be made elastic, and that all salaries, and annuities, and dividends will stretch to fit the prices and the fashions? . . .

"For consider, Mr Editor, our boys cost us £200 a year; then there is what my husband pays to his publisher, and there are his cigars, and his subscriptions—he has no indulgences except smoking and writing, and explaining everything, and something must be allowed for pleasure out of every income. I am sure my dress, and the girls', is not much of a pleasure, nor the parties that we must have white gloves and flys for; still less the parties we must have at home in return. These things may be very well for people who need not think of the expense; but do what I will, these items I have mentioned never stop at the middle of the fourth hundred, and it is easy to see (remembering the price of meat and grocery) that when rent and taxes and wages have been paid, we have barely enough left for our ordinary housekeeping; and as for giving anything away—the most helpful explanation I ever heard of from political economy is, that charity does harm.

"Well, all this difficulty of living comfortably on an income that used to be thought ample for people of the middle class comes, I am told, from the action of necessary laws, which it is ridiculous to quarrel with, and if I say anything to the contrary I am checked by being reminded that I am a woman, and must not expect to understand these things. (My husband leaves the accounts to me, else, ridiculous or not, I think there would be some quarrelling with the necessary laws.) But, Sir, since you have not checked me in letter-writing, what I want to know is, whether extravagant fashions, and habits out of keeping with one's station, are necessary laws. I say nothing about champagne. And whether the world is made on such a plan that people who cannot afford good sherry and claret must now-a-days, whether they like it or not, make matters worse by giving poor champagne at their tables. We do not consume a great deal of champagne at home; but nothing would help me more in making both ends meet, or save me more worry and labour, than a lightening of the demands for dress.

¶"And is it, pray, a necessary law—is it independent of everybody's will in the world, or the necessary action of everybody's will—that a woman's gown should drag at the very least half a yard on the ground, or else that it should be looped-up over a crinoline so as to make it indispensable that her underclothing should be expensively ornamental! My girls are not very silly, but they require experience to see that though every other young lady has an embroidered petticoat and muslin-work and striped stockings, besides a dress that drags like a peacock's tail when it is let down, their own lives might be endurable without such things. There is no hiding from them the fact that the backs of dresses shorter than the fashion are stared at by their own sex with more contempt than a long train of silk or poplin that is filled with dust.

" . . . In my own youth it was thought disgraceful for a woman to have dust about her person, and she was under no temptation to buy several extra yards of silk for the sake of spoiling them immediately. But now I see women, who otherwise have an air of respectability, raising a cloud of dust behind them as they walk, and seeming not to mind that their handsome moiré or grenadine is as full of dust as the sides of an emptied flour-bag are full of flour. I suppose every one knows that these elegant ladies have not all of them maids specially to attend to their dress, and even if they had, no amount of brushing could make their trailed dresses look quite clean again.

"A lady's wardrobe used to be all lavender and purity; and my mother had silk dresses of her grandmother's so free from stain that they were made into best frocks for me. I wonder what is the state of these ladies' wardrobes whose dresses sweep the streets. My girls fasten up their dresses when they walk abroad, but that does not prevent the expense of having long skirts in-doors. And of course the poor things like to go to dances as well as to other parties; naturally, they want pleasures suited to their age. Their father has his cigars and his explanations, and I am broad and clumsy now, and must now, in these difficult times, look for more pleasure than keeping the bills within compass, and seeing the children enjoy themselves and do well. But, as I said, the girls must go to dances; and it will not do now for them to have a simple muslin dress of moderate length, which may be washed and worn again and again. They would feel that they were tittered at as bread-and-butter Misses. They must have a certain style about them: a bunch of costly flowers in the front of the head and a bunch at the back; a large transparent skirt with bows and furbelows over a silk petticoat—what my husband calls a dress of great volume (but I am sure the largest volume he ever wrote has never paid for such a dress); then ear-rings, lack tuckers, bracelets, the finest French gloves, gossamer pocket-handkerchiefs, and delicate fans, to say nothing of shoes and stockings—and certainly their feet are very pretty, and my girls when they are dressed in this do not look like some others who seem to have stuck twenty pounds' worth of finery about them on purpose to expose their face and figure, which are God's handiwork, to all men's ridicule. Look at their features, Mr Editor, and you may see their Creator never meant them to have three large pink roses set on the top of them.

" . . . If this is national wealth, I wish I had lived a little earlier, so as to see only the time of national poverty, when people had pleasure in taking care and saving, that they might feel they had enough, and could get fond of the few things they wore and used, because they lasted a long while. To be sure, I have plenty of saving and taking care, but it is all for extravagance; it never makes me feel we have enough. And my children never get fond of their things, for nothing lasts long, or if it does it gets old-fashioned, and they are ashamed of it. I am afraid this sort of feeling may go deeper than sleeves and sashes, and that this generation may be unlearning some good feelings that used to make people tender to the old and uncomely, out of memory and faithful affection. If one has to think so very much of gawdy stuffs and new patterns, it stands to reason there can be little time for thinking about other things which will not be crushed up in the rag-bag when next year comes.

"Perhaps you will say, Why, then, if you are a sensible woman, do you go on doing what you know is objectionable? But O! Sir, society is 'too many' for me. It is not likely that a stout woman, who is nothing particular in any way, and whose daughters have grown up with a will of their own, can make the world bend to her notions . . . there are a great many of our fellow-country-men whose wives and daughters have not only no trimmings, but no proper dinner. These questions are always tangling themselves with gimps, and gauzes, and prices, and weekly bills . . .

Your puzzled correspondent,

SACCHARISSA"

The Influence of Rationalism: Lecky's History

(pp 43-55)

History of the Rise and Influence of the Spirit of Rationalism in Europe, by William Edward Hartpole Lecky (2 vols.)

In this generally admiring, signed review, GE picks out for special notice Lecky's chapters on witchcraft and on persecution. She wryly notes the current fashion for spiritualists as a substitute (and with less cruel results) for the broomstick-riding beldames of yore. She summarizes Lecky's account of the evolution of ideas on the supernatural, citing **Bodin** and **Montaigne**. She praises Lecky's discussion of persecution and the reasons it seemed in its day justified, but she is very critical of other aspects of the work. In conclusion, she deplores his failure to conjure with the growth of rigorous physical science as a concomitant and explanation of the rise of Rationalism.

The Work Reviewed

" . . . there are clever, fair-minded men, who will write books for [the general reader—*see Topicon* M:Intellectual life—*reading*],—men very much above him in knowledge and ability, but not too remote from him in their habits of thinking, and who can thus prepare for him infusions of history and science that will leave some solidifying deposit, and save him from a fatal softening of the intellectual skeleton. Among such serviceable writers, Mr [William Edward Hartpole] Lecky's 'History of the Rise and Influence of the Spirit of Rationalism in Europe' entitles him to a high place. He has prepared himself for its production by an unusual amount of well-directed reading; he has chosen his facts and quotations with much judgment; and he gives proof of those important moral qualifications—impartiality, seriousness, and modesty." 44

—*spiritualism:* "It is felt preposterous to think of spiritual agencies in connection with ragged beldames soaring on broomsticks, in an age when it is known that mediums of communication with the invisible world are usually unctuous personages dressed in excellent broadcloth, who soar above the curtain-poles without any broomstick, and who are not given to unprofitable intrigues." 46

"No undiscovered natural laws, no names of 'respectable' witnesses are invoked to make us feel our presumption in questioning the diabolic intimacies of that obsolete old woman, for it is known now that the undiscovered laws, and the witnesses qualified by the payment of income-tax, are all in favor of a different conception—the image of a heavy gentleman in boots and black coat-tails foreshortened against the cornice." 46

—dogmatism: " . . . dogmatic Protestantism, holding the vivid belief in Satanic agency to be an essential of piety, would have felt it shame to be a whit behind Catholicism in severity against the devil's servants. **Luther**'s sentiment was that he would not suffer a witch to live (he was not much more merciful to Jews); and, in spite of his fondness for children, believing a certain child to have been begotten by the devil, he recommended the parents to throw it into the river." 48

"The torch must be turned on the worst errors of heroic minds—not in irreverent ingratitude, but for the sake of measuring our vast and various debt to all the influences which have concurred, in the intervening ages, to make us recognize as detestable errors the honest convictions of men who, in more individual capacity and moral force, were very much above us." 48

—persecution: "Persecution, [Lecky] shows, is not in any sense peculiar to the Catholic Church; it is a direct sequence of the doctrines that salvation is to be had only within the Church, and that erroneous belief is damnatory—doctrines held as fully by Protestant sects as by the Catholics; and in proportion to its power, Protestantism has been as persecuting as Catholi-cism. He maintains, in opposition to the favorite modern notion of persecution defeating its own object, that the Church, holding the dogma of exclusive salvation, was perfectly consequent, and really achieved its end of spreading one belief and quenching another by calling in the aid of the civil arm.

"Who will say that Governments, by their power over institutions and patronage, as well as over punishment, have not power also over the interests and inclinations of men, and over most of those external conditions into which subjects are born, and which make them adopt the prevalent belief as a second nature? Hence, to a sincere believer in the doctrine of exclusive salvation, Governments had it in their power to save men from perdition; and wherever the clergy were at the elbow of the civil arm, no matter whether they were Catholic or Protestant, persecution was the result.

" 'Compel them to come in,' was a rule that seemed sanctioned by mercy, and the horrible sufferings it led men to inflict seemed small to minds accustomed to contemplate, as a perpetual source of motive, the eternal unmitigated miseries of a hell that was the inevitable destination of a majority amongst mankind." ¶54-5

—effect of physical science: see Topicon: M:Science*—effect on miracles*

Jean Bodin, "the famous writer on government and jurisprudence, whose 'Republic,' **Hallam** thinks, had an important influence in England, and furnished 'a store of arguments and examples that were not lost on the thoughtful minds of our country-men.' In some of his views he was original and bold; for example, he anticipated **Montesquieu** in attempting to appreciate the relations of government and climate. Hallam inclines to the opinion that he was a Jew, and attached Divine authority only to the Old Testament.

"But this was enough to furnish him with his chief data for the existence of witches and for their capital punishment; and in the account of his 'Republic' given by Hallam, there is enough evidence that the sagacity which often enabled him to make fine use of his learning was also often entangled in it, to temper our surprise at finding a writer on political science of whom it could be said that, along with Montesquieu, he was 'the most philosophical of those who had read so deeply, the most learned of those who had thought so much,' in the van of the forlorn hope to maintain the reality of witchcraft. It should be said that he was equally confident of the unreality of the Copernican hypothesis, on the ground that it was contrary to the tenets of the theologians and philosophers and to common-sense, and therefore subversive of the foundations of every science." ¶49-50

Sir Thomas Browne, "who far surpassed **Glanvil** [*sic*] in magnificent incongruity of opinion, and whose works are the most remarkable combination existing, of witty sarcasm against ancient nonsense and modern obsequiousness, with indications of a capacious credulity." 53

Michel de Montaigne. " . . . came Montaigne, whose sceptical acuteness could arrive at negatives without any apparatus of method. A certain keen narrowness of nature will secure a man from many absurd beliefs which the larger soul, vibrating to more manifold influences, would have a long struggle to part with. And so we find the charming, chatty Montaigne—in one of the brightest of his essays, 'Des Boiteux,' where he declares that, from his own observation of witches and sorcerers, he should have recommended them to be treated with curative hellebore—stating in his own way a pregnant doctrine, since taught more gravely.

"It seems to him much less of a prodigy that men should lie, or that their imaginations should deceive them, than that a human body should be carried through the air on a broomstick, or up a chimney, by some unknown spirit. He thinks it a sad business to persuade one's self that the test of truth lies in the multitude of believers —'en une presse où les fols surpassent de tant les sages en nombre.' " ¶51

Also mentioned

[relatively distinguished historical or literary figures are in Index X or XI]

Buckle, hostile views on Scotch Protestantism 49
Trois Echelles, a supposed sorceress pardoned by Charles IX 51

Address to Working Men, by Felix Holt

(pp 1-11)

[pp 169-83 in the 1894 Crowell ed.; citations are to these pages]

Disraeli's Reform Bill of 1867 passed in July of that year. He came to Edinburgh and spoke on the subject, and Blackwood, struck by the timeliness of Eliot's novel *Felix Holt,* asked her to write for his magazine "an address to the Working Men on their new responsibilities," as though spoken by her leading character. She was pleased to oblige, but wrote from her conservative convictions and concerns: Most modern editions of the novel include the complete address in an Appendix, so we limit ourselves here to a few characteristic extracts.

"FELLOW WORKMEN—I am not going to take up your time by complimenting you. It has been the fashion to compliment kings and other authorities when they have come into power, and to tell them that, under their wise and beneficent rule, happiness would certainly overflow the land. But the end has not always corresponded to that beginning. If it were true that we who work for wages had more of the wisdom and virtue necessary to the right use of power than has been shown by the aristocratic and mercantile classes, we should not glory much in that fact, or consider that it carried with it any near approach to infallibility." 169

—*the record:* "Any nation that had within it a majority of men—and we are the majority—possessed of much wisdom and virtue, would not tolerate the bad practices, the commercial lying and swindling, the poisonous adulteration of goods, the retail cheating, and the political bribery, which are carried on boldly in the midst of us." 169

—*example:* " . . . if we had discerned better between good and evil, if the multitude of us artisans, and factory hands, and miners, and laborers of all sorts, had been skilful, faithful, well-judging, industrious, sober—and I don't see how there can be wisdom and virtue anywhere without those qualities—we should have made an audience that would have shamed the other classes out of their share in the national vices. We should have had better members of Parliament, better religious teachers, honester tradesmen, fewer foolish demagogues, less impudence in infamous and brutal men; and we should not have had among us the abomination of men calling themselves religious while living in splendor on ill-gotten gains." 169

—*indignation:* "Indignation is a fine war-horse, but the war-horse must be ridden by a man: it must be ridden by rationality, skill, courage, armed with the right weapons, and taking definite aim." 171

—*the body:* " . . . no society is made up of a single class: society stands before us like that wonderful piece of life, the human body, with all its various parts depending on one another, and with a terrible liability to get wrong because of that delicate dependence. We all know how many diseases the human body is apt to suffer from, and how difficult it is even for the doctors to find out exactly where the seat or beginning of the disorder is. That is because the body is made up of so many various parts, all related to each other, or likely all to feel the effect if any one of them goes wrong. It is somewhat the same with our old nations or societies." 173

—*classes:* "No society ever stood long in the world without getting to be composed of different classes." 173

—*analogy to irrigation:* "Just as in that case I spoke of before, the irrigation of a country, which must absolutely have its water distributed or it will bear no crop; there are the old channels, the old banks, and the old pumps, which must be used as they are until new and better have been prepared, or the structure of the old has been gradually altered. But it would be fool's work to batter down a pump only because a better might be made, when you had no machinery ready for a new one: it would be wicked work, if villages lost their crops by it." 174

—*the franchise:* "Our getting the franchise will greatly hasten that good end in proportion only as every one of us has the knowledge, the foresight, the conscience, that will make him well-judging and scrupulous in the use of it. The nature of things in this world has been determined for us beforehand, and in such a way that no ship can be expected to sail well on a difficult voyage, and reach the right port, unless it is well manned: the nature of the winds and the waves, of the timbers, the sails and the cordage, will not accommodate itself to drunken, mutinous sailors." 175

—*first reform bill:* "After the reform Bill of 1832 I was in an election riot, which showed me clearly, on a small scale, what public disorder must always be; and I have never forgotten that the riot was brought about chiefly by the agency of dishonest men who professed to be on the people's side." 175

—*no hurry:* "I am a Radical; and, what is more, I am not a Radical with a title or a French cook or even an entrance into fine society. I expect great changes, and I desire them. But I don't expect them to come in a hurry, by mere inconsiderate sweeping. A **Hercules** with a big besom is a fine thing for a filthy stable, but not for weeding a seed-bed, where his besom would soon make a barren floor." 177

—*the common estate:* " . . . a wealth over and above buildings, machinery, produce, shipping, and so on, though closely connected with these; a wealth of a more delicate kind, that we may more unconsciously bring into danger, doing harm and not knowing that we do it. I mean that treasure of knowledge, science, poetry, refinement of thought, feeling, and manners, great memories, and the interpretation of great records, which is carried on from the minds of one generation to the minds of another. This is something distinct from the indulgences of luxury and the pursuit of vain finery; and one of the hardships in the lot of working men is that they have been for the most part shut out from sharing in this treasure." 178

—*ignorance:* "No political institution will alter the nature of Ignorance, or hinder it from producing vice and misery. Let Ignorance start how it will, it must run the same round of low appetites, poverty, slavery, and superstition. Some of us know this well—nay, I will say, feel it; for knowledge of this kind cuts deep; and to us it is one of the most painful facts belonging to our condition that there are numbers of our fellow-workmen who are so far from feeling in the same way, that they never use the imperfect opportunities already offered them for giving their children some schooling, but turn their little ones of tender age into bread-winners, often at cruel tasks, exposed to the horrible infection of childish vice." 179

—*children:* "It is true enough that there is a low sense of parental duties in the nation at large, and that numbers who have no excuse in bodily hardship seem to think it a light thing to beget children—to bring human beings, with all their tremendous possibilities, into this difficult world—and then take little heed how they are disciplined and furnished for the perilous journey they are sent on without any asking of their own. This is a sin shared in more or less by all classes; but there are sins which, like taxation, fall the heaviest on the poorest, and none have such galling reasons as we working men to try and rouse to the utmost the feeling of responsibility in fathers and mothers." 180

—*our unions:* "Let us demand from the members of our Unions that they fulfil their duty as parents in this definite matter, which rules can reach. Let us demand that they send their children to school, so as not to go on recklessly breeding a moral pestilence among us, just as strictly as we demand that they pay their contributions to a common fund, understood to be for a common benefit. While we watch our public men, let us watch one another as to this duty, which is also public, and more momentous even than obedience to sanitary regulations." 180

—*slow wisdom:* "To get the chief power into the hands of the wisest, which means to get our life regulated according to the truest principles mankind is in possession of, is a problem as old as the very notion of wisdom. The solution comes slowly, because men collectively can only be made to embrace principles, and to act on them, by the slow stupendous teaching of the world's events. Men will go on planting potatoes, and nothing else but potatoes, till a potato disease comes and forces them to find out the advantage of a varied crop. Selfishness, stupidity, sloth, persist in trying to adapt the world to their desires, till a time comes when the world manifests itself as too decidedly inconvenient to them." 181

—*class disparities:* "Many of the highest uses of life are in their [the endowed classes'] keeping; and if privilege has often been abused, it has also been the nurse of excellence. Here again we have to submit ourselves to the great law of inheritance. If we quarrel with the way in which the labors and earnings of the past have been preserved and handed down, we are just as bigoted, just as narrow, just as wanting in that religion which keeps an open ear and an obedient mind to the teachings of fact, as we accuse those of being who quarrel with the new truths and new needs which are disclosed in the present. The deeper insight we get into the causes of human trouble, and the ways by which men are made better and happier, the less we shall be inclined to the unprofitable spirit and practice of reproaching classes as such in a wholesale fashion. Not all the evils of our condition are such as we can justly blame others for; and, I repeat, many of them are such as no change of institutions can quickly remedy. To discern between the evils that energy can remove and the evils that patience must bear, makes the difference between manliness and childishness, between good sense and folly. " 182

Ambrose [**Ambroise**] **Paré**. "For the thousands of years, down to the middle of the sixteenth century since **Christ**, that human limbs had been hacked and amputated, nobody knew how to stop the bleeding except by searing the ends of the vessels with red-hot iron. But then came a man named Ambrose Paré, and said, 'Tie up the arteries!' That was a fine word to utter. It contained the statement of a method—a plan by which a particular evil was forever assuaged." 181

—*concluding:* "I am addressing a mixed assembly of workmen, and some of you may be as well or better fitted than I am to take up this office. But they will not think it amiss in me that I have tried to bring together the considerations most likely to be of service to us in preparing ourselves for the use of our new opportunities. I have avoided touching on special questions. The best help towards judging well on these is to approach them in the right temper, without vain expectation, and with a resolution which is mixed with temperance." 182-3

Reviews and Notes

The observant reader of the previous section, Essays and Reports, will have noticed that frequently an Essay will begin with the citation of a recently published work, apparently intended to be the subject of a Review. Why, then, is it classified as an Essay? It has long been a convention in Eliot scholarship that her important nonfiction, like the seven items chosen by Charles Lewes for his posthumous edition of Eliot's complete works (discussed on page 3), must be considered Essays, even if they take off from an event like the recent (sometimes not so recent) publication of a cited work.

The fact is that in these "Essays," Eliot goes well beyond the usual purview of a book review and gets into ramifications of the subject under discussion which are original with her and not necessarily very closely connected with the work which started the trouble. On the other hand, out of the sixty-eight items of published nonfiction we have been able to assemble, a good many (we have decided there are thirty—there is no objective way to certainty in this) are clearly not important examples of the Eliot intellectual imagination but rather are competent reports of the arrival of noteworthy items of literature more or less serious, and descriptions of them.

Pieces like this we term Reviews (or Notes) and present them below:

Reviews and Notes

Coventry *Herald and Observer* **QM**
October 30, 1846

Quinet and Michelet

Christianity in its Various Aspects, by Edgar Quinet
The Jesuits, by Edgar Quinet and Jules Michelet
Priests, Women and Families, by Jules Michelet

We give in its entirety George Eliot's first published book review, as transcribed for us by the indispensable David Parker at the Colindale archive in London. He helped us with the following piece as well.

"These publications are three of a series of translations from contemporary French authors which, on the whole, form a not unwelcome addition to our rapidly increasing stock of cheap literature. It is true that a translation can never be more than a second best vehicle for an author's thoughts, and the more abundant his excellencies, the more does he suffer from this method of presentation—the finer the nectar, the greater the risk in transferring it from one vessel to another. But an acquaintance with foreign modes of thought, especially on the greater questions which occupy the human mind, is too important an element in the true enlightenment of a nation, to be dispensed with until all English readers shall have faculties or leisure to become linguists.

¶"These remarks apply very forcibly to the works before us. The authors suffer perhaps more than in the average degree from the translating process; but notwithstanding this disadvantage, it is well that ordinary readers should have the means of knowing what writers so influential in their own country have to say on subjects of universal interest. Still, though we can thus approve the introduction of these works to the English public, they are far from obtaining our unqualified admiration. While they exhibit much fervid eloquence, expansiveness of view, and ardour for human liberty and human progress, they are too vague and allusive to be very rich in instruction to persons less informed than their authors, and they have the fault, perhaps inevitable to works of an antagonistic character, of putting statements too broadly, and painting facts in too strong light and shadow. Moreover, all the philosophy of the writers has not delivered them from an almost ridiculous excess of *amour de la patrie*, which leads them to represent the French people as a sort of second chosen race, who alone have the mission to propagate, by pen and sword, the truth which is to regenerate nations. But national egotism is the last foible on which we English must allow ourselves to be severe.

"Whatever may be the reception of the above works amongst us, the friends of Jesuitism have done them the honour of showing the most vehement indignation, and alarm at their tendency, while, on the other hand, their authors have been warmly supported by those who think that France and Christendom in general have reason to regret the revival of the Society of Jesus in 1814. MM. Michelet and Quinet are, as they are fond of telling their readers, brothers not only in office, but in opinion, sharing the same views so intimately and completely, that whenever the one speaks or writes, he knows himself to be expressing the mind of the other; and one of the works before us, 'The Jesuits,' is a visible sign of this unity, being the joint production of the two friends.

¶"It consists of two series of lectures—the first, by M. Michelet, too declamatory and general to be considered for anything but a *viva voce* delivery, to an audience who shared in the excitement that produced 'long interruption' of the speaker, by 'applause, murmurs, and violent language.' The second course, by M. Quinet, is of more intrinsic value, containing a rapid and well-marked sketch of the origin and fortunes of the Society of Jesus, the nature of its discipline and constitution, its missions, political agency, and relation to theology and philosophy. With a candid acknowledgement of the true genius and enthusiasm which gave birth to the idea of the Society in the mind of its founder, of the pure earnestness and simple faith which carried a **Xavier** from India to Japan, and from thence to the shores of China, compelling from the inhabitants of those strange lands the tribute of veneration for him as a holy man—M. Quinet shows that the system of **Loyola** runs counter to the grand law which God has impressed on all nature—the production and development of life; that wherever it presides there must be moral, social, and intellectual death; its first aim being to annihilate in its agents, and consequently in those on which they act, all spontaneity, all will. Let man become as a corpse, *ut cadaver*, were the death-bed words of Loyola—let him be as a staff in the hands of an old man, *senis baculus*, which is taken up and cast away again at pleasure; and one of the rules in his Spiritual Exercises is equally startling: '*If authority declares that what seems to be white is black, affirm it to be black.*'

"Michelet's 'Priests, Women, and Families,' is more special, in its object, and much more likely to be extensively read. The author selects from history and biography samples of the effects of religious direction, by which he means a spiritual superintendence over individuals of a closer and more rigid character than that of the confessor. He gives some melancholy proofs of the too undeniable fact, that women have ever been the victims and instruments of priestly despotism, and in the latter part of the work he dilates especially on the baneful influence of the director on the peace of domestic life. There is certainly much truth very cogently stated in the form both of facts and principles in this work of Michelet's; but we confess that to us, loving, as we do, to dwell in the serene atmosphere of admiration for mankind, its perusal has been exquisitely painful, and with all deference to the author's experience and judgment, we advise his readers to bear in mind, that there is a large amount of truth to be urged in vindication of the defendant, which Michelet, as counsel for the other party, is not to be expected to state. We have not space for many quotations, but we give the following as rather a happy illustration of the power of habit:—

" 'I read once in an old story what is really affecting, and significant. It was about a woman, a wandering princess, who, after many sufferings, found for her asylum a deserted palace in the midst of a forest. She felt happy to repose there, and remaining some time: she went to and fro from one large empty room to another, without meeting with any obstacle; she thought herself alone and free. All the doors were open; only at the hall-door, no one having passed through since herself, the spider had woven his web in the sun, a thin, light, and almost invisible net-work; a feeble obstacle, which the princess, who wishes at last to go out, thinks she can remove without difficulty. She raises the web; but there is another behind it, which she also raises without trouble. The second conceals a third; that she must also raise—strange! here are four, no five! or rather six—and more beyond Alas! how will she get rid of so many? She is already tired. No matter! she perseveres; by taking breath a little she may continue. But the web continues too, and is ever renewed with a malicious obstinacy. What is she to do? She is overcome with fatigue and perspiration, her arms fall by her sides. At last, exhausted as she is, she sits down on the ground, on that insurmountable threshold; she looks mournfully at the aerial obstacle fluttering in the wind, lightly and triumphantly. Poor princess! poor fly! now you are caught! But why did you stay in that fairy dwelling, and give the spider time to spin the web?' "

"Too much credit cannot be given to Messrs. Longmans and Co, for the style in which these publications are got up. As regards paper, type, and form, we think them superior to any cheap issue of popular literature that has hitherto appeared, and we trust that the spirited publishers will follow up their praiseworthy commencement in this department of the public service."

The Comic History of England

The Comic History of England, by Gilbert A. À Beckett

"Mr. Gilbert A. À Beckett is well known as a writer who can find matter for fun and drollery where, to others, such a discovery would appear as hopeless as the extracting of sunbeams from cucumbers. The 'Comic History of England' is not likely to diminish his reputation in this line. It teems with that rich species of *double entendre* which not only amuses by the presentation of incongruity, but at the same time conveys sly and pungent satire. The illustrations by **Leech** indicate that there is as racy a wit in the artist as in the author. We recommend the work to unfortunate students with short memories, who have never been able to engrave on their mental tablets the events of English History, especially those 'battles of kites and crows' as **Milton** called them—the struggles of the Saxon Heptarchy. We assure them that they will not be able to forget either Mr. G. A. À Beckett's narrative, or Mr. Leech's graphic commentary."

Froude's *The Nemesis of Faith*

"On certain red-letter days of our existence, it happens to us to discover among the *spawn* of the press, a book which, as we read, seems to undergo a sort of transfiguration before us. We no longer hold heavily in our hands an octavo of some hundred pages, over which the eye laboriously travels, hardly able to drag along with it the restive mind: but we seem to be in companionship with a spirit, who is transfusing himself into our souls, and is vitalizing them by his superior energy, that life, both outward and inward, presents itself to us for higher relief, in colours brightened and deepened—we seem to have been bathing in a pool of Siloam, and to have come forth reeling. The books which carry this magic in them are the true products of genius, and their influence, whether for good or evil, is to the influence of all the respectable results of mere talent and industry, as the mighty Nile to the dykes which receive and distribute its heaven-fed waters.

¶"Such a book is *The Nemesis of Faith.* We are sure that its author is a bright particular star, though he sometimes leaves us in doubt whether he be not a fallen 'son of the morning.' Much there is in the work of a questionable character: yet more which hardly falls within the scope of a newspaper editor's notice: but its trenchant remarks on some of our English conventions, its striking sketches of the dubious aspect which many chartered respectabilities are beginning to wear under the light of this nineteenth century, its suggestive hints as to the necessity of recasting the currency of our religion and virtue, that it may carry fresh and bright the stamp of the age's highest and best idea—these have a practical bearing, which may well excite the grave, perhaps the alarmed attention of some important classes among us. We will resign the work into the hands of judges of more ability, and more unquestioned credentials, only quoting one or two passages as a slight sample for our readers. Surely there is work for our augurs when a Clergyman writes thus of his co-ordinates:—"

GE here extracts two paragraphs attacking the Clergy for their worldly values and preoccupation with comfort, and for their indifference to and ignorance of the Poor and their needs. A second shorter passage argues that the arrival of the printing press has made moot the role and purpose of the Clergy in the pulpit, and perhaps better so.

The Life of John Sterling
(pp 247-51)

The Life of John Sterling, by Thomas Carlyle (1851)

"As soon as the closing of the Great Exhibition afforded a reasonable hope that there would once more be a reading public, 'The Life of Sterling' appeared. A new work by Carlyle must always be among the literary births eagerly chronicled by the journals and greeted by the public. In a book of such parentage we care less about the subject than about its treatment, just as we think the 'Portrait of a Lord' worth studying if it come from the pencil of a **Vandyck**." 247

"[Sterling's] intellect was active and rapid, rather than powerful, and in all his writings we feel the want of a stronger electric current to give that vigour of conception and felicity of expression, by which we distinguish the undefinable something called genius; while his moral nature, though refined and elevated, seems to have been subordinate to his intellectual tendencies and social qualities, and to have had itself little determining influence on his life." 247-8

"The impression of his intellectual power on his personal friends seems to have been produced chiefly by the eloquence and brilliancy of his conversation; but the mere reader of his works and letters would augur from them neither the wit, nor the *curiosa felicitas* of epithet and imagery, which would rank him with the men whose sayings are thought worthy of perpetuation in books . . . . The public, then, since it is content to do without biographies of much more remarkable men, cannot be supposed to have felt any pressing demand even for a single life of Sterling; still less, it might be thought, when so distinguished a writer as **Archdeacon Hare** had furnished this, could there be any need for another." 248

"Carlyle here shows us his 'sunny side.' We no longer see him breathing out threatenings and slaughter as in the Latter-Day Pamphlets, but moving among the charities and amenities of life, loving and beloved—a *Teufelsdröckh* still, but humanized by a *Blumine* worthy of him." 249

"Its comparatively tame scenes and incidents gather picturesqueness and interest under the rich lights of Carlyle's mind. We are told neither too little nor too much; the facts noted, the letters selected, are all such as serve to give the liveliest conception of what Sterling was and what he did; and though the book speaks much of other persons, this collateral matter is all a kind of scene-painting, and is accessory to the main purpose." 249

—conclusion: "This 'Life of Sterling' is a touching monument of the capability human nature possesses of the highest love, the love of the good and beautiful in character, which is, after all, the essence of piety. The style of the work, too, is for the most part at once pure and rich; there are passages of deep pathos which come upon the reader like a strain of solemn music, and others which show that aptness of epithet, that masterly power of close delineation, in which, perhaps, no writer has excelled Carlyle." 250-1

The Art of the Ancients
(pp 257-8)

Torso. The Art, Artists, and Art-Remains of the Ancients, by Adolf Stahr (first part)

This careful and detailed review takes the reader sequentially through Stahr's survey of Greek sculpture. GE notes the controversy on the question whether the art of the Greeks was altogether indigenous or had been derived from Egyptian models. She pooh-poohs scholars who see no further than the end of their noses and insist on the truth of what they already know or think they know. She and Stahr clearly incline toward the evolution of art, as of much else, from eastern influence moving westward.

"The books of which a reviewer can say that he has read every word, and has laid them down wishing for more, are far from being as plentiful as blackberries, especially in German literature. Professor Stahr's *Torso,* however, is one of these exceptional books: we have read it from beginning to end with delight, and are eager for the second part, which is yet to appear. The name of Adolf Stahr is well known in Germany, and not unknown in England, as that of a writer who unites thorough scholarship with refined taste, and who has that rare mastery of the unwieldy German language which makes his works charm by their form as well as their matter. There is not a trace of pedantry in his books; you perceive his knowledge as you perceive the daylight, by the clearness with which objects are presented to you . . . . His pre-eminent talent lies in description both of natural scenery and works of art; he has not only an intense susceptibility to the beautiful, but he is in possession of the magic word which will convey his impression to the mind of the reader. These excellent qualities are remarkably exhibited in his latest and yet uncompleted work . . . . It is more historical and descriptive than disquisitional; condensed enough to serve as an introductory manual for those who have the opportunity of immediately studying ancient sculpture, and yet so full and vivid in its descriptions, and so philosophic in its mode of considering the development of art, that it may be read with lively interest in a country town, far away from all casts and museums . . . .

"After general considerations on the progress of Greek art from **Dædalus** to **Phidias**, and from Phidias to **Hadrian**, and on the criteria of relative antiquity, the author commences his descriptive survey of the principal remains of Hellenic sculpture—those remains which best illustrate the ideals of the successive epochs. The Gate of Lions at Mycenæ, and the reliefs at Samothrace representing **Agamemnon** seated on a throne accompanied by two heralds, bear strong traces of the abstract Egyptian manner: the one herald, for example, being the repetition of the other. So do the Lycian sculptures, consisting of from sixty to seventy statues in a sitting posture, which formed the avenue to a temple; the perfect parallelism of the feet, the stiff posture of the arms, the straight lines of the drapery, everything is Egyptian in style . . . .

"To the chapter on **Praxiteles** follows a long and valuable discourse on the Social Position of the Artist in Greece, and another on the relation between Art and Freedom. Then comes a highly interesting survey of ancient Portrait sculpture; and finally, this first part of the work closes with a consideration of the Colouring and Nudity of Greek statues. We are glad to find Professor Stahr insisting that in the highest period of Greek art the colouring of statues was not guided by the barbaric idea of producing illustrations, but by a fine sense of relief in colours, an opinion which we have advanced in these columns."

A discussion of the complete work is at page 98.

Westward Ho!

(pp. 474-5)

Westward Ho! Or, the Voyages and Adventures of Sir Amyas Leigh, Knight, of Burrough, in the county of Devon, in the reign of Her Most Glorious Majesty Queen Elizabeth. Rendered into modern English by Charles Kingsley

"There are two points of view under which a book like this may be examined. One may try its purpose, and inquire how far it is wise in what it advocates; or one may consider it simply as a work of art, and investigate its claims to pictorial excellence. So, **Dr Johnson**, in his *Life of Akenside*, begins his criticism by saying—'With the philosophical or religious tenets of the author I have nothing to do; my business is with his poetry.' And so, likewise, the critic of a picture of the 'Annunciation' would pronounce on its merit, without troubling himself whether the orthodox view of the 'Annunciation' was correct or not.

"It would, however, be peculiarly unjust to Mr Kingsley to look at this work only as an historical picture. We well know that he had other designs in writing it than the merely producing a novel. It so happens that novels in our age contribute to the formation of public opinion. Mr Kingsley, who knows that, and has many of the talents of a novelist, uses the novel (as some religious bodies use secular tunes) for his own objects as a churchman. He is a preacher and painter in one. He aims at catching by fiction those who are out of his pulpit range. He is a lucky priest to be able to exercise his faculties in this way.

¶"In Scotland we fear that his Presbytery would have silenced or dismissed him long ago. But it is a characteristic of the Church of England—and nobody will accuse the *Leader* of being bigoted in her favour—that she constantly produces popular writers—many of them, indeed, such as reflect by their gravity no great additional dignity on the venerable institution. [**John**] **Skelton** and Bishop [**Joseph**] **Hall**, two of our earliest satirists, were of her. Then, [**Jonathan**] **Swift** the terrible, and [**Lawrence**] **Sterne**, and [**Charles**] **Churchill**, and **Peter Pindar** [**John Wolcot**], and **Sydney Smith**! How much jolly 'profane' literature we owe to these parsons! Add, as members of the rival Church, [**François**] **Rabelais** and

[**Desiderius**] **Erasmus**—and it will be seen at once that Europe owes its best laughter to its spiritual guides. We mention these facts to vindicate Mr Kingsley in the eyes of those sour and stern persons who may think novel-writing no proper employment for a clergyman. We say it is a great advantage to Mother Church to have a son who can write a successful novel. Mr Kingsley has done more for her by his novels than even he himself (not to mention inferior men) could do by his sermons. We, ourselves, never heard Mr Kingsley preach, but we have read his books—and of these books none has given us more pleasure than the one before us.

"Now to begin with the 'purpose,' which, as we have said, is the great matter with Mr Kingsley. It is plain enough. The reign of **Bess** was great and glorious. Everybody was religious in the days of Bess. It was a grand time. England then represented light, freedom, and truth; Spain the Pope, despotism, and the devil. The great Armada fight in 1588 was 'Britain's Salamis.' . . . Here you have the 'views ' of this Novel. It is written altogether from that standing point, and Mr Kingsley hammers away at his favourite subjects of detestation as heartily as **Francis Drake** hammered at the Spanish fleet. For he is, before everything else, a 'hearty' writer, and notably pugnacious. Indeed, if he will excuse our familiarity, we will venture to say that two influences more than any other seem to have made him the writer he is—the influence of **Thomas Carlyle**—and that of—Thomas Cribb!

"To carry out these views, then, Mr Kingsley centres his interest round one Amyas Leigh, a Devonshire gentleman, and one of the great sea-adventurers of that period who so excellently represent its spirit. **Goethe** speaks of the age of **Shakspeare** as 'a great and energetic time.' Now, energy is precisely the word which describes the Elizabethan age. There is a burning vitality to be seen in everything it produced, from the colonies to its songs. Nowhere is it more seen than in its naval history, and it was wise of Mr Kingsley to choose that for the most prominent feature. Round Amyas other portraits are hung—the courtier, gallant, chivalrous, graceful,—the Jesuit—the Spanish Don—the merchant— the gentleman—all typical figures and careful studies. The author has broken from the routine habit of painting only court figures and known incidents. A commonplace man would have brought in Elizabeth at every turn, swearing her usual oath, and boxing people's ears. Mr Kingsley gives us the life of England, as it has formed that which still exists. A homely reality distinguishes the book—earnestness dashed by colloquial ease . . . . [long extract follows].

"The consistency of bluff Amyas is well preserved throughout the story. The plot we do not feel called on to describe. Those who have read or are going to read the book don't require it; and for others, it would have but a faint interest. We shall select a few characteristic bits of writing, such as can be enjoyed without much reference to the context." [Another extract includes a graphic description of Francis Drake.]

GE wrote another review of the Kingsley book, which appeared in the first *Belles Lettres* section she wrote for the *Westminster Review*. *See* BL 1.

Belles Lettres
(pp 288-307)

Westward Ho!, or, The Voyages and Adventures of Sir Amyas Leigh, Knight, of Burrough, in the County of Devon, in the Reign of Her Most Glorious Majesty Queen Elizabeth, rendered into Modern English by Charles Kingsley.

"Every one who was so happy as to go mushrooming in his early days, remembers his delight when, after picking up and throwing away heaps of dubious fungi, dear to naturalists but abhorred of cooks, he pounces on an unmistakeable mushroom, with its delicate fragrance and pink lining tempting him to devour it there and then, to the prejudice of the promised dish for breakfast. We speak in parables, after the fashion of the wise, amongst whom Reviewers are always to be reckoned. The plentiful dubious fungi are the ordinary quarter's crop of novels, not all poisonous, but generally not appetizing, and certainly not nourishing; and the unmistakeable mushroom is a new novel by Charles Kingsley." 288

"It seemed too long since we had any of that genuine description of external nature, not done after the poet's or the novelist's recipe, but flowing from spontaneous observation and enjoyment [word omitted?] any of that close, vigorous painting of out-door life, which serves as myrrh and rich spices to embalm much perishable theorizing and offensive objurgation—too long since we had a taste of that exquisite lyrical inspiration to which we owe—

'O, Mary! go and call the cattle home
Along the sands of Dee.' " 288

"After courses of 'psychological' novels (very excellent things in their way), where life seems made up of talking and journalizing, and men are judged almost entirely on 'carpet consideration,' we are ready to welcome a stirring historical romance, by a writer who, poet and scholar and social reformer as he is, evidently knows the points of a horse and has followed the hounds, who betrays a fancy for pigs, and becomes dithyrambic on the virtues of tobacco. After a surfeit of **Hebes** and **Psyches**, or Madonnas and **Magdalens**, it is a refreshment to turn to **Kiss**'s **Amazon** . . . this ruddy and, now and then, rather ferocious barbarism . . . is singularly compounded in Mr

Kingsley with the susceptibility of the poet and the warm sympathy of the philanthropist . . . . " 288

"In these two points—his fierce antagonism and his perpetual hortative tendency—lie, to our thinking, the grand mistakes which enfeeble the effect of all Mr Kingsley's works, and are too likely to impede his production of what his high powers would otherwise promise—a fiction which might be numbered among our classics. Poet and artist in a rare degree, his passionate impetuosity and theological prepossessions inexorably forbid that he should ever be a philosopher; he sees, feels, and paints vividly, but he theorizes illogically and moralizes absurdly." 289

"We abstain on principle from telling the story of novels, which seems to us something like stealing geraniums from your friend's flower-pot to stick in your own button-hole: you spoil the effect of his plant, and you secure only a questionable ornament for yourself." 290

"Where his prepossessions do not come into play, where he is not dealing with his model heroes, or where the drama turns on a single passion or motive, he can scarcely be rivalled in truthfulness and beauty of presentation; for in clothing passion with action and language, and in the conception of all that gives local colouring, he has his best gifts to aid him." 291

"His view of history seems not essentially to differ from that we have all held in our childish days, when it seemed perfectly easy to us to divide mankind into the sheep and the goats, when we devoutly believed that our favourite heroes, **Wallace** and **Bruce**, and all who fought on their side, were 'good,' while **Edward** and his soldiers were all 'wicked;' that all the champions of the Reformation were of unexceptionable private character, and all the adherents of Popery consciously vicious and base. Doubtless the Elizabethan age bore its peculiar fruit of excellence, as every age has done which forms a nodus, a ganglion, in the historical development of humanity—as the age of **Pericles** produced the divinest sculptures, or the age of the Roman Republic the severe grandeur of Roman law and Roman patriotism, or as the core of the Middle Ages held the germ of chivalrous honour and reverential love. Doubtless the conquest of the Spanish Armada was virtually the triumph of light and freedom over darkness and bondage. What then?" 292

Thomas Carlyle. " . . . no sooner does [**Kingsley**] get astride [his hobby horse], than he becomes a feeble imitator of Carlyle's *manège,* and attempts to put his wooden toy to all the wonderful paces of the great Scotchman's fiery Tartar horse . . . Mr Kingsley's impetuosity and **Boanerges**' vein give him an affinity for Carlyle's faults—his one-sided judgment of character and his undiscriminating fulminations against the men of the present as tried by some imaginary standard in the past . . . . [Kingsley] has not that piercing insight which every now and then flashes to the depth of things, and alternating as it does with the most obstinate one-sidedness, makes Carlyle a wonderful paradox of wisdom and wilfulness; he has not that awful sense of the mystery of existence which continually checks and chastens the denunciations of the **Teufelsdröckh**; still less has he the rich humour, the keen satire, and the tremendous word-missiles, which Carlyle hurls about as **Milton**'s angels hurl the rocks." 289

Sir Walter Scott, "who remains the unequalled model of historical romancists, however they may criticize him." 290

Constance Herbert, by Geraldine E. Jewsbury.

"Miss Jewsbury has created precedents for herself which make critics exacting towards her. We measure her work by her own standard, and find it deficient; when if measured by the standard of ordinary feminine novelists, it would perhaps seem excellent." 294

"An easy, agreeable style of narrative, some noble sentiments expressed in the quiet, unexaggerated way that indicates their source to be a deep spring of conviction and experience, not a mere rain-torrent of hearsay enthusiasm, with here and there a trait of character or conduct painted with the truthfulness of close observation, are merits enough to raise a book far above the common run of circulating library fiction; but they are not enough to make a good novel, or one worthy of Miss Jewsbury's reputation." 294

Thorney Hall: a Story of an Old Family, by Holme Lee

" . . . it has no pretension to be anything else than a story of ordinary life, with its inward and outward trials, its mistakes and misfortunes . . . those who are looking out for a one-volumed novel, which will not disturb the initiation of the digestive process, and is likely, by-and-by, to lull them into their siesta, will find 'Thorney Hall' unexceptionable for their purpose." 296

Our World; or, the Democrat's Rule, by Justia, a Knownothing.

" . . . an American novel which will attract only those readers who can be induced to linger over scenes more painful than the most painful in 'Uncle Tom's Cabin,' by any slighter motive than a stern necessity for becoming acquainted with the facts of a special case." 296

Married Women

". . . milk-and-water triviality . . . . We suppose there is still a public for novels like this among the clients of the circulating libraries in provincial towns; and, after all, an interest in such feeble creations is better than blank *ennui* or indulgence in acrid gossip." 296

Brittany and La Vendée. Tales and Sketches, by Emile Souvestre

"Emile Souvestre is deservedly a favourite writer in England . . . . The beautiful paper and type, and the convenient size of the volume, make these pleasant tales seem all the more readable—in happy contrast with the getting up of German books which you can only read *in spite* of the fact that they fall to pieces before you have turned over half-a-dozen pages." 297

Poems, by Matthew Arnold

"Our first impression from a poem of Mr Arnold's—and with some persons this is the sole impression—generally is, that it is rather tame and prosaic. The thought is always refined and unhackneyed, sometimes new and sublime, but he seems not to have found the winged word which carries the thought at once to the mind of the reader; his poems do not come to us like original melodies, which are beautiful facts that one never thinks of altering any more than a pine-tree or a river; we are haunted by the feeling that he might have said the same thing much better. But when, simply for the sake of converse with a nature so gifted and cultivated as Mr Arnold's, we linger over a poem which contains some deep and fresh thought, we begin to perceive poetic beauties—felicities of expression and description, which are too quiet and subdued to be seized at the first glance. You must become familiar with his poems before you can appreciate them as poetry, just as in the early spring you must come very near to the woods before you can discern the delicate glossy or downy buds which distinguish their April from their winter clothing." 297

" . . . we should point to 'Resignation,' and to 'The Last Glen,' and 'Typho' in 'The Harp-player on Ætna,' as favourable specimens of the author's power in two directions—the expression of exquisite sensibility united with deep thought, in which he reminds us of **Wordsworth**, and the revivifying of antique conceptions by freshly-felt descriptions of external nature and masterly indications of permanent human feeling, after the manner of **Tennyson**." 298

Poetical Works of Geoffrey Chaucer, Robert Bell, ed.

"The notes are brief and really enlightening. Mr Bell does not incessantly invite your eye to the bottom of the page in order to expatiate on something quite beside the question; but wherever you are conscious of fogginess, you find a reference to a note which detains you from the text only just so long as is necessary." 300

Poems, by Arthur M. Morgan

The Transcript, and other Poems, by William Ball

" . . . the Reviewer must resignedly expect as so much inevitable chickweed or dandelion which will spring up round the heliotropes and anemones." 300 *See Topicon* LC:Poet and Poetry—*bad*

Echoes of the War, and other Poems, by Henry Sewell Stokes

"[These] are unpretending rhymes, which seem to be the sincere response of a warm British heart to the tales of noble deeds, and nobly endured suffering, which have come to us from the Crimea. The poem on Inkermann is an easy, spirited ballad of the kind we wish our war poets had hit on more frequently, instead of the highflown metaphysical strain." 301

Passing Thoughts, by James Douglas, of Cavers

"The 'Passing Thoughts' on **Goethe** and **Rousseau** were certainly not worth arresting, but those on Italy show some largeness of view and some feeling for the beautiful." 301

The History of Woman, and Her Connexion with Religion, Civilization, and Domestic Manners, from the Earliest Periods, by C. W. Fullom

"We use this fable [of the braying ass] to intimate why we show less tolerance to Mr C. W. Fullom than to many other utterly unqualified authors who come under our notice." 301

" . . . the 'History of Woman' 'offers a forcible instance of what has to be surmounted in the journey of life,'—by a devoted reviewer." 302

Ménandre. Etude Historique et Littéraire sur la Comédie et la Société Grecques, by Guillaume Guizot, "a study of Menander, in which M. Guillaume Guizot very ably popularizes the labours of **Meineke**. **Lessing**'s fable of the blind hen industriously scratching up the grain which the alert cock forthwith appropriates, retains its application to the laborious German scholar, and his facile interpreter the Frenchman." 302

"The devices of barren critics have always been the same: first, Menander was too young; then he was a plagiarist; then he held the pernicious doctrines of **Epicurus**; then his life was immoral. Everything was easier to prove than that he had written bad comedies. Menander avenged himself by asking **Philemon**: 'Do you not sometimes blush when your comedies are preferred to mine?' and the next age avenged him by placing him at the head of all comic dramatists. The celebrated critic, **Aristophanes**, ranked him even next to **Homer**; his comedies were performed at private banquets as well as on the stage, and, four centuries after Menander's day, **Plutarch**, in an enthusiastic eulogy, said, that at such banquets they were equally acceptable to the graver judgment of the sober guests and the rather riotous spirits of the winebibbers. It was the critic Aristophanes, by the way, who applied to Menander the graceful compliment, which has since been so often borrowed, and paid to forgotten immortals: 'O Menander! O Life! which of you has imitated the other?' " 303

Aristophanes. "The ancient comedy, represented by Aristophanes, occupied itself almost entirely with political subjects: it was a dramatised criticism and satire of public men and public measures—the acted 'Punch' or 'Charivari' of Athens. The characters were either personifications in which there was the most daring combination of extravagant fancy with acutely portrayed reality, or outrageous caricatures of well-known individuals; personal attack was its essence; the public weal was the only thing it held sacred." 304

Tolla, by Edmond About

" 'Tolla' is a perfectly charming tale, by M. Edmond About, a young writer already known by an interesting book of travel in Greece. The incidents of this little story . . . are very simple, but they are made of absorbing interest by the artistic mastery with which the writer transports us beneath the skies of Italy, and shows us the life of the modern Italian grandee, or the romantic barbarism still existing in the Italian peasant; by the living, unexaggerated reality of the characters; and by the pure and tender spirit which breathes through the whole narrative, and tempers the French point and vivacity of the style." 306

"We hope and believe that 'Tolla' is only the first of many beautiful stories for which we shall have to thank M. Edmond About: a bit of virgin gold like this tells of a rich mine yet to be worked." 306

Nouvelles Danoisés, Xavier Marmier, transl.

"These . . . are nothing more than love stories of the very flimsiest texture, impressing one simply with the strong family resemblance there is between poor writers of all nations." 306

Miltona, by Théophile Gautier

"How is it that novels and tales are so often like the baskets of strawberries which tempt the thirsty pedestrian at Kew or elsewhere on a bright summer's day—all inviting, ripe, and fresh at the beginning, and, as you near the end, poor, crude and stale?" 306-7

Lord Brougham's Literature

Lives of Men of Letters and Science, Who Flourished in the Time of George III, by Lord Brougham

"It is a matter of very common observation that members of the 'privileged classes,' who, either from want of work or want of ability to do their proper work, find their time hang rather heavily on their hands, try to get rid of it by employments which, if not self-imposed, they would think rather pitiable. Kings and emperors have turned their hands to making locks and sealing-wax; ambassadresses have collected old stockings for the sake of darning them; and we knew a wealthy old gentleman who devoted himself to making pokers, which he presented to all the ladies of his acquaintance. It is generally presumed of such people that if they had brains to enable them to do anything better, they would prosecute this voluntary artisanship with less zeal; still, the case of these incapables is one to be charitably smiled at or sighed over, not gravely rebuked; we graciously accept the present of their lock or their poker and say no more about it.

¶"But it would be a different affair if these voluntary artisans were to set up shop—if, for example, Lord A, or Sir B. C., or any other of the tribe of wealthy Englishmen to whom foreigners give the generic title of *milord,* were not only to amuse himself with making boots, but were to hire a shop frontage, with plate glass, and exhibit his clumsy wares to the public with as much pomp and circumstance as if he were a very **Hoby** [boot and shoe maker in Pall Mall], thereby inducing snobbish people to set the fashion of wearing and crying up Lord A's boots, to the depreciation of really well-made articles, and to the great detriment both of human candour and the human foot. Political economists and bootmakers, lady-loves and orthopœdists, science and æsthetics, would vote the aristocratic **Crispin** a nuisance.

"A sufficiently close parallel to this hypothetic case is suggested by Lord Brougham's *Lives of Men of Letters,* the sight of which, republished in a cheap form, has, we confess, roused our critical gall. Relived from the labours of his chancellorship, Lord Brougham, we suppose, found a good deal of leisure on his hands; and how did he employ it? By taking to what we may call literary lock and poker-making—by writing third-rate biographies in the style of a literary hack! Biographies, too, of men whose lives had already been depicted in all sorts of ways, and presented to us in all sorts of lights—like **Prince Albert**'s face and legs.

¶"If we had found these 'Lives of Men of Letters' in a biographical dictionary we should perhaps have thought them about up to the average of the piece-work usually to be met with in such compilations; finding them, as we did more than ten years ago, in an *édition de luxe* adorned with portraits, and with Lord Brougham's name on the title-page, we felt some simmering indignation at such gratuitous mediocrities in a pretentious garb; and now that we see them in a cheaper reissue—as if there were any demand for these clumsy superfluities, these amateur locks and pokers—our indignation fairly boils over. We have not the slightest wish to be disrespectful to Lord Brougham. His name is connected with some of the greatest movements in the last half century, and in general, is on the side of the liberal and the just. But he has been a successful man; his reputation is fully equal to his merit; society is unanimous in pronouncing that he has done many things well and wisely; and there is, therefore, no reason why we should be reticent of our criticism where, in our opinion, he has done some things less wisely and *not* well.

"The first thing that strikes us in these *Lives* is the slovenliness of their style, which is thrown almost ludicrously into relief by the fact that many of Lord Brougham's pages are occupied with criticism of other men's style. The hard-run literary man, who is every moment expecting the knock of the printer's boy, has reason enough to renounce fastidiousness; but his lordship, in the elegant case of his library, with no call impending but that of the lunch or dinner-bell, might at least atone for the lack of originality by finish—might, if he has no jewels to offer us, at least polish his pebbles . . . .

" . . . But we must remember that when indignation makes reviews instead of Juvenalian verses, the result is not equally enjoyable by the reader. So we restrain our noble rage, and say good-by now and for ever to Lord Brougham's *Lives of Men of Letters,* hoping that the next time we meet with a production of his we may be able to express admiration as strongly as we have just now expressed the reverse."

Pinney gives the full text, and in an opening note quotes GE's defense of her attack on Brougham in a letter she wrote her friend Charles Bray on July 16, 1855.

Life and Opinions of Milton

(page 750)

An Account of the Life, Opinions, and Writings of John Milton, with an Introduction to Paradise Lost, by Thomas Keightley

"This volume on Milton has been a labour of love to Mr Keightley, and, as with all such labours where there is ability as well as love, the result is valuable. The biographical part is full without being prolix; all the accessible materials are well digested, and the evidence for questionable details carefully sifted: there are no bookmaking digressions from the history of Milton's life to the history of his period, but the reader finds as much illustrative information as is necessary. Those who are unacquainted with Milton's prose works may get a very fair idea of them from Mr Keightley's analysis and extracts: they may learn what were Milton's opinions, how he argued, and in what style he wrote prose; and perhaps in these days, when the chief place of study is the railway carriage, the majority of readers will be satisfied with this rapid *coup d'œil.* Mr Keightley does not seem to us to be always felicitous in his criticism of Milton's poems, but his comments, especially in the introduction to *Paradise Lost,* contain much that is highly suggestive.

"The principal phases and incidents of Milton's life are familiar to us all: the sentence of rustication passed on him at the university; the bright, idyllic days at Horton when his early poems were produced; the journey to Italy where he 'found and visited the famous **Galileo**, grown old, a prisoner'; the prosaic transition to school-keeping in London City and inharmonious marriage with **Mary Powell**; his Latin secretaryship; his second and third ventures in matrimony, and small satisfaction in his daughters; the long days of blindness in which the *Paradise Lost* was poured forth by thirty lines at a time when a friendly pen happened to be near; and the quiet closing years when he might be seen 'to sit in a coarse grey cloth coat at the door of his house in Bunhill Fields, in warm, sunny weather, to enjoy the fresh air, and so, as well as in his room, to receive the visits of people of distinguished parts as well as quality.'

"Less familiar, because less generally interesting, are Milton's religious opinions, which were not fully known until 1823, when Mr Lemon, during his researches in the Old State Paper-office, happened to lay his hands on a Latin manuscript which proved to be the Treatise on Christian Doctrine, known to have been written by Milton. In this treatise, we have a complete statement of Milton's theological and ethical views. That he was an Arian, a believer in free-will and in the universal efficacy of **Christ**'s death, had been already apparent to the understanding reader in the pages of *Paradise Lost;* the Calvinists, it was evident, could not claim him as their own. His famous work, too, on the *Doctrine and Discipline of Divorce,* had sufficiently announced his departure from the prevalent opinion on that subject. The more unexpected points in the treatise on Christian doctrine are the position that polygamy is permitted by the law of Christ; the rejection of infant baptism; and the materialistic view of the human soul, that 'man is not, according to the common opinion, made up and framed of two distinct and different natures, as of soul and body, but that the whole man is soul and the soul man.' Milton was anti-Puritan in his view of the Sabbath, concurring with **Luther** in regarding the Christian day of rest as a matter of expediency to be regulated by the civil government, not as a matter of divine authority."

GE discusses Milton's personal stake in the divorce question:

"There is much unreasonable prejudice against this blending of personal interest with a general protest. If we waited for the impulse of abstract benevolence or justice, we fear that most reforms would be postponed to the Greek Kalends, and in all matters where popular alarms and prejudices do not come into play, personal experience is considered the next qualification for bearing witness to an evil. The Athenians, so far from sharing this ultra-delicate notion of ours, that a man is not to appear in a cause for the very reason that he has an interest in it, would allow no man to bring a case of litigation into court unless he had a personal concern in that case: they distrusted all disinterested officiousness as much as we should distrust a man who set up shop purely for the good of the community."

GE quotes some of Milton's eloquent remarks on the sometimes deceptive "bashful muteness of a virgin" and the unexpected binding of a well-meaning man "to an image of earth and phlegm, with whom he looked to be the copartner of a sweet and gladsome society; and sees withal that his bondage is now inevitable: though he be almost the strongest Christian, he will be ready to despair in virtue, and mutiny against Divine Providence."

"A picture, alas! too often realised since the year 1644, when it was thus powerfully drawn. For want of a more modern pendant to Mrs [**Caroline**] **Norton**'s plea [concerning her husband's refusal to pay her allowance], it is worth while to take up Milton's, and consider what such a mind as his had to urge on the husband's side of this painful subject."

Michelet on the Reformation

(page 892)

La Réforme, by J. Michelet

"This volume on the Reformation, in which M. Michelet continues his History of France, is much more satisfactory to us than its predecessor on the *Renaissance.* It is less of a comment on history, and more of a history; it has less of theatrical effect and more of sober delineation. The student must not come to it for a close narration of details or for a presentation of documentary evidence, for M. Michelet, though writing from extensive and accurate knowledge, does not make it his object to communicate that knowledge itself, but so to use its digested results, that the reader may see as in a panoramic view the true significance and relations of men and events. But he will find on the whole a masterly survey, though he may wish that the writer would less frequently adopt the oracular style of the inspired prophet, and that he would more frequently indicate the significance and tendency of characters and events by special facts as well as by general statements.

"The historian could hardly have a grander and more varied subject to occupy his canvas. The birth of the French Reformation among the simple Vaudois of the Alps, the Austrian Empire under Charles V, representing the reaction against the Protestant movement, and the Turkish power forming a check on Austrian predominance, and in some degree lifting up the pressure of Catholicism from central Europe—these are the principal forces of which M. Michelet traces the agency. The individuals whom he depicts with the care and closeness of portraiture, are **Francis I**, whose romantic fortunes have led to so strange an idealisation of his gross and dastardly nature, his devoted and accomplished sister, **Margaret of Navarre**, the vicious queen-mother **Louise of Savoy**, and the **Constable Bourbon**. But instead of *telling* what M. Michelet has done, we shall perhaps do our readers better service if we translate a few of his frequent and picturesque passages, and thus *show* them something of what he has done."

GE then sets forth long quotations on Margaret of Navarre, The Turk in the Sixteenth Century, and The Villas of Italy.

German Mythology and Legend
(pp 917-18)

Odin, by Wolfgang Menzel
Bayerische Sagen und Bräuche (Bavarian Legends and Customs), by Friedrich Pander; second volume

"When **Tacitus** said of the Germans: 'They think it unfitting the majesty of the gods to confine them within walls, or to represent them under any human form'—'Ceterum nec cohibere parietibus deos, neque in ullam humani oris speciem assimilare, ex magnitudine coelestium arbitrantur.'—he probably committed a mistake something like our anthropomorphic interpretations of the actions of animals, and attributed to a lofty positive principle what was simply the result of circumstances chiefly negative. At the period when history first caught sight of the Northern tribes, they were already in the tumult of their great migrations, in which all the conditions necessary to the enshrining of a Religion in Art were wanting; and when the rush of nations southward began to subside, Christianity was already baptising German men and German ideas with new names.

¶"Thus it was that one of the grandest and most purely indigenous mythologies of the world had only an ideal, and ultimately a written existence, and was never solidified into intelligible monuments such as the giant structures and statues of Egypt, the marble temples and divinities of Greece, or the myriad pictures and churches of Christianity. It was for want of being thus perpetuated in plastic symbols that the Northern Mythology was so long neglected, and it is probably for the same reason that now, when ample materials for studying it are presented in a popular form, it fails to arrest attention except in minds of comprehensive culture. And yet the Odin religion has a strong attraction beyond its philosophic interest as a phase in the development of the human race: it has the poetic elements of power, terror, wildly capricious imagination, some tinges of pathos, and even a vein of humour. What is more grandly savage than the notion that the feast of the Walhalla and the tendance of the Valkyrien were for those alone who died in battle, while the feeble beings who allowed peaceful death to overtake them must do down to dim Helheim? What more pathetic than the story of Sigune's devotion to her husband the malignant Loki—how she perpetually holds a vessel to catch the viper's venom which would else drop on his face? What more fantastic extravagance than the rope that binds the terrible wolf Fenris, made, amongst other materials, of a maiden's beard and the sound of a cat's tread?

"To the many excellent works through which the student may make himself acquainted with the Northern Mythology, Menzel, the well-known historian, added, just before his recent death, an admirable monograph on Odin, in which he has not only assembled all the myths relating directly or indirectly to Odin, but has treated the subject in that widely philosophic and historical spirit which makes it far more than a study of Mythology. One of the points which he brings into due clearness and prominence, is the unmoral character of the German as of the Greek Mythology. The highest god, Odin, was by no means the highest because he was good: the German was as far from holding any distinct Dualism as the Greek. The world was to him a battlefield where the law was death to the weak; Odin was chiefly the personification of warlike force, and to be 'filled with the god' was to have that rage of the warrior which the appalled Romans named the *furor teutonicus.* Menzel also traces the reminiscences of Odin which still survive among the people—travestied in their course through twenty centuries; and this is not the least interesting part of his interesting book.

"Another field in the history of the German popular imagination is opened up to us in Panzer's diligent work on the Legends and Customs of Bavaria. Catholicism not only absorbs into itself all Pagan legend, but retains the popular mind at that stage in which it is the ever-teeming source of new legends; and Bavaria is of all countries the most prolific in these often pretty weeds of an untilled soil."

GE includes two bizarre extracts demonstrating the Teutonic imagination as it intersected with Christian saints and the miracles of Jesus.

This piece has not heretofore been reprinted, as far as we can determine.

Belles Lettres

(pp 596-615)

Maud, and other Poems, by Alfred Tennyson

"If we were asked who among contemporary authors is likely to live in the next century, the name that would first and most unhesitatingly rise to our lips is that of **Alfred Tennyson**. He, at least, while belonging emphatically to his own age, while giving a voice to the struggles and the far-reaching thoughts of this nineteenth century, has those supreme artistic qualities which must make him a poet for all ages.

"As long as the English language is spoken, the word-music of Tennyson must charm the ear; and when English has become a dead language, his wonderful concentration of thought into luminous speech, the exquisite pictures in which he has blended all the hues of reflection, feeling, and fancy, will cause him to be read as we read **Homer**, **Pindar**, and **Horace**.

"Thought and feeling, like carbon, will always be finding new forms for themselves, but once condense them into the diamonds of poetry, and the form, as well as the element, will be lasting. This is the sublime privilege of the artist—to be present with future generations, not merely through the indirect results of his work, but through his immediate creations; and of all artists the one whose works are least in peril from the changing conditions of humanity, is the highest order of poet, who has received—

'Aus Morgenduft gewebt und Sommenklarheit
Der Dichtung Schleier aus der Hand der Wahrheit.' " ¶596

—*Ulysses* " is a pure little ingot of the same gold that runs through the ore of the Odyssey. It has the 'large utterance' of the early epic, with that rich fruit of moral experience which it has required thousands of years to ripen." 597

—*Morte d'Arthur* "breathes the intensest spirit of chivalry in the pure and serene air of unselfish piety; and it falls on the ear with the rich, soothing melody of a *Dona nobis* swelling through the aisles of a cathedral." 597

—*Locksley Hall* "has become, like **Milton**'s minor poems, so familiar that we dare not quote it; it is the object of a sort of family affection which we all cherish, but think it is not good taste to mention." 597

—*The Gardener's Daughter:* "Then there are his idyls, such as the "Gardener's Daughter,'—works which in their kind have no rival, either in the past or present." 597

—*The Princess,* "too, with all that criticism has to say against it, has passages of inspiration and lyrical gems imbedded in it, which make it a fresh claim on our gratitude." 597

—*In Memoriam:* "But, last and greatest, came 'In Memoriam,' which to us enshrines the highest tendency of this age, as the Apollo Belvedere expressed the presence of a free and vigorous human spirit amidst a decaying civilization. Whatever was the immediate prompting of 'In Memoriam,' whatever the form under which the author represented his aim to himself, the deepest significance of the poem is the sanctification of human love as a religion." 597

—*Maud:* "We could not prevail on ourselves to say what we think of 'Maud,' without thus expressing our love and admiration of Tennyson . . . . [But] even seen in the light of the most reverential criticism, the effect of 'Maud' cannot be favourable to Tennyson's fame. Here and there only it contains a few lines in which he does not fall below himself. With these slight exceptions, he is everywhere saying, if not something that would be better left unsaid, something that he had already said better; and the finest sentiments that animate his other poems are entirely absent." 597

"While to his other poems we turn incessantly with new distress that we cannot carry them all in our memory, of 'Maud' we must say, if we say the truth, that excepting only a few passages, we wish to forget it as we should wish to forget a bad opera." 598

"It is possible, no doubt, to allegorize all this into a variety of edifying meanings; but it remains true, that the ground-notes of the poem are nothing more than hatred of peace and the Peace Society, hatred of commerce and coal-mines, hatred of young gentlemen with flourishing whiskers and padded coats, adoration of a clear-cut face, and faith in War as the unique social regenerator." 601

Life, Opinions, and Writings, of John Milton, by Thomas Keightley.

"From Tennyson we pass to a still greater poet, who also thought it worth while to print some verses . . . . An excellent introduction to Milton's works, together with a carefully-written biography, is given us in a compendious volume by Mr Keightly." 601-2

"The famous and often-quoted passages in Milton's prose are so splendid, that, like the prize-fruit at horticultural shows, they are apt to give a false notion of the average; and if we go to the places whence they are culled, we are surprised to find them so exceptional as they are. One source of obscurity and monotony—the great faults of his general style—was his supreme contempt for short sentences, amusingly expressed in his 'Apology for Smectymnuus,' where he says of his antagonist, 'Instead of well-sized periods, he greets us with a quantity of thumb-ring posies.' " 602

"[Keightley] is rather an exact and diligent than a fascinating critic, and is less apt at bringing into relief beauties of diction and sentiment than at setting the student right on a point of etymology or prosody; but this also is a good service, and is the one least often rendered in these days, when writers are more given to be eloquent on their personal impressions than to aid us in seeing the outward fact." 604 *See also* "Life and Opinions of Milton" from the *Leader,* pp 155-6.

The Life and Works of Goethe

(pp 1058-61)

Life and Works of Goethe: with Sketches of His Age and Contemporaries (From published and unpublished sources), by G. H. Lewes

Because of Lewes's association with the *Leader* as founder and major contributor, Eliot begins with a disclaimer, justified in the event by the paucity of her own remarks (though they work well enough as a "commercial" for her dear friend's effort) and the generosity of her direct quotation from the work. We extract her contribution in its entirety, to picture her loyal and skilful tribute to her beloved's most important literary work.

"For reasons which will be easily divined, we have received an injunction to deliver no judgment on this work, but simply to make the reader acquainted with its general character and purpose. Perhaps, if reviewers more frequently wrote under such an injunction, the public would not be a loser: readers would have smaller exercise for their faith (in critics), but they would have a compensating increase of knowledge.

"Some acquaintance with Goethe is felt to be indispensable in these days. Those who are unable to study him directly, find him mentioned by great authorities as the intellectual father, or grandfather of this age, which is said to be living chiefly on the ideas it has inherited from him. Accordingly, they are eager for some specific information as to what he has really done: they get translations of *Götz* and *Faust*, and *Egmont,* and *Tasso,* and lend a too reliant ear to 'Lines from the German of Goethe.' The result is, that they are in some wonderment how Goethe can be called the greatest of modern poets. They read translations of *Warhheit und Dichtung, Wilhelm Meister,* and the *Wahlvewandtschaften,* and while they find some wisdom and beauty which they understand and appreciate, they perhaps find much more which seems to them not at all wisdom or beauty, and they have generally a sense that a *clue* is wanted. For readers thus baffled, few books can be more interesting than one which will give them such a history of Goethe the Man as will throw light on Goethe the Writer—such a descriptive and analytical account of his works as will enable them to conceive the artistic merits which have won him the supreme place among modern poets, such a *natural history* of his various productions as will show how they were the outgrowth of his mind at different stages of its culture.

"Again, the real student of Goethe who has sought a commentary on his works in that huge mass of correspondence and criticism, and biographical material called *Goethe Literatur*—who has groaned over **Düntzer**, and nodded over **Viehoff**—who has felt the difficulty of reconciling conflicting statements and opinions about Goethe's character, and of discerning through the cloud of criticism and comment the true relation of the works to the man, will welcome the aid of any honest labourer in the same field, of any one who has diligently gone over this confused heap of documents, and not simply filed them chronologically, as the respectable Viehoff has done, but given a sort of balance-sheet, briefly exhibiting their relative importance. Such a student may be unable to concur in the point of view adopted, he may differ as to many conclusions, but the very extent of his knowledge will cause him to value a candid and intelligent opinion on a subject in which he has experienced the difficulty of forming such an opinion, and he will at least be interested to see presented in a panorama the way over which he has himself wearily travelled.

"Readers of Goethe's autobiography have, we imagine, generally been disappointed when they have found it abruptly break off while he is in the bloom of youth, and just before his entrance on his Weimar career. Many of them, too, have probably felt that it was for the most part something like an Italian landscape painted with a northern sky, and that it gave them little idea of what the writer was when the young blood was rushing through his veins, and the young enthusiasms impelled his lips and his pen. They have been tantalized by the abundance of wise dissertation on other men, and the paucity of details about himself, and, on the whole, they have felt that the autobiography has rather stimulated their curiosity than satisfied it.

¶"The means of satisfying that curiosity have been increasing with the lapse of years, through the publication of interesting portions of correspondence and contributions of narrative by the personal friends of Goethe, so that it is now possible for the biographer to fill in a multitude of details unnoticed in the autobiography, and to correct its too frigid colouring by the warm tints of his own early letters, and the light thrown by the testimony of early friends. In this way we may get a picture of Goethe's youthful life, of which the autobiography forms, indeed, a principle [*sic*] source, but only one among many sources. Such a picture it is Mr Lewes's object to give through the greater part of his first volume, in which his course is side by side with the autobiography. His work, he tells us in his preface, has been long on the anvil: it was commenced ten years ago, and during the interval we presume he has been on the watch for all information that might enrich his stock of materials or modify his conclusions.

¶"Having rewritten the first volume during a residence in Germany last winter, he has wrought into his narrative everything that he considers valuable in subsidiary documents, and fitted in fragmentary hints so as to render them significant. By this means he gives vividness and reality to Goethe's student-life at Leipzig and Strasburg, which seem so vague and distant in Goethe's own grave and allusive mode of telling the story. But the part of the youthful life which gains most in fullness and distinctness is the Wetzlar, or, rather the *Werther* period—thanks to the timely publication last year of the volume called *Goethe and Werther*, containing letters of Goethe, and illustrative documents, which bring into clear daylight his relation to **Charlotte Buff**, the heroine of *Werther*, and to her husband, **Kestner**, and show us, as by a daguerrotype, what the young Goethe of those days actually was—how ardent, ingenious, loving, and loveable. This was the period of the famous *Sturm und Drang* tendency, by which Goethe was just so far intoxicated as to be inspired with the greatest work that tendency produced—*Götz von Berlichingen.* Germany had not yet recovered from its astonishment at the bold innovation of this drama, when a new and yet stronger sensation was excited by the appearance of Werther. Mr Lewes thus sketches the characteristics of the period, of which *Götz* and *Werther* are the intensest expression:—

[Here appears a half-column of Lewes's prose commenting on *Götz.*]

"On the publication of *Werther* and the commencement of Goethe's world-wide fame, Mr Lewes pauses in his narrative to give a survey of German Literature up to this period, so that the reader who is not conversant with the subject may have a fair idea of Goethe's position in the intellectual history of his nation. Then he takes up the thread of his narrative, and shows us the young Literary Lion at Frankfort, the wild flirtation which gave rise to **Clairgo**, the warm beginning of the friendship with **Lavater**, and the more transient intimacy with the strange **Basedow**. The reader will be amused with the following portraits of these very heterogeneous friends:—

[Lewes's devastating portrait of Lavater is quoted in full at this point.]

"In contrast with these friendships, with grave philosophical speculations and lofty poetic projects such as the *Wandering Jew* and *Prometheus,* stands the romantic story of Goethe's attachment to *Lili,* which closes this *Sturm und Drang* period, and immediately precedes his departure for Weimar. Here the guidance of his Autobiography ceases, and for the remaining half century of Goethe's life, he himself only gives us occasional information in the *Italiänische Reise,* the *Campagne in Frankreich,* and the *Tag und Jahres-Hefte.* With the commencement of the Fourth Book, entitled the *Genialisch Period at Weimar,* we enter into entirely new scenes and new society, and Mr Lewes has done his best to make us at home in them by restoring for us the Weimar of the eighteenth century, and sketching the principal figures at its Court during the earlier years of Goethe's residence there.

¶"We have portraits (in words) of all the notabilities—not only those of widely-known fame, such as **Wieland**, **Herder**, the **Dowager Duchess Auralia**, **Karl August** and his **Duchess Luise**—but less conspicuous names among the *dramatis personæ* such as the little hump-backed maid-of-honour, **Mdlle. Göchhausen**, and the beautiful actress **Corona Schröter**. The most interesting points which this fourth book brings into relief in relation to Goethe's character are the noble friendship between him and Karl August, his attachment to the **Tran von Stein**, and his secret beneficence to the person known by the name of **Kraft**—a beneficence so far beyond anything which the motives even of benevolent people usually prompt, that it would probably seem incredible to many, if the evidence admitted of a doubt. They were gay and busy years, these early times at Weimar; gay with private theatricals, boar-hunting, skating parties by torchlight, and other diversions of that free and joyous kind. Private stages were then the rage in Germany; but, says M. Lewes:—

[Eliot gives half a column to Lewes's description of theatrical life in Weimar.]

"The Weimar gaiety was rather wild and boisterous at first, but on Goethe's part it was soon toned down into compatibility with official and literary diligence. *A propos* of this gradual transition, M. Lewes has some observations, which we quote because they tend to dissipate a very common misconception:—

[And she quotes Lewes on the way Goethe toned down his bohemian side to suit his diplomatic and business concerns. This extract occupies a full column.]

"Hitherto Goethe's works, though they had already given him a European fame, are in his biography subordinate to the history of his external life and the development of his intellect and character; but from this point the most important and interesting part of his life lies in his activity as an author. Before he went to Weimar, he had published or written, besides *Götz* and *Werther,* several dramatic pieces—the *Laune des Verliebten, Die Mitschuldigen,* Clavigo and Stella; and many plans and fragments, never completed, lay in his portfolio. Each of these Mr Lewes describes and discusses as they occur in the narrative, so that the history of Goethe's productive faculty forms one web with the history of his life. The first of his mature and greatest productions was the Iphigenia, and with the consideration of this work Mr Lewes opens his second volume. We quote the introductory observations in which he contests the opinion that the Iphigenia is a great play:—

[Now comes more than a full column on the differences between Greek and German tragedy.]

"We must pass over the journey to Italy, the criticism of **Egmont** and **Tasso**, and the story of *Christiane Vulpius* (though we would willingly have paused over this, because it, for the first time, gives us a distant idea of the woman who became Goethe's wife), to notice the chapter in which Mr Lewes presents a survey of Goethe's labours in Science. The reader will there find a full account, intelligible even to unscientific persons, of what Goethe really achieved in Botany and Comparative Anatomy and of what he *failed* to achieve in Optics. The chapter will be interesting to the psychological student as furnishing an example of the mode in which the poetic mind works in the region of positive science.

"The Sixth Book comprises the period of the Friendship with **Schiller**—a friendship which Goethe said made a new 'Spring' for him. It was during this period that he completed *Wilhelm Meister,* and the first part of *Faust*, wrote his unrivalled *Ballado*, and that most perfect of idyls, *Hermann und Dorothea*, and united with Schiller in schemes for the elevation of the drama in Germany; so that this sixth book is very various in its matter. We have a sketch of the Romantic School, against which Goethe and Schiller conducted a vigorous crusade, a criticism and analysis of the great works just mentioned, and an amusing chapter, telling the story of Goethe's career, as Intendant of the Theatre at Weimar. The last Book—'Sunset'—describes the circumstances of his marriage, his relation to *Bettina,* and his interviews with **Napoleon**, criticizes the *Wahlverwandtschaften* and the second part of *Faust,* discusses Goethe's politics and religion, and depicts the occupations and incidents of his closing years. It contains also a letter from **Thackeray**, very pleasantly describing the aspect of society in Weimar when he resided there as a youth, and the interview he had with Goethe. But we shall best use our remaining space by giving another quotation. It shall be the following passage from the comparison between Goethe and Schiller.

[Now comes another extended extract, describing the physical characteristics of the two poets and summarizing their interactive relationship, with analogies to classic myth. There is no other conclusion. Eliot allows the piece to close with the following from Lewes.]

> " '[Goethe and Schiller] were opposite and allied, with somewhat of the same differences and resemblances as are traceable in the Greek and Roman Mars. In the Greek Mythology the God of War had not the prominent place he attained in the Roman; and the Greek sculptors, when they represented him, represented him as the victor returning after conflict to repose: holding in his hand the olive branch, while at his feet sits Eros. The Roman sculptors, or those who worked for Rome, represented Mars as the God of War in all his terrors, in the very act of leading on to victory. But, different as these two conceptions were, they were both conceptions of the God of War; Goethe may be likened to the one, and Schiller to the other: both [*sic*] were kindred spirits united by a common purpose.' "

Belles Lettres
(pp 290-312)

Men and Women, by Robert Browning

"We never read **Heinsius** [Dutch scholar who edited the *Poetics*]—a great admission for a reviewer—but we learn from **M. Arago** that that formidably erudite writer pronounces **Aristotle**'s works to be characterized by a *majestic obscurity which repels the ignorant.* We borrow these words to indicate what is likely to be the first impression of a reader who, without any previous familiarity with Browning, glances through his two new volumes of poems. The less acute he is, the more easily will he arrive at the undeniable criticism, that these poems have a 'majestic obscurity' which repels not only the ignorant but the idle.

"To read poems is often a substitute for thought: fine-sounding conventional phrases and the sing-song of verse demand no co-operation in the reader; they glide over his mind with the agreeable unmeaningness of 'the compliments of the season,' or a speaker's exordium on 'feelings too deep for expression.' But let him expect no such drowsy passivity in reading Browning. Here he will find no conventionality, no melodious commonplace, but freshness, originality, sometimes eccentricity of expression; no didactic laying-out of a subject, but dramatic indication, which requires the reader to trace by his own mental activity the underground stream of thought that jets out in elliptical and pithy verse.

"To read Browning he must exert himself, but he will exert himself to some purpose. If he finds the meaning difficult of access, it is always worth his effort—if he has to dive deep, 'he rises with his pearl.' Indeed, in Browning's best poems he makes us feel that what we took for obscurity in him was superficiality in ourselves. We are far from meaning that all his obscurity is like the obscurity of the stars, dependent simply on the feebleness of men's vision. On the contrary, our admiration for his genius only makes us feel the more acutely that its inspirations are too often straitened by the garb of whimsical mannerism with which he clothes them. This mannerism is even irritating sometimes, and should at least be kept under restraint in *printed* poems, where the writer is not merely indulging his own vein, but is avowedly appealing to the mind of his reader.

"Turning from the ordinary literature of the day to such a writer as Browning, is like turning from **Flotow**'s music, made up of well-placed shreds and patches, to the distinct individuality of **Chopin**'s Studies or **Schubert**'s Songs. Here, at least, is a man who has something of his own to tell us, and who can tell it impressively, if not with faultless art. There is nothing sickly or dreamy in him: he has a clear eye, a vigorous grasp, and courage to utter what he sees and handles. His robust energy is informed by a subtle, penetrating spirit, and this blending of opposite qualities gives his mind a rough piquancy that reminds one of a russet apple. His keen glance pierces into all the secrets of human character, but, being as thoroughly alive to the outward as to the inward, he reveals those secrets, not by a process of dissection, but by dramatic painting . . . .

"Browning has no soothing strains, no chants, no lullabys; he rarely gives voice to our melancholy, still less to our gaiety; he sets our thoughts at work rather than our emotions. But though eminently a thinker, he is as far as possible from prosaic; his mode of presentation is always concrete, artistic, and, where it is most felicitous, dramatic." ¶ 290-1

GE here extracts extensively from 'Fra Lippo Lippi,' "a poem at once original and perfect in its kind." There follow allusions to 'Bishop Blougram's Apology,' 'Epistle of Karshish, the Arab physician,' 'Cleon,' and 'How it strikes a Contemporary,' with a short extract from 'In a Balcony,' which "is so fine, that we regret it is not a complete drama instead of being merely the suggestion of a drama."

" . . . generally, the greatest deficiency we feel in his poetry is its want of music. The worst poems in his new volumes are, in our opinion, his lyrical efforts; for in these, where he engrosses us less by his thought, we are more sensible of his obscurity and his want of melody. His lyrics, instead of tripping along with easy grace, or rolling with a torrent-like grandeur, seem to be struggling painfully under a burthen too heavy for them; and many of them have the disagreeable puzzling effect of a charade, rather than the touching or animating influence of song.

¶"We have said that he is never prosaic; and it is remarkable that in his blank verse, though it is often colloquial, we are never shocked by the sense of a sudden lapse into prose. **Wordsworth** is, on the whole, a far more musical poet than Browning, yet we remember no line in Browning so prosaic as many of Wordsworth's, which in some of his finest poems have the effect of bricks built into a rock. But we must also say that though Browning never flounders helplessly on the plain, he rarely soars above a certain table-land —a footing between the level of prose and the topmost heights of poetry. He does not take possession of our souls and set them aglow, as the greatest poets—the greatest artists do. We admire his power, we are not subdued by it.

¶"Language with him does not seem spontaneously to link itself into song, as sounds link themselves into melody in the mind of the creative musician; he rather seems by his commanding powers to compel language into verse. He has *chosen* verse as his medium; but of our greatest poets we feel that they had no choice: Verse chose them. Still we are grateful that Browning chose this medium: we would rather have 'Fra Lippo Lippi' than an essay on Realism in Art; we would rather have 'The Statue and the Bust' than a three-volumed novel with the same moral; we would rather have 'Holy Cross-Day' than 'Strictures on the Society for the Emancipation of the Jews.' " 295-6

The Poetical Works of Augustine Duganne

" . . . a sort of poetical flowered calico of which we feel sure that the manufacturer can produce any quantity to order. Here they will find a large volume of smooth versifying on unexceptionable sentiments, adorned with a portrait of the author, presenting unexceptionable features." 296

The Song of Hiawatha, by Henry Wadsworth Longfellow.

"[**Duganne**] informs us that Longfellow's fame will rest chiefly on the merits of his early and 'less pretending' lyrics, not foreseeing the appearance of 'Hiawatha,' which may rank with the 'Scarlet Letter,' as one of the two most indigenous and masterly productions in American literature.

"The coincidences of publication do not often present so striking a conjunction as that of 'Men and Women' and 'Hiawatha.' Browning's poems seem to smell of the warm south; they tell of pictures and statues, of the complex questions and the complex forms of life which belong to an old civilization. 'Hiawatha' brings us a breeze from the forest and the prairie; it has the simplicity, the purely narrative spirit, the child-like love of every outward detail, which belong to the primitive epic; it embalms the most human elements in the life and ideas of a race of hunters and warriors." (297)

"The metre which he has chosen, and which he manages with exquisite art, is, as those who are wise on such subjects tell us, derived from the ancient literature of Northern Europe, and its large, simple melody, is one of the greatest charms in the poem. Indeed, every time we look into the volume, this metre seems to have a stronger fascination for us. Longfellow has woven into it the Indian names of animals and other natural objects with great effect, almost always indicating their meaning beforehand; and they drop in here and there at the end of the lines with charming contrast, like the little bells of the tambourine in the accompaniment to a song. 'Hiawatha' must, we think, be equally delightful to childhood and maturity, as all poetry is that expresses primitive feelings and primitive forms of imagination. It is like flowers, and birds, and the colours of sunset, which may be looked at with equal pleasure by the child and the man; for though the man sees *more* in them, the child sees them with a fresher sense. We recommend mothers who love poetry, to read 'Hiawatha' aloud with their boys and girls." 297-8

Poems of Ten Years, by Mrs D. Ogilvy

Metrical Pieces, Translated and Original, by N. L. Frothingham

"[These works] belong to that dilettante class of productions which are not likely to have any greater result than that of giving refined occupation to the writer's leisure." 298

Agamemnon the King, A Tragedy, from the Greek of Æschylus, by William Blew

The Poetry of Creation, In Seven Parts, by Nicholas Michell.

"A far more elaborate work of learned leisure is Mr Blew's meritorious translation of the 'Agamemnon,' accompanied with abundant notes, which shew a quite curious acquaintance with recent literature. Mr Michell . . . seems to be a worthy follower of Mr **Robert Montgomery**; an intimation which may serve either as a warning or a recommendation, according to the taste of our readers." 299

Doctor Antonio, A Tale.

"It is a singular book; singular as the production of an Italian who writes English better than the vast majority of English authors, and singular as exhibiting undeniable originality and power amid the most ordinary commonplaces of fiction. The story and the incidents are so hackneyed that for a long while it was only the superiority of the writing which carried us forward; but as there was no mistaking the presence of a vigorous and remarkable mind, we read on in spite of the *incredulus odi* and the echoes of the circulating library." 299

"The writing, as we have intimated, is throughout idomatic [*sic*], vigorous, picturesque. The characters of Antonio and Lucy, especially the latter, are touched with extreme delicacy of observation, and are very unlike the characters usually found in novels. The Italian peasants, it may be supposed, are faithfully drawn, the artist being an Italian and showing a power of painting English character, with which he would necessarily be less familiar than with Italian. But we cannot admire the portrait of the Baronet. It appears to us essentially a caricature, and not consistent even as a caricature. There are Englishmen, doubtless, prouder and even more absurd to be met with on many a continental highway; our objection to this Baronet is not that he is proud and absurd, but that he is not a human being." 299-300

Gilbert Massenger, by Holme Lee.

"The writer . . . has excellent moral taste. There is no exaggeration in her sentiments, no impotent ambition in her style, and her narrative is easy and agreeable (we venture to use the feminine pronoun, because though the name is *epîcene,* the style of Holme Lee is unmistakeably feminine.)." 300

My First Season, by Beatrice Reynolds.

"Beatrice Reynolds, who, in 'My First Season,' gives us an episode in her life, is not only feminine, which may be a merit, she is also frothy, which must be a demerit." 300

"[There is] pert assumption that repels us . . . . " 301

Tolla. A Tale of Modern Rome, by Edmund About

"We have already given our opinion, in a previous number [July 1855], on the merits of this delightful tale—one of the few French fictions which can do no harm to the most inexperienced reader." 300-301

Villette, by Currer Bell

" . . . there is the cheap edition of 'Villette,' which we, at least, would rather read for the third time than most new novels for the first." 301

Faces in the Fire, by G. F. Pardon

"[It] is harmless . . . . After reading more than half . . . we should have pronounced it an elaborate, but extremely feeble imitation of **Dickens**, if we had not happened to turn to the preface, where the author tells us—'Though I may, unconsciously, have sometimes *adopted a style so natural and popular as that of Mr Dickens's (sic),* I have never, in my literary career, endeavoured to imitate his, or any other writer's, peculiarities of diction or incident.' We immediately remembered what important distinctions lie in a refined use of language, as **Pistol** long ago admonished us—'Steal! Convey, the wise it call!' " 301

Nach Amerika! Ein Volksbuch, by Friedrich Gerstäcker

"Readable novels are not among the most plentiful productions of the German press, and for this reason we the more emphatically recommend 'Nach Amerika' . . . . A rough indication of this writer's style may be gathered from the fact that he is called the 'German Boz'—a name which leads to a comparison, certainly very disadvantageous to Herr Gerstäcker, so far as all Dickens's great qualities are concerned, but not in the least disadvantageous to him in relation to invention of incident and cleverness of construction." 301

Romantische Märchen und Sagen, by Ludwig Bechstein
Aus der Gegenwart, a novel by Theodor König

"A very slight tasting . . . made us shrink from a repetition of the dose, and we give our experience to our readers for what they may think it worth." 301

The Greek Romances of Heliodorus, Longus, and Achilles Tatius, translated with notes by the Rev. Rowland Smith

" . . . Mr Bohn's edition [is] a book which will be welcomed by those who are fond of what we may call *comparative literature*—who like to trace every type of literary creation in its less developed forms." 301-2

Little Millie and her Four Places, by Margaret Maria Brewster

" . . . a story written for young servant girls. Besides the story, the small volume contains a variety of instructive matter . . . . Even those who do not share Miss Brewster's Evangelical point of view will see much that is valuable . . . . " 302

Walden; or, Life in the Woods, by Henry D. Thoreau

" . . . published last year, but quite interesting enough to make it worth while for us to break our rule by a retrospective notice—we have a bit of pure American life (not the 'go ahead' species, but its opposite pole), animated by that energetic, yet calm spirit of innovation, that practical as well as theoretic independence of formulæ, which is peculiar to some of the finer American minds.

"The writer tells us how he chose, for some years, to be a stoic of the woods; how he built his house; how he earned the necessaries of his simple life by cultivating a bit of ground. He tells his system of diet, his studies, his reflections, and his observations of natural phenomena. These last are not only made by a keen eye, but have their interest enhanced by passing through the medium of a deep poetic sensibility; and, indeed, we feel throughout the book the presence of a refined as well as a hardy mind.

"People—very wise in their own eyes—who would have every man's life ordered according to a particular pattern, and who are intolerant of every existence the utility of which is not palpable to them, may pooh-pooh Mr Thoreau and this episode in his history, as unpractical and dreamy. Instead of contesting their opinion ourselves, we will let Mr Thoreau speak for himself. There is plenty of sturdy sense mingled with his unworldliness." ¶302

Two fairly generous extracts are given.

Contributions to the Edinburgh Review, by Henry, Lord Brougham

"The subjects of these articles, which make three handsome octavo volumes, range under the heads of rhetoric, history, foreign policy, constitutional questions, political economy and finance, criminal law, physical science, and miscellaneous literature . . . concise and clear accounts of scientific experiments . . . .

"The historical articles are readable, anecdotic, and often indicative of special knowledge; but they are unorganized, often careless in their style, and have scarcely any of the qualities of permanent writing." 304

"The division of these volumes which most arrests us is that containing the Rhetorical articles. Here Lord Brougham writes with the fine appreciation of specific genius, and it is amazing to us how so able a critic of **Demosthenes**, **Cicero**, **Massillon**, and **Erskine**, can show so much heedlessness in his own manner of writing, and such frequent bad taste in his metaphors." 304

Léonardo da Vinci et son Ecole, by A. F. Rio

"M. Rio gives us a compact and interesting volume . . . . " 305

"Humanity is an ideal type, made up of fragments called men—some of them, it must be owned, very miserable chips indeed. But every now and then Nature puts this supreme type of hers into a small mould, and turns out humanity almost complete in the form of a single man—a man at once observant and speculative, practical and theoretic, artistic and reflective, grand in intellect, grand in feeling, and grand in physique.

"Such a man was Leonardo da Vinci. He was not only a painter who produced one of the sublimest pictures the world has ever seen, a sculptor, an architect, a musician, and a poet; he anticipated some of the grandest discoveries in physics, and there was hardly a department of science in which he had not aperçus, in which he did not throw out hypotheses and speculations; he was a first-rate civil and military engineer; he was a master of all personal accomplishments—of dancing, of horsemanship, and of fencing, which he raised to the rank of a science by writing the first treatise on it; with all his artistic delicacy of finger, he was so strong that he could twist the clapper of an enormous bell and bend a horse-shoe double: and this union of delicacy with strength was expressed in his face, which might serve as a model both for a genius and a sage.

"To crown all this, he was a man of noble and disinterested feeling, and of so sympathetic a nature that he would buy caged birds that he might have the pleasure of giving them their liberty: *aveva grandissimo animo,* says **Vasari**, *ed in ogni sua azione era generosissimo.*

"When Leonardo, in his thirtieth year, came to seek his fortune at Milan, he carried no testimonials from Florence, where his merits had been neglected by the Medici, but he addressed a letter to **Lodovico il Moro**, the reigning Duke of Milan, in which he stated his capabilities with the calm self-confidence of real power. 'I can carry through every kind of work in sculpture in clay, marble, and bronze; also in painting I can execute everything that can be demanded, as well as any one whosoever.'

"His achievements were not formed below his pretensions, and in this first residence at Milan he had ample scope for the exercise of his varied powers. Penetrated with the conviction that theoretic principle is a necessary basis of perfection in art, he founded and directed an Academy, the first institution of the kind in Italy, in which it was his object to further the investigation of all the great theoretic and practical questions in Art; and it was in the course of his instructions to his pupils in this academy that he wrote his Treatises on Perspective, on Light and Shadow, and on Painting.

"He was a diligent student of antiquity, and it was the object of his ardent hope that the discovery of some fresh treasures in ancient art and literature would throw light on the famous *canon* of **Polycletes** and on the true causes of the superiority of Greek Art. An interesting indication of this yearning exists in an epitaph, written for him during his life by a friend of his, apparently under his own inspiration, in which he styles himself simply 'the admirer of the ancients and their grateful disciple,' adding, 'One thing has been wanting to me, their science of proportions; I have done what I could, let posterity pardon me.'

Mirator veterum discipulusque memor
Defuit una mihi symmetria prisca, peregi
Quod potui: veniam da mihi, posteritas

"He was associated in the great work of carrying forward the creation of the Cathedral, the centre at once of national and princely interests, but a finer opportunity for his genius was given him in the commission to execute an equestrian statue of **Francesco Sforza**, the founder of the reigning dynasty. His passion for horses could here find a grand expression through his art, and his success was so complete, that when, after a delay of ten years, the clay model of the statue was exhibited to the public view, it was universally pronounced superior to every other work of the same kind.

"It was doubtless, says M. Rio, from having caught the last echoes of this contemporary judgment, that **Lodovico Dolce**, in his dialogue on painting, written half-a-century later, spoke of Leonardo as a sublime genius, always dissatisfied with his own works, excelling in everything, but exciting astonishment by his manner of representing horses—*supendissimo in far cavalli.* For, alas! Leonardo, having completed the creative part of his labour, deferred, in spite of the public importunity, giving his work a more durable form in bronze, and the model was utterly destroyed in the political troubles of 1499.

"A fate only a little less cruel awaited the sublime mural painting of the Last Supper, in the convent of Santa Maria delle Grazie, which he commenced immediately on finishing his equestrian statue, and in which he attained the highest conception of the Christ, as **Raphael** afterwards did of the Madonna. M. Rio tells us, that according to **Lomazzo**, who collected the traditions of Leonardo's own school, the head of Christ was the subject of long and deep meditation; the artist was continually absorbed in the contemplation of the Divinity, and his hand trembled whenever he began to paint this supreme object of art—a detail noticed by **Dante** in the devout painters of his time:—

Similemente operando all'artista
Ch'ha l'abito dell' arte *e man che trema.*

"M. Rio of course insists on the high degree in which idealism entered into Leonardo's method, and blames **Goethe**'s criticism as attributing a preponderance to naturalism, which is contradicted by the well-known answer that the artist gave to Lodovico il Moro, in excuse for his tardiness in execution—that it was not on earth he would seek his type of Christ. We are ready to wish that **Francis I** could have succeeded in his project of carrying this great mural painting into France, where it would have been at least safer from the barbarous neglects and injuries which have at last robbed it of all existence except in copies and engravings; for we fear that the recent report of its restoration by some chemical process was only the expression of a vain hope. The proximate cause to which the world owed the production of this masterpiece was the fact that the **Duchess Beatrice** made the church of Santa Maria delle Grazie her favourite place of devotion, and hence her husband lavished on this church and the adjoining convent every species of ornament that art could furnish.

"Another circumstance equally characteristic of the age gave rise to the next greatest picture of Leonardo, that of the Virgin seated on the lap of St Ann, singularly enough the only picture of his mentioned by the historian **Paulus Jovius**. In 1485, a mysterious image of this Virgin in the church of San Celso appeared suddenly to emit a splendid light in the presence of some hundred worshippers. The report of this miracle having spread, the scene of this 'divine manifestation' was crowded night and day with eager votaries, and the enthusiasm was so lasting, that even eleven years afterwards it was found necessary to construct an additional bridge to render less dangerous the perpetual flux and reflux of visitants, and finally to erect a larger and more magnificent church, for which ample funds were provided by the incessant offerings of the pious. It was for this new church that Leonardo painted his picture, now in the Belvedere gallery at Vienna. On the occupation of the Milanese by the enemy, Leonardo left Milan, and resided by turns at Florence and Rome. Once more he returned to Milan under the brilliant patronage of Francis I: and it was to this monarch that he owed a peaceful retreat in his old age, at Clou, near Amboise, where he died in 1519." ¶305-7

Voyage à Travers l'Exposition des Beaux-Arts (Peinture et Sculpture), by Edmond About

"The reader may fancy himself walking through the department of Fine Art in company with a friend who is extremely witty, extremely French, and in the end, perhaps, a little fatiguing by force of his perpetual epigrams. Truffles are good things; but we do not like everything served with truffles. M. About does not eminently possess, or at least exhibit, the happy power of describing pictures, but he has always something acute to say *à propos* of a picture, and if his criticism sometimes irritates us by its flimsiness, it has the airy smartness which we expect from flimsy things." 308

M. Tullii Ciceronis Orationes, with a commentary, by George Long

"Mr Long . . . is an excellent specimen of the editor as he should be. He spares no pains, and makes no pretensions to infallibility; when he meets with a difficulty, he says so, and when he can keep his readers out of one, he does so, with brief and pregnant comments." 310

"It was a maxim equally with the rising and the established orator to keep himself always before the eyes of the Roman people: by this pertinacity he came to eclipse his most formidable rival **Hortensius**, and to depose the king of the Forum. Hortensius loved fame; but he loved ease also, the luxuries of his villa at Tusculum, the beautiful shadow of his plane trees, his carp-ponds and his peacocks. Cicero, at least during two-thirds of his career, loved fame alone, and wooed her with an obstinacy equal to that of the miser or the lover. He was as deeply and constantly engaged in civil as in criminal cases, and took as much pains to recover for his clients the title of an estate, or the value of a bond or mortgage, as he bestowed in driving **Verres** into exile, or **Lentulus** and **Cathegus** to the Carcer Tullianum." 310-11

The Shaving of Shagpat

(pp 15-17)

The Shaving of Shagpat, an Arabian Entertainment, by George Meredith

"No act of religious symbolism has a deeper root in nature than that of turning with reverence towards the East. For almost all our good things—our most precious vegetables, our noblest animals, our loveliest flowers, our arts, and religions and philosophical ideas, our very nursery tales and romances, have travelled to us from the East. In an historical as well as in a physical sense, the East is the Land of the Morning. Perhaps the simple reason of this may be, that when the earth first began to move on her axis her Asiatic side was towards the sun—her Eastern cheek first blushed under his rays. And so this priority of sunshine, like the first move in chess, gave the East the precedence though not the pre-eminence in all things; just as the garden slope that fronts the morning sun yields the earliest seedlings, though those seedlings may attain a hardier and more luxuriant growth by being transplanted. But we leave this question to wiser heads—

Felix qui potuit rerum cognoscere causas*

(Excuse the novelty of the quotation.) We have not carried our reader's thoughts to the East that we may discuss the reason why we owe it so many good things, but that we may introduce him to a new pleasure, due, at least indirectly, to that elder region of the earth. We mean 'The Shaving of Shagpat,' which is indeed an original fiction just produced in this western island, but which is so intensely Oriental in its conception and execution, that the author has done wisely to guard against the supposition of its being a translation, by prefixing the statement that it is derived from no Eastern source, but is altogether his own.

" 'The Shaving of Shagpat,' is a work of genius, and of poetical genius. It has none of the tameness which belongs to mere imitations manufactured with servile effort or thrown off with simious facility. It is no patchwork of borrowed incidents. Mr Meredith has not simply imitated Arabian fictions, he has been inspired by them; he has used Oriental forms, but only as an Oriental genius would have used them who had been 'to the manner born.' **Goethe**, when he wrote an immortal work under the inspiration of Oriental studies, very properly called it *West-östliche*—West-eastern—because it was thoroughly Western in spirit, though Eastern in its forms.

¶"But this double epithet would not give a true idea of Mr Meredith's work, for we do not remember that throughout our reading we were once struck by an incongruity between the thought and the form, once startled by the intrusion of the chill north into the land of the desert and the palm. Perhaps more lynx-eyed critics, and more learned Orientalists, than we, may detect discrepancies to which we are blind, but our experience will at least indicate what is likely to be the average impression. In one particular, indeed, Mr Meredith differs widely from his models, but that difference is a high merit: it lies in the exquisite delicacy of his love incidents and love scenes. In every other characteristic—in exuberance of imagery, in picturesque wildness of incident, in significant humour, in aphoristic wisdom, the 'Shaving of Shagpat' is a new Arabian Night. To two thirds of the reading world this is sufficient recommendation.

"According to Oriental custom the main story of the book—The Shaving of Shagpat—forms the setting to several minor tales, which are told, on pretexts more or less plausible, by the various *dramatis personæ*. We will not forestall the reader's pleasure by telling him who Shagpat was, or what were the wondrous adventures through which Shibli Bagarag, the wandering barber, became Master of the Event and the destroyer of illusions, by shaving from Shagpat the mysterious identical which had held men in subjection to him. There is plenty of deep meaning in the tale for those who cannot be satisfied without deep meanings, but there is no didactic thrusting forward of moral lessons, and our imagination is never chilled by a sense of allegorical intention predominating over poetic creation.

¶"Nothing can be more vivid and concrete than the narrative and description, nothing fresher and more vigorous than the imagery. Are we reading how horsemen pursued their journey? We are told that they 'flourished their lances with cries, and jerked their heels into the flanks of their steeds, and stretched forward till their beards were mixed with the tossing manes, and the dust rose after them crimson in the sun.' Is it a maiden's eyes we are to see? They are 'dark, under a low arch of darker lashes, like stars on the skirts of storm.' Sometimes the images are exquisitely poetical, as when Bhanavar looks forth 'on the stars that were above the purple heights and the *blushes of inner heaven that streamed up the sky*'; sometimes ingenious and pithy: for example, 'she clenched her hands an instant with that feeling which knocketh a nail in the coffin of a desire not dead.' Indeed, one of the rarest charms of the book is the constant alternation of passion and wild imaginativeness with humour and pithy, practical sense. Mr Meredith is very happy in his imitation of the lyrical fragments which the Eastern tale-tellers weave into their narrative, either for the sake of giving emphasis to their sententiousness, or for the sake of giving a more intense utterance to passion, a loftier tone to description."

At this point, GE provides a long quotation, mostly in poetry, from the story of *Bhanavar the Beautiful,* which she considers "the brightest gem among the minor tales, and perhaps in the whole book." She then gives an example of Meredith's humour in prose, with the *Punishment of Khipil the Builder.* Her review ends without further remark. *And see* BL 4

*"*Happy is the man who has been able to learn the causes of created things*"
—Virgil

Rachel Gray

(page 19)

Rachel Gray. A Tale founded on Fact. By Julia Kavanagh

"Rachel Gray is not a story of a fine lady's sorrows wept into embroidered pocket-handkerchiefs, or of genius thrust into the background by toad-eating stupidity. It does not harrow us with the sufferings and temptations of a destitute needlewoman, or abash us by the refined sentiments and heroic deeds of navvies and ratcatchers. It tells the trials of a dressmaker who *could* get work, and of a small grocer, very vulgar, and not at all heroic, whose business was gradually swallowed up by the large shop over the way. Thus far 'Rachel Gray' is commendable: it occupies ground which is very far from being exhausted, and it undertakes to impress us with the every-day sorrows of our commonplace fellow-men, and so to widen our sympathies . . . .

" 'Rachel Gray' further professes to show how Christianity exhibits itself as a refining and consoling influence in that most prosaic stratum of society, the small shopkeeping class; and here is really a new sphere for a great artist who can paint from close observation, and who is neither a caricaturist nor a rose-colour sentimentalist.

"We wish we could say that Miss Kavanagh's judgment in choosing her subject has been equalled by her success in working it up. We do not feel that the story of 'Rachel Gray' brings any nearer to us the real life of the class it attempts to depict; still less that 'Rachel Gray's' piety gives the reader any true idea of piety as it exists in any possible dressmaker. It is an abstract piety, made up of humility, resignation, and devotion, feeding on **Milton**'s sonnets, and quite disembodied of sectarian idiom and all other fleshly weaknesses which are beneath Miss Kavanagh's own mind. Our own experience of what piety is amongst the uneducated has not brought us in contact with a Christianity which smacks neither of the Church nor of the meeting-house, with an Evangelicalism which has no *brogue;* and if, when Miss Kavanagh says that her tale is founded on fact, she means that the character of 'Rachel Gray' is a portrait, we are obliged to say that she has failed in making us believe in its likeness to an original. We are far from meaning that there are not feelings as essentially beautiful as Rachel Gray's to be met with amongst the uneducated, but the feelings run into a specific mould; they do not exhibit themselves as abstract virtues, but as qualities belonging to an individual character, of mixed moral nature and uncultured intellect. All this, perhaps, Miss Kavanagh knows as well as any; but either from too great haste to publish, or from unwillingness to give the requisite labour to her work, she has produced a book which might have been written in an ignorance both of heart and of life which we cannot impute to her. She even seems to be conscious herself of her failure towards the close of her volume, for she resorts to the very unartistic plan of telling the reader that he would be touched by the sorrows she describes, if they were depicted by an abler hand . . . . [extracts]

"The mere novel reader, who cares only for excitement or amusement, will find little attraction in 'Rachel Gray.' The story, as we have intimated, is of that quiet kind, which depends for its pathos and its humour on the delicate and masterly treatment of slight details, and in this sort of treatment it is altogether deficient. In our judgment, then, 'Rachel Gray' is a failure; and it is our disagreeable duty to say so, for the sake not only of the public but of the authoress, from whose talents and diligence we hope for better things to come."

History of German Protestantism

(page 140)

Internal History of German Protestantism since the Middle of the Last Century, by Dr. Kahnis. Translated from the German by the Rev. Theodore Meyer

"As naturalists tell us that the animals of the Old World are represented by analogous, but not by identical species in the New, so the various forms of religious opinion amongst us are represented by corresponding but not precisely similar forms in Germany. The Anglican Churchman is *ipso verbo* a purely English product; but his species has its German analogue in the extreme Lutheran party, which has been urged to a rigid and vehement assertion of its peculiar tenets by the unsuccessful attempt of the late and actual Kings of Prussia to effect a union between the two great branches of German Protestantism known as the Lutheran and Reformed Churches. The opinions of the 'High' Lutherans concerning the authority of the Church and the efficacy of the Sacraments, resemble, with a difference not, let us hope, absolutely fatal, those of our more geographically favoured Anglicans, and among the other indications of kinship, a certain arrogance of tone is not wanting. To this extreme Lutheran party belongs Dr Kahnis, the author of the compact History of German Protestantism of which we have the translation before us.

[GE quotes at length from the Kahnis discussion of rules of faith.]

"Having thus forewarned the reader of the point of view from which Dr. Kahnis' little book is written, we may recommend it to him, in the absence of better and equally accessible books on the same subject, as a useful and compendious survey. The information that can be given on so great a subject in about three hundred duodecimo pages is necessarily scanty, but it is rendered *un*-necessarily so by an unwise expenditure of space on gossiping biographical details, which ought to have no place in a rapid historical sketch. Dr Kahnis seems, especially, tempted to give such details when they are disadvantageous to those whom he regards as heterodox. An example of his bad taste in this way is his gratuitous mention of a private, and, as he deems, reprehensible relation of [**Friedrich**] **Schleiermacher**'s in early life. The other flaws which might be pointed out in the book are chiefly theoretic, and will be recognised as defects by those who share the author's theological position.

"We wish our criticism could stop here, but the injury that is constantly done to the reading public by the issue of defective translations, renews a duty for reviewers to allow no case of the kind to pass unnoticed. Theodore Meyer, as we gather from his preface to his translation, is German; it is not surprising, therefore, that his English should be inlaid with German idioms, but it *is* surprising that publishers who spend sums on the reproduction of foreign works should not be more eager to secure a respectable quality of translation . . . .

"Translators, as a class, seem to want impressing with the wholesome truth that whatever is worth doing at all is worth doing well. They are 'legions in the great intellectual traffic of the world'—a function not so high as that of the producers, but one which it is of manifest importance to have earnestly and honestly fulfilled."

The Poets and Poetry of America
(page 210)

The Poets and Poetry of America, by Rufus Wilmot Griswold

"A collection of 'Poems by Authors in their Teens' would not, we imagine, be very delightful reading. Here and there we might detect a form of originality which it would be interesting to compare with the fruit of the matured genius—here and there we might be startled by the precocious vigour or fertility of a **Shelley** or a **Keats**; but, generally, even genius is not original in its early efforts, and a song like 'Childe Harold' is preluded by faint chirpings like the 'Hours of Idleness.' The main characteristic of such a volume as we have imagined would be feeble and stiff imitation. It would have a psychological and biographical interest, but considered as poetry, it would be dreary.

"Something of the same character, and the same order of interest, belongs to Dr Griswold's large volume of selections from the American poets. It registers the progress of a poetic literature which may be said, figuratively speaking, to be in its *teens*—a literature which has hardly yet passed through the stage of Imitation, and is only beginning to put forth originating power. Viewed in this light it is a valuable addition to the library, and perhaps the sense of its acceptability is heightened by the very decided impression which a tolerably persistent reading is likely to leave—that, with two or three brilliant exceptions, it gives us quite as much as we want to know of the American poets. In more than six hundred double-columned pages, large octavo, there is room for quite satiating specimens of poets whom we may regard as the **Gottsched**s, the **Bodner**s, and the **Hagedorn**s of America. Mere specimens of [**William Cullen**] **Bryant** and [**Henry Wadsworth**] **Longfellow** will content no lover of poetry, but, happily, their entire works are easily accessible. The reader should be warned, too, that the 'Fable for Critics,' a satirical poem by **James Russell Lowell**, shows a much higher order of talent than would be inferred from the samples given in this volume of the writer's sentimental poetry.

"Some of the names in Dr Griswold's collection are likely to surprise the English reader, who has been accustomed to associate them with graver business in life and literature than that of verse writing. It seems that **John Quincy Adams** not only perpetrated, but printed, a great deal of very indifferent verse. [**George**] **Bancroft**, too, has published 'Poems,' which are about the grade of second-rate album verses—at least, if we may trust Dr Griswold's judgment for giving us fair specimens. Perhaps we ought to allow individual poets the benefit of a doubt as to the validity of that judgment, and admit that they may have written very fine things, which Dr Griswold has strangely neglected in favour of the very common-place things he has inserted. Still his volume, as a whole, may be presumed to present a fair average of American poetry; and certainly, with the exception of the two poets for whom we have already intimated our admiration, and of one or two flashes of originality—such as **Edgar Poe**'s 'Raven,'—it is poetry difficult to read and easy to forget. Mr **Bayard Taylor** arrests us more than most of his fellow poets. 'The Phantom' is a charming bit of simple pathos, and 'Kubleh,' a story in which an Arabian mare is the heroine, is finely told, and tempts us to quote a passage . . . .

"Dr Griswold's labours have not been confined to selection. He opens with a brief survey, including fragmentary specimens, of American poetry before the Revolution, and throughout the volume the selections from each poet are preceded by a slight biographical and critical sketch. His narrative is rather bold, and his criticism has the opposite defect of being more rhetorical than judicious; still, we have to be grateful to him for his diligence in putting together a useful summary of facts. If our readers share our previous ignorance, they will perhaps be interested, as we were, to learn through Dr Griswold that 'Home, Sweet Home' was written by an American—the dramatist **Payne** . . . .

"Before quitting Dr Griswold's volume we ought to mention that it contains some well-executed portraits and is altogether a handsome book. The portrait of Bryant, from a daguerreotype, is particularly fine; the refined moral expression of the head perfectly corresponds with the spirit of his poetry."

Westminster Review LXV
April 1856 **BL 4**

Art and Belles Lettres
(pp 625-50)

Modern Painters, by John Ruskin. Volume 3

"Our table this time does not, according to the favourite metaphor, 'groan' under the light literature of the quarter, for the quarter has not been very productive; but, in compensation, we ourselves groan under it rather more than usual, for the harvest is principally of straw, and few grains of precious corn remain after the winnowing. We except one book, however, which is a rich sheaf in itself, and will serve as bread, and seed-corn too, for many days. We mean the new volume of Mr Ruskin's 'Modern Painters,' to which he appropriately gives the subordinate title, 'Of Many Things.' It may be taken up with equal pleasure whether the reader be acquainted or not with the previous volumes, and no special artistic culture is necessary in order to enjoy its excellences or profit by its suggestions.

"Every one who cares about nature, or poetry, or the story of human development—every one who has a tinge of literature, or philosophy, will find something that is for him and that will 'gravitate to him' in this volume. Since its predecessors appeared, Mr Ruskin has devoted ten years to the loving study of his great subject—the principles of art; which, like all other great subjects, carries the student into many fields. The critic of art, as he tells us, 'has to take *some* note of optics, geometry, geology, botany, and anatomy; he must acquaint himself with the works of all great artists, and with the temper and history of the times in which they lived; he must be a fair metaphysician, and a careful observer of the phenomena of a natural scenery.' And when a writer like Mr Ruskin brings these varied studies to bear on one great purpose, when he has to trace their common relation to a grand phase of human activity, it is obvious that he will have a great deal to say which is of interest and importance to others besides painters.

"The fundamental principles of all just thought and beautiful action or creation are the same, and in making clear to ourselves what is best and noblest in art, we are making clear to ourselves what is best and noblest in morals; in learning how to estimate the artistic products of a particular age according to the mental attitude and external life of that age, we are widening our sympathy and deepening the basis of our tolerance and charity.

"Of course, this treatise 'Of many things' presents certain old characteristics and new paradoxes which will furnish a fresh text to antagonistic critics; but, happily for us, and happily for our readers, who probably care more to know what Mr Ruskin says than what other people think he *ought* to say, we are not among those who are more irritated by his faults than charmed and subdued by his merits. When he announces to the world in his Preface, that he is incapable of falling into an illogical deduction—that, whatever other mistakes he may commit, he cannot possibly draw an inconsequent conclusion, we are not indignant, but amused, and do not in the least feel ourselves under the necessity of picking holes in his arguments in order to prove that he is not a logical Pope.

"We value a writer not in proportion to his freedom from faults, but in proportion to his positive excellencies—to the variety of thought he contributes and suggests, to the amount of gladdening and energizing emotions he excites. Of what comparative importance is it that Mr Ruskin undervalues this painter, or overvalues the other, that he sometimes glides from a just argument into a fallacious one, that he is a little absurd here, and not a little arrogant there, if, with all these collateral mistakes, he teaches truth of infinite value, and *so* teaches it that men will listen?

"The truth of infinite value that he teaches is *realism*—the doctrine that all truth and beauty are to be attained by a humble and faithful study of nature, and not by substituting vague forms, bred by imagination in the mists of feeling, in place of definite, substantial reality. The thorough acceptance of this doctrine would remould our life; and he who teaches its application to any one department of human activity with such power as Mr Ruskin's, is a prophet for his generation.

"It is not enough simply to teach truth; that may be done, as all know, to empty walls, and within the covers of unsaleable books; we want it to be so taught as to compel men's attention and sympathy. Very correct singing of very fine music will avail little without a *voice* that can thrill the audience and take possession of their souls. Now, Mr Ruskin has a voice, and one of such power, that whatever error he may mix with his truth, he will make more converts to that truth than less erring advocates who are hoarse and feeble.

"Considered merely as a writer, he is in the very highest rank of English stylists. The vigour and splendour of his eloquence are not more remarkable than its precision, and the delicate truthfulness of his epithets. The fine *largo* of his sentences reminds us more of **De Quincy** [*sic*] than of any other writer, and his tendency to digressiveness is another and less admirable point of resemblance to the English Opium-eater. Yet we are not surprised to find that he does not mention De Quincy among the favourite writers who have influenced him, for Mr Ruskin's style is evidently due far more to innate faculty than to modifying influences; and though he himself thinks that his constant study of Carlyle must have impressed itself on his language as well as his thought, we rarely detect this. In the point of view from which he looks at a subject, in the correctness of his descriptions, and in a certain rough flavour of humour, he constantly reminds us of **Carlyle**, but in the mere tissue of his style, scarcely ever." ¶625-7

GE in her essay takes us through the four criteria of great art as set forth by Ruskin: 1) the choice of great subjects; 2) the love of beauty; 3) sincerity, i.e., truth; and 4) invention. She then elucidates the False Ideal, first in religious and then in profane art, and goes on to the "Pathetic Fallacy."

"With that intense interest in landscape which is a peculiar characteristic of modern times, is associated the 'Pathetic Fallacy'—the transference to external objects of the spectator's own emotions, as when **Kingsley** says of the drowned maiden—

They rowed her in across the rolling foam—
The *cruel, crawling foam.*

"The pleasure we derive from this fallacy is legitimate when the passion in which it originates is strong, and has an adequate cause. But the mental condition which admits of this fallacy is of a lower order than that in which, while the emotions are strong, the intellect is yet strong enough to assert its rule against them; and 'the whole man stands in an iron glow, white hot, perhaps, but still strong, and in nowise evaporating; even if he melts, losing none of his weight.' Thus the poets who delight in this fallacy are chiefly of the second order—the reflective and perceptive—such as **Wordsworth**, **Keats,** and **Tennyson**; while the creative poets, for example, **Shakspeare**, **Homer**, and **Dante**, use it sparingly." 631

Torso, by Adolf Stahr Volume 2

"The second volume . . . completes, in moderate compass, a survey of Greek sculptural art from its earliest dawn to what may be called its faint afterglow under the **Emperor Hadrian** . . . . " 633

GE reviews the historical subject-matter of the book, from classic Greek through Alexandrian, Etruscan, and Roman times. *See* AAG.

The History of Greek Artists, by Dr Heinrich Brunn

" . . . valuable and elaborate . . . . " 638

The History of the Painters of All Nations, by M. Charles Blanc

"This promise of comprehensiveness is not fulfilled, for the volume contains the lives of a few painters only, belonging to the German, Dutch, Spanish, and French schools. Some of the lives are well-written, the illustrations varying in value, from the respectable to the worthless—from the tolerably fresh to the quite worn-out stock engraving; indeed, the book seems to have been constructed on the same principle of using up fragments, as the housewife's economical pie." 638

The Shaving of Shagpat. An Arabian Entertainment by George Meredith

"[The book] is distinguished from the common run of fictions, not in being an imitation, but in the fact that its model has been chosen from no incidental prompting, from no wish to suit the popular mood, but from genuine love and mental affinity. Perhaps we ought to say that it is less an imitation of the 'Arabian Nights' than a similar creation inspired by a thorough and admiring study." 638

"We confess to having felt rather a languishing interest towards the end of the work; the details of the action became too complicated, and our imagination was rather wearied in following them. But where is the writer whose wing is as strong at the end of his flight as at the beginning? Even **Shakspeare** flags under the artificial necessities of a dénouement." 639 *See also* SS

After Dark, by Wilkie Collins in two volumes.

" . . . ingeniously conceived possibilities . . . tales, all, except one, previously published in 'Household Words,' but now for the first time cleverly put into a common setting, which heightens their effect." 639

"Since **Mrs Crowe** has ceased to write, Mr Wilkie Collins seems to be without a rival in the skilful movement of a ghost or murder story, and he knows how to give the thrill of terror, without mingling that sort of offence to refined sensibilities which causes terror to pass into horror and disgust. Three admirable stories of this class are, 'The Terribly Strange Bed,' 'Gabriel's Wedding,' and 'The Yellow Mask,' and we commend them as short, strong draughts to any one who has been nauseated by the copious drawing-room slip-slop of three -volumed novels like 'Laura Gay,' or 'Olive Hastings.' The author of 'After Dark' seeks his moving incidents in modern life, and he usually, in the end, interprets the supernatural into the natural." 640

"**Edgar Poe**'s tales were an effort of genius to reconcile the two tendencies—to appal the imagination and yet satisfy the intellect; and Mr Wilkie Collins, in this respect, often follows in Poe's track, though, to our thinking, he succeeds best when he pays no tribute to rationalism, but gives the rein to his faculty for what the Germans call the *schauderhaft,* which means, in general, whatever makes one's flesh creep." 640

La Bohême Galante, by Gérard de Nerval

"There are still plenty of readers left who abhor the explanatory, and doat on what can never be accounted for. To such readers we recommend 'La Main Enchantée,' an eerie story (scene, Paris, time, the reign of Henry the Fourth), by poor Gérard de Nerval. It forms only a small part of a small posthumous volume recently published under the title 'La Bohême Galante', a medley of literary sketches, poems, tales, and dramatic criticisms." 640-1

Sagenkränzlein aus Tirol, by Martin Meyer ("Wreath of Tyrolese Legends")

"It seems to speak well for the virtue of the Tyrolese, that Satan cuts an extremely poor figure in their Saga—that he seems indeed to have the reputation of being somewhat of a blockhead, the popular mind of Tyrol thus jumping with the conclusion of sage philosophers, that sin is in fact supreme stupidity." 641

Bilder aus dem orientalischen Kriege: Eine Folge historischer Romane aus unsern Zeit, by Max Von Riedwald

"We are always ready to listen to the Germans when they have a legend to tell us; no people better acquainted than they with the manners and conversation of web-footed dwarfs, nixies, and Kobolds. The regions of the air, as Jean Paul says, are their peculiar inheritance—the regions of the hypothetic and unreal. But the nearer the German romancer approaches *terra-firma* and every-day life, the less likely he is to be endurable . . . he thinks he can improve on the natural granite by daubing it with his stucco." 642

De l'Amour, by Stendhal (Henri Beyle)

"The tale we mean is called 'Ernestine, ou la Naissance de l'Amour'; it is no more than thirty pages long, but in that short space, and at the expense of only half an hour's reading, we have the story of a naive girlish passion, given with far more finish, that is, with more significant detail, than most of our writers can achieve by the elaboration of three volumes . . . . The form of the book is repulsive; it is, in fact, a collection of notes . . . . But renouncing a continuous reading of what has no proper continuity, and dipping in here and there, one alights on fragments of excellent sense and caustic observation." 642

"For though Beyle would have, 'as far as possible, exactly the same education given to girls as to boys,' he has no encouragement for the *femme auteur,* at least he regards that phenomenon as not very desirable, until feminine culture shall have become too general for a woman to suppose that *some* culture is a sufficient outfit for authorship. In the meantime, he advises a woman to write on two conditions only: that she contributes to maintain her family by it, or that she keeps the fact a secret even from her friends—conditions, which we fancy, would considerably thin the ranks of the authoresses; perhaps not without compensating advantages to the world. Since, however, in spite of all discouragements, from the days of Faust until now, the number of silly *men* who rush into print has been constantly on the increase, we see no reason to think that silly women will follow a different law." 643

The Heroes: or Greek Fairy Tales for My Children, by the Rev. Charles Kingsley

"Fortunately, in the absence of more **Miss Edgeworth**s and **Harriet Martineau**s, there is every now and then a man of genius, who is also a happy father, and thinks it worth while to write delightful stories for boys and girls, as well as for men and women . . . . The 'Heroes' he has chosen are **Perseus**, the Argonauts, and **Theseus**; and he tells about them so charmingly, that we have read his tales from beginning to end almost as eagerly as they can have been read by the 'Rose, Maurice and Mary,' for whom they were expressly written." 643

The Iliad of Homer, faithfully Translated into unrhymed English, by Francis Newman

"Every one will admit that, in spite of **Chapman**, **Pope**, **Southey**, and **Cowper**, Homer yet waits for a translator who shall be to the English mind what **Voss** is to the German. Voss, we think, solved the translator's problem: he produced a version of Homer which was simple, faithful, and yet satisfactory to the ear; but he had the advantage of writing in a language which lends itself with facility to hexameters." 643-4

GE faithfully quotes Professor Newman's explanation of his choice of metre and stress, and she gives a copious illustration of the result. But she nowhere indicates whether or not she agrees with or likes what he has achieved.

Recollections of the Table Talk of Samuel Rogers, to which is added *Porsoniana*

"What admirable energy and perseverance it must require to produce a translation of the 'Iliad,' in the midst of other important avocations, may be inferred from Porson's declaration that it would take him ten years to give a literal prose translation of Homer." 645

Flowers and Flower-gardens, by David Lester Richardson

"He wishes to stimulate the love of gardening not only among the English in India, but among the wealthy natives, in the hope that so civilizing a taste may spread downwards to the poorer classes, and of course his book is accommodated to the meridian under which he writes. But people in England who care for what we may call garden-literature, will find a great deal to interest them in these results of Mr Richardson's studies and experience." 645

GE now notices several Bohn-published works in the classics and modern English literature: **Quintilian**, **Hesiod**, **Callimachus**, **Theognis** among the ancient writers; **Burke** and **Addison** of the more recent period; and the third volume of the 'Noctes Ambosianæ.'

Bad Poetry

" 'With poetry second-rate in *quality* no one ought to be allowed to trouble mankind . . . . All inferior poetry is an injury to the good, inasmuch as it takes away the freshness of rhymes, blunders upon and gives a wretched commonalty to good thoughts; and, in general, adds to the weight of human weariness in a most awful and culpable manner.' So says Mr Ruskin, and we thank him for lending his voice to a protest of which there is every day more urgent need.

"Formerly we used to hear that the unsaleability of bad poems imposed a wholesome check on their publication; but it is clear now, from the constantly increasing supply that there is a demand somewhere—that beneath the active imbecility of those who write feeble poetry there is a lower deep—namely, the passive imbecility of those who read it. Some one has suggested that the bad poets buy and read each other, and thus form a sort of corporation which threatens to outvote the good sense and good taste of society, and set up balderdash as the ideal of literature.

"It is easy to see how such a corporation may become a terrible majority. Almost all men who have any literary talent or ambition write verse before they are twenty; they disdain any but the highest prizes, and will try for nothing short of epic or dramatic fame. Those who do not begin their career in this way are rare exceptions, and for the most part men of rare, because thoroughly determinate, faculty.

"But after twenty, the literary aspirants branch off into three distinct classes: first, the true poets, who witch the world with noble song; secondly, the men of real ability, who have early discovered that they are not poets, and in whom some other power than that of versifying has begun to assert itself; thirdly, the men who have too little intellect and too much vanity to know that their poems are bad, and who have no faculty strong enough to constitute a true vocation, which may divert them from their false vocation of poetizing.

"Some of this class, however, if we may believe their prefaces, are aware that the quality of their poems is not high, but they entertain the opinion that feeble verses are acceptable and edifying to mankind; they presume that people well choose to nourish themselves with the crude and insipid fruit of a currant bush, when the rich clusters of the vine are at their elbow." ¶646-7

Garlands of Verse, by Thomas Leigh

"Here plain people must ask *what* is the impulse which irresistibly drove Mr Leigh . . . to carry his manuscripts to a publisher, to go through the very cooling process of correcting the sheets, to choose a binding for them, and invite the attention of the public to them by advertisement? A man who knows that he sings badly may indeed have a musical impulse to sing in private, but such an 'impulse' would hardly drive him to undertake a solo part in Exeter Hall. Verse is not like bread—so indispensable that it must be made of sawdust and chopped thistles if no better material is to be had." 647

Poems, by W. R. Cassels

"We are inclined to think that Mr W. R. Cassels is one of those to whom the 'better days' are likely to come. His small volume . . . is remarkably free from affectation, and there is occasionally a bit of quiet grace or, as in 'The Raven,' a pregnant idea not sufficiently worked up which indicate that a little more patience would have enabled him to produce something that would remain as a distinct possession in the reader's memory." 648

The Isles of Loch Awe, and other Poems of my Youth, by Philip Gilbert Hamerton

"This fact of the writer's youthfulness makes the manly, healthy simplicity of his descriptive poetry all the more remarkable. He does not cast about for scenes remote from his experience, but describes the scenes he has lived among, and the unstrained thoughts and feelings they have suggested to him, now and then varying his descriptions with a local legend. Wordsworth seems to be his model, and unlike young imitators generally, he seems to have the most affinity for his model's best characteristics." 648

Poems, by James Ballantyne

"[These] are principally written in Lowland Scotch; and where this dialect does not become unintelligible to those who 'have not the privilege to be born north of the Tweed,' it has somewhat of the elevating effect common to all unfamiliar languages. At least, it is in this way we account to ourselves for the fact that Mr Ballantyne's Scotch poems are more readable to us than his English ones . . . [when he] 'gets him to his English,' he is as commonplace and insipid as more southern versifiers." 648

The Poetical Works of Thomas Aird

"**Coleridge**'s sublime 'Hymn in the Vale of Chamouni,' was an audacious plagiarism from a German poetess; but Coleridge did his plundering grandly; he was like the white-headed American eagle which swoops down with force enough to seize the whole prey from his fellow, and soar with it unmutilated in its beak. Now, Mr Aird and other poets of his quality, merely nibble and pilfer, and then mash up the fragments they have appropriated into an artificial whole. One would have thought that after Coleridge, **Shelley**, and **Byron**, writers of verse would not be eager to take Mont Blanc for a subject; but Mr Aird is nothing daunted by such predecessors, and he gives us ten or twelve quatrains on the 'monarch of mountains.' " 648-9

Man in Paradise: a Poem, in Six Books, with Lyrical Poems by John Edmund Reade

"It is impossible to deny to Mr Reade the merit of having a capacious memory for poetical phrases and images, which he appears to shake together until they are in what the printers call a state of 'pie,' and then to take them as they come uppermost, and arrange them into various metres. The result is that, read sonorously and with significant emphasis, his verses may startle the unwarned ear with the promise of poetry, as the shooting of stones from a cart may sometimes give an absent person the idea that it thunders." 649

GE's final segment is, to a modern reader, a rather breathtaking surprise.

"We have still said nothing of [three more books of poetry by Englishmen] or of another American production which, according to some Transatlantic critics, is to initiate a new school of poetry. This is a poem called 'Leaves of Grass,' and, instead of criticising it, we will give a short extract, typical in every respect, except that it contains none of the very bold expressions by which the author indicates his contempt for the 'prejudices' of decency.

A child said, What is the grass? fetching it to me with full hands;
How could I answer the child? . . . I do not know what it is any more than he.
I guess it must be the flag of my disposition, out of hopeful green stuff woven.
Or I guess it is the handkerchief of the Lord,
A scented gift and remembrancer designedly dropped,
Bearing the owner's name someway in the corners, that we may see and remark, and say Whose?

Or I guess the grass is itself a child . . . the produced babe of the vegetation.

Or I guess it is a uniform hieroglyphic,
And it means, Sprouting alike in broad zones and narrow zones,
Growing among black folks as among white,
Kanuck, Tuckahoe, Congressman, Cuff, I give them the same, I receive them the same.

And now it seems to me the beautiful uncut hair of graves.

* * * *

I think I could turn and live a while with the animals . . . they are so placid and self-contained,
I stand and look at them sometimes half the day long.

They do not sweat and whine about their condition,
They do not lie awake in the dark and weep for their sins,
They do not make me sick discussing their duty to God,
Not one is dissatisfied . . . not one is demented with the mania of owning things,
Not one kneels to another of his kind that lived thousands of years ago.
Not one is respectable or industrious over the whole earth.

The essay ends here. No mention of the author's name; not a word more.

The Court of Austria

(pp 352-3)

Memoirs of the Court, Aristocracy, and Diplomacy of Austria, by Dr. E. Vehse; translated from the German by Franz Demmler (2 vols.)

"Dr Vehse's long series of volumes entitled *The History of the German Courts since the Reformation,* has created a great sensation among two classes in Germany, neither of them, indeed, the most highly intellectual in the nation. One of these is the reading, but not well-read, class, and the other the royal—for in Germany royal families are numerous enough to form a class. No books are more constantly 'out' when you ask for them at the circulating libraries in Germany; and almost every division of the series has been in its turn forbidden by the censorship of one or other of the German Courts. In most of the German States, too, the presence of the author was even less tolerated than that of his books, and at last he is expiating a little extra audacity or extra carelessness in relation to the Court of Würtemberg by a six months' imprisonment.

"What, then, is the character of these books which have the double honour of being at once popular and proscribed? Are they attractive to the popular reader because they are written with the fascinating talent of a **Macaulay** or dangerous to royalty because they are charged with democratic ideas? Neither the one more the other. Dr Vehse's memoirs are simply collections of historical (and sometimes perhaps unhistorical) facts and anecdotes, brought together with considerable industry, but without much art; and in many cases, being little more than a patch-work of extracts from a variety of sources, more or less accessible to the common reader.

¶"The ostensible reason for their proscription is, that they narrate a few falsehoods; the real reason, probably, is that they narrate a great many inconvenient facts, casting anything but a favourable light on hereditary royalty and aristocracy: that is the reason of their attractiveness for the public. Dr Vehse's books sate curiosity, whereas German histories generally will satisfy nothing but the most philosophic and self-denying search after knowledge. He is neither a philosopher, an historian, nor a good writer; but simply a man who has a taste for historical details, and who has fallen on a vein of inquiry which affords abundant material for popular compilations. There is no trace of a peculiar animus against royalty and aristocracy in his books. He merely does not 'believe in the great as people believe in ghosts,' and he looks on kings, queens, and dukes and duchesses in the same light in which we most of us look at our common fellow-mortals—namely, as objects of unrestrained gossip. It is to Dr Vehse's credit that, holding this point of view, he has abstained from making his memoirs of courts and aristocracies more of a *chronique scandaleuse,* and that the worst fault he can be accused of is a too hasty and careless redaction of his materials.

"The *Memoirs of the Court of Austria* are amongst the most important of Dr Vehse's series, occupying, in the original, eleven volumes. Having made our acquaintance with them in that original form, we can appreciate the advantage now offered to readers, of an excellent English edition, reduced, by the omission of uninteresting lists of officials, to the convenient size of two moderate octavo volumes, and in every way made more appetising by its new dress. For, Dr Vehse is one of those writers who have nothing to lose by translations; and, in the present case, we have a translator who understands his business, and has performed it carefully. In this form, the work is likely to be almost as popular in England as in Germany, for it presents that compromise between amusement and 'instruction' so precious to the members of Book Clubs.

"And the history of the Austrian court and aristocracy from the days of the half-wise, half-cracked **Max** until those of **Francis Joseph**, is eminently picturesque, and eminently edifying, too, if it be edifying to have abundant demonstrations of **Oxenstierna**'s rather misty observation to his son—'Son, with how little wisdom the world is governed.' For, to the list of governors, with little wisdom, the House of Hapsburg can furnish as handsome a contingent as any royal house in Europe: the greater number of its precious scions being, apparently, Nature's experiments in the production of the utmost amount of imbecility with the utmost amount of despotic, self-assertion, and obstinate bigotry.

¶"One redeeming point there was in the very worst of them—the love of music and the arts, and the exceptions to the imbecility of the later Hapsburgs—**Maria Theresa** and her son **Joseph**—are among the most fascinating characters in history. The grandeur of the Austrian Empire and its importance in the scales of European power, lift the smallest details about the *personnel* of its court quite above that character of gossip which belongs to some of Dr Vehse's volumes on the petty courts of Germany. A semi-idiot, who happens to be named of Hapsburg, has a passion for hunting, and the consequence is a series of the most important vicissitudes in the history of Europe.

"One of the most striking facts made evident in Dr Vehse's volumes is the wholesale apostacy [*sic*] of the Austrian aristocracy. In no country affected by the Reformation, has 'conversion' been so palpably an affair of selfish calculation as in Austria proper. First, the prospect of sharing the Church lands was an irresistible bait held out by Protestantism, and carried over the Austrian aristocracy in shoals. In 1596, says Dr Vehse, when **Ferdinand** (afterwards emperor) celebrated Easter in his capital of Grätz, he was almost the only one who took the sacrament, according to the Romish rite, there being not more than three Papists besides him in the town.

¶"In the whole of the arch-duchy of Austria there were, of all the noble houses, only five, in Carinthia seven, and in Styria not more than one that had remained Papists. When the tide turned, after the Thirty Years' War, the re-conversions were equally wholesale."

The review now extracts Vehse's depiction of **Prince Eugene** and a description and an anecdote on the great **Kaunitz**.

"This kind of anecdotic sketching is abundant in the book, and, as it is connected with a continuous survey of the fortunes of the Austrian Empire, readers will be at once amused, and put in possession of a general conception of Austrian history, which is likely to be acceptable to the great majority."

GE made a far more extensive report on the Vehse volumes a year earlier in the *Westminster Review*. *See* page 30.

Margaret Fuller's Letters from Italy

(page 475)

At Home and Abroad; or, Things and Thoughts in America and Europe, by Margaret Fuller Ossoli

Massachusetts-born Margaret Fuller, transcendentalist and feminist, had become noted for her influential tract, *Women in the Nineteenth Century* (1845) when she moved to Italy to interest herself in the Italians' struggle for independence. She married a follower of **Mazzini**, the **Marquis Ossoli**, with whom she was drowned en route from Leghorn to New York in 1852. Their vessel was wrecked just short of reaching harbour. Her magnetism and passion caught George Eliot's imagination. She is mentioned frequently in GE's work.

"Every reader of Margaret Fuller's Life must have felt the superiority of the letters she wrote from Italy over her earlier journals and correspondence. A straining after some unattained effect had given way to calm vigour, and magniloquence to noble simplicity. It was clear that the blossoming time of her nature had come. Her affections had been drawn into their proper channel; her intellect had found its proper soil in the deep rich loam of European civilization, and her wide sympathies had found a grand definite object in the struggles of the Italian people.

"In the present volume of selections from her writings, edited by her brother, it is again the letters written from Italy which chiefly arrest us. They have indeed a double value, a value not only biographical, but historical. A description, however fragmentary and imperfect, of the events in Rome from 1847 to 1849, written on the spot by a foreign resident who could both feel and think forcibly, must have an interest quite apart from any special interest in the writer. It will bring those events nearer to the imagination of the ordinary reader, and help him to make a picture of what has hitherto perhaps been a rough diagram in his mind; and to the historical in search materials it is likely to contribute some valuable touches. These letters from Italy were written, apparently with haste and with many interruptions, for the *New York Tribune*. They have no great merit considered as literature, and we could probably have afforded to neglect them, if Margaret Fuller's manuscript *History of the Italian Revolution* had been rescued from the waves; but being, as they are, the only result left to us of her experience and observation in Rome, they are precious.

"Though believing thoroughly in the excellent intentions of Pius IX, she had from the first no faith in the permanence of such paradoxes as a liberal Pope and reforming Romanism . . . .

"In her remonstrances with her countrymen for their want of sympathy for the struggling Italians, she mentions an appeal which ought to go home to the English conscience as well as the American. 'Some of the lowest of the people,' she says, 'have asked me, "Is it not true that your country had a war to become free?" "Yes." "then why do they not feel for us?" '

"She observed what went forward in the Roman streets with the feeling of an artist, as well as of one who 'loved the people well,' and her descriptions have often a fine mixture of the pathetic and the picturesque. [That] of the departure of **Garibaldi** and his soldiers, after the French had taken possession of Rome, is perhaps the finest of all . . . ."

The review extracts passages of observation and critical commentary on the indifferent behaviour and unsympathetic attitudes of both the English and the Americans toward the Italians in their efforts to be free.

Belles Lettres and Art
(pp 257-78)

This segment of GE's critical writings lacks any central focus of interest. It exemplifies her competent work, uninspired by its subject-matter and engaged in for the pay it earned.

The Vicar of Wakefield

"[It] is never threadbare, though we began to read it when we were eight years old, and have been reading it, in quotations and pictures, ever since; it is as inexhaustible as a really fine melody." 258

Perversion

"It has not the elements of a good novel. The story is uninteresting; the character-sketching is approximative, coarse, and often feeble; the satire is without *finesse;* there is little appeal to the emotions; and the power of dramatic representation is entirely absent. The general characteristic of the first two volumes and half the third, is unamiable dulness, occasionally relieved by unamiable cleverness—something like a heavy cake flavoured with the wrong spice." 259

"The impression likely to be left by 'Perversion' is not so much that only Christians are good, as that most men are good for nothing . . . . " 261

"The moral odour of the book is bad. There is the readiest imputation of the worst motives to all kinds of people; and it is clear that in the writer's view Christian charity has nothing to do with abstinence from abusing and slandering such men as Goethe and Carlyle." 261

" . . . we see in [the 'writing'] no felicity of phrase or epithet, no epigrammatic salt, no concrete vigour—nothing that distinguishes the style of the superior writer from that of the merely educated and facile contributor." 261

Beyminstrė

"[It] depends for its interest on the delineation of quiet provincial life; it belongs to that genus of novels in which **Miss Austen** and **Balzac** have given us too high a standard to allow of our being easily satisfied . . . unhappily he has not the art of making us believe in his characters . . . . Still, we got to the end of 'Beyminstre' without much effort, especially as the interest of the story is intensified towards the close.

"We can hardly say so much for *Maurice Elvington,* which begins rather smartly, but becomes gradually dull, and occasionally dismal." 262

Les Contemplations, by Victor Hugo

"There are touches in these poems [on the death of his daughter] such as real affection and real sorrow only can inspire; and every heart that has known a great loss will feel itself in sympathy with the poet, and will thank him for letting others share in this exquisite expression of his grief. The cold winds of calamity and death sweep over us all; but it is only the poets amongst us from whom they call forth delicious tones like these, and such tones ought not to die out unheard." 262

Shadows of the Past, by Lionel H. Holdreth

" . . . a small collection of poems . . . which, without showing any remarkable power or originality, are pleasing because they have an air of genuineness as well as refinement; they seem to have been suggested by real experience, and not to spring from the vague determination to write poetry." 264

Grace and Remembrance, by F. Girard

" . . . a little volume which opens with a series of poems addressed to **Shakspeare**, against which we have nothing to say except that we feel none the richer for reading them: they have no particular fault, but we feel that we are listening to an echo, and not a voice." 264

Lonely Hours, by Caroline Giffard Phillipson

"[Her] verses can hardly be said to have either song or sense in them, but rather, jingle and nonsense . . . a new and enlarged edition, accompanied with a portrait conveying a very high idea of her personal charms—charms which we can only regard as a kind compensation of Nature for the imbecility exhibited in her verses." 264

The Poetical Works of Edmund Peel "has been long enough before the public to dispense with our criticism." 264

Gabriel, by Bessie Rayner Parkes

"It recalls the chief incidents of **Shelley**'s life, and apparently it is Shelley's wife who is supposed, almost throughout, to be the speaker. This is a disadvantage, since it raises a demand for psychological verisimilitude which Miss Parkes has not satisfied." 264-5

Life's a Dream: The Great Theatre of the World, from Calderon, with an essay by Richard Chenevix Trench

"As among the uninitiated, then, we must confess that the translations in this volume do not in the least help to convince us that Calderon merits the high position Mr Trench assigns to him as a poet Now and then there occurs a rather graceful passage which is rendered more felicitously than usual, but the general texture of the translations seems to us extremely poor . . . . " 266

Essays, Biographical and Critical: chiefly on English Poets, by David Masson

"[It] derives a value . . . from the admirable biography of **Chatterton**, now for the first time published in its enlarged form . . . . Here is a biography told without exaggeration, without any unwarranted use of hypothetic incidents, yet surpassing the most highly-wrought fiction in its power over our emotions . . . . To this advantage which the true story of a remarkable life has over fiction, are added, in Mr Masson's life of Chatterton, the vivid reproduction of details, the psychological insight, and the wise charity which are amongst the most important characteristics of a good biography." 267

Briefe von Schiller's Gattin an einem vertrauten Freund

"Genius is the proximate cause of great books, the remote cause of big books . . . . "

"The letters are simple, friendly notes written to **Knebel**, detailing the current nothings of the day." 269

Madame de Chevreuse et Madame de Hautefort. Nouvelles Etudes sur les Femmes Illustres du XVII siècle, by Victor Cousin

"This writer has latterly relinquished philosophy for literature; and few readers will complain when, instead of a hash of German metaphysics, they get a piquant dish of semi-historical biography." 270

"**Marie de Rohan** [Duchesse de Chevreuse] was a beautiful, impetuous, restless, intriguing duchesse, who 'loved much, and—many,' and who espoused the political ambitions of her lovers, sharing their perils, aiding their schemes, and making herself an influence dreaded by **Richelieu** and **Mazarin**."

At Home and Abroad; or, Things and Thoughts in America and Europe, by Margaret Fuller Ossoli

"It is very pleasing to read the warm testimony which a close observer like Margaret Fuller bears to the noble conduct of **Mazzini**, both in the days of revolutionary triumph and of revolutionary tribulation." 271

Thorwaldsen's Leben, by Just Mathias Thiele. Second instalment

" . . . it abounds in interesting details . . . the incidents which connect the exercise of Thorwaldsen's art with the beautiful Albanese girl, **Vittoria Cardoni** . . . .

"Sculptor after sculptor modelled her bust, and the painters, with **Horace Vernet** at their head, strove to do justice to her in portraits, of which there are no less than twenty-four in existence. But all confessed themselves vanquished in the contest, and unanimously declared that not one of them had seized the entire beauty of their model. The most curious fact, however, in this little history, is, that when the various busts and portraits were compared, there were scarcely two that bore any resemblance to each other—an additional proof that each man sees things not as they are, but as they appear through his peculiar mental media. Thorwaldsen tried his hand with the rest, but was not more successful." 272

The Lives and Works of Michael Angelo and Raphael, by R. Duppa and Quatremère de Quincy

"Another book which will be acceptable to those who delight in the biography of artists . . . . " 272

Critique et Littérature Musicales, by P. Scudo

"M. Scudo speaks exceedingly well of his own book in his Preface . . . . He is equally in admiration of his own authorship in the Introduction . . . . After this, one is surprised to find him opening with a personal attack on **Liszt**, who is evidently his favourite aversion—we should imagine for reasons rather private than public, since M. Scudo is vague when he treats of Liszt's faults as a musician, and is only particular on his dress and demeanour, his white gloves, and the cut of his hair. The criticism is bitter rather than poignant." 272

" . . . a series of articles, moderately agreeable and instructive, on music and musical artists." 273

The History and Antiquities of St David's, by William Basil Jones and Edward Augustus Freeman

"The description of the cathedral in this work is accompanied by numerous and admirable engravings. The history is elaborate, but never trivial or tedious and it is altogether a book well written and well illustrated." 274

Modern Painters, Vol. IV, by John Ruskin

"It has all the transcendant merits and all the defects of its predecessor; it contains an abundance of eloquent wisdom and some eloquent absurdity; it shows a profound love and admiration for the noble and the beautiful, with a somewhat excessive contempt or hatred for what the writer holds to be the reverse of noble and beautiful." 274

Sections on Turner's topography, light and mystery are followed by a discourse on Mountain Beauty. GE quotes Ruskin extensively but largely without comment.

The Lover's Seat

(pp 735-6)

The Lover's Seat. Kathemérina or Common Things in Relation to Beauty, Virtue, and Truth, by Kenelm Henry Digby

"We lent the *Lover's Seat* to two lady friends of very different ages, and they assured us it was a 'delightful book;' a fact worth mentioning because it shows that whatever objections may be made to Mr Digby's work from a critical point of view, there is a class of readers with whom it is likely to find acceptance. And since it is every where inspired by rare refinement and moral elevation, since it is obviously the production of a man who is both morally and intellectually more entitled to ask an audience for his opinions than ninety-nine writers out of a hundred, the larger the audience he finds, the better.

"It is now many years since Mr Kenelm Digby became known to the public through his authorship of the *Broad Stone of Honour,* and by the mediæval enthusiasm manifested in that work, made comprehensible as well as noteworthy his subsequent conversion to Catholicism. It is desirable to recollect these biographical particulars in connexion with the *Lover's Seat,* because they render all the more remarkable the fine spirit of tolerance and charity which is the strongest characteristic of the book. Converts or 'perverts' are proverbially virulent, but the author is one of those exceptional persons who learn by their own variations to tolerate and comprehend the variations of others.

"But, setting aside the admirable sentiments by which for a time the *Lover's Seat* throws our critical spirit into abeyance, and measuring the book simply by the demands of literary art, we are obliged to say that it is deficient in some most important requisites. The writer, apparently, like many men of various and extensive reading, has a note-book which, as **Southey** said of his own, is 'like an urn under the arm of a river-god;' and the existence of this note-book is, we imagine, the proximate cause of the two volumes now offered to the public. For the *Lover's Seat* is a mosaic of quotations inlaid in a comparatively small portion of material from the writer's own pen, at least if we accept all the anonymous quotations as genuine, and do not suppose them to be put in this form merely as a device of style. Such a device would be a particularly unfortunate one, for the incessant citation renders the book wearisome for continuous reading, while the absence of any precise classification prevents it from being available as a repertory of extracts.

¶"Another great mistake in the structure of the book is the dimly indicated velleity towards dialogue, in the supposition that the long discourses which form the successive chapters are uttered at the 'Lover's Seat' either *to* a pair of lovers or by the lover of the more honourable gender to his companion; for the writer appears to vacillate in his plan. This ghost of a dramatic intention sometimes appears too ludicrously in company with the very *adagio* and essay-like style of the writer, that it would be extremely easy to satirize the *Lover's Seat,* and make it appear a silly, twaddling book. But 'everything has two handles,' and sympathy and veneration for just and noble sentiments are so much better things than satire, that we prefer holding up to our readers the more admirable aspect of Mr Digby's work, and selected from it some passages which will give a fair idea of its merits.

"One habit which we particularly relish in the writer is the felicity with which he extracts lessons of indulgence and kindliness from Scriptural passages and incidents, which have been far from yielding such honey to the majority of those who make an equally diligent use of the Bible . . . . "

The first extract GE gives us at this point seems bewilderingly *inapropos,* in that it contains no reference to scripture whatever. A second long extract cites the story of the Samaritan and expounds at great length on lessons of love to be drawn from **Charles Dickens**'s *The Old Curiosity Shop.* A third very long extract discusses **Cromwell**'s Parliament and Protestant intolerance, and "that supposed paradox, a tolerant Catholic."

The review strikes this writer as oddly careless and inconsistent. It nowhere demonstrates or discusses the supposed "deficiencies" of Digby's book, nor does it give much of an indication of the reasons why "the larger the audience he finds, the better."

Ferny Combes

(page 787)

Ferny Combes: a Ramble after Ferns in the Glens and Valleys of Devonshire, by Charlotte Chanter

"Ferny Combes! The very words are a treat to us in warm weather, and make us feel cooler as we write them. Everyone who has been in Devonshire knows that a *Combe* is a vale or glen—an opening between the hills, sometimes so wide that a town can nestle in it, sometimes so narrow that nothing but a rivulet can make its cunning way along the hollow, and sometimes threaded by a winding lane, where you may either look at the grand curtain of hills all round you, or let your eye fall on the slate-built bank beside you, every yard of which is a study for a painter like **Hunt**—an enchanting confusion of starry flowers, delicate trefoil, and long, waving fronds.

"And among all the lovely things that grow along the lanes and on the hills of Devonshire, Ferns are some of the loveliest. There is this additional temptation to their study, that they may be dried without losing their beauty, and that, as Mrs Chanter tells us, the collector 'has but to open his "Fern-book," and the forms of his favourites appear before him as green and graceful as when they hung by the mountain torrent, or waved in some quiet, shady lane, bringing back to remembrance pleasant summer rambles amid lovely scenes, making the heart swell with gladness at the recollection of the forms of beauty and purity on which he has been permitted to gaze.' Moreover, the most dismal London drawing-room stared at by 'naked-eyed' houses, and in which no flowers will flourish, may have a wreath of poetry brought into it by a glass-case of living ferns, looking always fresh and happy, as you return from 'take the dust' in Hyde Park, or even when you light the gas at mid-day in a November fog. Hear Mrs Chanter's practical directions to those who have not many shillings to spare on superfluities—

[There follows a lesson on maintaining ferns in a drawing-room, through the use of a cover, case or bell-glass to maintain evenness of temperature and the right level of humidity.]

"But we must tell our readers more particularly what this pretty book is, from which we have been quoting. It is a little volume of not much more than a hundred pages, containing not only a description of Devonshire ferns with eight excellent illustrations, but also, as an introduction to this more special matter, a charming sketch of an excursion through the finest and least known districts of Devon, whither, very frequently, only your own horse or carriage can take you. We can wish for nothing pleasanter at this moment in the way of excursions, than to find ourselves in North Devon, in that guarantee of respectability, a gig, and making the very tour along which Mrs Chanter has carried us in imagination. A very agreeable companion she is in this imaginary tour, for there is an ardour in her enjoyment of nature, and a happy way of describing and narrating, which is the less surprising when one knows that she is a sister of **Charles Kingsley**.

"One great attraction in the tour described by Mrs Chanter—at least to those who shudder at watering places which leave only a general impression of eyes and flounces and bad German bands—is that it takes you to scenes where the delicious sounds of Nature are not drowned or scared away, and where her beauties are not all ticketed with a price. England is not quite transformed into continuous tea-gardens.

[Now we get extracts on the inns of Devonshire (not always accommodating) and the hills and crags of Dartmoor. Not a word about ferns (nor even about combes), but much charming travelogue.]

"One thing we wish Mrs Chanter had not done at the opening of her book— namely, argue with certain persons who may inquire 'What is the advantage of knowing the names of a set of weeds which are of no use to any one?' Argument is far too great a compliment to pay to people who can take no interest in a plant unless they can be told that it will cure the cholic, or that it tastes well when boiled and served up with sauce. When her pretty little book reaches a second edition, as it deserves to do, we hope she will re-write her first three pages, and give it a more worthy opening than pedagogical remarks, rather questionable in their logic, to people who are not likely to profit by her remarks even if they were less questionable."

Recollections of Heine

(pp 811-12)

Heinrich Heine. Erinnerungen von Alfred Meissner (Recollections of Heinrich Heine, by Alfred Meissner)

"Poor is the base habit of us mortals generally, to enjoy things first and find fault with them afterwards, to reap some pleasant fruit from other men's doings and then cry out against them as misdoings. Thus we, after running through these *Recollections of Heine* with considerable interest, and gathering from them several details which enable us to correct or fill up the picture of him in our imagination, are inclined, now we lay down Herr Meissner's book, to blame him for falling into the temptation of bookmaking, and diluting into a volume the matter which might easily have been conveyed in an article. But since, after all, the volume is a small one, and is written agreeably enough, we repress our critical impulse, and prefer noticing with satisfaction the at once sympathetic and impartial spirit in which these *Recollections* are written.

¶"Herr Meissner is himself a poet, and what is more, a poet with whom Heine never quarrelled; during several long visits to Paris he was a frequent visitor, and in the intervals a constant correspondent of Heine's; and he saw him both alone and in the society of others at different stages of his seven years' lingering death; so that he gives us the experience of an appreciatory friend, and not the gossip of a tourist or a lion-hunter. The fact that this experience was always personally agreeable to himself has not prevented him from forming a sober estimate of Heine, and he does not discredit his own testimony by indiscriminating laudation. Considering his opportunities, we might have expected a greater amount of positive material in these *Recollections,* if we had not remembered how fragmentary and often incommunicable are the particulars from which we build up our conception even of many whom we call our intimate friends. Herr Meissner, however, has the power of reproducing such particulars with considerable vividness, and from his successive sketches, for which he assures us he has not drawn on his memory, but on notes carefully made while a scene or conversation was fresh in his mind, the reader may very well gather an idea of Heine's habits and *entourage* at different epochs during the later years of his life.

"Nothing could be more common-place than Heine's Paris home—three small rooms on the third story, moderately furnished, and looking on a narrow, dimly-lighted court. The sitting-room had the usual white marble chimney-piece, with the inevitable Parisian mirror and vases filled with artificial flowers; and this chimney-piece was the most striking object in the room. All that seemed exceptional about this home was, that when you knocked at the door, it was opened by an old pock-marked negress, in a motley silk turban, and you heard the screaming of a parrot from Madame Heine's room."

Now come extracts describing Heine's wife, the simple and loyal Matilda, his consideration for his aged mother in Germany, and his attitude toward the Jews. We provide the last, for its historical importance as a reliable rendering by the faithful, diligent Meissner:

'You hear, my dear Meissner, how I almost in one breath ridicule and compassionate the Jews; in fact, they appear to me at once ludicrous and venerable. I could not devote myself to them entirely, as Gabriel Riesser and others have done; I united myself with no party, whether republicans or patriots, Christians or Jews. I have this in common with all artists who write not for enthusiastic moments, but for centuries—not for one land, but for the world—not for one race, but for mankind. It would be absurd and petty in me if, as people pretend, I had ever been ashamed of being a Jew; but it would be just as ridiculous if I declared myself to be a Jew . . . . As I was born to deliver over the bad and the rotten, the false and the foolish, to eternal ridicule, so it is equally in my nature to feel what is sublime, to admire what is great, and to venerate whatever has true life.'

¶'Heine had spoken the last words with deep earnestness, and had become thoughtful. But, as if laughter must always resume its wonted seat on his lips, he added, playfully, 'If our little friend Weill comes to see us soon, you shall have another proof of my piety towards primitive Mosaism. Weill was formerly a singer in the synagogue; he has a fine bell-like tenor, and chants the old songs of Judah in all their traditional purity, from their earliest monotonous simplicity to their latest point of Old Testament finish. My good wife, who has no notion that I am a Jew, was not a little amazed when she heard this strange musical lament, this shaking and quavering. When Weill began his first song, Minko the dog crept under the sofa, and Cocotte the parrot tried to hang himself between the bars of his cage. "Monsieur Weill! Monsieur Weill!" Matilda cried out, in alarm, "don't carry the joke too far!" Weill went on. Matilda turned to me and said, "Henry, tell me what songs are these?" "They are our German national songs," I answered; and I have obstinately persisted in this assertion.'

"Heine, to the last, wrote everything himself, except his letters. Paper and pencil lay before him, and as he was able, he wrote in a large hand his latest poems and his yet unpublished Memoirs. When he was tired, or indisposed to work, his wife read to him such light things as **Dumas**'s novels; but he also went through a great deal of serious reading, especially in physiology, anatomy, and pathology. He made himself familiar with the most elaborate works bearing on his own disease. 'My studies,' he used to say, 'will certainly not be of much use to me. At the utmost, they will enable me to give lectures in heaven, in order to demonstrate to my audience how poorly the physicians on earth know how to treat diseases of the spine.' On another occasion, he said, 'My nerves are so utterly shattered, that I am sure at the Exposition they would win the great gold medal for pain and misery.'

"Few friends bear such a test of constancy as a seven years' illness, especially in a great city, and one is not surprised that the visits to Heine's sick room became fewer and farther between as the years wore on. One day, when **Berlioz** was announced, Heine exclaimed, 'What! some one coming to see me! Berlioz is always original!' But in the very last months Heine was soothed by the visits of a new friend, a young lady of 'unusual intellectual powers,' and it is touching to read his notes to her, some of which Herr Meissner has been permitted to publish. We will quote one—and it must be our last quotation—written at the beginning of January, 1856:—

> Dearest *Mouche!* I am very suffering, and vexed to death, and the lid of my right eye falls, so that I can hardly write any more. But I love you and think of you, sweetest one! The novel has not bored me, and it gives good hopes for the future—you are not so stupid as you look! Charming you are beyond all measure, and therein my soul delights. Shall I see you to-morrow? A sort of weeping *malaise* overpowers me. My heart gapes spasmodically. These *bâillements* are intolerable. I wish I were dead! Deepest anguish, thy name is—HEINRICH HEINE."

GE's proficiency in German and her love of poetry combined to make her England's principal advocate of the works of Heinrich Heine. She wrote four articles on the poet. See HH, HBS, and HP.

Felice Orsini

(page 835)

The Austrian Dungeons in Italy: Narrative of Fifteen Months' Imprisonment and Final Leap from the Fortress of S. Giorgio, by Felice Orsini. Translated from the unpublished manuscript by J. Meriton White

"If **De Foe** were alive again, and had to rewrite his *History of the Devil,* he could hardly add a more striking supplementary chapter than one on Austrian prisons and Austrian tribunals in Italy, and among all the *mémoires pour* [illegible] that he might consult, he could hardly find anything more to his purpose than this little book, in which Felice Orsini, now happily safe in London, tells us the story of his imprisonment and the terrible contingencies of his escape. It has not the literary charm belonging to **Silvio Pellico**'s narrative, which we have known as a young student of Italian, in blissful ignorance of Austrian policy, to take for a romance, and devour it with a culpable reliance on 'guessing' instead of the dictionary. For though the matter of Felice Orsini's narrative is everywhere of great interest, it is thrown together with little art, and the early part is so desultory in its arrangement, that it reads like hasty notes. But it has one grave source of superior influence on the reader, namely, that it recounts *recent* facts—it sets before us Austrian prisons and tribunals as they are in the present day, and does not allow us to get rid of painful sympathy by conjecturing that things are different now.

"Felice Orsini was born, he tells us, in 1819. He is a man of education, and was brought up under prosperous circumstances. His ostensible profession was to have been the law, but, as with so many others of his countrymen, the main thrust of his life has been conspiracy against the Austrian Government, an object which, when it has succeeded, men will call heroism, but until then folly. His experience as a political prisoner began when he was only three-and-twenty, and this beginning was anything but a mild one, for, not to mention other particulars, in a journey from Pesaro to Rome, he was taken among thieves, who were all huddled with him in open court, from which, in arrest, they travelled for seventeen days. From this first imprisonment of two years' duration, he was liberated by the general amnesty decreed upon the accession of Pius IX, and from that time up to the moment of his last arrest, his life was a story of futile conspiracy, detentions and proscription.

¶"But in the present little volume, he merely indicates this earlier part of his career, and reserves his space for a minute account of his last fifteen months' imprisonment and his amazing escape, frequently digressing, however, for the sake of illustrating more completely the Austrian mode of treating political offenders. Stories of escapes from durance are always thrilling, and the escape of Felice Orsini is among the most thrilling we remember. For us commonplace people who have never 'set our lives upon the hazard of a die,' there is always an air of incredibility about these stories, and we are apt to suspect that the narrator has magnified or dressed up his adventures. But such a suspicion is not only ungenerous, it is unintelligent. It is in the nature of a great risk to convert an ordinary event into a crisis: let a drunken man lie asleep on a railway, and some ordinary event which delays a train for five minutes, so that the man is roused in time to walk away, will seem a 'providence,' a 'coincidence,' and wherever a man is in a state of continuous danger, as when he undertakes to rescue a child from a burning house, every breath of wind that beats the flame from him will seem marvellously timed.

¶"So it is with attempts at escape from prison: we think the coincidences amazing—incredible—when nothing happens but would be altogether usual, if the fact of risk and danger were not co-existent. We will not forestal the interest of the reader in Orsini's narrative by telling it in brief, but there is one little trait in it which we are tempted to notice, because it shows the value of that sort of practical knowledge which is so notably wanting in 'polite' education. In calculating all the casualties of his escape, Orsini of course remembered the probability of his falling down stunned; but he also remembered—and this would not be at all 'of course' with most men—that the first sensation experienced on recovering sensibility is intense thirst. Hence he took care to provide himself with an orange. He was stunned twice, and each time he relieved his consequent thirst with half an orange.

"Since the publication of Silvio Pellico's narrative, Austria has somewhat alleviated the treatment of her political prisoners. The bastinado is rarely administered, and is disavowed by the officials, and the *carcere durissimo* is abolished. Felice Orsini was allowed to receive money from his family, and to purchase even luxuries of diet, and he might, if he chose, have fattened himself into a plethoric subject for the hangman. Still there are frightful hardships to be endured in most cases, though the worst features in the Austrian system at present seem to lie less in physical cruelty than in the unscrupulous devices and slow tortures of the judicial process, which has no other object than to prove the prisoner guilty in the end, and in the meantime to entrap him into avowals that will compromise so many of his friends as possible. Two examples of the pretexts on which Italians are arrested, and the amount of evidence on which they are detained and condemned, we will quote, referring the reader to Orsini's volume for still more striking but more lengthy illustrations . . . . "

The rest of the piece is given up to extracts from Orsini's book, providing examples of the arbitrary severity and injustice of the Austrian tribunals, who repeatedly arrested the innocent and put them to severe penalties for nothing more than having been acquainted with someone who turned out to be a suspected person.

Belles Lettres
(pp 566-82)

"Every reader of **Lessing**'s 'Laokoon' remembers his masterly distinction between the methods of presentation in poetry and the plastic arts—the acumen and the aptness of illustration with which he shows how the difference in the materials wherewith the poet and painter or sculptor respectively work, and the difference in their mode of appeal to the mind, properly involve a difference in their treatment of a given subject. **Virgil** adds to the effect of his description by making his Laocoon shriek with agony; the words, *clamores horrendos ad sidera tollit,* do not suggest a distorted mouth, but simply intensify in our imagination the conception of suffering.

"But the sculptor did not attempt to render this detail, because he could have given us nothing else than the distorted mouth, which would have been rigid ugliness, exciting in us no tragic emotion. And the same fine instinct which has here guided the sculptor to a different method of treatment from that of the epic poet, is needed in the dramatist. 'It is one thing,' says Lessing, 'to be told that some one shrieked, and another to hear the shriek itself.' The narrative is a suggestion, and addresses the imagination only; but the dramatic representation attacks the sense. On the other hand, the poet would be under an equal mistake if he adopted all the symbolism and detail of the painter and sculptor, since he has at his command the media of speech and action, and it is the absence of these which their symbolism is intended to supply." ¶566

England in Time of War, by Sydney Dobell

"But Mr Dobell's iteration, instead of escaping him as an inevitable climax, is an elaborate appliance by which he undertakes to make words perform the functions of musical notes; and he sometimes even surpasses in monotony the 'burthen' of the early English and Scottish ballads. For example, we have more than a page of stanzas varying no more from each other than the two following:—

'Oh the wold, the wold,
Oh the wold, the wold!

Oh the winter stark,
Oh the level dark
On the wold, the wold, the wold!
'Oh the wold, the wold,
Oh the wold, the wold!
Oh the mystery
Of the blasted tree
On the wold, the wold, the wold!'

"Iteration is a necessity to the primitive mind, because there is no other resource for the expression of persistent emotion: thought or art is not yet complex enough to clothe the same feeling in a perpetually varied form. But under a condition of high culture, this primitive monotony becomes intolerable; and when a modern writer recurs to it, the only impression he is likely to produce on his readers is, that he is inadequate to the expression of his idea through his proper medium of thought-suggesting speech, and that, unable to attain an effect by genuine art, he resorts to a mere trick; as angry people who are unable to say cutting things, fall to making faces." 567

"We are not enthusiastic admirers either of Mr Dobell or of the school of poetry to which he belongs, but we can at least see that he is a man of deep thought and sensibility, essentially a poet, and earnest though aberrant in the pursuit of his art;—in fact, a man who is not to be extinguished either by **Mr Gilfillan**'s praise or **Mr Gigadibs'** condemnation." 568

"We have three other volumes of recent verse before us. The best is *St Bartholomew's Day, and other Poems*—unaffected, and not ungraceful." —by Stewart Lockyer.

"The Rev. Archer Gurney's *Songs of Early Summer* are robustly commonplace, like a bed of marigolds."

Mrs Machell's *Poems and Translations* "are passable *vers de société*, such as, doubtless, 'friend will flatter, prudent foes forbear.'

"We confess that these modern verses have not tempted us to linger so long over them as the selection of *Early Ballads, Illustrative of History, Traditions, and Customs* edited by Robert Bell—a well-chosen selection, both for interest and variety." 570-1

Dred; a Tale of the Great Dismal Swamp, by Harriet Beecher Stowe

" . . . for the last three weeks there have been men, women, and children reading it with rapt attention—laughing and sobbing over it—lingering with delight over its exquisite landscapes, its scenes of humour, and tenderness, and rude heroism—and glowing with indignation at its terrible representation of chartered barbarities. Such a book is an uncontrollable power, and critics who follow it with their objections and reservations—who complain that Mrs Stowe's plot is defective, that she has repeated herself, that her book is too long and too full of hymns and religious dialogue, and that it creates an unfair bias—are something like men pursuing a prairie fire with desultory watering-cans.

"In the meantime, 'Dred' will be devoured by the million, who carry no critical talisman against the enchantments of genius. We confess ourselves to be among the million, and quite unfit to rank with the sage minority of Fadladeens. We have been too much moved by 'Dred' to determine with precision how far it is inferior to 'Uncle Tom'; too much impressed by what Mrs

Stowe *has* done to be quite sure that we can tell her what she ought to have done. Our admiration of the book is quite distinct from any opinions or hesitations we may have as to the terribly difficult problems of Slavery and Abolition—problems which belong to quite other than 'polite literature.' Even admitting Mrs Stowe to be mistaken in her views, and partial or exaggerated in her representations, 'Dred' remains not the less a novel inspired by a rare genius—rare both in intensity and in range of power." ¶571

"Inventions in literature are not as plentiful as inventions in the paletôt and waterproof department, and it is rather amusing that we reviewers, who have, for the most part, to read nothing but imitations of imitations, should put on airs of tolerance towards Mrs Stowe because she has written a second Negro novel, and make excuses for her on the ground that she perhaps would not succeed in any other kind of fiction . . . . But whatever else she may write, or may not write, 'Uncle Tom' and 'Dred' will assure her a place in that highest rank of novelists who can give us a national life in all its phases—popular and aristocratic, humorous and tragic, political and religious." 572

"The strength of Mrs Stowe's own religious feeling is a great artistic advantage to her here; she never makes you feel that she is coldly calculating an effect, but you see that she is all a-glow for the moment with the wild enthusiasm, the unreasoning faith, and the steady martyr-spirit of Dred, of Tiff, or of Father Dickson. But with this, she has the keen sense of humour which preserves her from extravagance and monotony; and though she paints her religious negroes *en beau,* they are always specifically negroes—she never loses hold of her characters, and lets dramatic dialogue merge into vague oratory. Indeed, here is her strongest point: her dramatic instinct is always awake; and whether it is the grotesque Old Tiff or the aërial Nina, the bluff sophist Father Bonim or the gentlemanly sophist Frank Russell, her characters are always like themselves; a quality which is all the more remarkable in novels animated by a vehement polemical purpose." 572

It is Never Too Late to Mend, by Charles Reade

" . . . also a remarkable fiction, and one that sets vibrating very deep chords in our nature . . . " 573

" . . . there are fine situations, fine touches of feeling, and much forcible writing; especially while the scene is in the Gaol, the best companion who drops in you will probably regard as a bore, and will become earnest in inviting to remain only when you perceive he is determined to go." 573

"[It] is one of the exceptional novels to be read not merely by the idle and the half-educated, but by the busy and the thoroughly informed." 574

"Nevertheless, Mr Reade's novel does not rise above the level of cleverness: we feel throughout the presence of remarkable talent, which makes effective use of materials, but nowhere of the genius which absorbs material, and reproduces it as a living whole, in which you do not admire the ingenuity of the workman, but the vital energy of the producer.

"Doubtless there is a great deal of nonsense talked about genius and inspiration, as if genius did not and must not labour; but, after all, there remains the difference between the writer who thoroughly possesses you by his creation, and the writer who only awakens your curiosity and makes you recognise his ability; and this difference may as well be called 'genius' as anything else. Perhaps a truer statement of the difference is, that the one writer is himself thoroughly possessed by his creation—he lives *in* his characters; while the other remains outside them, and dresses them up." 574

"Here lies the fundamental contrast between Mrs Stowe's novel and Mr Reade's. Mrs Stowe seems for the moment to glow with all the passion, to quiver with all the fun, and to be inspired with all the trust that belong to her different characters; she attains her finest dramatic effects by means of her energetic sympathy, and not by conscious artifice. Mr Reade, on the contrary, seems always self-conscious, always elaborating a character after a certain type, and carrying his elaboration a little too far—always working up to situations, and over-doing them." 574

". . . the Jew Isaac Levi, who is a mosaic character in more senses than one . . . . " 575

Young Singleton, by Talbot Gwynne

"Throughout the novel the situations are at once striking and natural, and the characters are all specific; yet, notwithstanding these merits, it does not impress us as a success. The outline is vigorous, but the filling up is often feeble; the story shows a power of construction without an adequate power of detail, and it reminds us of a play schemed by an able dramatist but written by an inefficient collaborator." 575

Bertha, by Frederika Bremer

" . . . perhaps there is hardly another instance of fictions so eagerly read in England which have left so little trace in English literature as Miss Bremer's. No one quotes them, no one alludes to them: and grave people who have entered on their fourth decade, remember their enthusiasm for the Swedish novels among those intellectual 'wild oats' to which their mature wisdom can afford to give a pitying smile. Yet how is this? For Miss Bremer had not only the advantage of describing manners which were fresh to the English public; she also brought to the description unusual gifts—lively imagination, poetic feeling, wealth of language, a quick eye for details, and considerable humour, of that easy, domestic kind which throws a pleasant light on every-day things." 576

"One reason, we think, why Miss Bremer's novels have not kept a high position among us is, that her luxuriant faculties are all overrun by a rank growth of sentimentality, which, like some faint-smelling creeper on the boughs of an American forest, oppresses us with the sense that the air is unhealthy." 576

"Another reason why Miss Bremer's novels are not likely to take rank among the permanent creations of art, is the too confident tone of the religious philosophy which runs through them. When a novelist is quite sure that she has a theory which suffices to illustrate all the difficulties of our earthly existence, her novels are too likely to illustrate little else than her own theory." 576

"Women have not to prove that they can be emotional, and rhapsodic, and spiritualistic; every one believes that already. They have to prove that they are capable of accurate thought, severe study, and continuous self-command." 578

Erlsmere, by L. S. Lavenu

"[It] is a book of remarkable promise. It bears the stamp of unusual insight and culture, and of a mind that possesses some important qualifications of the novelist." 578

" . . . compound words which are innovations without being acquisitions." 578

"Nevertheless, the author of 'Erlesmere' is one of that minority among novelists to whom such readers will say, 'More, give me more.' Her first attempt is not in itself satisfactory, but it creates a belief in her powers." 579

Stories of an Old Maid, related to her Nephews and Nieces, by Mme Emile de Girardin, translated by Alfred Elwes

"The book is very elegantly got up, with abundant pictures, and is a present that we envy any aunt or uncle the pleasure of bestowing." 579

Bacon's Essays; with Annotations, by R. Whately, Archbishop of Dublin

"If we were captiously inclined, we might complain that these annotations are so often made up of citations from the Archbishop's own writings; but a veteran writer has his privileges as well as a veteran talker who recites his own *mots,* or a veteran general who is a little too fond of fighting his battles 'o'er again.' Quite a charming quality in these annotations is their abundance of appropriate and easy illustration . . . . " 579

Essays Critical and Imaginative, by Prof. Wilson

"We found this volume delightful reading when we were in need of that best of all relaxations, an intellectual laugh; and to any one who is the least peevish or dull, we recommend a dose of Wilson's hearty, rollicking humour. . . . " 581

Geschichten der Postischen National Literatur der Hebräer, by Dr Ernst Meier

"It is pleasant to get a serious German work of which we can see the end; for German writers too often oblige us to pay a heavy premium for the thoroughness with which they do their work, by making us wait an indefinite space of time between a first and second volume; and sometimes, indeed, the *erster theil* remains to the end in a state of melancholy bachelorhood." 582

Belles Lettres

(pp 306-26)

Aurora Leigh, by Elizabeth Barrett Browning

"**Foster**, the essayist, has somewhere said that the person who interests us most is the one that most gives us the idea of *ample being*. Applying this remark to books, which are but persons in a transmigrated form, we discern one grand source of the profound impression produced in us by 'Aurora Leigh.' Other poems of our own day may have higher finish, or a higher degree of certain poetic qualities; but no poem embraces so wide a range of thought and emotion, or takes such complete possession of our nature. Mrs Browning is, perhaps, the first woman who has produced a work which exhibits all the peculiar powers without the negations of her sex; which superadds to masculine vigour, breadth, and culture, feminine subtlety of perception, feminine quickness of sensibility, and feminine tenderness. It is difficult to point to a woman of genius who is not either too little feminine, or too exclusively so. But in this, her longest and greatest poem, Mrs Browning has shown herself all the greater poet because she is intensely a poetess." 306

"The most striking characteristic of 'Aurora Leigh' . . . is that its melody, fancy, and imagination—what we may call its poetical *body*—is everywhere informed by a *soul*, namely, by genuine thought and feeling. There is no petty striving after special effects, no heaping up of images for their own sake, no trivial play of fancy run quite astray from the control of deeper sensibility; there is simply a full mind pouring itself out in song as its natural and easiest medium." 307

'This mind has its far-stretching thoughts, its abundant treasure of well-digested learning, its acute observation of life, its yearning sympathy with multiform human sorrow, its store of personal domestic love and joy; and these are given out in a delightful alternation of pathos, reflection, satire playful or pungent, and picturesque description, which carries us with swifter pulses than usual through four hundred pages, and makes us sorry to find ourselves at the end." 307

Craigcrook Castle, by Gerald Massey

"Perhaps no poet of the present day has a more exuberant fancy than Mr Massey; but he rarely shows any higher power than fancy. The majority of his poems are like children's May-garlands, bright with flowers which have no root and are only artificially woven into close contact." 310

" . . . Mr Massey's imagery is rarely derived from any deeper relations than those which lie in the fleeting impressions of a susceptible organization and the capricious combinations of an active fancy. We are not insensible to the charm of this imagery, and are anxious duly to recognise Mr Massey's remarkable endowment of fancy; but it is an endowment which, unless it be pruned and made subordinate to riper intellectual and moral activity, will be just as fatal as a deficiency." 310-11

A Song in Prose to the Westminster Owl

—"on the Criticism of the Westminster Review of July, 1856 [Eliot's review], of 'Lonely Hours,' Poems by Caroline Gifford Phillipson."

"Mrs Phillipson is the authoress of a volume of poems entitled 'Lonely Hours,' which we briefly but advisedly characterized, some months back, as 'sentimental doggerel.' We did not follow up the severity of this opinion by the further severity of quotation, and we have no longer the lady's poems at hand to supply this omission." 312

Bothwell. A Poem. In Six Parts. By W. Edmonstone Aytoun

" 'Bothwell' is modelled on the poetical-historical tales of **Scott**, with the disadvantageous difference of being a story told in a monologue supposed to be uttered by Bothwell when a prisoner in the fortress of Malmoe . . . . The easy spirited rhymes carry the reader along like a cantering steed, and with one who applies neither a high nor an irrelevant standard . . . we can understand that 'Bothwell' may be a favourite poem." 315

Friedrich Halm's Werke

"The poems are very various and pleasing; the sentimental lyrics especially are often felicitously turned; and readers of ample leisure who read all poets, major, minor, and minim, may spend some agreeable hours over Halm's 'Werke.' " 315

Geschichte der Deutschen National-Literatur, by A. F. C. Vilmar

"Apropos of German poetry, we recommend very strongly to those readers who require a really popular and informing book on German literature, Vilmar's . . . . The survey of the mediæval literature is what many English students have desired and sought for in vain in numerous histories of German literature—a *direct account* of the chief poems, and not a dissertation upon them." 315

Rouman Anthology; or, Selections of Rouman Poetry, ancient and modern, Mr Stanley, ed. (poems of Moldavia and Wallachia)

"Of the forty-five poems in Mr Stanley's volumes, only seventeen are translated into English. The whole are printed in Rouman, which bears a strong resemblance to the Latin—not surprising in the language of a people who trace their descent from the legionaries of **Trajan** and **Aurelian**." 316

"But the Latinity of the Rouman language has for more than four centuries been concealed under the barbaric disguise of the Cyrillic alphabet, introduced by the priests of the Greek Church to defeat the attempts of the Popes to unite their flocks with the Church of Rome, and since maintained by Russian influence as a bond connecting the Rouman with the Sclavonic races." 316

"It is impossible to read many of these poems without feeling that love of country—love of the very soil—is the ruling passion of the writers and of the audience they address. We meet with comparatively little of this in English poetry; with much in Scotch; and the 'Adieu to Moldavia,' which is the last of the English translations, reminds us forcibly of the well-known passage in the sixth canto of the 'Lay of the Last Minstrel,' by the intensity of the love of country which it exhibits." 318

Seven Lectures on Shakespeare and Milton, by Samuel Taylor Coleridge; J. Payne Collier, ed.

"This is a very heterogeneous performance, and one which will greatly surprise the majority of persons attracted to it by Coleridge's name." 319

" . . . we greatly doubt the policy which dictated the republication of these Lectures. Coleridge was not so great a man that every scrap of his must needs be interesting; indeed, the public is already in possession of volumes published by himself which it declines to read; and these scraps of lectures would scarcely gain admittance into any good periodical if they were now offered as original articles." 320

Essays, Critical and Imaginative, by Professor Wilson

"It is for the sake of poetical criticism that we chiefly value the second volume of Professor Wilson's Essays, which contains the memorable article on **Tennyson**, written in 1832—an article at once severe and generous: severe in its criticism, generous in its appreciation. The criticism is in Wilson's most characteristic vein, both humorous and poetical." 320

Kathie Brande, a Fireside History of a Quiet Life, by Holme Lee

"Her last work . . . is distinguished from the generality of women's novels by its absence of affectation, maudlin sentimentality, and dogmatic assertions on philosophical, political, and religious points. It is, moreover, nicely written; but, as a story, it is neither new nor entertaining." 320

"When the imagination is actively creating unusual characters and startling incidents, we do not so closely scrutinize probability and truthful representation; but when the imagination moves amidst ordinary realities, if it does not realize them vividly, the result is inevitable weariness." 321-2

Tender and True: a Colonial Tale

"[It] is not a novel of the sickly sentimental order . . . It is really an unaffected attempt to exhibit the trials and vicissitudes of married life and married love. There is no fine writing in it, no pretension to any kind of loftiness . . . . The writer has a real sense of character, which is especially visible in her conception of the husband wife, whose domestic life forms the main thread of the story. But, though her intention is everywhere such as to indicate a well-balanced nature, it is not borne out by any vigorous artistic power." 322

Deverell: a Novel

"In 'Deverell' we are in the highest society—Lord Henry Travers, Lord Malvern, Lord Shirley Mansfield; and among ladies in all styles of beauty, the dark and passionate with 'billowing' eyelids, the severe and classical with braided tresses, the consumptive ethereal, and the auburn-haired domestic. Moreover, there is abundance of fine writing, and an original use of language. For example: 'My father said little consecutively. Buried in a long train of thought, he appeared to reveal it only in part, when in the *protracted category* he would relate some anecdote, some incident, some generous impulse &c.' And of the proud passionate beauty we read, that her 'filled eye rolled inwardly to feed on her heart.' There is, apparently, a large public for this kind of writing . . . . " 322-3

Stories by an Archæologist and his Friends

"[The book] is a mistake of an accomplished man, who has abundant knowledge rare enough to be worth communicating, but who has unhappily chosen a vehicle quite unfitted both for his powers and his purpose. Fiction is art, and like all other art ought not to be undertaken in the absence of an artistic impulse. What should we say to a man who became a painter simply that he might familiarize the public with mediæval costumes? . . . **Walter Scott** was full of historical and antiquarian knowledge; but he was pre-eminently a story-teller, an artist in fiction. He did not write 'Ivanhoe' in order to instruct us in the condition of England in the feudal times, or in the relation of the Saxon to his Norman conqueror; but, having a dramatic imagination, his knowledge of the feudal period necessarily organized itself into dramatic presentation."

Aus Herder's Nachlass, ungedruckte Briefe, Heinrich Düntzer and F. G. v. Herder, eds.

"We opened this Correspondence with peculiar eagerness, which was proportionately disappointed." 323

"The publication is a mistake. What, indeed, could be expected of a publication committed to the stupendous dulness of Herr Düntzer, who has constituted for himself a parasitic existence on *Goethe-Literatur,* much to the affliction of all readers of the said *Literatur?*" 324

M. Tullii Ciceronis Orationes, with a commentary by George Long

"These are the contents of a volume which the much-reading public will not probably care for, but which scholars and learners will prize." 324-5

"[We] have merely to repeat our commendations of [Long's] pains, perspicuity, and conciseness. What can be known of Cicero's text or times he strives to know and explain; what cannot be regained for knowledge he does not seek to define or explain away. His candid admissions of ignorance inspire his readers with trust in his knowledge. He is not the most gracious or genial of commentators, but he is a very honest and plain-spoken one." 325

Archias "in short, was a Greek lion, who, to Latin ears, roared like any nightingale; having, it seems, the good gift of persuading the Luculli and other noble Romans that they and their fathers were the very salt of the earth. His talent appears to have lain in improvisation principally, and, though he also wrote and published verses, we have probably no great loss in their absence. And even here is a useful illustration of Roman life in the later days of the Commonwealth. A Greek *improvisatore* was welcomed in great houses as a great singer is in our own days. He lived at rack and manger among statesmen and generals, and there was scrambling and pulling of togas to get possession of him." 326

History, Biography, Voyages and Travels

With this issue of the *Westminster,* George Eliot said farewell to journalism until eight years later, when she published several small pieces in other magazines. This summary reflects her only chore under the above rubric, and it must have been a chore, for almost nothing with any colour or interest can be derived from these comments.

Life in Ancient India, by Mrs Speir: "elegant, yet solid volume"

"Mrs Speir writes not only with genuine love of her subject, but with a vigour, a clearness, and an unpretentious thoroughness which raise her quite above the level of dilettantism." 289

The Social History of the People of the Southern Counties of England in Past Centuries, from the researches of George Roberts

The Eighteenth Century; or Illustrations of the Manners and Customs of our Grandfathers, by Alexander Andrews

The Popular History of England; an illustrated History of Society and Government from the Earliest Period to our Own Times, by Charles Knight

The Northmen in Cumberland and Westmoreland, by Robert Ferguson

Reformation in Italy Reformation in Spain, by Thomas M'Crie

"M'Crie belongs to that higher class of writers to whose earnestness, thoroughness, and genuine research we turn for relief from the superficial, second-hand showiness of books written from a transient impulse, in order to supply only a transient need." 295

Life of Cornelius Agrippa von Nettesheim, Doctor and Knight, commonly known as a Magician, by Henry Morley

The Girlhood of Catherine de' Medici, by T. A. Trollope

"It is the girlhood only of Catherine which is here related, and the details of that girlhood are so scanty that the book necessarily becomes history flavoured with biography to about the same amount as **Falstaff**'s sack was flavoured with bread; but those who are fonder of sack than of bread will not complain." 297

The Life and Correspondence of Major-General Sir John Malcolm, G. C. B., late Envoy to Persia, and Governor of Bombay, by John William Kaye

Mémoires du Duc de Raguse de 1792 a 1732 [Marshal Marmont]

Memorials of the Lineage, Early Life, Education, and Development of the Genius of James Watt, by George Williamson

Records of Longevity; with an introductory Discourse on Vital Statistics, by Thomas Bailey

The Discovery of the North-West Passage by H.M.S. Investigator, Captain R. M'Clure, 1850-1854, ed. Commander Sherard Osborne

Arctic Explorations in the Years 1853, 1854, and 1855, by Elisha Kent Kane

"Hoping to recur to Dr Kane's remarkable work, we felt the less regret at leaving it for the present, with an emphatic recommendation to the reader's attention. Simply as a story of heroism, it would be fascinating; but that story, lying as it does among some of the most terribly magnificent scenes of nature, and being connected with objects dear to science, touches our intellectual and moral enthusiasm alike." 304

There are notes on guidebooks for Egypt (the **deLesseps** researches), Australia, Tasmania, New Zealand.

Flemish Interiors, in which a story is told of a Scotch newspaper reporter's conversion on hearing the sermons of **Cardinal Manning**

"Observe the climax: not only a sceptic, but a hardened one—and not of a common hardness, but the hardness of a newspaper reporter, accustomed to consider all sermons from a short-hand point of view; further, not merely a reporter, but a *Scotch* reporter, who may be supposed to represent the last stage of flintiness; and this superlative hardness reduced to perfect Catholic softness already by the *third* sermon: no need of the fourth!" 306

The Grammar of Ornament

(pp 124-5)

The Grammar of Ornament, by Owen Jones, Architect

The new *Fortnightly Review*, founded by Anthony Trollope among others, had a policy requiring that all contributions be signed. So, as with "The Influence of Rationalism," we can rely for an attribution, not on prior or our own scholarship, but on the printing of the author's name at the bottom of her review!

"The inventor of movable types, says the venerable **Teufelsdröckh**,* was disbanding hired armies, cashiering most kings and senates, and creating a whole new democratic world. Has any one yet said what great things are being done by the men who are trying to banish ugliness from our streets and our homes, and to make both the outside and inside of our dwellings worthy of a world where there are forests, and flower-tressed meadows, and the plumage of birds; where the insects carry lessons of colour on their wings, and even the surface of stagnant pool will show us the wonder of iridescence and the most delicate forms of leafage? They, too, are modifying opinions, for they are modifying men's moods and habits, which are the mothers of opinions, having quite as much to do with their formation as the responsible father—Reason. Think of certain hideous manufacturing towns where the piety is chiefly a belief in copious perdition, and the pleasure is chiefly gin. The dingy surface of wall pierced by the ugliest windows, the staring shop-fronts, paper-hangings, carpets, brass and gilt mouldings, and advertising placards, have an effect akin to that of malaria; it is easy to understand that with such surroundings there is more belief in cruelty than in beneficence, and that the best earthly bliss attainable is the dulling of the external senses.

¶"For it is a fatal mistake to suppose that ugliness which is taken for beauty will answer all the purposes of beauty; the subtle relation between all kinds of truth and fitness in our life forbids that bad taste should ever be harmless to our moral sensibility or our intellectual discernment; and—more than that—as it is probable that fine musical harmonies have a sensitive influence over our bodily organization, it is also probable that just colouring and lovely combinations of lines may be necessary to the complete well-being of our systems apart from any conscious delight in them. A savage may indulge in discordant chuckles and shrieks and gutturals, and think that they please the gods, but it does not follow that his frame would not be favourably wrought upon by the vibrations of a grand church organ. One sees a person capable of choosing the worst style of wall-paper become suddenly afflicted by its ugliness under an attack of illness. And if an evil state of blood and lymph usually goes along with an evil state of mind, who shall say that the ugliness of our streets, the falsity of our ornamentation, the vulgarity of our upholstery, have not something to do with those bad tempers which breed false conclusions?

"On several grounds it is possible to make a more speedy and extensive application of artistic reform to our interior decoration than in our external architecture. One of these grounds is that most of our ugly buildings must stand: we cannot afford to pull them down. But every year we are decorating interiors afresh, and people of modest means may benefit by the introduction of beautiful designs into stucco ornaments, paper-hangings, draperies, and carpets. Fine taste in the decoration of interiors is a benefit that spreads from the palace to the clerk's house with one parlour.

"All honour, then, to the architect who has zealously vindicated the claim of internal ornamentation to be a part of the architect's function, and has laboured to rescue that form of art which is most closely connected with the sanctities and pleasures of our hearths from the hands of uncultured tradesmen. All the nation ought at present to know that this effort is peculiarly associated with name of Mr. Owen Jones: and those are most disposed to dispute with the architect about his colouring, must at least recognise the high artistic principle which has directed his attention to coloured ornamentation as a proper branch of architecture. One monument of his effort in this way is his 'Grammar of Ornament,' of which a new and cheaper edition has just been issued.

¶"The one point in which it differs from the original and more expensive edition, viz. the reduction in the size of the pages (the amount of matter and number of plates are unaltered) is really an advantage: it is now a very manageable folio, and when the reader is in a lounging mood may be held easily on the knee. It is a magnificent book; and those who know no more of it than the title, should be told that they will find in it a pictorial history of ornamental design from its rudimentary condition as seen in the productions of savage tribes, through all the other great types of art—the Egyptian, Assyrian, ancient Persian, Greek, Roman, Byzantine, Arabian, Moresque, Mahommedan-Persian, Indian, Celtic, Mediæval, Renaissance, Elizabethan, and Italian. The letter-press consists, first, of an introductory statement of fundamental principles of ornamentation—principles, says the author, which will be found to have been obeyed more or less instinctively by all nations in proportion as their art has been a genuine product of the national genius; and, secondly, of brief historical essays, some of them contributed by other eminent artists, presenting a commentary on each characteristic series of illustrations, with the useful appendage of bibliographical lists.

"The title 'Grammar of Ornament' is so far appropriate that it indicates what Mr Owen Jones is most anxious to be understood concerning the object of his work, namely, that it is intended to illustrate historically the application of principles, and not to present a collection of models for mere copyists. The plates correspond to examples in syntax, not to be repeated parrot-like, but to be studied as embodiments of syntactical principles. There is a logic of form which cannot be departed from in ornamental design without a corresponding remoteness from perfection; unmeaning, irrelevant lines are as bad as irrelevant words or clauses, that tend no whither. And as a suggestion towards the origination of fresh ornamental design, the work concludes with some beautiful drawings of leaves and flowers from nature, that the student, tracing in them the simple laws of form which underlie an immense variety in beauty, may the better discern the method by which the same laws were applied in the finest decorative work of the past, and may have all the clearer prospect of the unexhausted possibilities of freshness which lie before him, if, refraining from mere imitation, he will seek only such likeness to existing forms of ornamental art as arises from following like principles of combination.

GEORGE ELIOT"

*A leading figure in Carlyle's *Sartor Resartus*

Essays of George Eliot
Not Published
in her Lifetime

There appears to be more than one school of thought on the meaning of the word "essay," as we have noted above in another connection. Some scholars class as essays GE's journal entries such as "Recollections of Ilfracombe," and "How I Came to Write Fiction." But we exclude here this kind of personal note-taking as reportage not carrying any weight of reflection or analysis. Gordon S. Haight, in his monumental edition of GE's Letters, includes these reports, though they are not "letters" in any usual sense.

Essays of George Eliot Not Published in Her Lifetime

Two Forgotten Essays

We found these two essays in bound manuscript and transcribed them at Princeton University Library's Department of Rare Books and Collections. They are undated, and there is no internal evidence to suggest when Eliot wrote them, although the handwriting is obviously mature, clear, and beautiful and resembles the calligraphy of the later years of her life. We have supplied bracketed titles and numbered the pieces for reference. For more than a year we thought we had uncovered something no scholar had previously unearthed, and the failure of the ORC to refer to these pieces was a seemingly strong confirmation of this impression. But at the last moment we learned of the work of Professor K. K. Collins, who published the essays under the rubric, "Questions of Method: Some Unpublished Late Essays," in *Nineteenth Century Fiction,* Vol. 35, No.3, Special Issue: George Eliot, 1880-1980 (Dec., 1980), at pp 385-405. Had she included Eliot's name in her title, this excellent piece of work would presumably have been noticed, usefully indexed, and accepted easily into the canon of George Eliot's *oeuvre.*

1. [Thoughts on Anthropology]

*"Es ist dafür gesorgt dass die Bäume nicht in den Himmel wachsen** says the German proverb: in other words, everything on this Earth has its limits which may not be surpassed. Even imagination which used to be in high repute for its immensity, is seen nowadays to be no more than a worker in mosaics, owing every one of its glinting fragments & every type of its impossible vastnesses to the small realm of experience; nay, finds herself beaten by discovery & sits amazed, like a sorceress outdone. And discovery? That too must end somewhere & under the name of Knowledge has long been recognized as a mere parenthesis in a context of irremovable darkness. Even

*"Care is taken that trees do not grow into the sky"—epigraph to Part III of Goethe's *Aus Meinem Leben: Dichtung und Wahrheit*

the ravings of madness & the vagaries of wilful nonsense have their logical limits. 'They all fell to playing at catch as catch can till the gunpowder ran out at the heels of their boots,' may be compared to a zigzag made of straight lines & measurable angles, or a sinuousity which however wildly looped is inevitably made up of curves.

¶"To be plain, it is obvious enough that a being like man, having a certain shape, certain modes of movement, certain forms of sense & certain unchangeable wants must continue to be determined & limited by these in all his inventions, however far the progress of the ages may carry him; & also that different groups of human beings, though in the very beginning of their existence sundered from each other, must inevitably fall upon the same devices for self-preservation, communication & analogical representation. They might have in no single case the same name for the same thing, but over a certain range their speech would be made up of like sounds, & they would of necessity have much agreement in the metaphorical development of their speech, above & below, light & dark, fast & slow, warm & cold, sweet & sour, hard & soft, smooth & rough, heavy & light, noisy & still, cloudy & clear, wet & dry, far & near, and so on, would be the same qualities for each group, & the words expressing them would be transformed from the external to the internal, from the visible & palpable to the invisible & imaginary.

¶"In short, their languages would be to a good extent translatable: they would be different media of ideas held in common. Their grammar must have corresponding elements, however differently rendered, since the main elements of grammar are simply indispensable facts of human existence: that I am not you, that he is neither of us, that the sky is still the sky though it may be either bright & sunny or dark & starry, that my hand is still my hand though it may be hot or cold. Change, active & passive, distinction of persons, of substance & quality, are wrought into the experience of every sensitive animal, & where the power of language exists make part of its earliest stimuli, however imperfectly represented in words.

"It would be the same with their clothing where climate forced them into clothing. Tunic & toga, the closer constant garment & the looser occasional covering, would be found out in the same latitude though on different sides of the world, & if a head covering were taken, one sees that it must be of a shape to stick on, which shape in relation to human skulls, through the extremes of brachycephalous & dolichocephalous, could not vary widely in fundamental character.

¶"Indeed, looking at costumes through all the caprices of wealthy fashion in the rolling centuries, one sees the restraining influence of such simple facts as our four limbs & trunk, for with all the extravagance that would clearly have gone any possible length the changes are in trivial accessories. Apart from the great division of breeched and unbreeched which seems to have been at first a matter of climate, one sees a comparative anatomy in all varieties of apparel. The dress coat & waistcoat of the present day are a tunic of which the fore part has been injudiciously cut away to supply another form of frontage, & under-garments are mere reduplications. Breeches, hosen, gaiters, stockings, are easily convertible: what is unchangeable is the human leg.

¶"One may safely say that while the human race lasts, there will be no wide departure from the typical long or short tunic, the *braccae* full or narrow, the head-covering of the skull-cap or high-crowned genus, with more or less or nothing of brim. It will never be the general fashion of communities for one man to carry twenty chimney-pots one above another on his head—not because the effect would be ugly, for this would not, we know, be a *vera causa,* but because the human balance in walking could not sustain that height of absurdity. Nor will ladies ever be able to go beyond a certain height in the heels of their boots while they have to keep their toes on the ground. To everything human there are limits, & let folly pay invention never so high, inventors in dress will radically be doing the same thing over again, covering four limbs, a trunk & a skull so as to leave a certain power of movement withal.

"Well, all this is very simple; but I wish it were borne in mind & practically applied in the investigation & discussion of origins. For then we should not see that irrational exclusiveness of theory which insists on interpreting the resemblances between the mythologies & legends of different peoples as a result of tradition or identity of descent. Likeness in the connexion & representation of facts is what we should expect over a large range of experience even in tribes the most remote from each other & with no traceable alliance through descent. Cup-shaped vessels & sharp-edged implements; terror & worship or attempted propitiation of visible or imaginary powers—of mountains, trees, animals, fire & storm; ways of accounting for things as due to the will & activity of beings curiously or monstrously different from men, & yet fundamentally like them: these & other forms of human apprehension might be found all over the world without, surely, compelling us to the supposition that they all proceed from one nest of speech & practice. What we should be surprised at is a novelty like the boomerang.

"But the likeness would in a great proportion of cases be analogical & not direct. There are many animals to whom a more or less anthropomorphic view would attribute cunning: stories of cunning arising independently would be likely to have corresponding incidents, with various animals taken as the agents. I cannot be persuaded that what is the *nodus* in the story of the Fisherman for getting rid of the alarming Djinn, in the Arabian Nights, namely, that Cunning masters Strength by piquing Strength to take some position or form in which it can be the easy prey of Cunning, must have been born exclusively in Asia. I should have more confidence in the probability that this idea would spontaneously arise in many different communities than I should have in the circuitous tracing of etymological derivations through mutations of vocal sounds which might or might not have happened in a particular instance, however conceivable or deducible on general grounds.**

"But in the investigation of origins & derivations there is another principle to be borne in mind besides this of limitation. It is that in whatever concerns the life of man there is a constantly increasing complexity or interaction of various conditions, so that similar phenomena may often be produced by a different concurrence of facts & events & that you can hardly find any phenomenon which is not a highly mixed product. Surely it is as unreasonable to explain mythology exclusively by the personification of natural forces as by the deification of kings & heroes or the symbolical exoteric teaching of priests; but in considering the tendencies of man in society an unprejudiced judgment sees ground for accepting all these agencies in various proportions according to time & circumstance.

"Is the interpretation of man's past life on Earth according to the method of **Sir Charles Lyell** in geology, namely, on the principle that all changes were produced by agencies still at work, thoroughly adequate & scientific?

Or must we allow, especially in the earlier periods, for something incalculable by us from the data of our present experience? Even within comparatively near times & in kindred communities how many conceptions & fashions of life have existed to which our understanding & sympathy has no clue!"

[*Eliot's footnote*] **Here is one example of the fallacious estimate of evidence among the learned. To prove that certain mutations might possibly have occurred—they being according to discernible operative laws—is not a proof that they occurred here or there even in instances of a direct & simple kind: much less can it fairly be taken as such proof where the transmutations are of a number & complexity to themselves require a strain of belief for the acceptance of such a series as having actually occurred."

2. [A Note on Truth in Art]

"Portrait painters may conceal the age of their sitters & deck them in fancy garments, but the living subject is less successful in the corresponding attempt. Indefatigable Time models as well as colours & of his work everybody is a connoisseur. A woman's face beautified by an excellent master will have an ideal truth; but when the same face is beautified by her own fingers in the decorative way with rouge-pot & henna, such truth as it presents is too often of a grimly real kind not sought for by the colourist.

¶"And even with regard to the great portrait painters there is a balance of advantages in two possible methods. Let none decry ideal portraits seeing that these must include our most precious pictures of sacred types. But on the other hand we are glad to have **Rembrandt**'s mother, **Bellini**'s old Doge **Holbein**'s **Archbishop Warham**, nay, **Titian**'s **Philip II** in all his shuffling viciousness of expression, from his wispy yellow hair to his ill-fitting yellow slippers. Let us see how mankind might be made lovelier: but let us also see what they are & have been without fastidious selection.

"It is the same with the histories of men. We cannot afford to part with heroic forms as they have been seen in the high imagination of poets. But it is good that the narrator should also if possible follow the example of those greatest painters who not only painted the finest ideal types they were capable of beholding, but also painted severely veracious likenesses, taking their models as they were with all their facial irregularities & wrinkles & presenting them in their habit as they lived.

"It is an old bias to suppose that we can delight in conceiving men as they ought to be only by shutting our eyes to what they are & that otherwise we shall not believe in their having those elements or qualities which can make them grow towards what they ought to be. Looked at closely this notion seems to hold in it the utmost possible scepticism as to human goodness, & is an indirect assertion that society is to be saved by silliness & pretence. Everybody can see what mischief would follow if we carried this kind of wilful illusion into our working of metals & our building of bridges.

¶"Among some peoples it has been held that fishes could be enticed by flattery & that a storm could be quieted by a present of tobacco. But it is now pretty well agreed in this quarter of the globe that we are the better off for knowing better the nature of fishes & storms & acting according to that knowledge. The mere fact that mankind has a conception of what is pure & lovely, might be fairly taken as a ground of faith in the human nature out of which the conception was born, & the proper attitude of faith is bravery."

Versification (1867)

This piece is referred to by Thomas Pinney in his *Essays of George Eliot* (p 431). He tells us that Bernard J. Paris published an article, "George Eliot's Unpublished Poetry," in *Studies in Philology,* LVI (July 1959), pp 439-558, in which he promised to publish the prose in the manuscripts with commentary in another article. We have not found this latter article.

We went to the Beinecke Library at Yale University and made the following transcription, working from a photocopy of pages from one of the Eliot notebooks. We now find it in CSP at II:185-91, its date given as 1869.

"The rule that English blank verse should consist of five iambi, may be compared with the rule that a bar of common time must consist of four crotchets or eight quavers. A poem of any length made up of verses invariably presenting five regular iambi would be about as high a style of composition as a sonata of which every bar presented eight quavers, without rest, without an appoggiatura, without any note of diverse value. Nothing higher than a jig or a 'patter' song can be constructed on this homogenous plan. High musical expression depends not only on the succession of tonic intervals; it depends equally on the adjustment of varying quantities given to the successive notes comprised within a bar or series of bars, In any high order of music, and even in rude music which gives voice to any passion deeper than childish merriment, a large proportion of these beats are perceived by the inward sense only, and are not represented in sounds that strike the tympanum.

"Though the rhythmic elements of fine verse cannot throughout their whole range be paralleled with the structure of fine music, because language is another and more complex medium than notes, yet, in their fundamental principles they are analogous. In both verse & music rhythmic & tonic relations are used as a means of moving men's souls by the adjustment of those relations to the bias of passionate experience, i.e. to the accumulated associations of certain modes of sound with ease & struggle, consent or resistance, joy or sorrow, awe or triumph, calmness or rage. But in every art that reaches a high degree of practice, the use of the medium discloses new & newer relations in that medium, so that the artist in his turn confers fresh associations & enriches that sensibility of the multitude which originally made all the wealth of his art.

"Our English blank verse having had the good fortune to be written by poets & not by carpenters ('Scit tendere versum non secus, ac si oculoo rubricam dirigat uno;' Persius Sat 1 67*) the ten syllable, five iambi rule was never regarded as an absolute type; & even in the sense of five beats or accents it was departed from by the best writers in some of their most effective passages. The five iambi theory was always a background for licenses. [**Thomas**] **Campion** [1567-1620], a contemporary of **Shakspeare**—'Sweet Master Campion' he was called in 1595, but in 1675 he had sunk into 'a writer of no extraordinary fame'—undertaking to lay down rules for the writing of English blank verse, begins by allowing to the 'licentiate iambic' a spondee in the first or second place, forbidding it in the third or fifth; & in the second or fourth place allowing a tribrach or dactyl, or even by way of exception an anapest. But he presently relaxes all these exceptions for a still greater freedom—sees no reason why a trochee should not come in the first place, so that it be not followed by an iambus, which, 'beginning with a single short syllable, & the other ending before with the like, would too much *drink up the verse* if they came immediately together.' Therefore, says he, let your initial trochee be followed by a spondee, a dactyl, or a tribrach. And finally he shows examples where what he mistakenly calls a tribrach 'may be very formally taken' in the fifth place.

"But while 'Sweet Master Campion' was giving poor verses of his own to illustrate these kind indulgences, Master Shakspeare & Master [**John**] **Fletcher** [1579-1625] were asking leave of no authority but their own ears & their own sensibility to pregnant speech, while they produced 'licentiate iambics' which the world still accepts as types of excellence in blank verse. If then we want to know what elements the form of verse must or may consist of, the surest way will be to examine the best passages of the best masters—to inquire what the great poets have done rather than what small gentlemen have said that poets ought to do.

"Careful study will discover that there are certain conditions which are never departed from in a passage of thoroughly fine blank verse: conditions which cannot be departed from without a loss of power: and power over the minds of men is in this case the measure of perfection. 'Whatsoever form of words,' says that virile writer **Samuel Daniel** [1563-1619], 'Whatsoever form of words doth move, delight, and sway the affections of men, in what Scythian sort soever it be disposed or uttered, that is true number, measure, eloquence, & the perfection of speech: which .... hath as many shapes as there be tongues and nations in the world, nor can with all the tyrannical rules of Idle Rhetoric be governed otherwise than custom & present observation will allow.'

"But these conditions of power are such as can least be fulfilled by the carpenter measurement, & the greater part are such as cannot be well stated in the form of rules. There are no rules that will cover all the requirements of fine writing except the one rule, that fine writing demands a fine writer.

"The most rigorous conditions of fine blank verse are such as conciliate the rhythmical movement with the demands of forcible declamation, pregnant expression, fully marked meaning. Time, accent, melodic utterance, have to be so inwrought with the emphasis, the tones, the gradations of rapidity which belong to the passionate or intellectual intention of the verse, that the versification shall be to the meaning as the mythical wings to the strong quadruped.

"All valid rules—all rules not voluntarily assumed for the mere pleasure of bondage—must have a psychological or physical basis. They must be founded either on physical necessities, or on an organic bias which habit has made a necessity, or on a firmly established sense of relations which is not natural merely but permanently human. Many have given themselves trouble to write poems after the shape of wings, arrows, hearts or flowers, but posterity has not greatly thanked them, any more than it has thanked the confectioners who shaped the sugar and pastry of our ancestors into castles & armed knights, into shepherds, shepherdesses & their flocks, or other mimicries that pleased the fancy of the time. Every irregularity is good if it can be shown to be [deletion of 'of'] the secret of a higher pleasure than the unbroken observance of a rule. Fortunate irregularities are discoveries in art: they are the stages of its development & go on living according to a natural selection.

"But there are certain conditions of blank verse which may be safely taken as rules having an organic or psychological validity. The accented syllable in the last foot must never be so mean as to mar the effect of the delicate pause or hiatus which should be felt at the end of every verse. There should be no ending which throws the impetus of the whole verse on some understrapper—some 'of' or 'for' having no more than the ordinary value of a preposition, & no ending which causes the hiatus to occur after any word depending for its value on the word that follows it . . . related to it as the handle to the blade. Take as examples to be avoided these verses from **Byron**'s 'Cain.'

'I look
Around me on a world which I deem nothing *with*
Thoughts which arise within me as if *they*
Could conquer all things.'

or,

'I lean no more on superhuman aid
It hath no power upon the past, or *on*
The future, till the past be gulfed in darkness——'

If Shakspeare in one of his best moods had been writing these last three lines, which are vigorous and poetic enough in expression though spoiled by the feebleness of the second ending, they would probably have come from his pen in this way:

'I lean no more on superhuman aid
It hath no power upon the past, or for the future.
Until the past be gulfed in darkness—'

leaving the verse shorter than rule would make it, but not therefore unmelodious, because it is simply a curtailed verse & carries the ear musically to a pause, just as the curtailed verse in the lines—"

'Light thickens; and the crow
Makes wing to the rooky wood;
Good things of day begin to droop and drowse;
While night's black agents to their prey do rouse.'

Here we are not obliged to [**George**] **Steevens** [1736-1800] or any other verse-carpenter who will nail two more feet to the second line. In those verses of Byron's, we cannot help thinking that if the poet had been Shakespeare he would have left a longish pause after 'future' which would have pushed on the feet of the following line, and made it complete to his inward ear. Again, in *Lear* we have a thoroughly grand piece of declamation with curtailed verses:

'It may be so, my Lord.—
Hear, Nature, hear; dear Goddess, hear!
Suspend thy purpose, if thou didst intend
To make this creature fruitful!
Dry up in her the organs of increase;
And from her derogate body never spring
A babe to honour her!'

Not but that Shakespeare himself in his bad, careless moods, wrote verses with feeble endings enough to give him in this matter too his usual supremacy.

"It is not needful that all endings should be of equal weight: on the contrary this would not be tolerable in a poem of much length, and variety in this respect is often a source of greater enjoyment. But the declamatory grandeur of weighty endings is heard in such passages as this from *Samson Agonistes:*

'Nothing is here for tears; nothing to wail
Or knock the breast; no weakness, no contempt,
Disprase or blame; nothing but well and fair,
And what may quiet us in a death so noble!'

Where a light syllable at the end of a verse produces a fine effect, it usually belongs to a trisyllable of weight and beauty. In any case, it must be a word—or a syllable belonging to a word—which can carry well an occasionally conferred dignity.

"The pronunciation of words must not be forced to suit the exigencies of metre. There ought to be no violence done to any custom of the ear which is so far rooted as to give its arbitrariness an air of necessity.

"The pauses must be so used as to subserve at once musical variety and force of meaning. *This concurrence being secured,* there is no point in the verse where the pause may not sometimes occur—the effect of certain pauses which should be kept infrequent, gaining by that very infrequency. Thus, in the last place:

'Rich conceit
Taught thee to make vast Neptune weep for aye
On thy low grave on faults forgiven. *Dead*
Is the noble Timon.'

'Loud as from numbers without number, *sweet*
As from blest voices uttering joy.'

In the first place, when also weight in the foot marked off by the pause is essential—in this case the foot which precedes, not follows, the pause:

'His heart
Distends with pride, and hardening in his strength
Glories; for never since created man
Met such embodied force.' " [*End*]

---

*"Our poet knows how to draw his lines straight as if he were directing a ruddle cord with one eye shut." [CSP is the source of this translation.]

Notes on Form in Art (1868)

This work was found at Yale University and first published in 1963 by Thomas Pinney in his *Essays of George Eliot.* He reports obtaining the permission of the then copyright-owner, Mrs E. Carrington Ouvry, granddaughter of George Henry Lewes, and we are grateful to her grandson, Jonathan Ouvry, for allowing us to reproduce the piece here. We reviewed the work (it is in photocopy) at Yale, and the date 1868 is GE's notation.

"Abstract words & phrases which have an excellent genealogy are apt to live a little too much on their reputation & even to sink into dangerous imposters that should be made to show how they get their living. For this reason it is often good to consider an old subject as if nothing had yet been said about it: to suspend one's attention even to revered authorities & simply ask what in the present state of our knowledge are the facts which can with any congruity be tied together & labelled by a given abstraction.

"For example, to any but those who are under the dire necessity of using the word & cannot afford to wait for a meaning, it must be more fruitful to ask, what relations of things can be properly included under the word Form as applied to artistic composition, than to decide without any such previous inquiry that a particular work is wanting in form, or to take it for granted that the works of any one period or people are the examples of all that is admissible in artistic form.

"Plain people, though indisposed to metaphysical subtleties, can yet understand that Form, as an element of human experience, must begin with the perception of separateness, derived principally from touch [*note* of which the other senses are modifications], & that things must be recognized as separate wholes before they can be recognized as wholes composed of parts, or before these wholes again can be regarded as relatively parts of a larger whole.

"Form, then, as distinguished from merely massive impression, must first depend on the discrimination of wholes & then on the discrimination of parts. Fundamentally, form is unlikeness, as is seen in the philosophic use of the word Form in distinction from Matter; & in consistency with this fundamental meaning, every difference is form. Thus, sweetness is a form of sensibility, rage is a form of passion, green is a form both of light & of sensibility. But with this fundamental discrimination is born in necessary antithesis the sense of wholeness or unbroken connexion in space & time: a flash of light is a whole compared with the darkness which precedes & follows it; the taste of sourness is a whole & includes parts or degrees as it subsides. And as knowledge continues to grow by its alternative processes of distinction & combination, seeing smaller & smaller unlikenesses & grouping or associating these under a common likeness, it arrives at the conception of wholes composed of parts more & more multiplied & highly differenced, yet more & more absolutely bound together by various conditions of common likeness or mutual dependence.

¶"And the fullest example of such a whole is the highest example of Form: in other words, the relation of multiplex interdependent parts to a whole which is itself in the most varied & therefore the fullest relation to other wholes. Thus, the human organism comprises things as diverse as the finger-nails & tooth-ache, as the nervous stimulus of muscle manifested in a shout, & the discernment of a red spot on a field of snow; but all its different elements or parts of experience are bound together in a more necessary wholeness or more inseparable group of common conditions than can be found in any other existence known to us. The highest Form, then, is the highest organism, that is to say, the most varied group of relations bound together in a wholeness which again has the most varied relations with all other phenomena.

"It is only in this fundamental sense that the word Form can be applied to Art in general. Boundary or outline & visual appearance are modes of form which in music & poetry can only have a metaphorical presence. Even in the plastic arts form obviously, in its general application, means something else than mere imitation of outline, more or less correctness of drawing or modelling—just as, with reference to descriptive poetry it means something more than the bare delineation of landscape or figures. Even those who use the phrase with a very dim understanding, always have a sense that it refers to structure or composition, that is, to the impression from a work considered as a whole. And what is a structure but a set of relations selected & combined in accordance with the sequence of mental states in the constructor, or with the preoccupation of a whole which he has inwardly evolved?

¶"Artistic form, as distinguished from mere imitation, begins in sculpture & painting with composition or the selection of attitudes & the formation of groups, let the objects be of what order they may. In music it begins with the adjustment of tones & rhythm to a climax, apart from any direct imitation. But my concern is here chiefly with poetry which I take in its wider sense as including all literary production of which it is the prerogative & not the reproach that the choice & sequence of images & ideas—that is, of relations & groups of relations—are more or less not only determined by emotion but intended to express it. I say more or less; for even the ravings of madness include multitudinous groups & sequences which are parts of common experience; & in the range of poetry we see wide distances of degree in the combination of emotive force with sequences that are not arbitrary & individual but true & universal, just as the guiding emotion varies from an idiosyncracy [*sic*] only short of madness to a profoundly human passion which is or must come to be the heritage of all mankind. Sometimes the wider signification of poetry is taken to be fiction or invention as opposed to ascertained external fact or discovery. But what is fiction other than an arrangement of events or feigned correspondences according to predominant feeling? We find what destiny pleases; we make what pleases us—or what we think will please others.

"Even taken in its derivative meaning of outline, what is form but the limit of that difference by which we discriminate one object from another?—a limit determined partly by the intrinsic relations or composition of the object, & partly by the extrinsic action of other bodies upon it. This is true whether the object is a rock or a man; but in the case of the inorganic body, outline is the result of a nearly equal struggle between inner constitution & the outer play of forces; while in the human organism the outline is mainly determined by the intrinsic relation of its parts, & what is called fitness, beauty or harmony in its outline & movements is dependent on the inward balance. The muscular strength which hurls, the muscular grace which gives a rhythmic movement to half a dozen balls, show a moving outline of which the chief factors are relations within the body; but the line with which a rock cuts the sky, or the shape of a boulder, may be more due to outer forces than to inner constitution.

¶"In ordinary language, the form of a stone is accidental. But the true expression of the difference is, that the wholeness of the stone depends simply on likeness of crystallization & is merely a wholeness of mass which may be broken up into other wholes; whereas the outline defining the wholeness of the human body is due to a consensus or constant interchange of effects among its parts. It is wholeness not merely of mass but of strict & manifold dependence. The word consensus expresses that fact in a complex organism by which no part can suffer increase or diminution without a participation of all other parts in the effect produced & a consequent modification of the organism as a whole.

"By this light, forms of art can be called higher or lower only as the same principle as that on which we apply these words to organisms; viz. In proportion to the complexity of the parts bound up into one indissoluble whole. In Poetry—which has this superiority over all the other arts, that its medium, language, is the least imitative, & is in the most complex relation with what it expresses—Form begins in the choice of rhythms & images as signs of a mental state, for this is a process of grouping or association of a less spontaneous & more conscious order than the grouping or association which constitutes the very growth & natural history of mind. *Poetry* begins when passion weds thought by finding expression in an image; but *poetic form* begins with a choice of elements, however meagre, as the accordant expression of emotional states. The most monotonous burthen chanted by an Arab boatman on the Nile is still a beginning of poetic form.

"Poetic form was not begotten by thinking it out or framing it as a shell which should hold emotional expression, any more than the shell of an animal arises before the living creature; but emotion, by its tendency to repetition, i.e. rhythmic persistence in proportion as diversifying thought is absent, creates a form by the recurrence of its elements in adjustment with certain given conditions of sound, language, action, or environment. Just as the beautiful expanding curves of a bivalve shell are not first made for the reception of the unstable inhabitant, but grow & are limited by the simple rhythmic conditions of its growing life.

"It is a stale observation that the earliest poetic forms arose in the same spontaneous unreflecting way—that the rhythmic shouts with clash of metal accompanying the huntsman's or conqueror's course were probably the nucleus of the ballad epic; that the funeral or marriage sing-song, wailing or glad, with more or less violent muscular movement & resonance of wood or metal made the rude beginnings of lyric poetry. But it is still worth emphasis that this spontaneous origin is the most completely demonstrated in relation to a form of art which ultimately came to be treated more reflectively than any other—the tragic & comic drama.

"A Form being once started must be & by cease to be purely spontaneous: the form itself becomes the object & material of emotion, & is sought after, amplified and elaborated by discrimination of its elements till at last by the abuse of its refinement it preoccupies the room of emotional thinking; & poetry, from being the fullest expression of the human soul, is starved into an ingenious pattern-work, in which tricks with vocables take the place of living words fed with the blood of relevant meaning, & made musical by the continual intercommunication of sensibility & thought.

"The old phrases should not give way to scientific explanation, for speech is to a great extent like sculpture, expressing observed phenomena & remaining true in spite of **Harvey** & **Bichat**.

"In the later development of poetic fable the *anagnorisis* tends to consist in the discernment of a previously unrecognized *character,* & this may also form the *peripateia*, according to **Aristotle**'s notion that in the highest form the two coincide." [Pinney considers that this reference is to a plot element in *Felix Holt:* Harold Transome's discovery at the end of the book that he is illegitimate and that his father is the despised manipulator and embezzler Jermyn.]

"Leaves from a Note-book"

[so captioned by Charles Lee Lewes]

The following essays, never published in GE's lifetime, saw the light of day as the result of the editorship of Charles Lee Lewes, son of GE's dear friend, who did the work of bringing forward reflections composed by the great lady which might otherwise have remained obscure for a time. His introductory comments are from his edition, published four years after her death, of seven major essays. These pieces were included.

> The opportunity afforded by this republication seemed a suitable one for giving to the world some "notes", as George Eliot simply called them, which belong to a much later period [than the seven Essays he publishes], and which have not been previously published. The exact date of their writing cannot be fixed with any certainty, but it must have been some time between the appearance of "Middlemarch" and that of "Theophrastus Such". They were probably written without any distinct view to publication—some of them for the satisfaction of her own mind; others perhaps as memoranda, and with an idea of working them out more fully at some later time. It may be of interest to know that, besides the "notes" here given, the note-book contains four which appeared in "Theophrastus Such", three of them practically as they there stand; and it is not impossible that some of those in the present volume might also have been so utilised had they not happened to fall outside the general scope of the work. The marginal titles are George Eliot's own, but for the general title, 'Leaves from a Note-book', I am responsible.
>
> —Charles Lee Lewes

To facilitate reference elsewhere in this work, we have provided a number for each separate item to which GE gave a caption. Because these works are not often reprinted, we have provided them complete.

1. Authorship

"To lay down in the shape of practical moral rules courses of conduct only to be made real by the rarest states of motive and disposition, tends not to elevate but to degrade the general standard, by turning that rare attainment from an object of admiration into an impossible prescription, against which the average nature first rebels and then flings out ridicule. It is for art to present images of a lovelier order than the actual, gently winning the affections, and so determining the taste. But in any rational criticism of the time which is meant to guide a practical reform, it is idle to insist that action ought to be this or that, without considering how far the outward conditions of such change are present, even supposing the inward disposition towards it. Practically, we must be satisfied to aim at something short of perfection—and at something very much further off it in one case than in another. While the fundamental conceptions of morality seem as stationary through ages as the laws of life, so that a moral manual written eighteen centuries ago still admonishes us that we are low in our attainments, it is quite otherwise with the degree to which moral conceptions have penetrated the various forms of social activity, and made what may be called the special conscience of each calling, art or industry. While on some points of social duty public opinion has reached a tolerably high standard, on others a public opinion is not yet born; and there are even some functions and practices with regard to which men far above the line in honourableness of nature feel hardly any scrupulosity, though their consequent behaviour is easily shown to be as injurious as bribery, or any other slowly poisonous procedure which degrades the social vitality.

"Among those callings which have not yet acquired anything near a full-grown conscience in the public mind is Authorship. Yet the changes brought about by the spread of instruction and the consequent struggles of an uneasy ambition, are, or at least might well be, forcing on many minds the need of some regulating principle with regard to the publication of intellectual products, which would override the rule of the market: a principle, that is, which should be derived from a fixing of the author's vocation according to those characteristics in which it differs from the other bread-winning professions. Let this be done, if possible, without any cant, which would carry the subject into Utopia away from existing needs. The guidance wanted is a clear notion of what should justify men and women in assuming public authorship, and of the way in which they should be determined by what is usually called success. But the forms of authorship must be distinguished; journalism, for example, carrying a necessity for that continuous production which in other kinds of writing is precisely the evil to be fought against, and judicious careful compilation, which is a great public service, holding in its modest diligence a guarantee against those deductions of vanity and idleness which draw many a young gentleman into reviewing, instead of the sorting and copying which his small talents could not rise to with any vigour and completeness.

"A manufacturer goes on producing calicoes as long and as fast as he can find a market for them; and in obeying this indication of demand he gives his factory its utmost usefulness to the world in general and to himself in particular. Another manufacturer buys a new invention of some light kind likely to attract the public fancy, is successful in finding a multitude who will give their testers for the transiently desirable commodity, and before the fashion is out, pockets a considerable sum: the commodity was coloured with a green which had arsenic in it that damaged the factory workers and the purchasers. What then? These, he contends (or does not know or care to contend), are superficial effects, which [it] is folly to dwell upon while we have epidemic diseases and bad government

"The first manufacturer we will suppose blameless. Is an author simply on a par with him, as to the rules of production?

"The author's capital is his brain-power—power of invention, power of writing. The manufacturer's capital, in fortunate cases, is being continually reproduced and increased. Here is the first great difference between the capital which is turned into calico and the brain capital which is turned into literature. The calico scarcely varies in appropriateness as to quality, no consumer is in danger of getting too much of it, and neglecting his boots, hats, and flannel-shirts in consequence. That there should be large quantities of the same sort in the calico manufacture is an advantage: the sameness is desirable, and nobody is likely to roll his person in so many folds of calico as to become a mere bale of cotton goods, and nullify his sense of hearing and touch, while his morbid passion for Manchester shirtings makes him still cry 'More!' The wise manufacturer gets richer and richer, and the consumers he supplies have their real wants satisfied and no more.

"Let it be taken as admitted that all legitimate social activity must be beneficial to others besides the agent. To write prose or verse as a private exercise and satisfaction is not social activity; nobody is culpable for this any more than for learning other people's verse by heart if he does not neglect his proper business in consequence. If the exercise made him sillier or secretly more self-satisfied, that, to be sure, would be a roundabout way of injuring society; for though a certain mixture of silliness may lighten existence, we have at present more than enough.

"But man or woman who publishes writings inevitably assumes the office of teacher or influencer of the public mind. Let him protest as he will that he only seeks to amuse, and has no pretension to do more than while away an hour of leisure or weariness—'the idle singer of an empty day'—he can no more escape influencing the moral taste, and with it the action of the intelligence, than a setter of fashions in furniture and dress can fill the shops with his designs and leave the garniture of persons and houses unaffected by his industry.

"For a man who has a certain gift of writing to say, 'I will make the most of it while the public likes my wares—as long as the market is open and I am able to supply it at a money profit—such profit being the sign of liking'—he should have a belief that his wares have nothing akin to the arsenic green in them, and also that his continuous supply is secure from a degradation in quality which the habit of consumption encouraged in the buyers may hinder them from marking their sense of by rejection; so that they complain, but pay, and read while they complain. Unless he has that belief, he is on a level with the manufacturer who gets rich by fancy-wares coloured with arsenic green. He really cares for nothing but his income. He carries on authorship on the principle of the gin-palace.

"And bad literature of the sort called amusing is spiritual gin.

"A writer capable of being popular can only escape this social culpability by first of all getting a profound sense that literature is good-for-nothing, if it is not admirably good: he must detest bad literature too heartily to be indifferent about producing it if only other people don't detest it. And if he has this sign of the divine afflatus within him, he must make up his mind that he must not pursue authorship as a vocation with a trading determination to get rich by it. It is in the highest sense lawful for him to get as good a price as he honourably can for the best work he is capable of; but not for him to force or hurry his production, or even do over again what has already been done, either by himself or others, so as to render his work no real contribution, for the sake of bringing up his income to the fancy pitch. An author who would keep a pure and noble conscience, and with that a developing instead of degenerating intellect and taste, must cast out of his aims the aim to be rich. And therefore he must keep his expenditure low—he must make for himself no dire necessity to earn sums in order to pay bills.

"In opposition to this, it is common to cite **Walter Scott**'s case, and cry, 'Would the world have got as much innocent (and therefore salutary) pleasure out of Scott, if he had not brought himself under the pressure of money-need? I think it would—and more, but since it is impossible to prove what would have been, I confine myself to replying that Scott was not justified in bringing himself into a position where severe consequences to others depended on his retaining or not retaining his mental competence. Still less is Scott to be taken as an example to be followed in this matter, even if it were admitted that money-need served to press at once the best and the most work out of him: any more than a great navigator who has brought his ship to port in spite of having taken a wrong and perilous route, is to be followed as to his route by navigators who are not yet ascertained to be great.

"But after the restraints and rules which must guide the acknowledged author, whose power of making a real contribution is ascertained, comes the consideration, how or on what principle are we to find a check for that troublesome disposition to authorship arising from the spread of what is called Education, which turns a growing rush of vanity and ambition into this current? The well-taught, an increasing number, are almost all able to write essays on given themes, which demand new periodicals to save them from lying in cold obstruction. The ill-taught—also an increasing number—read many books, seem to themselves able to write others surprisingly like what they read, and probably superior, since the variations are such as please their own fancy, and such as they would have recommended to their favourite authors; these ill-taught persons are perhaps idle and want to give themselves 'an object'; or they are short of money, and feel disinclined to get it by a commoner kind of work; or they find a facility in putting sentences together which gives them more than a suspicion that they have genius, which, if not very cordially believed in by private confidants, will be recognised by an impartial public; or finally, they observe that writing is sometimes well paid, and sometimes a ground of fame or distinction, and without any use of punctilious logic, they conclude to become writers themselves.

"As to these ill-taught persons, whatever medicines of a spiritual sort can be found good against mental emptiness and inflation—such medicines are needful for *them.* The contempt of the world for their productions only comes after their disease has wrought its worst effects. But what is to be said to the well-taught, who have such an alarming equality in their power of writing 'like a scholar and a gentleman'? Perhaps they, too, can only be cured by the medicine of higher ideals in social duty, and by a fuller representation to themselves of the processes by which the general culture is furthered or impeded."

2. Judgments on Authors

"In endeavouring to estimate a remarkable writer who aimed at more than temporary influence, we have first to consider what was his individual contribution to the spiritual wealth of mankind? Had he a new conception? Did he animate long-known but neglected truths with new vigour, and cast fresh light on their relation to other admitted truths? Did he impregnate any ideas with a fresh store of emotion, and in this way enlarge the area of moral sentiment? Did he by a wise emphasis here, and a wise disregard there, give a more useful or beautiful proportion to aims or motives? And even where his thinking was most mixed with the sort of mistake which is obvious to the majority, as well as that which can only be discerned by the instructed, or made manifest by the progress of things, has it that salt of a noble enthusiasm which should rebuke our critical discrimination if its correctness is inspired with a less admirable habit of feeling?

"This is not the common or easy course to take in estimating a modern writer. It requires considerable knowledge of what he has himself done, as well as of what others had done before him, or what they were doing contemporaneously; it requires deliberate reflection as to the degree in which our own prejudices may hinder us from appreciating the intellectual or moral bearing of what on a first view offends us. An easier course is to notice some salient mistakes, and take them as decisive of the writer's incompetence; or to find out that something apparently much the same as what he has said in some connection not clearly ascertained, had been said by somebody else, though without great effect, until this new effect of discrediting the other's originality had shown itself as an adequate final cause; or to pronounce from the point of view of individual taste that this writer for whom regard is claimed is repulsive, wearisome, not to be borne except by those dull persons who are of a different opinion.

"Elder writers who have passed into classics were doubtless treated in this easy way when they were still under the misfortune of being recent—nay, are still dismissed with the same rapidity of judgment by daring ignorance. But people who think that they have a reputation to lose in the matter of knowledge, have looked into cyclopædias and histories of philosophy or literature, and possessed themselves of the duly balanced epithets concerning the immortals. They are not left to their own unguided rashness, or their own unguided pusillanimity. And it is this sheeplike flock who have no direct impressions, no spontaneous delight, no genuine objection or self-confessed neutrality in relation to the writers become classic—it is these who are incapable of passing a genuine judgment on the living. Necessarily. The susceptibility they have kept active is a susceptibility to their own reputation for passing the right judgment, not the susceptibility to qualities in the object of judgment. Who learns to discriminate shades of colour by considering what is expected of him? The habit of expressing borrowed judgments stupifies [*sic*] the sensibilities, which are the only foundation of genuine judgments, just as the constant reading and retailing of results from other men's observations through the microscope, without ever looking through the lens oneself, is an instruction in some truths and some prejudices, but is no instruction in observant susceptibility; on the contrary, it breeds a habit of inward seeing according to verbal statement, which dulls the power of outward seeing according to visual evidence.

"On this subject, as on so many others, it is difficult to strike the balance between the educational needs of passivity or receptivity, and independent selection. We should learn nothing without the tendency to implicit acceptance; but there must clearly be a limit to such mental submission, else we should come to a stand-still. The human mind would be no better than a dried specimen, representing an unchangeable type. When the assimilation of new matter ceases, decay must begin. In a reasoned self-retraining deference there is as much energy as in rebellion; but among the less capable, one must admit that the superior energy is on the side of the rebels. And certainly a man who dares to say that he finds an eminent classic feeble here, extravagant there, and in general over-rated, may chance to give an opinion which has some genuine discrimination in it concerning a new work or a living thinker—an opinion such as can hardly ever be got from the reputed judge who is a correct echo of the most approved phrases concerning those who have been already canonised."

3. Story-telling

"What is the best way of telling a story? Since the standard must be the interest of the audience, there must be several or many good ways rather than one best. For we get interested in the stories life presents to us through divers orders and modes of presentation. Very commonly our first awakening to a desire of knowing a man's past or future comes from our seeing him as a stranger in some unusual or pathetic or humorous situation, or manifesting some remarkable characteristics. We make inquiries in consequence, or we become observant and attentive whenever opportunities of knowing more may happen to present themselves without our search. You have seen a refined face among the prisoners picking two in gaol; you afterwards see the same unforgetable [*sic*] face in a pulpit: he must be of dull fibre who would not care to know more about a life which showed such contrasts, though he might gather his knowledge in a fragmentary and unchronological way.

"Again, we have heard much, or at least something not quite common, about a man whom we have never seen, and hence we look round with curiosity when we are told that he is present; whatever he says or does before us is charged with a meaning due to our previous hearsay knowledge about him, gathered either from dialogue of which he was expressly and emphatically the subject, or from incidental remark, or from general report either in or out of print.

"These indirect ways of arriving at knowledge are always the most stirring even in relation to impersonal subjects. To see a chemical experiment gives an attractiveness to a definition of chemistry, and fills it with a significance which it would never have had without the pleasant shock of an unusual sequence such as the transformation of a solid into gas, and *vice versâ*. To see a word for the first time either as substantive or adjective in a connection where we care about knowing its complete meaning, is the way to vivify its meaning in our recollection. Curiosity becomes the more eager from the incompleteness of the first information. Moreover, it is in this way that memory works in its incidental revival of events: some salient experience appears in inward vision, and in consequence the antecedent facts are retraced from what is regarded as the beginning of the episode in which that experience made a more or less strikingly memorable part. 'Ah! I remember addressing the mob from the hustings at Westminster—you wouldn't have thought that I could ever have been in such a position. Well, how I came there was in this way——'; and then follows a retrospective narration.

"The modes of telling a story founded on these processes of outward and inward life derive their effectiveness from the superior mastery of images and pictures in grasping the attention—or, one might say with more fundamental accuracy, from the fact that our earliest, strongest impressions, our most intimate convictions, are simply images added to more or less of sensation. These are the primitive instruments of thought. Hence it is not surprising that early poetry took this way—telling a daring deed, a glorious achievement, without caring for what went before. The desire for orderly narration is a later, more reflective birth. The presence of the Jack in the box affects every child: it is the more reflective lad, the miniature philosopher, who wants to know how he got there.

"The only stories life presents to us in an orderly way are those of our autobiography, or the career of our companions from our childhood upwards, or perhaps of our own children. But it is a great art to make a connected strictly relevant narrative of such careers as we can recount from the beginning. In these cases the sequence of associations is almost sure to overmaster the sense of proportion. Such narratives *ab ovo* are summer's-day stories for happy loungers; not the cup of self-forgetting excitement to the busy who can snatch an hour of entertainment.

"But the simple opening of a story with a date and necessary account of places and people, passing on quietly towards the more rousing elements of narrative and dramatic presentation, without need of retrospect, has its advantages which have to be measured by the nature of the story. Spirited narrative, without more than a touch of diligence here and there, may be made eminently interesting, and is suited to the novelette. Examples of its charm are seen in the short tales in which the French have a mastery never reached by the English, who usually demand coarser flavours than are given by that delightful gaiety which is well described by **La Fontaine** as not anything that provokes fits of laughter, but a certain charm, an agreeable mode of handling which lends attractiveness to all subjects even the most serious. And it is this sort of gaiety which lays around the best French novelettes. But the opening chapters of the 'Vicar of Wakefield' are as fine as anything that can be done in this way.

"Why should a story not be told in the most irregular fashion that an author's idiosyncrasy may prompt, provided that he gives us what we can enjoy? The objections to **Sterne**'s wild way of telling 'Tristram Shandy' lie more solidly in the quality of the interrupting matter than in the fact of interruption. The dear public would do well to reflect that they are often bored from the want of flexibility in their own minds. They are like the topers of 'one liquor.' "

4. Historic Imagination

"The exercise of a veracious imagination in historical picturing seems to be capable of a development that might help the judgment greatly with regard to present and future events. By veraçious imagination, I mean the working out in detail of the various steps by which a political or social change was reached, using all extant evidence and supplying deficiencies by careful analogical creation. How triumphant opinions originally spread—how institutions arose— what were the conditions of great inventions, discoveries, or theoretic conceptions—what circumstances affecting individual lots are attendant on the decay of long-established systems—all these grand elements of history require the illumination of special imaginative treatment.

¶"But effective truth in this application of art requires freedom from the vulgar coercion of conventional plot, which is become hardly of higher influence on imaginative representation than a detailed 'order' for a picture sent by a rich grocer to an eminent painter—allotting a certain portion of the canvas to a rural scene, another to a fashionable group, with a request for a murder in the middle distance, and a little comedy to relieve it. A slight approximation to the veracious glimpses of history artistically presented, which I am indicating, but applied only to an incident of contemporary life, is 'Un paquet de lettres' by **Gustave Droz**. For want of such real, minute vision of how changes come about in the past, we fall into ridiculously inconsistent estimates of actual movements, condemning in the present what we belaud in the past, and pronouncing impossible processes that have been repeated again and again in the historical preparation of the very system under which we live. A false kind of idealisation dulls our perception of the meaning in words when they relate to past events which have had a glorious issue: for lack of comparison no warning image rises to check scorn of the very phrases which in other associations are consecrated.

"Utopian pictures help the reception of ideas as to constructive results, but hardly so much as a vivid presentation of how results have been actually brought about, especially in religious and social change. And there is the pathos, the heroism often accompanying the decay and final struggle of old systems, which has not had its share of tragic commemoration. What really took place in and around **Constantine** before, upon, and immediately after his declared conversion? Could a momentary flash be thrown on **Eusebius** in his sayings and doings as an ordinary man in bishop's garments? Or on **Julian** and **Libanius**? There has been abundant writing on such great turning-points, but not such as serves to instruct the imagination in true comparison. I want something different from the abstract treatment which belongs to grave history from a doctrinal point of view, and something different from the schemed picturesqueness of ordinary historical fiction. I want brief, severely conscientious reproductions, in their concrete incidents, of pregnant movements in the past."

5. Value in Originality

"The supremacy given in European cultures to the literatures of Greece and Rome has had an effect almost equal to that of a common religion in binding the Western nations together. It is foolish to be for ever complaining of the consequent uniformity, as if there were an endless power of originality in the human mind. Great and precious origination must always be comparatively rare, and can only exist on condition of a wide massive uniformity. When a multitude of men have learned to use the same language in speech and writing, then and then only can the great masters of language arise. For in what does their mastery consist? They use words which are already a familiar medium of understanding and sympathy in such a way as greatly to enlarge the understanding and sympathy. Originality of this order changes the wild grasses into world-feeding grain. Idiosyncrasies are pepper and spices of questionable aroma."

6. To the Prosaic All Things Are Prosaic

" 'Is the time we live in prosaic?' 'That depends: it must certainly be prosaic to one whose mind takes a prosaic stand in contemplating it.' 'But it is precisely the most poetic minds that most groan over the vulgarity of the present, its degenerate sensibility to beauty, eagerness for materialistic explanation, noisy triviality.' 'Perhaps they would have had the same complaint to make about the age of **Elizabeth**, if, living then, they had fixed their attention on its more sordid elements, or had been subject to the grating influence of its everyday meannesses, and had sought refuge from them in the contemplation of whatever suited their taste in a former age.' "

7. "Dear Religious Love"

"We get our knowledge of perfect Love by glimpses and in fragments chiefly—the rarest only among us knowing what it is to worship and caress, reverence and cherish, divide our bread and mingle our thoughts at one and the same time, under inspiration of the same object. Finest aromas will so often leave the fruits to which they are native and cling elsewhere, leaving the fruit empty of all but its coarser structure!"

8. We Make Our Own Precedents

"In the times of national mixture when modern Europe was, as one may say, a-brewing, it was open to a man who did not like to be judged by the Roman law, to choose which of certain other codes he would be tried by. So, in our times, they who openly adopt a higher rule than their neighbours, do thereby make act of choice as to the laws and precedents by which they shall be approved or condemned, and thus it may happen that we see a man morally pilloried for a very customary deed, and yet having no right to complain, inasmuch as in his foregoing deliberative course of life he had referred himself to the tribunal of those higher conceptions, before which such a deed is without question condemnable."

9. Birth of Tolerance

"Tolerance first comes through equality of struggle, as in the case of Arianism and Catholicism in the early times—**Valens**, Eastern and Arian, **Valentinian**, Western and Catholic, alike publishing edicts of tolerance; or it comes from a common need of relief from an oppressive predominance, as when **James II** published his Act of Tolerance towards non-Anglicans, being forced into liberality towards the Dissenters by the need to get it for the Catholics. Community of interest is the root of justice; community of suffering, the root of pity; community of joy, the root of love."

10. Felix qui non potuit

"Many feel themselves very confidently on safe ground when they say: It must be good for man to know the Truth. But it is clearly not good for a particular man to know some particular truth, as irremediable treachery in one whom he cherishes—better that he should die without knowing it.

"Of scientific truth, is it not conceivable that some facts as to the tendency of things affecting the final destination of the race might be more hurtful when they had entered into the human consciousness than they would have been if they had remained purely external in their activity?"

11. Divine Grace: A Real Emanation

"There is no such thing as an impotent or neutral deity, if the deity be really believed in, and contemplated either in prayer or meditation. Every object of thought reacts on the mind that conceives it, still more on that which habitually contemplates it. In this we may be said to solicit help from a generalisation or abstraction. **Wordsworth** had this truth in his consciousness when he wrote (in the Prelude):

> Not general truths, which are themselves a sort
> Of elements and agents, Under-powers
> Subordinate helpers of the living mind—

Not indeed precisely in the same relation, but with a meaning which involves that wider moral influence."

12. "A Fine Excess." Feeling is Energy

"One can hardly insist too much, in the present stage of thinking, on the efficacy of feeling in stimulating to ardent co-operation, quite apart from the conviction that such co-operation is needed for the achievement of the end in view. Just as hatred will vent itself in private curses no longer believed to have any potency, and joy, in private singing far out among the woods and fields, so sympathetic feeling can only be satisfied by joining in the action which expresses it, though the added 'Bravo!' the added push, the added penny, is no more than a grain of dust on a rolling mass. When students take the horses out of a political hero's carriage, and draw him home by the force of their own muscle, the struggle in each is simply to draw or push, without consideration whether his one arm be really needful to the effect. It is under the same inspiration that abundant help rushes towards the scene of a fire, rescuing imperilled lives, and labouring with generous rivalry in carrying buckets. So the old blind **King John** of Bohemia at the battle of Creçy [*sic*] begged his vassals to lead him into the fight that he might strike a good blow, though his own stroke, possibly fatal to himself, could not turn by a hair's-breadth, the imperious course of victory.

"The question, 'Of what use is it for me to work towards an end confessedly good?' comes from that sapless kind of reasoning which is falsely taken for a sign of supreme mental activity, but is really due to languor, or incapability of that mental grasp which makes objects strongly present, and to a lack of sympathetic emotion. In the 'Spanish Gypsy' Fedalma says—

> The grandest death! to die in vain—for Love
> Greater than sways the forces of the world.

Referring to the image of the disciples throwing themselves, consciously in vain, on the Roman spears. I really believe and mean this—not as a rule of general action, but as a possible grand instance of determining energy in human sympathy, which even in particular cases, where it has only a magnificent futility, is more adorable, or as we say divine, than unpitying force, or than a prudent calculation of results. Perhaps it is an implicit joy in the resources of our human nature which has stimulated admiration for acts of self-sacrifice which are vain as to their immediate end. **Marcus Curtius** was probably not imagined as concluding to himself that he and his horse would so fill up the gap as to make a smooth *terra firma*. The impulse and act made the heroism, not the correctness of adaptation. No doubt the passionate inspiration which prompts and sustains a course of self-sacrificing labour in the light of soberly estimate results gathers the highest title to our veneration, and makes the supreme heroism. But the generous leap of impulse if needed too to swell the flood of sympathy in us beholders, that we may not fall completely under the mastery of calculation, which in its turn may fail of ends for want of energy got from ardour. We have need to keep the sluices open for possible influxes of the rarer sort."

The Taxonomy

The Taxonomy

(all references are to the Fiction: *see* Index to this Volume for references to the Nonfiction)

Index I

Characters by Surname

Title figures are highlighted in SOLID CAPS—and, for novellas, short stories and sketches, SOLID CAPS—and **bold**. Other Principals are in SOLID CAPS and SOLID CAPS. "Also mentioned" are in smaller type. *Italics* indicate a figure in internal fiction, e. g., a character in a book referred to. Though limited to fictional figures in most cases, this Index includes historical figures in *Romola* given roles in the intricate plot. To locate a figure in a work, go to the chapter on that work and follow the alphabetical arrangement. All references to the Nonfiction are in the Indexes at the back of this volume.

Arrowpoint, Admiral; a forebear DD
Arrowpoint, Mr; completely conventional: married a fortune DD
—Mrs; even more conventional; ridiculous dresser; inherited a fortune DD
—Catherine; very intelligent: to be the wife of Klesmer DD
Ascoli, Cecco d'; reputed to have burned for excessive brains R
Askern, Mr; surgeon who attended Tom Tulliver's foot MF
Assher, the late baronet, particular about his shirts GL
—Lady; old flame of Sir Christopher Cheverel GL
—Beatrice; death took her fiancé GL
Astorga, father of good singing DD
Avis, who took too much sugar TS 13

B

Bacon, Miss; a beauty AB
Badgers, the; of Hilbury and a good family FH
Bagster, Mr; Parliamentary candidate MM
Baird, Mr; who preached in a little church SF
Baker, Will; a bull terrier who had strayed AB
Baldwin, tax-gatherer MM
Bale (or Beale), Kester; an old farmer AB
Ballard, Mrs; schoolmistress MM
Bambridge, a horse-dealer MM
Banks, the bailiff for Sir Hugo Mallinger DD
—Mrs; his wife DD
Banks, the bailiff at Transome Court FH
Bantam, Sir Hong Kong; slow and insignificant TS 11
Barabbas, a disreputable life TS 16
BARDI, BARDO de'; blind scholar with a devoted daughter R
—Bernardino (Dino); became Fra Luca R
—ROMOLA di; Florentine aristocrat, wife, and survivor R
BARTON, REV. AMOS, fortunes blighted by human failings, misfortune **SF**
—AMELIA (MILLY); well-beloved wife: her death was a major tragedy SF
—Chubby, a small sister put upon by Dickey SF
—Dickey (Richard), the second son, a boisterous boy of five; an engineer SF
—Patty, the eldest; sweet and grave-faced, already taking on duties SF
—Sophy, asked to carry books steadily SF
—Walter, the baby (one year) SF
Bass, Trapping; a poacher MM
Bates, the head gardener at Cheveral Manor GL
Batt & Cowley, a law firm FH
Bazley, agent for Lord Brackenshaw DD
Beale, Molly; a rough old virago JR
Beaton, Margaret; who married a Tulliver and bore Mr Tulliver MF
Beaucaire, Seneschal de; a favorite of the French king R
Beck, Mrs; lodging-house keeper MM
BEDE, Thias; carpenter gone to the dogs of drink AB
—Lisbeth, his wife; dotes on her eldest AB
—ADAM, carpenter and lover AB
—DINAH (*née* Morris), the preacher no longer preaches AB
—Addy, sturdy two-year-old AB
—Lisbeth, just over four AB
—Seth, his brother, loyal and devoted despite his unrequited love AB

Beevor, Captain; who dragged his wife around MM
—Mrs; step-daughter of Lord Grinsell MM
Bellamy, butler to Sir Christopher Cheverel GL
—Mrs; housekeeper bringing comfort GL
Benevieni, Girolamo [H]; mystical poet in Florence R
—Antonio; a great master of the chirugic art R
Benghi, Ser; figure in a story R
Best, Mrs; housekeeper for the Donnithornes AB
Bethell, a driver employed by Squire Donnithorne AB
Bincome, who sold his farm on the Ripple to Pivart MF
Blakesley, Justice; local magistrate MM
Blarney, Lord; allegedly known to the Countess SF
Blenny, who once lived at Offendene DD
Blethers, Viscount; a landlord GL
Blick, Dr; predecessor to Mr Irwine AB
Blick, Dr; of Flitton SM
Blough, Lord; his kitchen much admired DD
Bodkin, a bank clerk fired for being a Dissenter FH
Bombus, a bouncing, aggressive author TS 14
Bond, a churchwarden with Mr Hackit SF GL
—Tommy, graduated into corduroys and brass buttons GL
Bott, a tenant with good brick-making clay on his land MM
Bovis, conscious of the question of sugar TS 13
—Mrs; strongly in favour of sugar TS 13
Bowyer, a singer of comic songs MM
Brackenshaw, Lord; middle-aged peer DD
—Lady; with two girls and a boy DD
—Beatrice, Lady; not old enough to hunt DD
—Maria, Lady; not old enough to hunt DD
Bradwell, a farmer needing Adam Bede's help AB
Brady, a dealer in horse-tack JR
Brand, the Shepperton doctor obnoxious to Mr Pilgrim SF
Brecon, with a double first DD
Brent, head-gardener FH
Bretton, Mrs; the late: her large house would suit Rosamond MM
Brewitt, blacksmith DD
Brick, Mrs; wide-awake old woman very fond of snuff SF
Bridmain, Mr; retired bachelor half-brother studied the art of conversation SF
Briggs, a groom at Freshitt MM
Brimstone, brickmaker who got religion AB
Brincey, Michael (otherwise Mike Brindle); a witness in the Holt trial FH
Brindle, Mike (sobriquet for Michael Brincey), a trial witness FH
Brinley, Mrs; the carpenter's wife JR
Britton, Luke, sr; a poor and careless farmer AB
—Luke, his son; attracted by Hetty Sorrel AB
BROOKE, Arthur, uncle and easygoing guardian to two girls MM
—DOROTHEA (DODO); dreamy, idealistic sister MM
—CELIA (KITTY); practical, sensible younger sister MM
Brooks, Mr; an old man in need of a comforter GL
Brumby, Dick; childhood friend of Bob Jakin's MF
Brumley, litigant represented by John Waken MF

Bryce, a horseman interested in the Cass horse SM
Buchan, tavern philosopher and a saddler DD
Bucks, Mrs; with a cork leg; a customer for Bob Jakin MF
Budd, Mr; small scandalous bachelor JR
Bugle, lady's maid at Offendene DD
BULSTRODE, NICHOLAS; banker with a disgrace to hide MM
—HARRIET (*née* Vincy); loyal to the death MM
—Ellen; a daughter treated by Lydgate MM
—Kate; a little young for marriage MM
Bult, strong party man; eligible for Catherine Árrowpoint's hand DD
Bunch, to be hanged as a sheep-stealer MM
Bunney, Master; gardener MM
Burchiello, formerly a barber in Florence R
Burge, Jonathan; carpenter and builder in Hayslope AB
—Mary, his daughter; interested in Adam Bede AB
Butterworth, Elias Baptist; a minor prophet of vegetarianism MP
Button, Betty; a Dissenting sympathizer FH
Butts, Sally; who had to sell her mangle JR
Butzkoff, German scientist TS 3
Buzzard, who might have written something TS 11
Bycliffe, Maurice Christian; the heir to the true Transome interests FH
—Mrs Annette (*née* LeDru), separated from him and impoverished FH
—Esther, a baby; raised by her mother and the Rev. Lyon FH
Bygate, lawyer AB
Byles, Luke; a reader prejudiced against Evangelicals JR
Byles, the butcher MM

C

Cachalot, M.; scientist TS 3
Cadwallader, Rev. Humphrey MM
—Elinor (*née* De Bracy) MM
—the youngest daughter, age 5 MM
Calcondila, Demetrio [H]; scholar of Greek civilization, now in Milan R
Calderino (Domizio Calderini) [H]; Florentine scholar R
Calibut, former partner in a warehouse with Nolan FH
Callum, clerk to Caleb Garth MM
CALVO, BALDASSARRE; vengeful father of Tito Melema R
Cambini, Andrea; with rumours about convicted Mediceans R
Caparra, Niccolò; blacksmith R
Capponi, Piero [H]; strong Florentine Republican R
Carp, who did not write enhusiastically about Casaubon's work MM
Carpe, Rev; the pluralistic Vicar of Shepperton SF
Carr; the late; incompetent his last three years MF
Carrol, Mr Irwine's butler AB
Carter, Mrs; cook at Tipton Grange MM
CASAUBON, REV. EDWARD; scholar on a hopeless project MM
—DOROTHEA (*née* BROOKE), supportive, critical, disillusioned MM
Cass, Squire; a hard, insensitive father: the greatest man in Raveloe SM
—Bob; the youngest son SM
—Dunstan (Dunsey); younger brother and a profligate SM

—Godfrey; son and heir, who fails to acknowledge his daughter SM
—Molly (Farren), his unacknowledged wife; drunken mother of Eppie SM
—Eppie (Hepzibah), unacknowledged infant SM
—Nancy (*née* Lammeter), his elegant, childless wife SM
—other, younger sons SM
Casson, a landlord of extraordinary adiposity AB
Catulus, a younger scientist who attacks Merman TS 3
Ceccone, Ser [H]; notary and spy R
Cei, Francesco [H]; Florentine poet R
Cennini, Piero; scholar in Florence R
—Bernardo; innovative printer R
—Domenico, goldsmith R
Chaloner, Mrs; the rector's wife BJ
Charisi, Daniel; profoundly observant Jew DD
—Mrs; of Portuguese Jewish background DD
—Leonora; who rejected Judaism for an opera career; married a prince DD
Cherry, Mrs; lady's maid FH
Chesher, remembered for radical cures MM
Chester, working boy at the Donnithorne estate AB
CHETTAM, Lady; dowager conscious of health issues MM
—Sir James; first wooed Dorothea, then made a practical choice MM
—CELIA; happy wife and ecstatic mother; Dorothea's sister MM
—baby Arthur, a natural cynosure MM
Cheverel, Sir Anthony; a distinguished forebear GL
—Lady, hanging opposite him GL
—Sir Christopher; Bart. GL
—Henrietta, Lady; his wife GL
Chevreuil, who came over with the Conqueror GL
Chichely, Mr; middle-aged bachelor MM
Chowne, a neighbouring farmer AB
—Mrs; not held in high opinion by Mrs Poyser AB
Choyce, a tenant on the Donnithorne estate AB
Christian, Maurice (an alias: he is Henry Scaddon); high-level manservantFH
Chubb, William; a remarkable publican FH
Cioni, Ser [H]; Florentine notary R
Clement, Sir James; a poor baronet FH
Clemmens, a Brassing solicitor who drew a Featherstone will MM
Cleve, Mrs; her trustee let a shop BJ
Cleves, Rev. Martin; sympathetically presented true Christian gentleman SF
Cliff, former tailor; a horseman SM
—Cliff son, who died SM
Clint, Emily; she married John Waken and bore Philip MF
Clintock, Rev.; the archdeacon DD
—the younger; a scholar and an admirer of womankind DD
Clintup, diffident but distinguished nurseryman MM
Clout, Colin; narrator and idealist (an eloquent voice of the author) MP
Cohen, Mrs: don't talk about her daughter DD
—Ezra; self-satisfied shopman and money-lender DD
—Addy, his wife; brightly dressed young woman DD
—Adelaide Rebekah; little girl who charms Deronda DD
—Eugenie Esther, black-eyed toddler DD

—Jacob Alexander, already a businessman at six	DD
Coleman, whose house needed a doctor	MM
Cook, Phib; who left her evening washtub	JR
Cooper, Timothy; labourer with his savings in a stocking	MM
Corsini, Luca [H]; Florentine lawyer	R
Corvus, lately flattered by Morcas	TS 8
Cosimo, Piero di [H]; Florentine artist	R
Coulter, Ann; she had an idiot child	SM
Cowley, law partner with Batt	FH
Cox, lawyer for Squire Cass	SM
Crabbe, the glazier	MM
Crabtree, a Hayslope farmer	AB
Crackenthorp, Mr; rector	SM
—Mrs; a small blinking woman	SM
Cragstone, Lady; a gambler	DD
Craig, gardener at the Chase	AB
Crake, Sir James; Master of the Harriers	MF
Cramp, Mrs; charwoman	SF
Cranage, Chad; the blacksmith	AB
—Ben ('Wiry Ben'); a dancer	AB
—Bessy, his daughter; flamboyant	AB
Cranch, Martha (*née* Featherstone); soft speaker, but hopeful	MM
—Tom, her son; arrived to watch his uncle	MM
Crane, outdoor servant at Offendene	DD
Crespi, an artist	TS 9
Crewe, Mr; a curate	JR
—Mrs; who carried spare dinners to the sick and hungry	JR
Crichley, a portraitist	MM
Crickley, the rector who has the living Mr Gilfil will inherit	GL
Croly, Mrs; a celebrated beauty	MM
Crombeck, Lord; in the market for a good horse	SM
Cronaca, oraclar bystander	R
Croop, tavern philosopher and a shoemaker	DD
Crow, the high constable of Treby	FH
Crowder, tenant farmer behind in his rent	FH
—his brother	FH
Crowe, the widow	NE 1
Crowse, unimpressive cleric	MM
Crypt, Zephaniah; a testator	BJ
Cuff, Jacob; an ornament of the pot-house	FH
Cushats, the; invited to Grandcourt	DD
Cuttler, Miss; who inherited a fortune and married Arrowpoint	DD
Czerlaski, Countess Caroline (formerly Bridmain); beautiful, experienced	SF
—Count, the late; had had wonderful escapes and gave dancing lessons	SF

D

Dacey, Lord; with a lawsuit AB
—Lady; fretted over the lawsuit AB
—son, who lost badly to the Prince of Wales AB
Dagge, Joel; blacksmith's son DD
—Sally, who twice dislocated her shoulder DD
Dagley, tumble-down farmer MM
—Mrs; overworked; no pleasure in life MM
—Jacob, who killed a leveret MM
Dalton, a coachman AB
Dane, William; Dissenter, hypocrite, thief and traitor SM
Darleigh, Squire; had the Dodson sisters to dances in their youth MF
Davilow, Captain; a bad actor and good riddance DD
—Fanny; mother of Gwendolen (by first marriage), Mrs Gascoigne's sister DD
—Alice, daughter of the second marriage DD
—Bertha, her sister DD
—Fanny, another sister DD
—Isabel, the youngest; alarming memory and inconvenient DD
Dawes, driver for Robert Dempster JR
DEANE, MR; father of the family MF
—Susan, mother of the family (*née* Dodson) MF
—LUCY, daughter; cousin of Maggie and Tom Tulliver MF
Debarry, Sir Maximus, Bart.; staunch Tory FH
—Lady; mountain of satin and lace FH
—Harriet, elder daughter whose forte was general knowledge FH
—Selina, radiant girl of twenty FH
—Rev. Augustus; his brother, the old-fashioned aristocratic clergyman FH
—Lady Mary, his wife FH
—Philip, their scrupulous son FH
De Bracy, the family of Mrs Cadwallader MM
De Coursy; hero of a book by Miss Pratt JR
DEMPSTER, Mamsey, destructive mother-in-law JR
—ROBERT; a lawyer, despicable, abusive husband and bully JR
—**JANET**; troubled wife turned to drink JR
Denner, maiden name of Mrs Transome's trusted retainer Mrs Hickes FH
Dent, a game-keeper AB
DERONDA, DANIEL; raised an English gentleman, chooses to be a Jew DD
Dibbitts, an apothecary MM
Dibbs, elector with cautious views FH
Dickison, landlord at the Marquis of Granby MF
Dill, a barber MM
Dingall, a grocer AB
—Mrs; a sensible woman AB
Dix, a miller on the same stream with the Dorlcote Mill MF
DODSONS, the; a highly respectable family MF
—daughters married to a Deane, a Glegg, a Pullet, and a Tulliver MF
—a brother who had a mole, and died MF
—the late father of the four sisters MF
Dolby, architect for the Shepperton church SF
Dollop, Mrs; landlady at the Tankard MM

DONNITHORNE, Squire	AB
—Lydia, his sister	AB
—CAPTAIN ARTHUR, his son; gives in to temptation; tragedy follows	AB
Dover, a silversmith	MM
Dovizi, Bernardo of Bibbiena [H]; witty participant in politics	R
—Piero, Ser [H]; his brother less favorably regarded	T
Dow, the hereditary printer in Treby	FH
Dowlas, a farrier	SM
Downes, Bill; excellent stone-sawyer	AB
Downes, Kit; lives in a small house with a large family	MM
D'Oyley, a cleric formerly at Treddleston	AB
Dredge, debater on Reform	FH
Drumlow, a cleric who liked a drop on a cold morning	SM
Dugong, German scientist	TS 3
Duke, Rev. Archibald; dyspeptic and evangelical; heavy meat breakfasts	SF
Dummilow, Job; got a warm coat as a present	AB
Duncan, Archie; he blurted out the truth to Sarah Dunkirk	MM
Dunkirk, rich pawnbroker, not inquisitive as to source of goods he bought	MM
—Mrs; simple, credulous; once a widow a prey to Bulstrode	MM
—Sarah, daughter who ran away on principle; went on the stage	MM
—a son who died	MM
Dunn, a draper	JR
—Mary, his daughter	JR
Durfeys; the family who held the entailed Transome estate	FH
Dymock, a dark curate	DD
Dymock and Halliwell, lawyers for Harold Transome	FH
E	
Ely, Mr; charistmatic cleric good at presiding at dinner	SF
Euphorion, a comfortable plagiarist	TS 11
F	
Farebrother, Mrs; a distinguished old lady	MM
—Henrietta Noble, a sister	MM
—Rev. Camden, her son; impecunious, skilled at games, in love	MM
—Winifred, his sister	MM
Farquhar, Mr; the secondary squire of the parish	SF
—Mrs; fond of Milly Barton	SF
—Miss Arabella, observant of defects in speech	SF
—Miss Julia; both sisters snobbish and critical	SF
Farren, Molly; secretly married to Godfrey Cass; a mother	SM
Father Clement, protagonist in a book for the new library	JR
Faulkner, who bought a horse from Bambridge	MM
FAUX, Jonathan; a father with seven sons	BJ
—Mrs; a saving and forgiving mother	BJ
—DAVID; diligent confectioner, unscrupulous son	BJ
—**JACOB**; an idiot brother who is very inconvenient	BJ
—Jonathan, the eldest brother	BJ
Fawkes, Bessie; she died leaving children	SM
Fawks, Bill; gave Bob Jakin a terrier instead of drowning it	MF
Featherstone, Peter; rich and rude	MM
—Jane, a sister, married name Waule	MM
—Jonah, a brother, not successful	MM

—Martha, a sister; married name Cranch MM
—Rigg; heretofore unacknowledged son (Rigg his former surname) MM
—Solomon, a successful brother MM
Felix, Minutius; a Such acquaintance TS 1
Fellowes, Mr; rector, magistrate, successful manipulator always in a feud SF
Fenn, who bequeathed to his daughter his unfortunate looks DD
—Juliet; bad profile but fine archer DD
Ferravecchi, Bratti; street vendor in Florence R
Ficino, Marsilio [H]; Platonic philosopher R
Filmore, a nonentity LV
—Mrs; in silk and cashmere LV
Filmore, surgeon's assistant FH
Filmore, of Corpus Christi College FH
Firniss, Miss; schoolmistress at Laceham MF
Fitchett, formerly a footman, now a field-hand SF
Mrs Fitchett, the lodge-keeper's wife MM
Fitzadams, the; of the Worcestershire branch DD
Flavell, a Methodist preacher MM
Fletcher, a lady's maid LV
Fletcher, a law-clerk MM
Fletcher, lessee of collieries DD
Fodge, Poll (Mary Higgins); a rebellious occupant of the workhouse SF
—son with a sniffle SF
Ford, Hiram; a waggoner MM
Ford, a Staffordshire patriarch GL
Fothergill, Miss; she became Mrs Prettyman BJ
—sister who married a London mercer BJ
Fortinbras, Lord; Calibut's son-in-law FH
Fowler, on an outlining farm; having trouble with the rent SM
Franco, Matteo [H]; sceptic and poet R
Fraser, tutor and secretary to Sir Hugo Mallinger DD
Freely, a sallow swain for Penelope Palfrey BJ
Freke, Rev.; a brick-and-mortar incumbent MM
French, Mrs; housekeeper to Sir Hugo Mallinger DD
Fripp, Dame; a mourner for Mr Gilfil GL
Fugleman, who pontificates on the 'Iliad' TS 5
Fulke, in the Colonial Office MM
Fullilove, timber merchant in Grimworth BJ
—Miss: timber-merchant's daughter BJ
Furley, who held the mortgage on the Dorlcote Mill property MF
Furness, Mr; poetical curate plucked at Cambridge SF

G

Gabbadeo, Mastre; doctor R
Gaddi, Francesco [H]; distrusted his own French R
Gadsby, yeomanry captain DD
—Mrs; once a kitchen maid and still spoke like one DD
Gambit, Mr; a medical practitioner not of the highest order MM
Ganymede, perennial youth TS 12
—wife considerably older than he TS 12
Gardner, Maria; tall girl attentive to her hair JR
Garnett and his son: an example for Mr Tulliver in his plans for Tom MF

Garratt, a lady's maid at Freshitt MM
Garstin, Peter; candidate for Parliament FH
GARTH, CALEB; utterly trustworthy innocent MM
—Mrs Susan; staunch, intelligent, educated wife and mother MM
—Alfred, whose tuition had been saved for MM
—Ben; energetic young male with a bow and arrow MM
—Christy, who likes books better than business MM
—Jim, five years away from getting into business MM
—Letty, not careful with her elbows MM
—MARY, who holds out for a husband who is a man MM
GASCOIGNE, HENRY; kind, wise uncle and clergyman, good father DD
—Nancy, his wife; sister of Fanny Davilow DD
—Anna, his daughter; devoted partisan of her brother DD
—Edwy, a daughter DD
—Lotta, who went blackberrying DD
—Rex; son who falls into desperate unrequited love DD
—Warham, studying for India with a Wanchester 'coach' DD
Gaskin, provincial corn-dealer DD
Gate, Mrs; at the large carding-mill BJ
Gawaine a friend of Arthur Donnithorne's AB
Gawcome, lessee of collieries DD
Gedge, landlord of the Royal Oak AB
Gell, a new partner in Guest & Co. MF
Gibbs, Miss Janet; single lady of fifty, liberal with the cream at tea SF
Gibbs, John; waggoner hired by Mr Tulliver; he died MF
Gibbs, valet on a yacht DD
Gibson, a schoolmate who fought Tom Tulliver to make him share MF
Gideon, tavern philosopher and optical instrument-maker DD
Giles, unsuccessful candidate MM
GILFIL, MR; clergyman with a romance in his past SF GL
—MRS. Caterina (Tina), *née* Sarti GL
Gills, a stone-cutter FH
Glasher, Colonel; an Irish officer who would not grant a divorce DD
—Lydia; mistress and never-to-be wife of Grandcourt DD
—son by the Colonel; abandoned by his mother at three, dead at five DD
—Henleigh, her son; to be the heir; Grandcourt's son DD
—three daughters, children of Grandcourt DD
GLEGG, MR; retired wool-stapler MF
—JANE, his wife (*née* Dodson); a formidable personality MF
Goby, Mrs; had money in trust before her marriage MM
Godwin, a doctor AB
Goffe, a tenant farmer at Rabbit's End FH
Gogoffs, the; invited to the Grandcourts DD
Goodrich, the drawing-master MF
Goodwin, tavern philosopher and wood-inlayer DD
Gore, a sly lawyer MF
Gottlib, a banker FH
Grainger, a patient MM
Grampian, Lord; close to Bishop Mompert DD
Grampus, scientist TS 3
Grampus, a colonial governor MM
Granby, the host of a dinner-party SF

GRANDCOURT, HENLEIGH MALLINGER; cruel, calculating husband DD
—GWENDOLEN, surprised and unhappy wife DD
GRANT, Bertha; the admired prospective wife of two brothers LV
Grapnell & Co., who failed for a million DD
Grattan lad, who shot his mother in an accident; rescued by Mr Kenn MF
Graves, Miss; governess DD
Gray, Mrs; milliner to Mrs Pullet MF
Griffin, lady's maid to Lady Assher GL
Griffins, the; threatened with no more coals if they audited a preacher MM
Grinsell, Lord; step-father of Mrs Beevor MM
—his second wife, Mrs Teveroy MM
Gripp & Co., Middlemarch publishers MM
Gruby, a shopkeepeer JR
Guccio, one of a group of gossipers R
Guest senior; wealthy businessman MF
—Stephen, son; engaged to Lucy Deane but loves Maggie Tulliver MF
—the Misses Guest, his sisters MF
Gunn, the Misses; they showed their shoulders fashionably SM

H

Hackbutt, a rich tanner of fluent speech MM
—Mrs; who had to receive Mrs Bulstrode at an awkward time MM
—Fanny, who took lessons with Susan Garth MM
Hackit, a shrewd, substantial man; his advice on crops is always good SF GL
—Mrs; sharp-tongued and epigrammatic; fond of Dickey Barton SF GL
Halliwell, law partner with Dymock FH
Halm-Eberstein, Prince DD
—Princess Leonora; mother of Deronda DD
—five children by the Prince DD
Hanmer, an engineer MM
Hardy, Jim; coal-carrier JR
Hardy, Justice AB
Harfager, Clara; with a portion MM
HARLETH, the late father; of high family DD
—GWENDOLEN; a spoiled beauty DD
—Lady Molly, a forebear DD
Hart, Doctor; not surprised at Captain Wybrow's sudden decease GL
Hartopp, Mrs Bessie; distraught at losing her home GL
Hautboy, who is pleased to consider Chaucer a great poet TS 5
Hawkins, Brother; with a high tenor FH
Hawkins, a factory manager for Harold Transome FH
Hawley, Frank; lawyer and town-clerk MM
—Arabella, who went into a consumption MM
—his son, a good hand with the cue MM
Haxey, Job; weaver in St Ogg's MF
Haynes, who wanted to rent Offendene DD
Heron, Rev. Arthur; keeping a brood together GL
—Oswald (Ozzy); keeps a menagerie GL
Herons, the; of Fenshore and a good family FH
Hibbert, Miss; who sang at the Asshers' GL
Hickes, a neat machine of a butler FH
—Mrs (*née* Denner); faithful retainer of Mrs Transome FH

Hicks, coarse but knowledgeable medical man	MM
Higgins, Mrs; an elderly widow "well left"	GL
Hinze, obsequious conversationalist	TS 5
Holdsworth, Michael; he ploughed on a Sunday	AB
Hollis, invited to the Grandcourts'	DD
—Lady Flora; a lively house-guest	DD
HOLT, the late purveyor of nostrums; originally a weaver	FH
—Mrs Mary; aggrieved at her son	FH
—FELIX; social activist who falls in love	FH
Hood, Jim; the bassoon-man	SF
Hoopoe, a scholar at John's	TS 11
Hopkins, a meek-mannered draper	MM
Horner, Rev. Mr; given to tippling and quarrelling with his wife	JR
Horrock, veterinarian	MM
Hutchins, manservant to Grandcourt	DD
Hyndmarsh, grocer of St Ogg's	MF
I	
IRWINE, Mrs; elegant lady and fond mother	AB
—REV. ADOLPHUS; kind-hearted rector and son	AB
—Anne, his invalid sister	AB
—Kate, a sister caring for Anne	AB
J	
Jacobs, local schoolmaster	MF
Jacobson, believed to be Jewish and thought unpleasant	TS 18
Jakin, Mrs; dreadfully fat	MF
—Bob, her son; boyhood friend of Tom Tulliver's	MF
—Prissy, his wife	MF
—Maggie, two months' old baby	MF
Jarrett, a village carpenter	DD
Jay, Betty; with a good sense of smell	SM
Jebb, Bishop; whose memoirs Mr Ely is reading	SF
Jeffries, groom and driver at Offendene; departed	DD
Jenning, who wrote a poem on croquet	DD
Jennngs, Mrs; town-bred and ignorant of mourning customs	GL
JERMYN, MATTHEW; lawyer, manipulator, embezzler	FH
—eldest daughter, having a birthday	FH
—Louisa, his daughter	FH
Jerome, Thomas; parishioner in good standing	JR
—Mrs Susan, about sixty	JR
—Lizzie, a grandchild	JR
Jesson, a shopkeeper	JR
Jetsome, put in charge of the Dorlcote Mill, but drank	MF
Jodson, who died, leaving a house available	DD
Johns, Mr; mentor to Rev. Barton	SF
Johns, preaching with a solemn twang at a Baptist chapel in the lowest suburbs	TS 9
Johnson, John; election manipulator	FH
Johnson, Mr Brooke's gamekeeper	MM
Jonas, a good-natured dyer	MM
Jortin, who owns a mare	SM

Joyce, a farmer of superior information FH
K
Kalonymos, Joseph; the Jewish conscience of the Alcharisis DD
—sons, all successful and none of them wanderers DD
Keating, a horseman SM
Keck, manager of the 'Trumpet,' a newspaper MM
Kell, Mrs; housekeeper at the Grange MM
Kemp, Brother; a bass voice FH
Kench, the constable SM
Kenn, Dr; kindhearted clergyman MF
—Mrs, his wife, in poor health MF
—baby, age three MF
Kibble, purveyor of silverware MM
Kimble, Mr; the village doctor SM
—Mrs, who is sister to Squire Cass SM
Klesmer, Julius; great musician who married Catherine Arrowpoint DD
Knott, Daniel; coachman GL
—Mrs Dorcas, his wife GL
—Baby, apathetic at the moment GL
—Bessie, age three GL
—Daniel the younger, age nine GL
Knowles, a wagon-driver AB
L
Labron, a political agent FH
Ladbrook, Mrs; attending a dancing party SM
—Miss; more conservative than the Gunn sisters in fashion SM
LADISLAW, Julia; a grandmother on the father's side MM
—her son, and Will's father; married Sarah Dunkirk MM
—WILL; a cousin of Mr Casaubon, lover of Dorothea MM
Lakin family, in deep distress JR
Lamb, Jonathan; old parish clerk JR
Lamb, Leonard; tutor to Raffles MM
Lambert, a Dissenter FH
Lammeter, senior; from the north SM
— Mr; soberest and best man in the countryside SM
—Mrs; *née* Osgood SM
—Nancy; the belle of the town, and Godfrey Cass's love SM
—Priscilla, her self-subordinating sister SM
Landino, Cristoforo [H]; scholar R
Landor, old Mr; the wealthy banker JR
—Benjamin; a meagre business as a lawyer SF JR
—Mrs; the attorney's wife SF
—Ben Landor JR
—Eustace JR
—Miss; the belle of Milby JR
Langen, Baron; with Gwendolen under protection DD
—Baroness; she plays a sober game DD
Laniger, with a temper but no repartee TS 8
LAPIDOTH, thief, mendicant, humiliated embarrassment to his children DD
—Sara, a long-suffering wife who died bereft of her daughter DD

—EZRA (MORDECAI); Jewish idealist and dreamer DD
—MIRAH, his sister; to be the wife of Daniel Deronda DD
Larcher, Edwin; an eminent carrier MM
—Mrs; whose children got the measles MM
—Caius; young man about town MM
LATIMER, fond, bereaved father LV
—Alfred, handsome, athletic heir; he dies LV
—unnamed son, parapsychologically gifted; he sees his own death LV
—Bertha (*née* Grant); a marriage marred by cordial hatred LV
Lawe, Lady; mother DD
—Miss; handsome but eclipsed by Gwendolen DD
Ledru, Annette; the late wife of Rev. Rufus Lyon; mother of Esther FH
Leek, a farmer near Offendene DD
Lemon, Mrs; schoolmistress MM
Lenoni, Dominic; courier and factotum to Harold Transome FH
Lentulus, surprised by his own originality TS 4
Leo, Joseph; Viennese composer DD
Leonardi, Camillo [H]; discreet medical practitioner R
Letherall, phrenologist who examined Latimer LV
Leyburn, Miss; daughter of the Member for the County; a prospect for Stephen Guest MF
Limp, a meditative shoemaker MM
Lingon, Rev. John (Parson Jack); of Little Treby, Mrs Transome's brother FH
—Lady Fanny; of good family, now very careful about money FH
—Lady Sara, sister-in-law, whose husband went jealously mad FH
Linnet, Mrs; an assiduous reader of religious works JR
—Miss Mary; an old maid JR
—Rebecca, her sister; not nearly so well-regarded JR
Linter, Lady Sarah; a horseback rider GL
Lippus, bleary-eyed TS 1
Liret, Monsieur; Vaulois clergyman and tutor to the Brooke sisters MM
Loligo, scientist TS 3
Lovegood, steward to Sr James Chettam MM
Lowme, an elderly Lothario JR
—Mrs; who is confined to her room JR
—Bob, with beautiful whiskers JR
—the Misses; who will be out JR
Luca Antonio, a relative of Monna Brigida R
Luff, a Grimworth draper BJ
Lukyns, the; guests at the Jermyns' for dinner FH
—Miss; who drove out in a gig FH
Lundy, Bob; a butcher SM
Lunn, known only as Sally's father BJ
—Sally; old flame of the confectioner's BJ
Lush, Thomas Cranmer; factotum and dependant on Grandcourt DD
LYDGATE, TERTIUS; doctor with high dreams MM
—ROSAMOND (*née* VINCY); very beautiful and very willful MM
—Godwin, Sir, Bart.; an uncle MM
—Captain, the son; whose riding with Rosamond led to a miscarriage MM
—Charles, his brother; a respectable cleric MM
—Mengan, Mrs; daughter of the baronet MM

LYON, REV. RUFUS; did not tell his daughter everything for a long time FH
—Mrs Annette (*née* Ledru, first married name Bycliffe)
—ESTHER; unexpectedly an heiress: she is her daughter, not his FH

M

MACARTHY, wanderer dies leaving collection of MSS for the narrator NE 1
Macchiavelli [*sic*], Niccolò de' [H]; political observer in Florence R
Macey, clerk of the parish SM
—Solomon; first fiddler in the countryside SM
—grandfather, who made livery SM
Mackworth, part of the gambling scene at Leubronn DD
MacWheeble, Baillie; a toadying snob in a study of snubbing NE 5
Madeley, Dr; physician from Rotherby SF JR
Mainwaring, Fred Vincy's schoolmate MM
Makepiece, an election agent FH
Malam, Justice SM
Malingre, Huges le; ancestor DD
Mallinger, Sir Francis; a forebear who made an ill-advised settlement DD
Mallinger, Henleigh; a forebear who married Miss Grandcourt DD
MALLINGER, SIR HUGO; foster father to Deronda; Grandcourt's uncle DD
—Lady Louisa (*née* Raymond); humiliated to have had no sons DD
—Lady Annabel, who had singing lessons with Mirah DD
—Lady Theresa, in need of dentistry DD
Manetti, Sibilla; at whose house Tessa found refuge R
Mantrap, Sir Gavial; fraudulent financier TS 16
Markham, steward at Cheverel Manor GL
MARNER, SILAS; a weaver and a lonely man SM
—baby Marner, Silas's little sister, who died in infancy SM
—Hepzibah (Eppie), a foundling raised by Silas (actual surname Cass) SM
Marrables, tavern philosopher and laboratory assistant DD
Marriott, Ellen; about to be confirmed JR
Marshall, a jeweller DD
Martin, Sally; deformed and afflicted with consumption JR
Maruffi, Fra Salvestro; Romola's designated confessor R
Marullo [H]; painter R
Maskery, Will; wheelwright AB
—Mrs; of Methodist inclination AB
Maso of Brescia, maker of beautiful mesh armor R
MASSEY, BARTLE; misogynist and schoolmaster AB
Mawmsey, Mr; an exceptional grocer MM
—Mrs; a fertile mother MM
Maxum, Old; pauper patriarch SF
Medici, Lorenzo de' [H]; the great leader of Florence R
—Giovanni; Cardinal [H] R
—Piero, younger son [H] R
Medlicote, Lord; a benefactor of the hospital MM
Medwin, a law clerk correspondent of Jermyn's; *sub rosa* FH
Megalosaurus, that greatest of fossils TS 3
Megatherium, Lord; a connection of Mrs Cadwallader's MM
MELEMA, TITO; scholar, husband, disloyal foster son; received his death R
Melibœus, of sartorial uncertainty TS 13
Mengan, Mrs; Baronet Lydgate's daughter, sister to the Captain MM

Mercer, Joseph; read to at home by Miss Eliza JR
Merman, Proteus; conveyancer and innovator TS 3
—Julia, a loyal wife TS 3
Merry, Miss (Jocosa); governess and companion to the Davilow girls DD
Merula, Rev., to whom a writing was attributed by Columba TS 11
Methurst, Lady Alicia; who got heart trouble when her uncle died FH
Meunier, Charles; an innovative medical experimenter LV
Meunier, Mme.; a schoolmistress DD
Meyrick, an engraver of some distinction; deceased DD
—Mrs; warmhearted mother, loving Mirah DD
—Amy, one of three daughters DD
—Hans, schoolfellow of Deronda's; in love with Myra Lapidoth DD
—Kate, another of the three DD
—Mab, the musical one DD
Microps, scientific researcher TS 3
Middleton, Mr; the actual curate DD
Miller, tavern philosopher and exceptional second-hand bookseller DD
Mills, butler at the Chase AB
Minchin, Dr; a good diagnostician MM
Mitchell, coachman to Sir Maximus Debarry FH
Mixtus, well-informed and kind TS 9
Moffat, an auctioneer who died BJ
Moggs, Luke; head miller at the Dorlcote Mill MF
—Mrs; hospitable to the Tulliver children MF
Mole, Mrs; who bought a mound of jelly BJ
Mompert, Bishop; not narrow in public matters DD
—Mrs; in need of a governess (Gwendolen ducked) DD
Monas, author of one book TS 15
Mordax, ardent in intellectual work TS 8
Morgan, Miss; governess at the Vincys' MM
MORRIS, DINAH; Methodist preacher; beloved of Adam Bede AB
Morteira, Leonora; aunt of Leonora Charisi DD
Morton, the late; a businessman MF
Moss, Mr; unsuccessful farmer MF
—Gertrude, his wife; sister of Mr Tulliver MF
—Baby, who knew her own mind MF
—children, who worshipped their cousin Maggie Tulliver MF
—Georgy, who ran for his father MF
—Lizzy, seven, looking very shy MF
—Willy, who was called to hold Mr Tulliver's horse MF
Mott, the village gardener; now retiring SM
Muscat, cheese-maker FH
—Mrs; a Dissenting parishioner FH
—young son, who sighs after Esther FH

N
Nardi, Jacopo [H]; a writer on Savonarola R
Narwhal, Lord; scientist TS 3
Nash, Nancy; charwoman MM
Nash, a bone-setter DD
Naumann, Adolf; painter in Rome MM
Neff, Felix; memoirist whose book is being covered in the new library JR
Nero, Bernardo del [H]; the godfather of Romola R
Nisbett, a retailer of gossip SF
Noble, Henrietta, charitable sister of Mrs Farebrother; admired Ladislaw MM
Nolan, Baruch; retired London hosier FH
—Mrs; (*née* Pendrell), thought to have ruined herself by her marriage FH
Nuttwood, Mr; grocer FH
—Mrs; a Dissenting parisioner FH
O
Oates, Sally; the cobbler's wife SM
—Jinny; a daughter SM
Oca, Capo d'; with trumpets for a tournament R
Olding, John; labourer and witness AB
Oldinport, Mr; cousin and predecessor Squire in bad odour with tenantry GL
—Lady Felicia; a delicate odour of Indian roses in church GL
—successor Squire, a kind-hearted contributor to the Rev. Barton SF
Oliver, the local M.P., a Peelite MM
Osgood, Mr; a fine old family SM
—Mrs; elderly lady much admired for her dancing SM
—Miss; courted and won by Mr Lammeter SM
—Gilbert, Nancy Lammeter's first cousin; his proposal was declined SM
Ottley, Molly's (Poyser kitchen-maid) former employer AB
P
Pack, retained to make political trouble FH
Paine, Mat; clerk to Robert Dempster JR
Palfrey, who could not easily change his mind BJ
—Mrs; flattered by a visit BJ
—brother who was friends with Towers BJ
—Miss Letitia, a daughter of a prouder style than Penny's BJ
—Miss Penelope; a daughter the object of matrimonial intentions BJ
—sister engaged for a year and a half BJ
—Squire; a forebear much respected BJ
Parrot, whose heifer was driven off GL
—Mrs; commiserating GL
—Bessie, age three GL
—Selina, who postponed her wedding GL
Parry, Mr; a popular preacher who preceded Mr Barton SF GL
Partridge, whose effects were sold at auction MF
Pash, tavern philosopher and watchmaker DD
Paston, Mr; the old minister at Lantern Yard SM
Patch, Ned; a pedlar FH
Patch, the old parish clerk who went out to sing carols MF
Patten, Mrs; childless old lady now rich through spending nothing SF GL
—late husband SF

Pazzini, La; a kind-hearted virago GL
Peacock, who sold his practice to Lydgate MM
Pegwell, a corn-factor MM
Pelley, whose bank failed (Tom was able to warn Guest & Co. in time) MF
Pendrell; banker who will hire only adherents of the established church FH
—Mrs; eager to hear Sherlock debate Rufus Lyon FH
Pentreath, Lord; invited to meet the Grandcourts DD
—Lady; relaxed social observer DD
Pepin, vivacious author TS 14
Pepper, Mrs; a customer of Bob Jakin's pack MF
Perry, a butler LV
Pettifer, Mrs; a widow helpful in illness GL
Philemon, with ambivalent and contradictory reports of Euphemia TS 13
Phipps, amiable and laconic banker JR
—Mrs; the banker's wife suspicious of the Countess Czerlaski SF JR
—Miss; stumpy and unsuccessful in her dress SF
—Ned; kneeling in church and whispering JR
Pickard, Rev.; an Independent preacher GL
Pico della Mirandola [H}, Renaissance luminary R
Pike, a scholar who finds Mr Casaubon's work ridiculous MM
Pilgrim, Mr; the doctor from a nearby market town SF JR
Pilulus: recommended avoiding sugar TS 13
Pink, a saddler and political observer FH
Pinkerton, a parliamentary incumbent MM
Pippin, Miss; passionately in love with Pumpkin MM
Pittman, an old lawyer JR
—four daughters, the Misses JR
Pivart, farmer with irrigation plans upstream of the Dorlcote Mill MF
Plessy, Lord; who played dominoes in bed MM
Plymdale, not liking being called "a servile crawler" MM
—Mrs Selina; falcon-faced wife MM
—Ned; one of the good matches in town MM
Poinçon, Miss; Lausanne schoolmistress MM
Poliziano (Politian), Angelo [H]; scholar and lecturer in Florence R
Pomfret, Mrs; whose house Hetty says she visits for lessons AB
Pontanus (or Merula) [H]; poet R
Porpesse, M.; French scientist TS 3
Porter, Sir William; his named dropped by the Countess SF
—Lady; a friend of the countess Czerlaski SF
Poulter, the village schoolmaster at St Ogg's MF
Powderell, a retired ironmonger MM
—Samuel, his brother MM
Powers, Bill; natural leader among beer-drinkers JR
POYSER, old Martin; the grandfather AB
—MARTIN; farmer and pater familias AB
—MRS RACHEL; with a tongue that is never idle AB
—Charlotte (Totty) Poyser, adored toddler AB
—Marty, age nine AB
—Tommy, age seven AB
Pratt, Richard; a medical man JR
—Miss; kept her brother's house for him: a confirmed old maid JR
—Eliza, his daughter, her niece JR

—Joshua; illegitimate son of Peter Featherstone: the principal heir	MM
Riley, engineer, auctioneer, appraiser, advisor to Mr Tulliver	MF
—daughter, now an underteacher at Miss Firniss's	MF
Robins, Clara; puzzled on the status of clergymen	JR
Robinson, an attorney	DD
Robisson, former employer of Mrs Abel	MM
Rodd, a Baptist minister	BJ
Rodney, Jem; the town mole-catcher	SM
Roe, Mr; travelling preacher	AB
Rose, Rev. Mr; his doctrine was a little too high	JR
Rose, Timothy; a gentleman farmer	FH
—Mrs; his helpmeet	FH
Rosemary, creator of a sculpture called "Babes in the Wood"	TS 5
Rucellai, Bernardo [H]; Florentine well-connected political figure	R
—Camilla [H], his wife; subject to hysterical possession	R
Ryde, Mr; succeeded Mr Irwine as rector; more stringent, not well loved	AB
S	
Sadler, a mercer with a good damask	MM
Salkeld, a friend of Arthur Donnithorne's	AB
Salt, associated with seagoing trade; a supercargo	MF
Salt, a wool-factor	FH
—Mary, who married Tiliot	FH
Salt, Jim ('Sandy Jim'); proud of his boy	AB
—Bess, his wife ('Timothy's Bess')	AB
—baby, heavy	AB
—Ben ('Timothy's Bess's Ben'), sturdy young man of five	AB
Salviati, Marco; adherent of Savonarola	R
Sampson, coach proprietor	FH
San Severino, Count di; purchaser of the Bardi collection	R
Sandeman, Squire in Tilston	JR
Sargent, Mr; who has just been given a living	SF
Sarti, singer who lost his voice; kept alive through copying	GL
—Signora; who had three children and died of fever	GL
—Caterina; a beautiful voice and a frail, soon departed wife	GL
—two children who died of fever	GL
Sasso, Meo di; bringing wonderful news when his horse broke down	R
Satchell, timber manager for Squire Donnithorne	AB
—Mrs; her dairy management criticized	AB
SAVONAROLA, GIROLAMO [H]; charismatic religious reformer	R
Scaddon, Henry; *alias* Maurice Christian	FH
Scala, Bartolommeo [H]; secretary of the Florentine republic	R
Scales, house-steward and head butler	FH
Schmidt, a German courier	LV
Scrogg, county historian	DD
Semper, a poor but frequent public speaker	TS 13
Sforza, Ludovico [H]; splendid patron of Leonardo	R
Shark, a younger scientist who attacks Merman	TS 3
Sharp, Mrs; lady's maid to Lady Cheverel	GL
Sherlock, Rev. Theodore; too shy for a debate	FH
Short, Mrs; owner of Camp Villa; landlady to Countess Czerlaski	SF
Shrike, who made an erroneous attribution	TS 11
Simeon, Mr; mentor to Amos Barton at Cambridge	SF

Stubb, who has an exaction against Mrs Strype's drying-ground MM
Stultus, Rev. Anylatus; a figure in a study on snubbing NE 5
SUCH, THEOPHRASTUS, who receives impressions TS
—Clarissa, his wife TS 10
Sutton, Mrs; died at last of dropsy MF

T

Tacco, Maestro; a doctor from Padua R
Taft, Mrs; inclined to draw wrong conclusions MM
Taft, old feyther AB
—Billy, the village idiot AB
—Mum, his son; a tacturn carpenter AB
Tantripp, a lady's maid MM
Tapir, Lord; a connection of Mrs Cadwallader's MM
Tarbett, Mr; who preached at the Shepperton church GL
Teedman, Dame; at whose school Nancy Lammeter received an education SM
Tegg, the shoemaker's son MM
Tench, scholar whose ridicule Mr Casaubon feared MM
Teveroy, Mrs; Lord Grinsell's second wife MM
Theron, a writer ignored TS 14
Thesiger, Mr; moderate evangelical minister MM
Tholer, Tom ('Tom Saft'), half-witted AB
—Bob; for whom a coffin was arranged AB
Tholoway, Ben; a powerful thresher AB
Thomson, Liza; a housemaid at the Phipps' JR
Thrupp, clerk at the bank JR
Tibbitts, Mrs; washerwoman BJ
Tiliot, with a famous gin; now looks down on former associates FH
—Mrs (the former Mary Salt); now risen with her husband FH
Tilt, with a distorted mouth MF
Timpson, a useful man in the parish of St Ogg's MF
Tod, Josh; innkeeper at the Holly Bush AB
Toller, a long-established medical practitioner MM
—Harry, his brother; a brewer MM
—Sophy, a well-regarded daughter, engaged to Ned Plymdale MM
Tomlinson, a rich miller JR
—the Misses, his three daughters JR
Tomms, Jacob; young man in the tailoring line SF
Tooke, Mrs; to whom Janet Dempster carried parcels JR
Tookey, Mr; deputy clerk of the parish SM
Torbits, the; in debt MM
Tornabuoni, Lorenzo [H]; politic supporter of the Medici R
Torrington, Captain; invited to the Grandcourts' DD
—Mrs; to come with her husband DD
Torry, James; a miller connected to Guest & Co MF
—Mrs: would not consider Maggie for a governess MF
—Miss; intermediary MF
Toucan, of Magdalen, who might have written something TS 11

U

Ubique, criticised by Semper for inept public speaking TS 13
Unit, Miss; turning up her nose at the putative Guest couple MF

V

Vaiano, Florentine conjuror and illusionist R
Valla, Lorenzo [H]; a severe scholar R
Valori, Francesco [H]; Florentine liberal politician R
Vendernoodt, society observer DD
Vibrio, a critic TS 15
Vigo, Mrs; had been a reader and secretary to eminence MM
VINCY, Walter; Mayor of the town, comfortable in business MM
—Mrs Lucy; an innkeeper's daughter; a sister the late Mrs Featherstone MM
—Bob, who irritated his sister Rosamond MM
—FRED; a brother in love with Mary Garth MM
—MARY, married at last with three children MM
—Louisa, a precious toddler MM
—ROSAMOND; decides Dr Lydgate is the man MM
—clergyman brother, now deceased MM
Volvox, a literary critic TS 15
Vulcany, Mrs; observer of Gwendolen Harleth DD
Vyan, a schoolmate of Fred Vincy MM

W

Wace, the brewer and a keen observer FH
Wagstaff, Mrs; who kept lodgings where Mr Tryan lived JR
Wakefield, Jim ('Gentleman Wakefield') AB
Wakem, John; lawyer of questionable ethics MF
—Emily, the late, sweet wife and mother (*née* Clint) MF
—Philip, his crippled son, who loves Maggie Tulliver MF
—other sons, including a favourite MF
Wall, Mary; she became Mrs Holt FH
Walsh, Mr; a new curate for Paddiford JR
Walsingham, Mrs; mother of the present Mrs Truberry MM
Warren, Mr; Sir Christopher Cheverel's venerable valet GL
Watling, Lord; favors black angus SF
Waule, the late; a warm (tight) man MM
—Jane (*née* Featherstone); rich and watchful MM
—Elizabeth, a daughter MM
—Joanna, a daughter MM
—John, her son, age twenty-three MM
—Rebecca, a daughter MM
Webbe, medical man from Carbsley MM
Wengstein, Princess; with whom Countess Czerlaski is acquainted SF
West, a wool factor AB
Whale, Scrag; explorer TS 3
Whale, Professor Sperm N.; scientist TS 3
Wiener, pawnbroker and moneychanger at Leubronn DD
Williamson Sarah; Methodist preacher AB
Willis, head game-keeper FH
Willoughby, Miss; a high-born schoolfellow of Rosamond Vincy MM
Wimple, vicar at Shuttleton FH
Wimple, Miss; a patient of Dr Minchin's MM
Winship, auctioneer in the sale of the Dorlcote mill MF

Commentary

We count 747 different surnames in the above listing of over 1,100 figures in the works. In twenty-six cases, a surname is re-used in a different work, but only in one case (Dolly Winthrop in SM) for a character of any importance; in fact, in almost every case these are "Also mentioned" people. It is evident that George Eliot made a systematic, successful effort to avoid using a name of any significance more than once. She was more thorough in this policy than either of her contemporaries Charles Dickens and Anthony Trollope (we have not analyzed Thackeray on this point). Only three times did she repeat a name more than once. Here are the repeats we found:

Banks
Blick
Byles
Downes
Dymock
Filmore
Fletcher (3)
Ford
Gibbs (3)
Grampus
Hawkes
Heron
Johns
Johnson
Lamb
Nash
Patch
Pratt
Rose
Salt (3)
Spratt
Taft
Townley
Tucker
Winthrop
Wright

Historical Sources of Characters

Scholars have given considerable attention to the question of the degree to which Eliot modeled her characters on real people. We have little to add, except the inspiration of David Faux, to these conjectures, but we summarize them here for convenient reference. In most instances the modeling was more general than particular.

Romola di Bardi	Barbara Leigh Smith Bodichon (1827-91), artist, educationist and active feminist; perhaps Eliot's closest friend
Amos Barton SF	Rev. John Gwyther, Curate of Chilvers Coton 1831-41 [GSH 211]
Adam Bede AB and Caleb Garth MM	Many of the admirable qualities of these two characters were observed by Eliot in her own father Robert Evans (1773-1849)
Celia Brooke	Chrissey Evans, Eliot's elder and much prettier sister
Dorothea Brooke	Margaret Fuller Ossoli, ardent and well-known feminist and strong sympathizer with the Italian revolt against Austrian oppression
Rev. Carpe SF	Rev. George Hake, Vicar of Chilvers Coton, with livings at Rocester and Ellastone, Staffordshire [GSH 217]
Edward Casaubon MM	Dr Robert Herbert Brabant (1781-1866), who had been working for years when Eliot first knew him on a "great work" which would endeavor to prove the absence of the supernatural in the life of Jesus and the early days of the Christian Church
Sir Christopher Cheverel GL	Sir Roger Newdigate (1719-1806), who remodeled his home, Arbury Hall, in Gothic style
Lucy Deane MF	Christiana Evans ("Chrissey"), Eliot's elder sister (1814-59)
Janet Dempster JR	Mrs Nancy Wallington Buchanan, the daughter of Eliot's Nuneaton schoolmistress
Robert Dempster JR	James William Buchanan (1792-1846), Nuneaton lawyer
The Dodson sisters MF	Eliot's mother, *née* Pearson, had several sisters, her aunts
David Faux BJ	The Weimar confectioner Rabenhorst (3M)
Mr Gilfil GL	Rev. Bernard Gilpin Ebdell, who baptized GE
Felix Holt FH	Perhaps Gerald Massey (1828-1907), self-educated socialist and poet, and perhaps John Chapman (1821-94), one of Eliot's most important friends and mentors
Julius Klesmer DD	Anton Rubenstein (1829-94), flamboyant Jewish pianist
Rev. Rufus Lyon FH	Rev. Francis Franklin, the Baptist minister in Coventry whose daughters ran the school George Eliot attended there
Bartle Massey	This very name was borne by a teacher in Mr Evans' village
Mordecai (Ezra Cohen) DD	Emanuel Deutsch (1829-73), scholar and popularizer in England of the Talmud and other Jewish studies
Dinah Morris AB	Eliot's 'Aunt Samuel' (Mrs Samuel Evans), who was one of the early Methodist travelling woman preachers, and who visited and prayed with a woman condemned to die for infanticide
Gritty Moss MF	Chrissey Evans (see Lucy Deane) had to endure much financial worry and leaned both on Mary Ann and their brother Isaac, particularly after her struggling husband's death, leaving her with a large brood of children
The Oldinports SF GL	The Newdigate family of Arbury Hall, near Nuneaton
Hetty Sorrel AB	Mary Voce, visited by Eliot's Aunt Samuel in Nottingham gaol before her execution for infanticide
Rev. Edgar Tryan JR	Rev. John Edmund Jones, curate of Stockingford
Tom and Maggie Tulliver MF	Eliot's own relationship with her elder brother Isaac Evans was clearly the basis of much in the Tullivers' mutual love, impatience, judgment, and pain
Philip Wakem MF	François D'Albert Durade, Swiss artist who painted Eliot —*see* frontispiece to Volume I

Essay

Parallels and Echoes: Eliot Revisits Eliot

While she was assiduous in avoiding repetitions of character surnames (see previous Index), George Eliot repeated herself in her fictional plots far more than her contemporaries did. This is the more evident because she wrote only eight full length works of fiction. A carping critic might feel that she could have worked harder on this aspect of her craft. It will be seen in the following brief synopses that only in her autobiographical novel MF does Eliot manage to avoid some of the romantic clichés of the novels of sensation (foundlings finding fortunes, guilty secrets, narrow escapes of foreign beauties, shocking discoveries when the Will is opened) common in her time.

Childhood and children

Baby in jeopardy: The lost and bereft Hetty Sorrel AB gives birth to an infant daughter, whom she covers over in a quasi-burial and abandons at first. When she returns, it is too late.

The infant Fedalma SG is found by Spaniards in a gypsy encampment after a battle, with no parents visible. She is raised by aristocrats and later learns of her background.

When the drunken Molly Farren SM falls asleep and dies in the snow, her infant daughter miraculously finds her way to a fireside, where the myopic weaver Silas Marner at first mistakes her for his stolen gold.

Annette Ledru Bycliffe FH is discovered in desperate straits with her baby daughter. The Rev. Rufus Lyon takes both under his protection.

Brother and Sister—and Death: Tom Tulliver MF and the younger Maggie are close to autobiography. After a generally halcyon childhood during which the girl worships her big brother, the two draw apart when Tom, the stronger personality, harshly judges Maggie's reckless conduct with a man. He has lectured her and lectured her, to no avail, as he sees it. Maggie is present at Tom's death, which she shares.

Romola R is the younger sister of the judging and obsessive Bernardino (Dino) de' Bardi. They have lived apart since Dino chose a monk's vocation. On his deathbed, he sends for her and utters a dire warning against a romantic entanglement. Romola is present at Dino's death. To her sorrow, her persistence in her love leads to deep disappointment, as Dino had predicted.

Mirah Lapidoth DD has long been separated from her religiously enthusiastic brother Ezra (Mordecai), but they find each other, and Mordecai dies in his sister's presence. Mirah is devoted to her brother and deeply respects his views. Her marriage is just what he would have wished.

Daughter fled to the stage: Sarah Dunkirk MM runs away from a father who bends the law. To live, she turns to the stage.

Mirah Lapidoth DD has been abducted by her father. She loses all contact with her mother and brother . Lapidoth tries to make her his meal-ticket in the theatre but she escapes him and returns to London to search for her mother.

Leonora Alcharisi DD has rejected her father's strict Jewish way of life and gone on the stage with enormous success. She marries a prince.

Early Scars: The character flaws of Tito Melema R, primarily deviousness, insincerity, and a lack of trust in and loyalty to older father figures, appear to have been engendered by his horrific and dangerous first seven years as an abandoned and unvalued waif on the streets of Naples.

The inability of Gwendolen Harleth DD to love a man may have had its roots in her mistreatment in early years by a step-father. *See* page 317.

Tito Melema was not vindictive or cruel, but he disliked any unpleasantness and would dissemble, sneak and lie to avoid it; Gwendolen Harleth "liked to make her penances easy" DD 3.

Ignorance of origins: In four of Eliot's eight major fictional works, the essential plot element is a protagonist's ignorance of his or her parenthood.

Eppie Marner SM is informed as she is about to be married of her parentage. She does not allow the news to affect her plans.

Fedalma SG learns from her father of her gypsy origins and obligations. She accepts her fate, perhaps contrary to probability, a decision which leads to the destruction of the man she had planned to marry and to her father's death.

Esther Lyons FH makes the happy discovery that she is an heiress, through a father she never knew, though she decides at last to forgo the status and wealth to which she is entitled. In the same work Harold Transome learns the unpalatable truth of his father's identity only at the end of the story.

Daniel Deronda DD has been raised by a man he thinks must be his father. He discovers his Jewish origins only after an accidental encounter in a European synagogue leads to the intervention of his grandfather's loyal friend and his mother's forced confession.

Rescue and Renunciation: A toddler walks into Silas Marner's SM life and transfigures it. He names and raises little Eppie, who cleaves with unquestioning loyalty to him despite a later offer of status and wealth. She marries the town gardener.

Baldassare Calvo R rescues the seven-year-old orphaned street urchin Tito Melema and raises and protects him. Tito treacherously renounces his foster- father. Through his own efforts he achieves status and wealth but overreaches and dies at Calvo's hand.

The Rev. Rufus Lyon FH raises little Esther after her mother dies. She turns out to be an heiress, but, like Eppie Marner, she declines status and wealth, remains loyal to her foster-father and marries rough diamond Felix Holt, the mentor and man of her life.

Youth

Assignations: Heir to the manor Arthur Donnithorne AB and the bewitching Hetty Sorrel, a dairy-maid, find each other irresistible and meet in a summer-house more than once too often. Adam Bede, who loves Hetty, accidentally learns of their trysts and intervenes violently.

Philip Wakem MF and Maggie Tulliver get in the habit of finding each other in a forsaken spot, but her brother Tom puts two and two together and waylays them. Only his language is violent, as Philip has been crippled in a childhood accident.

The Squire's eldest, Godfrey Cass SM, has entangled himself with Molly Farren and, having seduced her, in a quixotic burst of fancy has married her. Their meetings are not described in the novel, and the secret is nearly perfectly kept, though a younger brother knows.

Child bride: Tina Sarti GL has been taken under the wing of Rev. Maynard Gilfil, who deeply loves her. Tina, however, is on the rebound from a passionate relationship with a man who rejected her and then died; she herself has not long to live.

Tessa R has been rescued from dire circumstance by Tito Melema, to whom she naively believes she has been married. He makes a home for her. She lacks intellect and any perceptible life of the mind, but she cares to the extent of her ability for their offspring.

Annette Ledru FH has been rescued from privation and imminent catastrophe by the Rev. Rufus Lyon, who loves her and persuades her to marry him. She has not long to live. Like Tessa, she lacks intelligence and any sense of the world, but she adores her little daughter Esther, who is only five years old when she dies.

Guilty secrets: Arthur Donnithorne's AB dalliance with Hetty Sorrel is a secret from the world until Adam Bede accidentally finds it out. She keeps the secret of her pregnancy to the point of its inevitable tragedy. Her unwillingness to tell the truth nearly leads her to the gallows.

Godfrey Cass SM has married beneath him, to put it mildly. He keeps the existence of drunken Molly Farren from his father, but his brother knows. His own fatherhood is another secret he bears until confession to his wife at last.

Tito Melema R alone bears the knowledge of his treachery to his foster-father. His determination that his conduct remain a secret is a principal preoccupation for him during most of the novel and a major engine of the plot.

The quasi-criminal past of the ostentatiously religious Bulstrode MM is a constant strain on his conscience, and his engineering the death of the man who knows his secret is nearly his undoing.

Yoked to an idiot husband and a feckless son, Mrs Transome FH allows herself to accept the wooings of the family lawyer and has a son by him. Harold's parentage is a burden she bears alone, as Matthew Jermyn regards it as his ace in the hole. His covert embezzlements, and his complicity in the unjust imprisonment of the young Bycliffe are pangs to his conscience. Maurice Christian conceals his true identity and unsavoury past. M

Overeducation: Mr Tulliver MF ambitiously consigns his son Tom to a clergyman schoolmaster, who inflicts Latin and the like on the ill-adapted young man. Mr Tulliver had hoped for a son of sufficient education to battle his enemies in the courts; in fact he gets better than that, for Tom's courage and good sense stand him in good stead once his father's bankruptcy forces him out on his own.

Walter Vincy MM, the Mayor of the town, has sent his son Fred to Cambridge and is very unhappy when he fails to take his degree. Fred is footloose until he gains redemption through the love of a good woman and her father's trust in him. By going to work for Caleb Garth he loses "class" but gains self-respect.

Rescuing swain: she's foreign: Mr Gilfil GL and the Italian Tina Sarti; Rufus Lyon FH and the French Annette; Daniel Deronda DD and the Jewess Mirah Lapidoth, whom he rescues from suicidal drowning in the Thames.

Parentage

Failed father: Thias Bede AB is a ne'er-do-well drunkard who cannot fulfill his tasks in the family carpentry shop. He dies by drowning while drunk.

Mr Tulliver's MF failures are not as a father but as a businessman. His hot temper and combative nature lead him to financial disaster and finally to death. He has done little to provide for his children, but they get on.

Fearing disgrace and the loss of the lady he loves, Godfrey Cass SM lets his chance to claim his daughter slip away.

Tito Melema's R Greek father, whoever he was, either died young or was completely indifferent to the welfare of his son, who was found abandoned on the streets of Naples by the man who took him in and raised him.

Dunkirk's MM quasi-criminal line of work, that of a pawnbroker who does not hesitate to deal in stolen goods, alienates his daughter Sarah, who runs away to escape contamination.

Maurice Bycliffe FH is betrayed and wronged. He dies in prison, his wife and child effectively abandoned to privation.

Lapidoth DD has kidnapped his daughter and tried to live on what she can earn. When she escapes him, he finds her again, then steals—and steals away.

Foster-father: Martin Poyser AB raises his wife's niece Hetty Sorrel as his own, directing and controlling her as a father, though ultimately she eludes him and, he feels, disgraces him.

Silas Marner SM devotedly nurtures little Eppie, who had materialised on his hearth. His loving care is rewarded.

Baldassarre Calvo R rescues little Tito Melema, aged seven, from the streets of Naples, but when both are captured by pirates he is abandoned by his foster-son. He seeks revenge and finally achieves it, dying in the process.

The Rev. Rufus Lyon FH, after the death of his wife Annette, raises and educates her daughter Esther as his own. For a long time he allows her to believe he is her father but eventually he reveals the truth as he knows it.

Arthur Brooke MM, whose brother has died, raises his two daughters Dorothea and Celia as his own.

Sir Hugo Mallinger DD, at the behest of a woman he loves but who will not marry him, devotedly and generously raises her son as an English gentleman, Daniel Deronda. He has earned Deronda's loyalty, but ultimately he sees him choose his blood heritage and become a practicing Jew.

Missing mother: Of the seven novels and SG, only MF lacks this plot element.

Hetty Sorrel's mother AB is invisible, having made a bad marriage. The absence of any guidance from this source is a quiet engine in the plot.

Fedalma SG, who turns out to be a gypsy princess, has been found with no parents in evidence and raised in the town castle by its matriarch. The father reappears, but never the mother.

Eppie's SM drunken mother dies in the snow while Eppie is still a toddler. It is apparent she would have been of little use to her daughter had she survived.

Romola R lost her mother years ago. Maternal wisdom here, too, might have made a difference.

The Brooke sisters MM have lost both parents and are raised by their uncle. Dorothea's lack of common sense might have been mitigated by a present mother; certainly her guardian Arthur Brooke lacks it too.

Esther Lyon FH lost her mother when she was five. She misses the influence a mother might have had, though she learns valuable lessons from an unlikely source: the practical idealist Felix Holt.

Mirah Lapidoth DD lost her mother when her father abducted her, and she has died before Mirah can return.

Daniel Deronda's mother DD, the opera star Leonora Alcharisi, has consigned him to be raised by one of her lovers. Ultimately she is obliged to reveal herself and confess her renunciation of her son. In the process she introduces him to his missing Jewish heritage.

Parents unknown: Fedalma SG has never known who her actual parents were, having been found abandoned in a gypsy encampment.

Eppie Marner SM has never known who her parents were until her father Godfrey Cass at last comes to see and claim her.

Esther Lyon FH has grown up in total ignorance of her father's identity until her foster-father at last reveals the truth—as far as he knows it.

Daniel Deronda DD has grown up in total ignorance of his parentage. But for the accident of his being recognized by his grandfather's friend, this would have continued.

Unexpectedly an heiress: Eppie Marner SM is told she is the daughter of the local squire, who had fudged his chance to claim her as an infant. Esther Lyon FH turns out to be the proper heiress of an estate through her father, long since departed; Both girls decline their patrimonies and choose to marry in the class in which they have grown up.

Plot similarities continue in the way the two girls are visited by those who would impart the wonderful news of their new fortunes in life. Godfrey Cass and his wife, the former Nancy Lammeter, call on Eppie Marner; Harold Transome and his mother make a similar call on Esther. Eppie's decision is quick and decisive; Esther accepts an invitation to visit Transome Court and only determines to reject her good fortune after much reflection.

When her father finds and claims her, Fedalma SG discovers her heritage as the daughter of and heiress to gypsy leadership, fated to lead in her turn.

Character Parallels

Actresses with a hypnotic effect: The story of Tertius Lydgate MM and his idol Mme Laure, who deliberately kills her husband because the life he wants her to lead bores her, is very funny but not characteristic of Eliot's art. The Princess Leonora Halm-Eberstein DD in her life as Leonora Alcharisi, opera star, was followed throughout her career by men and wooed vainly until the fatal moment when she believed she had lost her voice.

Dying brother of religious vocation: Romola's brother Dino R (Bernardino; now Dominican monk Fra Luca), has summoned his sister to hear a warning and promptly dies.

Mirah Lapidoth's brother Ezra (Mordecai) DD, a devout and passionate Jewish advocate of independence and freedom for Jews in their homeland, comes to his end with his sister and her beloved Daniel Deronda beside him. DD

Egoism in a beautiful woman: Rosamond Vincy's MM indomitable insensitivity and self-concern lead to the trivialization of her husband's career. The spoiled and arrogant Gwendolen Harleth DD finds her comeuppance in the brutal egotism of her husband Grandcourt.

Experienced older man: Arthur Brooke MM and Sir Hugo Mallinger DD, both land-owning country magnates, pride themselves on having tried many things and going beyond the routine. Both are generous and exceptionally good-natured but not all that acute.

Feminine naiveté: Dorothea Brooke's MM idealistic infatuation for her imagined scholarly knight, Edward Casaubon, is described perfectly in the next novel: "How can one feel anything else than pity for a young creature like that—full of unused life—ignorantly rash—hanging all her blind expectations on that remnant of a human being"—in DD 35, this is Deronda's soliloquy on Gwendolen and Henleigh Grandcourt.

Living on in another: Her father, the gypsy king Zarca, SG III asks Fedalma, "Shall I live in you When the earth covers me?" Mordecai DD is counting on his living on in Daniel Deronda as he works for the independence and freedom of the Jewish people.

Losing lover tells: Rosamond Vincy MM, deeply hurt by Will Ladislaw's indifference to her, tells Dorothea Brooke Ladislaw loves her alone. This is crucial to Dorothea, whose revived hopes permit her to open to Will when he comes to her.

Hans Meyrick DD, who has long been besotted by love for Mirah Lapidoth, tells Daniel Deronda that he, Daniel, possesses Mirah's heart, a crucial piece of news which emboldens Deronda to speak to her at last.

These revelations are both critically timed. They are not uttered in a spirit of self-abnegation but essentially out of frustration and a bitter acceptance that the speaker's dreams have been just that.

A parallel but differently motivated revelation occurs when Adam Bede's AB mother Lisbeth tells the blind young lover about Dinah Morris's feelings for him. Once he grasps the facts, he does not hesitate.

Male mentor: It is revealing that George Eliot, the great feminine author of her day, barely touches on the possibility of feminine teaching and leadership. The exception, Dolly Winthrop SM, gives good down-home coaching in the care and feeding of the young.

On the other hand, we have Felix Holt FH and his dominance over Esther Lyon, and Daniel Deronda's DD moral ascendancy over Gwendolen Harleth: "It is one of the secrets in that change of mental poise which has been fitly named conversion, that to many among us neither heaven nor earth has any revelation till some personality touches theirs with a peculiar influence, subduing them into receptiveness." DD 35

Compare Savonarola and Romola R. For most of the novel, Romola submits to the monk's guidance and moral leadership. Only when he does nothing to save her uncle from execution is she disillusioned.

Melancholy servitor: Lyddy to the Lyons FH and Miss Merry (ironically 'Jocosa') to the Davilows DD are morose as a matter of habit and attitude. They are the only servants, except Jenner FH given enough dimension for us to see their gloom.

Miraculous power gone: Savonarola R near the end of his career finds himself, in words which describe Gwendolen Harleth as she faces taking a humble governess's post: "To be a queen disthroned is not so hard as some other down-stepping: imagine one who had been made to believe in his own divinity finding all homage withdrawn, and himself unable to perform a miracle that would recall the homage and restore his own confidence" DD 26

Parson's wife of good family, now parsimonious: The "brilliant" Lady Fanny Lingon (her maiden name; she is of the distinguished family from which Mrs Transome had come), "being married to a country parson, became so niggardly that she had gone about almost begging for fresh eggs from the farmers' wives." FH 40 She finds an echo more substantial than her own first note in Mrs Cadwallader MM, of the DeBracys, whose aristocratic background contrasts remarkably with her present status as the wife of the lovable, gentle Rev. Humphrey Cadwallader. Her willingness to negotiate with and beat down her rustic neighbours when in the market for produce is proverbial.

Power of music: Little Caterina (Tina) Sarti GL, from a largely disregarded indigent dependant, becomes a figure to be reckoned with when her great singing talent appears.

Stephen Guest's MF singing and admiration of his accompanist, Maggie Tulliver, is the start of her trouble with her heart and leads to her disastrous foray on the water.

Rosamond Vincy's MM imitative facility at the piano makes an early breach in Tertius Lydgate's vow not to become involved with the opposite sex.

The great musician Julius Klesmer DD has earned the love of Catherine Arrowpoint, heiress, without his even realizing it. His audition of Mirah Lapidoth will lead to great things for her.

On a more mythological plane, compare Jubal's LJ power with the lyre he has invented and Juan's SG powers on the lute.

—the Voice is Gone: The great opera-singer Armgart AR loses her voice and for a time struggles in a moral crisis. Another opera-singer, Leonora Alcharisi DD, after a great career, loses her voice and, in despair, marries a prince and has six children. Her voice comes back too late.

Religious exhortation: Dinah Morris AB is fervent with and for Hetty Sorrel; Fra Girolamo Savonarola R overwhelms Romola Bardi; Maggie Tulliver's MF discovery of Thomas à Kempis brings great comfort in a moment of trial; Mordecai's R messianic pleas for the Jewish people and their proper destiny deeply move Daniel Deronda

Yearning for an acolyte: Tito Melema R seems to fill the bill for Romola's blind, frail scholar father, Bardo de' Bardi; Deronda DD truly fulfills the fondest dreams of a feeble scholar, near to death, the Jew Mordecai. Tito betrays the old man's trust, but Deronda is true to his bond.

Plot Echoes

Death in the garden: Captain Wybrow GL dies suddenly of heart failure. He is discovered on the path by Tina, his rejected lover; Mr Casaubon MM dies suddenly of heart failure and is discovered by Dorothea, the wife he has essentially rejected, collapsed at a table

Destiny imposed by birth: Fedalma SG follows her gypsy origins when her father tells her who she is. After her father's death and her lover's disgrace she leads her people onto the ships which will take them to Africa.

Daniel Deronda DD, when finally told of his Jewish heritage, proposes to and marries the Jewess he loves and taking her with him follows his destiny to the Middle East.

Guardianship mishandled: Arthur Brooke MM, formally guardian of his nieces Dorothea and Celia, seems to have been grossly negligent in negotiating Dorothea's marriage settlement. Mr Casaubon's ability to disinherit his wife if she marries a specific male not to his liking is inconceivable had Brooke been paying attention, no matter how feckless and idealistic Dorothea might have been in her anticipation of wedded bliss.

An experienced man of the world, the Rev. Henry Gascoigne DD should have protected his niece Gwendolen Harleth far better than he did. Grandcourt's will leaves her a comparative pittance and discloses an embarrassing familial situation the reverend had had adequate reason to suspect.

Mountain pass escape forestalled: Gwendolen Grandcourt, DD in a dream is summoned back to her duty to her chosen husband and her life by the one man who can influence her, Daniel Deronda. Romola R in an episode which is no dream is stopped and turned back by Savonarola from her flight from Rome over the hills. She must take up again her duties in to the poor and, perhaps, to her husband Tito Melema.

Will disappointments: Mr Casaubon's MM will punishing his widow if she marries Will Ladislaw shocks her uncle and feckless guardian Arthur Brooke, who should have been alert.

Peter Featherstone's MM will shocks everyone, especially Fred Vincy, whom he had given strong ground to believe would inherit richly.

Grandcourt's DD niggardly provision for his widow, Gwendolen, deeply aggrieves her guardian Gascoigne and sympathizer Sir Hugo Mallinger, who had discounted ugly rumours about his liaison with a lady he never married but who is now shown to have borne his heir. *See* Essay, page 297.

Index II

Given Names of Surnamed Characters

(excluding the names in *Romola*)

Male

Interestingly, there is not a single "George" in the works of George Eliot, loving consort of George Henry Lewes: only one unimportant "Georgy." Eponymous names are in **Bold**.

Aaron Winthrop	SM
Adam Bede	AB
Addy (Adam) Bede	AB
Adolphus Irwine	AB
Alfred Garth	MM
Alfred Lattimer	LV
Alfred Naumann	MM
Alfred Phipps	JR
Amos Barton	SF
Anthony Cheverel	GL
Anthony Wybrow	GL
Archibald Duke	SF
Archie Duncan	MM
Arthur Brooke	MM
Arthur Chettam	MM
Arthur Donnithorne	AB
Arthur Heron	GL
Augustus Purwell	GL
Bartle Massey	AB
Ben Cranage	AB
Ben Garth	MM
Ben Landor the younger	JR
Ben Salt	AB
Ben Tholoway	AB
Ben Winthrop	SM
Benjamin Landor	JR
Bill Downes	AB
Bill Fawks	MF
Bill Powers	JR
Billy Taft	AB
Bob Cass	SM
Bob Jakin	MF
Bob Lowme	JR
Bob Tholer	AB
Bob Vincy	MM
Caius Larcher	MM
Caleb Garth	MM
Camden Farebrother	MM
Chad Cranage	AB
Charles Lydgate	MM
Charles Meunier	LV
Christopher Cheverel	GL
Christy Garth	MM
Daniel Charisi	DD
Daniel Deronda	DD
Daniel Knott the younger	GL
Daniel Knott	GL
David Faux	BJ
Dick Brumby	MF
Dickey Barton	SF
Dominic Lenoni	FH
Dunstan Cass	SM

Durfey Transome	FH
Edgar Raymond	DD
Edgar Tryan	JR
Edmund Bridmain	SF
Edward Casaubon	MM
Edwin Larcher	MM
Ephraim Alcharisi	DD
Eustace Landor	JR
Ezra Cohen	DD
Ezra Lapidoth	DD
Felix Holt	FH
Francis Mallinger	DD
Frank Hawley	MM
Fred Barton	SF
Fred Vincy	MM
Gavial Mantrap	TS
Georgy Moss	MF
Gil Tranter	AB
Gilbert Osgood	SM
Godfrey Cass	SM
Godwin Lydgate	MM
Hans Meyrick	DD
Harold Transome	FH
Harry Toller	MM
Harry Transome	FH
Henleigh Mallinger	DD
Henleigh Mallinger Grandcourt	DD
Henry Gascoigne	DD
Henry Scaddon	FH
Henry Scaddon, the first	FH
Hiram Ford	MM
Hong Kong Bantam	TS
Huges de Malingre	DD
Hugh Crow	FH
Hugo Mallinger	DD
Humphrey Cadwallader	MM
Jacob Alexander Cohen	DD
Jacob Cuff	FH
Jacob Dagley	MM
Jacob Faux	BJ
Jacob Storey	AB
Jacob Tomms	SF
Jacob Wright	JR
James Chettam	MM
James Clement	FH
James Crake	MF
James Putty	FH
James Torry	MF
Jasper Stiwell	GL
Jem Rodney	SM
Jim Garth	MM
Jim Hardy	JR
Jim Hood	SF
Jim Salt	AB
Jim Wakefield	AB
Job Dummilow	AB
Job Haxey	MF
Job Tudge	FH
Joel Dagge	DD
John Assher	GL
John Gibbs	MF
John Johnson	FH
John Justus Transome	FH
John Lingon	FH
John Olding	AB
John Raffles	MM
John Snell	SM
John Wakem	MF
Jonathan Burge	AB
Jonathan Lamb	JR
Joseph Kalonymos	DD
Joseph Leo	DD
Joseph Mercer	JR
Josh Tod	AB
Joshua Rann	AB
Julius Klesmer	DD
Kester Beale	AB
Kit Downes	MM
Leonard Lamb	MM
Luke Britton	AB
Luke Britton senior	AB
Luke Byles	JR
Luke Moggs	MF
Martin Cleves	SF
Martin Poyser	AB
Martin Poyser senior	AB
Marty Poyser	AB
Mat Paine	JR
Matthew Jermyn	FH
Maurice Christian	FH
Maurice Christian Bycliffe	FH
Maximus Debarry	FH
Maynard **Gilfil**	SF
Michael Brincey	FH
Michael Holdsworth	AB
Mike Brindle	FH
Mike Holdsworth	AB
Minutius Felix	TS
Mum Taft	AB
Ned Patch	FH
Ned Phipps	JR
Ned Plymdale	MM
Nicholas Bulstrode	MM
Oswald Heron	GL
Ozzy Heron	GL
Peter Featherstone	MM
Peter Garstin	FH
Philip Debarry	FH

Female

Fanny Lingon	FH
Felicia Oldinport	GL
Flora Hollis	DD
Gertrude Moss	MF
Gwendolen Harleth (Grandc'rt)	DD
Harriet Bulstrode	MM
Harriet Debarry	FH
Henrietta Cheverel	GL
Henrietta Noble	MM
Hepzibah (Eppie) Marner	SM
Hester (Hetty) Sorrel	AB
Hetty Sorrel	AB
Isabel Davilow	DD
Jane Glegg	MF
Jane Waule	MM
Janet Dempster	JR
Janet Gibbs	MF
Jinny Oates	SM
Joanna Waule	MM
Julia Farquhar	SF
Julia Ladislaw	MM
Julia Merman	TS 3
Juliet Fenn	DD
Kate Bulstrode	MM
Kate Irwine	AB
Kate Meyrick	DD
Laura Stelling	MF
Leonora Charisi	DD
Leonora Morteira	DD
Letitia Palfrey	BJ
Letty Garth	MM
Lisbeth Bede	AB
Lisbeth Bede, the younger	AB
Lizzie Jerome	JR
Lizzy Moss	MF
Louisa Jermyn	FH
Louisa Mallinger	DD
Louisa Stelling	MF
Louisa Vincy	MM
Lucy Deane	MF
Lucy Vincy	MM
Lydia Donnithorne	AB
Lydia Glasher	DD
Mab Meyrick	DD
Maggie Jakin	MF
Maggie Tulliver	MF
Margaret Beaton	MF
Maria Gardner	JR
Martha Cranch	MM
Mary Burge	AB

Mary Debarry	FH
Mary Dunn	JR
Mary Garth (Vincy)	MM
Mary Holt	FH
Mary Linnet	JR
Mary Salt	FH
Milly Barton	SF
Mirah Lapidoth	DD
Molly Beale	JR
Molly Farren (Cass)	SM
Molly Harleth	DD
Nancy Gascoigne	DD
Nancy Lammeter	SM
Nancy Nash	MM
Patty Barton	SF
Patty Richards	GL
Penelope Palfrey	BJ
Phib Cook	JR
Poll Fodge	SF
Priscilla Lammeter	SM
Prissy Jakin	MF
Rachel Poyser	AB
Rebecca Linnet	JR
Rebecca Waule	MM
Rosamond Vincy (Lydgate)	MM
Sally Butts	JR
Sally Dagge	DD
Sally Lunn	BJ
Sally Martin	JR
Sally Oates	SM
Sally Rann	AB
Sara Lapidoth	DD
Sara Lingon	FH
Sarah Dunkirk	MM
Sarah Linter	GL
Sarah Stone	AB
Sarah Williamson	AB
Selina Debarry	FH
Selina Parrot	GL
Selina Plymdale	MM
Sophy Barton	SF
Sophy Pullet	MF
Sophy Toller	MM
Susan Deane	MF
Susan Garth	MM
Susan Jerome	JR
Theresa Mallinger	DD
Tina Sarti (Gilfil)	GL
Totty Poyser	AB
Winifred Farebrother	MM

Index III

Archetypal, Allegorical, and Facetious Names; Aliases and Sobriquets

Jocosa, Gwendolyn Harleth's name for governess Merry	DD 3
John Presbyter, figment alleged to have founded Presbyterian religion	JR 1
Josiah Smith, prototype name	DD 33
Kitty, her sister's affectionate name for Celia Brooke	MM 50
Kunz, type of German peasant	NH 129
La Pazzini, shopkeeping virago in Milan	GL 3
Lentulus (implying lens-shaped), unadmiring of others' achievement	TS 4
Loligo (meaning cuttlefish), a scientist	TS 3
Madonna Gozzoviglia, the madonna of gluttony and revelry	R 39
Margery, archetypal farmer's wife	FH 2 ep
Megatherium, Lord; a highly regarded scientist	MM 6
Minutius Felix, acquaintance of Theophrastus Such	TS 1
Mixtus, philanthropic commercial man	TS 9
Mordax, determined that he already knows everything	TS 8
Mum Taft, laconic carpenter	AB 1
Naldo, the name Tito Melema calls himself with his mistress Tessa	R 34
Narwhal, Lord (sea unicorn)	TS 3
Old Joshway (Joshua Rann, parish clerk)	AB 2
Old Maxum, proper name unknown; a workhouse denizen	SF 2
Pike, in a school of scholars with Carp and Tench	MM 29
Pilulus, opposed to eating sugar	TS 13
Pine-apple, the noble young wooer of Camelia	FH 3
Placidia, inclined to useless small mendacities	FF
Poll Fudge (Mary Higgins), workhouse denizen	SF 2
Porpesse (porpoise—in French)	TS 3
Proteus Merman, unoffending lawyer with a startling scientific idea	TS 3
Pummel, valet and factotum	TS 8
Queasy, employer of cook with predilection for fat in the soup	SL
Sacharissa, or Saccharissa, a nome-de-plume for writing to the editor	FF
Sally Lunn, girlfriend of a confectioner	BJ
San Buonvino, the patron saint of good wine	R 39
Sandy Jim (Jim Salt), a carpenter	AB 1
Scintilla, pretty and lively wife	TS 9
Scrag Whale, a scientist and explorer	TS 3
Semper, inclined to public speaking	TS 13
Shark, contentious writer of articles	TS 3
Silly Caleb, an idiot harassed by boys	JR 4
Silly Jim, a young man afflicted with hydrocephalus	SF 2
Skunk, a scholar	TS 11
Sperm N. Whale, Professor	TS 3
Spike, who might at times sit alone in the same room with his books	TS 7
Tapir, Lord	MM 6
Tench, in a school of scholars with Carp and Pike	MM 29
Theophrastus Such, a bachelor who observes mankind	TS
Timothy's Bess (Bessy Salt)	AB 2
Timothy's Bess's Ben (Ben Salt)	AB 2
Tom Saft (Tom Tholer), half-witted farm labourer	AB 53
Toucan, a scholar	TS 11
Touchwood, a man of bad temper	TS 6
Trapping Bass, a poacher	MM 84
Triptolemus Yellowley, Scottish agriculturist and admirer of Virgil	NH
Triton, Lord	MM 54
Vandyke duchess, Hans Meyrick's name for Gwendolen Harleth	DD 52
Wandering Jew, the; Klesmer's facetious name for himself	DD 22
Wiry Ben (Ben Cranage), a carpenter	AB 1
Zephaniah Crypt, a beneficient testator	BJ
Ziphius (a bottle-nosed dolphin), a scientist	TS 3

—and many more usages of less obvious wit in *Theophrastus Such*

Index IV

Male Characters: Occupations and Activities

It is apparent that George Eliot made a conscious effort to include a wide range of occupations, particularly when she describes gatherings of males in taverns and political contexts. The result is a great number of trades, used to identify particular individuals but often without any other mention than the name of the activity ("bell-hanger," "glazier," etc.). Even allowing for this frequent lip-service to male endeavours, the contrast in their number with those of women is remarkable: 184 specific trades and activities for men; 31 for women (Index VI). Figures mentioned in *Romola,* even though historical, are included. Figures in SG, though unprovided with surnames in many cases, are also here.

Pendrell, won't employ Dissenters FH
Mr Phipps SF
Pulley who failed MF

Barber
Burchiello, Nello's predecessor R
Dill with a long score at the pub MM
Nello, center of Florence life R

Bell-hanger
Spicer, in Lowick Gate MM

Bishop
unnamed, all Greek and greediness FH
Jebb, who wrote memoirs SF
Mompert, a position for Gwendolen DD

Blacksmith
Brewitt, who loves it DD
Niccolò Caparra R
Dagge, whose son helped Rex DD
Chad Cranage AB

Boatman
unnamed witness of Grandcourt death DD

Bookseller (secondhand)
Ezra (Mordecai) Lapidoth DD
Miller, exceptionally knowledgeable DD
Ram, Jewish and unobtrusivve DD

Boy, employed
Chester, who does chores for gardener AB
Harry, told to feed the rabbits MF
Joseph, an auctioneer's assistant MM
Tom, assistant to Caleb Garth MM

Brewer
Harry Toller, observing Lydgate MM
Wace, against Reform FH

Brickmaker
'Brimstone,' a Methodist AB

Builder
Caleb Garth, a failure MM

Businessman *and see* Merchant (13)
Bob Dakin, rising rapidly MF
Mr Deane, in trade and warehousing MF
Garnett, example for Tulliver MF
Peter Garstin, mining company FH
Gell, new partner in Guest & Co. MF
Grapnell & Co., failed for a million DD
Guest sr; wealthy and snobbish MF
Hickes, for the Transomes FH
Mixtus, successful in commerce TS 9
Morton, the late MF
Tiliot, who devised a famous gin FH
Mr Timpson, influential MF
Tom Tulliver, from a standing start MF

Butcher
Byles, whose bill ran on and on MM
Bob Lundy, jolly and smiling SM
Woods, needed something on his bill SF

Butler
Bellamy GL
Carrol, for Rev. Irwine AB
Mills, at the Chase AB
Perry alarmed by the housekeeper LV
Pratt, to the Brookes MM
Scales, house-steward, head butler FH

Carpenter
Adam Bede AB
Seth Bede AB
Brinley JR
Jonathan Burge, master AB
Ben Cranage AB
Jarrett, the village practitioner DD
Jim Salt (Sandy Jim) AB
Mum Taft AB

Charity-man
Jacob Cuff, liked the pothouse FH

Cheese-maker
Muscat; and a deacon FH

Church reader
Luke Byles JR
Joshua Rann, rich bass voice AB

Churchwarden
Mr Bond SF
Mr Budd, despite colourful reputation JR
Mr Hackit SF

Civil servant
Aquila TS 11
Fulke, in the Colonial office MM
Grampus, colonial governor MM
Bartolommeo Scala, Secretary R
Touchwood, with a bad temper TS 6

Clergyman (59)
Mr Baird SF
Amos Barton, curate SF
Rev. Blick, Mr Irwine's predecessor AB
Rev. Humphrey Cadwallader MM
Rev. Carpe, Vicar of Shepperton SF
Rev. Edward Casaubon MM
Martin Cleves, parish priest SF
Rev. Clintock, archdeacon DD
Mr Crackenthrop, rector SM
Mr Crewe, curate JR
Mr Crichley, rector GL
Mr Crowse, empty face, empty head MM
Rev. Augustus DeBarry, rector FH
Mr D'Oyley, once at Treddleston AB
Mr Drumlow, taking a drop SM
Rev. Archibald Duke SF
Mr Dymock, a dark curate DD
Mr Ely, parson SF
Rev. Camden Farebrother MM
Mr Fellowes, rector SF
Rev. Freke, brick, mortar incumbent MM
Mr Furness SF
Rev. Henry Gascoigne DD
Mr Gaskin, rector DD
Rev. Maynard Gilfil, vicar SF GL
Rev. Arthur Heron GL
Rev. Mr Horner JR
Rev. Adolphus Irwine, rector and vicar AB
Mr Johns, at Gun Street Chapel SF
Dr Kenn, kindhearted MF
Rev. John Lingon
Charles Lydgate, D. D. Tertius' uncle MM
Rev. Rufus Lyon, independent FH
Proteus Merman, conveyancer TS 3
Rev. Merula TS 11
Mr Middleton, actual curate DD
Mr Parry, the late incumbent SF JR
Mr Paston, minister in Lantern Yard SM
Rev. Mr Pickard, Independent GL
Mr Prendergast, nonresident rector JR

Palfrey, farmed his own land BJ
Parrot, who lost his heifer GL
Pivart, needing water for irrigation MF
Martin Poyser AB
Trent, dairy-maid's employer AB
Yoddrell, a farm near Frick MM

Farrier
Dowlas, conversing in a bar SM

Fisherman
Gianni, who owned a large boat, but died R

Footman
Fitchett, in the Oldinport family SF
Jabez, at Transome Court FH
John, at the Jermyns' FH

Gambler
unnamed worn-out libertine DD
unnamed London tradesman DD
Italian, impassive at Leubronn DD
Lassman, plunged; lost others' funds DD
Mackworth, part of the scene DD
Vandernoodt, conversational DD

Gamekeeper
Dent AB
Johnson, for Brooke MM
Willis, head at Treby Manor FH

Gardener
Bates, at Cheveral Manor GL
Brent, head FH
Master Bunney, putting in seeds MM
Craig, head at the Chase AB
David, groom at the vicaage GL
Mott, village gardener retiring SM
Tozer, stiff-jointed now SF
Aaron Winthrop to succeed Mott SM

Gentleman farmer
Arthur Brooke MM
Mr Pullet MF
Timothy Rose, spontaneous servility FH
Lord Watling SF

Glazier
Crabbe, who groped dimly in the news MM

Goldsmith
Domenico Cennini, in Florence R

Grocer
Dingall AB
Hyndmarsh, at St Ogg's MF
Mawmsey, exceptional MM
Nuttwood, a deacon FH
Prettyman, respectable BJ

Groom
Albizzi, for Dianola in Florence R
Briggs, at Freshitt MM
David, gardener at the vicarage GL
Jeffries, at Offendene; left DD
John, a dolt the Squire keeps on AB
John, to Sir James Chettam MM
Wright, for Arthur Brooke MM

Hair-dresser
Rappit, from St Ogg's MF

Health remedies purveyor
the late Holt: equivocal benefits FH

Historian
Jacopo Nardi, who wrote of Savonarola R
Antonio Panhormita, humanist R
Giovanni Villani R

Horse-dealer
Bambridge, prosperous MM

Hosier
Barush Nolan, retired from London FH

Hospital board (13)
Arthur Brooke, landowner and new MM
Bulstrode, chairman and treasurer MM
Hackbutt, a rich tanner MM
Frank Hawley, lawyer and town-clerk MM
Larcher, eminent carrier MM
Tertius Lydgaste, newly involved MM
Dr Minchin, surgeon MM
Plymdale, not a Servile Crawler MM
Powderell, retired ironmonger MM
Doctor Sprague, surgeon MM
Rev. Edward Thesiger MM
Mr Toller, medical practitioner MM
Mr Wrench, medical practitioner MM

Host
Mr Arrowpoint DD
Rev. Mr Ely SF
Granby, for a dinner party SF

Householder
Coleman, needed a doctor's visit MM
Gian Fantoni, aided Romola R

Innkeeper: *see* Landlord

Inquisitor
Arbués, in Aragon SG

Investor
Furley, held mortgage on the mill MF
Bob Jakin, trade and speculation MF
Salt, a reference for Jakin MF
Tom Tulliver, with Jakin MF

Ironmonger
Bratti Ferravecchi, street hawker R
Powderell, retired MM

Jeweller
Marshall, at Wanchester DD

Journalist
S. Catulus, articles on science TS 3
Keck, manager of the 'Trumpet' MM
Will Ladislaw MM
Loligo, abusive articles TS 3
Shark, abusive, eloquent articles TS 3
Vibrio, playful notices TS 15

Justice, *and see* Magistrate
Hardy: an information on a dead baby AB
Malam, of capacious mind SM

Laboratory assistant
Marrables, pub philosopher DD

Labourer
Timothy Cooper, lived alone MM
John Olding, a witness in Hetty's trial AB

Land-agent
Bazley, for Lord Brackenshaw DD
Caleb Garth: good work, little charge MM

Landlord (Publican)
Casson of the Donnithorne Arms AB
William Chubb, the Benefit Club FH
Dickison, at the Marquis of Granby MF
Mr Gedge, of the Royal Oak AB
Lorenzo, a tavern host SG
John Snell, of neutral disposition SM

Captain Arthur Donnithorne AB
Gadsby, yeomanry captain DD
Colonel Glasher DD
Hassan, leader of gypsy soldiers SG
Captain Lopez SG
Poulter, retired; teaching drill to boys MF
Duke Silva, commanding his troops SG
Colonel Townley, travelling incognito AB
Captain Anthony Wybrow GL

Miller
Dix, on the same stream as Tulliver MF
Jetsome, hired to manager MF
Sircome, of eminence FH
Tomlinson JR
Tulliver MF

Mining
Mike Brindle, one of the heads FH
Fletcher, colliery lessee DD
Gawcome, colliery lessee DD
Pack, taking the lead at elections FH

Mole-catcher
Jem Rodney

Money-changing
Ephraim Alcharisi DD

Monk (12)
Fra Bartolommeo (formerly Baccio, painter) R
Fra Cristoforo, confessor R
Fra Domenico, follower of Savonarola R
Fra Guiliano, Franciscan R
Fr. Isidor, fanatic brother of the Duke SG
Fra Luca (Bernardino de' Bardi) R
Fr. Marcos, confessor SG
Fra Mariano, preached against Savonatola R
Fra Salvestro Maruffi, confessor R
Fra Francesco di Puglia, preacher R
Girolamo Savonarola R
Ambrosio Traversari, vicar-general of order R

Mountebank
Roldan, street entertainer SG
Vaiano, street-conjuror R

Musician
Maestro Albani, singing teacher GL
Astorga, singing's foster-father DD
Jim Hood, the church's bassoon-man SF
Juan, lutenist and minstrel SG
Julius Klesmer, great DD
Joseph Leo, singing teacher in Vienna DD
Pablo, street singer of great talent SG
Sarti, *primo tenore* for one season GL

Notary
Ser Ceccone, spying for the Mediceans R
Ser Cioni R

Nurseryman
Clintop MM

Optical instrument maker
Gideon, a pub philosopher DD

Packman
Bob Jakin MF

Painter (12)
Baccio, who became a monk R
Piero di Cosimo R
Crespi, an artist TS 9
Critchley, a portraitist MM
Domenico Ghirlandaio R
Giotto de Bondone R
Leonardo da Vinci R
Lorenzo di Credi, portraitist R
Michelangelo Buonarotti R
Alfred Naumann in Rome MM
Antonio Pollajuolo R
Raffaelle (Raphael) R
Andrea del Sarto, frescoist R

Parish clerk
Jonathan Lamb JR
Macey SM
Patch, who goes out to sing carols MF
Spicer, a shoemaker MM
Tookey, deputy SM

Pawnbroker
Ezra Cohen, doing Deronda a service DD
Dunkirk, rich receiver of stolen goods MM
Wiener, at Leubronn DD

Pedlar (and Packman)
Ned Patch, good drinking pot FH

Pew-opener
Zachary, at Malthouse Yard FH

Poacher
Trapping Bass MM
'Brimstone' AB
Jem Rodney SM
Tommy Trounsem (the last Transome) FH

Poet
Girolamo Benevieni, mystic R
Burchiello, also a barber R
Francesco Cei, popular figure R
Matteo Franco R
Mr Furness SF
Jenning, four cantos on croquet DD
Marullo, Greek soldier-poet R
Pontanus (Merula) R

Political activist (21)
Alberti, a Radical in Florence R
Bult, an esteemed party man DD
Piero Capponi, for a Republic R
Piero Dovizi, Medicean R
Piero Guicciardini, moderate R
Felix Holt, with the working-man FH
John Johnson, fomenting riot FH
Domenico Mazzinghi, partisan of Savonarola R
Fra Michele, Carthusian lay brother R
Nerli, a Radical R
Bernardo del Nero R
Pazzi, a Radical R
Giannozzo Pucci, Medicean R
Luigi Pulci R
Gian Battista Ridolfi R
Niccolò Ridolfi R
Bernardo Rucellai, Medicean R
Marco Salviati with a small army R
Dolfo Spini, inclined to violence R
Lorenzo Tornabuoni, Medicean R
Harold Transome, running as Radical FH

Political advisor
Will Ladislaw (Arthur Brooke) MM

Preacher
Apollos TS 9
Flavell, knocked down a hare MM
Johns, in a Baptist chapel TS 9

Caleb Garth MM
Lovegood, to Sir James Chettam MM
Markham, at Cheverel Manor GL
Satchell, does not know timber AB
Scales, house-steward, head butler FH
Stone-breaker
Tudge, grandfather of Job FH
Stone-sawyer
Bill Downes, studying reading AB
Gills, a stone-cutter FH
Student
Jacob Storey, teenager and reading AB
Supercargo
Salt; on ship taking Tulliver's goods MF
Surgeon's Assistant
Filmore, well turned-out FH
James; married employer's niece AB
Surveyor
Caleb Garth MM
Tailor
Cliff, in London; not proud of it SM
Macey, also parish clerk SM
Nanni, political reformer R
Jacob Tomms SF
Tanner
Hackbutt, knowledgeable MM
Tax-gatherer
Baldwin, part of Bulstrode gossip MM
Teacher (and see Schoolmaster)
unnamed; piano to Rosamond MM
Filmore of Corpus Christi FH
Goodrich, drawing-master MF
Leonard Lamb, of Finsbury MM
Mr Simeon, at Cambridge SF
Town-clerk
Frank Hawley, a lawyer MM
Tutor
Joannes Crisola, at the court of Naples R
Fraser, to Daniel Deronda DD
Stillfox, to Rex Gascoigne DD
Valet
Gibbs, on a yacht DD
Dominic Lenoni, to Harold Transome FH
Pummel, to Theophrastus Such TS 8
Pym, to Arthur Donnithorne AB
Turvey, to Sir Hugo Mallinger DD
Mr Warren (Sir Christopher Cheverel) GL
Veterinarian
Horrock, respected judge of horses MM
Waggoner
unnamed; aided Hetty on her way AB
Hiram Ford, a dim notion of London MM
John Gibbs, hired by Mr Tulliver; died MF
Knowles, a driver AB
Waiter
Radcliffe, at the Red Lion bar JR
Warehouse proprietor
Calibut, colleague of Nolan's FH
Baruch Nolan FH
Wastrel
Dunstan (Dunsey) Cass SM
Macarthy NE 1
Durfey Transome, wild half-natural FH
Jim Wakefield, an idle life AB
Watchmaker
Felix Holt; also clocks FH
Pash, pub philosopher DD
Prowd, mentor to Felix Holt FH
Weaver
John Haxey: tablecloths for Tullivers MF
Holt, before turning to nostrums FH
Silas Marner of Raveloe SM
Whart clerk
Stoew, replacing absent Tom Tulliver MF
Tom Tulliver, in his early stages MF
Wheelwright
Will Maskery AB
Ben Winthrop SM
Wine-merchant
Gunn, of Lytherly SM
Mr Tiliot, spirit-merchant FH
Wool-beater
Goro, with a fat cheek R
Wool-stapler
Mr Glegg, retired MF
Wool factor
Salt, a bilious man FH
West, based in Rosseter AB
Wood inlayer
Goodwin, pub philosopher DD
Yacht captain
Angus, for Grandcourt DD

Essay

George Eliot and the Law

George Eliot from her earliest fiction displayed no reluctance to deal with lawyers and the law. We have counted seventeen lawyers and law-firms in her work, a number which cannot compare with sixty clergymen, but the total exceeds that of most of the rest of the professions and occupations represented in the *oeuvre*. It is not the quantity of lawyering in her work, however, that inspires this essay, but rather the surprising ineptitude and carelessness with which this brilliant woman sometimes dealt with legal issues.

Janet's Repentance. Eliot's first lawyer is no credit to his calling: Robert Dempster is a drunk, a wife-abuser, a bully, and, after an initial success in the law thanks to his aggressive unscrupulousness, dead of *delirium tremens*. We do not see him in law practice.

Adam Bede. Hetty Sorrel is tried for infanticide and convicted. We see something of the proceedings and hear witnesses, but the lawyers involved are anonymous. Bartle Massey reports to Adam:

> " ' . . . they're slow, they're slow; and there's the counsel they've got for her puts a spoke in the wheel whenever he can, and makes a deal to do with cross-examining the witnesses, and quarrelling with the other lawyers. That's all he can do for the money they give him . . . he's a 'cute fellow, with an eye that 'ud pick the needles out of the hay in no time. If a man had got no feelings, it 'ud be as good as a demonstration to listen to what goes on in court . . . . ' " AB 42

Hetty is silent, out of pride and shame, and she does not tell her story. Eliot states that, while a witness was allowed to speak to the defendant's good character, this had to stand in the stead of the plea for mercy, "which her own counsel would have made if he had been allowed to speak for her—a favour not granted to criminals in those stern times." AB 42

When Hetty confesses at last, just before her execution, to the saintly Dinah Morris, we realize that her crime had not warranted the death penalty: it was manslaughter through negligence, at worst. Eliot is silent on the point, though she tells the story clearly. Curiously, she refrains from commenting on how Hetty's silence has made a death sentence unavoidable. At the last moment, Hetty's lover brings a reprieve: transportation instead of the gallows.

The Mill on the Floss. Mr Tulliver's struggles litigating water rights are a ground of the plot of Eliot's second novel. His adversary, the unethical attorney John Wakem, gets the better of him and takes over his mill. There is no courtroom scene, no legal action, but the adverse consequences of Tulliver's last lawsuit drive him to bankruptcy and shatter his morale. He gets a chance to chastise his enemy later and does so with enthusiasm, but the effort brings him quickly to his death. Eliot comments on the bankruptcy process:

> ". . . the taxing-masters had done their work like any respectable gunsmith conscientiously preparing the musket that, duly pointed by a brave arm, will spoil a life or two. Allocaturs, filing of bills in Chancery, decrees of sale, are legal chain-shot or bomb-shells that can never hit a solitary mark but must fall with widespread shattering. So deeply inherent is it in this life of ours that men have to suffer for each other's sins, so inevitably diffusive is human suffering, that even justice makes its victims, and we can conceive no retribution that does not spread beyond its mark in pulsations of unmerited pain." MF III 7

Felix Holt. There is plenty of evidence that George Eliot sometimes was very careful in working out a plot where a tricky legal question was involved. FH is the prime example: here arcane questions of Future Interests, as they used to be called in Law School, had to be vetted and approved by an expert attorney, Frederick Harrison, who guided Eliot meticulously through the complex web she had decided to weave. It is so tricky, hardly any reader, not also a legal expert, is likely to understand it—or to care. But the *dénouement* depends on the fact that a cast-away named Tommy Trounsem gets killed in an election riot, and by his death terminates the rights his forebear Thomas Transome had sold to the Durfeys (now known as the Transomes, though they are not the Transomes). These rights, since the estate was entailed, could only be alienated temporarily, that is, only so long as there was a living heir who could have taken the property but for the alienation.

And there is a true heir of the Transome interests, which had devolved upon a family called Bycliffe: this is a Bycliffe daughter whose father had died while unjustly incarcerated for asserting his rights (he was found, falsely, to have committed fraud in doing so—a verdict abetted by the novel's villain, Matthew Jermyn). Esther Lyon is the daughter of the sad man who died, and her identity, once brought to light, makes her the only legal heir and owner of the Transome estate. The putative heir and owner, Harold Transome, will have to quit the property in any event, for Eliot has compounded his plight by making him by birth illegitimate (he is Jermyn's natural son) and not even the Durfey-Transome he thought he was—and the world knows it.

She is silent, and doubtless ignorant through never asking, on the fascinating question of what will happen to the estate since Harold cannot hold it. If his putative father, the senile, helpless old Transome, were competent to do so, he could formally adopt or acknowledge Harold and so perhaps solve the problem. But in the circumstances Eliot has crafted, we are left in the dark. The Attorney General's office will have to do some research to find the next heir. Eliot simply doesn't go there.

Harrison advised Eliot on the details of the trial of Felix Holt for manslaughter, after the death of a constable during the election riots Holt had attempted to prevent and then to deflect. We have no quibble with the way she deals with the flow of witnesses and evidence, and Esther's rising up to speak for her man is moving and very effective—not only for the reader but for the men listening, who gather later to plan an appeal for Holt's deliverance.

In her Introduction to the Penguin edition (1995), Lynda Mugglestone speaks of "Eliot's well-known concern for accuracy," and certainly it is clear that in the case of FH the result partly vindicates the remark. But there later came instances of her dealings with law where the same comment could not be made, and the prime examples occur in her perhaps greatest novel, *Middlemarch.*

Middlemarch. The testamentary law treatments in the novel are to say the least inept, as regards Edward Casaubon's absurd codicil, and clumsy in the case of the farce of Featherstone. Featherstone first:

We are in early 1830. The mortally ill Peter Featherstone has spent the last months of his life entertaining himself by teasing his hovering relations over his Will. Through the lucky chance of manganese found on his property, his power to so torment sisters, brothers, cousins, nephews and nieces (there is no living spouse) has been materially increased. He tells Mary Garth he has made two Wills and that he plans to burn one of them. Apparently he intends thereby to reinstate the other, earlier one he has decided he prefers. But with ironic poetic justice, Mary refuses to cooperate: she will do nothing not in the presence of witnesses. She refuses to be bribed. The old man is frantic but too weak to take matters into his own hands. He is dead by morning.

On the question of cancelling a validly executed Will there were different rules in common law, ecclesiastical law, and equity in Eliot's time. The question is whether such a cancellation or destruction without more revives a previous Will. The subsequent Will would have had language revoking all previous Wills: could actions or words vacate such a revocation? Certainly Mary was right to insist there be witnesses, particularly when it is discovered at the Will reading that her intended husband was the major beneficiary of the prior Will. But because Featherstone has changed his mind too late and is helpless to prevent his last dispositions from taking effect, Fred will end a relatively poor man, happily married and working honestly for a living.

The Wills are read. The family solicitor Mr Standish is present to announce that the Will he drew, dated August 9, 1825, names Fred Vincy (Mary's swain) the legatee of the munificent cash sum of £10,000, with the residuary estate—primarily land, buildings and furniture—going to one Rigg, an illegitimate son whose existence has never been suspected by all those relations. Then the lawyer draws from the chest another, more recently dated Will (July 20, 1826), which, revoking the Will he has just read, effectually leaves the funds originally designated for Fred Vincy to a charitable corporation intended to build housing for the unfortunate. Rigg's bequest stands. The Wills are so disappointing to those assembled that there is an outcry, but Standish states that his colleague Clemmens, who drew the later Will, has enclosed a letter buttressing its status. There is nothing to be done. There is no mention of the witnesses to either Will, and we must assume their signatures were in good order and unimpeachable.

Probably the most significant aspect of all this, though Eliot does not mention it, is the escape Mary Garth, by her integrity and caution, has had. If Featherstone had succeeded in destroying the newer Will, drawn by a living, credible solicitor, it is to be anticipated that Mr Clemmens would have turned up and made very serious trouble for Mary with his evidence concerning that Will. Her naked word that Featherstone had ordered her to bring it to him and had destroyed it himself would have suffered through the evident fact that she has benefitted, through the bequest to her beloved Fred, and her conviction for fraud would not have been unlikely. Fred's bequest would likely have been annulled, and the two lovers would have been sadly discomfited. It seems strange that Eliot would forgo the interest of a discussion of Mary's escape, but it is possible it did not occur to her.

Eliot also omits any allusion to the cold-bloodedness of Featherstone, who had made his Wills five and four years respectively before he presided over the circus of his relations gathered around his death-bed, and who had teased and tantalized Fred Vincy, and made him jump through a variety of hoops, all the while knowing that his second and dispositive Will left him nothing. The whole scenario is improbable and repellent, but, we would have thought, too remarkable to let pass without remark.

Some time after the Will readings, the Rev. Farebrother comes to give Mary comfort, lest she blame herself for depriving Fred of his £10,000: " 'I mean, that your action made no real difference to Fred's lot. I find that the first will would not have been legally good after the burnng of the last; it would not have stood if it had been disputed, and you may be sure it would have been disputed. So, on that score, you may feel your mind free.' " MM 52 He does not explain, nor does Eliot, but we can be comfortably in agreement with him.

Now, as to the Casaubon codicil: we never read it, but we are told more than once—first in a disgruntled conversation between Sir James Chettam and Dorothea's uncle Arthur Brooke; then, in a conversation between Dorothea and her sister Celia—that Mr Casaubon has attempted to disinherit Dorothea if she marries Will Ladislaw, his cousin, of whom he has been furiously jealous. In the first instance, Chettam speaks:

> " 'I say that [Casaubon] has most unfairly compromised Dorothea. I say that there never was a meaner, more ungentlemanly action than this—a codicil of this sort to a will which he made at the time of his marriage with the knowledge and reliance of her family—a positive insult to Dorothea . . . .
>
> " . . . 'But I believe Casaubon was only jealous of [Ladislaw] on Dorothea's account, and the world will suppose that she gave him some reason; and that is what makes it so abominable—coupling her name with this young fellow's.' "
>
> Brooke makes a reply:
>
> " 'Well, it would have been worse if he had made the codicil to hinder her from marrying again at all, you know.'
>
> " 'I don't know that,' said Sir James. 'It would have been less indelicate.'
>
> " 'One of poor Casaubon's freaks! That attack upset his brain a little. It all goes for nothing. She doesn't want to marry Ladislaw.'
>
> " 'But this codicil is framed so as to make everybody believe that she did.' " MM 39

Most of the ensuing conversation is an argument over Chettam's wish to see Will Ladislaw removed from the scene. Brooke finally convinces him that this would look as though her friends did not trust Dorothea where Ladislaw was concerned.

Later, Celia takes matters into her own hands, to apprise Dorothea at last of what her late husband has done.

> " 'I can see what you are thinking of as well as can be, Dodo,' said Celia. 'You are waiting to find out if there is anything uncomfortable for you to do now, only because Mr Casaubon wished it. As if you had not been uncomfortable enough before. And he doesn't deserve it, and you will find that out. He has behaved very badly. James is as angry with him as can be. And I had better tell you, to prepare you.'
>
> " 'Celia,' said Dorothea, entreatingly, 'you distress me. Tell me at once what you mean.' It glanced through her mind that Mr Casaubon had left the property away from her—which would not be so very distressing.
>
> " 'Why, he has made a codicil to his will, to say the property was all to go away from you if you married—I mean—'
>
> " 'That is of no consequence,' said Dorothea, breaking in impetuously.
>
> " 'But if you married Mr Ladislaw, not anybody else,' Celia went on with persevering quietude. 'Of course that is of no consequence in one way—you never *would* marry Mr Ladislaw; but that only makes it worse of Mr Casaubon . . . .
>
> " 'James says so. He says it is abominable, and not like a gentleman. . . . It is as if Mr Casaubon wanted to make people believe that you would wish to marry Mr Ladislaw—which is ridiculous. Only James says it was to hinder Mr Ladislaw from wanting to marry you for your money—just as if he ever would think of making you an offer.' " MM 50

Eliot was perhaps well-advised not to give us the text, because, from the facts she did (and did not) supply, there is no way such a provision could have stood any legal examination. In those times a husband could totally disinherit his wife (though "highly satisfactory" settlements, such as we are told Mr Casaubon had made, would presumably have forestalled this), but the codicil would have been nugatory as described. Leaving aside the unlikelihood that Casaubon could have violated those settlements (Chettam has told us he made a Will leaving his estate to Dorothea at the time he signed them), for the codicil to have been effective there would have had to be trustees appointed with the power to take away Dorothea's inheritance if she married Ladislaw, no matter how far off in the future such an event might occur. We are not told how Casaubon's Will otherwise read: presumably the estate would then go to his remaindermen (though none are named), and if none then by the laws of intestacy to his surviving next of kin, presumably Ladislaw!

Furthermore, a codicil could not be just written out in the dead of night by a solitary testator: it was subject, then as now, to the same requirements for witnessing that a Will is. The only solicitor mentioned in MM is old Mr Standish. There is no hint anywhere that he ever visited Mr Casaubon, or that Mr Casaubon visited him. There is no hint that he knew, at the time or at any time later, about the codicil. And we can expect that he would have remonstrated with Casaubon over it if he had been asked to officiate. And there is no hint that the codicil bore the signatures of witnesses. Who would they have been? Pratt and Tantripp, the two domestics? It is inconceivable that these two excellent people would not have blurted something out after Casaubon's death.

All in all, in *Middlemarch* George Eliot allowed herself a level of laziness and indifference to detail which is incomprehensible, especially given the central importance of the punitive codicil to the later workings-out of the plot.

Daniel Deronda. The only legal issue here revolves around Henleigh Grandcourt's Will, by which, if at the time of his death his wife Gwendolen had had no son, the estate would go, except for a small annuity for his widow, to his illegitimate son by Lydia Glasher.

The anomalous feature here is that this Will apparently did not violate the original marriage settlements. But given Grandcourt's strong, and Gwendolen's credulous advisor's weak, position at the time of the wedding, this is not very surprising. Grandcourt had committed to maintain his wife's family, and he was allowed to have his own way in everything else. Furthermore, he had made a point of being sure that Gwendolen knew in advance what his Will contained, by sending his flunky Lush to tell her about it in detail. She was sincerely pleased that Lydia's boy would benefit and indifferent to the question of her own wealth.

Her former guardian, the Rev. Henry Gascoigne, is disillusioned in Grandcourt, embarrassed and very unhappy when he realized what had been done, but he has to admit to himself that he did not attempt before the marriage to confirm or contradict the rumours he had heard about Grandcourt's prior life.

Rex Gascoigne, who has broken his heart over Gwendolen, is reading law, and he makes the only significant general statement on the subject Eliot has in the *oeuvre:*

> " 'You don't repent the choice of the law as a profession, Rex?' said his father.
>
> " 'There is no profession I would choose before it,' said Rex. 'I should like to end my life as a first-rate judge, and help to draw up a code. I reverse the famous dictum—I should say, "Give me something to do with making the laws, and let who will make the songs." '
>
> " 'You will have to stow in an immense amount of rubbish, I suppose—that's the worst of it,' said the Rector.
>
> " 'I don't see that law-rubbish is worse than any other sort. It is not so bad as the rubbishy literature that people choke their minds with. It doesn't make one so dull. Our wittiest men have often been lawyers. Any orderly way of looking at things as cases and evidence seems to me better than a perpetual wash of odds and ends bearing on nothing in particular. And then, from a higher point of view, the foundations and the growth of law make the most interesting aspects of philosophy and history.' " DD 58

Eliot speaks of the Law as "a profession where much that is noxious may be done without disgrace." FH 21 And she tells us, through the magniloquent Rufus Lyon, that Felix Holt thinks it " 'a profession wherein a man may without shame seek to justify the wicked for reward, and take away the righteousness of the righteous from him.' " FH 38

But this is as far as we need to go with Eliot and the Law.

Index V

Male Characters: Relationships and Characteristics

Peter Garstin FH
Giles, unsuccessful MM
Harold Traansome, running as Radical FH
Cardplayer
Rev. Camden Farebrother, for money MM
Child
unnamed, fascinated by Dinah Morris AB
Addy Bede, Adam's child) AB
Jacob Alexander Cohen, six DD
Glasher boy, five DD
Georgy Moss; ran for his father MF
Willy Moss; asked to hold the horse MF
Edgar Raymond, age four DD
Ben Salt, five (Timothy's Bess's Ben) AB
Job Tudge, five, Felix Holt's pet FH
Tom Tulliver MF
Aaron Winthrop, seven SM
Childhood friend (Schoolfellow)
Dick Brumby, leathered by Bob Jakin MF
Bill Fawks: gave Jenkin a pup
Gibson, schoolmate of Tom Tulliver's MF
Bob Jakin (Tom Tulliver) MF
Spouncer, fought Tom for a share MF
Gil Tranter, who fought Adam, lost AB
Tom Tulliver (Bob Jakin) MF
Clubman
Lentulus, a man of leisure TS 4
Convert
Philip DeBarry, to Catholicism (later) FH
Daniel Deronda, to his Jewishness DD
Coursing enthusiast (greyhound racing)
Mr Chichely, middle-aged bachelor MM
Walter Vincy MM
Cousin(s)
unnamed, blameless Brassing citizens MM
Abbott, of the Dodson sisters
Edward Casaubon and Will Ladislaw MM
Lucy Deane (the Tulliver children) MF
Rex Gascoigne (Harleth, Davilows) DD
Tertius Lydgate and the Captain MM
Mr Oldinport GL
Gilbert Osgood, proposed to Nancy SM
Tradgett, would inherit after Arthur AB
Tom Tulliver (Lucy Deane) MF
Dancer
Bob Cass, a hornpipe SM
Bed Cranage (Wiry Ben) AB
Deaf
Old Maxum SF
Old Feyther Taft AB
Deceased
Thias Bede, drunk in a brook AB
Maurice Christian Bycliffe FH
Rev. Edward Casaubon, suddenly MM
Cliff son; his death undid his father SM
Count Czerlaski SF
Captain Davilow, unmissed DD
Dodson, brother of the sisters MF
Squire Donnithorne AB
Peter Featherstone MM
Mr Gilfil, thirty years ago GL
Harleth, in a hunting accident DD
Alfred Latimer, the elder son and heir LV
Latimer, before the reader's eyes LV
Macarthy, leaving manuscripts NE
Mr Patten SF
John Raffles, questionably MM
Bob Tholer: a coffin ordered AB
Tucker, impetuous constable FH
Tulliver, in bed after a struggle MF
Tom Tulliver, by drowning MF
Waulé, a warm man MM
Capt. Anthony Wybrow, heart trouble GL
Deranged
Cliff father, after his son's death SM
Dilettante
Will Ladislaw, studying abroad MM
Macarthy, high æsthetic sensibility NE
Disablility
Carr, in second childhood MF
Bartle Massey AB
Silly Jim, with hydrocephalus SF
Squire Sandeman, with a clubfoot JR
Tom Tholer, half-witted AB
Mr Transome, half-witted FH
Philip Wakem, crippled in accident MF
Dissenter
Brother Hawkins FH
Thomas Jerome JR
Brother Kemp FH
Lambert, a house near the preaching FH
Rev. Rufus Lyon, eloquent debater FH
Muscat, with his wife FH
Nuttwood, a grocer FH
Samuel Powderell, of purple cheeks MM
Dog-owner
Will Baker, with a bull terrier AB
Bulstrode, with watch-dog Blucher MM
Squire Cass: deer-hound Fleet SM
—Snuff, a brown spaniel SM
Cheverel: blood-hound Rupert GL
Cowper, a spaniel named Beau DD
Countess Czerlaski: Jet, spaniel SF
Dagley: Fag, a sheep-dog MM
Arthur Donnithorne, tiny spaniel Trot AB
the Garths: Brownie, a mongrel MM
the Garths: Fly, black-and-tan terrier MM
Mr Gilfil: Ponto, old brown setter GL
Grandcourt: water-spaniel Fetch DD
Grandcourt: Fluff, a tiny Maltese DD
Rev Irwine: Juno, brown setter AB
—pug, who is part of the family AB
Bob Jakin: Mumps, bull-terrier MF
Latimer, blind Newfoundland Caesar LV
Bartle Massey, the pregnant Vixen AB
the Poysers: Growler, watchdog AB
—Trip, black-and-tan terrier AB
Tullivers: Yap, brown, white terrier MF
Drinker
Jacob Cuff, pothouse ornament FH
Dagley, speaking truth to power MM
Rev. Drumlow; of a cold morning SM
Rev. Mr Horner JR
Mr Pilgrim, doctor much entertained JR
Poulter: gin necessary for firmness MF
Robisson, Mrs Abel's former employer MM
Salkeld, refuge in daily port AB
Tommy Trounsem FH

Heir
Godfrey Cass, got the estate at last SM
Captain Arthur Donnithorne AB
Glasher boy, named in Grandcourt will DD
Henleigh Grandcourt, potential DD
Stephen Guest: major business MF
Harold Transome; Durfey died FH

Horseman
Bryce, unsavoury sort SM
Dunstan Cass, very unsavoury sort SM
Godfrey Cass, likes horses SM
Cliff, thought of nothing but hunting SM
Cliff son, forced to it; afraid of it; died SM
Lord Cromleck SM
Faulkner; a horse from Bambridge MM
Jortin, who owns a mare SM
Keating riding with Bryce, Dunstant SM
Alfred Latimer, to fatal result LV
Fred Vincy, easily gulled MM

Husband
Mr Arrowpoint DD
Banks, bailiff for Sir Hugo DD
Rev. Amos Barton SF
Captain Beevor, dragged wife around MM
Bellamy GL
Bovis TS 13
Lord Brackenshaw DD
Nicholas Bulstrode, got a Vincy MM
Bulstrode: deceived Mrs Dunkirk MM
Maurice Christian Bycliffe (Annette) FH
Rev. Humphrey Cadwallader MM
Rev. Edward Casaubon (Dorothea) MM
Godfrey Cass (Molly Farren *sub rosa*) SM
Godfrey Cass (Nancy Lammeter) SM
Daniel Charisi DD
Sir James Chettam (Celia Brooke) MM
Sir Anthony Cheverel GL
Chowne, a farmer AB
Ezra Cohen DD
Mr Crackenthorp SM
Dagley, indigence inclined to drink MM
Mr Deane, who married a Dodson MF
Rev. Augustus DeBarry FH
Sir Maximus DeBarry FH
Robert Dempster, abusive GL
Kit Downes, crowded family MM
Dunkirk, questionable profession MM
Mr Farquhar SF
Filmore, a nonentity LV
Caleb Garth, lucky in Susan MM
Rev. Henry Gascoigne DD
Maynard Gilfil; she died GL
Colonel Glasher, refused divorce DD
Mr Glegg, who married a Dodson MF
Mr Gogodd, invited to the Grandcourts DD
Hackbutt, knowledgeable tanner MM
Hackit, substantial man SF
Prince Halm-Eberstein DD
Hickes, butler married to Denner FH
Rev. Mr Horner, a quarreller JR
Bob Jakin (Prissy) MF
Thomas Jerome (Susan) JR
Dr Kenn MF
Dr Kimble SM
Ladislaw, from Poland MM
Baron Langen, at Leubronn DD
Latimer (Bertha Grant)—hatred LV
Rev Lingon (Lady Fanny—or Arabella) FH
Tertius Lydgate, unintentionally MM
Rev. Rufus Lyon; she died FH
Will Maskery AB
Proteus Merman TS 3
Mixtus (Scientilla) TS 9
Luke Moggs MF
Bishop Mompert DD
Muscat, a cheese-maker FH
Baruch Nolan FH
Nuttwood, a grocer FH
Oates (wife Sally) SM
Mr Oldinport GL
Mr Palfrey BJ
Pendrell, banker devoted to C of E FH
Lord Pentreath DD
Plymdale MM
Mr Pullet MF
Timothy Rose FH
Sir Jasper Sitwell GL
Mr Spike, an elector TS 7
Dr Sprague MM
Walter Stelling MF
Theophrastus Such (Clarissa) TS 10
Transome, half-witted and useless FH
Tucker, constable who died in riot FH
Mr Tulliver (Bessy) MF
Walter Vincy (Lucy) MM
Ben Winthrop (Dolly) SM
Woodcock, impressed by beauty SF

In debt
Tertius Lydgate MM
The Torbits MM
Fred Vincy, owes Caleb Garth MM

Jew
Ephraim Alcharisi, acquiescent DD
Daniel Charisi, adamant DD
Ezra Cohen, happy shopkeeper DD
Jacob Alexander Cohen, his son DD
Daniel Deronda, at last DD
Joseph Kalonymos, wanderer DD
Kalonymos sons; wealthy in Mainz DD
Julius Klesmer, great musician DD
Ezra (Mordecai) Lapidoth, enthusiast DD
Pash, watchmaker and philosopher DD
Ram, a downtrodden bookseller DD
Wiener, pawnbroking at Leubronn DD
Youth, selling Deronda a book DD

Jilted
Silas Marner (Sarah) SM

Lover
James Chettam (Dorothea Brooke) MM
Rex Gascoigne (Gwendolen Harleth) in vain DD
Maynard Gilfil (Tina Sarti) GL
Henleigh Grandcourt (Mrs Glasher) DD
Will Ladislaw (Dorothea Casaubon) MM
Tertius Lydgate inflamed: Mme Laure MM
Silas Marner (Sarah, servant girl) SM
Pumpkin, putatively, with Miss Pippin MM
Theophrastus Such, perpetual silence TS
Capt. Anthony Wybrow (Tina Sarti) GL

Step-father
Captain Donilow (Gwendolen) DD
Lord Grinsell (Mrs Beevor) MM
Student
Brecon, with a double first DD
Daniel Deronda—Cambridge DD
Rex Gascoigne—Oxford DD
Warham Gascoigne—Wanchester DD
Hans Meyrick—Cambridge DD
Tom Tulliver, privately MF
Testator
Rev. Edward Casaubon MM
Zephaniah Crypt BJ
Peter Featherstone MM
Henligh Mallinger Grandcourt DD
John Justus Transome: difficult will FH
Titled
Sir John Assher, Bart. GL
Sir Hong Kong Bantam TS 9, 11
Sir Christopher Cheverel, Bart. GL
Sir James Chettam MM
Sir James Clement, Bart. FH
Sir James Crake, Master of Harriers MF
Sir Maximus Debarry FH
Sir Godwin Lydgate, Bart. MM
Sir Gavial Mantrap TS 16
Sir William Porter SF
Sir Jasper Sitwell GL
Uncle
Sir Christopher Cheverel (Wybrow) GL
Mr Deane (the Tulliver children) MF
Sir Maximus DeBarry (Harriet, Selina) FH
Peter Featherstone, of Cranch, Waule MM
Henry Gascoigne (Gwendolen, etc.) DD
Mr Hackit (Tom Stokes) GL
Rev. John Lingon (Harold Transome) FH
Charles Lydgate, D. D. (Tertius) MM
Sir Godwin Lydgate (Tertius) MM
Sir Hugo Mallinger (Grandcourt) DD
Moss (Tulliver children) MF
Martin Poyser (Hetty Sorrel) AB
Tulliver (Lucy Deane, Moss children) MF
Walter Vincy (sundry) MM
Ward
Daniel Deronda (de facto) DD
Maynard Gilfil (Cheverel) GL
Widower
Rev. Amos Barton SF
Squire Cass: she has left a vacancy SM
Peter Featherstone MM
John Wakem MF
Witness
unnamed old man, at Hetty's trial AB
Michael Brincey (or Brindle) on Felix FH
John Olding, labourer, at Hetty's trial AB
Wooer
Adam Bede (Hetty Sorrel, Dinah Morris)
Seth Bede (Dinah Morris) AB
young Luke Britton (Hetty Sorrel) AB
James Chettam (Dorothea Brooke) MM
Craig, gardener (Hetty Sorrel) AB
Ben Cranage (his cousin Bessy) AB
David Faux (Penelope Palfrey) BJ
Rex Gascoigne (Gwendolen) in vain DD
Maynard Gilfil (Tina Sarti) GL
Henleigh Grandcourt (Gwendolen) DD
Stephen Guest (Maggie Tulliver) MF
Felix Holt, indirectly (Esther Lyon) FH
Tertius Lydgate: Mme Laure MM
John Towers (Penelope Palfrey) BJ
Harold Transome (Esther Lyon) FH
Philip Wakem (Maggie Tulliver) MF
Anthony Wybrow (Beatrice Assher) GL
Youth
Daniel Deronda, with a future DD
Ganymede TS 12
Rex Gascoigne DD
Stephen Guest MF
Felix Holt FH
Eustace Landor, nearly of age JR
Caius Larcher MM
Hans Meyrick, needing help in school DD
Ned Plymdale MM
Spilkins, a young Slender in the town MM
Tom Tulliver MF
Philip Wakem MF

Index VI

Female Characters: Occupations and Activities

Mrs French, for Sir Hugo DD
Hester, old and hum-backed, for Bates GL
Mrs Kell, at the Grange MM
Martha, for Mr Gilfil GL
Mrs Startin, at Offendene DD

Housewife
Amelia (Milly) Barton SF
Rosamond Lydgate MM
Mary Garth Vincy MM
Mrs Phipps, skinny in the kitchen JR

Landlady
Mrs Dollop: the Tankard, MM
Mrs Short: Camp Villa SF
Mrs Spilkins, at the Cross-Keys FH

Leech-keeper
Dame Fripp, called in to nurse GL

Lodging-house keeper
Mrs Adam, observant DD
Mrs Beck (Mr Bowyer a tenant) MM

Milliner
Mrs Gray, serving Aunt Pullet MF

Musician
Madame Alcharisi, opera singer DD
Catherine Arrowpoint, amateur DD
Gwendolen Harleth, amateur only DD
Miss Hibbert: sang at the Asshers' GL
Mirah Lapidoth, fine singer DD
Rebecca Linnet, in demand for songs JR
Mab Meyrick, good accompanist DD
Tina Sarti, a wonderful singer GL
Rosamond Vincy, fine rote pianist MM

Nymph
Hieria, hamadryad NE 4
Idione, hamadryad NE 4

Parishioner
Dame Fripp, sent great piece of bacon GL
Mrs Hackit, who liked the sermons GL
Mrs Higgins, disapproving levity GL
Mrs Muscat, Dissenter FH
Mrs Nuttwood, Dissenter FH
Mrs Patten GL

Patient
Gregarina, had cholera TS 15
Arabella Hawley, a consumption MM
Miss Wimple (Dr Minchin) MM

Pauper
Poll Fodge SF

Preacher
Dinah Morris, travelling Methodist AB

Roughneck
Molly Beale, brawny virago JR
Dame Ricketts JR

Schoolfellow
Rosamond Vincy, Miss Willoughby MM

Schoolmistress
Mrs Ballard: girls process in twos MM
Miss Firniss, at Laceham on the Floss MF
Mrs Lemon; Rosamond at her school MM
Mme Meunier (Gwendolen) DD
Mme Poinçon, in Lausanne MM
Dame Tedman, had Nancy Lammeter SM
Miss Townley JR

Secretary
Mrs Vigo, reader to royalty MM

Shopkeeper
Sarah Stone: tobacco, snuff, tea AB

Student
Fanny Hackbutt, with Susan Garth MM
Lady Theresa Mallinger, voice lessons DD

Teacher
Susan Garth, experienced MM
Esther Lyon, of French FH
Riley daughter, under-teacher MF

Washerwoman
Sally Butts; had to sell her mangle JR
Phib Cook JR
Mrs Strype, Mr Bulstrode a partisan MM
Mrs Tibbits BJ

Witness
Esther Lyon, for Felix Holt FH
Sarah Stone, shopkeeper: Hetty's trial AB

Index VII

Female Characters: Relationships and Characteristics

the Miss Guests MF
the Miss Gunns SM
Gwendolen Harleth (Mrs Davilow) DD
Louisa Jermyn, vulgar FH
Bessie Knott GL
Miss Ladbrook, in fashion cautious SM
Nancy and Priscilla Lammeter SM
Miss Landor, the belle of Milby JR
Mirah Lapidoth, father embarrassing DD
Miss Lawe, of Lady Lawe; outshone DD
Esther Lyon, Bycliffe and LeDru FH
Annabel and Theresa Mallinger DD
Mrs Mengan (Sir Godwin Lydgate) MM
Mab, Kate and Amy Meyrick DD
Jimmy Oates SM
Penelope Palfrey BJ
Miss Phipps JR
the four Misses Pittman JR
Charlotte (Totty) Poyser AB
Sophy Toller MM
the three Misses Tomlinson JR
Maggie Tulliver MF
Miss Turnbull, snubbing Maggie MF
Rosamond and Louisa Vincy MM
Rebecca, Joanna, Elizabeth Waule MM

Daughter, foster
Eppie Cass; by the weaver she visited SM
Esther Lyon, (Rev. Rufus) unknowing FH

Daughter-in-law
Janet Dempster (Mamsey); suffering JR

Deaf
Mrs Crewe JR

Deceased
Amelia (Milly) Barton SF
Mrs Bretton: her house would suit MM
Molly Farren (Cass); died in snowdrift SM
Hieria, her tree cut down NE
Mrs Sutton, pleurisy MF
Maggie Tulliver, by drowning MF

Disability
Ann Irwine, chronically ill AB
Miss Kirke, a spinal complaint MF
Sally Martin, deformed and tubercular JR

Dog-owner
Brooke girls: Monk, great St Bernard MM
Lucy Deane: Lolo, a little dog who died MF
—Minny, a King Charles spaniel MF
Eppie Marner: Snap, brown terrier SM
Mrs Transome: Moro, King Charles FH
—Nimrod, black retriever FH
—Puff, old Blenheim spaniel FH

Drinking problem
Janet Dempster; under great pressure JR
Dolly Farren, hopeless drunkard SM

Engaged
Alice, lady's maid, to Bridmain SF
Dorothea Brooke, to Mr Casaubon MM
Lucy Deane, to Stephen Guest MF
Mary Garth, finally, to Fred Vincy MM
Penelope Palfrey, to David Faux BJ
Penelope Palfrey, to Freely BJ
Miss Selina Parrot AB
Sarah, to Silas Marner; broke it off SM
Sophy Toller (Ned Plymdale) MM
Rosamond Vincy (Tertius Lydgate) MM

Fallen woman
Lucy, seduced by Edgar Tryan JR

Flaunter
Bessy Cranage, frightened by sermon AB
Deb Traunter JR

Granddaughter
Lizzie Jerome (Thomas) JR
Gwendolen Harleth (Armyn) DD
Nancy and Priscilla Lammeter SM
Maggie Tulliver, like grandmother MF

Grandmother
Mrs Cohen, won't speak of a daughter DD
Lady Molly Harleth (Gwendolen) DD
Mrs Tulliver senior; fine, dark-eyed MF

Half-sister
Countess Caroline Czerlaski SF
Gwendolen Harleth (Davilow sisters) DD

Heiress
Mrs Arrowpoint (*née* Cuttler) DD
Dorothea Brooke—if MM
Sarah Dunkirk, of dirty wealth MM
Esther Lyon, unexpectedly FH

Jewess
Mrs Charisi DD
Addy Cohen DD
Adelaide Rebekah Cohen DD
Eugenie Esther Cohen DD
Mirah Lapidoth DD

Jilt
Sarah, servant-woman (Silas Marner) SM

Jilted
Lucy Deane (Stephen Guest) MF
Tina Sarti (Anthony Wybrow) GL

Maid, hopeful
Mary Burge (Adam Bede) AB
Bessy Cranage (Adam Bede) AB
Mirah Lapidoth (Daniel Deronda) DD
Miss Pippin (Mr Pumpkin) MM
Rosamond Vincy (Lydgate) MM

Married twice
Mrs Davilow (Harleth the first) DD

Mistress
Lydia Glasher (Grandcourt) DD
Mrs Rigg, frog features (Featherstone) MM

Mother
Leonora Alcharisi (Daniel Deronda) DD
Mrs Arrowpoint (Catherine) DD
Lady Assher (Beatrice) GL
Amelia (Milly) Barton SF
Lisbeth Bede (Adam and Seth) AB
Lady Brackenshaw (two girls, a boy) DD
Harriet Bulstrode (Ellen and Kate) MM
Annette LeDru Bycliffe, abandoned FH
Celia Chettam, with new baby MM
Lady Clementina (nine daughters) DD
Ann Coulter, with an idiot child SM
Martha Cranch (*née* Featherstone) MM
Fanny Davilow (formerly Harleth) DD
Susan Deane (Lucy) MF
Mamsey Dempster, pernicious JR
Mrs Farebrother (Camden) MM
Molly Farren (Cass), a little baby SM
Susan Garth (two girls, four boys) MM

Bessy Tulliver (*née* Dodson) MF
Maggie Tulliver (Tom) MF
Lucy Vincy, late Mrs Featherstone MM
Rosamond and Louisa Vincy MM
Jane Waule (*née* Featherstone) MM
Rebecca, Joanna, Elizabeth Waule MM
Mrs Wybrow, Sir Christopher Cheverel GL

Sister-in-law
Harriet Bulstrode (Lucy Vincy) MM
Lucy Vincy—and old Featherstone MM

Spinster
Sister Allen, in decline AB
Lydia Donnithorne AB
Winifred Farebrother, elder sister MM
Janet Gibbs SF
Clara Harfager, with a portion MM
Ann Irwine AB
Miss Kate Irwine AB
Mary Linnet, amiable JR
old Miss Lukyn FH
Miss Phipps, stumpy and poor dresser SF
Miss Pratt JR

Step-daughter
Mrs Beevor (Lord Grinsell) MM
Gwendolen Harleth, abused DD

Titled
Lady Dacey AB
Lady DeBarry FH
Lady Molly Harleth, grandmother DD
Lady Flora Hollis, a lively curiosity DD
Lady Lawe, an outshone daughter DD
Lady Fanny Lingon, married a parson FH
Lady Sara Lingon, mad husband FH
Lady Louisa Mallinger DD
Lady Alicia Methurst, inherited FH
Lady Pentreath, grace in age DD
Lady Porter, alleged friend of Czerlaski SF
Lady Betty Transome FH
Princess Wengstein SF
Lady Wyvern FH

Town-bred
Mrs Jennings, improper mourning GL

Ward
Celia Brooke (uncle Arthur Brooke) MM
Dorothea Brooke (Arthur Brooke) MM

Widow
Lisbeth Bede (Thias drowned) AB
Dorothea Casaubon
Countess Caroline Czerlaski SF
Fanny Davilow (Mr Harleth is dead) DD
Sarah Dunkirk, too trusting MM
Gwendolen Grandcourt DD
Mrs Bessie Hartopp, to be dispossessed GL
Mary Holt (*née* Wall): nostrums are out FH
Mrs Patten, wealthy by no spending SF
Mrs Pettifer, caregiver in illness JR
Mrs Renfrew, colonel's widow MM
Mrs Steene, a bit of a drinker AB
Mrs Tucker, will get a pension FH

Wife
Mrs Abel, puzzled but forgot it MM
Leonora Alcharisi (Ephraim) DD
Mrs Arrowpoint (*née* Cuttler) DD
Lady Assher, to a baronet GL
Mrs Banks, wife of Sir Hugo's bailiff DD
Amelia (Milly) Barton SF
Lisbeth Bede (Thias, who died) AB
Mrs Beevor, married the captain MM
Mrs Bellamy GL
Mrs Bovis TS 13
Lady Brackenshaw DD
Mrs Brimley, carpenter's wife JR
Harriet Bulstrode (*née* Vincy) MM
Elinor Cadwallader (*née* De Bracy) MM
Dorothea Casaubon
Nancy Cass, sadly childless SM
Mrs Charisi DD
Celia Chettam MM
Henrietta Lady Cheverel GL
Mrs Chowne, not especially wise AB
Addy Cohen (Ezra) DD
Mrs Crackenthorp SM
Lady Dacey AB
Mrs Dagley, too poor for church MM
Fanny Davilow (Captain is gone) DD
Mrs Susan Deane MF
Lady DeBarry (Sir Maximus) FH
Lady Mary DeBarry (the rector) FH
Janet Dempster JR
Denner (Mrs Hickes) FH
Mrs Dingall, grocer's wife AB
Mrs Farquhar SF
Molly Farren (Cass), hidden SM
Felicia, unnerved by deference TS 5
Mrs Filmore LV
Mrs Gadsby, a yeomanry captain DD
Susan Garth MM
Nancy Gascoigne (Rev. Henry) DD
Mrs Gilfil (Tina Sarti) GL
Lydia Glasher, was refused a divorce DD
Mrs Jane Glegg MF
Mrs Goby, money in trust MM
Mrs Gogoff, a giantess spoils the room DD
Gwendolen Grandcourt DD
Mrs Hackbutt, weighed with scandal MM
Mrs Hackit GL
Princess Leonora Halm-Eberstein DD
Mrs Lucy Heron GL
Prissy Jakin MF
Mrs Susan Jerome (Thomas) JR
Mrs Kenn, an invalid MF
Mrs Kimble, wife of the doctor SM
Julia Ladislaw: husband Polish MM
Baroness Langen, inveterate gambler DD
Sara Lapidoth DD
Bertha Latimer (*née* Grant)—hatred LV
Arabella Lingon (? parson Lingon) FH
Lady Fanny Lingon (parson Lingon) FH
Lady Sara Lingon, mad husband FH
Rosamond Lydgate MM
Annette LeDru Lyon FH
Lady Louisa Mallinger (*née* Raymond) DD
Mrs Maskery AB
Julia Merman, heroically loyal TS 3
Mrs Moggs, hospitable MF
Mrs Mompert, position for Gwendolen DD
Mrs Muscat, husband makes cheese FH
Mrs Nolan, Baruch's helpmeet FH

Grandcourt and Gwendolen are Courting

Essay

The Elephant in the Parlor: Child-abuse in *Daniel Deronda*

There will be those who, reading what follows, may be inclined to sneer: "Today it is the fashion to speculate about child-abuse, to apply Freudian theory to everything." But it is worth remembering that some scholars now believe that Freud, working with patients who told him of abominations at the hands of parents and other adults, did not believe their stories and prudishly concluded that this was all fantasy life growing out of id and libido. Now, we recognize that at least some of those poor people were recounting actual occurrences. Perhaps Eliot had a similar blind spot, perhaps not, but we are convinced that, whether deliberately or not, she traced accurately and convincingly in an unfortunate adult the buried trauma of an abused infant.

The striking and surprising scene between Gwendolen Harleth and Rex Gascoigne, when he professes his love (perhaps callow, but desperately sincere) and she flies into an hysterical fit, is the culmination of a series of little hints pointing to a tragedy never described but, in our view, *the* central engine of the action and explanation of the behaviour of a very attractive, conflicted, extremely spoiled, erratic, and vulnerable heroine. We argue that this behaviour, including Gwendolen's sleep disorders, sudden hysterics, fears of being alone at night, and apparent inability to love a man in a normal way, is explained by a history of the sexual abuse of a prepubescent, beautiful girl by her recreant step-father, Captain Davilow.

Did Eliot consciously or unconsciously posit a dreadful past for her heroine? We will brave the reader's raised eyebrow. We ask only that that reader keep an open mind and consider the evidence we assemble below, for there is quite a lot, and it cannot all be coincidental or inadvertent. Here is the sequence of clues we have noticed (all emphases are ours):

The first reference to Captain Davilow, Gwendolen Harleth's step-father, occurs at the beginning of the novel, as Gwendolen is approaching a new home at Offendene—once, we are told, the abode of dowager countesses. This prior use suits Gwendolen very well, as her family considers itself in the "border-territory of rank" and well-suited to a house which "no beholder could suppose to [have been] inhabited by retired tradespeople."

This new accession of circumstance "appeared suddenly possible on the death of her step-father Captain Davilow, who had for the last nine years joined his family only in a brief and fitful manner, enough to reconcile them to his long absences; but she cared much more for the fact than for the explanation. All her prospects had become more agreeable in consequence . . . . She would probably have known much more about her father but for an incident which happened when she was twelve years old. Mrs Davilow had brought out, as she did only at wide intervals, various memorials of her first husband, and while showing his miniature to Gwendolen recalled with a fervour . . . the fact that that dear papa had died when his little daughter was in long clothes. Gwendolen, immediately thinking of the unlovable step-father whom she had been acquainted with the greater part of her life *while her frocks were short,* said—

" 'Why did you marry again, mamma? It would have been nicer if you had not.'

"Mrs Davilow coloured deeply, a slight convulsive movement passed over her face, and straightway shutting up the memorials she said, with a violence quite unusual in her—

" 'You have no feeling, child!'

"Gwendolen, who was fond of her mamma, felt hurt and ashamed, and had never since dared to ask a question about her father." DD 3

During the initial inspection of Offendene, the youngest Davilow girl, Isabel, opens a panel in the wainscoting.

"The opened panel had disclosed the picture of an upturned dead face from which an obscure figure seemed to be fleeing with outstretched arms. 'How horrible!' said Mrs Davilow, with a look of mere disgust; but Gwendolen shuddered silently, and Isabel, a plain and altogether inconvenient child with an alarming memory, said—

" 'You will never stay in this room by yourself, Gwendolen.' " DD 3

Gwendolen is furious. She demands that the panel be shut and locked, and if there is no key one must be made and given to her. Her face is "flushed in reaction from her chill shudder."

Later, in her room, she vows to her mother, " 'I have made up my mind not to let other people interfere with me *as they have done.*' " There is *never any explanation* of what specifically she is talking about. "Mrs Davilow [was] conscious that she had always been seen under a cloud as poor dear Fanny, who had made a sad blunder with her second marriage . . . . " DD 3

Her uncle Gascoigne remarks after dinner to his wife that Gwendolen " 'has been under a disadvantage with such a father-in-law,' " but there is no reason to suppose he suspects anything really untoward.

In the next chapter, there is more of the same, and one begins to think that Eliot must mean something by it. Gwendolen's charm and wilfulness, to which even waiters automatically pay obeisance, mark her out. She is the eldest daughter, "towards whom her mamma had always been in an apologetic state of mind *for the evils brought on her by a step-father.*" DD 4 Again, there is no explanation. *Evils?* We are left to our imaginations, and where do they lead?

The mysterious panel is the center of the next incident, during the performance of charades at the house.

" . . . the movable panel, which was on a line with the piano, flew open on the right opposite the stage and disclosed the picture of the dead face and the fleeing figure, brought out in pale definiteness by the position of the wax-lights. Every one was startled, but all eyes in the act of turning towards the opened panel were recalled by a piercing cry from Gwendolen, who stood without change of attitude, but with a change of expression that was terrifying in its terror. She looked like a statue into which a soul of Fear had entered: her pallid lips were parted; her eyes, usually narrowed under their long lashes, were dilated and fixed. Her mother, less surprised than alarmed, rushed towards her . . . the touch of her mother's arm had the effect of an electric charge. Gwendolen fell on her knees and put her hands before her face. She was still trembling, but mute, and it seemed that she had self-consciousness enough to aim at controlling her signs of terror, for she presently allowed herself to be raised from her kneeling posture and led away, while the company were relieving their minds by explanation." DD 6

Eliot at first gives us no way to diagnose the reasons for this striking overreaction. Gwendolen "had shown her susceptibility to terror. She wondered at herself in these occasional experiences, which seemed like a brief remembered madness, an unexplained exception from her normal life; and in this instance she felt a peculiar vexation that her helpless fear had shown itself, not, as usual, in solitude, but in well-lit company." But then Eliot explores more deeply and comes to a point where we seem to be invited to insert our own interpretation.

"What she unwillingly recognized, and would have been glad for others to be unaware of, was that liability of hers to fits of spiritual dread, though this fountain of awe within her had not found its way into connection with the religion taught her or with any human relations. She was ashamed and frightened, as at what might happen again, in remembering her tremor on suddenly feeling herself alone, when, for example, she was walking without companionship and there came some rapid change in the light. Solitude in any wide scene impressed her with an undefined feeling of immeasurable existence aloof from her, in the midst of which she was helplessly incapable of asserting herself . . . .

"To her mamma and others her fits of timidity or terror were sufficiently accounted for by her 'sensitiveness' or the 'excitability of her nature;' but these explanatory phrases required conciliation with much that seemed to be blank indifference or rare self-mastery. Heat is a great agent and a useful word, but considered as a means of explaining the universe it requires an extensive knowledge of differences; and as a means of explaining character 'sensitiveness' is in much the same predicament."

We come now to the moment when Rex Gascoigne speaks. Eliot has set the stage explicitly as a halcyon moment when the two ride together on a beautiful morning. Rex's evident idealization of the beautiful Gwendolen takes an ominous turn introduced by the faint intimation, "For *some* of the goodness which Rex believed in was there." Eliot's powerful evocation of childhood and its dangers makes the blood run cold:

"Goodness is a large, often a prospective word; like harvest, which at one stage when we talk of it lies all underground, with an indeterminate future: is the germ prospering in the darkness? At another, it has put forth delicate green blades, and by-and-by the trembling blossoms are ready to be dashed off by an hour of rough wind or rain. Each stage has its peculiar blight, and *may have the healthy life choked out of it by a particular action of the foul land which rears or neighbours it,* or *by damage brought from foulness afar.*" DD 7

What in the world is she talking about? *Foulness?* What intimation of 'foulness' have we had or have a basis to infer?

"Gwendolen was perfectly aware that her cousin was in love with her; but she had no idea that the matter was of any consequence, having never had the slightest visitation of painful love herself. She wished the small romance of Rex's devotion to fill up the time of his stay at Pennicote, and to avoid explanations which would bring it to an untimely end. Besides, she objected, *with a sort of physical repulsion,* to being directly made love to. With all her imaginative delight in being adored, there was a certain fierceness of maidenhood in her." DD 7

Gwendolen, intoxicated by the sights and sounds of the hunt, follows, and Rex tries to do so, but his horse stumbles and breaks his knees. Rex is thrown and dislocates his shoulder. He is helped home, but the next day he walks to Offendene to make his avowals. "The perception that poor Rex wanted to be tender made her curl up and harden like a sea-anemone at the touch of a finger."

" 'Pray don't make love to me! I hate it.' She looked at him fiercely.

"Rex turned pale and was silent, but could not take his eyes off her, and the impetus was not yet exhausted that made her eyes dart death at him. Gwendolen herself could not have foreseen that she should feel in this way. It was all a sudden, new experience to her . . . the life of passion had begun negatively in her. She felt passionately averse to this volunteered love."

" 'Is that the last word you have to say to me, Gwendolen? Will it always be so?'

"She could not help seeing his wretchedness and feeling a little regret for the old Rex who had not offended her. Decisively, but with some return of kindliness, she said—

" 'About making love? Yes. But I don't dislike you for anything else.'

"There was just a perceptible pause before he said a low 'good-bye.' And passed out of the room. Almost immediately after, she heard the heavy hall-door bang behind him.

"Mrs Davilow too had heard Rex's hasty departure, and presently came into the drawing-room, where she found Gwendolen seated on the low couch, her face buried, and her hair falling over her figure like a garment. She was sobbing bitterly. 'My child, my child, what is it?' cried the mother, who had never before seen her darling struck down in this way, and felt something of the alarmed anguish that women feel at the sight of overpowering sorrow in a strong man; for the child had been her rule. Sitting down by her with circling arms, she pressed her cheek against Gwendolen's head, and then tried to draw it upward. Gwendolen gave way, and letting her head rest against her mother, cried out sobbingly, 'Oh mamma, what can become of my life? there is nothing worth living for!'

" 'Why, dear?' said Mrs Davilow. Usually she herself had been rebuked by her daughter for involuntary signs of despair.

" 'I shall never love anybody. *I can't love people.* I hate them.'

" 'The time will come, dear, the time will come.'

" Gwendolen was more and more convulsed with sobbing; but putting her arms round her mother's neck with an almost painful clinging, she cried brokenly, '*I can't bear any one to be very near me but you.*'

"Then the mother began to sob, for this spoiled child had never shown such dependence on her before: and so they clung to each other." DD 7

There is a report that a bachelor of good fortune has come to the area for the hunting. Of course, it is to be supposed that he is in want of a wife. Gwendolen professes herself amused and indifferent. Her badinage with her mother leads to a riposte.

" 'I declare when your aunt and I were your age we knew nothing about wickedness. I think it was better so.'

" 'Why did you not bring me up in that way, mamma?' said Gwendolen. But immediately perceiving in the crushed look and rising sob that she had given a deep wound, she tossed down her hat and knelt at her mother's feet, crying—

" 'Mamma, mamma! I was only speaking in fun. I meant nothing.'

" 'How could I, Gwendolen?' said poor Mrs Davilow, unable to hear the retractation, and sobbing violently while she made the effort to speak. 'Your will was always too strong for me—if everything else had been different.'

"This disjointed logic was intelligible enough to the daughter [if not to the reader]. 'Dear mamma,. I don't find fault with you—I love you,' said Gwendolen, really compunctious. 'How can you help what I am? Besides, I am very charming. Come, now.' Here Gwendolen with her handkerchief gently rubbed away her mother's tears. 'Really—I am contented with myself. I like myself better than I should have liked my aunt and you. How dreadfully dull you must have been!'

"Such tender cajolery served to quiet the mother, as it had often done before after like collisions. Not that the collisions had often been repeated at the same point; for in the memory of both *they left an association of dread* with the particular topics which had occasioned them. Gwendolen dreaded the unpleasant sense of compunction towards her mother, which was the nearest approach to self-condemnation and self-distrust that she had known; and Mrs Davilow's timid maternal conscience dreaded whatever had brought on the slightest hint of reproach." DD 9

With the arrival on the scene of Mr Grandcourt and Gwendolen's demonstration of archery prowess, the plot of the novel gains momentum, and we find fewer references to any unsavoury past of Gwendolen's. Instead, it is Grandcourt's unsavory past which moves center-stage. Learning of it, Gwendolen flees to the continent. Then word reaches her that her family is ruined. She returns to Offendene and broods in the railway station. "Events might turn out anyhow, and *men were hateful.* Yes, men were hateful. Those few words were filled out with *very vivid memories.*" DD 21 We are given nothing with which to fill in this mysterious phrase.

Gwendolen consults the great musician Klesmer on her potential for the stage and is disabused. She must accept the post of governess with a bishop's family. She greets the Gascoignes cordially. "She had no gratuitously ill-starred feeling, or egoistic pleasure in making men miserable. *She only had an intense objection to their making her miserable.*" DD 24 There has been no antecedent explanation of this sentence, as usual.

Grandcourt pursues and wins Gwendolen. The day of the wedding arrives. Gwendolen is now to be a bride, and the bride of a masculine man of will who can be expected to assert his conjugal rights promptly. Gwendolen reflects.

> "Was it alone the closeness of this fulfilment which made her heart flutter? Or was it some dim forecast, *the insistent penetration of suppressed experience,* mixing the expectation of a triumph with the dread of a crisis? Hers was one of the natures in which exultation inevitably carries an infusion of dread ready to curdle and declare itself." 31

We won't keep beating the reader over the head, except with italics.

A miserably unhappy period of months of marriage leads at last to a trip to the Mediterranean, where Grandcourt's tormenting of his bride continues with his insistence on her accompanying him in a small boat while his yacht is being refurbished. The boom sweeps; the sail knocks him into the water; he calls for a rope; Gwendolen is frozen; he drowns. She tells Deronda the story. It seems that she has identified Grandcourt with her "father-in-law," that is to say, Captain Davilow.

> " 'I was full of rage at being obliged to go—full of rage—and I could do nothing but sit there like a galley-slave. And then we got away—out of the port—into the deep—and everything was still—and we never looked at each other, only he spoke to order me—and the very light about me seemed to hold me a prisoner and force me to sit as I did. *It came over me that when I was a child I used to fancy sailing away into a world where people were not forced to live with any one they did not like—I did not like my father-in-law to come home.* And now, I thought, just the opposite had come to me. I had stept into a boat, and my life was a sailing and sailing away—gliding on and no help—always into solitude with *him,* away from deliverance. And because I felt more helpless than ever, my thoughts went out over worse things—I longed for worse things—I had cruel wishes—I fancied impossible ways of—I did not want to die myself; I was afraid of our being drowned together. If it had been any use I should have prayed—I should have prayed that something might befall him. I should have prayed that he might sink out of my sight and leave me alone. I knew no way of killing him there, but I did, *I did kill him in my thoughts.'* " DD 56

Gwendolen's inability to evade Grandcourt's courtship, despite her knowledge of his past, recalls the fear and helplessness the little girl would have felt when her step-father came for her in the night. At some level she recognized *and responded to* the selfishness, the cruelty, the egotism, the ruthlessness, the dominance she had known before. Childish terror and impotence, hypnotized bridal compliance, frozen powerlessness when her demonic wish comes true and she is appalled by her seeming magical power. She can gain no comfort from the poetic justice visited on her cruel master.

We are left to imagine what she will do now with her life, and to wonder whether it is conceivable that she will gain emotional health sufficiently to accept Rex's love. We fear it cannot be. Gwendolen's psychic development has been forever stunted. Deronda's marriage deprives her, not of a loving husband, but of a protector and mentor who would keep her from wreaking more vengeance, inflicting more misery, on the world and on herself.

Index VIII

Pet and Other Animal Names

Nägeli, one of the miller's cows at St. Märgen	AG 59
Nimrod, a fine old black retriever, in residence at Transome Court	FH 1, 40
Old Brown, a sober horse at the Hall Farm	AB 22
Ponto, Mr Gilfil's old brown setter	GL 1
Primrose, Mr Gascoigne's grey nag; of ecclesiastical habits	DD 7
Puff, an old and peevish Blenheim spaniel at Transome Court	FH 7
Pug, part of the Irwine family	AB 16
Rattler, a horse in the Donnithorne stable	AB 12
Rupert, Sir Christopher Cheverel's pet blood-hound	GL 2
Saad, the noisy dog of Hinda's, who died	SG III
Sally, a meek short-horn at the Hall Farm	AB 18
Seneca, a solemn mastiff leaning on his master Lorenzo's knee	SG I i
Sindbad, Lucy Deane's chestnut horse	MF VI 1
Snap, a knowing brown terrier in the Marner household	SM 16
Snuff, the Cass family's brown spaniel	SM 3
Speckle, steady old grey horse owned by Mr Lammeter	SM 17
Tancred, Stephen Guest's great bay horse	MF VI 11
Toby, a mongrel whose mother acts in the Punch show	MF IV 3
Tortoise, a cat in the Garth family	MM 24
Trip, a black and tan terrier at the Hall Farm	AB 6
Trot, a tiny spaniel, inseparable companion to Meg	AB 12
Veilchen, one of the miller's cows at St. Märgen	AG 59
Vixen, a bitch of indeterminate breed: very short legs and two puppies	AB 21
Wildfire, Godfrey Cass's fine hunter, which Dunsey rides to death	SM 3
Yap, a brown and white terrier resident at the Mill on the Floss	MF I 4
Yarico, Grandcourt's beautiful black horse	DD 27

Index IX

Localities Mentioned in the Fictional Works

Great Britain

Houndsley, site of a horse-fair MM 23
Ilsley, a rail connection MM 68
Loamford AB 11 FH 41 MM 58
Middlemarch (q.v.) MM
Norburne AB 12
Oakbourne, a carrier stop AB 11, 36
Riverston, near Middlemarch MM 56
Rosseter AB 6
Tipton MM 26
Treddleston AB 2
Wartson Wake AB 10
Willow Brook, the AB 10
London JR 2
Bedford Row (Johnson) FH 17, 30, *E*
Blackfriars Bridge DD 20, 38
Brompton (Mordecai) DD 46, 62
Chelsea (Meyrick) DD 16, 37, 40
Chelsea Stairs DD 40
Colman Street DD 20
Crystal Palace DD 34
Gower Street JR 18
Grosvenor Square DD 44
Holborn DD 33, 40
Knightsbridge DD 62
Lambeth DD 20
Marble Arch DD 52
Newgate prison MM 74
Park Lane (Mallinger) DD 17, 28, 45
Regent Street DD 39
Rotten Row DD 33, 48
St Mary Axe DD 33
Whitehapel DD 33
Lowick (F), near Middlemarch MM 2
Frick, a hamlet MM 56
Halsell Common MM 37
Halsell Wood MM 46
Luckreth (F) near St Ogg's MF VI 13
Lytherly (the Miss Gunns) (F) SM 11
Market Bewley MF I 7
Melspring (F) MM 84
Middlemarch, Loamshire (F) MM
Blindman's Court MM 69
Bride Street MM 64
Lowick Gate (the Lydgates) MM 27
Parley Street MM 45
Slaughter Lane MM 45
St Peter's Place (Ned Plymdale) MM 64
Three Crofts, part of Stone Court MM 32
Milby (F) SF 2
The Bridge Way JR 4
Butcher's Lane JR 3
Dog Lane JR 4
Friar's Gate JR 2
Orchard Street (the Dempsters) JR 4
Paddiford Common JR 2
Redhill Road JR 25
Tucker's Lane JR 4
Molton (F) LV 2
Mudport, Lincolnshire [Brassing] MF I 2
Newcastle MF VI 5 FH *I*, 11, 37
North Loamshire (F) FH *I*
Duffield FH 2, 20, 28
Hathercote FH 31
Leek Malton FH 20
Little Treby FH *I*
Loamford Gaol (Felix Holt) FH 33
Malthouse Yard (Rev. Rufus Lyon) FH 3
Sproxton FH 3, 5, 11
New Pits FH 11
Old Pits FH 11
Pitchley District FH 17
Treby Magna FH *I*
Hobb's Lane FH 33
King Street FH 31, 33
Park Street FH 33
Pod's End FH 20
Pollard's End FH 28
Northumberland BJ 2
Norton AB 37
Nottingham FH *I*
Paddiford Common (F) JR 1
Prison Street, near Lantern Yard SM 21
Pumpiter (Vorticella; F) TS 15
Putney DD 17
Quallingham (Sir Godwin Lydgate) MM 36
—in the North of England
Raveloe (Silas Marner), central England SM
Richmond 3M 167
river Ripple [river Idle] MF
Ripstone, a market town GL 2
Rodham (F) BJ 2
Rotherby (F) SF 8 GL 1
Royston Baths SM 17
Sark TS 15
Scarborough, on the coast MF VII 4
Scotland MF VI 13
Sheffield TS 17 WM 170
Shepperton (F) SF *passim.*
Shetland Isles NH 143
Shoe Lane, near Lantern Yard SM 21
Skipper's Lane, southern port town FH 6
Sloppeter (F) GL 4
Southampton FH 6 DD 7
St Ogg's (F)
—[Gainsborough, Lincolnshire] MF I 1
Danish St (grocer Hyndmarsh) MF III 7
Dorlcote Mill, on the Ripple MF I 1
Dunlow Common (gypsies) MF I 11
Dunlow Lane MF I 11
Fibb's End MF V 2
Kennel Yard (Bob Jakin's world) MF I 6
River Street (Guest & Co.) MF III 5
Tofton Ferry MF V 7
Tofton Road MF I 12
Stony Stratford AB 36
Stonyshire (F; Derbyshire)
Littleshaw (Trounsem) FH 28, 29, 35
Sloman's End AB 54
Snowfield (Cromford) AB 3
Stoniton AB 35
Church Lane (Sarah Stone) AB 43
Hetton Coppice AB 43
Tedd's Hole, two miles out AB 43
Staffordshire GL 21
Stratford-on-Avon AB 36
Sydenham HH 46
Tarley, parish next to Raveloe (F) SM 1
Tetterley (F) SF 6

Elsewhere

Italian Locations Mentioned in *Romola*

Spanish Locations Mentioned in *The Spanish Gypsy*

Index X

Historical Figures Mentioned in the Fiction

[includes passing references in the Nonfiction; for major references *see* pp 647ff]
[For authors and composers *see* Index XI]

B

Baccio, Florentine painter, later became Fra Bartolommeo	R 49
Bacon, Francis, Baron Verulam, Viscount St Albans (1561-1626); statesman, lawyer	FH 30
Barbara, Santa (3d or 4th c.); supposedly imprisoned in tower to avoid contamination	MM 10
Barbarossa: *see* Frederick I	
Bardo de' Bardi, of the Florentine Bardo banking family, ruined by an English king	R 5 ff
Bartolomeo, Michelozzo di (1396-1472), Florentine architect	R *P*
Bartolommeo, Fra (Bartolommeo della Porta; 1472-1517), Florentine painter	R 25, 49
Baxter, Richard (1615-91); Puritan minister during the Civil War in England	FH 6
Baylem Pierre (1647-1706); Protestant philosopher and critic	IR 118
Ben Azai, either a Jewish teacher of Roman times, or an 8th century biblical scholar	DD 46
ben Chananja, Joshua; Jewish spiritual leader after Jerusalem fell to the Romans	DD 40
ben Maimon, Moses (12th c.); Jewish philosopher and teacher: *see* Maimonides	DD 43
Benevieni, Girolamo (15th c.); mystic poet of the Italian renaissance	R 25
Bentham, Jeremy (1748-1832); deviser of the political and ehtical theory of Utility	PY 38
Bichat, Marie François Xavier (1771-1802); French anatomist and physiologist	MM 15
Bismarck, Otto Eduard Leopold, Prince of (1815-98); unifier of Prussia	DD 48
Blessington, Margaret Power, Lady (1789-1849); novelist and socialite	MM 27
Blucher, General Gebbard Leberecht von (1742-1819); saved the day at Waterloo	MF I 7 NH 150
Bolingbroke, Henry St John 1st Viscount (1678-1751); prime minister to Queen Anne	DD 52 ET 448 SN 446
Bonaparte, Charles Louis Napoleon (1808-73); emperor of the French 1852-70	BJ 1
Bonsi, Domenico (15th c.); Florentine delegate in treaty negotiaton with France	R 29
Bopp, Franz (1791-1867); German philologist	TS 11
Borgia, Cesare (1476-1507); soldier and patron of the arts	DD 48 ep
Borgia, Lucrezia (1480-1510); reputation for wantonness and crime is mostly legend	LV 1
Borrow, George (1803-81); writer, correspondent, Bible Society agent	MM 32
Bosanquet, Mary (1739-1812); first woman Wesleyan preacher, later Mrs Fletcher	AB 8, 51
Bossuet, Jacques Bénigne (1627-1704); bishop, writer, famous preacher	MM 3
Bouddha (Buddha), Gautama Siddartha, Prince (c563-483 BC); founder of Buddhism	DD 37
Bourdaloue, Louis (1632-1704); French Jesuit preacher	MF II 1
Bracchiolini, Poggio (1380-1459); humanist, discoverer of several ancient texts	R 5
Bright, John (1811-89); Radical British statesman and orator	SG (intro)
Brougham, Henry Peter, Baron Brougham and Vaux (1778-1868); politician	FH 5 MM 38
Broussais, François Joseph Victor (1772-1838); French physician and lecturer	MM 10
Brown, Robert (1773-1858); eminent British botanist	MM 17
—author of "Microscopic Observations on the Pollen of Plants" (1828)	
Bruce, James (1730-1794); African explorer	MM 9
Bruce, Robert (1274-1329); King of Scots 1306-29; victor at Bannockburn	MF II 3, 4, 6 DD 16
Brunelleschi, Filippo (1377-1446), Florentine architect	R *P*, 3
Bruno, Leonardo (15th c.), Florentine scholar	R 20
Brunswick family, from whom English monarchs descended	TE 92
Bryant, Jacob (1715-1804); British antiquary and scholar of mythology	MM 22
Buonarotti, Michelangelo (1475-1564; sculptor, painter, poet	R 20
Buondelmonte, Christoforo (1385-1430); created a book of 70 maps of Greek islands	R 6
Burdett, Sir Francis (1770-1844); a populist Radical MP; campaigned for Reform	FH 1, 30
Burke, Edmund (1729-97); statesman and author, often in Parliament	MM 46
Burke, William (executed 1829); murderer by suffocation to sell cadavers	FH 16 MM 45
Burleigh, Lord; the title-holder in 1719 when Edward Young was in his employ	PY 7
Burleigh, William Cecil Lord (1520-98); for forty years Elizabeth's chief minister	FH 43

C

Calderini, Domizio (1446-78); humanist and professor of rhetoric at Rome	R 12
Caligula (Gaius Julius Caesar Germanicus; 12-41); Roman emperor 37-41	TS 18
Calvin, John (1509-64); Protestant reformer, founded a theocracy in Geneva	FH 23
Canaletto,Giovanni (1697-1768); painter of Venetian architecture; etcher	LV 1
Capponi, Piero (1446-96); Florentine soldier and patriot	R 25
Caravaggio (Michelangelo Merisi; 1573-1610); painter of religious subjects	S 46

R

S

Index XI

Biblical, Literary, Musical, and Mythological References

Part 1: Authors and Composers

Arne, Thomas	(1710-78)	composer	
The Tempest		—incidental music	MF VI 7
"Sweet Echo"	1740	text from Milton's *Comus*	DD 16
Arnold, Matthew	(1822-88)		JS BL 1
Athenaeus of Naucratis	(c.200 AD)		
Deipnosophistae		—citing Theophrastus for an anecdote on misplaced laughter	TS 10
Auber, Daniel-François-Esprit	(1782-1871)	composer	
La muette de Portici	1828	—to the English, *Masaniello*	MF VI 7
Bach, Johann Sebastian	(1685-1750)		S 12
Chaconne			S 4
Bacon, Sir Francis	(1561-1626)	first baron Verulam	GL 4 DD 44 TS 5
Essays	1597-1625		BL 6
Bailey, Nathan	(d c1742)		
Universal Etymological Dictionary	1721	A forerunner of Samuel Johnson	MM 15 AB 19
Balfe, Michael William	(1808-1870)	composer	
The Maid of Artois	1836		MF VI 6
Balzac, Honoré de	(1799-1850)		BJ 1
Baudelaire, Charles	(1821-67)	—his name is not mentioned	TS 16
Les Fleurs du mal	1857	—quotations are not direct	TS 16
Baxter, Richard	(1615-91)		
The Saint's Everlasting Rest	1650		MF VII 3
Beaumont, Sir Francis *and* ***John Fletcher*** (q.v.)	(1584-1616) (1579-1625)	*The Maid's Tragedy* (1610-11)	MM 1 ep
Beethoven, Ludwig van	(1770-1827)		AR 1 CA 313
"Per pietà non dirmi addio"		*Ah Perfido* (Opus 65)	DD 32, 45
"Herz, mein Herz"		—setting Goethe's poem *Neue Liebe, neues Leben*	DD 66
Fidelio	1805		AR 3
Bell, Currer		pen-name of Charlotte Brontë	SN 460
Villette	1853		BL 3
Bellini, Vincenzo	(1801-35)		DD 5
La sonnambula	1831	*Ah! perchè non posso odiarti*	MF VI 7
Bickerstaffe, Isaac	(1753?-1808)		MM 2
The Hypocrite (1769)		Mawworm, a pious hypocrite	MM 2
Blair Hugh	(1718-1800)		
Lectures on Rhetoric and Belles Lettres	1784		MF III 5
Blake, William			
Songs of Innocence		"The Divine Image"	MM 76 ep
Songs of Experience		"The Clod and the Pebble"	MM 25 ep
Blessington, Lady	(1789-1849)	Margaret Power, novelist	MM 27
Boccaccio, Giovanni	(1313-75)	a collector, among other things	R 5
The Decameron	1349-51	Maestro Simone	R 16
	V ii	Costanze	R 61
	X vii	The maid who loved a king; the story retold in GE's poem	HL

		—the slough of Despond	MM 79 ep
		—the verdict against Faithful	MM 85 ep
		—the Delectable Mountain	TS 1
		Christiana	MF I 5
		—the river over which there is no bridge	MF I 5
		Apollyon	MF I 11
		Mr Greatheart	MF I 11
			JR 10
			AB 14, 19
Burke, Edmund	(1729-97)		FH 1 DD 44
A Philosophical Enquiry into the Origin of our Ideas of the Sublime and the Beautiful	1757		JR 3
Reflections on the Revolution in France	1790	"But the age of chivalry is gone"	MF IV 3
Burns, Robert	1759-96		
Auld Lang Syne			FH 31
O whistle and I will come to thee, my lad			FH 31
A Red, Red Rose	1794	*A melody that's sweetly pitched in tune*	FH 46
Burton, Robert	(1577-1640)	*Anatomy of Melancholy* (1621-51)	MM 5 ep
Butler, Joseph	(18th c.)	Theologian	DD 44
Butler, Samuel	(1613-80)	*Hudibras* (1663)	TT
Byron, George Gordon Lord	(1788-1824)		MF IV 3 FH 5, 27 MM 9 DD 11, 16 HH 56
		—and Greece	TS 18
Childe Harold's Pilgrimage	1812-18		FH 5
The Corsair	1813	Miss Medora	FH 5 BJ 2
The Giaour	1813	The Giaour	FH 43 TS 4
		—term means a non-Moslem	DD 61
The Siege of Corinth	1816		BJ 2
The Dream	1816		FH 5
Manfred	1817		FH 5
The Two Foscari	1821	The elder Foscari, the doge	DD 51
Calderon de la Barca, Pedro	1600-81	Great Spanish dramatist	BL 5
Callimachus	(305-240 BC)	Alexandrian poet	R 5
Campbell, Thomas	(1777-1844)		
The Pleasures of Hope	1799		TS 4
Carlyle, Thomas	(1795-1881)		TS 15 TC BL 1
Sartor Researtus	1833-4	Teufelsdröckh, Blumine	JS TC GO
On Heroes and Hero-Worship	1840		TC
Latter-Day Pamphlets	1850		JS TC
The Life of John Sterling	1851		JS
Cei, Francesco	(1471-1505)	Florentine poet	R 8, 13
Cervantes Saavedra, Miguel de	(1547-1616)		HH 50 CA 331
Don Quixote	1605, 1615		MM 2 ep TS 15
Chamfort, Sébastien	(1741-94)	—tales, dramas, maxims	HH 46

La Divina Commedia	1314-1321	Virgil	DD 58 FH *I*
Inferno		The Malebolge: eighth circle	R 29, 45 TS 8
	IV 112	*Spirti magni con occhi tardi e gravi*	DD 36
	IV 131	*The master of those who know* —a reference to Aristotle	DD 23
	VI 106-8	*Ritorna à mia scienza . . .*	DD 55 ep
	XXIX 43-4	*Lamenti saettaron me diversi*	DD 50
	XXX ii 150	*E cortesia fù, lui esser villano*	TS 13
Purgatorio	IV 88-90	*Questa montagna è tale . . .*	DD 64 ep
	V 133-6	Madonna Pia	DD 54
	XV	*Quando l'anima mia tornò di fuori . . .*	TS 13
	XXI, p. 104	*Con viso che tacendo dicea . . .*	R 6
And see Gioacchino Rossini		*Nessun maggior dolore* *Che ricordarsi del tempo felice* *Nella miseria*	DD 17
de Beaumont, Mme Leprince			
Contes des Fées	1785	The ring that pricked the finger when duty is forgotten	SM 15
de Castres, Sabatier	(late 18th c.)		
La Solitaire des Pyrénées	(1802)	Jeanne de Montmorenci	MM 31
Defoe, Daniel	(1660-1731)		
Robinson Crusoe	1719	Robinson Crusoe	BJ 2
The History of the Devil	1726		MF I 3
Dekker, Thomas	(?1570-1632)		
Patient Grissel	1603		DD 4
De la Mothe-Fénélon, François de Salignac	(1651-1715)	*see* Fénélon, below	
de Musset, Alfred	(1810-57)		
"Une Bonne Fortune"		*Nous causâmes longtemps . . .*	MM 22 ep
De Quincey, Thomas	(1785-1859)		
Confessions of an English Opium Eater	1822		MM 10
"The Nation of London"	1834		TS 2
Descartes, René	(1596-1650)	French philosopher, mathematician	DD 44 TS 4
de Staël, Mme	(1766-1817)		
Corinne (1807)		Corinne	MF V 4 MM 14
Dickens, Charles	(1812-70)		
The Posthumous Papers of the Pickwick Club	1836-7	Sam Weller	SF 6 V&S
Nicholas Nickleby	1839	Mr Curdle	IR 120
		Miss Squeers	SN 457
Little Dorrit	1857	Mrs Plornish	NH 126
Dobell, Sydney	(1824-74)		
England in Time of War	1856		BL 6
Donizetti, Domenico Gaetano	(1797-1848)	composer	
Lucrezia Borgia	1833	Duke Alphonso	DD 45, 52
Donne, John	(1572-1631)	"The Undertaking"	MM 39 ep
		"The Good Morrow"	MM 83 ep

Acis and Galatea	1732, 1740	"Hush ye pretty warbling choir"	MF I 9
		"Love in her eyes sits playing"	MF V 3
Giordigiani, Luigi	(1806-60)	composer	DD 32
Glanvill, Joseph	(1636-80)		
Scepsis Scientifica			IR 115
Gluck, Christoph Willibald	(1714-87)	opera composer	MM 7 CA 313 AR 1
Orfeo ed Eurydice (1762)		Orpheus	AR 1
Che farò senza Eurydice?			GL 2, 20
		—a candid bust of him is at Weimar	3 M 156
Goethe, Johann Wolfgang von	(1749-1832)		MM 22 HH 46, 60 NH 150 3M 160 LWG
Faust		—double prologue referred to	DD 1 ep
	I	Mephistopheles	DD 5, 48 CB 579
	II 1.1		MM 81 ep
Römische Elegien			3M 161
Zweignung			TT
West-östlicher Divan	1819		DD 39 ep
Wilhelm Meister	1795-6, 1827		TS 5
Wilhelm Meister's Apprenticeship	1795-6	Mariana, Philina, Lothario	MW
"Die Lustigen von Weimar"			3M 164
The Golden Rule	*Matthew* 7:12	*Therefore all things whatsoever ye would that men should do to you, do you even so to them: for this is the law and the prophets*	TS 1
Goldsmith, Oliver	(?1730-74)		
The Vicar of Wakefield (1766)	1764	Olivia and Sophia Primrose	MM 14, 57 BL 5
"Edwin and Angelina"		song	TS 13
"I found that no genius in another could please me . . . "		*The Vicar of Wakefield* 20	MM 29 ep
"The Traveller"		*These little things are great to little man*	MM 63 ep
An History of the Earth and Animated Nature	1774		MF I4
Gray, Thomas	(1716-71)		
Elegy Written in a Country Churchyard	1751	*"E'en in our ashes live their wonted fires*	AM
The Bard	1757	*Ruin seize thee, ruthless King*	TS 4
Guinicelli, Guido	(13th c.)		
canzone, translated by Dante Gabriel Rossetti		*Al cor gentil sempre ripara amore . . . .*	DD 61 ep
Guizot, François Pierre	(1787-1874)	*C'est beaucoup que le jugement des hommes . . . .*	MM 38 ep DD 44 HH 63
ha-Levi, Jehuda	(1075-1141)	major Jewish poet	DD 38, 42
Handel, George Frederick	(1685-1759)	composer	CB 705
Acis amd Galatea —text by John Gay	1717	masque "Oh ruddier than the cherry"	TS 3

Hook, Theodore	(1788-1841)	the Fashionable Novel	MF II 4
Horace (Quintus Horatius Flaccus)	(65-8 BC)		R 5, 39 TS 4, 15
		Philip Francis: *A Poetical Translation of the Works of Horace* (1743-6)	LV 1
Sunt qui non habeant . . .		attributed by GE; not traced	R 5
Hugo, Victor	(1802-85)		HH 63
L'Homme qui rit	III 9		MM 86 ep
Notre Dame de Paris	1831		TS 14
Les Contemplations	1856		BL 5
Hume, David	(1711-76)	philosopher	TE 92
Ibn Gebirol	(11th c.)	Spanish-Jewish poet	DD 33
Irving, Washington	(1783-1859)		
The Sketch Book	1820	under penname, Geoffrey Crayon, Gent.	MF VI 2
Isaiah*, the prophet*	(8th c. BC)		TS 5
James VI *of Scotland*	(1566-1625)	became James I of England	
The Essays of a Prentise, in the Divine Art of Poesis (1585)		A woman's *'makdom and her fairness'*	MM 15
Jewsbury, Geraldine R.	(1812-80)		
Constance Herbert	1855		BL 1
Johnson, Samuel	(1709-84)		TS 8 PY 5 HH 47
Rasselas, Prince of Abyssinia	1759		JR 3 MF IV 3 MM 15, 61
		astronomer	TS 14
The Rambler		series of essays	MM 51
"The Vanity of Human Wishes"		*Let observation with extensive view / Survey mankind, from China to Peru*	MM 51
Johnstone, Charles	(?1719-1800)		
Chrysal, or the Adventures of a Guinea (1760-65)			MM 15
Jonson, Ben	(1572-1637)		
To Celia		*Drink to me only with thine eyes . . .*	MF VI 13
Every Man in His Humour	1598		MM 11 ep
Josephus, Flavius	(c38-100)	*A History of the Jews*	MM 12
Juvenal	(c60-136)		R 3
1st Satire 3: 73-74		*Ingenium velox, audacia . . .*	R 3
Satires X 356		*Orandum est ut sit mens sana in corpore sano*	TS 13
Kalkbrenner, Frédéric	(1785-1849)	pianist, composer	HH 63
Keats, John	(1795-1821)		
Lamia	1818		DD 1
Sonnet on Seeing the Elgin Marbles			DD 43 ep
Keble, John	(1792-1866)	hymnologist: "The Christian Year" (1827)	MF IV 3, VI 9 MM 48
Ken, Thomas	(1637-1711)	bishop and hymnist	
"Awake my soul"	1674	The Morning Hymn	AB 1
"Glory to Thee, My God, This Night"	1674	The Evening Hymn	AB 18

Macaulay, Thomas Babington	(1800-59)		TS 16 CA 304
Machiavelli, Niccolò	(1469-1527)		R *passim.*
The Prince	1513		DD 48 ep
Macpherson, James	(1736-96)	—fabricator of "Ossian"	TS 4
Maimon, Salomon	(18th c.)	Jewish philosopher	
Lebensgeschichte			DD 33
Mangnall, Richmal	(1769-1820)		
Mangnall's Questions: Historical and Miscellaneous Questions for the Use of Young People (1800); became a staple in schools			BJ 2
Marcus Aurelius Antoninus	(121-180)	Roman emperor; Stoic philosopher	
Meditations	XI 35		DD 57 ep
Marlowe, Christopher	(1564-93)		DD 5
Tamburlaine	1587-8		FH 6 ep MM 22
Martineau, Harriet	(1802-76)		SN 460
Mason, William	(1725-97)	*On Self-Knowledge*	JR 3
Massinger, Philip	(1583-1640)		
A New Way to Pay Old Debts	(1633)	Sir Giles Overreach	MM 12
Menander	(342-292 BC)		MGC BL 1
Periceiromene		Glycera	TS 1
Mendelssohn, Felix	(1809-47)	German composer	DD 22
Meredith, George	(1828-1909)		
The Shaving of Shagpat	1856		SS BL 4
Metatasio, Abbé Pietro	(1698-1782)	Poet, opera librettist	CA 323
Meyerbeer, Giacomo	(1791-1864)	opera composer	DD 11, 45 HH 58
Mill, John Stuart	(1806-73)		SN 459
On Liberty	1859		TS 18
Milton, John	(1608-1674)	"liberal air"	FH 6, 27 LOM LV 1 BL 2 MM 1, 29, 34 PY 9
Comus (212-13)	1637	*O, welcome, pure-eyed Faith . .*	DD 65 ep
Areopagitica	1644		DD 37 TS 15
		"a potency of life in them"	DD 60
Paradise Lost	1667	Raphael, the "affable archangel"	MM 3 ep
I 291		"spotty globe"	AB 2
III 1. 44		"human face divine"	FH 30
III 690-691		Uriel	NE MM 41
IV 788-91		Ithuriel	DD 61
Paradise Regained	1671		
III 82		"Great benefactors of mankind, deliverers"	DD 41
Samson Agonistes 1721-4 (the final chorus)	1671	*Nothing is here for tears, nothing to wail . . .*	DD 70
—his daughters read to him			MM 7
—looking for his portrait in a spoon			MM 10
Molière			HH 48, 50

Qui veut délasser hors de propos, lasse		"Who diverts himself aimlessly tires of diversion"—*Pensées*	MM 30 ep
Pausanias	(2d c.)	geographer and historian	
Itinerary		description of Messena	R 38
Pepys, Samuel	(1633-1703)	Diarist	CA 304
Petrarch	(1304-74)	—and Laura	R 49 MM 37
Rerum Familiarum		*Libri medullitus delectant . . .*	R 5
		Optimam feminam nullam . . .	R 5
Spirto gentil			R *E*
—Burning of the Vanities			R 49
Phaedrus	(1st c. BC)	—transl. Aesop into Latin	TS ep
Fables	II 5	*gratis anhelans, multa agendo nihil agens*	TS 14
Pindar	(522-443 BC)	Greek lyric poet	PY 11
Piozzi, Hester Lynch	(1741-1821)	*Anecdotes of the late Samuel Johnson* (1878)	MM 25
Plato	(c.428-c. 348 BC)		R *P*, 39 TS 4, 5 TE 93
Apology		Socrates	TS 10
Phaedrus		"What motive has a man to live, if not for the pleasures of discourse?"	DD 32
Plautus, Titus Maccius	(254-184 BC)		
Aulularia			R 5
Bacchides	III iii 50	*haud consimili ingenio*	FH 17
Pliny *the Elder (Gaius Plinius Secundus)*	AD 23-79		DD 58
Historia Naturalis	VII xl 131	*nemo mortalium omnibus . . .*	FH 17
Plutarch	(c50-c125)		LV 1
The Bravery of Women	XIII	"The Women of Phocis"	DD 17
Poliziano (Politian), Angelo Ambrogini	(1454-94)	Florentine poet and professor in Greek and Latin	R 3, 5
Miscellanea		Chariclo, Teiresias, Pallas, Minerva	R 5
Orfeo		*Ciascun segue, o Bacco, te: Bacco, Bacco, evoè, evoè!* —"Each one of us follows you, Bacchus/Hurrah, hurrah!"	R 39
Pope, Alexander	(1688-1744)		DD 5 MM 51 PY 5
Essay on Man (1733)			MM 18
II		*Vice is a monster of so frightful mien . . . .*	V&S
IV 203-4		*Worth makes the man, and want of it the fellow; The rest is all but leather or prunella*	MM 43
		Atticus, Sporus	PY 25
Prodicus	4th c BC		
"The Choice of Hercules"			MM 18
Pucci, Antonio	(1301-90)	Florentine poet	R 1
Pucci, Luigi	(15th c.)		
La proprietà di mercato vecchio		*E vedesi chi perde . . .*	R 1
Pulci, Luigi	(1432-84)	Dombruno	R *P*, 16

An die Freude			DD 18
Don Carlos	1787	Princess of Eboli	DD 52
Schubert, Franz	(1797-1828)	composer	DD 22, 32, 36
	"Schubert too wrote for silence: half his work/Lay like a frozen Rhine till summers came/That warmed the grass above him. Even so!'/His music lives now with a mighty youth."		AR 5
Scott, Sir Walter	(1771-1832)		MF IV 3 MM 27, 39, 57 ep TS 2 LNB 1
prefaces of several novels		Dr Jonas Dryasdust	DD 36
Waverly	1814	Edward Waverly	MM 14
		Flora MacIvor	MF V 4 MM 14
Guy Mannering	1815	Dominie Sampson	MF III 5
		Dandie Dinmont Counsellor Paulus Pleydell	NH 133
		Lucy Bertram	MF III 5
The Antiquary	1816	Miss Wardour	DD 44
		Luckie Mucklebackit	NH 125
Old Mortality	1816	The Covenanters	NE DD 46
		Habakkuk Mucklewrath	DD 46
The Heart of Midlothian	1818	Mr Saddletree	NH 133
Ivanhoe	1819		MM 32, 57
		Rebecca	MF V 4 DD 17, 32
The Pirate	1821	Minna Troil	MF V 1, 4
		Brenda and Minna	MM 14
		Mordaunt Merton	MM 14
		Clement Cleveland	MF V 1 MM 14
The Fortunes of Nigel	1822	Alsatia, a sanctuary	MF I 8
The Talisman	1825	Saladin	MF II 4
Woodstock	1826	Holdenough	FH 14
The Fair Maid of Perth	1828	Hal o' the Wynd (Henry Smith)	MF II 4
Anne of Geierstein	1829		MM 32
"The Two Drovers"			NH 125
William and Helen	Transl. German ballad	Leonore (eponymous heroine of G. A. Bürger's *Leonore*)	MF I 11
Scribe, Augustin Eugène	(1791-1861)	playwright	DD 11
Sedley, Sir Charles	(?1639-1701)		
Not, Celia, that I juster am	(1702)		MM 16 ep
Shakspeare, William	(1564-1616)		DD 5, 16, 20 TS 5, 10, 15 LV 1 HH 50
All's Well That Ends Well	I I 80	"bright particular star"	NF
Antony and Cleopatra	V ii	"My desolation does begin"	DD 53 ep
As You Like It		Orlando	MM 31
		"Sudden and quick in quarrel"	MM 60
		Rosalind —and Celia	DD 14 TS 10
Coriolanus	I i	*His nature is too noble . . .*	FH 30 ep

Henry VIII	II iii	*Come pat betwixt too early and too late*	DD 22
	III ii 298-99	*How much, methinks, I could despise this man*	MM 42 ep
Julius Caesar		Brutus	FH 2 TS 5
	II ii	*Mischief, thou art afoot.*	FH 33 ep
King John	II I 438-41	*He is the half part of a blessèd man* *Left to be finishèd by such as she* *And she a fair divided excellence* *Whose fulness of perfection lies in him*	FH 44
	III I (?)	*A woman naturally born to fears*	FH 9 ep
		Faulconbridge	DD 37
King Lear	V iii	*Her voice was ever soft, / Gentle and low, an excellent thing in woman.*	FH 5 TS 5, 10
		King Lear and the Fool	TS 15
		Edmund of Gloster	DD 37
King Richard II	II ii	GE gives "*with* nothing trembles": it is "*at* nothing"	FH 9 ep
	IV i	*Give sorrow leave a while . . .*	FH 13 ep
Macbeth	I i 11-12	*Fair is foul and foul is fair,* *Hover through the fog and filthy air*	TS 16
	I vii 4-7	*That but this blow* *Might be the be-all and the end-all here*	TT
	I vii 21-23	"Pity, that 'newborn babe' . . . did not 'stride the blast' on this occasion."	MM 29
	II iii 108-9	*Who can be wise, amazed, temp'rate and furious,* *Loyal and neutral in a moment? No man.*	DD 4
Measure for Measure	II i 17-18	*'Tis one thing to be tempted . . .*	MM 66 ep
	II i 125-30	*'Twas in the Bunch of Grapes*	MM 71 ep
The Merchant of Venice —Lorenzo and Jessica	V I 56-7	*Soft stillness and the night* *Become the touches of sweet harmony*	TT
The Merry Wives of Windsor		Slender	MM 60
		Falstaff	FH 31
A Midsummer Night's Dream	I v	"the poet's eye in a fine frenzy"	DD 5
	IV ii	*. . . the play is marred*	FH 24 ep
		Puck	HH 62
Much Ado About Nothing	III i		DD 5 ep
Othello		Desdemona	MM 8 GL 4 BJ 2
	III iii 91-2	*Perdition catch my soul, but I do love thee* [GE has it "her"]	DD 6
	III iii 354-5	*Farewell the plumèd troops and the big wars / That makes ambition virtue*	TS 10

Sinclair, Catherine	(1800-64)	novelist and philanthropist	SN 459
Sismondi, Léonard Simond de	(1773-1842)		
L'Histoire des républiques italiennes du Moyen-Age	1809-18		DD 16
Smith, Adam	(1723-1790)	*An Inquiry into the Nature and Causes of the Wealth of Nations* (1776)	MM 2
Smollett, Tobias	(1721-71)		
Roderick Random	1748		MM 30
Humphry Clinker	1771		MM 30
Solomon		reputed author of *Proverbs*	MM 17
	Proverbs 27:15	*A contonual dropping in a very rainy day and a contentious woman are alike.*	AB 4
Sophocles	(496-406 BC)		SF 4 AB 5 TS 16 MP 52
Antigone		*My way is to share my love, not share my hate*	DD 32
		Antigone, Eteocles, Polynices, Creon	AM
Ajax		*Yet it becomes a man . . .*	FH 42 ep
	II 507-11	the slaughtered sheep	MF I 7
Electra		*Thou says it, and not I . . .*	FH 42 ep
Œdipus the King			MF I 13
Southey, Robert	(1774-1843)		FH 7
Thalaba the Destroyer	1801		FH 1
Life of Wesley	1820	Alexander Knox	DD 20 ep
History of the Peninsular War	1823-32		MM 2
Life of Cowper	1832-37		MF VI 2
Spence, Joseph	(1699-1768)		
Anecdotes	1726—		PY 8
Spenser, Edmund	(c1522-99)		
Shephearde's Calendar	1579	"August" ll 77-84	DD 7 ep
The Faërie Queene	1590, 1596	Philemon	TS 13
Spinoza, Baruch (Benedict)	(1632-77)		DD 38
Spontini, Gaspare	(1774-1851)		HH 63
Steele, Richard	(1672-1729)		
"Inkle and Yarico"	1711	*The Spectator* 3/11/1711	BJ 1
Stendhal (Henri Beyle)	(1788-1842)		
Ernestine, ou la Naissance de l'Amour	1856		BL 4
Sterne, Laurence	(1713-68)		HH 76
Tristram Shandy	1759-60		RND 3
A Sentimental Journey through France and Italy	1767		DD 19 ep
Stowe, Harriet Beecher	(1811-96)		SN 457
Dred; A Tale of the Great Dismal Swamp	1856		BL 6
Sue, Eugène	(1804-57)	—prolific novelist of the French underworld	NH 126
Suetonius (Gaius Suetonius Tranquillus)	(75-160)		
De vita Caesarum		Titus and Berenice	DD 37

Micromégas			HH 48
Candide	1759	"the best of all possible worlds"	TS 17
Wagner, Richard	(1813-83)		LW
Walpole, Horace	(1717-97)		CA 304
Wesley, Charles	(1707-88)	Hymnist, brother of John	
"Dark and cheerless is the morn"		Verses from "Christ, Whose Glory Fills the Skies"	AB 38
"Eternal Beam of Light Divine"			AB 50
Wesley, John	(1703-91)	Evangelist, hymnist	AB 50
"Its streams the whole creation reach"	1780	"Thy Ceaseless, Unexhausted Love"—a hymn	AB 2
Whitman, Walt	(1819-92)		
Leaves of Grass	1856 (first intimation)		BL 4
Vocalism		*Surely whoever speaks to me in the right voice, him or her I shall follow . . . .*	DD 29 ep
Wieland, Christoph Martin	(1733-1813)	—writer, first translator of Shakspeare into German	3M 154
Wier, John	(16th c.)	—physician and writer	
De Prestigiis Dæmonum			IR 114
Wither, George	(1588-1667)		
Fidelia	1619	*Shall I wasting in despair*	MF VI 7
Wooton, Sir Henry	(19th c.)		
"The Character of a Happy Life"	1861		MM 56 ep
Wordsworth, William	(1770-1850)		MM 2 TS 2 HH 73
The Reverie of Poor Susan	1797; pub 1800	"Poor Susan"	NH 125
The Prelude VIII 608-15	1798-9; 1805	*The human nature unto which I felt that I belonged . . .*	DD 69 ep
	I 151-3	*Nor general truths . . .*	LNB 11
Lyrical Ballads	1798		FH 1
"A Poet's Epitaph"	1799; pub 1800	*And you must love him ere to you / He will seem worthy of your love*	DD 47 ep
Michael, a Pastoral Poem	1800	*A child, more than all other gifts* *That earth can offer to declining man,* *Brings hope with it, and forward-looking thoughts.*	SM ep
"London, 1802"	1802; pub 1807	*His heart / The lowliest duties on itself did lay*	MM 52 ep
"Three Years She Grew"	1799; pub 1800	*And beauty born of murmuring sound* *Shall pass into her face*	SM 19
"The Affliction of Margaret"	1801/04; pub1807	*I question things and do not find . . .*	DD 24 ep

Part 2: Others' Figures, Quotations, and Works

(Our work on the Biblical quotations from AB owes a major debt to Hugh Osborne's notes in the Modern Library edition)

See also the Supplement to this Part 2 at page 390

Aaron	*Exodus* 4:14ff	Moses's spokesman	MF V 2
	Numbers 17:8	*. . . and behold, the rod of Aaron for the house of Levi was budded, and brought forth buds, and bloomed blossoms, and yielded almonds*	TS 3
Abel	*Genesis* 4:4	*And Abel, he also brought of the firstlings of his flock and of the fat thereof. And the Lord had respect unto Abel and to his offering:*	TE 83
Abiram	*Psalms* 106:17	*The earth opened and swallowed up Dathan, and covered the company of Abiram*	JR 2
	Numb. 16 *passim.*	*see* Korah	TS 18
Abraham	*Genesis* 12ff	founder of Israel	MM 31 SG I i
Achilles	*The Iliad*		MF II 4 DD 6 FH 14
Adam	*Genesis*	the first man	AB 21 FH 44, 49 MM 15
Agag	*I Samuel 15*	king of the Amelekites spared by Saul, killed by Samuel	R 52
Agrippa	*Acts* 25:13	—his wife was Berenice	DD 37
Sir Andrew Aguecheek	*Twelfth Night*	"I was adored once"	MF VI 3
"airs from heaven"		*see* William Shakspeare Part 1	
Ajax	Greek myth	"Ignorance is a painless evil"	GL 3
—and the slaughtered sheep		*see* Sophocles Part 1	MF I 7
Alcestis	Greek myth	wife of Admetus of Thessaly; her sacrifice saved his life	R 13
" 'all the plagues o' Egypt' "	*Exodus* 8-12		AB 32
" 'Am I my brother's keeper?' "	*Genesis* 4:9	*And the Lord said unto Cain, Where is Abel thy brother? And he said, I know not: Am I my brother's keeper?*	AB 8
Amadis de Gaulle		—in the Middle Ages very popular chivalric romance in Spain and Portugal	HL 100
Amaryllis		the beloved of shepherds: *see* Theocritus Part 1	DD 15
"ambition one with social virtue"	*Othello*	*see* Shakspeare Part 1	TS 10
Amphitryon	Greek myth	husband cuckolded by Zeus; the result was Hercules	SF 6 ET 80
"And after we had seen the vision"	*Acts* 16:10	*And after he had seen the vision, immediately we endeavoured to go into Macedonia . . .*	AB 3

"Auld Langsyne [*sic*]		*see* Robert Burns Part 1	
Aurora	Roman myth	Goddess of the dawn	R 17
Baal	*Judges* 2	false idol to the Israelites	DD 35
Babylonian Talmud (*Babli*)		The more important of two	DD 62
Bacchante	Greek myth	female followers of Bacchus	R 32
Bacchus	Greek myth	god of wine and revelry	GL 4 R 4
Balaam	*Numbers* 21, 22		FH 5
"baptism of fire"	*Matthew* 3:11	*I indeed baptize you with water unto repentance: but he that cometh after me is mightier than I, whose shoes I am not worthy to bear: he shall baptize you with the Holy Ghost, and with fire*	AB 42
Colonel Bath		*see* Henry Fielding Part 1	AB 50
Batti, batti	Mozart	*Don Giovanni*	MM 16
Baxter's 'Saints' Everlasting Rest'	1650	by Richard Baxter, a moderate, rational Puritan divine	MF I 12
" 'bear the burthen and the heat of the day' "	*Matthew* 20:12	*Saying, These last have wrought but one hour, and thou hast made them equal unto us, which have borne the burden and heat of the day.*	AB 11
"beauty born of murmuring sound"		*see* William Wordsworth Part 1	SM 19
The Beggar's Opera		*see* John Gay Part 1	
"When the heart of a man is oppressed with care"			AB 12
"Begone dull care"	Air		MF VI 2
Benjamin	*Genesis* 35:18		FH 37
Berenice (**Bernice**)	*Acts* 25:13	—wife of Agrippa II	DD 37
Bia	Greek	personification of coercion	DD 38 ep
Bildad the Shuhite	*Job* 2:11, 8	one of Job's comforters	FH 40
" 'the birds o' the air' "	*Matthew* 6:26	*Behold the fowls of the air: for they sow not, neither do they reap, nor gather into barns; yet your heavenly Father feedeth them. Are ye not much better than they?*	AB 6
"bitter herbs, eat with"	*Exodus* 12:8	*And they shall eat the flesh in that night, roast with fire, and with unleavened bread; and with bitter herbs they shall eat it.*	MF IV 1
"Black-eyed Susan"		air	MM 16
Blair's Rhetoric		*see* Hugh Blair Part 1	MF III 5
"a blind Pharisee"	*Matthew* 23:26	*The blind Pharisee, cleanse first that which is within the cup and platter, that the outside of them may be clean also.*	AB 5
Boanerges	*Mark* 3:17	"sons of thunder": surname of the Apostles James and John	TE 96
Bouddha (Buddha)		Buddhism's central figure	MM 50
"bread without scarceness"	*Deut.* 8:9	*A land wherein thou shalt eat bread without scarceness . . .*	AB 8
Brenda Troil		*see* Sir Walter Scott Part 1	

The Creation		*see* Franz Joseph Haydn Part 1	MF VI 1
Creüsa	Greek myth	She married Jason, supplanting Medea, who caused her death with a poisoned dress	DD 36
Crispin		Patron saint of bootmakers	LB
"the cup we must drink of with him"	*Matthew* 20:23	. . . *Ye shall drink indeed of my cup, and be baptized with the baptism that I am baptized with* . . .	AB 30
Cupid	Roman myth	son of Venus, a god of love	R 7, 18 PY 25
Cupid and **Psyche**		*see* Apuleius Part 1	
Cush	*Genesis* 10:6-8	a son of Ham, father of Nimrod	MM 22, 34
Cybele	Classic myth	Goddess of love in Phrygia	SG I i
Da quel giorno in quà ch'amor m'accese *Per lei son fatto e gentile e cortese*	*see* **Luigi Pulci** Part 1	"From the day on which love set me on fire/ Through her I have been made gentle and courteous"	R 8
Dagon		Philistine fish-deity	MM 20, 49 CA 334
Dandie Dinmont	*Guy Mannering*	*see* Scott Part 1	
Daniel	*Daniel* 6:16-23	in the den with the lions	AB 22
—"the little horn"	*Daniel* 7:8	*I considered the horns, and, behold, there came up among them another little horn, before whom there were three of the first horns plucked up by the roots: and, behold, in this horn were eyes like the eyes of man, and a mouth speaking great things.*	FH 41
Daphnis	Greek myth	son of Hermes; raised by nymphs; invented pastoral poetry	MM 50 DD 14, 32 ep CB 325
Darby and Joan	The Joys of Love Never Forgot" (1735)	*Old Darby, with Joan by his side* *You're often regarded with wonder* *He's dropsical, she is sore-eyed* *Yet they're never happy asunder*	TS 2
"Dark and cheerless is the morn"		*see* Charles Wesley Part 1	
"a dark bottomless pit"	*Revelation* 9:1-2	. . . *and to him was given the key of the bottomless pit.* *And he opened the bottomless pit* . . .	AB 2
"the darkness is as noonday"	*Isaiah* 58:10	*And if thou draw out thy soul to the hungry, and satisfy the afflicted soul: then shall thy light rise in obscurity, and thy darkness be as the noon-day*	AB 45

Don Quixote		*see* Cervantes Part 1	TS 13 LV 1
Dorcas	*Acts* 9.36	virtuous woman	MM 3
Dr Jonas Dryasdust		*see* Sir Walter Scott Part 1	DD 36
"dumb dog"	*Isaiah* 56:10	*His watchmen are blind: they are all ignorant, they are all dumb dogs, they cannot bark; sleeping, lying down, loving to slumber.*	AB 5
E cortesia fù, lui esser villano —in Cocytus in the 9th circle	*see* Dante Part 1	"To be rude to him [Fra Albergo] was courtesy"	TS 13
E vedesi chi perde con gran soffi *E bestemmiar colla mano alla mascella* *E ricever e dar di molti ingoffi.*	*see* Luigi Pucci Part 1	"And you see someone who lets loose with a mighty breath, and swearing with his hand on his jaw, and receiving and giving many blows"	R 1
"an earthly affection"	*Coloss.* 3:2	*Set your affection on things above, not on things on the earth*	AB 51
Ecclesiasticus 19.10		*If thou hast heard a word . . .*	MM 69 ep
Eden	*Genesis*	—the first garden	SG I ii
Edmund of Gloster	*King Lear*	*see* Shakspeare Part 1	DD 37
Edom	*Psalms* 108:9	*Moab is my washpot: over Edom will I cast out my shoe; over Philistia will I triumph.*	DD 23 ep
	Numbers 20		DD 60
Edwin and **Angelina**		*see* Goldsmith Part 1	TS 13
Egeria	Greek myth	a death goddess	NE 2
"an egg, an apple, or a nut"	Proverb	—"you may eat after a slut"	AB 2
Eli	*1st Samuel* 3:8	*And the Lord called Samuel again the third time. And he arose and went to Eli, and said, Here am I, for thou didst call me. And Eli perceived that the Lord had called the child.*	FH 5
Eli, sons of	*1st Samuel* 2:12, 3:13, 4:4, 11	*Now the sons of Eli were sons of Belial; they knew not the Lord*	R 24
Elihu the Buzite	*Job* 32-37		FH 5
Elijah	*I Kings* 18	—and the priests of Baal	R 65 DD 47
Endymion	Greek myth	perpetual youth, perpetual sleep	R 8
Enna	Classic myth	—the valley where Proserpine was picking flowers when Pluto abducted her to Hades	DD 64
"enough and to spare"	*Luke* 15:17	*And when he came to himself, he said, How many hired servants of my father's have bread enough and to spare, and I perish with hunger!*	AB 49
Erinna	Greek myth	Poetess who died in youth when chained by her mother to a spinning-wheel; a symbol of female suppression	DD 51 ep
Eros	Greek myth	the god of Love	MM 36
		a first kiss	AB 13
Esau	*Genesis* 25, 27	"rash, warm-hearted nature" —sold his inheritance	AB 50 FH 29

Flying Dutchman	legend		DD 54
"For I could wish that myself were accursed from Christ"	*Romans* 9:3-5	[GE renders these verses accurately]	TS 18
"For that fine madness"		*see* Michael Drayton Part 1	DD 5
Foscari		*see* Byron Part 1	
"from my rising up"	*Lamentations* 3:63	*Behold their sitting down, and their rising up; I am their musick.*	AB 3
"frosty Caucasus"		*see* William Shakspeare Part 1 *Richard II*	MF VI 9
Furies	Greek myth	Three snake-headed goddesses who punished those who would otherwise escape	DD 31
Gabriel, the angel	*Luke* 1:26		DD 37, 42 SG II ii
Gallio —Proconsul of Achaia before whom Corinthian Jews accused Paul	*Acts* 18:12-17	15: *But if it be a question of words and names, and of your law, look ye to it; for I will be no judge of such matters.*	FH 38
Ganymede	Greek myth	abducted by an eagle	AB 30
Geoffrey Crayon		*see* Washington Irving Part 1	MF VI 2
Giant Python	Greek myth	—killed by Apollo	MF VI 9
The Giaour		*see* George Gordon Lord Byron Part 1	FH 43
"ginger is hot in the mouth"	*see* Shakspeare Part 1	*Twelfth Night*	R 35
Glycera	*see* Menander Part 1	*see also* Index III	TS 1
"go ye first [*no*] to the lost sheep of Israel"	*Matt.* 10:6	*Go rather to the lost sheep of Israel*	TS 18
"God rest you, merry gentlemen"	carol		SM 10
Gog and Magog	*Revelations* 20.8	Nations led by Satan at Armageddon	MM 48 TE 96
"gold, incense and myrrh"	*Matt.* 2:11	*. . . and when they had opened their treasures, they presented unto him gifts; gold, and frankincense, and myrrh.*	AR 1
Golgotha	*Matt.* 27:33-4	*And when they were come unto a place called Golgotha, that is to say, a place of a skull, They gave him vinegar to drink mingled with gall: and when he had tasted thereof, he would not drink.*	PY 4
Goliath	*I Sam.* 17:4	Philistine giant soldier	MF II 3
"the good seed might fall on that soil"	*Luke* 8:8	*And other [seed] fell on good ground, and sprang up, and bare fruit an hundredfold*	AB 8
Gorgons	Classic myth	Three sisters with snakes for hair: their glance turned a man to stone	BJ 1
"gratis anhelans, multa agendo nihil agens"	*see* Phaedrus Part 1	"Out of breath about nothing, with much ado doing nothing"	TS 14
"great drops of sweat"	*Luke* 22:44	*And being in an agony he prayed more earnestly: and his sweat was as it were great drops of blood falling down to the ground.*	AB 2

Hector	*Iliad*	Trojan hero	MF II 4, V 2
Hecuba	*Iliad*	Wife of Priam, Hector's mother; many sorrows	MF V 2 FH 39 SG I ii
Helen	Greek myth	she launched a thousand ships	GL 4
Hercules	Greek myth	—the ultimate strong man, who achieved twelve labours	MF VI 1 R 7 SG I i MM 66 3M 155 WM 177
—in the court of the Omphale			CA 325
Hermes	Greek myth	thief, trickster, messenger	R 3 FH 4
Hermione		*see* Shakspeare Part 1	
Herod	*Luke* 23:11	*And Herod with his men of war set him at nought, and mocked him, and arrayed him in a gorgeous robe, and sent him again to Pilate.*	R 29 FH 38
Herodias	*Mark* 6:19-20	*For John had said unto Herod, It is not lawful for thee to have thy brother's wife. Therefore Herodias had a quarrel against him, and would have killed him: but she could not.*	SG I ii
Hezekiah	*2d Kings* 16, 18		FH 5
"the hills to which they had first lifted up their eyes"	*Psalms* 121:1	*I will lift up mine eyes unto the hills, from whence cometh my help.*	TS 2
"him who denied thee"	*Luke* 22:61	*And the Lord turned, and looked upon Peter. And Peter remembered the word of the Lord, how he had said unto him, Before the cock crow, thou shalt deny me thrice.*	AB 45
"His blood be upon us . . . "	*Matt.* 27:25	*Then answered all the people, and said, His blood be on us, and on our children.*	TS 18
"His soul was exceeding sorrowful"	*Mark* 14:34	*And saith unto them, My soul is exceeding sorrowful unto death: tarry ye here, and watch.*	AB 2
Holofernes	*Judith* 4	—Nebuchadnezzar's general, who was decapitated by Judith	S 134
"Home, sweet home"		air	MM 12
Horae Paulinae		*See* William Paley Part 1	MF III 5
"a horror of great darkness"	*Genesis* 15:12	*And when the sun was going down, a deep sleep fell upon Abram; and, lo, an horror of great darkness fell upon him.*	AB 2
Hotspur	1 Henry IV	*see* Shakspeare Part 1	MF I 3 V 7
"I came not to call the righteous"	*Luke* 5:32	*I came not to call the righteous, but sinners to repentance.*	AB 2, 51
"I came to seek and to save"	*Luke* 19:10	*For the son of man is come to seek and to save that which was lost.*	AB 2

Ishmaelite	*Genesis* 37:27	an outcast or a rebel	FH 37 DD 16
Isis	Egyptian myth	*Queen of the gods; consort of Osiris; goddess of love*	SG V
"Its streams the whole creation reach"		*see* John Wesley Part 1	
Jack the Giantkiller		figure in a fairy tale	MF I 11
Jacob	*Genesis* 29:20	worked seven years for Rachel	AB 3, 21, 25
Jael, who destroyed Sisera	*Judges* 4:17-21		MF I 4
"jangled and out of tune"	*Hamlet*	*see* Shakspeare Part 1	TS 9
Janus	Roman myth	the two-faced god	DD 52
Jason	Greek myth	he used and deserted Medea	DD 36
Jeanne de Montmorenci		*see* Sabatier de Castres Part 1	MM 31
Jehovah		Old Testament name for the one God	TS 18
Jehu the son of **Nimshi**	*2 Kings* 9:20		AB 36
Jericho	*Joshua* 6:20	its walls fell before the sound of trumpets	SF 2
Jeshurun (an affectionate term for Israel the nation)	*Deut.* 32:15	*But Jeshurun waxed fat, and kicked: thou art waxen fat, thou art grown thick, thou art covered with fatness*	DD 42
Jesus of Nazareth		New Testament	CC
Job	*Job*		FH 40 PY 28
Joe Miller		—he of the joke-book	JR 3
John the Baptist	*John* 1:6-8		R 5 FH 6, 43
" 'joined to the lord' "	*1 Cor.* 6:17	*But he that is joined unto the Lord is one spirit*	AB 8
John Gilpin	ballad	*see* Cowper Part 1	TS 18
Jonah	*Jonah*		R 16
Jonathan	*1 Sam.* 18	son of Saul; devoted to David	SM 1
Joseph, the patriarch —his ring and robe	*Genesis* 37-50		AB 8, 30 FH 5
Jove	Greek myth	head of the gods	AB 30 DD 45
Jubal	*Genesis* 4:21		LJ
Judah	*Genesis* 37:26		FH 37
Judas Iscariot	*John* 13:2 *Luke* 22:48	who betrayed Jesus the betraying kiss	R 4 DD 61 TS 8 SG I ii SG IV iii LJ 228
Epistle of Jude			SF 6
	9	*Yet Michael the archangel, when contending with the devil he disputed about the body of Moses, durst not bring against him a railing accusation, but said, The Lord rebuke thee.*	FH 43
Judith	*Apocrypha*	a Donatello statue: *see* Holofernes	R 8 S 133
Judy	folk-lore	Punch's helpmeet in pantomime	MM 32
Juliet		*see* Shakspeare Part 1	

Lazarus	*John* 11:43-44	*And when he thus had spoken, he cried with a loud voice, Lazarus, come forth.* *And he that was dead came forth . . . .*	R 52
Leonore		*see* Sir Walter Scott Part 1	MF I 11
"leather and prunella"		*see* Alexander Pope Part 1	MM 43
"the length of every man's foot"	Ref: Hercules	*ex pede Herculem*	MF I 7
"Let brotherly love continue"	*Hebrews* 13:1		AB 22
"let the eyes of the blind be opened"	*Isaiah* 35:5	*Then the eyes of the blind shall be opened, and the ears of the deaf shall be unstopped*	AB 45
Lethe	Greek myth	—the Hades river, immersion in which causes forgetfulness	SM 2 R 68
"the letter was a mere obstruction to the Spirit"	*2 Cor.* 3:6	*Who also hath made us able ministers of the new testament; not of the letter, but of the spirit: for the letter killeth, but the spirit giveth life.*	AB 21
" 'letting 'em slap you i' the face' "	*Matthew* 5:39	*. . . but whosoever shall smite thee on thy right cheek, turn to him the other also.*	AB 49
Leviathan	*Psalms* 74:14	*Thou breakest the heads of leviathan in pieces, and gavest him to be meat to the people inhabiting the wilderness.*	DD 52 CB 53
	Job 41:1-2	*Canst thou draw out leviathan with an hook? or his tongue with a cord which thou lettest down?* *Canst thou put an hook into his nose? Or bore his jaw through with a thorn?*	BJ 2
"And, like the Parthian, wound us as they fly"	—not traced		JR 2
"looking before and after"	*Hamlet*	*see* Shakspeare Part 1	TS 2
Lothario			JR 2
"Love they neighbour as thyself"	*Mark* 12:31	*And the second is like, namely this, Thou shalt love thy neighbour as theyself. There is none other commandment greater than these.*	AB 18
"a lover of self"	*2 Timothy* 3:2	*For men shall be lovers of their own selves . . .*	AB 51
Lucifer			MF VI 1 MM 16
Lucrezia Borgia		*See* Gaetano Donizetti Part 1	DD 45
Lungi dal caro bene	Song	By Giuseppe Sarti (1729-1802); a standard student's exercise	MM 43
The Margites	6th or 7th c. BC	A comic poem of misadventures on the wedding night, once attributed to Homer	R 6
Mars	Roman myth	the god of war	R 5, 8, 18, 29
Martha and **Mary**	*John* 11:1		AB 6
Mary Magdalen			GL 4

Miriam	*Exod.* 15:20-21	*And Miriam the prophetess, the sister of Aaron, took a timbrel in her hand; and all the women went out after her with timbrels and with dances. And Miriam answered them, Sing ye to the Lord, for he hath triumphed gloriously; the horse and his rider hath he thrown into the sea.*	SG I ii
"mirror held up to nature"	*see* Shakspeare Part 1	*Hamlet*	TS 1
Mizraim	*Genesis* 10:6, 13	a son of Ham	MM 22, 34
Moloch, a Canaanite god	*Amos* 5:26	*But ye have borne the tabernacle of your Moloch and Chiun your images, the star of your god, which ye made to yourselves.*	TS 18
Mordaunt Merton		*see* Sir Walter Scott Part 1	
Mordecai	*Esther* 2:5		DD 34
Moses	*Exodus*		AB 50 FH 5 MM 31 DD 16, 63 ep, 63 PI DM TE 94
—and the burning bush	*Exodus* 3:2		AB 8
"the meekest of men"	*Numbers* 12:3	*(Now the man Moses was very meek, above all the men which were upon the face of the earth.)*	AB 50 MF I 12
Moses, trotz seiner Befeindung der Kunst. —*see* Heinrich Heine Part 1		"Despite his hostility to art, Moses was none the less himself a great artist and possessed the true spirit of an artist. But this artistic spirit, in him as in his Egyptian fellow-countrymen, was directed towards the colossal and the indestructible. Yet he did not, like the Egyptians, create works of art out of brick and granite; rather, he built human pyramids, he chiselled human obelisks, he took a poor tribe of shepherds and created from it a people that would equally defy the centuries . . . he created Israel."	DD 63 ep
"on the mountains . . . thy feet were beautiful"	*Isaiah* 52:7	*How beautiful upon the mountains are the feet of him that bringeth good tidings, that publisheth peace . . . .*	LJ 764-5
Murr the Cat		*see* E.T.A. Hoffmann Part 1	

	Acts 10:15, 28	*And the voice spake unto him again the second time, what God hath cleansed, that call not thou common.* *And he said unto them . . . God hath shewed me that I should not call any man common or unclean.*	TS 10
Philemon		*see* Spenser Part 1	TS 13
Philistia, "be thou glad of me!"	*Psalms* 60:8	*Philistia, triumph thou because of me.*	DD 13 ep
Philoctetes	Greek myth	wounded in the foot, he was abandoned on an island because of its stench	MF II 6
Phoebus Apollo	Greek myth	god of the sun	R 4
Piacer e popone Vuol la sua stagione	Italian proverb	"Pleasure and melons/Want the same weather"	MM 7 ep
Pilate	*see* Herod		R 29 SG IV iii
The Pilgrim's Progress		*see* John Bunyan Part 1	
"Pity, that 'newborn babe' "		*see* Shakspeare Part 1 *Macbeth*	MM 29
Pleiades	Greek myth	seven daughters of Atlas	R 13
Pluto	Greek myth	king of the underworld	R 12
"the poet's eye in a fine frenzy rolling"		*see* Shakspeare Part 1 *A Midsummer Night's Dream*	DD 5
Polypheme	*The Odyssey*	Cyclops	MF II 3 CB 706
Pontius Pilate	*Matthew* 27:24	*When Pilate saw that he could prevail nothing, but that rather a tumult was made, he took water, and washed his hands before the multitude, saying, I am innocent of the blood of this just person: see ye to it.*	FH 38
"a poor woman . . . sitting at a well"	*John* 4:7	*There cometh a woman of Samaria to draw water: Jesus saith unto her, Give me to drink.*	AB 2
Poseidon	Greek myth	god of the seas	R 6
"pray without ceasing"	*1 Thess.* 17		AB 47
"pressed him daily"	*Judges* 16:16	*And it came to pass, when she pressed him daily with her words, and urged him, so that his soul was vexed unto death;*	FH 30
Priam	Greek myth	king of Troy; lost the war	R 4
Prince Camaralzaman		*see Arabian Nights*	
Prodigal Son	*Luke* 15:11-32		MF I 4
Promethean tone		—a tone of disappointed heroic ambition	DD 24
Prometheus	Greek myth	he stole fire for man to use	DD 16 ep, 38 ep PY 4
"prophetic soul of the wide world"	Sonnet 107	*see* Shakspeare Part 1	TS 2
"the prophet's chariot of fire"	*2 Kings* 2:11	*. . . behold, there appeared a chariot of fire, and horses of fire, and parted them both asunder; and Elijah went up by a whirl-wind into heaven.*	LV 1

"richly to enjoy"	*1 Tim.* 6:17	*. . . nor trust in uncertain riches, but in the living God, who giveth us richly all things to enjoy*	AB 49
Richter, Johann Paul (Jean Paul)	(1763-1825)		HH 49
Ritorna à mia scienza Che vuol, quanto la cosa è più perfetta Più senta il bene, e così la doglienza.	*see* Dante Part 1	"Remember what your theologians teach: the more a thing is perfect, the more it must feel happiness, and thus also pain"	DD 55 ep
"the river over which there is no bridge"		*see* John Bunyan Part 1	MF I 5
Robin Hood		legendary outlaw	MF I 11 DD 11
Robinson Crusoe		*see* Defoe Part 1	BJ 2
Romeo	*Romeo and Juliet*	*see* Shakspeare Part 1	DD 31 ep
Rosalind	*As You Like It*	*see* Shakspeare Part 1	DD 14
"Roy's Wife of Aldivalloch"	Song		GL 4
"Ruin seize thee, ruthless King"	*The Bard*	*see* Thomas Gray Part 1	TS 4
" 'a rushing mighty wind' "	*Acts* 2:2	*And suddenly there came a sound from heaven as of a rushing mighty wind, and it filled all the house where they were sitting.*	AB 17
Rumpelstiltskin	nursery tale		MM 63
Saddletree	*The Heart of Midlothian*	*see* Scott Part 1	
"Sadness is a kind of mirth/So mingled as if mirth did make us sad/And sadness merry"	*The Two Noble Kinsmen*	*see* Shakspeare Part 1	TS 15
Samson	*Judges* 13-16		GL 4
—putting a riddle	*Judges* 14:12		MF I 5, II 3 FH 5
Samuel	*1 Samuel* 12	his dying speech to the people	AB 51
	1 Samuel 3:8	revelation to the boy Samuel	FH 5
		400 years after Moses	PI
"the sane mind in the sane body"	*Satires X*	*see* Juvenal Part 1	TS 13
Sara (Sarah)	*Genesis*	wife of Abraham	MM 3
"showed a spirit of unbelief"	*Genesis* 18:12	*Therefore Sarah laughed within herself, saying, After I am waxed old shall I have pleasure, my lord being old also?*	FH 4
Satan		the Devil; chief of evil spirits	TS 2
Saul	*1 Sam.* 18ff	—enmity against David	FH 16
"save to the uttermost"	*Hebrews* 7:25	*Wherefore he is able also to save them to the uttermost that come unto God by him . . .*	AB 45
"See the print of the nails"	*John* 20:25	*. . . Except I shall see in his hands the print of the nails, and put my finger into the print of the nails, and thrust my hand into his side, I will not believe.*	AB 2

St Paul	1 *Cor.* 7:34	*. . . she that is married careth for the things of the world, how she may please her husband.*	AB 3
	1 *Tim.* 3:2	*A bishop then must be blameless, the husband of one wife . . .* .	FH 6
	1 *Tim.* 5:14	*Women marry, bear children, guide the house, give none occasion to the adversary to speak reproachfully.*	AB 3
—a tent-maker	*Acts* 18:3		FH 5
—metaphysical subtleties			CC
		Did he know the Greek poets?	TS 11
St Peter		—Judaic narrowness	CC
St Philip	*Acts* 8:38	*And he commanded the chariot to stand still; and they went down into the water, both Philip and the eunuch: and he baptized him.*	R 6
"stinging adders"	*Proverbs* 23:32	*At the last it biteth like a serpent, and stingeth like an adder.*	AB 2
"stone that has been rolled away from the sepulchre"	*Matthew* 28:2	*And behold, there was a great earthquake: for the angel of the Lord descended from heaven, and came and rolled back the stone from the door, and sat upon it.*	AB 51
Strephon	folk story	conventional male lover	MM 3
"Sudden and quick at [should be "in"] quarrel		*see* Shakspeare Part 1 *As You Like It*	MM 60
"sufficient for the day"	*Matthew* 6:34	*. . . Sufficient unto the day is the evil thereof*	AB 30
"Take no thought for the morrow"	*Matthew* 6:34	*Take therefore no thought for the morrow: for the morrow shall take thought for the things of itself . . .*	AB 4
" 'taking off your cloak and giving it to 'em' "	*Matthew* 5:40	*And if any man will sue thee at the law, and take away thy coat, let him have thy cloak also.*	AB 49
Talents, five or two	*Matthew* 25:14-29	14. *For the kingdom of heaven is as a man travelling into a far country, who called his own servants, and delivered unto them his goods.* 15. *And unto one he gave five talents, to another two, and to another one; to every man according to his several ability; and straightway took his journey . . . .*	HH 52
Tannhäuser	Teutonic myth	prisoner in the toils of Venus	**DD 22**
Tartarus	Greek myth	the underworld	MM 10 SG I ii
Telemachus	Greek myth	son of Ulysses	DD 22
Télémaque		*see* François Fénélon Part 1	MF IV 3 FH 10
Teraphim	*Judges* 17:5, 18:14-20	molten images: household gods forcibly taken from Micah	MF III 2 ch title
Teufelsdröckh	*Sartor Resartus*	*see* Thomas Carlyle Part 1	

Ulysses	Homeric hero		MF I 9, II 3 SF 4, 14 R 39 DD 22
"unrecumbent sadness"		*see* William Cowper Part 1	MF II 2
Uriel		*see* John Milton Part 1	NE
Urim and Thummin (properly Thummim)	*Exodus* 28:30	*And thou shalt put in the breastplate of judgment the Urim and the Thummim: and they shall be upon Aaron's heart, when he goeth in before the Lord . . . .*	CB 144
Uzziah	*Isaiah* 6:1	King of Judah (781-40 BC)	**TS 13**
Valentine and Orson		old French romance	AB 19
The Valley of Humiliation	John Bunyan	*Pilgrim's Progress*	MF IV book title
Venus	Roman myth	goddess of love	R 7, 16, 18
Vestiges of the Natural History of Creation	1844	—published anonymously; in 1884 its author was revealed to have been Robert Chambers (1802-71), Scottish publisher	TS 11 TE 93
The Vicar of Wakefield		*see* Oliver Goldsmith Part 1	MM 57
Virgin Mary			MM 76
Voi che sapete	Mozart	*The Marriage of Figaro*	MM 16
Vulcan	Greek myth	god of the forge	3M 162 CA 317
Waverly		*see* Sir Walter Scott Part 1	
"ways of pleasantness"	*Proverbs* 3:17	*Her [wisdom's] ways are ways of pleasantness, and all her paths are peace.*	BJ 1
"We could never see him . . . "	*Romans* 1:20	*For the invisible things of him from the creation of the world are clearly seen, being understood by the things that are made*	AB 2
"We should be o' one heart and o' one mind"	*Acts* 4:32	*And the multitude of them that believed were of one heart and of one soul . . .*	AB 3
"What come ye out for to see? A prophetess?"	*Matthew* 11:9	*But what went ye out for to see? A prophet? Yea, I say unto you, and more than a prophet*	AB 1
"Wheat and Tares"	*Matthew* 13:24-30	parablé	MF V book title
"When first I saw thy face"		song	MM 46
"where you lay down and rose up again"	*Psalms* 139:2	*Thou knowest my downsitting and mine uprising, thou understandest my thought afar off.*	AB 45
"whether our prologue be in heaven or on earth"		*see* Goethe Part 1	DD 1 ep
"Whether we live or die, we are in the presence of God"	*Romans* 14:8	*For whether we live, we live unto the Lord: and whether we die, we die unto the Lord: whether we live therefore, or die, we are the Lord's.*	AB 45 TE 98

Supplement

"And Jacob served seven years for Rachel"	*Genesis* 29:20	*And Jacob served seven years for Rachel; and they seemed unto him but a few days, for the love he had to her.*	AB 3
"And all the people said, Amen"	*I Chron* 16:36	*Blessed be the Lord God of Israel for ever and ever, And all the people said, Amen, and praised the Lord*	FH 4
"And they all wept sore, and fell upon Paul's neck"	*Acts* 20:37	*And they all wept sore, and fell on Paul's neck, and kissed him*	AB 15
"How often would I have gathered you"	*Luke* 13:34	*O Jerusalem, Jerusalem, which killest the prophets, and stonest them that are sent unto thee; how often would I have gathered thy children together, as a hen doth gather her brood under her wings, and ye would not!*	AB 2
"human admiration, hope, and love"	*The Excursion*	*see* Wordsworth Part 1	
"human face divine"	*see* John Milton Part 1		
"I also could speak as ye do"	*Job* 16:4		FH 37 ep
"the lusts of the flesh and the pride of life"	*1 John* 2:16	*For all that is in the world, the lust of the flesh, and the lust of the eyes, and the pride of life, is not of the Father, but is of the world.*	AB 5
Mænad	Greek myth	a Bacchante—infuriated	R 38 AR 1
		see Plutarch Part 1	DD 17
Maid Marian	folk legend	companion to Robin Hood	DD 11
"Make them glad according to the days"	*Psalms* 90:15	*Make us glad according to the days wherein thou hast afflicted us, and the years wherein we have seen evil.*	AB 51
Mrs Malaprop	*The Rivals*	Richard Brinsley Sheridan	MFW
Malebolge	*see* Dante Part 1		R 29
"Man of Sin"	*2 Thess.* 2:3	*Let no man deceive you by any means: for that day shall not come, except there come a falling away first, and that man of sin be revealed, The son of perdition.*	TE 99
"Man of Sorrows"	*Isaiah* 53:3	*He is despised and rejected of men; a man of sorrows, and acquainted with grief*	AB 51
Mambrino, Golden Helmet of	Cervantes	*Don Quixote*	MM 2 ep
" 'My God, my God!' he cries"	*Matthew* 27:46	*And about the ninth hour Jesus cried with a loud voice, saying, Eli, Eli, lama sabachthani? That is to say, My God, my God, why hast thou forsaken me?*	AB 2

Sophia Primrose		*see* Oliver Goldsmith Part 1	
Sophia Western		*see* Henry Fielding Part 1	
The Speaker		*see* William Enfield Part 1	MF II 3
"The spirit of the lord is upon me"	*Luke* 4:18	*The Spirit of the Lord is upon me, because he hath anointed me to preach the gospel to the poor; he hath sent me to heal the broken-hearted, to preach deliverance to the captives, and recovering of sight to the blind, to set at liberty them that are bruised.*	AB 2
St George	legend	slayer of the dragon	MF I 11
St John		evangelist; disciple	CC R 4
St John, Revelation of	New Testament		MM 1

Index XII

Boroughs, Church Designations, Hostelries, Houses, Farms and Estates, Hunts and Hunting Venues, Periodicals, Schools, and Theatres

Boroughs

Church Designations

Pennicote Recxtory (Mr Gascoigne)	DD 3
Salem Chapel, Milby	JR 2
Shepperton Church (Mr Gilfil, Vicar; later Carpe; Amos Barton, curate)	SF 1 GL 1, 21
Shuttleton (Wimple the vicar)	FH 23
St Botolph's church (Camden Farebrother), Middlemarch	MM 16
St Paul's Criss (Hugh Latimer [H])	MM 50
St Peter's church, Middlemarch (Mr Thesiger, rector)	MM 16
St Peter's parish, Middlemarch (Mr Tyke is curate in a chapel of ease)	MM 18
St Ursula parish	MF I 3
Tipton and Freshitt parish, "a village church hardly larger than a parlour" (Humphrey Cadwallader, Rector)	MM 1, 34
Tripplegate parish (Martin Cleves)	SF 6
Welwyn rectory (Edward Young)	PY 12
Whittlecombe parish (Mr Pugh, curate)	SF 6
Witherington (Mr Bagshawe)	SF 6
Zion Independent chapel	GL 1

Companies and Associations

Association for the Prosecution of Felons (Mr Hackit presiding)	GL 1
Guest & Co., commercial firm in St Ogg's	MF III 5

Hostelries

Albergo dell' Italia, Genoa (Princess Halm-Eberstein)	DD 50
Anchor Tavern (Salt a customer)	MF V 2
Babboons, the (*Bertucce*), Florence	R 10
Bear and Ragged Staff, in the Bridge Way at Milby	JR 4
Belle Sauvage, London	FH 6
Black Swain, King's Lorton (Mr Poulter frequented it for its gin)	MK II 4
Blue Bull, Middlemarch (Dagley dined a little too well)	MM 39, 60
Blue Cow, at the Old Pits, Sproxton	FH 11
Bramcote (Fowler), a farm tenancy of Squire Cass of Raveloe	SM 3
Cartwright's restaurant	MM 2
Cross-Keys, in Pollard's End, Treby Magna (Tommy Trounsem's hangout)	FH 28
Crown, Duffield (in the Whig Debarry interest)	FH 30
Czarina Hotel, Leubronn	DD 2, 15
Donnithorne Arms, Hayslope (Mr Casson)	AB 2
Erbprinz, Weimar	3M 153
Fox and Hounds, Duffield (in the Radical Harold Transome interest)	FH 30
Golden Keys, Wanchester	DD 13
Golden Lion, St Ogg's	MF III 3
Green Dragon, Middlemarch; in the Conservative interest (billiards also)	MM 18, 51, 66
Green Man, Tucker's Lane, Milby	JR 4
Green Man, Windsor	AB 36
Hand and Banner, where Mordecai sometimes goes	DD 40
Holly Bush, Hayslope (Josh Tod), down by the Stone Pits	AB 1, 2
Hôtel des Bergues, Geneva	LV 1
Jolly Colliers, Shepperton	SF 7
Marquess of Granby (Basset parish; Dickison's)	MF I 8
Marquis of Granby, Treby Magna (Tory), with a market dinner in high repute	FH 2, 19
'Master Michael's Inn,' St Märgen	AG 149
Oldinport Arms	GL 1
Railway Inn, smewhere near Offendene	DD 21
Rainbow, Raveloe (Mr Snell, landlord)	SM 1
Ram Inn, Treby Magna (Whig); engaged for the Radical interest	FH 7, 19
Red Lion, Batherley	SM 8
Red Lion, Houndsley	MM 23
Red Lion, Milby	JR 1

Houses, Farms, and Estates

Shrubs, the (Nicholas Bulstrode), on the London road out of Middlemarch	MM 60
Stone Court, Lowick parish (Peter Featherstone)	MM 11
Tipton Grange (Arthur Brooke)	MM 1
Tiptop (Sir Gavial Mantrap)	TS 16
Topping (Sir Hugo Mallinger)	DD 29
Treby Manor (Sir Maximus Debarry; invaded by a mob)	FH 7, 33
The Twentylands (the late Mrs Sutton)	MF I 7
The Warrens (Lammeter)	SM 6
The White House (Thomas Jerome)	JR 8

Hunts and Hunting Venues

North Loamshire	FH 2, 47
Three Barns, a rendezvous of the Wessex Hunt	DD 7
Wessex	DD 7

Periodicals

Allgemeine Zeitung	HH 63
Candelabrum	TS 15
Christian Observer	SF 2
Church Clock, Pumpiter	TS 15
Clerical Gazette	DD 7
Cockaleekie *Advertiser*	TS 15
Crompton Argus	JR 3
Duffield Watchman (Liberal)	FH 8, 44
Evangelical Magazine	FH 6
Faublas	GL 2
Gentleman's Magazine	GL 2 PY 19
Goodwin Sands *Opinion*	TS 15
Hearts and Diamonds, a society magazine	DD 52
Independent Monitor, Pumpiter	TS 15
Keepsake, a literary annual, sentimentally illustrated	MM 27
Laceham Courier	MF VI 13
Land's End *Times*	TS 15
Latchgate Argus	TS 15
Manchester *Guardian*	DD 7
Medley Pie, Pumpiter	TS 15
Middlemarch *Pioneer*, which Arthur Brooke buys for Will Ladislaw to run	MM 30
Middlemarch *Trumpet*	MM 37
North Loamshire Herald (Conservative)	FH 1, 4, 8, 47
The Patriot, a Radical and Dissenting journal [H]	FH 24
Penllwy *Universe*	TS 15
The Pulpit	SF 3
Pumpiter *Gazette and Literary Watchman*	TS 15
Pumpshire Post, Pumpiter	TS 15
Rapporteur scientifique et historique	TS 3
Record	SF 2
The 'Regulator'	TS 4
Rotherby Guardan	JR 25
Selten-erscheinende Monat-schrift ("Infrequently appearing monthly journal") —Hayrick for the insertion of Split Hairs	TS 3
The *Times*	DD 61
Twaddler's Magazine	MM 17

Schools

Theatres

Glossary

(including Italian words and phrases found in *Romola*)
(*see also* Index XI, Part 2)

adytum	the innermost part of the temple; the secret shrine whence oracles are delivered LV 1
aigrette	ornamental crest of feathers (of the egret commonly) or gems R 26
Alexandrians	members of a school of philosophy which flourished in Alexandria from 30 BC to 642, allied to later Stoicism MM 10
Allocaturs	certificates allowing costs given at the end of a legal action MF III 7
andate con Dio	"go with God" R 14
Anonimo	anonymous figure R 3
Antinomian	Christian who believed that moral laws were superseded by faith and grace DD 45
antiphrasis	figure of speech seen in rhetoric, wherein words are used to contradict the ostensible meaning FH 22
Apulian Greek	spoken in the southeast Italian province of Apulia (Puglia today) when it was a part of greater Greece in the 8th to 4th centuries BC R 3
Arcivescovo	archbishop R 46
Arian heresy	rejected the doctrine of the Trinity DD 52
Arimaspians	*not traced* SF 3
Arnolfo, church of	*see* Santa Croce R *P*
Ausonia	an alternative name for the Italian peninsula GL 3
Bacco trionfante	triumphant Bacchus R 25
Badia bell-tower	part of the church of San Stefano (Benedictine), Florence, reconstructed in 1294
Baie!	"what a joke!" R 18
the Baptist	John the Baptist R 5
bechetto	a cap with a sash; alternatively a hood R *P*
befana	a corruption of *epifania* (Ephiphany): name given to the grotesques in black-face carried around on Twelfth Night, representing the magi R 12
bel erudito	goodlooking and knowledgeable person R 3
bella zazzera	beautiful long hair R 3
bello giovane	beautiful young man R 2
berlingozzi	doughnuts consumed especially during Carnival before Lent R 14
Bitter Waters	perhaps a reference to the bitter waters of Marah: *Exodus* 15:23 AB 40
Boeotian	a reference to the bucolic district of Boeotia in Greece, whose inhabitants, by literary convention, are considered exceptionally ignorant, if not stupid GL 1

Bösewichtl	soundrel (German) DD 23
Bosjesman	Afrikaans for bushman DD 28
boto (voto) caduto	a votive image R 1
Brummagem	from "Birmingham," and intended to suggest something cheap, tawdry, flamboyant, perhaps counterfeit (false coins were once manufactured there)
butties	petty mining contractors: interfacing between the miners and the proprietors FH 11
Cabbala	the esoteric doctrine of early Jewish mystics, which later became a systematic body of thought DD 38
Calcio	a sreet boys' game; a kind of football R 10
calenture	a disease characterized by bouts of hysteria, delusions, or delirium: it was said to afflict sailors in tropic seas, enticing them to throw themselves overboard to sink in what they imagined would be green fields, rather than the ocean MF II 1
capo d'opeera	masterpiece R 8
cassone	chest R 18
il cavallo	horse R 16
cenci e vetri	"rags and [broken] glass" R 1
ceri	wax tapers R 8
cerretano	street magician, or travelling salesman of spurious medicines R 10, 16
Chalybes	a tribe noted for its blacksmiths, on the Euxine (Black Sea) in Pontus MM 83
Chapel of ease	satellite to the principal house of worship in the parish MM 18
Che miracolo	"What a miracle!" R 1
Chi abbaratta	"Who wants to exchange?" R 1
Chicktaws	probably the Choctaw Indians of the American West JR 4
chuppa	canopy held over a Jewish bride and bridegroom DD 66
cicalata	idle chatter R 6
comparse	walk-on actress: minor roles DD 23
comprachico	"vendor of children"; refers to the practise of disfiguring or maiming children to make them serviceable beggars TS 8
Concords, three	the basic agreements between words as parts of speech: number, gender and case
confetti	confections; candies, as sugared almonds R 28
contadina	countrywoman R 16
Corso	a horse race in Florence R 11
culex	gnat R 7
cupping	a technique for drawing blood, intended to suppress fever MM 10
dal tetto in su	*non credere dal detto in su:* "not believing in anything from the roof upwards"—that is agnostic, lacking belief in the supernatural R *P*
damigella	young girl R 6
Delectus	a selection of passages from various authors for translation: usually Latin or Greek, used in school
deschi	stalls in the open market at Florence R 1
Il Diavolo	the Devil R 16
dignità	an outstanding characteristic; a "glory" R 1
Dissent	term applied to those not adhering to the established church: Methodists and Evangelicals. MM 9
dono infelice della bellezza	"the inconvenient gift of beauty" GL 10
dunque	"therefore" R 18
è falso	"it is false" R 1
è vero	"it is true" R 1
Eagre	a tidal wave of unusual height, caused by a tidal rush up a narrowing estuary MF I 5

Ebbene	"Well, then" R 1
Eleusinian mysteries	the secrets of the goddess of the harvest, Demeter, which were the subject of ceremonial observances at Eleusis, in Attica MP 46
energumen	one possessing unnatural powers; one possessed by the Devil LV 1
eruditi	scholars R 3
Fediddio!	a mild expletive referring to God R 8
Feme sole	legal term for an unmarried woman DD 21
ferri vecchi	"old iron" R 1
Fesulean	native of Fiesole, a town in the hills north of Florence R 1
fibula	a brooch of early design, looking like a large safety pin R 63
Fierucola	"little fair" in Florence, to which the "fierucoloni"—women from the neighbourhood—brought their wares R 13
figuola mia	"my child" R 12
fra converso	lay brother R 11
Frate Predicatore	"preaching brother"—the Dominicans are known as the Order of Preachers R *P*
Frati minori	Franciscan religious order R *P*
Frati serviti	Servite order, devoted to the service of the Virgin Mary R 1
Fu tutt' uno	it's all the same R 12
Galligaskins	long, loose breeches MM 46
Gallio-like	not traced GL 1
Gan Eden	Paradise DD 52
gattuccio	Tom-cat: a good mouser R 1
gentianella	name for sseveral species of gentian: intense blue flower FH 31
Ghibellines	supporters of the Holy Roman emperors in struggles with the Pope R 8
giostra	joust R 8
Giotto's tower	the campanile of the Florence cathedral, architect Giotto de Bondone; the work was begun in 1334 R *P*
Giovane mio	"my handsome young man" R 9
Gnaffè	"By my faith!" R 3
Good Men of St Martin	a Florentine league organized to aid persons in reduced circumstances (i.e., the poor of good family) R 12
Gwelfs	supporters of the popes in Rome R 8
hendecasyllable	a line of eleven-syllable poetry (a classical Latin form) R 7
Hesperus	the evening star DD 52
himation	a long garment, draped over the left shoulder and reaching the ankles; worn in ancient Greece TS 2
Hyperion	the sun DD 52
Iddio non paga il Sabato	"God does not pay on a Saturday"—the wages of sin may be delayed R *P*
Ingenia acerrima Florentina	"brilliant, clever, sharp Florentines" (quoted or misquoted, by GE, from Macchiavelli's *History of Florence*) R 17
Jacobinical	refers to the Jacobites, who favoured the restoration of Charles II and were considered supporters of Roman Catholicism JR 1
Jew's stone	crystallized iron pyrite, or marcasite; an amulet of Gnostic design usually carved on an inferior stone and once thought the work of the ancient Hebrews R 7
Karaites	they represented a Jewish scholarship tradition which emphasized the written word and the rigorous application of logical reasoning to doctrine; the school developed beginning in the 8th century DD 63
kittle-kattle to shoe	a skittish horse which will be difficult to get to stand for shoeing DD 25
la cugina	the cousin (female) R 12
Ladyday	March 25: the Feast of the Annunciation; one of four quarter-days on which tenancies usually begin and end, and financial arrangements are settled. MF I 2
Lasso	alas! R 16

Lauds	morning prayer service R 32
"Leg-plaiter"	"The image comes from the way bovine animals walk, setting their hooves down one in front of the other and seeming thus almost to cross their legs at every step."—Bert G. Hornback MM 11
Levantine coast	on the southern side of the western Mediterranean
lippi	persons of limited vision R 6
loggia	a roofed terrace, often sitting on the roof of a residence R 5
lucco	a long, pleatless robe, reaching to the feet R *P*
Madonna Annunziata	a painting of the Virgin Mary in the church of the Santissima Annunziata in Florence, thought to have special powers R *P*
Magdalen	a woman from Magdala; usually the reference is to the so-called Mary Magdalen, whose name never appears in the Bible R 3
Magna Grecia	southern Italy, originally occupied by the Greeks R 5
Manichaeism	a religious system dominant from the third to the fifth century, founded by one Manes, or Manichaeus, which held that Good and Evil (God and Satan) were both eternal principles and equally powerful. MF I 3
marmi	marbles (as of the steps in front of Florentine churches) R *P*
Marzocco	a stone lion, the emblem of the Republic of Florence R 1
marzolino	a cheese made in Florence in the month of March R 1
Merry-Andrew	entertainer at a country fair, dressed as a clown MM 12
Messer Domeneddio	a vulgar term for God (*Signore di dio)* R 3
Messer San Michele	St Michael R 1
mezuza	parchment with the scriptural commandments listed; placed in a container and attached to the doorway of a house or room DD 51
mi pare	"it seems to me" R 1
Michaelmas	September 29: one of four quarter-days (*see* Ladyday)
Midrash	"teaching," i.e. the body of a long tradition of Hebrew scripture interpretation, beginnng about 400 BC and, since about 200 AD, developed by individual rabbis in theological and moral analysis DD 61
Midsummer Day	June 24: one of four quarter-days (*see* Ladyday)
Modus	*modus decimundi:* a cash payment in lieu of a tithe MM 38
Modus	short for *modus vivendi,* a means of living: applicable to a local minister's receipts from his parishioners in lieu of tithe on produce FH 6
Mongibello	Mount Aetna, Sicily R 1, 45
Moravian Brethren	German evangelical religious sect founded in 1722 by followers of the Hussite tradition; the movement strongly influenced John Wesley. MM 6
Morbidezza	a style of painting demonstrating delicacy and softness (a critics' term) MM 9
muoio di fame	"dying of [vanishing with] hunger" R 2
murrain	an epizootic in cattle; a general term for pestilence in other animals and crops R 2
Nazarene school	a school of German painters akin to the later pre-Raphaelites. MM 19
Netto di specchio	"not registered as a debtor"—not subject to disqualification for election to public office R 1
niello	ornamental material of sulphur and copper, silver, or lead, used in decoration of metallic works of art R 12
novità	innovation R 60
novella da calze	good news—good enough to warrant a reward R 43
nozze	marriage R 20
obolus	one-sixth of an Athenian drachma, but effectively of no value R 2
old Puritan	John Bradford (1510-55) remarked, on seeing some criminals being led to execution, "There but for the grace of God goes John Bradford." TS 14
opici	barbarians R 6

opodeldoc	a soothing liniment, usually with a soap base, and perhaps containing camphor and rosemary FH 30
palagi e case grande	"palaces and great houses" R 5
Palazzo Vecchio	Florence's central governmental building; the seat of the *Signoria* R *P*
Pali	the language in which the canonical texts of Buddhism were originally written
palii	velvet or brocade banners R 8
palio	banner, awarded to the winner of a race R 16
panno di garbo	"cloth of courtesy"—clothing in high current fashion R 1
Paphlagonia	an ancient Roman province on the Black Sea MM 83
parentado	relationship R 5
Parergon	Supplemental or secondary work (pl. parerga) MM 29
paterini	dualist heretics who believed in two Gods: Jesus of the soul and the spiritual world, and the god of Abraham and the Old Testament who created the material, evil world R 8
patrigno	step-father R 20
pazzarella	crazy little friend R 10
il pelo nell' uovo	*cercare il pelo nell' uovo*—to be highly discerning or fastidious R 3
peplos	in ancient Greece, a loose outer robe worn by women R 8
peripateia (or peripeteia)	a sudden and violent change of fortune or circumstances BJ 2
pestilenza	"Plague on it!" R 8
Piagnoni	"weepers," originally applied derogatively to the followers of Savonarola; later an accepted designation for them R 12
pian, piano	"softly, slowly" R 3
pievano	parish priest R 10, 68
Pinzochera	an uncloistered Franciscn nun R 12, 36
Podestà	judge brought in from another city to mediate disputes R 8
popolani	commoners who rose to noble status through success in trade; they, and not the patricians, ran the city government R 5
popoli grassi	leaders of the commercial classes R 1
port wine, bark	wine mixed with powdered Cinchona bark, a source of quinine, as a remedy for fever
prophylactic rings	set in jewels thought to have medicinal and protective qualities R 5
Proposto	spokesman or moderator R 8
Prunella	material used in the cassocks of priests MM 43 *See* Index XI Part 1: Alexander Pope
Pyrrhic dance	devised by Pyrrichos, a Dorian: danced in full armour to a flute AB 8
pythoness	a woman possessed by a god or spirit; a soothsayer or witch, The Witch of Endor was one. Pythonesses whirled and writhed under their possessor's driving force. MF I 4
Quaresima	Lent, in the Catholic church calendar R 12
Quattrini bianchi	"white farthings"—small change: about four cents R 1
Qui nacque il divino Poeta	"Here was born the divine poet" (Dante) R 1
Rabbanites	members of the original school of Jewish scholarship which emphasied oral traditions in interpreting the Talmud; distinguished from the Karaites DD 63
ragazza	young girl R 10
raggia come stelle per sereno	"radiant as the stars in a clear sky" (Pulci) R 3
rallentando	slowing down FH 4
Revising Barrister	an official instituted after the 1832 Reform Act to ensure an accurate voter list, based on those prepared by parish overseers or town clerks: he dealt with applications for additions and deletions FH 20
rigattiere	junk-dealer R 30

romor	insurrection R 16
rotten nut	Hugh Osborne (Modern Library paperback ed.) suggests that this is a "schoolmasterly" phrase, evoking a standard Latin quotation assigned for memorization: *Teruncio seu vitiosa nuce non emerim*—"I would not buy it for a farthing or a rotten nut," from *Eton Latin Grammar* AB 40
Ruach-ha-kodesh	Hebrew: "the breath of divine thought" DD 40
Sadducee	member of a small, wealthy, aristocratic and materialistic Jewish religious sect AB 8
sajo	tunic R 6
Salic Law	a penal code established by the Salic Franks, it mandated exclusion of daughters from inheriting real property FH 6
San Giovanni	the feast of John the Baptist, June 24—a common date on which to formalize business transactions in 15th c. Florence R 1
Santa Croce	Franciscan church in Florence renovated and enlarged in 13th & 14th cs.; Arnolfo di Cambio believed to have been the architect R *P*
Satanasso	Satan R 8, 29
sbirro	policeman R 16
scagliola	plaster-work of Italian origin designed to imitate various kinds of stone FH 1
scapulary	part of a friar's habit, the cloak covered the shoulders front and back, with an opening for the head, or an attached hood R 10
scarsella	large leather purse R 36
scholia	explanatory notes or comments developed researching an author R 12
Ser Saccente	"Mr Know-it-all" R 46
sgherro	killer for hire R 3
shechinah	or *shekinah:* the Divine Presence dwelling among the cherubim GL 7 R 24
Shemah	the six Bible verses beginning at *Deuteronomy* 6:4, which summarize the core Jewish faith
Seven Sages	In ancient Greece (about 620-550 BC), they were Bias, Chilon, Cleobulus, Periander, Pittacus, Solon, and Thales MM 6
shophar	ram's horn blown on ceremonial Jewish occasions to call to repentance and remembrance (i.e., on the Day of Atonement) DD 42
Signoria	the elected city council of Florence, residing in the *Palazzo Vecchio* R *P*
Sirius	the dog-star DD 44 ep
"small quick-eyed man"	Filippo Brunelleschi, who completed the cathedral dome in Florence in 1436 R *P*
Socinians	A sect founded by Lælius and Faustus Socinus, Italian theologians; it denied the divinity of Christ SF 3
solco torto, sacco dritto	"a crooked furrow can yield a full sack" R 45
soughing tiles	tiles for drainage FH 43
sposalizio	betrothal ceremony R 20
sposi	the engaged couple R 20
Stella Maris	"star of the sea"—the Virgin Mary as patron saint of sailors DD 37
Stoicism	Athenian school of philosophy founded by Zeno in 300 BC, named for the great Athenian *Stoa,* or hall, where Zeno lectured MM 10
Supralapsarian	member of a sect which believed that before the Fall God had already chosen those who were to be saved DD 52
"Swing"	Captain Swing was a name signed to letters threatening mayhem in 1830, when riots by unemployed farm workers destroyed machinery TS 10
tabellario	post-man R 45
Tedesco	a German R 3
tephillin	container with a parchment bearing scriptural texts; worn on head and arm by Jewish men in prayer DD 51

thyrsus	symbol of Bacchus: the god or his followers carried this staff or spear, tipped with a pine cone R 6
tithe-pig	a reference to the old way the local minister was paid by farmers, who committed a tenth of their produce, sometimes in the form of a pig FH 6
Tracts for the Times	a series of pamphlets published 1833-41, espousing the ideas of the "Oxford Movement," led by John Henry Newman (1801-90), Richard Hurrell Froude (1803-36), John Keble (1792-1866), and Edward Bouverie Pusey (1800-82), holding that the Anglican Church was the true custodian of the Catholic faith since its split from Rome, and promulgating Catholic thought and practice in the Church of England. AB 52
Trebbiano	Italian wine R 46
Tripitaka	not traced; MP 47
truncis naribus	literally "truncated nostrils": refers to the typical damage to the noses of ancient busts and statues R *P*
tussis	cough R 16
Urim and Thummim	certain objects, the nature of which is not known, worn in or upon the breastplate of a Jewish priest in his most solemn approach to the tabernacle of the Lord, through which the will of Jehovah was made known. The literal meaning of the words is "lights and perfections," or "the shining and the perfect" CB 144
Va!	"Go on!" "go to"—or, today, perhaps "geddoudahere!" R 1
Vedas	the four ancient sacred books of the Hindus MP 47
Vendidad	not traced; MP 47
vermocane	the staggers: a disease affecting cattle R 16
Vinaigrette	an aromatic sachet carried by women in case of a fainting spell GL 11
vino di sotto	"wine from below"—inferior wine R 3
virtuosi colpi	honourable wounds (in the front, not the back of the body R *P*
Voluntarism	A principle which held that churches should be supported by voluntary contributions rather than by exactions (tithes) or the State. FH *I*
Waldenses	Adherents of a religious sect formed about 1170. It rejected papal authority; later associated with the Protestant Reformation. MM 2
wandering Jew	the Jew who, in legend, taunted Christ on the cross and thereafter spent eternity seeking a resting-place without success DD 22
zazzera	head of hair R 45
Zecca	the Mint R 8
zoccoli	wooden sandals R 43

Words and Thoughts in the Complete Works

Sayings of the Characters

'affection is the broadest basis of good in life' DD 35

'almanac for the Millennium, making an' DD 32

'antediluvian point of view' DD 52

'Antinomian, is she an' DD 45

'antiphrasis, Ciceronian' FH 22

'Arabs who are being inspired with a new zeal' DD 42

'When you get me a good man made out of *arguments,* I will get you a good dinner with reading you the cookery-book.' MM 17

'Arno run broth and stand by without dipping your finger, you're not the one to see the' R 14

'Art must intensify' DD 37

'An ass may bray a good while before he shakes the stars down.' R 50

'beautiful and the best thing it must be true, If people have thought what is the most' DD 37

'Beauty is of very little consequence in reality.' MM 12

'Beauty is part of the finished language by which goodness speaks.' R 19

'Before I bring words to market I should like to see 'em a bit scarcer' FH 7

'bimbo, I'll show you the' R 33

'blameless people are always the most exasperating' MM 12

'a blind Florentine is a match for two one-eyed men' R 1

'bloodhounds, All's virtue that cheats' SG II ii

'boast of nausea as proof of a strong inside, they might as well' FH 27

'Book of Mormon would never have answered in Hebrew, the' DD 40

'breed is stronger than pasture' SM 11

'buffalo in the snow, he can see a' R 8

'Burn burn indiscernibly into that which shall be which is my love and not me.' DD 61

'butlers, great houses must have great' FH 7

'the child 'ull grow like grass i' May, bless it' SM 14

'a clergyman should have no quarrels' FH 2

'clever stupidity to have only one sort of talent—like a carrier-pigeon' MF V 3

'comfortable as wet chickens' R 12

'common-sense in an ounce of miserliness, always a few grains of.' MM 6

'common-sense in it, the world would be a poor place if there were nothing but' DD 46

'Many things are true which only the *commonest* minds observe.' MM 5

'compliment can be eloquent except as an expression of indifference, no' MF VI 2

'conceited people carry their comfort about with them' MF V 4 'contempt contributes greatly to the elegance of life, A little' LV 2

'crows else you'll set others watching, don't seem to be on the look-out for' FH 1

'dairy if folks want a bit o' worrit to make the days pass, there's nothing like a' SM 17

'days long as pig's chitterlings' MF III 6

'debtor that thinks himself free? Who is so base as the' R 40

'Delian god' CB 748

'dissimulation is never immoderate, effective' R 39

'dissimulation treachery, we have our limits beyond which we call' R 3

'dithyrambic fine excess' S 122

'Hev a *dog*, Miss—they're better friends nor any Christian' MF IV 3

'If *donkeys* set to work to sing, you're pretty sure what the tune'll be.' AB 21

'drunkenness and darkness go better together than drunkenness and daylight.' AB 22

'dulness of things is a disease in ourselves, I think what we call the' DD 35

'easiest way to deceive a poet is to tell him the truth, the' LV 2

'eat eggs in Lent and the snow will melt' R 16

'elenchus makes a yoke, no dull' CB 781

'empty sacks 'ull never stand upright' MF I 8

'faites votre jeu, mesdames et messieurs' DD 1 [a surprising mistake: the expression, addressing a crowd, is *Faîtes vos jeux*]

'faithful heart is faithfulness, the deepest hunger of a' SG V

'fear about with one, it's like carrying' R 26

'glory of the cross is an illusion the sorrow is only the truer, if the' R 69

'a green Yule makes a fat churchyard.' SF 5

'the grey colt may chance to kick like his black sire' MF II 6

'harebrained and light-hearted, you've never been' AB 16

'[he] knows meal from bran' MF II 2

'he's all Greek and greediness' FH 2

'He remembers nothin' but his own inside—an' I wish it 'ud gripe him MF I 4

'he's a tool with a smooth handle' R 45

'he who bids for nuts and news may chance to find them hollow' R 1

'Heaven might be made of voices, I have often fancied' DD 32

'the heavy end will get downmost' FH 20

'honest men will have small hire to pay, he who will be captain of none but' R 45

'horse to tread on a dog when you're backing out of the way but it goes through you when it's done, You don't mean your' MM 40

'Husbands are an inferior class of men who require keeping in order' MM 86

'husbands as if they wanted to sell 'em, they praise their' SM 17

'I am as unnecessary as a chimney-ornament' FH 9

'I believe that people are almost always better than their neighbours think' MM 72

'I cannot take a good for myself that has been wrung out of their misery' MF VI 14

'I have not many years left at the bottom of my sack for them to rob me of' R 54

'I know how many legs go into one boot' R 12

'I like too well to feel admired but compliments never make me feel that' MF VI 2

'I put my ears down and wagged my tail at that stroking' FH 5

'I shan't be put off wi' spoon-meat afore I've lost my teeth' MF I 3

'I should require your words to be what your face and form are—always among the meanings of a noble music' DD 11

'If I want to believe in Jesus Christ I must shut my eyes for fear I should see a parson' FH 30

'if a man takes to tongue-work it's all over with him' FH 20

'if a nag is to throw me let him have some blood' FH 20

'If there's good anywhere we've need of it' SM 10

'If you want to slip into a round hole you must make a ball of yourself' MF III 5

'I'll never pull my coat off before I go to bed' MF I 3

'I'm a Dutchman' MF I 4

'I'm no better nor a tilted bottle I arn't—I can't stop mysen when once I begin' MF VI 4

'impetuosity about trifles has a freezing influence that would cool the baths of Nero, your' R 48

'it's not a pumpkin I carry on my shoulders' R 1

'I've been taking peas for paternosters' R 70

'Jewess who has not fault? How can an ugly Christian who is always dropping her work convert a beautiful' DD 32

'kills a man so soon as having nobody to find fault with but himself, there's nothing' SM 17 'knighthood, It is my' FH 32

'God A'mighty sticks to the *land*. He promises land, and He gives land, and He makes chaps rich with corn and cattle.' MM 12

'legs like bladders' MF I 7

'legs into twisted hose, thou hast got thy' R 63

'lessons not to sing, many of our girls nowadays want' DD 36

'Life was never anything but a perpetual see-saw between gravity and jest' R 8

'the light vehicle of a weighty moral' JR 3

'logician who described the pavement of the bottomless pit' R 39

'I don't *love* you' MF I 5

'love finds the need it fills' AR V

'lucky eel that escapes skinning, it is a' FH 1

'lymph oozing from your pores as if it were mere vulgar moisture, It is pitiful to see your learned' R 16

'to manage men one ought to have a sharp mind in a velvet sheath' R 39

'megatherium, injustice to the' DD 52

'Men have no memories in their hearts' FH 35

'Men know best about everything, except what women knew better' MM 72

'Men may cure themselves off the face of the land without knowing it.' MM 46

'mind is an enemy to beauty' R 45

'Miserliness is a capital quality to run in families; it's the safe side for madness to dip on' MM 6

'They've got the *money* for it,' as the girl said of her mistress who made herself ill with pickled salmon JR 25 [A Wellerism!]

'money's a good egg; and if you've got money to leave behind you lay it in a warm nest' MM 12

'a mother's love is like a tree that has got all the wood in it from the very first it made' DD 32

'mouse to have a nose that takes note of wax or tallow, I am not a' FH 5

'no amount of wishing will fill the Arno or turn a plum into an orange' R 48

'no better an imitation of men than if they were onions with bulbs uppermost' R 49

'no pleasure for old women unless they get it out of tormenting others, there's' FH 1

'nobody's luck is pulled only by one string' FH 1

'nose will do to be miserable with in this world, any' DD 3

'not nohow' thinking that where negatives were good the more you had of them the better FH 28

'nothing 'ud be a lesson to us if it didn't come too late, perhaps' AB 18

'oat-cake ran too much to bone instead of brains' AB 21

'old maids' husbands are al'ys well-managed' SF 5

'One *must* either die or get old' R 51

'Our people wandered before they were driven.' DD 60

'a packman can do wi' a small 'lowance o' church: it tastes strong; there's no call to lay it on thick' MF VII 1

'Palingenesis means telegraphs and measure of the rate at which the stars move' CB 729-9

'a park without fine timber is no better than a beauty without teeth and hair' FH 1

'particular lies may speak a general truth' SG I v

'poem without reading it as to know a sermon without listening, not so easy to know a' DD 5

'poets no more think the truth stale than they think the light of the moon stale R 16

'padding, life wants' MM 13

'people are not expected to be large in proportion to the houses they live in like snails' MV VI 2

'pleasure has cramped dwelling in our souls/ And when full Being comes must call on pain/To lend it liberal space.' AR I

'praise a cat to sell a horse' MM 46

'A prig is a fellow who is always making you a present of his opinions' MM 11

'processions, there has been no great people without' R 8

'puddle that was proud of standing alone while the river rushed by' R 8

'If one is not to get into a *rage* sometimes, what is the good of being friends?' MM 12

'riddle? What can promote innocent mirth and virtue more than a good' MM 60

'ridiculous rancour worthy only of wandering savages' MF VI 8

'Saint Anybody is a bad saint to pray to' DD 32

'the salt-shops were open when you came into the world' R 1

'Satan was a blunderer who made a stupendous failure' R 60

'satisfied wth the pleasant lust of arrogance, he is' R 16

'scandal too much to wish to repeat it, I despise hearing' MM 12

'science whose soul is explanation halts with hostile front at mystery' CB 227-8

'second size—pig-potato like' FH 28

'she will never die now because she is so well-dried' R 33

'Sin that's hidden's half forgiven' R 33

'All choice of words is *slang*. It marks a class' MM 11

'snout upward like a pig under an oak-tree, with your' R 1

'sorrow without duty—bitter herbs and no bread with them' R 40

'sorrowing is your sauce; you can do nothing without it' DD 31

'Souls have complexions too; what will suit one will not suit another' MM 1

'steal the keys from snoring destiny and make the prophets lie, He is of those who' SG I iii

'stone bed with the wind for a curtain, sleeping on a' R 1

'There's a *story* as when the mill changes hands the river's angry' MF III 9

'The strongest calf must have something to suck at' AB 21

'tears are no good: they put out the fire within' R 53

'thank a man for not being a rogue or a noodle, are you to? R 28

'toad said to the harrow, she'll come back presently as the' R 10

'traitors must see their interest in betraying, even' R 54

'trout-stream, It's a very good quality in a man to have a' MM 8

'trust a man let him be a bachelor, if you' AB 23

'truth in wine and some in gin and muddy beer, There's' FH 28

'two things not to be hidden: love and a cough' R 6

'ugliness is past its bloom, make conquests when our' SF 6

'unwritten poems in cipher on my face, I carry my' R 45

'use his gun to bring down your game and then beat the thief with the butt-end' FH 2

'veracity is a plant of paradise' R 45

'a very good fellow, but pulpy; he will run into any mould, but he won't keep shape' MM 8

'visions are the creators and feeders of the world' DD 40

'walking like a procession, she has that way of' R 13

'water [weeping] pays no tax' GL 2

'Water's a very particular thing—you can't pick it up with a pitchfork.' MF II 2

'We don't ask what a woman does—we ask whom she belongs to.' MF VI 8

'Wet your granny!' SF 3

'wheaten flour has to be accounted for' DD 20

'when the stool's rotten enough, no matter who sits in it' SF 5

'the wine and the sun will make vinegar without any shouting to help them' R 63

'wisdom a yearning after nothingness' CB 540

'wise as a calf with water on its brain, you are about as' R 63

'A woman's love is always freezing into fear' FH 39

'women think walls are held together with honey' R 28

'years as the Tuscans say are made for the letting of houses' DD 10

'you are come into the trap for your cheese, I fear me' R 16

'You come as opportunely as cheese on macaroni' R 4

'You're like a tipsy man as thinks every body's had too much but himself' MF I 12

'The *young* ones have always a claim on the old ones to help them forward.' MM 56

From the Narration

The Absurd is taken as an excellent juicy thistle by many constituitions TS 2

accident is but the touch of fire where there is oil and tow, the effective MM 56

acute deductive reasoning for keeping a man in the dark, there is nothing like IR 113

admiration, the glow of mingled undefined sensibilities forming DD 1

adytum LV 1

Aldebaran is a bright star TS 8 SG II ii

alligator, looked as neutral as an DD 15

allotropic condition HH 74

alone and for some women also, in the ages since Adam's marriage it has been good for some men to be FH 44

Anger and jealousy can no more bear to lose sight of their objects than love. MF I 1

another man's shortcomings, very little MM 21

antipode of all enthusiasm called 'a man of the world', that DD 40

Apocalypse, commentator on the FH 37

appetency towards antithetic apothegm PY 22

ardent woman's need to rule beneficently by making the joy of another soul MM 37

ardour broods over a prompt deed the deed seems to start forth with independent life, when young MM 37

Art is the nearest thing to life NH 125

auricula MF I 4

autumnal unripeness of his authorship MM 42

avatar of perfect wisdom and beauty, transient MF VI 11

axioms are not [our servants'], our SL

bachelor, with the usual shallowness of a young MM 17

badinage and lyrism had turned explosive MM 82

batrachian, dubiously complimentary to the blameless R 16

beaming timidity with which a man almost always addresses a pretty woman. JR 3

beating of the heart which makes existence seem simply a painful pulsation, that terrible MF III 1

Belgian railway-horn shows praiseworthy intentions inadequately fulfilled SF 2

birthright is sharp duty, many of us complain that half our DD 37

bloated and worldly Prelacy FH 3

blows are sarcasms turned stupid FH 30

Bodily haste and exertion usually leave our thoughts very much at the mercy of our feelings and imaginations AB 4

Body and mind must renew their force to suffer as well as to enjoy GL 6

Bosjesman DD 28

brazen horse, rise into the air on a DD 44

bread-crumb—the neutral basis needful for the plums and spice, society's TS 4

break of day, a form of struggle before DD 32

breeze to move gently like a social spirit among ears of uncut corn, enough DD 13

Brevity is justified at once to those who readily understand and to those who will never understand LV 2

brother simply as a spectator, no man can know his TS 1

caliginosity DD 37

canary-bird, the uncritical awe of an elegant-minded MM 20

candid people have their secrets, and secrets leave no lines in young faces AB 22

caressed mollusc MF II 4

the casuists have become a by-word of reproach MF VII 2

a cat wandering incognito MF I 6

Catholics than of the fossil mammals, rural Englishmen had hardly known more of FH *I*

causticity of tongue MF I 7

celestial breasts/charitable ladies MF VI 9

change in her like that of a glacier after sunset, there was a DD 54

change in Mary's face was chiefly determined by the resolve not to show any change, A certain MM 12

character too is a process and an unfolding MM 15

charcoal of ancestral sermons, diamonds of [poem] had been slowly condensed from the PY 4

Cherokees TS 1

chimeras begotten by imperfect learning on original incapacity, hideous TS 3

chosen nose, a broad low hat surmounting his DD 32

Christian Carnivora who formed the funeral procession MM 35

Christmas with the snowy hair and ruddy face MF II 2

classical, none but the ancients can always be MM 16

coarse kindness is at least better than coarse anger FH 9

cockatrices who have ceased to bite MF VI 12

Cohen you might as well advertise for two undescribed terriers, if the name was DD 20

common-sense which is able to accept momentous doctrines without any eccentric agitation, that MM 1

Comparison, our precious guide TS 13

condiment in domestic life DD 35

condiments or conduct, approve MF I 6

confidant escapes believing too little in his penetration and too much in his discretion? Who that has a DD 47

confidences are sometimes blinding even when they are sincere MF VI 3

conjecture is constantly guided by feeling R 39

connoisseur might have seen points MF I 7

conscience—a fear which is the shadow of justice—a pity which is the shadow of love DD 35 ep

consequences are determined not by excuses but by actions, Pity that AB 29

constant in her affection towards a baseless opinion as towards an erring lover, as SM 11

constructed of musical strings, as though she were MF VI 7

contradictory discoveries, close and diligent looking at living creatures even through the best microscope will leave room for new and FH 22

convenience—admirable branch system from the main line of self-interest JR 10

coughing fashion which was felt to be a privilege of his rank, ponderous SM 9

courtesy, sweet flower of SM 9

coxcombry, he had no R 9

cravat tied very tight on some higher principle than mere personal ease MF I 7

cried a little/trickling quiet way MF I 8

on *critical* occasions all moments seem comfortably remote until the last MM 51

dawn after we have looked away from it to the grey west, new radiance like the R 17

death, the great Reconciler AB 4

Our *deeds* are like children born to us; they live and act apart from our will R 16

Our *deeds* determine us as much as we determine our deeds AB 29

it is one thing to like *defiance* and another thing to like its consequences. MM 46

desire to conquer is itself a sort of subjection, the DD 10

despair if often only the painful eagerness of unfed hope, what we call MM 51

Destiny stands by sarcastic with our *dramatis personæ* folded in her hand MM 11

deuce, never referred knowledge of discreditable doings to any high power than the MM 40

difficulty of carring out a resolve we secretly long will be unnecessary MM 60

disthroned, a queen DD 26

He *distrusted* her affection; what loneliness is more lonely than distrust? MM 44

disturbing doctrine that it was not the duty of the rich to be luxurious for the sake of the poor R 39

The tale of the *Divine* Pity was never yet believed from lips that were not felt to be moved by human pity JR 18

divine presence stirring those inarticulate sensibilities which are our deepest life R 37

Djinn, an enslaved DD 38

the double soul which belongs to dreamers who answer questions MM 59

downy patience SM 14

drifting depends on something besides the currents when the sails have been set beforehand DD 27

dyspepsia SL

dyspeptic puritans MF II 2

eager theorising of ages is compressed as in a seed in the momentary want of a single mind R 17

earth to the solar system in general, the obligations of the TS 11

easier and pleasanter to recognize the old than to account for the new, it is R *P*

ebbing life, the strange, far-off look which belongs to SF 8

écarté, less competent to win at FH 14

edification which belongs to the inexplicable, that peculiar FH 11

effect as sure as roundness in the dewdrop MP 288-9

effeminate futilities MF VI 9

effervescence of the mind which we call fun, that delicious NH 124

embryonic wings, larger possibilities of her nature lay folded and crushed like R 27

emotion as a cunningly-carved crab-tree walking-stick, as much AB 12

emotion was at the acute point where it is not distinguishable from sensation DD 48

emptiness of all things from politics to pastimes is never so striking to us as when we fail in them, the DD 16

English had little foreignness except its fluency, his DD 5

epicurean urchins GL 1

Mahometanism, converted to FH 1

make men moral something more is requisite than to turn them out to grass, to NH 124

If a *man* could not love and be wise, surely he could flirt and be wise MM 27

the man was no more than the boy writ large with an extensive commentary FH 8

The man who let the mere anticipation of discovery choke him was simply a man of weak nerves R 16

manners must be very marked indeed before they cease to be interpreted by preconceptions either confident or distrustful MM 2

Mant's Bible SM 17

marital habit of not listening very closely MF I 2

marriage must be a relation either of sympathy or of conquest R 48

meanings we know depend on the key of interpretation, all DD 6

medical impartiality SM 11

melodies die out, like the pipe of Pan, with the ears that love them and listen for them AB 18

memento of solemnities, pale-faced SM 11

memory, the fresh and fresh vividness which belongs to emotive DD 19

memory has as many moods as the temper, and shifts its scenery like a diorama MM 53

men lose the dread of death in the clash of battle R 52

men who are apt to see in their own interest or desires a motive for other men's actions, there are MF III 1

metaphysic mind MF VI 7

a mind in the grasp of terrible anxiety is not credulous of easy solutions FH 42

mind there was not room enough for luxuries to look small in, in her MM 69

mind, motes from the mass of a magistrate's MM 2

mingled seed must bear a mingled crop MF V 7

mispronunciation against which the direct experience of eye and ear is often powerless, a long-standing TS 12

mob, all things except reason and order are possible with a R 67

Mohammedans in well-tolerated companionship with Christian cavaliers R 14

money was a good egg, and should be laid in a warm nest MM 32

Our *moods* are apt to bring with them images which succeed each other like the magic-lantern pictures of a doze MM 20

Moral vulgarity cleaved to him like an hereditary odour FH 9

A mother dreads no memories—those shadows have all melted away in the dawn of baby's smile GL 21

motive could any man really have except his own interest? What R 57

mumbo-jumbo, a sort of DD 28

musician in your house is a privilege of wealth, to have a first-rate DD 22

mutual speech, we see a very little way before us in R 48

nature never makes men who are at once energetically sympathetic and minutely calculating." FH 33

Nature that great tragic dramatist AB 4

necessity does the work of courage R 67

Nemesis is lame, but she is of colossal stature like the gods JR 13

The Nereid in sea-green robes DD 1

nethermost sediment in her mental shallows MM 12

neutrals not distressed to discern some folly in martyrs and some judiciousness in the men who burnt them R 55

the new force which belongs to a last opportunity AB 38

nidus for inconsistent beliefs TE 84

no kind of conscious obedience not an advance on lawlessness, There is R 49

no man not exceptionally feeble will endure being thwarted by his wife R 48

no story is the same to us after a lapse of time: we who read it are no longer the same interpreters AB 54

noise wanted he was the dog for it, if there was any MF I 4

notions and scruples were like spilt needles, making one afraid of treading, or sitting down, or even eating. MM 2

nullifidian [skeptic], a pink and white MM 4

objurgatory domestic eloquence: JR 10

obliged to 'run away'—a course as dark and dubious as a balloon journey SM 2

occiput TS 11

omniscience, perfect scheming demands R 63

one thing to love the fruits of treachery and another to love traitors, it is R 57

onion rubbed with spices, he was like an SF 2

onyx cameo, it was as clear to him as an DD 17

onyx, her long brown eyes glancing bright as a wave-washed DD 4

openness which is the sweet fresh air of our moral life, that DD 33 opodeldoc FH 30

oriental sunlight in their blood TS 18

own pure thoughts in [his eyes] as we read letters in happy dreams, she only read her R 17

pagans of his time, one of the few, frank R 15

Pain, the great lord of mortals R 38

painted figure looking as if it had been boned for a pie R 8

palsy of distrust R 30

parents' misery has made parents' wickedness WM 180

the passionate serenity of perfect love FH 44

a passionate woman's love is always overshadowed by fear GL 4

pasture her mind upon them, seek out the sadder elements of life and SM 10

patriarch, some young men since the DD 32

pedagogue, reflected confidence of the MM 10

Would not love see returning *penitence* afar off, and fall on its neck and kiss it? MM 21

People who live at a distance are naturally less faulty than those immediately under our own eyes MF III 3

percussive butcher's boy DD 58

peremptory hunger of the soul MF IV 2

periphrase, copious supply of words which often led him into FH 2

periphrases, polite R 52

perversity of a Desdemona MM 8

piety lies in punishing DD 60 ep

Pinzochera R 36

phiz MF I 5

phosphorous, mind active as MM 6

pleasure of guessing which active minds notoriously prefer to ready-made knowledge, that MR I 10

pleasure of a restriction is the pleasure of breaking it, the only great MF I 10

Plymouth Brother JR 10

poetry was only literature, where FH 44

poison is feeble against the sense of thirst, the fear of LV 1

the poisoned garment on him, the victim writhes under torture but has no thought of coming death GL 12

political economy, that never-explained science which was thrust as an extinguisher over all her lights MM 2

poor relations, a human dignity which can afford to acknowledge DD 17

poor relations are undeniably irritating MF I 8

popularity is the most complex and self-multiplying of echoes JR 26

porcine cheeks, large FH 20

positive physical oppression at the heart that sometimes accompanies a sudden mental pang MF VI 7

Possible is always the ultimate master of our efforts and desires, the TS 7

praiseworthy past of Pitt and high prices MF IV 1

pretences turn our lives into sorry dramas, such FH 32

pride only helps us to be generous; it never makes us so, any more than vanity makes us witty MM 8

prime minister, he had as little of his own way as if he had been a MM 36

probabilities which never occur, one of those endless things called DD 32

prophecy is the most gratuitous, Among all forms of mistake MM 10

Public opinion, in these cases, is always of the feminine gender MF VII 1

Public spirit can never be wholly immoral since its essence is care for a common good R *P*

puerile impulses or questionable inward fumes R 57

pursuant gaze convalescent persons often have for those who have tended them MF III 8

rack and manger, he lived at BL 7 326

Red Indians expected smallpox, expected it as little as the innocent JR 2

Reformation where a man can afford to do without it can hardly be other than genuine DD 9

religion of chapel-goers, which appeared to run in families, like asthma MF IV 1

resurrection into a new world DD 8

retina, red drapery spreading itself everywhere like a disease of the MM 20

rhythmic empire, musical vibrations with a R 12

rich find it easy to live married and apart, the LV 2

right in great memorable moments is perhaps the thing we need most desire for ourselves, to be FH 32

rinforzando, with a constant SF 2

ripeness beneath the sun has a further stage less esteemed in the market MF II 4

romance as most lives have between the ages of teetotum and tobacco, his life had SF 1

beneficent harness of *routine* enables silly men to live respectably and unhappy men to live calmly MM 66

The Rubicon was insignificant to look at: its significance lay entirely in invisible conditions MM 82

ruminant animal, he was as genuine a character as any MM 20

sacrifice that was not unpleasant, equal to any R 31

safety is a god that sometimes makes very grim demands, a man's own R 60

scholiast, experienced theologian or learned FH *I*

Sclavonic race NH 129

sea-anemone at the touch of a finger, made her curl up and harden like a DD 7

sea-lion plunges and swims TS 1

search the faintest suggestions have peculiar significance, to one anxiously in R 55

one's *self-satisfaction* is an untaxed kind of property which it is very unpleasant to find depreciated MM 16

shaken trust in God and man which is little short of madness to a loving nature, that SM 1

the shallowness of a water-nixie's soul may have a charm till she becomes didactic MM 64

there is no *shamefacedness* in a sad parting MM 62

sheep will face about a little when she has lambs, even a MF I 6

shyness only wears off in the absence of their elders, boys' MF II 3

shyness, that peculiar intimacy which consists in MM 27

sightless beauty which tells that the vision is all within, that FH 45

silence, we should die of that roar which lies on the other side of MM 20

silent sunny fields and pastures seemed filled with a natural joy that had no reproach for theirs MF VI 13

Sirius SG II ii

At sixteen the mind that has the strongest affinity for fact cannot escape illusion and self-flattery MF III 5

a skein is tangled there is nothing like snatching hastily at a single thread, for getting a strong impression that MF I 8

the solemn unspeakable kiss of a life-long parting AB 46

a solvent of feeling R 52

sophistry will nullify long struggle and bring the defeat we love better than victory MF V 3

as the *sore* palate findeth grit, so an uneasy consciousness heareth innuendoes MM 31

sorrow was more bearable now hatred was gone AB 48

soul full of unspoken evil and unacted good JR 16

The soul of man when it gets fairly rotten will bear you all sorts of poisonous toadstools MM 40

souls live on in perpetual echoes MM 16

how much of human *speech* is mere purposeless impulse or habit AB 5

spoken once is a tyrannous reason for speaking again, to have DD 32

spontaneous servility FH 20

spurned beauty, anger on account of MF VI 9

squirrel-like enjoyment of nuts at discretion R 34

stone hut was made a soft nest SM 14

stucco ornaments of which the substance was never worth anything FH 1

subdued by a general mealiness MF I 4

submit like all strong souls when she felt no valid reason for resistance, ready to R 20

suffusive pinkness of a healthy Briton on the central table-land of life DD 22

sunlight stole through boughs and played about them like a winged thing R 10

sustenance in the first few words of love, There is a wonderful amount of AB 54

sweep of her long tresses across her cheek seems to vibrate through the hours, the simple R 34

swims much better and takes his performances as a matter of course, A panting man thinks himself a clever swimmer; but a fish FH 24

sympathies are the very life and substance of our wisdom, human R 15

sympathy is but a living again through our own past in a new form JR 18

the tasting of joys wrung from crushed hearts MF VI 14

tautology, getting entangled in what is elegantly called DD 48

One likes to be done well by in every *tense,* past, present, and future MM 35

terrible handwriting of human destiny, illness and death SF 9

thickest ice of theory, The tides of the divine life in man move under the PY 40

thinking to be either premature or behindhand, it is the trick of DD 64

thought the strong angel with the implacable brow, eager R 10

thwarted energy subsides into a shudder. MM 42

Time itself were pausing, an unchanging stillness as if FH *I*

The *Topicon*

The *Topicon*

Captions, and Their Locations in the *Topicon*

A	Ages of Man
B	Body
FL	First and Last Things
FM	Fellow Man, in Relation
GB	Great Britain
GP	Government and Politics
H	Humankind in Activity
LC	Letters and Communication
LM	Love, Marriage, and the Sexes
M	Mind
N	Nature
RW	Germany and the Rest of the World
S	Spirit and Moral Qualities
SR	Self-Revelation
TP	Three Professions
TT	Transportation and Travel

Dorothea finds her Husband in the Garden

Ages of Man

"But were another childhood-world my share,
I would be born a little sister there." BS 154

"In the morning of life, work; in the mid-day,
give counsel; in the evening, pray." R 12

Adolescence

—*change:* "Perhaps she was growing out of that childhood to which common things have rareness, and all objects look larger. Perhaps from henceforth the whole world was to be meaner for her." FH 45

—*inspiration:* " . . . as the long stream of white-robed youthfulness, with its little red crosses and olive wreaths, had gone to the Duomo at dawn this morning to receive the communion from the hands of **Savonarola**, it was a sight of beauty; and, doubtless, many of those young souls were laying up memories of hope and awe that might save them from ever resting in a mere vulgar view of their work as men and citizens.

"There is no kind of conscious obedience that is not an advance on lawlessness, and these boys became the generation of men who fought greatly and endured greatly in the last struggle of their Republic." ¶R 49

—*predicted:* " 'Job's limbs will get lanky; this little fist, that looks like a puff-ball and can hide nothing bigger than a gooseberry, will get large and bony, and perhaps want to clutch more than its share; these wide blue eyes that tell me more truth than Job knows, will narrow and narrow and try to hide truth that Job would be better without knowing; this little negative nose will become long and self-asserting, and this little tongue . . . hardly bigger than a rose-leaf, will get large and thick, wag out of season, do mischief, brag and cant for gain or vanity, and cut as cruelly, for all its clumsiness, as if it were a sharp-edged blade.' " FH 22

—*quarrel:* "We learn to restrain ourselves as we get older. We keep apart when we have quarrelled, express ourselves in well-bred phrases, and in this way preserve a dignified alienation, showing much firmness on one side, and swallowing much grief on the other. We no longer approximate in our behaviour to the mere impulsiveness of the lower animals, but conduct ourselves in every respect like members of a highly civilised society." MF I 5

Ancestor

—*ancient spirits:* "(Doubtless some of these danced in their youth, doubted of their own vocation, and found their own times too modern.)" DD 36

—*debt to them:* "Acknowledge debt to that laborious life
Which, sifting evermore the mingled seeds,
Testing the Possible with patient skill,
And daring ill in presence of a good
For futures to inherit, made your lot
One you would choose rather than end it, nay,
Rather than, say, some twenty million lots
Of fellow-Britons toiling all to make
That nation, that community, whereon
You feed and thrive and talk philosophy." CB 556-565

—descendants: "And it was agreed on all hands that the habits of posterity would be very surprising to ancestors, if ancestors could only know them." R 39

—gallery: "Two rows of these descendants, direct and collateral, females of the male line, and males of the female, looked down in the gallery over the cloisters on the nephew Daniel as he walked there: men in armour with pointed beards and arched eyebrows, pinched ladies in hoops and ruffs with no face to speak of; grave-looking men in black velvet and stuffed hips, and fair, frightened women holding little boys by the hand, smiling politicians in magnificent perruques, and ladies of the prize-animal kind, with rosebud mouths and full eyelids, according to **Lely**; then a generation whose faces were revised and embellished in the taste of **Kneller**; and so on through refined editions of the family: types in the time of **Reynolds** and **Romney**, till the line ended . . . . " DD 16

—innovation: "One wonders whether the remarkable originators who first had the notion of digging wells, or of churning for butter, and who were certainly very useful to their own time as well as ours, were left quite free from invidious comparison with predecessors who let the water and the milk alone, or whether some rhetorical nomad, as he stretched himself on the grass with a good appetite for contemporary butter, became loud on the virtue of ancestors who were uncorrupted by the produce of the cow; nay, whether in a high flight of imaginative self-sacrifice (after swallowing the butter) he even wished himself earlier born and already eaten for the sustenance of a generation more *naïve* than his own." TS 2

—national: " . . . the historian guides us rightly in urging us to dwell on the virtues of our ancestors with emulation, and to cherish our sense of a common descent as a bond of obligation. The eminence, the nobleness of a people depends on its capability of being stirred by memories, and of striving for what we call spiritual ends—ends which consist not in immediate material possession, but in the satisfaction of a great feeling that animates the collective body as with one soul. A people having the seed of worthiness in it must feel an answering thrill when it is adjured by the deaths of its heroes who died to preserve its national existence; when it is reminded of its small beginnings and gradual growth through past labours and struggles, such as are still demanded of it in order that the freedom and wellbeing thus inherited may be transmitted unimpaired to children and children's children, when an appeal against the permission of injustice is made to great precedents in its history and to the better genius breathing in its institutions." TS 18

Baby

—aunt: " . . . to an aunt who does not recognise her infant nephew as Bouddha, and has nothing to do for him but to admire, his behaviour is apt to appear monotonous, and the interest of watching him exhaustible." MM 54

—calm: "She was perfectly quiet now, but not asleep—only soothed by sweet porridge and warmth into that wide-gazing calm which makes us older human beings, with our inward turmoil, feel a certain awe in the presence of a little child, such as we feel before some quiet majesty or beauty in the earth or sky—before a steady glowing planet, or a full-flowered eglantine, or the bending trees over a silent pathway." SM 13

—power: "Let even an affectionate *Goliath* get himself tied to a small tender thing, dreading to hurt it by pulling, and dreading still more to snap the cord, and which of the two, pray, will be master?" SM 14

—punishment: "Sorely was poor Silas puzzled . . . by the incompatible demands of love. Dolly Winthrop told him that punishment was good for Eppie, and that as for rearing a child without making it tingle a little in soft and safe places now and then, it was not to be done." SM 14

—stolen: " 'Suppose the stolen offspring of some mountain tribe brought up in a city of the plain, or one with an inherited genius for painting, and born blind—the ancestral life would lie within them as a dim longing for unknown objects and sensations, and the spell-bound habit of their inherited frames would be like a cunningly-wrought musical instrument, never played on, but quivering throughout in uneasy mysterious moanings of its intricate structure that, under the right touch, gives music.' " DD 63

—transcending alchemy: "When Marner's sensibility returned, he continued the action which had been arrested, and closed his door, unaware of the chasm in his consciousness, unaware of any intermediate change, except that the light had grown dim, and that he was chilled and faint. He thought he had been too long standing at the door and looking out. Turning towards the hearth, where the two logs had fallen apart, and sent forth only a red uncertain glimmer, he seated himself on his fireside chair, and was stooping to push his logs together, when, to his blurred vision, it seems as if there were gold on the floor in front of the hearth. Gold!—his own gold—brought back to him as mysteriously as it had been taken away!

"He felt his heart begin to beat violently, and for a few moments he was unable to stretch out his hand and grasp the restored treasure. The heap of gold seemed to glow and get larger beneath his agitated gaze. He leaned forward at last, and stretched forth his hand; but instead of the hard coin with the familiar resisting outline, his fingers encountered soft warm curls. In utter amazement, Silas fell on his knees and bent his head low to examine the marvel: it was a sleeping child—a round, fair thing, with soft yellow rings all over its head. Could this be his little sister come back to him in a dream—the little sister whom he had carried about in his arms for a year before she died, when he was a small boy without shoes or stockings? That was the first thought that darted across Silas's blank wonderment.

"*Was* it a dream? He rose to his feet again, pushed his logs together, and, throwing on some dried leaves and sticks, raised a flame; but the flame did not disperse the vision—it only lit up more distinctly the little round form of the child, and its shabby clothing. It was very much like his little sister. Silas sank into his chair powerless, under the double presence of an inexplicable surprise and hurrying influx of memories. How and when had the child come in without his knowledge? He had never been beyond the door. But along with that question, and almost thrusting it away, there was a vision of the old home and the old streets leading to Lantern Yard—and within that vision another, of the thoughts which had been present with him in those far-off scenes. The thoughts were strange to him now, like old friendships impossible to revive; and yet he had a dreamy feeling that this child was somehow a message come to him from that far-off life: it stirred fibres that had never been moved in Raveloe—old quiverings of tenderness—old impressions of awe at the presentiment of some Power presiding over his life; for his imagination had not yet extricated itself from the sense of mystery in the child's sudden presence, and had formed no conjectures of ordinary natural means by which the event could have been brought about.

"But there was a cry on the hearth: the child had awaked, and Marner stooped to lift it on his knee. It clung round his neck, and burst louder and louder into that mingling of inarticulate cries with 'mammy' by which little children express the bewilderment of waking. Silas pressed it to him, and almost unconsciously uttered sounds of hushing tenderness, while he bethought himself that some of his porridge, which had got cool by the dying fire, would do to feed the child with if it were only warmed up a little.

"He had plenty to do through the next hour. The porridge, sweetened with some dry brown sugar from an old store which he had refrained from using for himself, stopped the cries of the little one, and made her lift her blue eyes with a wide quiet gaze at Silas, as he put the spoon into her mouth. Presently she slipped from his knee and began to toddle about, but with a pretty stagger that made Silas jump up and follow her lest she should fall against anything that would hurt her. But she only fell in a sitting posture on the ground, and began to pull at her boots, looking up at him with a crying face as if the boots hurt her.

"He took her on his knee again, but it was some time before it occurred to Silas's dull bachelor mind that the wet boots were the grievance, pressing on her warm ankles. He got them off with difficulty, and baby was at once happily occupied with the primary mystery of her own toes, inviting Silas, with much chuckling, to consider the mystery too. But the wet boots had at last suggested to Silas that the child had been walking on the snow, and this roused him from his entire oblivion of any ordinary means by which it could have entered or been brought into his house.

"Under the prompting of this new idea, and without waiting to form conjectures, he raised the child in his arms, and went to the door. As soon as he had opened it, there was the cry of 'mammy' again, which Silas had not heard since the child's first hungry waking. Bending forward, he could just discern the marks made by the little feet on the virgin snow, and he followed their track to the furze bushes. 'Mammy!' the little one cried again and again, stretching itself forward so as almost to escape from Silas's arms, before he himself was aware that there was something more than the bush before him—that there was a human body, with the head sunk low in the furze, and half-covered with the shaken snow." ¶SM 12

"Marner took her on his lap, trembling with an emotion mysterious to himself, at something unknown dawning on his life. Thought and feeling were so confused within him, that if he had tried to give them utterance, he could only have said that the child was come instead of the gold—that the gold had turned into the child." SM 14

Boy

—judging: "A boy's sheepishness is by no means a sign of overmastering reverence: and while you are making encouraging advances to him under the idea that he is overwhelmed by a sense of your age and wisdom, ten to one he is thinking you extremely queer. The only consolation I can suggest to you is, that the Greek boys probably thought the same of **Aristotle**. It is only when you have mastered a restive horse, thrashed a drayman, or have got a gun in your hand, that these shy juniors feel you to be a truly admirable and enviable character." MF I 9

Child and Childhood

"Childhood has no forebodings; but then, it is soothed by no memories of outlived sorrow." MF I 9

—bachelor's: " 'A bachelor's children are always young: they're immortal children—always lisping, waddling, helpless, and with a chance of turning out good.' " FH 22

—being little: "I grieved/To part forever from that little girl/And all her happy world so near the ground." SG I iii

—carried high: "What little child ever refused to be comforted by that glorious sense of being seized strongly and swung upward? I don't believe *Ganymede* cried when the eagle carried him away, and perhaps deposited him on *Jove*'s shoulder at the end." AB 30

—childhood's end: "They had gone forth together into their new life of sorrow, and they would never more see the sunshine undimmed by remembered cares. They had entered the thorny wilderness, and the golden gates of their childhood had for ever closed behind them." MF II 7

" . . . the lizard's egg, that white rounded passive prettiness, had become a brown, darting, determined lizard." FH 1

"Some children, even younger than Daniel, have known the first arrival of care, like an ominous irremovable guest in their tender lives, on the discovery that their parents, whom they had imagined able to buy everything, were poor and in hard money troubles." DD 16

—disowned: " 'And disowning your own child because of a *mésalliance* is something like disowning your own eye: everybody knows it's yours, and you have no other to make an appearance with.' " DD 35

—doll: " . . . every sweet woman, who has begun by showering kisses on the hard pate of her bald doll, creating a happy soul within that woodenness from the wealth of her own love." MM 20

—punished: "This was the trunk of a large wooden doll, which once stared with the roundest of eyes above the reddest of cheeks, but was not entirely defaced by a long career of vicarious suffering. Three nails driven into the head commemorated as many crises in Maggie's nine years of earthly struggle; that luxury of vengeance having been suggested to her by the picture of **Jael** destroying **Sisera** in the old Bible. The last nail had been driven in with a fiercer stroke than usual, for the Fetish on that occasion represented aunt Glegg. But immediately afterwards Maggie had reflected that if she drove many nails in, she would not be so well able to fancy that the head was hurt when she knocked it against the wall, nor to comfort it, and make believe to poultice it when her fury was abated; for even aunt Glegg would be pitiable when she had been hurt very much, and thoroughly humiliated, so as to beg her niece's pardon. Since then, she had driven no more nails in, but had soothed herself by alternately grinding and beating the wooden head against the rough brick of the great chimneys that made two square pillars supporting the roof. That was what she did this morning on reaching the attic, sobbing all the while with a passion that expelled every other form of consciousness—even the memory of the grievance that had caused it." MF I 3

—free of fear: " . . . and then he falls
To dreamy picturing of sunny days
When he himself was a small big-cheeked lad
In some far village where no heroes came,
And stood a listener 'twixt his father's legs
In the warm fire-light, while the old folk talked
And shook their heads and looked upon the floor;
And he was puzzled, thinking life was fine—
The bread and cheese so nice all through the year
And Christmas sure to come. Oh that good time!
He, could he choose, would have those days again
And see the dear old-fashioned things once more." MP 246-57

—griefs: "Very trivial, perhaps, this anguish seems to weather-worn mortals who have to think of Christmas bills, dead loves and broken friendships, but it was not less bitter to Maggie—perhaps it was even more bitter—than what we are fond of calling antithetically the real troubles of mature life. 'Ah, my child, you will have real troubles to fret about by and by, is the consolation we have almost all of us had administered to us in our childhood, and have repeated to other children since we have been grown up." MF 7

—forgotten: "We have all of us sobbed so piteously standing with tiny bare legs above our little socks, when we lost sight of our mother or nurse in some strange place, but we

can no longer recall the poignancy of that moment till we weep over it, as we do over the remembered sufferings of five or ten years ago. Every one of those keen moments has left its trace and lives in us still, but such traces have blent themselves irrecoverably with the firmer texture of our youth and manhood; and so it comes that we can look on at the troubles of our children with a smiling disbelief in the reality of their pain." MF I 7

—remembering: see M:Memory*—childhood griefs*

—halcyon morning: "It was one of their happy mornings. They trotted along and sat down together with no thought that life would ever change much for them: they would only get bigger and not go to school, and it would always be like the holidays; they would always live together and be fond of each other, and the mill with its booming—the great chestnut-tree under which they played at houses, their own little river, the Ripple, where the banks seemed like home, and Tom was always seeing the water-rats, while Maggie gathered the purple plumy tops of the reeds which she forgot and dropped afterwards; above all, the great Floss along which they wandered with a sense of travel, to see the rushing spring tide—the awful Eagre—come up like a hungry monster, or to see the Great Ash which had once wailed and groaned like a man—these things would always be just the same to them. Tom thought people were at a disadvantage who lived on any other spot of the globe, and Maggie when she read about *Christiana* passing 'the river over which there is no bridge' always saw the Floss between the green pastures by the Great Ash." MF I 5

—hero-worship: "Children demand that their heroes should be fleckless, and easily believe them so: perhaps a first discovery to the contrary is hardly a less revolutionary shock to a passionate child than the threatened downfall of habitual beliefs which makes the world seem to totter for us in maturer life." DD 16

—idealized: " . . . the boy moved him with that idealising affection which merges the qualities of the individual child in the glory of childhood and the possibilities of a long future." DD 38

—legitimacy: "The average man may regard this sensibility on the question of birth as preposterous and hardly credible; but with the utmost respect for his knowledge as the rock from which all other knowledge is hewn, it must be admitted that many well-proved facts are dark to the average man, even concerning the action of his own heart and the structure of his own retina. A century ago he and all his forefathers had not had the slightest notion of that electric discharge by means of which they had all wagged their tongues mistakenly; any more than they were awake to the secluded anguish of exceptional sensitiveness into which many a carelessly-begotten child of man is born." DD 37

—little sister: "But were another childhood-world my share,/I would be born a little sister there." *Brother and Sister:* the complete cycle is at page 698

—mother's preference: " 'Nay, I'n got no daughter o' my own—ne'er had one—an' I warna sorry, for they're poor queechy things, gells is; I allays wanted to ha' lads, as could fend for theirsens.' " AB 10

—in nature: "We could never have loved the earth so well if we had had no childhood in it—if it were not the earth where the same flowers come up again every spring that we used to gather with our tiny fingers as we sat lisping to ourselves on the grass—the same hips and haws on the autumn hedgerows—the same redbreasts that we used to call 'God's birds' because they did no harm to the precious crops. What novelty is worth that sweet monotony where everything is known and *loved* because it is known?" MF I 5

—occasion for pious mischief: "To coerce people by shame, or other spiritual pelting, into the giving up of things it will probably vex them to part with, is a form of piety to which the boyish mind is most readily converted; and if some obstinately wicked men got enraged and threatened the whip or the cudgel, this also was exciting." R 49

—parental love: "A weaver who finds hard words in his hymn-book knows nothing of abstractions; as the little child knows nothing of parental love, but only knows one face and one lap towards which it stretches its arms for refuge and nurture." SM 2

—pawn: "If Sir Hugo in his bachelorhood had been beguiled into regarding children chiefly as a product intended to make life more agreeable to the full-grown, whose convenience alone was to be consulted in the disposal of them—why, he had shared an assumption which, if not formally avowed, was massively acted on at that date of the world's history. . . . " DD 59

—philosophy's lesson: "The true philosopher . . . gathers his rule of conduct, not from the suggestions of appetite, not from the dictates of expediency, but from the indications of man's highest destiny, to be found in those faculties of his nature which may be justly said to be more than human, since they might belong to conditions of being far less limited than those of man. Self-renunciation, submission to law, trust, benignity, ingenuousness, rectitude—these are the qualities we delight most to witness in the child, and these are the qualities which most dignify the man." NE 3

—promise: "When they did meet, she remembered her promise to kiss him, but, as a young lady who had been at a boarding-school, she knew now that such a greeting was out of the question, and Philip would not expect it. The promise was void like so many other sweet, illusory promises of our childhood: void as promises made in Eden before the seasons were divided, and when the starry blossoms grew side by side with the ripening peach—impossible to be fulfilled when the golden gates had been passed." MF II 7

—something new: "All who remember their childhood remember the strange vague sense, when some new experience came, that everything else was going to be changed, and that there would be no lapse into the old monotony." R 10

—sorrows: "These bitter sorrows of childhood! —when sorrow is all new and strange, when hope has not yet got wings to fly beyond the days and weeks, and the space from summer to summer seems measureless." MF I 5

—uncontrollable: see H:Deed(s)—*irrevocable*

Family

—poor relations: "Poor relations are undeniably irritating: their existence is so entirely uncalled for on our part, and they are almost always very faulty people." MF I 8

—resemblance: "Family likeness has often a deep sadness in it. Nature, that great tragic dramatist, knits us together by bone and muscle, and divides us by the subtler web of our brains; blends yearning and repulsion; and ties us by our heartstrings to the beings that jar us at every moment. We hear a voice with the very cadence of our own uttering the thoughts we despise; we see eyes—ah! so like our mother's—averted from us in cold alienation; and our last darling child startles us with the air and gestures of the sister we parted from in bitterness long years ago. The father to whom we owe our best heritage—the mechanical instinct, the keen sensibility to harmony, the unconscious skill of the modelling hand—galls us, and puts us to shame by his daily errors; the long-lost mother, whose face we begin to see in the glass as our own wrinkles come, once fretted our young souls with her anxious humours and irrational persistence." AB 4

—bequeathed: "Surely, considering the importance which is given to such an accident in female offspring, marriageable men, or what the new English calls 'intending bridegrooms,' should look at themselves dispassionately in the glass, since their natural selection of a mate prettier than themselves is not certain to bar the effect of their own ugliness." DD 11

Father and Fatherhood

—envied: "Dissatisfaction seated musingly on a childless hearth, thinks with envy of the father whose return is greeted by young voices—seated at the meal where the little heads rise one above another like nursery plants, it sees a black care hovering behind every one of them, and thinks the impulses by which men abandon freedom, and seek for ties, are surely nothing but a brief madness." SM 17

—idleness: "The Squire's life was quite as idle as his sons', but it was a fiction kept up by himself and his contemporaries in Raveloe that youth was exclusively the period of folly, and that their aged wisdom was constantly in a state of endurance mitigated by sarcasm." SM 9

—likeness: "The likeness was that of outline, which is always most striking at the first moment; the expression had been wrought into the strongest contrast by such hidden or inconspicuous differences as can make the genius of a **Cromwell** within the outward type of a father who was no more than a respectable parishioner." DD 66

Funeral

—elaborate: "There were pall-bearers on horseback, with the richest scarves and hatbands, and even the under-bearers had trappings of woe which were of a good well-priced quality. The black procession, when dismounted, looked the larger for the smallness of the churchyard; the heavy human faces and the black draperies shivering in the wind seemed to tell of a world strangely incongruous with the lightly-dropping blossoms and the gleams of sunshine on the daisies." MM 34

—grief: "[He] took out his white handkerchief again with a sense that in any case there would be affecting passages, and crying at funerals, however dry, was customarily served up in lawn." MM 35

Hearth and Home

—household gods: " . . . Silas would not consent to have a grate and oven added to his conveniences: he loved the old brick hearth as he had loved his brown pot—and was it not there when he had found Eppie? The gods of the hearth exist for us still; and let all new faith be tolerant of that fetishism, lest it bruise its own roots." SM 16

Maturity

—aging: " 'The days and the months pace over us like restless little birds, and leave the marks of their feet backwards and forwards, especially when they are like birds with heavy hearts—then they tread heavily.' " DD 20

—*defeated:* "It is something cruelly incomprehensible to youthful natures—this sombre sameness in middle-aged and elderly people whose life has resulted in disappointment and discontent, to whose faces a smile becomes so strange that the sad lines all about the lips and brow seem to take no notice of it, and it hurries away again for want of a welcome. 'Why will they not kindle up and be glad sometimes?' thinks young elasticity. 'It would be easy, if they only liked to do it.' And these leaden clouds that never part are apt to create impatience even in the filial affection that streams forth in nothing but tenderness and pity in the time of more obvious affliction." MF IV 2

—*dissatisfied:* "I suppose it is the way with all men and women who reach middle age without the clear perception that life never *can* be thoroughly joyous: under the vague dulness of the grey hours, dissatisfaction seeks a definite object, and finds it in the privation of an untried good." SM 17

—*female enhancements:* "A widow at fifty-five whose satisfaction has been largely drawn from what she thinks of her own person, and what she believes others think of it, requires a great fund of imagination to keep her spirits buoyant." R 51

—*pessimistic:* "A man nearly fifty who is not always quite well is seldom ardently hopeful: he is aware that this is a world in which merit is often overlooked." FH 12

—*sixties:* "[He] was at a time of life when, notwithstanding the fashionable retardation of most things from dinners to marriages, a man's hopefulness is apt to show signs of wear, until restored by second childhood." DD 15

—*source of guidance:* "The middle-aged, who have lived through their strongest emotions, but are yet in the time when memory is still half passionate and not merely contemplative, should surely be a sort of natural priesthood whom life has disciplined and consecrated to be the refuge and rescue of early stumblers and victims of self-despair: most of us at some moment in our young lives, would have welcomed a priest of that natural order in any sort of canonicals or uncanonicals, but had to scramble upwards into all the difficulties of nineteen entirely without such aid . . . . " MF VI 9

Mother and Motherhood

—*absent:* "For the Squire's wife had died long ago, and the Red House was without that presence of the wife and mother which is the fountain of wholesome love and fear in parlour and kitchen . . . . " SM 3

—*with babies:* " 'But what's the use of talking to a woman with babbies?' continued Bartle, 'she's, got no conscience—no conscience—it's all run to milk.' " AB 21

—*children grown:* "It is a fact perhaps kept a little too much in the background, that mothers have a self larger than their maternity, and that when their sons have become taller than themselves, and are gone from them to college or into the world, there are wide spaces of their time which are not filled with praying for their boys, reading old letters, and envying yet blessing those who are attending to their shirt-buttons." FH 8

—*and daughter:* "Looking at the mother, you might hope that the daughter would become like her, which is a prospective advantage equal to a dowry—the mother too often standing behind the daughter like a malignant prophecy—'Such as I am, she will shortly be.' " MM 24

—*disregarded:* " 'I don't know who would be a mother if she could foresee what a slight thing she will be to her son when she is old.' " FH 2

—*and growing boy:* "I have often wondered whether those early Madonnas of **Raphael**, with the blond faces and somewhat stupid expression, kept their placidity undisturbed when their strong-limbed strong-willed boys got a little too old to do without clothing. I think they must have been given to feeble remonstrance, getting more and more peevish as it became more and more ineffectual." MF I 2

—*intolerant:* "Splendid old ladies, who take a long time to dress in the morning, have often slight sympathy with sickly daughters." AB 5

—*mother love:* "The mother's love is at first an absorbing delight, blunting all other sensibilities; it is an expansion of the animal existence; it enlarges the imagined range for self to move in: but in after years it can only continue to be joy on the same terms as other long-lived love—that is, by much suppression of self, and power of living in the experience of another." FH 1

" 'A mother's love, I often say, is like a tree that has got all the wood in it, from the very first it made.' " DD 32

" 'Friendships begin with liking or gratitude —roots that can be pulled up. Mother's love begins deeper down.' " DD 32

—*motherhood:* "Mighty is the force of motherhood! says the great tragic poet to us across the ages, finding, as usual, the simplest words for the sublimest fact . . . . It transforms all things by its vital heat: it turns timidity into fierce courage, and dreadless defiance into tremulous submission [*GE has the latter backwards*]; it turns thoughtlessness into foresight, and yet stills all anxiety into calm content; it makes selfishness become self-denial, and gives even to hard vanity the glance of admiring love." JR 13

—observing a bachelor: "Notable mothers, who knew what it was to keep children 'whole and sweet'; lazy mothers, who knew what it was to be interrupted in folding their arms and scratching their elbows by the mischievous propensities of children just firm on their legs, were equally interested in conjecturing how a lone man would manage with a two-year-old child on his hands, and were equally ready with their suggestions: the notable chiefly retelling him what he had better do, and the lazy ones being emphatic in telling him what he would never be able to do." SM 14

—pain: " 'Oh, my dear, mothers are made to like pain and trouble for the sake of their children.' " DD 52

Old age

—bereavement: " . . . a sorrow had come—the sorrow of old age, which suffers the more from the crushing of its pride and its hopes, in proportion as the pride and hope are narrow and prosaic . . . . It is a dreary thing to live on doing the same things year after year, without knowing why we do them. Perhaps the tragedy of disappointed youth and passion is less piteous than the tragedy of disappointed age and worldliness." LV 2

—countenance: " 'I think all lines of the human face have something either touching or grand, unless they seem to come from low passions. How fine old men are, like my godfather! Why should not old women look grand and simple?' " R 51

"She stood before a tall mirror, going close to it and looking at her face with hard scrutiny, as if it were unrelated to herself. No elderly face [she is 56] can be handsome, looked at in that way; every little detail is startlingly prominent, and the effect of the whole is lost. She saw the dried-up complexion, and the deep lines of bitter discontent about the mouth." FH 1

—fact: " 'One *must* either die or get old.' " R 51

—feelings: " 'It is foolish to say people can't feel much when they are getting old. Not pleasure, perhaps—little comes. But they can feel they are forsaken—why, every fibre in me seems to be a memory that makes a pang. They can feel that all the love in their lives is turned to hatred or contempt.' " FH 39

—happy: " . . . only showing her emotion by that flush in the cheeks and brightness in the eyes which give an old woman a touching momentary identity with her far-off youthful self. . . . " MM 52

—longevity: "It is octogenerians whose four-score years have had no greater epochs than marriage and meal-times, that are likely to be most solicitous as to the possibility of prolonging life and making up by quantity for what is wanting in quality." HB 302

—looking on: " 'Things look dim to old folks: they'd need have some young eyes about 'em, to let 'em know the world's the same as it used to be.' " SM concl

—potation: " . . . gin-and-water, like obesity, or baldness, or the gout, does not exclude a vast amount of antecedent romance, any more than the neatly executed 'fronts' which you may some day wear, will exclude your present possession of less expensive braids. Alas, alas! we poor mortals are often little better than wood-ashes—there is small sign of the sap, and the leafy freshness, and the bursting buds that were once there; but wherever we see wood-ashes, we know that all that early fullness of life must have been. I, at least, hardly ever look at a bent old man, or a wizened old woman, but I see also, with my mind's eye, that Past of which they are the shrunken remnant, and the unfinished romance of rosy cheeks and bright eyes seems sometimes of feeble interest and significance, compared with that drama of hope and love which has long ago reached its catastrophe, and left the poor soul, like a dim and dusty stage, with all its sweet garden scenes and fair perspectives overturned and thrust out of sight." GL 1

—sight: " 'Old men's eyes are like old men's memories; they are strongest for things a long way off.' " R 31

—sorrowful: see S:Joy and Sorrow—*sorrow in old age*

—tears: " . . . there gathered some of those hard tears which just moisten elderly eyes. . . . " R 51

—watchful: " . . . the quiet *outward* glance of healthy old age, which, disengaged from any interest in an inward drama, spies out pins upon the floor, follows one's minutest motions with unexpectant purposeless tenacity, watches the flickering of the flame or the sun-gleams on the wall, counts the quarries on the floor, watches even the hand of the clock, and pleases itself with detecting a rhythm in the tick." FH 15

—and youth: "He gave Deronda the monitory and slightly suspicious look with which age is apt to commit any object to the keeping of youth." DD 60

Old Maid

—contrasts: "Miss Pratt was an old maid; but that is a no more definite description than if I had said she was in the autumn of life. Was it autumn when the orchards are fragrant with apples, or autumn when the oaks are brown, or autumn when the last yellow leaves are fluttering in the chill breeze? The young ladies in Milby would have told you that the Miss Linnets were old maids, but the Miss Linnets were to Miss Pratt what the apple-scented September is to the bare, nipping days

of late November. The Miss Linnets were in that temperate zone of old-maidism, when a woman will not say but what if a man of suitable years and character were to offer himself, she might be induced to tread the remainder of life's vale in company with him; Miss Pratt was in that arctic region where a woman is confident that at no time of life would she have consented to give up her liberty, and that she has never seen the man whom she would engage to honour and obey. If the Miss Linnets were old maids, they were old maids with natural ringlets and embonpoint, not to say obesity; Miss Pratt was an old maid with a cap, a braided 'front', a backbone and appendages." JR 3

—*alternative:* "Most of us who have had decent parents would shrink from wishing that our father and mother had been somebody else whom we never knew; yet it is held no impiety, rather, a graceful mark of instruction, for a man to wail that he was not the son of another age and another nation, of which also he knows nothing except through the easy process of an imperfect imagination and a flattering fancy." TS 2

—*beloved:* " . . . this question of wishing to be rid of one's contemporaries associates itself with my filial feeling, and calls up the thought that I might as justifiably wish that I had had other parents than those whose loving tones are my earliest memory, and whose last parting first taught me the meaning of death. I feel bound to quell such a wish as blasphemy." TS 2

Parents

—*thunderstruck:* "The decisive word had been spoken: there was no doubt concerning the end willed by each: there only remained the way of arriving at it, and Catherine determined to take the straightest possible. She went to her father and mother in the library, and told them that she had promised to marry Klesmer.

"Mrs Arrowpoint's state of mind was pitiable. Imagine **Jean Jacques**, after his essay on the corrupting influence of the arts, waking up among children of nature who had no idea of grilling the raw bone they offered him for breakfast with the primitive flint knife; or **Saint Just**, after fervidly denouncing all recognition of pre-eminence, receiving a vote of thanks for the unbroken mediocrity of his speech, which warranted the dullest patriots in delivering themselves at equal length. Something of the same sort befell the authoress of 'Tasso,' when what she had safely demanded of the dead **Leonora** was enacted by her own Catherine.

"It is hard for us to live up to our own eloquence, and keep pace with our winged words, while we are treading the solid earth and are liable to heavy dining. Besides, it has long been understood that the proprieties of literature are not those of practical life. Mrs Arrowpoint naturally wished for the best of everything. She not only liked to feel herself at a higher level of literary sentiment than the ladies with whom she associated; she wished not to be below them in any point of social consideration. While Klesmer was seen in the light of a patronised musician, his peculiarities were picturesque and acceptable; but to see him by a sudden flash in the light of her son-in-law gave her a burning sense of what the world would say. And the poor lady had been used to represent her Catherine as a model of excellence.

"Under the first shock she forgot everything but her anger, and snatched at any phrase that would serve as a weapon.

" 'If Klesmer has presumed to offer himself to you, your father shall horsewhip him off the premises. Pray, speak, Mr Arrowpoint.'

"The father took his cigar from his mouth, and rose to the occasion by saying, 'This will never do, Cath.'

" 'Do!' cried Arrowpoint, 'who in their senses ever thought it would do? You might as well say poisoning and strangling will not do. It is a comedy you have got up, Catherine. Else you are mad.'

" 'I am quite sane and serious, mamma, and Herr Klesmer is not to blame. He never thought of my marrying him. I found out that he loved me, and loving him, I told him I would marry him.'

" 'Leave that unsaid, Catherine,' said Mrs Arrowpoint, bitterly. 'Every one else will say it for you. You will be a public fable. Every one will say that you must have made the offer to a man who has been paid to come to the house—who is nobody knows what—a gypsy, a Jew, a mere bubble of the earth.'

" 'Never mind, mamma,' said Catherine, indignant in her turn. 'We all know he is a genius—as **Tasso** was.'

" 'Those times were not these, nor is Klesmer Tasso,' said Mrs Arrowpoint, getting more heated. 'There is no sting in *that* sarcasm, except the sting of undutifulness.'

" 'I am sorry to hurt you, mamma. But I will not give up the happiness of my life to ideas that I don't believe in and customs I have no respect for.'

" 'You have lost all sense of duty, then? You have forgotten that you are our only child—that it lies with you to place a great property in the right hands?'

" 'What are the right hands? My grandfather gained the property in trade.'

" 'Mr Arrowpoint, *will* you sit by and hear this without speaking?'

" 'I am a gentleman, Cath. We expect you to marry a gentleman,' said the father, exerting himself.

" 'And a man connected with the institutions of this country,' said the mother. 'A woman in your position has serious duties. Where duty and inclination clash, she must follow duty.'

" 'I don't deny that,' said Catherine, getting colder in proportion to her mother's heat. 'But one may say very true things and apply them falsely. People can easily take the sacred word duty as a name for what they desire any one else to do.'

" 'Your parents' desire makes no duty for you, then?'

" 'Yes, within reason. But before I give up the happiness of my life——'

" 'Catherine, Catherine, it will not be your happiness,' said Mrs Arrowpoint, in her most raven-like tones.

" 'Well, what seems to me my happiness—before I give it up, I must see some better reason than the wish that I should marry a nobleman, or a man who votes with a party that he may be turned into a nobleman. I feel at liberty to marry the man I love and think worthy, unless some higher duty forbids.'

" 'And so it does, Catherine, though you are blinded and cannot see it. It is a woman's duty not to lower herself. You are lowering yourself. Mr Arrowpoint, will you tell your daughter what is her duty?'

" 'You must see, Catherine, that Klesmer is not the man for you,' said Mr Arrowpoint. 'He won't do at the head of estates. He has a deuced foreign look—is an unpractical man.'

" 'I really can't see what that has to do with it, papa. The land of England has often passed into the hands of foreigners—Dutch soldiers, sons of foreign women of bad character:—if our land were sold to-morrow it would very likely pass into the hands of some foreign merchant on 'Change. It is in everybody's mouth that successful swindlers may buy up half the land in the country. How can I stem that tide?'

" 'It will never do to argue about marriage, Cath,' said Mr Arrowpoint. 'It's no use getting up the subject like a parliamentary question. We must do as other people do. We must think of the nation and the public good.'

" 'I can't see any public good concerned here, papa,' said Catherine. 'Why is it to be expected of an heiress that she should carry the property gained in trade into the hands of a certain class? That seems to me a ridiculous mish-mash of superannuated customs and false ambition. I should call it a public evil. People had better make a new sort of public good by changing their ambitions.'

" 'That is mere sophistry, Catherine,' said Mrs Arrowpoint. 'Because you don't wish to marry a nobleman, you are not obliged to marry a mountebank or a charlatan.'

" 'I cannot understand the application of such words, mamma.'

" 'No, I daresay not,' rejoined Mrs Arrowpoint, with significant scorn. 'You have got to a pitch at which we are not likely to understand each other.'

" 'It can't be done, Cath,' said Mr Arrowpoint, wishing to substitute a better-humoured reasoning for his wife's impetuosity. 'A man like Klesmer can't marry such a property as yours. It can't be done.'

" 'It certainly will not be done,' said Mrs Arrowpoint, imperiously. 'Where is the man? Let him be fetched.'

" 'I cannot fetch him to be insulted,' said Catherine. 'Nothing will be achieved by that.'

" 'I suppose you would wish him to know that in marrying you he will not marry your fortune,' said Mrs Arrowpoint.

" 'Certainly; if it were so, I should wish him to know it.'

" 'Then you had better fetch him.'

"Catherine only went into the music-room and said, 'Come': she felt no need to prepare Klesmer.

" 'Herr Klesmer,' said Mrs Arrowpoint, with a rather contemptuous stateliness, 'it is unnecessary to repeat what has passed between us and our daughter. Mr Arrowpoint will tell you our resolution.'

" 'Your marrying is quite out of the question,' said Mr Arrowpoint, rather too heavily weighted with his task, and standing in an embarrassment unrelieved by a cigar. 'It is a wild scheme altogether. A man has been called out for less.'

" 'You have taken a base advantage of our confidence,' burst in Mrs Arrowpoint, unable to carry out her purpose and leave the burthen of speech to her husband.

"Klesmer made a low bow in silent irony.

" 'The pretension is ridiculous. You had better give it up and leave the house at once,' continued Mr Arrowpoint. He wished to do without mentioning the money.

" 'I can give up nothing without reference to your daughter's wish,' said Klesmer. 'My engagement is to her.'

" 'It is useless to discuss the question,' said Mrs Arrowpoint. 'We shall never consent to the marriage. If Catherine disobeys us we shall disinherit her. You will not marry her fortune. It is right you should know that.'

" 'Madam, her fortune has been the only thing I have had to regret about her. But I must ask her if she will not think the sacrifice greater than I am worthy of.'

" 'It is no sacrifice to me,' said Catherine, 'except that I am sorry to hurt my father and mother. I have always felt my fortune to be a wretched fatality of my life.'

" 'You mean to defy us, then?' said Mrs Arrowpoint.

" 'I mean to marry Herr Klesmer,' said Catherine, firmly.

" 'He had better not count on our relenting,' said Mrs Arrowpoint, whose manners suffered from that impunity in insult which has been reckoned among the privileges of women.

" 'Madam,' said Klesmer, 'certain reasons forbid me to retort. But understand that I consider it out of the power either of you or of your fortune to confer on me anything that I value. My rank as an artist is of my own winning, and I would not exchange it for any other. I am able to maintain your daughter, and I ask for no change in my life but her companionship.'

" 'You will leave the house, however,' said Mrs Arrowpoint.

" 'I go at once,' said Klesmer, bowing and quitting the room.

" 'Let there be no misunderstanding, mamma,' said Catherine; 'I consider myself engaged to Herr Klesmer, and I intend to marry him.'

"The mother turned her head away and waved her hand in sign of dismissal.

" 'It's all very fine,' said Mr Arrowpoint, when Catherine was gone; 'but what the deuce are we to do with the property?'

" 'There is Harry Brendall. He can take the name.'

" 'Harry Brendall will get through it all in no time,' said Mr Arrowpoint, relighting his cigar." DD 22

Young girl

—spiteful: " 'Is that Miss Gardner's head?' 'Yes,' said Maria, amiable and stuttering, and no match for Ellen in retort; 'th—th—this is my head.' 'Then I don't admire it at all!' was the crushing rejoinder of Ellen, followed by a murmur of approval among her friends. Young ladies, I suppose, exhaust their sac of venom in this way at school. That is the reason why they have such a harmless tooth for each other in afterlife." JR 5

Young man

—finding purpose: "His early-wakened sensibility and reflectiveness had developed into a many-sided sympathy, which threatened to hinder any persistent course of action: as soon as he took up any antagonism, though only in thought, he seemed to himself like the Sabine warriors in the memorable story—with nothing to meet his spear but flesh of his flesh, and

objects that he loved. His imagination had so wrought itself to the habit of seeing things as they probably appeared to others, that a strong partisanship, unless it were against an immediate oppression, had become an insincerity for him His plenteous, flexible sympathy had ended by falling into one current with that reflective analysis which tends to neutralise sympathy.

"Few men were able to keep themselves clearer of vices than he; yet he hated vices mildly, being used to think of them less in the abstract than as a part of mixed human natures having an individual history, which it was the best of his mind to trace with understanding and pity. With the same innate balance he was fervidly democratic in his feeling for the multitude, and yet, through his affections and imagination, intensely conservative, voracious of speculations on government and religion, yet loath to part with long-sanctioned forms which, for him, were quick with memories and sentiments that no argument could lay dead.

"We fall on the leaning side; and Deronda suspected himself of loving too well the losing causes of the world. Martyrdom changes sides, and he was in danger of changing with it, having a strong repugnance to taking up that clue of success which the order of the world often forces upon us and makes it treason against the common weal to reject. And yet his fear of falling into an unreasoning narrow hatred made a check for him: he apologised for the heirs of privilege; he shrank with dislike from the loser's bitterness and the denunciatory tone of the unaccepted innovator.

"A too reflective and diffusive sympathy was in danger of paralysing in him that indignation against wrong and that selectness of fellowship which are the conditions of moral force; and in the last few years of confirmed manhood he had become so keenly aware of this that what he most longed for was rather some external event, or some inward light, that would urge him into a definite line of action, and compress his wandering energy.

"He was ceasing to care for knowledge—he had no ambition for practice—unless they could both be gathered up into one current with his emotions, and he dreaded, as if it were a dwelling-place of lost souls, that dead anatomy of culture which turns the universe into a mere ceaseless answer to queries, and knows, not everything, but everything else about everything—as if one should be ignorant of nothing concerning the scent of violets except the scent itself for which one had no nostril.

"But how and whence was the needed event to come?—the influence that would justify partiality, and make him what he longed to be yet was unable to make himself—an organic part of social life, instead of roaming in it like a yearning disembodied spirit, stirred with a vague social passion, but without fixed local habitation to render fellowship real?

"To make a little difference for the better was what he was not contented to live without; but how to make it? It is one thing to see your road, another to cut it. He found some of the fault in his birth and the way he had been brought up, which had laid no special demands on him and given him no fixed relationship except one of a doubtful kind; but he did not attempt to hide from himself that he had fallen into a meditative numbness, and was gliding farther and farther from that life of practically energetic sentiment which he would have proclaimed (if he had been inclined to proclaim anything) to be the best of all life, and for himself the only life worth living.

"He wanted some way of keeping emotion and its progeny of sentiments—which make the savours of life—substantial and strong in the face of a reflectiveness that threatened to nullify all differences. To pound the objects of sentiment into small dust, yet keep sentiment alive and active, was something like the famous recipe for making cannon—to first take a round hole and then enclose it with iron; whatever you do keeping fast hold of your round hole. Yet how distinguish what our will may wisely save in its completeness, from the heaping of cat-mummies and the expensive cult of enshrined putrefactions?

"Something like this was the common undercurrent in Deronda's mind, while he was reading law, or imperfectly attending to polite conversation. Meanwhile he had not set about one function in particular with zeal and steadiness. Not an admirable experience, to be proposed as an ideal, but a form of struggle before break of day which some young men since the patriarch had had to pass through, with more or less of bruising if not laming." DD ¶32

—*unappreciative:* " . . . the genteel youths of Milby were chiefly come home for the midsummer holidays from distant schools. Several of us had just assumed coat-tails, and the assumption of new responsibilities apparently following as a matter of course, we were among the candidates for confirmation. I wish I could say that the solemnity of our feelings was on a level with the solemnity of the occasion, but unimaginative boys find it difficult to recognise apostolical institutions in their developed form, and I fear our chief emotion concerning the ceremony was a sense of sheepishness, and our chief opinion, the speculative and heretical position, that it ought to be confined to the girls. It was a pity, you will say; but it is the way with us men in other crises, that come a long while after confirmation. The golden moments in the stream of life rush past us, and we see nothing but sand; the angels come to visit us, and we only know them when they are gone." JR 5

Youth

—*at sea:* " . . . he was in another sort of contemplative mood perhaps more common in the young men of our day—that of questioning whether it were worth while to take part in the battle of the world: I mean, of course, the young men in whom the unproductive labour of questioning is sustained by three or five per cent on capital which somebody else has battled for." DD 17

—*being in the moment:* "While we are still in our youth there can always come, in our early waking, moments when mere passive existence is itself a Lethe, when the exquisiteness of subtle indefinite sensation creates a bliss which is without memory and without desire." R 68

—*despair:* "There is no hopelessness so sad as that of early youth, when the soul is made up of wants, and has no long memories, no superadded life in the life of others; though we who look on think lightly of such premature despair, as if our vision of the future lightened the blind sufferer's present." MF III 5

—*disappointment:* "She was in that first crisis of passionate youthful rebellion against what is not fitly called pain, but rather the absence of joy—that first rage of disappointment in life's morning, which we whom the years have subdued are apt to remember but dimly as part of our own experience, and so to be intolerant of its self-enclosed unreasonableness and impiety. What passion seems more absurd, when we have got outside it and looked at calamity as a collective risk, than this amazed anguish that I and not Thou, He, or She, should be just the smitten one? Yet perhaps some who have afterwards made themselves a willing fence before the breast of another, and have carried their own heart-wound in heroic silence—some who have made their latter deeds great, nevertheless began with this angry amazement at their own smart, and on the mere denial of their fantastic desires raged as if under the sting of wasps which reduced the universe for them to an unjust infliction of pain." DD 26

—*and fear:* "No, something else would happen—something *must* happen—to set her free from this dread. In young, childish, ignorant souls there is constantly this blind trust in some unshapen chance: it is as hard to a boy or girl to believe that a great wretchedness will actually befall them, as to believe that they will die." AB 35

—*and hope:* "If youth is the season of hope, it is often so only in the sense that our elders are hopeful about us; for no age is so apt as youth to think its emotions, partings, and resolves are the last of their kind. Each crisis seems final, simply because it is new. We are told that the oldest inhabitants in Peru do not cease to be agitated by the earthquakes, but they probably see beyond each shock and reflect that there are plenty more to come." MM 55

—*learning:* "There were many subjects in the world—perhaps a majority—in which she felt no interest, because they were stupid; for subjects are apt to appear stupid to the young as light seems dim to the old . . . . " DD 4

—*and love:* "It is only in that freshness of our time that the choice is possible which gives unity to life, and makes the memory a temple where all relics and all votive offerings, all worship and all grateful joy, are an unbroken history sanctified by one religion." FH 44

—*new thoughts:* "There was another day for her to think of him with unsatisfied resentment, mixed with some longings for a better understanding; and in our spring-time every day has its hidden growths in the mind, as it has in the earth when the little folded blades are getting ready to pierce the ground." FH 18

—*perspective of age:* " 'Youth thinks itself the goal of each old life;/Age has but travelled from a far-off time/Just to be ready for youth's service. Well!/It was my chief delight to perfect you." AR V

—*respectable:* "True, when a young man has a fine person, no eccentricity of manners, the education of a gentleman, and a present income, it is not customary to feel a prying curiosity about his way of thinking, or his peculiar tastes. He may very well be settled in life as an agreeable clever young fellow without passing a special examination on those heads. Later, when he is getting rather slovenly and portly, his peculiarities are more distinctly discerned, and it is taken as a mercy if they are not highly objectionable." DD 32

—*speculation:* "It was impossible to mistake her for a happy woman; and young speculation is always stirred by discontent for which there is no obvious cause. When we are older, we take the uneasy eyes and the bitter lips more as a matter of course." FH 40

—*temporary:* "That one cannot for any considerable number of years go on being youthful, girlishly handsome, and precocious, seems on consideration to be a statement as worthy of credit as the famous syllogistic conclusion, '**Socrates** was mortal.' " TS 12

Body

"From the British point of view masculine beauty is regarded very much as it is in the drapery business:—as good solely for the fancy department—for young noblemen, artists, poets, and the clergy." FH 29

Alcohol

—addiction confessed: " 'I hated wine and spirits because Robert drank them so; but one day when I was very wretched, and the wine was standing on the table, I suddenly . . . I can hardly remember how I came to do it . . . I poured some wine into a large glass and drank it. It blunted my feelings, and made me more indifferent. After that, the temptation was always coming, and it got stronger and stronger. I was ashamed, and I hated what I did; but almost while the thought was passing through my mind that I would never do it again, I did it. It seemed as if there was a demon in me always making me rush to do what I longed not to do. . . . I feel sure that demon will be always urging me to satisfy the craving that comes upon me, and the days will go on as they have done through all those miserable years. I shall always be doing wrong, and hating myself after—sinking lower and lower, and knowing that I am sinking.' " JR 18

—drink removed: "She was suffering, too, from the absence of the long-accustomed stimulus which she had promised Mr Tryan not to touch again. The poor thing was conscious of this, and dreaded her own weakness, as the victim of intermittent insanity dreads the oncoming of the old illusion." JR 21

—recovery: "Besides, her constitution, naturally healthy and strong, was every week tending, with the gathering force of habit, to recover its equipoise, and set her free from those physical solicitations which the smallest habitual vice always leaves behind it. The prisoner feels where the iron has galled him, long after his fetters have been loosed." JR 26

—in the country: " . . . in bucolic society five-and-twenty years ago, the human animal of the male sex was understood to be perpetually athirst, and 'something to drink' was as necessary a 'condition of thought' as Time and Space." SF 1

—escape: "Some have an emphatic belief in alcohol, and seek their *ekstasis* or outside standing-ground in gin . . . . " MF IV 3

—time of day: "To say that Mr Raffles' manner was rather excited would be only one mode of saying that it was evening." MM 53

Beauty

—archetypal: "Beauty has an expression beyond and far above the one woman's soul that it clothes, as the words of genius have a wider meaning than the thought that prompted them: it is more than a woman's love that moves us in a woman's eyes—it seems to be a far-off mighty love that has come near to us, and made speech for itself there; the rounded neck, the dimpled arm, move us by something more than their prettiness—by their close kinship with all we have known of tenderness and peace. The noblest nature sees the most of this *impersonal* expression in beauty (it is needless to say that there are gentlemen with whiskers dyed and undyed who see none of it whenever), and for this reason, the noblest nature

is often the most blinded to the character of the one woman's soul that the beauty clothes. Whence, I fear, the tragedy of human life is likely to continue for a long time to come, in spite of mental philosophers who are ready with the best receipts for avoiding all mistakes of the kind." AB 33

—conscious: "The vainest woman is never thoroughly conscious of her own beauty till she is loved by the man who sets her own passion vibrating in return." AB 14

—its enemy: " 'Ah, mind is an enemy to beauty! I myself was thought beautiful by the women at one time—when I was in my swaddling-bands. But now—oimè! I carry my unwritten poems in cipher on my face!' " R 45

—and goodness: " '. . . I love Tito too because he is so good. I see it, I feel it, in everything he says and does. And if he is handsome, too, why should I not love him the better for that? It seems to me beauty is part of the finished language by which goodness speaks.' " R 19

—kittenish: "There are various orders of beauty, causing men to make fools of themselves in various styles, from the desperate to the sheepish; but there is one order of beauty which seems made to turn the heads not only of men, but of all intelligent mammals, even of women. It is a beauty like that of kittens, or very small downy ducks making gentle rippling noises with their soft bills, or babies just beginning to toddle and to engage in conscious mischief—a beauty with which you can never be angry, but that you feel ready to crush for inability to comprehend the state of mind into which it throws you . . . Mrs Poyser, who professed to despise all personal attractions and intended to be the severest of mentors, continually gazed at Hetty's charms by the sly, fascinated in spite of herself; and after administering such a scolding as naturally flowed from her anxiety to do well by her husband's niece . . . she would often confess to her husband, when they were safe out of hearing, that she firmly believed, 'the naughtier the little huzzy behaved, the prettier she looked.' " AB 7

—masculine: "From the British point of view masculine beauty is regarded very much as it is in the drapery business:—as good solely for the fancy department—for young noblemen, artists, poets, and the clergy." FH 29

—misleading: "Every man under such circumstances is conscious of being a great physiognomist. Nature, he knows, has a language of her own, which she uses with strict veracity; and he considers himself an adept in the language. Nature has written out his bride's character for him in those exquisite lines of cheek and lip and chin, in those eyelids delicate as petals, in those long lashes curled like the stamen of a flower, in the dark liquid depths of those wonderful eyes. How she will dote on her children! She is almost a child herself, and the little pink round things will hang about her like florets round the central flower; and the husband will look on, smiling benignly, able, whenever he chooses, to withdraw into the sanctuary of his wisdom, towards which his sweet wife will look reverently, and never lift the curtain. It is a marriage such as they made in the golden age, when the men were all wise and majestic, and the women all lovely and loving." AB 15

"Before you despise Adam [Bede] as deficient in penetration, pray ask yourself if you were ever predisposed to believe evil of any pretty woman—if you ever *could* without hard head-breaking demonstration, believe evil of the *one* supremely pretty woman who has bewitched you. No: people who love downy peaches are apt not to think of the stone, and sometimes jar their teeth terribly against it." AB 15

—seen: "It is generally a feminine eye that first detects the moral deficiencies hidden under the 'dear deceit' of beauty . . . . " AB 15

—and ugliness: "He had really taken off the hat automatically, and if he had been an ugly man might doubtless have done so with impunity: ugliness having naturally the air of involuntary exposure, and beauty, of display." DD 35

—reassurance: "The desire to know that one has not looked an absolute fright during a few hours of conversation may be construed as lying within the bounds of a laudable benevolent consideration for others." MF VI 1

—social setting: "We perhaps never detect how much of our social demeanour is made up of artificial airs, until we see a person who is at once beautiful and simple: without the beauty we are apt to call simplicity awkwardness." MF VI 9

—sympathetic: " . . . the most powerful of all beauty is that which reveals itself after sympathy and not before it. There is a charm of eye and lip which comes with every little phrase that certifies delicate perception or fine judgment, with every unostentatious word or smile that shows a heart awake to others; and no sweep of garment or turn of figure is more satisfying than that which enters as a restoration of confidence that one person is present on whom no intention will be lost. What dignity of meaning goes on gathering in frowns and laughs which are never observed in the wrong

place; what suffused adorableness in a human frame where there is a mind that can flash out comprehension and hands that can execute finely! The more obvious beauty, also adorable sometimes—one may say it without blasphemy—begins by being an apology for folly, and ends like other apologies in becoming tiresome by iteration. . . . " DD 22

—*and taste:* " 'Taste, beauty, what are they
But the soul's choice towards perfect bias wrought
By finer balance of a fuller growth—
Sense brought to subtlest metamorphosis
Through love, thought, joy—the general human store
Which grows from all life's functions? As the plant
Holds its corolla, purple, delicate,
Solely as outflush of that energy
Which moves transformingly in root and branch.' " CB 831-9

—*two kinds:* "All honour and reverence to the divine beauty of form! Let us cultivate it to the utmost in men, women, and children—in our gardens and in our houses. But let us love that other beauty too, which lies in no secret of proportion, but in the secret of deep human sympathy. Paint us an angel, if you can, with a floating violet robe, and a face paled by the celestial light; paint us yet oftener a Madonna, turning her mild face upward and opening her arms to welcome the divine glory; but do not impose on us any aesthetic rules which shall banish work-worn hands, those heavy clowns taking holiday in a dingy pot-house, those rounded backs and stupid weather-beaten faces that have bent over the spade and done the rough work of the world—those homes with their tin pans, their brown pitchers, their rough curs, and their clusters of onions. In this world there are so many of these common, coarse people, who have no picturesque sentimental wretchedness! It is so needful we should remember their existence, else we may happen to leave them quite out of our religion and philosophy; and frame lofty theories which only fit a world of extremes." AB 17

Body

—*arm:* "Who has not felt the beauty of a woman's arm?—the unspeakable suggestions of tenderness that lie in the dimpled elbow and all the varied gently lessening curves down to the delicate wrist with its tiniest, almost imperceptible nicks in the firm softness. A woman's arm touched the soul of a great sculptor two thousand years ago, so that he wrought an image of it for the Parthenon which moves us still as it clasps lovingly the time-worn marble of a headless trunk. Maggie's was such an arm as that—and it had the warm tints of life." MF VI 10

—*deformity:* "Ugly and deformed people have great need of unusual virtues, because they are likely to be extremely uncomfortable without them: but the theory that unusual virtues spring by a direct consequence out of personal disadvantages, as animals get thicker wool in severe climates, is perhaps a little overstrained. The temptations of beauty are much dwelt upon, but I fancy they only bear the same relation to those of ugliness, as the temptation to excess at a feast, where the delights are varied for eye and ear as well as palate, bears to the temptations that assail the desperation of hunger." MF V 3

—*eyelash:* "Long dark eyelashes, now: what can be more exquisite? I find it impossible not to expect some depth of soul behind a deep grey eye with a long dark eyelash, in spite of an experience which has shown me that they may go along with deceit, peculation, and stupidity. But if, in the reaction of disgust, I have betaken myself to a fishy eye, there has been a surprising similarity of result. One begins to suspect at length that there is no direct correlation between eyelashes and morals; or else, that the eyelashes express the disposition of the fair one's grandmother, which is on the whole less important to us." AB 15

—*eyes:* "Our eyes are so constructed . . . that they take in a wide angle without asking any leave of our will . . . . " R 20

—*face:* "But Hetty's face had a language that transcended her feelings. There are faces which nature charges with a meaning and pathos not belonging to the single human soul that flutters beneath them, but speaking the joys and sorrows of foregone generations—eyes that tell of deep love which doubtless has been and is somewhere, but not paired with these eyes—perhaps paired with pale eyes that can say nothing; just as a national language may be instinct with poetry unfelt by the lips that use it." AB 26

"Poor Dorothea! Compared with her, the innocent-looking Celia was knowing and worldly-wise; so much subtler is a human mind than the outside tissues which make a sort of blazonry or clock-face for it." MM 1

—*animated:* "The deep blush, which had come when he first started up, gradually subsided; but his features kept that indescribable look of subdued activity which often accompanies a new mental survey of familiar facts." DD 16

—*blush:* "A blush is no language: only a dubious flag-signal which may mean either of two contradictories." DD 35

—*extraordinary:* " . . . you could hardly have seen his face thoroughly meeting yours without believing that human creatures had done nobly in times past, and might do more nobly in time to come. The finest childlike faces have this consecrating power, and make us shudder anew at all the grossness and basely-wrought griefs of the world, lest they should enter here and defile." DD 16

—*lip:* " . . . the Austrian lip [the Habsburgs tended to have an exaggerated, protruding lower lip] confers a grandeur of historical associations on a kind of feature which might make us reject an advertising footman." TS 1

—*reaction to news:* " . . . a great change came over her face—a flush and slight spasm of the features such as we see in people who hear some news that will require them to readjust their conceptions of the past." MF V 4

—*smile:* "Deronda ended with that bright smile which, beaming out from the habitual gravity of his face, seemed a revelation (the reverse of the continual smile that discredits all expression)." DD 63

—*traitor's:* " 'A perfect traitor should have a face which vice can write no marks on—lips that will lie with a dimpled smile—eyes of such agate-like brightness and depth that no infamy can dull them—cheeks that will rise from a murder and not look haggard. I say not this young man is a traitor: I mean, he has a face that would make him the more perfect traitor if he had the heart of one, which is saying neither more nor less than that he has a beautiful face, informed with rich young blood, that will be nourished enough by food, and keep its colour without much help of virtue.' " R 4

—*hair:* " . . . public feeling required the meagreness of nature to be dissimulated by tall barricades of frizzed curls and bows, never surpassed by any great race except the Feejeean." MM 3

"The young ladies who frizzed their hair, and gathered it all into large barricades in front of their heads, leaving their occipital region exposed without ornament, as if that, being a back view, was of no consequence, dreamed as little that their daughters . . . would turn all their hair the other way—that instead of threatening us with barricades in front, they would be most killing in retreat,

And, like the Parthian, wound us as they fly."

JR 2

"[She] was obliged to give way to her mother about her hair and submit to have the abundant black locks plaited into a coronet on the summit of her head after the pitiable fashion of those antiquated times." MF IV 3

" . . . the midway parting of his crisp hair, not common among English committee-men, formed a presumption against the ripeness of his judgment which nothing but a speedy baldness could have removed." TS 12

—*nose:* " ' . . . only, how about my nose, mamma? I think saints' noses never in the least turn up. I wish you had given me your perfectly straight nose; it would have done for any sort of character—a nose of all work. Mine is only a happy nose; it would not do so well for tragedy.'

" 'Oh, my dear, any nose will do to be miserable with in this world' . . . . " DD 3

—*physique:* " . . . a certain thin eagerness in his aspect was attributed to the life of the metropolis, where narrow space had the same sort of effect on men as on thickly-planted trees." FH 20

—*shoulders*

—*shrugged:* "I think that the rare Englishmen who have this gesture are never of the heavy type—for fear of any lumbering instance to the contrary, I will say, hardly ever; they have usually a fine temperament and much tolerance towards the smaller errors of men (themselves inclusive)." MM 40

—*skin:* "It is agreeable to keep a whole skin; but the skin still remains an organ sensitive to the atmosphere." R 57

—*sleep:*

—*in misery:* "She was every moment slipping off the level on which she lay thinking, down, down into some depth from which she tried to rise again with a start. Slumber was stealing over her weary brain: that uneasy slumber which is only better than wretched waking, because the life we seemed to live in it determines no wretched future, because the things we do and suffer in it are but hateful shadows, and leave no impress that petrifies into an irrevocable past." JR 16

Dress

—*appearance:* " 'I abstain from judging by the outward appearance only . . . . I myself have experienced that when the spirit is much exercised it is difficult to remember neckbands and strings and such small accidents of our vesture, which are nevertheless decent and needful so long as we sojourn in the flesh.' " FH 5

—*boots:* " . . . he had taken off his boots and put on slippers before he came upstairs. Whoever remembers how many things he has declined to do even for himself, rather than have the trouble of putting on or taking off his boots, will not think this last detail insignificant." AB 5

—*crinolines:* "I like to mark the time, and connect the course of individual lives with the historic stream, for all classes of thinkers. This was the period when the broadening of gauge in crinolines seemed to demand an agitation for the general enlargement of churches, ball-rooms, and vehicles. But Anna Gascoigne's figure would only allow the size of skirt manufactured for young ladies of fourteen." DD 8 *See* MH p126

—*fine:* "Nay I have none—
Never had better clothes than these you see
Good clothes are pretty, but one sees them best
When others wear them . . . . " AG 274-7

—*in grief:* "It is a pathetic sight and a striking example of the complexity introduced into the emotions by a high state of civilisation—the sight of a fashionably drest female in grief. From the sorrow of a Hottentot to that of a woman in large buckram sleeves, with several bracelets on each arm, an architectural bonnet and delicate ribbon-strings—what a long series of gradations! In the enlightened child of civilisation the abandonment characteristic of grief is checked and varied in the subtlest manner, so as to present an interesting problem to the analytic mind. If with a crushed heart and eyes half-blinded by the mist of tears, she were to walk with a too devious step through a door-place, she might crush her buckram sleeves too, and the deep consciousness of this possibility produces a composition of forces by which she takes a line that just clears the doorpost. Perceiving that the tears are hurrying fast, she unpins her strings and throws them languidly backward—a touching gesture, indicative, even in the deepest gloom, of the hope in future dry moments when cap-strings will once more have a charm. As the tears subside a little and with her head leaning backward at the angle that will not injure her bonnet, she endures that terrible moment when grief which has made all things else a weariness has itself become weary, she looks down pensively at her bracelets and adjusts their clasps with that pretty studied fortuity which would be gratifying to her mind if it were once more in a calm and healthy state." MF I 7

—*literary influence:* "Her reading had been more extensive than her sister's, embracing most of the fiction in Mr Procter's circulating library, and nothing but an acquaintance with the course of her studies could afford a clue to the rapid transitions in her dress, which were suggested by the style of beauty, whether sentimental, sprightly, or severe, possessed by the heroine of the three volumes actually in perusal. A piece of lace, which drooped round the edge of her white bonnet one week, had been rejected by the next; and her cheeks, which, on Whit Sunday, loomed through a Turnerian haze of network, were, on Trinity Sunday, seen reposing in distinct red outline on her shelving bust, like the sun on a fog-bank. The black velvet, meeting with a crystal clasp, which one evening encircled her head, had on another descended to her neck, and on a third to her wrist, suggesting to an active imagination either a magical contraction of the ornament, or a fearful ratio of expansion in Miss Rebecca's person." JR 3

—*morning:* "The perfect morning costume of that day [1832] differed much from our present ideal: it was essential that a gentleman's chin should be well propped, that his collar should have a voluminous roll, that his waistcoat should imply much discrimination, and that his buttons should be arranged in a manner which would now expose him to general contempt. And . . . there existed many other anomalies now obsolete, besides short-waisted coats and broad stiffeners." FH 16

—*swain's:* "Let but Pumpkin have a figure which would sustain the disadvantages of the short-waisted swallow-tail, and everybody felt it not only natural but necessary to the perfection of womanhood, that a sweet girl should be at once convinced of his virtue, his exceptional ability, and above all, his perfect sincerity." MM 3

—*young girls':* "Girls are so accustomed to think of dress as the main ground of vanity, that in abstaining from the looking-glass, Maggie had thought more of abandoning all care for adornment, than of renouncing the contemplation of her face." MF V 1

Food and Drink

" . . . every form of selfishness, however ab-stract and unhuman, requires the support of at least one meal a-day . . . . " DD 66

—*Christmas fare:* " . . . the plum-pudding was of the same handsome roundness as ever, and came in with the symbolic blue flames around it, as if it had been heroically snatched from the nether fires into which it had been thrown by dyspeptic puritans; the dessert was as splendid as ever with its golden ranges, brown nuts, and the crystalline light and dark of apple jelly and damson cheese . . . . " MF II 2

—*cream:* "No—most likely you are a miserable town-bred reader, who thinks of cream as a thinnish white fluid, delivered in infinitesimal penny-worths down area-steps . . . . You have a vague idea of a milch cow as probably a white-plaster animal standing in a butterman's window, and you know nothing of the sweet history of genuine cream . . . how it was this morning in the udders of the large sleek beasts, as they stood lowing a patient entreaty under the milking-shed; how it fell with a pleasant rhythm into Betty's pail, sending a delicious incense into the cool air, how it was carried into that temple of moist cleanliness, the dairy, where it quietly separated itself from the meaner elements of milk, and lay in mellowed whiteness, ready for the skimming-dish which transferred it to Miss Gibbs's glass cream-jug." SF 1

—*on a farm:* " . . . for were they not men who, on all the days of the year except Christmas Day and Sundays, ate their cold dinner, in a make-shift manner, under the hedgerows, and drank their beer out of wooden bottles—with relish certainly, but with their mouths towards the zenith, after a fashion more endurable to ducks than to human bipeds." AB 53

—*market dinner:* "But the talk was necessarily in abeyance until the more serious business of dinner was ended, and the wine, spirits, and tobacco raised mere satisfaction into beatitude." FH 20

—*peacock:* " . . . crowning glory of a well-spread table, a peacock cooked according to the receipt of **Apicius** for cooking partridges, namely with the feathers on, but not plucked afterwards, as that great authority ordered concerning his partridges; on the contrary, so disposed on the dish that it might look as much as possible like a live peacock taking its unboiled repose. Great was the skill required in that confidential servant who was the official carver, respectfully to turn the classical though insipid bird on its back, and expose the plucked breast from which he was to dispense a delicate slice to each of the honourable company, unless any one should be of so independent a mind as to decline that expensive toughness and prefer the vulgar digestibility of capon . . . .

"In fact, very little peacock was eaten; but there was the satisfaction of sitting at a table where peacock was served up in a remarkable manner, and of knowing that such caprices were not within reach of any but those who supped with the very wealthiest men." R 39

—*tea:* "Do you know the dulcet strength, the animating blandness of tea sufficiently blended with real farmhouse cream?" SF 1

—*whey: see* SOS:Memories—*childhood*

Furniture and Utensils

—*chaise longue:* " . . . sofas resembling a prolongation of uneasy chairs . . . . " MM 17

—*elegant:* " . . . the still life in the room, which seemed the stiller for its sober antiquated elegance, as if it kept a conscious, well-bred silence, unlike the restlessness of vulgar furniture." DD 12

—*pitchers:* " 'Good earthenware pitchers, sir!—of an excellent quaint pattern and sober colour.' " FH 20 ep

—*simple:* " . . . its interior was filled with objects always in the same places, which for the mother held memories of her marriage time, and for the young ones seemed as necessary and uncriticised a part of their world as the stars of the Great Bear seen from the back windows. Mrs Meyrick had borne much stint of other matters that she might be able to keep some engravings specially cherished by her husband; and the narrow spaces of wall held a world-history in scenes and heads which the children had early learned by heart. The chairs and tables were also old friends preferred to new. But in these two little parlours with no furniture that a broker would have cared to cheapen except the prints and piano, there was space and apparatus for a wide-glancing, nicely-select life, open to the highest things in music, painting, and poetry." DD 18

—*study:* " . . . the attorney sat surrounded with massive oaken bookcases, and other furniture to correspond, from the thickest-legged library-table to the calendar frame and card-rack. It was the sort of room a man prepares for himself when he feels sure of a long and respectable future." FH 21

—*tea service:* "Mrs Jerome's best tea-service was of delicate white fluted china, with gold sprigs upon it—as pretty a tea-service as you need wish to see, and quite good enough for chimney ornaments; indeed, as the cups were without handles, most visitors who had the distinction of taking tea out of them, wished that such charming china had already been promoted to that honorary position." JR 8

Gambling

—*addiction:* "[He] had not that specific disease in which the suspension of the whole nervous energy on a chance or risk becomes as necessary as the dram to the drunkard. . . . " MM 23

—*disliked:* " 'I think it would be better for men not to gamble. It is a besotting kind of taste, likely to turn into a disease. And, besides, there is something revolting to me in raking a heap of money together, and internally chuckling over it, when others are feeling the loss of it. I should even call it base, if it were more than an exceptional lapse. There are enough inevitable turns of fortune which force us to see that our gain is another's loss:—that is one of the ugly aspects of life. One would like to reduce it as much as one could, not get amusement out of exaggerating it.' " DD 29

—*flaw:* "For the vice of gambling lay in losing money at it." DD 1

—*morning after:* "A philosopher fallen to betting is hardly distinguishable from a Philistine under the same circumstances: the difference will chiefly be found in his subsequent reflections . . . . " MM 67

—*obsession:* "The gambling appetite is more absolutely dominant than bodily hunger, which can be neutralised by an emotional or intellectual excitation; but the passion for watching chances—the habitual suspensive poise of the mind in actual or imaginary play—nullifies the susceptibility to other excitation. In its final, imperious stage, it seems the unjoyous dissipation of demons, seeking diversion on the burning marl of perdition." DD 66

—*participants:* "But while every single player differed markedly from every other, there was a certain uniform negativeness of expression which had the effect of a mask—as if they had all eaten of some root that for the time compelled the brains of each to the same narrow monotony of action." DD 1

—*resort:* " . . . one of those splendid resorts which the enlightenment of ages has prepared for the same species of pleasure at a heavy cost of gilt mouldings, dark-toned colour and chubby nudities, all correspondingly heavy—forming a terrible condenser for human breath belonging, in great part, to the highest fashion, and not easily procurable to be breathed in elsewhere in the like proportion, at least by persons of little fashion." DD 1

—*ruin:* "Whatever Grandcourt had done, he had not ruined himself; and it is well known that in gambling, for example, whether of the business or holiday sort, a man who has the strength of mind to leave off when he has only ruined others, is a reformed character." DD 9

Hardship and Poverty

—*consciousness:* "How much more might such trifles tell on a young lady equipped for society with a fastidious taste, an Indian shawl over her arm, some twenty cubic feet of trunks by her side, and a mortal dislike to the new consciousness of poverty which was stimulating her imagination of disagreeables? . . . What was the good of living in the midst of hardships, ugliness, and humiliation?" DD 21

—*dreaded:* "A man of sixty, with an unsuspicious wife and daughters capable of shrieking and fainting at a sudden revelation, and of looking at him reproachfully in their daily misery under a shabby lot to which he had reduced them—with a mind and with habits dried hard by the years—with no glimpse of an endurable standing-ground except where he could domineer and be prosperous according to the ambitions of pushing middle-class gentility—such a man is likely to find the prospect of worldly ruin ghastly enough to drive him to the most uninviting means of escape. He will probably prefer any private scorn that will save him from public infamy or that will leave him money in his pocket, to the humiliation and hardship of new servitude in old age, a shabby hat, and a melancholy hearth, where the firing must be used charily and the women look sad. But though a man may be willing to escape through a sewer, a sewer with an outlet into the dry air is not always at hand. Running away, especially when spoken of as absconding, seems at a distance to offer a good modern substitute for the right of sanctuary, but seen closely, it is often found inconvenient and scarcely possible." FH 42

—*at first:* "The beginning of hardship is like the first taste of bitter food—it seems for a moment unbearable; yet, if there is nothing else to satisfy our hunger, we take another bite and find it possible to go on." AB 36

—*London house:* "Outside, the house looked very narrow and shabby, the bright light through the Holland blind showing the heavy old-fashioned window-frame; but it is pleasant to know that many such grim-walled slices of space in our foggy London have been, and still are the homes of a culture the more spotlessly free from vulgarity, because poverty has rendered everything like display an impersonal question, and all the grand shows of the world simply a spectacle which rouses no petty rivalry or vain effort after possession." DD 18

—*for a lover:* " 'I never felt it a misfortune to have nothing till now,' he said. 'But poverty may be as bad as leprosy, if it divides us from what we most care for.' " MM 54

—*vowed:* "It is possible (though not greatly believed in at present) to be fond of poverty and take it for a bride, to prefer scoured deal, red quarries, and whitewash for one's private surroundings, to delight in no splendour but what has open doors for the whole nation, and to glory in having no privilege except such as nature insists on; and noblemen have been known to run away from elaborate ease and the option of idleness, that they might bind themselves for small pay to hard-handed labour." DD 16

House

—*best kitchen:* " . . . as charming a room as best kitchens used to be in farmhouses which had no parlours—the fire reflected in a bright row of pewter plates and dishes; the sand-scoured deal tables so clean you longed to stroke them; the salt-coffer in one chimney-corner, and a three cornered chair in the other, the walls behind handsomely tapestried with flitches of bacon, and the ceiling ornamented with pendent hams." GL 19

—the Hall Farm

—dairy: "The dairy was certainly worth looking at: it was a scene to sicken for with a sort of calenture in hot and dusty streets —such coolness, such purity, such fresh fragrance of new-pressed cheese, of firm butter, of wooden vessels perpetually bathed in pure water; such soft colouring of red earthenware and creamy surfaces, brown wood and polished tin, grey limestone and rich orange-red rust on the iron weights and hooks and hinges." AB 7

—furnishing: "Yes, the house must be inhabited, and we will see by whom . . . . Put your face to one of the glass panes in the right-hand window: what do you see? A large open fireplace, with rusty dogs in it, and a bare-boarded floor; at the far end fleeces of wool stacked up; in the middle of the floor some empty corn-bags. That is the furniture of the dining-room. And what through the left-hand window? Several clothes-horses, a pillion, a spinning-wheel, and an old box wide open, and stuffed full of coloured rags. At the edge of this box there lies a great wooden doll, which, so far as mutilation is concerned, bears a strong resemblance to the finest Greek sculpture, and especially in the total loss of its nose. Near it there is a little chair, and the butt-end of a boy's leather long-lashed whip." AB 6

—gate: "Evidently that gate is never opened: for the long grass and the great hemlocks grow close against it; and if it were opened, it is so rusty, that the force necessary to turn it on its hinges would be likely to pull down the square stone-built pillars, to the detriment of the two stone lionesses which grin with a doubtful carnivorous affability above a coat of arms, surmounting each of the pillars. It would be easy enough, by the aid of the nicks in the stone pillars, to climb over the brick wall with its smooth stone coping; but by putting our eyes close to the rusty bars of the gate, we can see the house well enough, and all but the very corners of the grassy enclosure." AB 6

—house: "It is a very fine old place, of red brick, softened by a pale powdery lichen, which has dispersed itself with happy irregularity, so as to bring the red brick into terms of friendly companionship with the limestone ornaments surrounding the three gables, the windows, and the door-place. But the windows are patched with wooden panes, and the door, I think, is like the gate—it is never opened: how it would groan and grate against the stone floor if it were! For it is a solid, heavy, handsome door, and must once have been in the habit of shutting with a sonorous bang behind a liveried lackey, who had just seen his master and mistress off the grounds in a carriage and pair." AB 6

—past: "The history of the house is plain now. It was once the residence of a country squire, whose family, probably dwindling down to mere spinsterhood, got merged in the more territorial name of Donnithorne. It was once the Hall; it is now the Hall Farm. Like the life in some coast-town that was once a watering-place, and is now a port, where the genteel streets are silent and grass-grown, and the docks and warehouses busy and resonant, the life at the Hall has changed its focus, and no longer radiates from the parlour, but from the kitchen and the farmyard." AB 6

—signs of life: "But at present one might fancy the house in the early stage of a chancery suit, and that the fruit from that grand double row of walnut trees on the right hand of the enclosure would fall and rot among the grass, if it were not that we heard the booming bark of dogs echoing from great buildings at the back. And now the half-weaned calves that have been sheltering themselves in a gorse-built hovel against the left-hand wall, come out and set up a silly answer to that terrible bark, doubtless supposing that it has reference to buckets of milk." AB 6

—kitchen fire: "So Mrs Pettifer busied herself with rousing the kitchen fire, which was kept in under a huge 'raker'—a possibility by which the coal of the midland counties atones for all its slowness and white ashes." JR 15

—Offendene: "The season suited the aspect of the old oblong red-brick house, rather too anxiously ornamented with stone at every line, not excepting the double row of narrow windows and the large square portico. The stone encouraged a greenish lichen, the brick a powdery grey, so that though the building was rigidly rectangular there was no harshness in the physiognomy which it turned to the three avenues cut east, west, and south in the hundred yards' breadth of old plantation encircling the immediate grounds. One would have liked the house to have been lifted on a knoll, so as to look beyond its own little domain to the long thatched roofs of the distant villages, the church towers, the scattered homesteads, the gradual rise of surging woods, and the green breadths of undulating park which made the beautiful face of the earth in that part of Wessex. But though standing thus behind a screen amid flat pastures, it had on

one side a glimpse of the wider world in the lofty curves of the chalk downs, grand steadfast forms played over by the changing days.

"The house was but just large enough to be called a mansion, and was moderately rented, having no manor attached to it, and being rather difficult to let with its sombre furniture and faded upholstery. But inside and outside it was what no beholder could suppose to be inhabited by retired tradespeople: a certainty which was worth many conveniences to tenants who not only had the taste that shrinks from new finery, but also were in that border-territory of rank where annexation is a burning topic; and to take up her abode in a house which had once sufficed for dowager countesses gave a perceptible tinge to Mrs Davilow's satisfaction in having an establishment of her own." DD 3

—Stone Court, "looking as if it had been arrested in its growth toward a stone mansion by an unexpected budding of farm-building on its left flank, which had hindered it from becoming anything more than the substantial dwelling of a gentleman farmer. It was not the less agreeable an object in the distance for the cluster of pinnacled corn-ricks which balanced the fine row of walnuts on the right." MM 12

"The fine old place never looked more like a delightful home than at that moment, the great white lilies were in flower, the nasturtiums, their pretty leaves all silvered with dew, were running away over the low stone wall; the very noises all around had a heart of peace within them." MM 53

—study of a clergyman: "At the mention of a clergyman's study, perhaps, your too active imagination conjures up a perfect snuggery, where the general air of comfort is rescued from a secular character by strong ecclesiastical suggestions in the shape of the furniture, the pattern of the carpet, and the prints on the wall; where, if a nap is taken, it is in an easy-chair with a Gothic back, and the very feet rest on a warm and velvety simulation of church windows; where the pure art of rigorous English protestantism smiles above the mantelpiece in the portrait of an eminent bishop, or a refined Anglican taste is indicated by a German print from **Overbeck**; where the walls are lined with choice divinity in sombre binding, and the light is softened by a screen of boughs with a grey church in the background." JR 11

—tenant's cottage: " . . . this homestead called Freeman's End: the old house had dormer-windows in the dark-red roof, two of the chimneys were choked with ivy, the large porch was blocked up with bundles of sticks, and half the windows were closed with grey worm-eaten shutters about which the jasmine-boughs grew in wild luxuriance; the mouldering garden wall with hollyhocks peeping over it was a perfect study of highly-mingled subdued colour, and there was an aged goat (kept doubtless on interesting superstitious grounds) lying against the open back-kitchen door.

"The mossy thatch of the cow-shed, the broken grey barn-doors, the pauper labourers in ragged breeches who had nearly finished unloading a waggon of corn into the barn ready for early threshing, the scanty dairy of cows being tethered for milking and leaving one half of the shed in brown emptiness; the very pigs and white ducks seeming to wander about the uneven neglected yard as if in low spirits from feeding on a too meagre quality of rinsings—all these objects under the quiet light of a sky marbled with high clouds would have made a sort of picture which we have all paused over as a 'charming bit,' touching other sensibilities than those which are stirred by the depression of the agricultural interest, with the sad lack of farming capital, as seen constantly in the newspapers of that time." ¶MM 39

And see GB:Stately home

Infirmity

—blindness: " 'It is not mere bodily organs that I want: it is the sharp edge of a young mind to pierce the way for my somewhat blunted faculties. For blindness acts like a dam, sending the streams of thought backward along the already-travelled channels and hindering the course onward.' " R 5

—cause: " 'I am, as you perceive . . . totally blind: a calamity to which we Florentines are held especially liable, whether owing to the cold winds which rush upon us in spring from the passes of the Apennines, or to that sudden transition from the cool gloom of our houses to the dazzling brightness of our summer sun, by which the *lippi* are said to have been made so numerous among the ancient Romans; or, in fine, to some occult cause which eludes our superficial surmises.' " R 6

—deafness: " . . . one of the exceptionally meek deaf, who never expect to be spoken to . . . . " R 55

Jewelry

—emerald: " 'It is strange how deeply colours seem to penetrate one, like scent. I suppose that is the reason why gems are used in spiritual emblems in the Revelation of St John. They look like fragments of heaven. I think that emerald is more beautiful than any of them.' " MM 1

—family: "You know these jewels; they are precious signs
Of long-transmitted honor, heightened still

By worthy wearing; and I give them you—
Ask you to take them—place our house's trust
In her sure keeping whom my heart has found
Worthiest, most beauteous." SG I iii

—poisoned: " 'These diamonds, which were once given with ardent love to Lydia Glasher, she passes on to you. You have broken your word to her, that you might possess what was hers. Perhaps you think of being happy, as she once was, and of having beautiful children such as hers, who will thrust hers aside. God is too just for that. The man you have married has a withered heart . . . . You will have your punishment . . . .'

"Truly here were poisoned gems, and the poison had entered into this poor young creature.

"After that long while, there was a tap at the door and Grandcourt entered, dressed for dinner. The sight of him brought a new nervous shock, and Gwendolen screamed again and again with hysterical violence. He had expected to see her dressed and smiling, ready to be led down. He saw her pallid, shrieking as it seemed with terror, the jewels scattered around her on the floor. Was it a fit of madness?

"In some form or other the Furies had crossed his threshold." DD 31

—sapphire: "What is lovely seen
Priced as a tarif?—lapis lazuli,
Such bulk, so many drachmas: amethysts
Quoted at so much; sapphires higher still.
The stone like solid heaven in its blueness
Is what I care for, not its name or price." SG III

Money

—accumulation: " . . . the love of accumulating money grows an absorbing passion in men whose imaginations, even in the very beginning of their hoard, showed them no purpose beyond it. Marner wanted the heaps of ten to grow into a square, and then into a larger square; and ever added guinea, while it was itself a satisfaction, bred a new desire . . . the money had come to mark off his weaving into periods, and the money not only grew, but it remained with him. He began to think it was conscious of him, as his loom was, and he would on no account have exchanged those coins, which had become his familiars, for other coins with unknown faces. He handled them, he counted them, till their form and colour were like the satisfaction of a thirst to him . . . . " SM 2

—business: "He wished Hetty well, doubtless; but pray, how many of your well-wishers would decline to make a little gain out of you? Your landlady is sincerely affected at parting with you, respects you highly, and will really rejoice if any one else is generous to you; but at the same time she hands you a bill by which she gains as high a percentage as possible." AB 37

—craving: " . . . there is no escape from sordidness but by being free from money-craving, with all its base hopes and temptations, its watching for death, its hinted requests, its horse-dealer's desire to make bad work pass for good, its seeking for function which ought to be another's, its compulsion often to long for Luck in the shape of a wide calamity." MM 64

—debt

—expenditure: "Expenditure—like ugliness and errors—becomes a totally new thing when we attach our own personality to it, and measure it by that wide difference which is manifest (in our own sensations) between ourselves and others." MM 58

—insidious: "It was an inference with a conspicuous handle to it, and had been easily drawn by indifferent observers, that Lydgate was in debt; and he could not succeed in keeping out of his mind for long together that he was every day getting deeper into that swamp, which tempts men towards it with such a pretty covering of flowers and verdure. It is wonderful how soon a man gets up to his chin there—in a condition in which, in spite of himself, he is forced to think chiefly of release, though he had a scheme of the universe in his soul." MM 58

—name: " . . . men whose names were good for anything were usually pessimists, indisposed to believe that the universal order of things would necessarily be agreeable to an agreeable young gentleman." MM 23

—to be repaid: "Mrs Tulliver carried the proud integrity of the Dodsons in her blood, and had been brought up to think that to wrong people of their money, which was another phrase for debt, was a sort of moral pillory: it would have been wickedness, to her mind, to have run counter to her husband's desire to 'do the right thing' and retrieve his name . . . .

"These narrow notions about debt, held by the old-fashioned Tullivers, may perhaps excite a smile on the faces of many readers in these days of wide commercial views and wide philosophy, according to which everything rights itself without any trouble of ours—the fact that my tradesman is out of pocket by me is to be looked at through the serene certainty that somebody else's tradesman is in pocket by somebody else, and since there must be bad debts in the world, why, it is mere egoism not to like that we in particular should make them instead of our fellow-citizens. I am telling the history of very simple people, who had never had any illuminating doubts as to personal integrity and honour." MF IV 2

—*retention:* " . . . the most glutinously indefinite minds enclose some hard grains of habit; and a man has been seen lax about all his interests except the retention of his snuffbox, concerning which he was watchful, suspicious, and greedy of clutch." MM 1

—*saving:* "This inalienable habit of saving, as an end in itself, belonged to the industrious men of business of a former generation, who made their fortunes slowly, almost as the tracking of the fox belongs to the harrier—it constituted them a 'race,' which is nearly lost in these days of rapid money-getting, when lavishness comes close on the back of want. In old-fashioned times, an 'independence' was hardly ever made without a little miserliness as a condition, and you would have found that quality in every provincial district combined with characters as various as the fruits from which we can extract acid." MF I 12

Senses

—*hearing:* "I remember still the mingled trepidation and delicious excitement with which I was affected by the tramping of the horses on the pavement in the echoing stables, by the loud resonance of the grooms' voices, by the booming bark of the dogs as my father's carriage thundered under the archway of the courtyard, by the din of the gong as it gave notice of luncheon and dinner. The measured tramp of soldiery which I sometimes heard—for my father's house lay near a country town where there were large barracks—made me sob and tremble; and yet when they were gone past, I longed for them to come back again." LV 1

—*smell:* "[She] was left alone in the parlour amidst the lingering odours of the early dinner, not easily got rid of in that small house. Rich people, who know nothing of these vulgar details, can hardly imagine their significance in the history of multitudes of human lives in which the sensibilities are never adjusted to the external conditions. Esther always felt so much discomfort from those odours that she usually seized any possibility of escaping from them. . . . " FH 27

Sleep

—*inevitable:* "Arthur did not pass a sleepless night: he slept long and well. For sleep comes to the perplexed—if the perplexed are only weary enough." AB 29

Tobacco

—*pipe:* "Your impatient loquacious man has never any notion of keeping his pipe alight by gentle measured puffs; he is always letting it go nearly out, and then punishing it for that negligence." AB 21

Mind

Belief

—*faith:* "The faith that life on earth is being shaped
To glorious ends, that order, justice, love
Mean man's completeness, mean effect as sure
As roundness in the dew-drop—that great faith
Is but the rushing and expanding stream
Of thought, of feeling, fed by all the past.
Our finest hope is finest memory,
As they who love in age think youth is blest
Because it has a life to fill with love.
Full souls are double mirrors, making still
An endless vista of fair things before
Repeating things behind: so faith is strong
Only when we are strong, shrinks when we shrink.
It comes when music stirs us, and the chords'
Moving on some grand climax shake our souls
With influx new that makes new energies.
It comes in swellings of the heart and tears
That rise at noble and at gentle deeds—
At labors of the master-artist's hand
Which, trembling, touches to a finer end,
Trembling before an image seen within.
It comes in moments of heroic love,
Unjealous joy in joy not made for us—
In conscious triumph of the good within
Making us worship goodness that rebukes.
Even our failures are a prophecy,
Even our yearnings and our bitter tears
After that fair and true we cannot grasp;
As patriots who seem to die in vain
Make liberty more sacred by their pangs."
MP 286-315

—*martyrdom:* " '. . . what is martyrdom
But death-defying utterance of belief,
Which being mine remains my truth supreme
Though solitary as the throb of pain
Lying outside the pulses of the world?' " CB 306-10

Consciousness

—*double:* "Nay, so distinct sometimes is the working of a double consciousness within us, that Tito himself, while he triumphed in the apparent verification of his lie, wished that he had never made the lie necessary to himself—wished he had recognised his father on the steps—wished he had gone to seek him—wished everything had been different." R 39

"Are you unable to imagine this double consciousness at work within me, flowing on like two parallel streams which never mingle their waters and blend into a common hue? Yet you must have known something of the presentiments that spring from an insight at war with passion; and my visions were only like presentiments intensified to horror. You have known the powerlessness of ideas before the might of impulse; and my visions, when once they had passed into memory, were mere ideas—pale shadows that beckoned in vain, while my hand was grasped by the living and the loved." LV 1

"Thus Silva, inwardly debating, all his ear
Turned into audience of a twofold mind;
For even in tumult full-fraught consciousness
Had plenteous being for a self aloof
That gazed and listened, like a soul in dreams
Weaving the wondrous tale it marvels at."
SG III

—*dream:* " 'For in the painful linking together of our waking thoughts we can never be sure that we have not mingled our own error with the light we have prayed for; but in visions and dreams we are passive, and our souls are as an instrument in the Divine hand.' " R 15

—*happy:* "Happy dreams are pleasant, and they easily come to an end with daylight and the stir of life." R 18

—*images:* "Mordecai's mind wrought so constantly in images, that his coherent trains of thought often resembled the significant dreams attributed to sleepers by waking persons in their most inventive moments; nay, they often resembled genuine dreams in their way of breaking off the passage from the known to the unknown." DD 38

—future: "Who—if our consciousness is, as I have been given to understand, a mere stumbling of our organisms on their way to unconscious perfection—who shall say that those fittest existences will not be found along the track of what we call inorganic combinations, which will carry on the most elaborate processes as mutely and painlessly as we are now told that the minerals are metamorphosing themselves continually in the dark laboratory of the earth's crust?" TS 17

—noisy: " 'What demons so potent as molecular movements, none the less tremendously potent for not carrying the futile cargo of a consciousness screeching irrelevantly, like a fowl tied head downmost to the saddle of a swift horseman?' " TS 17

—painful: " . . . that higher consciousness which is known to bring higher pains." FH 2

—phantasies: "As a strong body struggles against fumes with the more violence when they begin to be stifling, a strong soul struggles against phantasies with all the more alarmed energy when they threaten to govern in the place of thought." R 36

—sensitized: "It is wonderful how much uglier things will look when we only suspect that we are blamed for them. Even our own persons in the glass are apt to change their aspect for us after we have heard some frank remark on their less admirable points, and on the other hand it is astonishing how pleasantly conscience takes our encroachments on those who never complain or have nobody to complain for them." MM 39

—shocked by terror: "It was not a long walk, but, for Tito, it was stretched out like the minutes of our morning dreams: the short spaces of street and piazza held memories, and previsions, and torturing fears, that might have made the history of months. He felt as if a serpent had begun to coil round his limbs." R 23

—slow: "Our consciousness rarely registers the beginning of a growth within us any more than without us: there have been many circulations of the sap before we detect the smallest sign of the bud." SM 7

—telepathically perceived: " . . . a microscopic vision, that showed all the intermediate frivolities, all the suppressed egoism, all the struggling chaos of puerilities, meanness, vague capricious memories, and indolent make-shift thoughts, from which human words and deeds emerge . . . . " LV 1

—vision of portent: "Romola, in the deep night, as I lay awake, I saw my father's room —the library—with all the books and the marbles and the leggio, where I used to stand and read; and I saw you—you were revealed to me as I see you now, with fair long hair, sitting before my father's chair. And at the leggio stood a man whose face I could not see. I looked, and looked, and it was a blank to me, even as a painting effaced; and I saw him move and take thee, Romola, by the hand; and then I saw thee take my father by the hand; and you all three went down the stone steps into the streets, the man whose face was a blank to me leading the way.

"And you stood at the altar in Santa Croce, and the priest who married you had the face of death; and the graves opened, and the dead in their shrouds rose and followed you like a bridal train. And you passed on through the streets and the gates into the valley, and it seemed to me that he who led you hurried you more than you could bear, and the dead were weary of following you, and turned back to their graves. And at last you came to a stony place where there was no water, and no trees or herbage; but instead of water, I saw written parchment unrolling itself everywhere, and instead of trees and herbage I saw men of bronze and marble springing up and crowding round you.

"And my father was faint for want of water and fell to the ground; and the man whose face was a blank loosed thy hand and departed: and as he went I could see his face; and it was the face of the Great Tempter. And thou, Romola, didst wring thy hands and seek for water, and there was none. And the bronze and marble figures seemed to mock thee and hold out cups of water, and when thou didst grasp them and put them to my father 's lips, they turned to parchment.

"And the bronze and marble figures seemed to turn into demons and snatch my father's body from thee, and the parchments shrivelled up, and blood ran everywhere instead of them, and fire upon the blood, till they all vanished, and the plain was bare and stony again, and thou wast alone in the midst of it. And then it seemed that the night fell and I saw no more . . . . Thrice times have I had that vision, Romola . . . . " ¶R 15

—vision of prophecy: " 'It seems to me a dream may mean whatever comes after it. As our **Franco Sacchetti** says, a woman dreams over-night of a serpent biting her, breaks a drinking-cup the next day, and cries out, "Look you, I thought something would happen—it's plain now what the serpent meant." ' " R 29

Consistency

—lacking: "To think with pleasure of his niece's husband having a large ecclesiastical income was one thing—to make a Liberal speech was another thing; and it is a narrow mind which cannot look at a subject from various points of view." MM 7

Deception

—the Devil's: "The fiend makes preparation his favourite object of mockery, that he may fatally persuade us against our best safeguard. He even meddles so far as to suggest our taking out waterproofs when he is well aware the sky is going to clear, foreseeing that the imbecile will turn this delusion into a prejudice against waterproofs instead of giving a closer study to the weather-signs." DD 37

—the mind's: "Men's minds have no hiding-place out of themselves—their affectations do but betray another phase of their nature." PY 21

Education

—a bright girl: "In the schoolroom her quick mind had taken readily that strong starch of unexplained rules and disconnected facts which saves ignorance from any painful sense of limpness, and what remained of all things knowable, she was conscious of being sufficiently acquainted with through novels, plays, and poems." DD 4

—college: " 'He says college mostly makes people like bladders—just good for nothing but t'hold the stuff as is poured into 'em.' " AB 16

—early 19th c.: "All this, you remember, happened in those dark ages when there were no Schools of Design, before schoolmasters were invariably men of scrupulous integrity, and before the clergy were all men of enlarged minds and varied culture. In those less favoured days, it is no fable that there were other clergymen besides Mr Stelling who had narrow intellects and large wants, and whose income, by a logical confusion to which Fortune, being a female as well as blindfold, is peculiarly liable, was proportioned not to their wants but to their intellect—with which income has clearly no inherent relation.

"The problem these gentlemen had to solve was to readjust the proportion between their wants and their income; and since wants are not easily starved to death, the simpler method appeared to be—to raise their income. There was but one way of doing this: any of those low callings in which men are obliged to do good work at a low price were forbidden to clergymen: was it their fault if their only resource was to turn out very poor work at a high price? Besides, how should Mr Stelling be expected to know that education was a delicate and difficult business? Any more than an animal endowed with a power of boring a hole through rock should be expected to have wide views of excavation.

"Mr Stelling's faculties had been early trained to boring in a strait line, and he had no faculty to spare. But among Tom's contemporaries whose fathers cast their sons on clerical instruction to find them ignorant after many days, there were many far less lucky than Tom Tulliver. Education was almost entirely a matter of luck—usually of ill-luck—during those distant days. The state of mankind in which you take a billiard-cue or a dice-box in your hand is one of sober certainty compared with that of old-fashioned fathers, like Mr Tulliver, when they selected a school or a tutor for their sons." ¶MF II 4

"Excellent men, who had been forced all their lives to spell on an impromptu phonetic system, and having carried on a successful business in spite of this disadvantage, had acquired money enough to give their sons a better start in life than they had had themselves, must necessarily take their chance as to the conscience and the competence of the schoolmaster whose circular fell in their way and appeared to promise so much more than they would ever have thought of asking for—including the return of linen, fork, and spoon.

"It was happy for them if some ambitious draper of their acquaintance had not brought up his son to the Church and if that young gentleman, at the age of four-and-twenty, had not closed his college dissipations by an imprudent marriage: otherwise, these innocent fathers desirous of doing the best for their offspring could only escape the draper's son by happening to be on the foundation of a grammar school as yet unvisited by commissioners where two or three boys could have all to themselves the advantages of a large and lofty building, together with a head-master, toothless, dim-eyed and deaf, whose erudite indistinctness and inattention were engrossed by them at the rate of three hundred pounds a head—a ripe scholar, doubtless, when first appointed; but all ripeness beneath the sun has a further stage less esteemed in the market." ¶MF II 4

—*labourer's:* "It was touching to see these three big men, with the marks of their hard labour about them, anxiously bending over the worn books, and painfully making out, 'The grass is green,' 'The sticks are dry,' 'The corn is ripe'—a very hard lesson to pass to after columns of single words all alike except in the first letter. It was almost as if three rough animals were making humble efforts to learn how they might become human." AB 21

"Some who follow the narrative of his experience may wonder at the midnight darkness of Mr Dagley; but nothing was easier in those times than for an hereditary farmer of his grade to be ignorant, in spite somehow of having a rector in the twin parish who was a gentleman to the backbone, a curate nearer at hand who preached more learnedly than the rector, a landlord who had gone into everything, especially fine art and social improvement, and all the lights of Middlemarch only three miles off.

"As to the facility with which mortals escape knowledge, try an average acquaintance in the intellectual blaze of London, and consider what that eligible person for a dinner-party would have been if he had learned scant skill in 'summing' from the parish-clerk of Tipton, and read a chapter in the Bible with immense difficulty, because such names as *Isaiah* or *Apollo* remained unmanageable after twice spelling. Poor Dagley read a few verses sometimes on a Sunday evening, and the world was at least not darker to him than it had been before. Some things he knew thoroughly, namely the slovenly habits of farming, and the awkwardness of weather, stock and crops, at Freeman's End—so called apparently by way of sarcasm, to imply that a man was free to quit it if he chose, but that there was no earthly 'beyond' open to him." ¶MM 39

—*lack of it:* "It was a time [the 1830s] when ignorance was much more comfortable than at present, and was received with all the honours in very good society, without being obliged to dress itself in an elaborate costume of knowledge: a time when cheap periodicals were not, and when country surgeons never thought of asking their female patients if they were fond of reading, but simply took it for granted that they preferred gossip: a time when ladies in rich silk gowns wore large pockets in which they carried a mutton bone to secure them against cramp." MF I 12

—*premature:* "As to the formation of a pure and correct taste by placing first-rate authors in the hands of boys, we think that result is quite an exceptional one; the ordinary effect is rather that of vulgarizing the finest products of genius by premature familiarity. Too early an intimacy with the highest, in any department, deadens the sensibility and robs the mature mind of its proper enjoyments. A child who has been taken to see the Alps at ten years of age is pitiable; he will never know the rush of thought and feeling which would have made the sight an epoch for his manhood." BL 2 603-4

—*private:* "But there are two expensive forms of education, either of which a parent may procure for his son by sending him as solitary pupil to a clergyman: one is, the enjoyment of the reverend gentleman's undivided neglect; the other is, the endurance of the reverend gentleman's undivided attention." MF II 1

—*refuge:* " . . . incompetent gentlemen must live, and without private fortune, it is difficult to see how they could all live genteelly if they had nothing to do with education or government." MF II 1

—*remembered:* " ' . . . all the learnin' *my* father ever paid for was a bit o' birch at one end and the alphabet at t' other.' " MF I 2

—*rote formula:* "Perhaps it was because teaching came naturally to Mr Stelling that he set about it with that uniformity of method and independence of circumstances which distinguish the actions of animals understood to be under the immediate teaching of nature. **Mr Broderip**'s amiable beaver, as that charming naturalist tells us, busied himself as earnestly in constructing a dam, in a room up three pairs of stairs in London, as if he had been laying his foundation in a stream or lake in Upper Canada. It was 'Binny's' function to build: the absence of water or of possible progeny was an accident for which he was not accountable.

"With the same unerring instinct Mr Stelling set to work at his natural method of instilling the Eton Grammar and **Euclid** into the mind of Tom Tulliver. This, he considered, was the only basis of solid instruction: all other means of education were mere charlatanism, and could produce nothing better than smatterers. Fixed on this firm basis, a man might observe the display of various or special knowledge made by irregularly educated people with a pitying smile: all that sort of thing was very well, but it was impossible these people could form sound opinions.

"In holding this conviction, Mr Stelling was not biassed, as some tutors have been, by the excessive accuracy or extent of his own scholarship, and as to his views about Euclid, no opinion could have been freer from personal partiality. Mr Stelling was very far from being led astray by enthusiasm, either religious or intellectual: on the other hand, he had no secret belief that everything was humbug. He thought religion was a very excellent thing, and **Aristotle** a great authority, and deaneries and prebends useful institutions, and Great Britain the providential bulwark of Protestantism, and faith in the unseen a great support of afflicted minds: he believed in all these things as a Swiss hotel keeper believes in the beauty of the scenery around him, and in the pleasure it gives to artistic visitors.

"And in the same way Mr Stelling believed in his method of education: he had no doubt that he was doing the very best thing for Mr Tulliver's boy. Of course, when the miller talked of mapping and summing in a vague and diffident manner, Mr Stelling had set his mind at rest by an assurance that he understood what was wanted; for how was it possible the good man could form any reasonable judgment about the matter? Mr Stelling's duty was to teach the lad in the only right way—indeed, he knew no other: he had not wasted his time in the acquirement of anything abnormal.

"He very soon set down poor Tom as a thoroughly stupid lad; for though by hard labour he could get particular declensions into his brain, anything so abstract as the relation between cases and terminations could by no means get such a lodgment there as to enable him to recognise a chance genitive or dative. This struck Mr Stelling as something more than natural stupidity: he suspected obstinacy, or at any rate, indifference, and lectured Tom severely on his want of thorough application. 'You feel no interest in what you're doing, sir,' Mr Stelling would say, and the reproach was painfully true . . . he only observed that Tom's faculties failed him before the abstractions hideously symbolised to him in the pages of the Eton Grammar, and that he was in a state bordering on idiocy with regard to the demonstration that two given triangles must be equal—though he could discern with great promptitude and certainty the fact that they *were* equal.

"Whence Mr Stelling concluded that Tom's brain being peculiarly impervious to etymology and demonstrations, was peculiarly in need of being ploughed and harrowed by these patent implements: it was his favourite metaphor, that the classics and geometry constituted that culture of the mind which prepared it for the reception of any subsequent crop. I say nothing against Mr Stelling's theory: if we are to have one regimen for all minds his seems to me as good as any other. I only know it turned out as uncomfortably for Tom Tulliver as if he had been plied with cheese in order to remedy a gastric weakness which prevented him from digesting it.

"It is astonishing what a different result one gets by changing the metaphor! Once call the brain an intellectual stomach, and one's ingenious conception of the classics and geometry as ploughs and harrows seems to settle nothing. But then, it is open to some one else to follow great authorities and call the mind a sheet of white paper or a mirror, in which case one's knowledge of the digestive process becomes quite irrelevant. It was doubtless an ingenious idea to call the camel the ship of the desert, but it would hardly lead one far in training that useful beast.

"O Aristotle! if you had had the advantage of being 'the freshest modern' instead of the greatest ancient, would you not have mingled your praise of metaphorical speech as a sign of high intelligence, with a lamentation that intelligence so rarely shows itself in speech without metaphor—that we can so seldom declare what a thing is, except by saying it is something else?

"Tom Tulliver being abundant in no form of speech, did not use any metaphor to declare his views as to the nature of Latin: he never called it an instrumentality of torture; and it was not until he had got on some way in the next half-year and in the Delectus, that he was advanced enough to call it a 'bore' and 'beastly stuff'. At present, in relation to this demand that he should learn Latin declensions and conjugations, Tom was in a state of as blank unimaginativeness concerning the cause and tendency of his sufferings, as if he had been an innocent shrew-mouse imprisoned in the split trunk of an ash tree in order to cure lameness in cattle.

"It is doubtless almost incredible to instructed minds of the present day that a boy of twelve, not belonging strictly to 'the masses' who are now understood to have the monopoly of mental darkness, should have had no distinct idea how there came to be such a thing as Latin on this earth: yet so it was with Tom. It would have taken a long while to make conceivable to him that there ever existed a people who bought and sold sheep and oxen and transacted the everyday affairs of life through the medium of this language, and still longer to make him understand why he should be called upon to learn it, when its connection with those affairs had become entirely latent. So far as Tom had gained any acquaintance with the Romans at Mr Jacobs' Academy, his knowledge was strictly correct, but it went no farther than the fact that they were 'in the New Testament.' And Mr Stelling was not the man to enfeeble and emasculate his pupil's mind by simplifying and explaining, or to reduce the tonic effect of etymology by mixing it with smattering, extraneous information such as is given to girls." ¶MF II 1

—science: "The popular lecturer on science comes before his audience with a selection of striking and apt experiments in readiness, and is silent as to the morning's preparation in the laboratory; and so the scholar, who would produce a work of general utility, must not drag his readers through the whole region of his own researches, but simply present them with an impressive *coup d'oeil.*" PI 359

—the thumb-screw: "It was the practice of our venerable ancestors to apply that ingenious instrument the thumb-screw, and to tighten and tighten it in order to elicit non-existent facts: they had a fixed opinion to begin with, that the facts were existent, and what had they to do but to tighten the thumb-screw? In like manner, Mr Stelling had a fixed opinion that all boys with any capacity could learn what it was the only regular thing to teach: if they were slow, the thumb-screw must be tightened—the exercises must be insisted on with increased severity, and a page of **Virgil** be awarded as a penalty, to encourage and stimulate a too languid inclination to Latin verse." MF II 4

—young girl's: "In the schoolroom her quick mind had taken readily that strong starch of unexplained rules and disconnected facts which saves ignorance from any painful sense of limpness, and what remained of all things knowable, she was conscious of being sufficiently acquainted with through novels, plays, and poems." DD 4

Genius

—development: "We know what a masquerade all development is, and what effective shapes may be disguised in helpless embryos.—In fact, the world is full of hopeful analogies and handsome dubious eggs called possibilities . . . . He held that reliance [on the intentions of the universe with regard to himself] to be a mark of genius, and certainly it is no mark to the contrary; genius consisting neither in self-conceit nor in humility, but in a power to make or do, not anything in general, but something in particular." MM 10

Habit and Tradition

—building character: see S:Character*—built from habit*

—feeling of security: "The sense of security more frequently springs from habit than from conviction, and for this reason it often subsists after such a change in the conditions as might have been expected to suggest alarm. The lapse of time during which a given event has not happened, is, in this logic of habit, constantly alleged as a reason why the event should never happen, even when the lapse of time is precisely the added condition which makes the event imminent. A man will tell you that he has worked in a mine for forty years unhurt by an accident as a reason why he should apprehend no danger, though the roof is beginning to sink . . . . " SM 4

—a loss: "Our habitual life is like a wall hung with pictures, which has been shone on by the suns of many years: take one of the pictures away, and it leaves a definite blank space, to which our eyes can never turn without a sensation of discomfort. Nay, the involuntary loss of any familiar object almost always brings a chill as from an evil omen; it seems to be the first finger-shadow of advancing death." JR 10

—repetition: "Have not men, shut up in solitary imprisonment, found an interest in marking the moments by straight strokes of a certain length on the wall, until the growth of the sum of straight strokes, arranged, in triangles, has become a mastering purpose? Do we not wile away moments of inanity or fatigued waiting by repeating some trivial movement or sound, until the repetition has bred a want, which is incipient habit?" SM 2

—tradition: "But perhaps large minds have been peculiarly liable to this fluctuation concerning the sphere of tradition, because, while they have attacked its misapplications, they have been the more solicited by the vague sense that tradition is really the basis of our best life. Our sentiments may be called organized traditions; and a large part of our actions gather all their justification, all their attraction and aroma, from the memory of the life lived, of the actions done, before we were born.

"In the absence of any profound research into psychological functions or into the mysteries of inheritance, in the absence of any comprehensive view of man's historical development and the independence of one age on another, a mind at all rich in sensibilities must always have had an indefinite uneasiness in an undistinguishing attack on the coercive influence of tradition." ¶IR 116-7

History

—unexpected: "History, we know, is apt to repeat herself, and to foist very old incidents upon us with only a slight change of costume. From the time of **Xerxes** downwards, we have seen generals playing the braggadocio at the outset of their campaigns, and conquering the enemy with the greatest ease in after-dinner speeches. But events are apt to be in disgusting discrepancy with the anticipations of the most ingenious tacticians; the difficulties of the expedition are ridiculously at variance with able calculations; the enemy has the impudence not to fall into confusion as had been reasonably expected of him; the mind of the gallant general begins to be distracted by news of intrigues against him at home, and, notwithstanding the handsome compliments he paid to Providence as his undoubted patron before setting out, there seems every probability that the *Te Deums* will be all on the other side." JR 10

Hope and Desire

"Our finest hope is finest memory,
As they who love in age think youth is blest
Because it has a life to fill with love." MP 292-4

—deceptive: "But Hope to him was like the brilliant west/Telling of sunrise in a world unknown . . . . " MP 264-5

—distinguished from certainty: "I have a knack of hoping, which is as good as an estate in reversion, if one can keep from the temptation of turning it into certainty, which may spoil all. My Hope wanders among the orchard-blossoms, feels the warm snow falling on it through the sunshine, and is in doubt of nothing; but, catching sight of Certainty in the distance, sees an ugly *Janus*-faced deity, with a dubious wink on the hither side of him, and turns quickly away." DD 52

" . . . Hope, that immortal delicious maiden, for ever courted, for ever propitious, whom fools have called deceitful, as if it were Hope that carried the cup of disappointment, whereas it is her deadly enemy Certainty, whom she only escapes by transformation." DD 52

—first impulse: "Quick souls have their intensest life in the first anticipatory sketch of what may or will be, and the pursuit of their wish is the pursuit of that paradisiacal vision which only impelled them, and is left farther and farther behind, vanishing for ever even out of hope in the moment which is called success." FH 6

—given up: "That famous ring that pricked its owner when he forgot duty and followed desire—I wonder if it pricked very hard when he set out on the chase, or whether it pricked but lightly then, and only pierced to the quick when the chase had long been ended, and hope, folding her wings, looked backward and became regret?" SM 15

—not given up: "But strong feeling unsatisfied is never without its superstition, either of hope or despair. Romola's was the superstition of hope: *somehow* she was to find that mother and the children." R 70

—prophecy fulfilled: " 'Second-sight' is a flag over disputed ground. But it is matter of knowledge that there are persons whose yearnings, conceptions—nay, travelled conclusions—continually take the form of images which have a foreshadowing power: the deed they would do starts up before them in complete shape, making a coercive type; the event they hunger for or dread rises into vision with a seed-like growth, feeding itself fast on unnumbered impressions. They are not always the less capable of the argumentative process, nor less sane than the commonplace calculators of the market: sometimes it may be their natures have manifold openings, like the hundred-gated Thebes, where there may naturally be a greater and more miscellaneous inrush than through a narrow beadle-watched portal." DD 38

—sought ideal: " . . . the words youth, beauty, refinement, Jewish birth, noble gravity, turned into hardly individual but typical form and colour: gathered from his memory of faces seen among the Jews of Holland and Bohemia, and from the paintings which revived that memory. Reverently let it be said of this mature spiritual need that it was akin to the boy's and girl's picturing of the future beloved; but the stirrings of such young desire are feeble compared with the passionate current of an ideal life straining to embody itself, made intense by resistance to imminent dissolution. The visionary form became a companion and auditor; keeping a place not only in the waking imagination, but in those dreams of lighter slumber of which it is truest to say, 'I sleep, but my heart waketh'—when the disturbing trivial story of yesterday is charged with the impassioned purpose of years." DD 38

—speaking: "And when Hope speaks and argues that the divine love has not forsaken him, it says nothing now of a great work to be done, but only says, 'Thou art not forsaken, else why is thy heart bowed in penitence? That too is a gift.' " R 71

—unreliable: "Hopes have precarious life.
They are oft blighted, withered, snapped sheer off
In vigorous growth and turned to rottenness.
But faithfulness can feed on suffering,
And knows no disappointment." SG III

—wish: ". . . when we take to wishing a great deal for ourselves, whatever we get soon turns into mere limitation and exclusion." DD 14

"Wishes are held to be ominous, according to which belief the order of the world is so arranged that if you have an impious objection to a squint, your offspring is the more likely to be born with one; also, that if you happened to desire a squint, you would not get it. This desponding view of probability the hopeful entirely reject, taking their wishes on good and sufficient security for all kinds of fulfilment. Who is absolutely neutral?" DD 33

Idea

—abstractions: "For abstractions are deities having many specific names, local habitations, and forms of activity, and so get a multitude of devout servants who care no more for them under their highest titles than the celebrated person who, putting with forcible brevity a view of human motives now much insisted on, asked what Posterity had done for him that he should care for Posterity?" TS 7

—actions: " 'For, look at it in one way, all actions men put a bit of thought into are ideas—say, sowing seed, or making a canoe, or baking clay; and such ideas as these work themselves into life and go on growing with it, but they can't go apart from the material that set them to work and makes a medium for them. It's the nature of wood and stone yielding to the knife that raises the idea of shaping them, and with plenty of wood and stone the shaping will go on. I look at it, that such ideas as are mixed straight away with all the other elements of life are powerful along with 'em. The slower the mixing, the less power they have. And as to the causes of social change, I look at it in this way—ideas are a sort of parliament, but there's a commonwealth outside, and a good deal of the commonwealth is working at change without knowing what the parliament is doing.' " DD 42

—appropriated: "True, some persons are so constituted that the very excellence of an idea seems to them a convincing reason that it must be, if not solely, yet especially theirs. It fits in so beautifully with their general wisdom, it lies implicitly in so many of their manifested opinions, that if they have not yet expressed it (because of preoccupation) it is clearly a part of their indigenous produce, and is proved by their immediate eloquent promulgation of it to belong more naturally and appropriately to them than to the person who seemed first to have alighted on it, and who sinks in their all-originating consciousness to that low kind of entity, a second cause. This is not lunacy, nor pretence, but a genuine state of mind very effective in practice, and often carrying the public with it, so that the poor **Columbus** is found to be a very faulty adventurer, and the continent is named after **Amerigo**." TS 11 *See* LC:Authorship *—plagiarism*

—crude: "Gwendolen's ideas were pitiably crude; but many grand difficulties of life are apt to force themselves on us in our crudity." DD 29

—and emotion: "After all has been said that can be said about the widening influence of ideas, it remains true that they would hardly be such strong agents unless they were taken in a solvent of feeling. The great world-struggle of developing thought is continually foreshadowed in the struggle of the affections, seeking a justification for love and hope." R 52

—influence: "Blessed influence of one true loving human soul on another! Not calculable by algebra, not deducible by logic, but mysterious, effectual, mighty as the hidden process by which the tiny seed is quickened, and bursts forth into tall stem and broad leaf, and glowing tasselled flower. Ideas are often poor ghosts; our sun-filled eyes cannot discern them; they pass athwart us in thin vapour, and cannot make themselves felt. But sometimes they are made flesh; they breathe upon us with warm breath, they touch us with soft responsive hands, they look at us with sad sincere eyes, and speak to us in appealing tones; they are clothed in a living human soul, with all its conflicts, its faith, and its love. Then their presence is a power, then they shake us like a passion, and we are drawn after them with gentle compulsion, as flame is drawn to flame." JR 19

—obsession: "It was no longer a hope; it was only that possibility which clings to every idea that has taken complete possession of the mind: the sort of possibility that makes a woman watch on a headland for the ship which held something dear, though all her neighbours are certain that the ship was a wreck long years ago." R 67

Imagination and Illusion

"We are all of us imaginative in some form or other, for images are the brood of desire. . . ." MM 34

—artificial aid: " 'Is he very much cut up, poor fellow?' Bartle added, taking out his spectacles and putting them on, as if they would assist his imagination." AB 40

—awe-inducing: "Impossible for men of duller fibre—men whose affection is not ready to diffuse itself through the wide travel of imagination, to comprehend, perhaps even to credit this sensibility of

Deronda's, but it subsisted, like their own dulness, notwithstanding their lack of belief in it. . . . " DD 60

—*enlightened:* " . . . that imagination that reveals subtle actions inaccessible by any sort of lens, but tracked in that outer darkness through long pathways of necessary sequence by the inward light which is the last refinement of Energy, capable of bathing even the ethereal atoms in its ideally illuminated space. He for his part had tossed away all cheap inventions where ignorance finds itself able and at ease: he was enamoured of that arduous invention which is the very eye of research, provisionally framing its object and correcting it to more and more exactness of relation; he wanted to pierce the obscurity of those minute processes which prepare human misery and joy, those invisible thoroughfares which are the first lurking-places of anguish, mania, and crime; that delicate poise and transition which determine the growth of happy or unhappy consciousness." MM 16

—*illusion:* "Even if high imagination were to be identified with illusion, there would be the same sort of difference between the imperial wealth of illusion which is informed by industrious submissive observation and the trumpery stage-property illusion which depends on the ill-defined impressions gathered by capricious inclination, as there is between a good and a bad picture of the Last Judgment." TS 13

"Our sweet illusions are half of them conscious illusions, like effects of colour that we know to be made up of tinsel, broken glass, and rags." LV 2

—*injuring another:* " . . . he had not occupied himself with the inconvenience and possible injury that his breach might occasion them; for this exercise of the imagination on other people's needs is not common with hopeful young gentlemen. Indeed we are most of us brought up in the notion that the highest motive for not doing a wrong is something irrespective of the beings who would suffer the wrong." MM 24

—*limited:* " . . . I am always glad to believe that the poverty of our imagination is no measure of the world's resources. Our posterity will no doubt get fuel in ways that we are unable to devise for them." TS 4

—*misunderstood:* "High imagination is often assigned or claimed as if it were a ready activity in fabricating extravagances such as are presented by fevered dreams, or as if its possessors were in that state of inability to give credible testimony which would warrant their exclusion from the class of acceptable witnesses in a court of justice; so that a creative genius might fairly be subjected to the disability which some laws have stamped on dicers, slaves, and other classes whose position was held perverting to their sense of social responsibility." TS 13

—*morbid:* "Many men have been praised as vividly imaginative on the strength of their profuseness in indifferent drawing or cheap narration:—reports of very poor talk going on in distant orbs; or portraits of Lucifer coming down on his bad errands as a large ugly man with bat's wings and spurts of phosphorescence; or exaggerations of wantonness that seem to reflect life in a diseased dream." MM 16

—*optimum:* " . . . a fine imagination, which is always based on a keen vision, a keen consciousness of what *is,* and carries the store of definite knowledge as material for the construction of its inward visions. Witness **Dante**, who is at once the most precise and homely in his reproduction of actual objects, and the most soaringly at large in his imaginative combinations. On a much lower level we distinguish the hyperbole and rapid development in descriptions of persons and events which are lit up by humorous intention in the speaker—we distinguish this charming play of intelligence which resembles musical improvisation on a given motive, where the farthest sweep of curve is looped into relevancy by an instinctive method, from the florid inaccuracy or helpless exaggeration which is really something commoner than the correct simplicity often depreciated as prosaic." TS 13

—*powerful:* " . . . it is worth repeating that powerful imagination is not false outward vision, but intense inward representation, and a creative energy constantly fed by susceptibility to the veriest minutiæ of experience, which it reproduces and constructs in fresh and fresh wholes; not the habitual confusion of provable fact with the fictions of fancy and transient inclination, but a breadth of ideal association which informs every material object, every incidental fact with far-reaching memories and stored residues of passion, bringing into new light the less obvious relations of human existence.

"The illusion to which it is liable is not that of habitually taking duck-ponds for lilied pools, but of being more or less transiently and in varying degrees so absorbed in ideal vision as to lose the consciousness of surrounding objects or occurrences; and when that rapt condition is past, the sane genius discriminates clearly between what has been given in this parenthetic state of excitement, and what he has known, and may count on, in the ordinary world of experience." ¶TS 13

—*prophetic:* "To glory in a prophetic vision of knowledge covering the earth, is an easier exercise of believing imagination than to see its beginning in newspaper placards, staring at you from a bridge beyond the cornfields, and it might well happen to most of us dainty people that we were in the thick of the battle of Armageddon without being aware of anything more than the annoyance of a little explosive smoke and struggling on the ground immediately about us." DD 33

—reflection: " . . . that agreeable after-glow of excitement when thought lapses from examination of a specific object into a suffusive sense of its connections with all the rest of our existence—seems, as it were, to throw itself on its back after vigorous swimming and float with the repose of unexhausted strength . . . . " MM 16

—visiting: " . . . imagination is a licensed trespasser: it has no fear of dogs, but may climb over walls and peep in at windows with impunity." AB 6

Intellectual life

—and affections: " 'To delight in doing things because our fathers did them is good if it shuts out nothing better; it enlarges the range of affection—and affection is the broadest basis of good in life.'

" 'Do you think so?' said Gwendolen, with a little surprise. 'I should have thought you cared most about ideas, knowledge, wisdom, and all that.'

" 'But to care about them is a sort of affection . . . . Call it attachment, interest, willingness to bear a great deal for the sake of being with them and saving them from injury. Of course it makes a difference if the objects of interest are human beings; but generally in all deep affections the objects are a mixture—half persons and half ideas —sentiments and affections flow in together.' " DD 35

—books: " [He] bought the books he heard spoken of, arranging them carefully on the shelves of what he called his library, and occasionally sitting alone in the same room with them." TS 7

—distractions: "Only those who know the supremacy of the intellectual life—the life which has a seed of ennobling thought and purpose within it—can understand the grief of one who falls from that serene activity into the absorbing soul-wasting struggle with worldly annoyances." MM 73

—reading: "For the most part, the general reader of the present day does not exactly know what distance he goes; he only knows that he does not go 'too far.' Of any remarkable thinker whose writings have excited controversy, he likes to have it said that 'his errors are to be deplored,' leaving it not too certain what those errors are: he is fond of what may be called disembodied opinions, that float in vapory phrases above all systems of thought or action; he likes an undefined Christianity which opposes itself to nothing in particular, an undefined education of the people, an undefined amelioration of all things: in fact, he likes sound views—nothing extreme, but something between the excesses of the past and the excesses of the present.

"This modern type of the general reader may be known in conversation by the cordiality with which he assents to indistinct, blurred statements: say that black is black, he will shake his head and hardly think it; say that black is not so very black, he will reply, 'Exactly.' He has no hesitation, if you wish it, even to get up at a public meeting and express his conviction that at times, and within certain limits, the radii of a circle have a tendency to be equal; but, on the other hand, he would urge that the spirit of geometry may be carried a little too far. His only bigotry is a bigotry against any clearly defined opinion; not in the least based on a scientific scepticism, but belonging to a lack of coherent thought—a spongy texture of mind, that gravitates strongly to nothing. The one thing he is stanch for is the utmost liberty of private haziness." IR 107-8

—scholarship domesticated: "It is well known that great scholars who have shown the most pitiless acerbity in their criticism of other men's scholarship, have yet been of a relenting and indulgent temper in private life; and I have heard of a learned man meekly rocking the twins in the cradle with his left hand, while with his right he inflicted the most lacerating sarcasms on an opponent who had betrayed a brutal ignorance of Hebrew. Weaknesses and errors must be forgiven—alas! they are not alien to us—but the man who takes the wrong side on the momentous subject of the Hebrew points must be treated as the enemy of his race." AB 14

—uneven results: "Intellect is no longer taken to be a ready-made dose of ability to attain eminence (or mediocrity) in all departments; it is even admitted that application in one line of study or practice has often a laming effect in other directions, and that an intellectual quality or special facility which is a furtherance in one medium of effort is a drag in another. We have convinced ourselves by this time that a man may be a sage in celestial physics and a poor creature in the purchase of seed-corn, or even in theorising about the affections; that he may be a mere fumbler in physiology and yet show a keen insight into human motives; that he may seem the 'poor Poll' of the company in conversation and yet write with some humorous vigour. It is not true that a

man's intellectual power is like the strength of a timber beam, to be measured by its weakest point." TS 8

Intuition

—subtlety: "It is well known to all experienced minds that our firmest convictions are often dependent on subtle impressions for which words are quite too coarse a medium." AB 34

—wish: " . . . she had sat in languid melancholy and suspense, fixing her mind on Will Ladislaw's coming as the one point of hope and interest, and associating this with some new urgency on Lydgate to make immediate arrangements for leaving Middlemarch and going to London; till she felt assured that the coming would be a potent cause of the going, without at all seeing how. This way of establishing sequences is too common to be fairly regarded as a peculiar folly in Rosamond. And it is precisely this sort of sequence which causes the greatest shock when it is sundered; for to see how an effect may be produced is often to see possible missings and checks, but to see nothing except the desirable cause, and close upon it the desirable effect, rids us of doubt and makes our minds strongly intuitive." MM 77

Knowledge and Ignorance

—dry: "There is hardly any contact more depressing to a young ardent creature than that of a mind in which years full of knowledge seem to have issued in a blank absence of interest or sympathy." MM 20

—fact: "For Fact, well-trusted, reasons and
persuades,
Is gnomic, cutting or ironical,
Draws tears, or is a tocsin to arouse—
Can hold all figures of the orator
In one plain sentence; has her pauses too—
Eloquent silence at the chasm abrupt
Where knowledge ceases." S 36-42

—how gained: "Do not philosophic doctors tell us that we are unable to discern so much as a tree, except by an unconscious cunning which combines many past and separate sensations; that no one sense is independent of another, so that in the dark we can hardly taste a fricassee, or tell whether our pipe is alight or not, and the most intelligent boy, if accommodated with claws or hoofs instead of fingers, would be likely to remain on the lowest form? If so, it is easy to understand that our discernment of men's motives must depend on the completeness of the elements we can bring from our own susceptibility and our own experience. See to it, friend, before you pronounce a too hasty judgement, that your own moral sensibilities are not of a hoofed or clawed character. The keenest eye will not serve, unless you have the delicate fingers, with their subtle nerve filaments, which elude scientific lenses, and lose themselves in the invisible world of human sensations." JR 11

—ignorance: " 'Ignorance,' says *Ajax,* 'is a painless evil'; so, I should think, is dirt, considering the merry faces that go along with it." GL 3

—its depth: "The depths of middle-aged gentlemen's ignorance will never be known, for want of public examinations in this branch." TS 7

—its power: "It is a common sentence that Knowledge is power, but who hath duly considered or set forth the power of Ignorance? Knowledge slowly builds up what Ignorance in an hour pulls down. Knowledge, through patient and frugal centuries, enlarges discovery and makes record of it; Ignorance, wanting its day's dinner, lights a fire with the record, and gives a flavour to its one roast with the burnt souls of many generations. Knowledge, instructing the sense, refining and multiplying needs, transforms itself into skill and makes life various with a new six days' work; comes Ignorance drunk on the seventh, with a firkin of oil and a match and an easy 'Let there not be'—and the many-coloured creation is shrivelled up in blackness.

"Of a truth, Knowledge is power, but it is a power reined by scruple, having a conscience of what must be and what may be; whereas Ignorance is a blind giant who, let him but wax unbound, would make it a sport to seize the pillars that hold up the long-wrought fabric of human good, and turn all the places of joy dark as a buried Babylon. And looking at life parcel-wise, in the growth of a single lot, who have a practised vision may not see that ignorance of the true bond between events, and false conceit of means whereby sequences may be compelled—like that falsity of eyesight which overlooks the gradations of distance, seeing that which is afar off as if it were within a step or a grasp—precipitates the mistaken soul on destruction?" ¶DD 21 ep

—imputed: "No premisses require closer scrutiny than those which lead to the constantly echoed conclusion, 'He must have known,' or 'He must have read.' I marvel that this facility of belief on the side of knowledge can subsist under the daily demonstration that the easiest of all things to the human mind is *not* to know and *not* to read. To praise, to blame, to shout, grin, or hiss, where others shout, grin, or hiss—these are native tendencies; but to know and to read are artificial, hard accomplishments, concerning which the only safe supposition is, that as little of them has been done as the case admits." TS 11

—learned in the morning: "All knowledge which alters our lives penetrates us more when it comes in the early morning: the day that has to be travelled with something new and perhaps for ever sad in its light, is an image of the life that spreads beyond. But at night the time of rest is near." FH 26

—suddenly useful: "It is a natural subject of self-congratulation to a man, when special knowledge, gained long ago without any forecast, turns out to afford a special inspiration in the present . . . . " FH 29

—suspect: "All cleverness, whether in the rapid use of that difficult instrument the tongue, or in some other art unfamiliar to villagers, was in itself suspicious: honest folk, born and bred in a visible manner, were mostly not overwise or clever—at least, not beyond such a matter as knowing the signs of the weather; and the process by which rapidity and dexterity of any kind were acquired was so wholly hidden, that they partook of the nature of conjuring." SM 1

Latin and Greek

—advice: "The truth is, unless a man can get the prestige and income of a Don and write donnish books, it's hardly worth while for him to make a Greek and Latin machine of himself and be able to spin you out pages of the Greek dramatists at any verse you'll give him as a cue. That's all very fine, but in practical life nobody does give you the cue for pages of Greek. In fact it's a nicety of conversation which I would have you attend to—much quotation of any sort, even in English, is bad. It tends to choke ordinary remark. One couldn't carry on life comfortably without a little blindness to the fact that everything has been said better than we can put it ourselves." DD 16

" 'What I wish you to get is a passport in life. I don't go against our university system: we want a little disinterested culture to make head against cotton and capital, especially in the House. My Greek has all evaporated: if I had to construe a verse on a sudden, I should get an apoplectic fit. But it formed my taste. I daresay my English is the better for it.' " DD 16

—starting-point: " . . . it was not entirely out of devotion to her future husband that she wished to know Latin and Greek. Those provinces of masculine knowledge seemed to her a standing-ground from which all truth could be seen more truly." MM 7

Meditation

—dealing with fear: " 'Turn your fear into a safeguard. Keep your dread fixed on the idea of increasing that remorse which is so bitter to you. Fixed meditation may do a great deal towards defining our longing or dread. We are not always in a state of strong emotion, and when we are calm we can use our memories and gradually change the bias of our fear, as we do our tastes. Take your fear as a safeguard. It is like quickness of hearing. It may make consequences passionately present to you. Try to take hold of your sensibility, and use it as if it were a faculty, like vision.' " DD 36

—mystic: " 'And that sound of my name was like the touch of a wand that recalled me to the body wherefrom I had been released as it were to mingle with the ocean of human existence, free from the pressure of individual bondage.' " DD 43

—not benign: "He spent the evening in the solitude of the smaller drawing-room, where, with various new publications on the table, of the kind a gentleman may like to have at hand without touching, he employed himself (as a philosopher might have done) in sitting meditatively on a sofa and abstaining from literature—political, comic, cynical, or romantic. In this way hours may pass surprisingly soon, without the arduous invisible chase of philosophy; not from love of thought, but from hatred of effort—from a state of the inward world, something like premature age, where the need for action lapses into a mere image of what has been, is, and may or might be; where impulse is born and dies in a phantasmal world passing in rejection even of a shadowy fulfilment. That is a condition which often comes with whitening hair and sometimes, too, an intense obstinacy and tenacity of rule, like the main trunk of an exorbitant egoism, conspicuous in proportion as the varied susceptibilities of younger years are stripped away." DD 28

—obedience: " 'One authority,
And only one, says simply this, Obey:
Place yourself in that current (test it so!)
Of spiritual order where at least
Lies promise of a high communion,
A Head informing members, Life that breathes
With gift of forces over and above
The *plus* of arithmetic interchange.' " CB 175-82

—perhaps dangerous: "But Grandcourt's hair, though he had not much of it, was of a fine sunny blond, and his moods were not entirely to be explained as ebbing energy. We mortals have a strange spiritual chemistry going on within us, so that a lazy stagnation or even a cottony milkiness may be preparing one knows not what biting or explosive material. The navvy waking from sleep and without malice heaving a stone to crush the life out of his still sleeping comrade, is understood to lack the trained motive which

makes a character fairly calculable in its actions; but by a roundabout course even a gentleman may make of himself a chancy personage, raising an uncertainty as to what he may do next, which sadly spoils companionship." DD 28

Memory

—*in bereavement:* " . . . she had forgotten his faults as we forget the sorrows of our departed childhood . . . . " AB 10

—*childhood griefs:* "Is there any one who can recover the experience of his childhood, not merely with a memory of what he did and what happened to him, of what he liked and disliked when he was in frock and trousers, but with an intimate penetration, a revived consciousness of what he felt then —when it was so long from one Midsummer to another?—what he felt when his schoolfellows shut him out of their game because he would pitch the ball wrong out of mere wilfulness; or on a rainy day in the holidays when he didn't know how to amuse himself and fell from idleness into mischief, from mischief into defiance, and from defiance into sulkiness; or when his mother absolutely refused to let him have a tailed coat that 'half,' although every other boy of his age had gone into tails already? Surely if we could recall that early bitterness, and the dim guesses, the strangely perspectiveless conception of life that gave the bitterness its intensity, we should not pooh-pooh the griefs of our children." MF I 7

—*compressed:* "The recollections of the past become contracted in the rapidity of thought till they sometimes bear hardly a more distinct resemblance to the external reality than the forms of an oriental alphabet to the objects that suggested them." LV 2

—*emotive:* "He sat up half the night, living again through the moments since he had first discerned Mirah on the river-brink, with the fresh and fresh vividness which belongs to emotive memory." DD 19

—*in a faint:* "It is a wonderful moment, the first time we stand by one who has fainted, and witness the fresh birth of consciousness spreading itself over the blank features, like the rising sunlight on the alpine summits that lay ghastly and dead under the leaden twilight. A slight shudder, and the frostbound eyes recover their liquid light; for an instant they show the inward semiconsciousness of an infant's, then, with a little start, they open wider and begin to look; the present is visible, but only as a strange writing, and the interpreter Memory is not yet there." GL 15

—*fertile:* "And as memory, when duly impregnated with ascertained facts, is sometimes surprisingly fertile, Mr Snell gradually recovered a vivid impression of the effect produced on him by the pedlar's countenance and conversation. He had a 'look with his eye' which fell unpleasantly on Mr Snell's sensitive organism." SM 8

—*first recovery:* "The earliest and the longest has still the mastery over us; and the only past that linked itself with those glazed unconscious eyes, was the past when they beamed on her with tenderness. She forgot the interval of wrong and jealousy and hatred—all his cruelty, and all her thoughts of revenge—as the exile forgets the stormy passage that lay between home and happiness and the dreary land in which he finds himself desolate." GL 15

—*inward life:* "Nothing had been outwardly altered there [in her boudoir], but while the summer had gradually advanced over the western fields beyond the avenue of elms, the bare room had gathered within it those memories of an inward life which fill the air as with a cloud of good or bad angels, the invisible yet active forms of our spiritual triumphs or our spiritual falls." MM 37

—*locale:* "Scenes which make vital changes in our neighbours' lot are but the background of our own, yet, like a particular aspect of the fields and trees, they become associated for us with the epochs of our own history, and make a part of that unity which lies in the selection of our keenest consciousness." MM 34

—*mother's:* "A mother dreads no memories —those shadows have all melted away in the dawn of baby's smile." GL 21

—*national:* "That the preservation of national memories is an element and a means of national greatness, that their revival is a sign of reviving nationality, that every heroic defender, every patriotic restorer, has been inspired by such memories and has made them his watchword, that even such a corporate existence as that of a Roman legion or an English regiment has been made valorous by memorial standards—these are the glorious commonplaces of historic teaching at our public schools and universities, being happily ingrained in Greek and Latin classics. They have also been impressed on the world by conspicuous modern instances." TS 18 *See* RW:Greece and RW:Italy

—*of pain:* " . . . pain must enter into its glorified life of memory before it can turn into compassion." MM 78

—*past in the present:* " . . . he felt the scenes of his earlier life coming between him and everything else, as obstinately as when we look through the window from a lighted room, the objects we turn our backs on are still before us, instead of the grass and the occurs only if the matter is not limited to administration alone as has, in some places, been the case. And here *particularly* the role of *Soviet construction* emerges as one and the same with the establishment of the new legality.

Are we now approaching such work? Unfortunately, we still are not. At the start of this article we saw how the "high" and responsible commission, instead of providing a directive in the area of civil law—a directive now more necessary than ever before—has gone to sleep until, they say, everything is under control and it will be apparent what to write, until we have *finally* come to a halt. Indeed, this can be drawn out until the complete victory of socialism—and then law itself will not be necessary. The "legislator" of the revolution should perhaps, like a model journalist, have in his portfolio material for an article in the event something important occurs. But, in any case, the revolutionary law, *barring a retreat*, must pave the way for a further advance. We took a step forward and learned to fear using the words "socialist," etc. in law. However, the problem does not lie in phraseology, but in content. For law is not simply an order; it regulates or protects a system of *social relationships*. Revolutionary law must also be approached in this sense. In bourgeois society, these relationships were realized anarchically and imperialistically within the framework of the norms of the Civil Code which, of course, provides only bare forms for "free contract" "social exchange of objects" (simply according to the forms of purchase and sale). Without restricting the working people, Soviet revolutionary law must in the future give defined, general directives for development to socialism. The economics of this development will be defined by the socialist state plan of production and distribution. But Soviet power will ensure the conduct of this plan both in the struggle *against* class enemies and in the struggle for strict social discipline, until "people become accustomed to observing the elementary rules of social intercourse . . . without force and without coercion" [Lenin 1917, p. 462]. These two tasks: struggle *against* . . . and struggle *for* . . . in essence constitute the two tasks of every revolution: destruction and creativity. In the Criminal Code, where these two aspects of the struggle have not been recognized and have been insufficiently separated, this division must henceforth be more clearly expressed. Of course both these tasks are intertwined, for even part of the working people ("subkulaks," "bourgeois yesmen") were under the *influence* of the class enemy. In the countryside, collectivization has brought about a great upheaval, depriving the estate-owner and then the kulak of his material power and creating the basis for the birth and growth of consciousness amongst the most backward farm worker, *under whose influence* the middle peasant also must fall in the future, before he is transformed into a conscious worker. This upheaval will, of course, be a long one; it requires time, intensified agitation, and a correct evaluation in the future of the so-called subkulak.

This upheaval in the countryside must entail another and even greater change in life-style: *the liberation of women and the family from the shameful survival from the times of slavery—the household family*. During dekulakization we had to his will; he had recovered the memory of all that part of his life which was closely enwrought with his emotions; and he had felt more and more constantly and painfully the uneasy sense of lost knowledge.

"But more than that—once or twice, when he had been strongly excited, he had seemed momentarily to be in entire possession of his past self, as old men doze for an instant and get back the consciousness of their youth: he seemed again to see Greek pages and understand them, again to feel his mind moving benumbed among familiar ideas. It had been but a flash, and the darkness closing in again seemed the more horrible; but might not the same thing happen again for longer periods?" ¶R 30

—decision: "But she came to the conclusion that she could not possibly call at Mrs Holt's.

"It followed that up to a few minutes past twelve, when she reached the turning towards Mrs Holt's, she believed that she should go home the other way; but at the last moment there is always a reason not existing before—namely, the impossibility of further vacillation. Esther turned the corner without any visible pause, and in another minute was knocking at Mrs Holt's door." FH 22

—defect of a sort: "A boy born with a deficient power of apprehending signs and abstractions must suffer the penalty of his congenital deficiency, just as if he had been born with one leg shorter than the other; a method of education sanctioned by the long practice of our venerable ancestors was not to give way before the exceptional dulness of a boy who was merely living at the time then present." MF II 4

—defiant: ". . . she was in that mood of defiance in which the mind loses sight of any end beyond the satisfaction of enraged resistance; and with the puerile stupidity of a dominant impulse includes luck among its objects of defiance. Since she was not winning strikingly, the next best thing was to lose strikingly." DD 1

—development: "The mind of a man is as a country which was once open to squatters, who have bred and multiplied and become masters of the land. But then happeneth a time when new and hungry comers dispute the land; and there is trial of strength, and the stronger wins. Nevertheless the first squatters be they who have prepared the ground, and the crops to the end will be sequent (though chiefly on the nature of the soil, as of light sand, mixed loam, or heavy clay, yet) somewhat on the primal labour and sowing." FH 8 ep

—differences: "No doubt men's minds differ in what we may call their climate or share of solar energy, and a feeling or tendency which is comparable to a panther in one may have no more imposing aspect than that of a weasel in another; some are like a tropical habitat in which the very ferns cast a mighty shadow, and the grasses are a dry ocean in which a hunter may be submerged; others like the chilly latitudes in which your forest-tree, fit elsewhere to prop a mine, is a pretty miniature suitable for fancy potting. The eccentric man might be typified by the Australian fauna, refuting half our judicious assumptions of what nature allows." TS 13

—disoriented: "Even people whose lives have been made various by learning, sometimes find it hard to keep a fast hold on their habitual views of life, on their faith in the Invisible, nay, on the sense that their past joys and sorrows are a real experience, when they are suddenly transported to a new land, where the beings around them know nothing of their history, and share none of their ideas—where their mother earth shows another lap, and human life has other forms than those on which their souls have been nourished." SM 2

"Under the shock of discovering her son's Radicalism, Mrs Transome had no impulse to say one thing rather than another; as in a man who had just been branded on the forehead all wonted motives would be uprooted." FH 1

—emanation: "There seems to be a subtle emanation from passionate natures like [**Savonarola**'s], making their mental states tell immediately on others; when they are absentminded and inwardly excited there is silence in the air." R 64

—enfeebled: " . . . his mind was dwelling upon her and her circumstances as feeble eyes dwell on lines and colours, trying to interpret them into consistent significance." R 50.

—escape: "Minds that have been unhinged from their old faith and love, have perhaps sought this Lethean influence of exile, in which the past becomes dreamy because its symbols have all vanished, and the present too is dreamy because it is linked with no memories." SM 2

—feelings intruding: "Our naked feelings make haste to clothe themselves in propositions which lie at hand among our store of opinions, and to give a true account of what passes within us something else is necessary besides sincerity, even when sincerity is unmixed." R 64

—healthy: "When we come to examine in detail what is the sane mind in the sane body, the final test of completeness seems to

be a security of distinction between what we have professed and what we have done; what we have aimed at and what we have achieved; what we have invented and what we have witnessed or had evidenced to us; what we think and feel in the present and what we thought and felt in the past." TS 13

—*impressions:* "Harold, like the rest of us, had many impressions which saved him the trouble of distinct ideas." FH 47

—*inchoate:* "His mind was crowded with images and conjectures, which were a language to his hopes and fears, just as we hear tones from the vibrations which shake our whole system." MM 69

—*inspiration:* "And do we not all agree to call rapid thought and noble impulse by the name of inspiration? After our subtlest analysis of the mental process, we must still say, as Dinah did, that our highest thoughts and our best deeds are all given to us." AB 10

—*interest:* " . . . it would take a long while to dull the curiosity of the five men on board, and reduce these handsome young strangers to that minor degree of interest which belongs, in a sailor's regard, to all objects nearer than the horizon." MF VI 13

—*judging probability:* "Probabilities are as various as the faces to be seen at will in fretwork or paperhanging: every form is there, from *Jupiter* to *Judy,* if you only look with creative inclination." MM 32

—*lacking ballast:* "In a mind where no strong sympathies are at work, where there is no supreme sense of right to which the agitated nature can cling and steady itself to quiet endurance, one of the first results of sorrow is a desperate vague clutching after any deed that will change the actual condition. Poor Hetty's vision of consequences, at no time more than a narrow fantastic calculation of her own probable pleasures and pains, was now quite shut out by reckless irritation under present suffering, and she was ready for one of those convulsive, motiveless actions by which wretched men and women leap from a temporary sorrow into a life-long misery." AB 31

—*moral questions:* "To the common run of mankind it has always seemed a proof of mental vigour to find moral questions easy, and judge conduct according to concise alternatives." R 64

—*mysterious inspiration:* " 'I don't think any of the strongest effects our natures are susceptible of can ever be explained. We can neither detect the process by which they are arrived at nor the mode in which they act on us. The greatest of painters [**Raphael**] only once painted a mysteriously divine child [in the *Sistine Madonna*]—he couldn't have told how he did it—and we can't tell why we feel it to be divine. I think there are stores laid up in our human nature that our understandings can make no complete inventory of. Certain strains of music affect me so strangely—I can never hear them without their changing my whole attitude of mind for a time, and if the effect would last I might be capable of heroisms.' " MF V 1

—*observation:* " . . . the respectable townsfolk there were not more given than mortals generally to any eager attempt at exactness in the representation to themselves of what did not come under their own senses." MM 15

—*opinion:* "Our pet opinions are usually those which place us in a minority of a minority amongst our own party:—very happily, else those poor opinions, born with no silver spoon in their mouths—how would they get nourished and fed?" FH 16

—*predisposition:* "To have a mind well oiled with that sort of argument which prevents any claim from grasping it, seems eminently convenient sometimes; only the oil becomes objectionable when we find it anointing other minds on which we want to establish a hold." R 63

—*primary:* "All sacred rules, imagined or revealed,

Can have no form or potency apart
From the percipient and emotive mind.
God, duty, love, submission, fellowship,
Must first be framed in man, as music is,
Before they live outside him as a law." CB 598-603

—*psyche:* "There is a great deal of unmapped country within us which would have to be taken into account in an explanation of our gusts and storms." DD 24

—*recrimination:* "All minds, except such as are delivered from doubt by dulness of sensibility, must be subject to this recurring conflict where the many-twisted conditions of life have forbidden the fulfilment of a bond. For in strictness there is no replacing of relations: the presence of the new does not nullify the failure and breach of the old. Life has lost its perfection: it has been maimed; and until the wounds are quite scarred, conscience continually casts backward, doubting glances." R 69

—*refuge:* "Yes, there was a sort of refuge which always comes with the prostration of thought under an overpowering passion: it was that expectation of impossibilities, that belief in contradictory images, which is still distinct from madness, because it is capable of being dissipated by the external fact." SM 5

—*resignation:* " 'Is it not right to resign ourselves entirely, whatever may be denied us?

I have found great peace in that for the last two or three years—even joy in subduing my own will.'

" 'Yes, Maggie,' said Philip, vehemently, 'and you are shutting yourself up in a narrow self-delusive fanaticism which is only a way of escaping pain by starving into dulness all the highest powers of your nature. Joy and peace are not resignation: resignation is the willing endurance of a pain that is not allayed—that you don't expect to be allayed. Stupefaction is not resignation: and it is stupefaction to remain in ignorance—to shut up all the avenues by which the life of your fellow-men might become known to you. I am not resigned: I am not sure that life is long enough to learn that lesson. You are not resigned: you are only trying to stupefy yourself.' " MF V 3

—restored: "That sense of mental empire which belongs to us all in moments of exceptional clearness was intensified for him by the long days and nights in which memory had been little more than the consciousness of something gone." R 38

—second thoughts: "Was there a motive at work under this strange reluctance of Arthur's which had a sort of backstairs influence, not admitted to himself? Our mental business is carried on much in the same way as the business of the State: a great deal of hard work is done by agents who are not acknowledged. In a piece of machinery, too, I believe there is often a small unnoticeable wheel which has a great deal to do with the motion of the large obvious ones. Possibly, there was some such unrecognised agent secretly busy in Arthur's mind at this moment—possibly it was the fear lest he might hereafter find the fact of having made a confession to the Rector a serious annoyance, in case he should *not* be able quite to carry out his good resolution? I dare not assert that it was not so. The human soul is a very complex thing." AB 16

—seeming stupidity: " . . . for getting a fine flourishing growth of stupidity there is nothing like pouring out on a mind a good amount of subjects in which it feels no interest." MF V 2

—and sensibility: "It is not force of intellect which causes ready repulsion from the aberration and eccentricities of greatness, any more than it is force of vision that causes the eye to explore the warts on a face bright with human expression; it is simply the negation of high sensibilities." R 44

—the sexes: "A man's mind—what there is of it—has always the advantage of being masculine—as the smallest birch-tree is of a higher kind than the most soaring palm—and even his ignorance is of a sounder quality." MM 2

—stricken: " . . . the paralytic obstruction was, little by little, losing its tenacity, and the mind was rising from under it with fitful struggles, like a living creature making its way from under a great snowdrift that slides and slides again, and shuts up the newly made opening." MF III 7

—in suffering: "Adam sat looking at the clock: the minute-hand was hurrying along the last five minutes to ten, with a loud hard indifferent tick, and Adam watched the movement and listened to the sound as if he had had some reason for doing so. In our times of bitter suffering, there are almost always these pauses, when our consciousness is benumbed to everything but some trivial perception or sensation. It is as if semi-idiocy came to give us rest from the memory and the dread which refuse to leave us in our sleep." AB 39

—tremor: " . . . she felt herself in the grasp of that tremor which does not disable the mind, but rather gives keener consciousness of a mind having a penalty of body attached to it." FH 46

—unbalanced—or not: "Certainly the seer, whether prophet, philosopher, scientific discoverer, or poet, may happen to be rather mad: his powers may have been used up, like *Don Quixote*'s, in their visionary or theoretic constructions, so that the reports of common-sense fail to affect him, or the continuous strain of excitement may have robbed his mind of its elasticity. It is hard for our frail mortality to carry the burthen of greatness with steady gait and full alacrity of perception. But he is the strongest seer who can support the stress of creative energy and yet keep that sanity of expectation which consists in distinguishing, as **Dante** does, between the *cose che son vere* [reality] outside the individual mind, and the *non falsi errori* [not false visions] which are the revelations of true imaginative power." TS 13

—undisciplined: "How trace the why and wherefore in a mind reduced to the barrenness of a fastidious egoism, in which all direct desires are dulled, and have dwindled from motives into a vacillating expectation of motives: a mind made up of moods, where a fitful impulse springs here and there conspicuously rank amid the general weediness? 'Tis a condition apt to befall a life too much at large, unmoulded by the pressure of obligation. *Nam deteriores omnes sumus licentiæ*, saith **Terence**, or, as a more familiar tongue might deliver it, *'As you like' is a bad finger-post.* " DD 25 ep

—*the unknown:* " . . . the human mind in that grassy corner had not the proverbial tendency to admire the unknown, holding rather that it was likely to be against the poor man, and that suspicion was the only wise attitude with regard to it." MM 56

—*untrained:* "People who pride themselves on the correctness of their reasoning have to suffer many mortifications. They are constantly finding that as a means of immediate influence their carefully-drawn conclusions are quite powerless by the side of a good bold fallacy. The majority of minds are no more to be controlled by strong reasons than plum-pudding is to be grasped by sharp pincers. The farther your thinker sees into the real relations of things, the closer he makes his sequences—the farther he will be from the possibility of carrying untrained minds along the path of his argument. Their conclusions are determined, not at all by close sequences, but by vague, habitual impressions and by chance associations." SL

—*visualization:* "The promptitude with which men will consent to touch red-hot iron with a wet finger is not to be measured by their theoretic acceptance of the impossibility that the iron will burn them: practical belief depends on what is most strongly represented in the mind at a given moment." R 64

—*volatile:* "For *Macbeth*'s rhetoric about the impossibility of being many opposite things in the same moment [*Macbeth* II iii], referred to the clumsy necessities of action and not to the subtler possibilities of feeling. We cannot speak a loyal word and be meanly silent, we cannot kill and not kill in the same moment; but a moment is room wide enough for the loyal and mean desire, for the outlash of a murderous thought and the sharp backward stroke of repentance." DD 4

—*wishful thinking:* "A dull mind, once arriving at an inference that flatters a desire, is rarely able to retain the impression that the notion from which the inference started was purely problematic." SM 4

Prejudice

—*impartiality:* " . . . our impartiality is kept for abstract merit and demerit, which none of us ever saw." MM 40

—*Jews:* "To take only the subject of the Jews: it would be difficult to find a form of bad reasoning about them which has not been heard in conversation or have been admitted to the dignity of print; but the neglect of resemblances is a common property of dulness which unites all the various points of view—the prejudiced, the puerile, the spiteful, and the abysmally ignorant." TS 18

—*mental squint:* " . . . [**Menander**] had no mental squint, which unhappily can co-exist with the most symmetrical pair of eyes." BL 1 304

—*religious:* "It appears that the Caribs, who know little of theology, regard thieving as a practice peculiarly connected with Christian tenets, and probably they could allege experimental grounds for this opinion." DD 19 *See* FM:Jews

—*sentiment:* " 'No man,' says a Rabbi, by way of indisputable instance, 'may turn the bones of his father and mother into spoons' —sure that his hearers felt the checks against that form of economy. The market for spoons has never expanded enough for any one to say, 'Why not?' and to argue that human progress lies in such an application of material. The only check to be alleged is a sentiment, which will coerce none who do not hold that sentiments are the better part of the world's wealth." DD 33 ep

—*type of mind:* "But to minds strongly marked by the positive and negative qualities that create severity—strength of will, conscious rectitude of purpose, narrowness of imagination and intellect, great power of self-control and a disposition to exert control over others—prejudices come as the natural food of tendencies which can get no sustenance out of that complex, fragmentary, doubt-provoking knowledge which we call truth. Let a prejudice be bequeathed, carried in the air, adopted by hearsay, caught in through the eye—however it may come, these minds will give it a habitation: it is something to assert strongly and bravely, something to fill up the void of spontaneous ideas, something to impose on others with the authority of conscious right: it is at once a staff and a baton. Every prejudice that will answer these purposes is self-evident." MF VI 12

Scholarship

—*ethics:* " 'Else, why have I refused the loan of many an annotated codex? Why have I refused to make public any of my translations? Why? But because scholarship is a system of licensed robbery; and your man in scarlet and furred robe who sits in judgment on thieves, is himself a thief of the thoughts and the fame that belong to his fellows.' " R 5

—*footnotes:* "The notes are brief and really enlightening. Mr Bell does not incessantly invite your eye to the bottom of the page in order to expatiate on something quite beside the question; but wherever you are conscious of fogginess, you find a reference to a note which detains you from the text only just so long as is necessary." BL 1 300

"He dreams footnotes; and they run away with all his brains." MM 8

—penalties: " ' . . . if your book contains novelties you will be charged with forgery; if my elucidations should clash with any principles of interpretation adopted by another scholar, our personal characters will be attacked, we shall be impeached with foul actions; you must prepare yourself to be told that your mother was a fish-woman, and that your father was a renegade priest or a hanged malefactor. I myself, for having shown error in a single preposition, had an invective written against me wherein I was taxed with treachery, fraud, indecency, and even hideous crimes. Such . . . are the flowers with which the glorious path of scholarship is strewed!' " R 6

And see SR:Scholarship

Science

—chemistry: "Doubtless a vigorous error vigorously pursued has kept the embryo of truth a-breathing: the quest of gold being at the same time a questioning of substances, the body of chemistry is prepared for its soul, and **Lavoisier** is born." MM 48

—effect on miracles: "Through some parts of his book [Lecky] appears to regard the grand characteristic of modern thought and civilization, compared with ancient, as a radiation in the first instance from a change in religious conceptions. The supremely important fact, that the gradual reduction of all phenomena within the sphere of established law, which carries as a consequence the rejection of the miraculous, has its determining current in the development of physical science, seems to have engaged comparatively little of his attention; at least, he gives it no prominence. The great conception of universal regular sequence, without partiality and without caprice—the conception which is the most potent force at work in the modification of our faith, and of the practical force given to our sentiments—could only grow out of that patient watching of external fact, and that silencing of preconceived notions, which are urged upon the mind by the problems of physical science." IR 120-1

—inquiry: " ' . . . the purest experiment in treatment may still be conscientious: my business is to take care of life, and to do the best I can think of for it. Science is properly more scrupulous than dogma. Dogma gives a charter to mistake, but the very breath of science is a contest with mistake, and must keep the conscience alive.' " MM 73

—limitations: "Science, detecting hydrogen
aflame
Outside our firmament, leaves mystery
Whole and untouched beyond; nay, in our blood
And in the potent atoms of each germ
The Secret lives—envelops, penetrates
Whatever sense perceives or thought divines.
Science, whose soul is explanation, halts
With hostile front at mystery." CB 221-8

—new theory: " . . . it appeared that the attack might possibly be held damaging, unless the ignorance of the author were well exposed and his pretended facts shown to be chimeras of that remarkably hideous kind begotten by imperfect learning on the more feminine element of original incapacity." TS 3

—and Philosophy: " 'Science, reasoning
On nature's order—they exist and move
Solely by disputation, hold no pledge
Of final consequence, but push the swing
Where **Epicurus** and the Stoic sit
In endless see-saw." CB 170-5

—and Poetry: "Men can do nothing without the make-believe of a beginning. Even Science, the strict measurer, is obliged to start with a make-believe unit, and must fix on a point in the stars' unceasing journey when his sidereal clock shall pretend that time is at Nought. His less accurate grandmother Poetry has always been understood to start in the middle; but on reflection it appears that her proceeding is not very different from his; since Science, too, reckons backwards as well as forwards, divides his unit into billions, and with his clock-finger at Nought really sets off *in medias res.* No retrospect will take us to the true beginning; and whether our prologue be in heaven or on earth, it is but a fraction of that all-presupposing fact with which our story sets out." DD 1 ep

—robotics: see H:Commerce and Industry

And see Education—*science*

Self-knowledge and Self-deception

—in infatuation: "Strange, that some of us, with quick alternate vision, see beyond our infatuations, and even while we rave on the heights, behold the wide plain where our persistent self pauses and awaits us." MM 15

—tradition believed in: "I have sometimes thought that this facility of men in believing that they are still what they once meant to be—this undisturbed appropriation of a traditional character which is often but a melancholy relic of early resolutions, like the worn and soiled testimonial to soberness and honesty carried in the pocket of a tippler whom the need of a dram has driven into peculation—may sometimes diminish

the turpitude of what seems a flat, barefaced falsehood. It is notorious that a man may go on uttering false assertions about his own acts till he at last believes in them: is it not possible that sometimes in the very first utterance there may be a shade of creed-reciting belief, a reproduction of a traditional self which is clung to against all evidence? There is no knowing all the disguises of the lying serpent." TS 13

Sensibility

—discernment: "To discern likeness amidst diversity, it is well known, does not require so fine a mental edge as the discerning of adversity amidst general sameness. The primary rough classification depends on the prominent resemblances of things: the progress is towards finer and finer discrimination according to minute differences.

"Yet even at this stage of European culture one's attention is continually drawn to the prevalence of that grosser mental sloth which makes people dull to the most ordinary prompting of comparison—the bringing things together because of their likeness. The same motives, the same ideas, the same practices, are alternately admired and abhorred, lauded and denounced, according to their association with superficial differences, historical or actually social: even learned writers treating of great subjects often show an attitude of mind not greatly superior in its logic to that of the frivolous fine lady who is indignant at the frivolity of her maid." TS 18

—poet's: "A poet pours forth his song and believes in the listening ear and answering soul, to which his song will be floated sooner or later. But the poet's sensibility without his voice—the poet's sensibility that finds no vent but in silent tears on the sunny bank, when the noonday light sparkles on the water, or in an inward shudder at the sound of harsh human tones, the sight of a cold human eye—this dumb passion brings with it a fatal solitude of soul in the society of one's fellow-men." LV 1

—rejection: "Deronda turned pale with what seems always more of a sensation than an emotion—the pain of repulsed tenderness." DD 51

—taste: " 'You said you didn't mind about people having right opinions so that they had good taste. Now I want you to see what shallow stuff that is . . . .

" 'But by opinions you mean men's thoughts about great subjects, and by taste you mean their thoughts about small ones: dress, behaviour, amusements, ornaments.'

" 'Well—yes—or rather, their sensibilities about those things.'

" 'It comes to the same thing; thoughts, opinions, knowledge, are only a sensibility to facts and ideas. If I understand a geometrical problem, it is because I have a sensibility to the way in which lines and figures are related to each other; and I want you to see that the creature who has the sensibilities that you call taste, and not the sensibilities that you call opinions, is simply a lower, pettier sort of being—an insect that notices the shaking of the table, but never notices the thunder.' " FH 10

Skepticism

—limits: "But skepticism, as we know, can never be thoroughly applied, else life would come to a standstill . . . . " MM 23

Superstition

—dread: "It is of such stuff that superstitions are commonly made: an intense feeling about ourselves which makes the evening star shine at us with a threat, and the blessing of a beggar encourage us. And superstitions carry consequences which often verify their hope or their foreboding." DD 29

—as to evil: " . . . with that superstitious impression which clings to us all, that if we expect evil very strongly it is the less likely to come . . . . " SM 8

—peasant's: " . . . a peasant can no more help believing in a traditional superstition than a horse can help trembling when he sees a camel." AB 4

Suspicion

—as to motive: "For there is nothing more widely misleading than sagacity if it happens to get on a wrong scent, and sagacity persuaded that men usually act and speak from distinct motives, with a consciously proposed end in view, is certain to waste its energies on imaginary game. Plotting covetousness and deliberate contrivance in order to compass a selfish end, are nowhere abundant but in the world of the dramatist: they demand too intense a mental action for many of our fellow-parishioners to be guilty of them.

"It is easy enough to spoil the lives of our neighbours without taking so much trouble: we can do it by lazy acquiescence and lazy omission, by trivial falsities for which we hardly know a reason, by small frauds neutralised by small extravagances, by maladroit flatteries and clumsily improvised insinuations. We live from hand to mouth, most of us, with a small family of immediate desires—we do little else than snatch a morsel to satisfy the hungry brood, rarely thinking of seed-corn or the next year's crop." MF I 3

Thought and Thinking

"It is the trick of thinking to be either premature or behindhand." DD 64

—*the absurd:* " . . . it is a narrow prejudice of mathematicians to suppose that ways of thinking are to be driven out of the field by being reduced to an absurdity. The Absurd is taken as an excellent juicy thistle by many constitutions." TS 2

—*another's:* "No chemical process shows a more wonderful activity than the transforming influence of the thoughts we imagine to be going on in another. Changes in theory, religion, admirations, may begin with a suspicion of dissent or disapproval, even when the grounds of disapproval are but matter of searching conjecture." DD 35

—*anticipation:* "Foreseeing, to men of Bulstrode's anxious temperament, is often worse than seeing; and his imagination continually heightened the anguish of an imminent disgrace." MM 68

—*brooding:* "But in her long solitary hours she brooded over her regretful thoughts about Dinah, till they had grown very near that point of unmanageable strength when thoughts are apt to take wing out of their secret nest in a startling manner." AB 51

—*and confectionery:* "Say what you will about the identity of the reasoning process in all branches of thought, or about the advantage of coming to subjects with a fresh mind, the adjustment of butter to flour, and of heat to pastry, is *not* the best preparation for the office of prime minister . . ." BJ 1

—*conflicting theory:* "When the robbery was talked of . . . the balance continued to waver between the rational explanation founded on the tinder-box, and the theory of an impenetrable mystery that mocked investigation. The advocates of the tinder-box-and-pedlar view considered the other side a muddle-headed and credulous set, who, because they themselves were wall-eyed, supposed everybody else to have the same blank outlook; and the adherents of the inexplicable more than hinted that their antagonists were animals inclined to crow before they had found any corn—mere skimming-dishes in point of depth—whose clear-sightedness consisted in supposing there was nothing behind a barn-door because they couldn't see through it; so that, though their controversy did not serve to elicit the fact concerning the robbery, it elicited some true opinions of collateral importance." SM 10

—*distracted:* "Bodily haste and exertion usually leave our thoughts very much at the mercy of our feelings and imagination." AB 4

"But to defer thought in this way was something like trying to talk down the singing in her own ears. The thought that is bound up with our passion is as penetrative as air—everything is porous to it; bows, smiles, conversation, repartee, are mere honey-combs where such thought rushes freely, not always with a taste of honey. And without shutting herself up in any solitude, Gwendolen seemed at the end of nine or ten hours to have gone through a labyrinth of reflection, in which already the same succession of prospects had been repeated, the same fallacious outlets rejected, the same shrinking from the necessities of every course." DD 48

—*inhibited by ingestion:* "But Christmas puddings, brawn, and abundance of spirituous liquors, throwing the mental originality into the channel of nightmare, are great preservatives against a dangerous spontaneity of waking thought." SM 10

—*logic:* "The driest argument has its hallucinations, too hastily concluding that its net will now at last be large enough to hold the universe. Men may dream in demonstrations, and cut out an illusory world in the shape of axioms, definitions, and propositions, with a final exclusion of fact signed Q.E.D. No formulas for thinking will save us mortals from mistake in our imperfect apprehension of the matter to be thought about. And since the unemotional intellect may carry us into a mathematical dreamland where nothing is but what is not, perhaps an emotional intellect may have absorbed into its passionate vision of possibilities some truth of what will be—the more comprehensive massive life feeding theory with new material as the sensibility of the artist seizes combinations which science explains and justifies. At any rate, presumptions to the contrary are not to be trusted. We must be patient with the inevitable makeshift of our human thinking, whether in its sum total or in the separate minds that have made the sum. **Columbus** had some impressions about himself which we call superstitions, and used some arguments which we disapprove; but he had also some true physical conceptions, and he had the passionate patience of genius to make them tell on mankind. The world has made up its mind rather contemptuously about those who were deaf to Columbus." DD 41

"What a blessing has a little false logic been to the world! Seeing that men are so slow to question their premises, they must have made each other much more miserable, if pity had not sometimes drawn tender conclusion not warranted by Major and Minor; if there had not been people with an amiable imbecility of reasoning which enabled them at once to cling to hideous beliefs, and to be conscientiously inconsistent with them in their conduct. There is nothing like acute deductive reasoning for keeping a man in the dark: it might be called the *technique* of the intellect, and the concentration of the mind upon it corresponds to that predominance of technical skill in art which ends in degradation of the artist's function, unless new inspiration and invention come to guide it." IR 113

—narrow theory: "Mr Lyon will perhaps seem a very simple personage, with pitiably narrow theories; but none of our theories are quite large enough for all the disclosures of time . . . . " FH 6

—night and morning: " . . . he went to sleep thinking that he had done with inward debating. But when he awoke in the still morning darkness he found it impossible to reawaken his evening thoughts; it was as if they had been tired out and were not to be roused to further work." SM 8

—opinion: "[Her] opinion was forming itself that very moment (as opinions will) under the heat of irritation." MM 3

—opinion of others: "Who can know how much of his most inward life is made up of the thoughts he believes other men to have about him, until that fabric of opinion is threatened with ruin?" MM 68

—the opposite: "It takes very little water to make a perfect pool for a tiny fish, where it will find its world and paradise all in one, and never have a presentiment of the dry bank. The fretted summer shade, and stillness, and the gentle breathing of some loved life near—it would be paradise to us all, if eager thought, the strong angel with the implacable brow, had not long since closed the gates." R 10

—and passions: " . . . there is no human being who having both passions and thoughts does not think in consequence of his passions—does not find images rising in his mind which soothe the passion with hope or sting it with dread." MM 47

—planning: "It is a peculiar test of a man's metal when, after he has painfully adjusted himself to what seems a wise provision, he finds all his mental precaution a little beside the mark, and his excellent intentions no better than miscalculated dovetails, accurately cut from a wrong starting-point. His magnanimity has got itself ready to meet misbehaviour, and finds quite a different call upon it." DD 37

—reasoning: " . . . Sinbad himself may have fallen by good-luck on a true description, and wrong reasoning sometimes lands poor mortals in right conclusions starting a long way off the true point, and proceeding by loops and zigzags, we now and then arrive just where we ought to be." MM 3

—unsanitized: "But these fine words with which we fumigate and becloud unpleasant facts are not the language in which we think. Deronda's thinking went on in rapid images of what might be . . . . " DD 19

—a weapon: "Vice was essentially stupid—a deaf and eyeless monster, insusceptible to demonstration: the Spirit might work on it by unseen ways, and the unstudied sallies of sermons were often as the arrows which pierced and awakened the brutified conscience; but illuminated thought, finely-dividing speech, were the choicer weapons of the Divine armoury, which whoso could wield must be careful not to leave idle." FH 15

Wisdom

—in judgment: "And to judge wisely I suppose we must know how things appear to the unwise; that kind of appearance making the larger part of the world's history." DD 29

—necessary ingredient: "The prevision that Fra Luca's words had imparted to Romola had been such as comes from the shadowy region where human souls seek wisdom apart from the human sympathies which are the very life and substance of our wisdom; the revelation that might have come from the simple questions of filial and brotherly affection had been carried into irrevocable silence." R 15

—recipe: "One cannot give a recipe for wise judgment: it resembles appropriate muscular action, which is attained by the myriad lessons in nicety of balance and of aim that only practice can give." TS 13

—and political reform: "But while still outside us, wisdom often looks terrible, and wears strange forms, wrapped in the changing conditions of a struggling world. It wears now the form of wants and just demands in a great multitude of British men: wants and demands urged into existence by the forces of a maturing world. And it is in virtue of this—in virtue of this presence of wisdom on our side as a mighty fact, physical and moral, which must enter into and shape the thoughts and actions of mankind—that we working men have obtained the suffrage. Not because we are an excellent multitude, but because we are a needy multitude." WM 181-2

—working slowly: "Wisdom stands outside of man and urges itself upon him, like the marks of the changing seasons, before it finds a home within him, directs his actions, and from the precious effects of obedience begets a corresponding love." WM 181

Spirit and Moral Qualities

"Who shall put his finger on the work of justice, and say, 'It is there'? Justice is like the Kingdom of God—it is not without us as a fact, it is within us as a great yearning." R 67

"The mere fact that mankind has a conception of what is pure and lovely, might be fairly taken as a ground of faith in the human nature out of which the conception was born; and the proper attitude of faith is bravery." EH 2

"Community of interest is the root of justice; community of suffering, the root of pity; community of joy, the root of love." LNB 9

Anger and Indignation

"Anger and jealousy can no more bear to lose sight of their objects than love." MF I 10

—*needing outlet:* "Yet proud wrath
Leaped in dark flood above the purer stream
That strove to drown it: Anger seeks its prey—
Something to tear with sharp-edged tooth and claw,
Likes not to go off hungry, leaving Love
To feast on milk and honeycomb at will.
Silva's heart said, he must be happy soon,
She being there; but to be happy—first
He must be angry, having cause." SG I iii

—*objective indignation:* "The danger of . . . judging of self by what one observes in others, if it is carried on with much impartiality and keenness of discernment, is that it has a laming effect, enfeebling the energies of indignation and scorn, which are the proper scourges of wrong-doing and meanness, and which should continually feed the wholesome restraining power of public opinion." TS 13

" . . . it is undeniable that a too intense consciousness of one's kinship with all frailties and vices undermines the active heroism which battles against wrong." TS 13

—*phlegmatic:* "That cold dislike which is the anger of unimpassioned beings was hardening within him." R 46

—*rage:* " . . . [speaking] with that vain effort which rage always makes, to throw as much punishment as it desires to inflict into words and tones, since blows are forbidden." MF VI 8

—*righteous:* "When a man is in a rage and wants to hurt another in consequence, he can always regard himself as the civil arm of a spiritual power, and all the more easily because there is real need to assert the righteous efficacy of indignation. I for my part feel with the [attacked], and should object all the more to their or my being lacerated and dressed with salt, if the administrator of such torture alleged as a motive his care for Truth and posterity, and got himself pictured with a halo in consequence." TS 8

—*unreflective:* "I respect the horsewhip when applied to the back of Cruelty, and think that he who applies it is a more perfect human being because his out-leap of indignation is not checked by a too curious reflection on the nature of guilt—a more perfect human being because he more completely incorporates the best social life of the race, which can never be constituted by ideas that nullify action." TS 13

Character

—*built from habit:* "Tito was experiencing that inexorable law of human souls, that we prepare ourselves for sudden deeds by the reiterated choice of good or evil which gradually determines character." R 23

"Our lives make a moral tradition for our individual selves, as the life of mankind at large makes a moral tradition for the race; and to have once acted nobly seems a reason why we should always be noble. But Tito was feeling the effect of an opposite tradition: he had won no memories of self-conquest and perfect faithfulness from which he could have a sense of falling." R 39

—*conceit:* "Our vanities differ as our noses do: all conceit is not the same conceit, but varies in correspondence with the minutiae of mental make in which one of us differs from another." MM 15

—*convenience conquers:* "But convenience, that admirable branch system from the main line of self-interest, makes us all fellow helpers in spite of adverse resolutions. It is probable that no speculative or theological hatred would be ultimately strong enough to resist the persuasive power of convenience: that a latitudinarian baker, whose bread was honourably free from alum, would command the custom of any dyspeptic Puseyite; that an Arminian with the toothache would prefer a skilful Calvinistic dentist to a bungler staunch against the doctrines of Election and Final Perseverance, who would be likely to break the tooth in his head; and that a Plymouth Brother, who had a well-furnished grocery shop in a favourable vicinage, would occasionally have the pleasure of furnishing sugar or vinegar to orthodox families that found themselves unexpectedly 'out of' those indispensable commodities.' " JR 10

—*cross-purposes:* "There are episodes in most men's lives in which their highest qualities can only cast a deterring shadow over the objects that fill their inward vision. Lydgate's tender-heartedness was present just then only as a dread lest he should offend against it, not as an emotion that swayed him to tenderness." MM 73

—*and destiny:* "For the tragedy of our lives is not created entirely from within. 'Character'—says **Novalis**, in one of his questionable aphorisms—'character is destiny.' But not the whole of our destiny. *Hamlet,* Prince of Denmark, was speculative and irresolute, and we have a great tragedy in consequence. But if his father had lived to a good old age, and his uncle had died an early death, we can conceive Hamlet's having married *Ophelia* and got through life with a reputation of sanity notwithstanding many soliloquies, and some moody sarcasms towards the fair daughter of *Polonius,* to say nothing of the frankest incivility to his father-in-law." MF VI 6

—*effect of temper:* "I doubt the possibility that a high order of character can coexist with a [bad] temper . . . . For it is of the nature of such temper to interrupt the formation of healthy mental habits, which depend on a growing harmony between perception, conviction, and impulse. There may be good feelings, good deeds—for a human nature may pack endless varieties and blessed inconsistencies in its windings—but it is essential to what is worthy to be called high character, that it may be safely calculated on, and that its qualities shall have taken the form of principles or laws habitually, if not perfectly, obeyed." TS 6

—*feeling of injury:* "The sense of an entailed disadvantage—the deformed foot doubtfully hidden by the shoe, makes a restlessly active spiritual yeast, and easily turns a self-centred, unloving nature into an Ishmaelite. But in the rarer sort, who presently see their own frustrated claim as one among a myriad, the inexorable sorrow takes the form of fellowship and makes the imagination tender." DD 16

" . . . there are some cases, and his was one of them, in which the sense of injury breeds—not the will to inflict injuries and climb over them as a ladder, but—a hatred of all injury." DD 16

—*formed by action:* "Our deeds determine us, as much as we determine our deeds; and until we know what has been or will be the peculiar combination of outward with inward facts, which constitutes a man's critical actions, it will be better not to think ourselves wise about his character. There is a terrible coercion in our deeds which may first turn the honest man into a deceiver, and then reconcile him to the change; for this reason—that the second wrong presents itself to him in the guise of the only practicable right. The action which before commission has been seen with that blended common-sense and fresh untarnished feeling which is the healthy eye of the soul, is looked at afterwards with the lens of apologetic ingenuity, through which all things that men call beautiful and ugly are seen to be made up of textures very much alike. Europe adjusts itself to a *fait accompli,* and so does an individual character. . . . " AB 29

—*human feeling:* "Yes! thank God; human feeling is like the mighty rivers that bless the earth: it does not wait for beauty—it flows with resistless force and brings beauty with it." AB 17

—*humility:* " . . . he was too simple and sincere a man to ape a sort of humility which would not have made him any the better if he had possessed it. Such pretences turn our lives into sorry dramas." FH 32

—*in the eyes of a beloved:* "Even much stronger mortals than Fred Vincy hold half their rectitude in the mind of the being they love best." MM 24

—*noble:* "The presence of a noble nature, generous in its wishes, ardent in its charity, changes the lights for us: we being to see things again in their larger, quieter masses, and to believe that we too can be seen and judged in the wholeness of our character." MM 76

"But it is given to us sometimes even in our everyday life to witness the saving influence of a noble nature, the divine efficacy of rescue that may lie in a self-subduing act of fellowship." MM 82

—not fixed: " 'Character is not cut in marble —it is not something solid and unalterable. It is something living and changing, and may become diseased as our bodies do.' " MM 72

—overt action: "A course of action which is in strictness a slowly-prepared outgrowth of the entire character, is yet almost always traceable to a single impression as its point of apparent origin . . . . " R 35

—self-distrusting: "It belongs to every large nature, when it is not under the immediate power of some strong unquestioning emotion, to suspect itself, and doubt the truth of its own impressions, conscious of possibilities beyond its own horizon." R 27

—shallow: "Shallow natures dream of an easy sway over the emotions of others, trusting implicitly in their own petty magic to turn the deepest streams, and confident, by pretty gestures and remarks, of making the thing that is not as though it were . . . she had been little used to imagining other people's states of mind except as a material cut into shape by her own wishes; and she believed in her own power to soothe or subdue.." MM 78

—strong: "A character at unity with itself— that performs what it intends, subdues every counteracting impulse and has no visions beyond the distinctly possible, is strong by its very negations." MF V 2

Christmas

—country village: "But in Raveloe village the bells rang merrily, and the church was fuller than all through the rest of the year, with red faces among the abundant dark-green boughs—faces prepared for a longer service than usual by an odorous breakfast of toast and ale. Those green boughs, the hymn and anthem never heard but at Christmas—even the Athanasian Creed, which was discriminated from the others only as being longer and of exceptional virtue, since it was only read on rare occasions—brought a vague exulting sense, for which the grown men could as little have found words as the children, that something great and mysterious had been done for them in heaven above and in earth below, which they were appropriating by their presence. And then the red faces made their way through the black biting frost to their own homes, feeling themselves free for the rest of the day to eat, drink, and be merry, and using that Christian freedom without diffidence." SM 10

—white: "Fine old Christmas with the snowy hair and ruddy face had done his duty that year in the noblest fashion, and had set off his rich gifts of warmth and colour with all the heightening contrast of frost and snow.

"Snow lay on the croft and river-bank in undulations softer than the limbs of infancy; it lay with the neatliest finished border on every sloping roof, making the dark-red gables stand out with a new depth of colour; it weighed heavily on the laurels and fir-trees till it fell from them with a shuddering sound; it clothed the rough turnip-field with whiteness and made the sheep look like dark blotches; the gates were all blocked up with the sloping drifts, and here and there a disregarded four-footed beast stood as if petrified 'in unrecumbent sadness;' there was no gleam, no shadow, for the heavens too were one still pale cloud—no sound or motion in anything but the dark river, that flowed and moaned like an unresting sorrow.

"But old Christmas smiled as he laid this cruel-seeming spell on the outdoor world, for he meant to light up home with new brightness, to deepen all the richness of indoor colour, and give a keener edge of delight to the warm fragrance of food: he meant to prepare a sweet imprisonment that would strengthen the primitive fellowship of kindred, and make the sunshine of familiar human faces as welcome as the hidden day-star. His kindness fell but hardly on the homeless—fell but hardly on the homes where the hearth was not very warm, and where the food had little fragrance; where the human faces had no sunshine in them, but rather the leaden, blank-eyed gaze of unexpectant want. But the fine old season meant well; and if he has not learnt the secret how to bless men impartially, it is because his father Time, with ever unrelenting purpose, still hides that secret in his own mighty, slow-beating heart." ¶MF II 2

Church

—art: " 'For as for them furrin churches as Sir Cristifer is so unaccountable mad after, wi' pictures o' men an' women a-showing themselves just for all the world as God made 'em, I think, for my part, as it's almost a sin to go into 'em.' " GL 4

—critic in Florence: " ' . . . I venture to tell you that your buildings smack too much of Christian barbarism for my taste. I have a shuddering sense of what there is inside— hideous smoked Madonnas; fleshless saints in mosaic, staring down idiotic astonishment and rebuke from the apse; skin-clad skeletons hanging on crosses, or stuck all over with arrows, or stretched on gridirons;

women and monks with heads aside in perpetual lamentation. I have seen enough of those wry-necked favourites of heaven at Constantinople. But what is this bronze door rough with imagery? These women's figures seem moulded in a different spirit from those starved and staring saints I spoke of: these heads in high relief speak of a human mind within them, instead of looking like an index to perpetual spasms and colic.' " R 3

—*Foxholm Parsonage.* "Nowhere was there a lawn more smooth-shaven, walks better swept, or a porch more prettily festooned with creepers, than at Foxholm Parsonage, standing snugly sheltered by beeches and chestnuts half-way down the pretty green hill which was surmounted by the church, and overlooking a village that straggled at its ease among pastures and meadows, surrounded by wild hedgerows and broad shadowing trees, as yet unthreatened by improved methods of farming." GL 20

—*Hayslope Church:* "I cannot say that the interior of Hayslope Church was remarkable for anything except for the grey age of its oaken pews—great square pews mostly, ranged on each side of a narrow aisle. It was free, indeed, from the modern blemish of galleries. The choir had two narrow pews to themselves in the middle of the right-hand row, so that it was a short process for Joshua Rann to take his place among them as principal bass, and return to his desk after the singing was over. The pulpit and desk, grey and old as the pews, stood on one side of the arch leading into the chancel, which also had its grey square pews for Mr Donnithorne's family and servants. Yet I assure you these grew pews, with the buff-washed walls, gave a very pleasing tone to this shabby interior, and agreed extremely well with the ruddy faces and bright waistcoats. And there were liberal touches of crimson toward the chancel, for the pulpit and Mr Donnithorne's own pew had handsome crimson-cloth cushions; and, to close the vista, there was a crimson altar-cloth, embroidered with golden rays by Miss Lydia's own hand." AB 18

—*congregation:* " . . . Mr Irwine was in the desk, looking benignly round on that simple congregation—on the hardy old men, with bent knees and shoulders perhaps, but with vigour left for much hedge-clipping and thatching; on the tall stalwart frames and roughly-cut bronzed faces of the stone-cutters and carpenters; on the half-dozen well-to-do farmers, with their apple-cheeked families; and on the clean old women, mostly farm-labourers' wives, with their bit of snow-white-cap border under their black bonnets, and with their withered arms, bare from the elbow, folded passively over their chests. For none of the old people held books—why should they? Not one of them could read. But they knew a few 'good words' by heart, and their withered lips now and then moved silently, following the service without any very clear comprehension indeed, but with a simple faith in its efficacy to ward off harm and bring blessing." AB 18

—*Knebley Church:* " . . . a wonderful little church, with a chequered pavement which had once rung to the iron tread of military monks, with coats of arms in clusters on the lofty roof, marble warriors and their wives without noses occupying a large proportion of the area, and the twelve apostles, with their heads very much on one side, holding didactic ribbons, painted in fresco on the walls." GL 1

—*congregation:* "The farmers' wives and children sat on the dark oaken benches, but the husbands usually chose the distinctive dignity of a stall under one of the twelve apostles, where, when the alternation of prayers and responses had given place to the agreeable monotony of the sermon, Paterfamilias might be seen or heard sinking into a pleasant doze, from which he infallibly woke up at the sound of the concluding doxology. And then they made their way back again through the miry lanes, perhaps almost as much the better for this simple weekly tribute to what they knew of good and right, as many a more wakeful and critical congregation of the present day." GL 1

—*Nunziata in Florence:* "The whole area of the great church was filled with peasant-women, some kneeling, some standing; the coarse bronzed skins, and the dingy clothing of the rougher dwellers on the mountains, contrasting with the softer-lined faces and white or red head-drapery of the well-to-do dwellers in the valley; who were scattered in irregular groups. And spreading high and far over the walls and ceiling there was another multitude, also pressing close against each other, that they might be nearer the potent Virgin. It was the crowd of votive waxen images, the effigies of great personages, clothed in their habit as they lived: Florentines of high name in their black silk lucco, as when they sat in council; popes, emperors, kings, cardinals, and famous condottieri with plumed morion seated on their chargers; all notable strangers who passed through Florence or had aught to do with its affairs—Mohammedans, even, in well-tolerated companionship with Christian cavaliers, some of them with faces blackened and robes tattered by the corroding breath of centuries, others fresh and bright in new red mantle or steel corselet, the exact doubles of the living. And wedged in with all these were detached arms, legs, and other members, with only here and there a gap where some image had been removed for public disgrace, or had fallen ominously, as **Lorenzo**'s had done six months before. It was a perfect resurrection-swarm of remote mortals and fragments of mortals, reflecting, in their varying degrees of freshness, the sombre dinginess and sprinkled brightness of the crowd below." R 14

—rectory: "The Rectory was on the other side of the river, close to the church of which it was the fitting companion: a fine old brick-and-stone house, with a great bow-window opening from the library on to the deep-turfed lawn, one fat dog sleeping on the door-stone, another fat dog waddling on the gravel, the autumn leaves duly swept away, the lingering chrysanthemums cherished, tall trees stooping or soaring in the most picturesque variety, and a Virginian creeper turning a little rustic hut into a scarlet pavilion. It was one of those rectories which are among the bulwarks of our venerable institutions—which arrest disintegrating doubt, serve as a double embankment against Popery and Dissent, and rally feminine instinct and affection to reinforce the decisions of masculine thought." FH 23

—rural: "[My father's] one extra living was a poor vicarage, with hardly fifty parishioners, and its church would have made a very shabby barn, the grey worm-eaten wood of its pews and pulpit, with their doors only half hanging on the hinges, being exactly the colour of a lean mouse which I once observed as an interesting member of the scant congregation, and conjectured to be the identical church mouse I had heard referred to as an example of extreme poverty. . . ." TS 2

—Shepperton Church

—now: "Shepperton Church was a very different-looking building five-and-twenty years ago. To be sure, its substantial stone tower looks at you through its intelligent eye, the clock, with the friendly expression of former days, but in everything else what changes! Now there is a wide span of slated roof flanking the old steeple; the windows are tall and symmetrical; the outer doors are resplendent with oak-graining, the inner doors reverentially noiseless with a garment of red baize; and the walls, you are convinced, no lichen will ever again effect a settlement on—they are smooth and innutrient as the summit of the Rev. Amos Barton's head, after ten years of baldness and supererogatory soap. Pass through the baize doors and you will see the nave filled with well-shaped benches, understood to be free seats; while in certain eligible corners, less directly under the fire of the clergyman's eye, there are pews reserved for the Shepperton gentility. Ample galleries are supported on iron pillars, and in one of them stands the crowning glory, the very clasp or aigrette of Shepperton church-adornment—namely, an organ, not very much out of repair, on which a collector of small rents, differentiated by the force of circumstances into an organist, will accompany the alacrity of your departure after the blessing, by a sacred minuet or an easy 'Gloria'." SF 1

—then: " . . . Shepperton Church as it was in the old days, with its outer coat of rough stucco, its red-tiled roof, its heterogeneous windows patched with desultory bits of painted glass, and its little flight of steps with their wooden rail running up the outer wall, and leading to the schoolchildren's gallery . . . .

"No benches in those days, but huge roomy pews, round which devout church-goers sat during 'lessons', trying to look anywhere else than into each other's eyes. No low partitions allowing you, with a dreary absence of contrast and mystery, to see everything at all moments, but tall dark panels, under whose shadow I sank with a sense of retirement through the Litany, only to feel with more intensity my burst into the conspicuousness of public life when I was made to stand up on the seat during the psalms or the singing." SF 1

Compassion, Consolation, Sympathy

—in bereavement: "And so there was earnest prayer—there was faith, love, and hope pouring itself forth that evening in the little kitchen. And poor aged fretful Lisbeth, without grasping any distinct idea, without going through any course of religious emotions, felt a vague sense of goodness and love, and of something right lying underneath and beyond all this sorrowing life." AB 10

—and calculation: " . . . nature never makes men who are at once energetically sympathetic and minutely calculating." FH 33

—after death: "But we have all a chance of meeting with some pity, some tenderness, some charity, when we are dead: it is the living only who cannot be forgiven—the living only from whom men's indulgence and reverence are held off, like the rain by the hard east wind." LV 1

—at death: "Then your charitable speeches may find vent; then you may remember and pity the toil and the struggle and the failure; then you may give due honour to the work achieved; then you may find extenuation for errors, and may consent to bury them." LV 1

—enlivening: "So pregnant is the divine hope of moral recovery with the energy that

fulfils it. So potent in us is the infused action of another soul, before which we bow in complete love." DD 65

—*personal need:* "Examining the world in order to find consolation is very much like looking carefully over the pages of a great book in order to find our own name, if not in the text, at least in a laudatory note: whether we find what we want or not, our preoccupation has hindered us from a true knowledge of the contents." TS 1

—*rejected:* "Caterina, like the rest of us, turned away from sympathy which she suspected to be mingled with criticism, as the child turns away from the sweetmeat in which it suspects imperceptible medicine." GL 2

—*rescue:* "The creature we help to save, though only a half-reared linnet, bruised and lost by the wayside—how we watch and fence it, and dote on its signs of recovery! Our pride becomes loving, our self is a not-self for whose sake we become virtuous, when we set to some hidden work of reclaiming a life from misery and look for our triumph in the secret joy—'This one is the better for me.' " DD 32

—*sympathy:* "He had never been in the presence of a sorrow and a self-despair that had sent so strong a thrill through all the recesses of his saddest experience; and it is because sympathy is but a living again through our own past in a new form, that confession often prompts a response of confession." JR 18

" . . . the one poor word which includes all our best insight and our best love." AB 50

—*virtue and relevance:* "But, for certain other elements of virtue, which are of more obvious importance to plain people—a delicate sense of our neighbor's rights, an active participation in the joys and sorrows of our fellowmen, a magnanimous acceptance of privation or suffering for ourselves when it is the condition of rescue for others—in a word, the widening and strengthening of our sympathetic nature—it is surely of some moment to contend, that they have no more direct dependence on the belief in a future state than the interchange of gases in the lungs on the plurality of worlds." PY 37

Confession

—*enabled:* "The impulse to confession almost always requires the presence of a fresh ear and a fresh heart; and in our moments of spiritual need, the man to whom we have no tie but our common nature, seems nearer to us than mother, brother, or friend. Our daily familiar life is but a hiding of ourselves from each other behind a screen of trivial words and deeds, and those who sit with us at the same hearth are often the furthest off from the deep human soul within us, full of unspoken evil and unacted good." JR 16

Conscience

—*compensation:* " 'One who has committed irremediable errors may be scourged by that consciousness into a higher course than is common. There are many examples. Feeling what it is to have spoiled one life may well make us long to save other lives from being spoiled.' " DD 36

—*individual:* "Our consciences are not all of the same pattern, an inner deliverance of fixed laws: they are the voice of sensibilities as various as our memories (which also have their kinship and likeness)." DD 41

—*the morning after:* "In bed our yesterdays are too oppressive: if a man can only get up, though it be but to whistle or to smoke, he has a present which offers some resistance to the past—sensations which assert themselves against tyrannous memories. And if there were such a thing as taking averages of feeling, it would certainly be found that in the hunting and shooting seasons regret, self-reproach, and mortified pride, weigh lighter on country gentlemen than in late spring and summer." AB 29

—*pervasive:* "Were uneasiness of conscience measured by extent of crime, human history had been different, and one should look to see the contrivers of greedy wars and the mighty marauders of the money-market in one troop of self-lacerating penitents with the meaner robber and cut-purse and the murderer that doth his butchery in small with his own hand. No doubt wickedness hath its rewards to distribute; but whoso wins in this devil's game must needs be baser, more cruel, more brutal than the order of this planet will allow for the multitude born of woman, the most of these carrying a form of conscience—a fear which is the shadow of justice, a pity which is the shadow of love—that hindereth from the prize of serene wickedness, itself difficult of maintenance in our composite flesh." DD 35 ep

—*retribution:* "Nemesis can seldom forge a sword for herself out of our consciences—out of the suffering we feel in the suffering we may have caused: there is rarely metal enough there to make an effective weapon. Our moral sense learns the manners of good society, and smiles when others smile; but when some rude person gives rough names to our actions, she is apt to take part against us." AB 29

Courage and Fortitude

—*adversity:* "The strongest heart will faint sometimes under the feeling that enemies are bitter, and that friends only know half its sorrows. The most resolute soul will now and then cast back a yearning look in treading the rough mountain path, away from the greensward and laughing voices of the valley." JR 8

—denial: "Stephen thought again that he was beginning to prevail—he had never yet believed that he should not prevail: there are possibilities which our minds shrink from too completely for us to fear them." MF VI 14

—dirty politics: "It requires a conviction and resolution amounting to heroism not to wince at phrases that class our foreshadowed endurance among those common and ignominious troubles which the world is more likely to sneer at than to pity." FH 17

—fearlessness: "We are not apt to fear for the fearless, when we are companions in their danger . . . . " MF VII 5

And see FM:The Sexes—*bravery*

Cruelty

—in life: "While the heart beats, bruise it—it is your only opportunity; while the eye can still turn towards you with moist timid entreaty, freeze it with an icy unanswering gaze; while the ear, that delicate messenger to the inmost sanctuary of the soul, can still take in the tones of kindness, put it off with hard civility, or sneering compliment, or envious affectation of indifference; while the creative brain can still throb with the sense of injustice, with the yearning for brotherly recognition—make haste—oppress it with your ill-considered judgments, your trivial comparisons, your careless misrepresentations." LV 1

—in marriage: "Cruelty, like every other vice, requires no motive outside itself—it only requires opportunity . . . . And an unloving, tyrannous, brutal man needs no motive to prompt his cruelty; he needs only the perpetual presence of a woman he can call his own. A whole park full of tame or timid-eyed animals to torment at his will would not serve him so well to glut his lust of torture; they could not *feel* as one woman does; they could not throw out the keen retort which whets the edge of hatred." JR 13

—transmitted: "For the wrong that rouses our angry passions finds only a medium in us; it passes through us like a vibration, and we inflict what we have suffered." JR 13

Duty

—the call:

CHAPTER XL

An Arresting Voice

"When Romola sat down on the stone under the cypress, all things conspired to give her the sense of freedom and solitude: her escape from the accustomed walls and streets; the widening distance from her husband, who was by this time riding towards Siena, while every hour would take her farther on the opposite way; the morning stillness, the great dip of ground on the roadside making a gulf between her and the sombre calm of the mountains. For the first time in her life she felt alone in the presence of the earth and sky, with no human presence interposing and making a law for her.

"Suddenly a voice close to her said—

" 'You are Romola de' Bardi, the wife of Tito Melema.'

"She knew the voice: it had vibrated through her more than once before; and because she knew it, she did not turn round or look up. She sat shaken by awe, and yet inwardly rebelling against the awe. It was one of those black-skirted monks who was daring to speak to her, and interfere with her privacy: that was all. And yet she was shaken, as if that destiny which men thought of as a sceptred deity had come to her, and grasped her with fingers of flesh.

" 'You are fleeing from Florence in disguise. I have a command from God to stop you. You are not permitted to flee.'

"Romola's anger at the intrusion mounted higher at these imperative words. She would not turn round to look at the speaker, whose examining gaze she resented. Sitting quite motionless, she said—

" 'What right have you to speak to me, or to hinder me?'

" 'The right of a messenger You have put on a religious garb, and you have no religious purpose. You have sought the garb as a disguise. But you were not suffered to pass me without being discerned. It was declared to me who you were: it is declared to me that you are seeking to escape from the lot God has laid upon you. You wish your true name and your true place in life to be hidden, that you may choose for yourself a new name and a new place, and have no rule but your own will. And I have a command to call you back. My daughter, you must return to your place.'

"Romola's mind rose in stronger rebellion with every sentence. She was the more determined not to show any sign of submission, because the consciousness of being inwardly shaken made her dread lest she should fall into irresolution. She spoke with more irritation than before.

" 'I will not return. I acknowledge no right of priests and monks to interfere with my actions. You have no power over me.'

" 'I know—I know you have been brought up in scorn of obedience. But it is not the poor monk who claims to interfere with you: it is the truth that commands you. And you cannot escape it. Either you must obey it, and it will lead you; or you must disobey it, and it will hang on you with the weight of a chain which you will drag for ever. But you will obey it, my daughter. Your old servant will return to you with the mules; my companion is gone to fetch him; and you will go back to Florence.'

"She started up with anger in her eyes, and faced the speaker. It was Fra Girolamo: she knew that well enough before. She was nearly as tall as he was, and their faces were almost on a level. She had started up with defiant words ready to burst from her lips, but they fell back again without utterance. She had met Fra Girolamo's calm glance, and the impression from it was so new to her, that her anger sank ashamed as something irrelevant.

"There was nothing transcendent in Savonarola's face. It was not beautiful. It was strong-featured, and owed all its refinement to habits of mind and rigid discipline of the body. The source of the impression his glance produced on Romola was the sense it conveyed to her of interest in her and care for her apart from any personal feeling. It was the first time she had encountered a gaze in which simple human fellowship expressed itself as a strongly-felt bond. Such a glance is half the vocation of the priest or spiritual guide of men, and Romola felt it impossible again to question his authority to speak to her. She stood silent, looking at him. And he spoke again.

" 'You assert your freedom proudly, my daughter. But who is so base as the debtor that thinks himself free?'

"There was a sting in those words, and Romola's countenance changed as if a subtle pale flash had gone over it.

" 'And you are flying from your debts: the debt of a Florentine woman; the debt of a wife. You are turning your back on the lot that has been appointed for you—you are going to choose another. But can man or woman choose duties? No more than they can choose their birthplace or their father and mother. My daughter, you are fleeing from the presence of God into the wilderness.'

"As the anger melted from Romola's mind, it had given place to a new presentiment of the strength there might be in submission, if this man, at whom she was beginning to look with a vague reverence, had some valid law to show her. But no—it was impossible; he could not know what determined her. Yet she could not again simply refuse to be guided; she was constrained to plead; and in her new need to be reverent while she resisted, the title which she had never given him before came to her lips without forethought.

" 'My father, you cannot know the reasons which compel me to go. None can know them but myself. None can judge for me. I have been driven by great sorrow. I am resolved to go.'

" 'I know enough, my daughter: my mind has been so far illumined concerning you, that I know enough. You are not happy in your married life; but I am not a confessor, and I seek to know nothing that should be reserved for the seal of confession. I have a divine warrant to stop you, which does not depend on such knowledge. You were warned by a message from heaven, delivered in my presence—you were warned before marriage, when you might still have lawfully chosen to be free from the marriage-bond. But you chose the bond; and in wilfully breaking it—I speak to you as a pagan, if the holy mystery of matrimony is not sacred to you—you are breaking a pledge. Of what wrongs will you complain, my daughter, when you yourself are committing one of the greatest wrongs a woman and a citizen can be guilty of—withdrawing in secrecy and disguise from a pledge which you have given in the face of God and your fellow-men? Of what wrongs will you complain, when you yourself are breaking the simplest law that lies at the foundation of the trust which binds man to man—faithfulness to the spoken word? This, then, is the wisdom you have gained by scorning the mysteries of the Church?—not to see the bare duty of integrity, where the Church would have taught you to see, not integrity only, but religion.'

"The blood had rushed to Romola's face, and she shrank as if she had been stricken. 'I would not have put on a disguise,' she began, but she could not go on—she was too much shaken by the suggestion in the Friar's words of a possible affinity between her own conduct and Tito's.

" 'And to break that pledge you fly from Florence: Florence, where there are the only men and women in the world to whom you owe the debt of a fellow-citizen.'

" 'I should never have quitted Florence,' said Romola, tremulously, 'as long as there was any hope of my fulfilling a duty to my father there.'

" 'And do you own no tie but that of a child to her father in the flesh? Your life has been spent in blindness, my daughter. You have lived with those who sit on a hill aloof, and look down on the life of their fellow-men. I know their vain discourse. It is of what has been in the times which they fill with their own fancied wisdom, while they scorn God's work in the present. And doubtless you were taught how there were pagan women who felt what it was to live for the Republic; yet you have never felt that you, a Florentine woman, should live for Florence. If your own people are wearing a yoke, will you slip from under it, instead of struggling with them to lighten it? There is hunger and misery in our streets, yet you say, "I care not; I have my own sorrows; I will go away, if peradventure I can ease them." The servants of God are struggling after a law of justice, peace and charity, that the hundred thousand citizens among whom you were born may be governed righteously; but you think no more of this than if you were a bird, that may spread its wings and fly whither it will in search of food to its liking. And yet you have scorned the teaching of the Church, my daughter. As if you, a wilful wanderer, following your own blind choice, were not below the humblest Florentine woman who stretches forth her hands with her own people, and craves a blessing for them; and feels a close sisterhood with the neighbour who kneels beside her and is not of her own blood; and thinks of the mighty purpose that God has for Florence; and waits and endures because the promised work is great, and she feels herself little.'

" 'I was not going away to ease and self-indulgence,' said Romola, raising her head again, with a prompting to vindicate herself. 'I was going away to hardship. I expect no joy: it is gone from my life.'

" 'You are seeking your own will, my daughter. You are seeking some good other than the law you are bound to obey. But how will you find good? It is not a thing of choice: it is a river that flows from the foot of the Invisible Throne, and flows by the path of obedience. I say again, man cannot choose his duties. You may choose to forsake your duties, and choose not have the sorrow they bring. But you will go forth; and what will you find, my daughter? Sorrow without duty—bitter herbs, and no bread with them.'

" 'But if you know,' said Romola, clasping her hands and pressing them tight, as she looked pleadingly at Fra Girolamo; 'if you know what it was to me—how impossible it seemed to me to bear it.'

" 'My daughter,' he said, pointing to the cord round Romola's neck, 'you carry something within your mantle; draw it forth, and look at it.'

"Romola gave a slight start, but her impulse now was to do just what Savonarola told her. Her self-doubt was grappled by a stronger will and a stronger conviction than her own. She drew forth the crucifix. Still pointing towards it, he said—

" 'There, my daughter, is the image of a Supreme Offering, made by Supreme Love, because the need of man was great.'

"He paused, and she held the crucifix trembling—trembling under a sudden impression of the wide distance between her present and her past self. What a length of road she had travelled through since she first took that crucifix from the Frate's hands! Had life as many secrets before her still as it had for her then, in her young blindness? It was a thought that helped all other subduing influences; and at the sound of Fra Girolamo's voice again, Romola, with a quick involuntary movement, pressed the crucifix against her mantle and looked at him with more submission than before.

" 'Conform your life to that image, my daughter; make your sorrow an offering: and when the fire of Divine charity burns within you, and you behold the need of your fellow-men by the light of that flame, you will not call your offering great. You have carried yourself proudly, as one who held herself not of common blood or of common thoughts; but you have been as one unborn to the true life of man. What! you say your love for your father no longer tells you to stay in Florence? Then, since that tie is snapped, you are without a law, without religion: you are no better than a beast of the field when she is robbed of her young. If the yearning of a fleshly love is gone, you are without love, without obligation.

" 'See, then, my daughter, how you are below the life of the believer who worships that image of the Supreme Offering, and feels the glow of a common life with the lost multitude for whom that offering was made, and beholds the history of the world as the history of a great redemption in which he is himself a fellow-worker, in his own place and among his own people! If you held that faith, my beloved daughter, you would not be a wanderer flying from suffering, and blindly seeking the good of a freedom which is lawlessness. You would feel that Florence was the home of your soul as well as your birthplace, because you would see the work that was given you to do there. If you forsake your place, who will fill it? You ought to be in your place now, helping in the great work by which God will purify Florence, and raise it to be the guide of the nations. What! the earth is full of iniquity—full of groans—the light is still struggling with a mighty darkness, and you say, "I cannot bear my bonds; I will burst them asunder; I will go where no man claims me"? My daughter, every bond of your life is a debt: the right lies in the payment of that debt; it can lie nowhere else. In vain will you wander over the earth; you will be wandering forever away from the right.'

"Romola was inwardly struggling with strong forces: that immense personal influence of Savonarola, which came from the energy of his emotions and beliefs; and her consciousness, surmounting all prejudice, that his words implied a higher law than any she had yet obeyed. But the resisting thoughts were not yet overborne.

" 'How, then, could Dino be right? He broke ties. He forsook his place.'

" 'That was a special vocation. He was constrained to depart, else he could not have attained the higher life. It would have been stifled within him.'

" 'And I too,' said Romola, raising her hands to her brow; and speaking in a tone of anguish, as if she were being dragged to some torture. 'Father, you may be wrong.'

" 'Ask your conscience, my daughter. You have no vocation such as your brother had. You are a wife. You seek to break your ties in self-will and anger, not because the higher life calls upon you to renounce them. The higher life begins for us, my daughter, when we renounce our own will to bow before a Divine law. That seems hard to you. It is the portal of wisdom, and freedom, and blessedness. And the symbol of it hangs before you. That wisdom is the religion of the Cross. And you stand aloof from it: you are a pagan; you have been taught to say, "I am as the wise men who lived before the time when the Jew of Nazareth was crucified." And that is your wisdom! To be as the dead whose eyes are closed, and whose ear is deaf to the work of God that has been since their time.

" 'What has your dead wisdom done for you, my daughter? It has left you without a heart for the neighbours among whom you dwell, without care for the great work by which Florence is to be regenerated and the world made holy; it has left you without a share in the Divine life which quenches the sense of suffering Self in the ardours of an ever-growing love. And now, when the sword has pierced your soul, you say, "I will go away; I cannot bear my sorrow." And you think nothing of the sorrow and the wrong that are within the walls of the city where you dwell: you would leave your place empty, when it ought to be filled with your pity and your labour. If there is wickedness in the streets, your steps should shine with the light of purity; if there is a cry of anguish, you, my daughter, because you know the meaning of the cry, should be there to still it. My beloved daughter, sorrow has come to teach you a new worship: the sign of it hangs before you.'

"Romola's mind was still torn by conflict. She foresaw that she should obey Savonarola and go back: his words had come to her as if they were an interpretation of that revulsion from self-satisfied ease, and of that new fellowship with suffering, which had already been awakened in her. His arresting voice had brought a new condition into her life, which made it seem impossible to her that she could go on her way as if she had not heard it; yet she shrank as one who sees the path she must take, but sees, too, that the hot lava lies there. And the instinctive shrinking from a return to her husband brought doubts. She turned away her eyes from Fra Girolamo, and stood for a minute or two with her hands hanging clasped before her, like a statue. At last she spoke, as if the words were being wrung from her, still looking on the ground.

" 'My husband . . . he is not . . . my love is gone!'

" 'My daughter, there is the bond of a higher love. Marriage is not carnal only, made for selfish delight. See what that thought leads you to! It leads you to wander away in a false garb from all the obligations of your place and name. That would not have been, if you had learned that it is a sacramental vow, from which none but God can release you. My daughter, your life is not as a grain of sand, to be blown by the winds; it is a thing of flesh and blood, that dies if it be sundered. Your husband is not a malefactor?'

"Romola started. 'Heaven forbid! No; I accuse him of nothing.'

" 'I did not suppose he was a malefactor. I meant, that if he were a malefactor, your place would be in the prison beside him. My daughter, if the cross comes to you as a wife, you must carry it as a wife. You may say, "I will forsake my husband," but you cannot cease to be a wife.'

" 'Yet if—oh, how could I bear——' Romola had involuntarily begun to say something which she sought to banish from her mind again.

" 'Make your marriage-sorrows an offering too, my daughter: an offering to the great work by which sin and sorrow are being made to cease. The end is sure, and is already beginning. Here in Florence it is beginning, and the eyes of faith behold it. And it may be our blessedness to die for it: to die daily by the crucifixion of our selfish will—to die at last by laying our bodies on the altar. My daughter, you are a child of Florence; fulfil the duties of that great inheritance. Live for Florence—for your own people, whom God is preparing to bless the earth. Bear the anguish and the smart. The iron is sharp—I know, I know—it rends the tender flesh. The draught is bitterness on the lips. But there is rapture in the cup—there is the vision which makes all life below it dross for ever. Come, my daughter, come back to your place.'

"While Savonarola spoke with growing intensity, his arms tightly folded before him still, as they had been from the first, but his face alight as from an inward flame, Romola felt herself surrounded and possessed by the glow of his passionate faith. The chill doubts all melted away; she was subdued by the sense of something unspeakably great to which she was being called by a strong being who roused a new strength within herself. In a voice that was like a law, prayerful cry, she said—

" 'Father, I will be guided. Teach me! I will go back.'

"Almost unconsciously she sank on her knees. Savonarola stretched out his hands over her; but feeling would no longer pass through the channel of speech, and he was silent." ¶R 40

Editor's note: we believe George Eliot chose to write Romola *so she could write this scene. She chose Savonarola as the figure through whom she would express her deepest spiritual—not necessarily religious—insights and her ideas of how her own life could most fruitfully and usefully be spent. The resultant enormous expenditure of mental and emotional effort made possible what we consider to be the greatest achievement of her life.*

—and love: "Why should she care about wearing one badge more than another, or about being called by her own name? She despaired of finding any consistent duty belonging to that name. What force was there to create for her that supremely hallowed motive which men call duty, but which can have no inward constraining existence save through some form of believing love?" R 61

—and passion: "The great problem of the shifting relation between passion and duty is clear to no man who is capable of apprehending it: the question, whether the moment has come in which a man has fallen below the possibility of a renunciation that will carry any efficacy, and must accept the sway of a passion against which he had struggled as a trespass, is one for which we have no master key that will fit all cases." MF VII 2 *See* FM:Censure—*judging.*

—routine: "What duty is made of a single difficult resolve? The difficulty lies in the daily unflinching support of consequences that mar the blessed return of morning with the prospect of irritation to be suppressed or shame to be endured. And such consequences were being borne by these, as by many other, heroic children of an unworthy father . . . . " DD 67

—sense awakened: "Our sense of duty must often wait for some work which shall take the place of dilettantism and make us feel that the quality of our action is not a matter of indifference." MM 46

—unpredictable: "But Duty has a trick of behaving unexpectedly—something like a heavy friend whom we have amiably asked to visit us, and who breaks his leg within our gates." MM 52

Egoism and Egotism

—absence unnoticed: "A man may, from various motives, decline to give his company, but perhaps not even a sage would be gratified that nobody missed him." MM 31

—amiability: "He had never been insulted on his own land before, and had been inclined to regard himself as a general favourite (we are all apt to do so, when we think of our own amiability more than of what other people are likely to want of us)." MM 39

—another's reverse: "Who has been quite free from egoistic escapes of the imagination picturing desirable consequences on his own future in the presence of another's misfortune, sorrow, or death? The expected promotion or legacy is the common type of a temp-

tation which makes speech and even prayer a severe avoidance of the most insistent thoughts, and sometimes raises an inward shame, a self-distaste, that is worse than any other form of unpleasant companionship" DD 58

—another's vow: " . . . people are apt to think that resolutions taken on their own behalf will be firm." R 18

—aroused: "It only proves that his arrogant egoism, set on fire, sends up smoke and flame where just before there had been the dews of fellowship and pity." TS 8

—awareness: "But on the point of knowing when we are disagreeable, our human nature is fallible. Our lavender-water, our smiles, our compliments, and other polite falsities, are constantly offensive, when in the very nature of them they can only be meant to attract admiration and regard." FH 29

—bad temper: "As people confess to bad memory without expecting to sink in mental reputation, so we hear a man declared to have a bad temper and yet glorified as the possessor of every high quality. When he errs or in any way commits himself, his temper is accused, not his character, and it is understood that but for a brutal bearish mood he is kindness itself. If he kicks small animals, swears violently at a servant who mistakes orders, or is grossly rude to his wife, it is remarked apologetically that these things mean nothing—they are all temper.

"Certainly there is a limit to this form of apology, and the forgery of a bill, or the ordering of goods without any prospect of paying for them, has never been set down to an unfortunate habit of sulkiness or of irascibility." TS 6

—'good fellow': "Let it be admitted, however, that a man may be 'a good fellow' and yet have a bad temper, so bad that we recognise his merits with reluctance, and are inclined to resent his occasionally amiable behaviour as an unfair demand on our admiration." TS 6

—social negative: "A man who uses his balmorals to tread on your toes with much frequency and an unmistakeable emphasis may prove a fast friend in adversity, but meanwhile your adversity has not arrived and your toes are tender. The daily sneer or growl at your remarks is not to be made amends for by a possible eulogy or defence of your understanding against depreciators who may not present themselves, and on an occasion which may never arise. I cannot submit to a chronic state of blue and green bruise as a form of insurance against an accident." TS 6

—benign: "An insane exaggeration of his own value . . . many would have counted this yearning, taking it as the sublimer part for a man to say, 'if not I, then another,' and to hold cheap the meaning of his own life. But the fuller nature desires to be an agent, to create, and not merely to look on: strong love hungers to bless, and not merely to behold blessing. And while there is warmth enough in the sun to feed an energetic life, there will still be men to feel, 'I am lord of this moment's change, and will charge it with my soul.' " DD 38

—at birth: "We are all of us born in moral stupidity, taking the world as an udder to feed our supreme selves." MM 21

—burned away: "It is in the nature of all human passion, the lowest as well as the highest, that there is a point where it ceases to be properly egoistic, and is like a fire kindled within our being to which everything else in us is mere fuel." R 30

—clumsy: " . . . the constant experience that temper and selfish insensibility will defeat excellent gifts—will make a sensible person shout when shouting is out of place, and will make a polished man rude when his polish might be of eminent use to him." FH 42

—confidence: "The most obstinate beliefs that mortals entertain about themselves are such as they have no evidence for beyond a constant, spontaneous pulsing of their self-satisfaction—as it were a hidden seed of madness, a confidence that they can move the world without precise notion of standing-place or lever." DD 23 ep

—consolations: "The consolations of egoism are simply a change of attitude or a resort to a new kind of diet which soothes and fattens it. Fed in this way it is apt to become a monstrous spiritual pride, or a chuckling satisfaction that the final balance will not be against us but against those who now eclipse us." TS 1

—discontent: "In my conscience I saw that the bias of personal discontent was just as misleading and odious as the bias of self-satisfaction. Whether we look through the rose-coloured glass or the indigo, we are equally far from the hues which the healthy human eye beholds in heaven above and earth below." TS 1

—domestic tyrant: "I remember having seen the same assiduous, apologetic attention awarded to persons who were not at all beautiful or unusual, whose firmness showed itself in no very graceful or euphonious way, and who were not eldest daughters with a tender, timid mother, compunctious at having to subject them to inconveniences. Some of them were a very common sort of men. And the only point of resemblance among them all was a strong determination

to have what was pleasant, with a total fearlessness in making themselves disagreeable or dangerous when they did not get it. Who is so much cajoled and served with trembling by the weak females of a household as the unscrupulous male—capable, if he has not free way a home, of going and doing worse elsewhere?" DD 4

—evil and good: "I dropped a form of consolation which seemed to be encouraging me in the persuasion that my discontent was the chief evil in the world, and my benefit the soul of good in that evil. May there not be at least a partial release from the imprisoning verdict that a man's philosophy is the formula of his personality?" TS 1

—giving comfort: "I suppose one reason why we are seldom able to comfort out neighbours with our words is that our goodwill gets adulterated, in spite of ourselves, before it can pass our lips. We can send black puddings and pettitoes without giving them a flavour of our own egoism, but language is a stream that is almost sure to smack of a mingled soil." SM 10

—guardian's new wife: " . . . he would find Lady Mallinger a new friend whom he would be sure to love—and much more to the usual effect when a man, having done something agreeable to himself, is disposed to congratulate others on his own good fortune, and the deducible satisfactoriness of events in general." DD 16

—having struck: "When the stricken person is slow to recover and look as if nothing had happened, the striker easily glides into the position of the aggrieved party; he feels no bruise himself, and is strongly conscious of his own amiable behaviour since he inflicted the blow." R 35

—hurt: "What man of us, in the first moments of a sharp agony, could ever feel that the fellow-man who has been the medium of inflicting it, did not mean to hurt us? In our instinctive rebellion against pain, we are children again, and demand an active will to wreak our vengeance on." AB 27

—and ideology: " . . . the egoism which enters into our theories does not affect their sincerity; rather, the more our egoism is satisfied, the more robust is our belief." MM 53

—of the imagination: " . . . we are all apt to fall into this passionate egoism of imagination, not only towards our fellow-men but towards God." DD 69

—literary: "Some gentlemen have made an amazing figure in literature by general discontent with the universe as a trap of dulness into which their great souls have fallen by mistake; but the sense of a stupendous self and an insignificant world may have its consolations." MM 64

—martyrdom: "That is the path we all like when we set out on our abandonment of egoism—the path of martyrdom and endurance, where the palm-branches grow, rather than the steep highway of tolerance, just allowance, and self-blame, where there are no leafy honours to be gathered and worn." MF IV 3

—moral: "The notion that duty looks stern, but all the while has her hand full of sugar-plums, with which she will reward us by-and-by, is the favourite cant of optimists, who try to make out that this tangled wilderness of life has a plan as easy to trace as that of a Dutch garden; but it really undermines all true moral development by perpetually substituting something extrinsic as a motive to action, instead of the immediate impulse of love or justice, which alone makes an action truly moral." BL 1 295

—needy: "She identified him with the struggling regenerative process in her which had begun with his action. Is it any wonder that she saw her own necessity reflected in his feeling? She was in that state of unconscious reliance and expectation which is a common experience with us when we are preoccupied with our own trouble or our own purposes. We diffuse our feeling over others, and count on their acting from our motives." DD 65

—negativity: "We often enough mistake our own negations for a negation out of ourselves, as purblind people are apt to think the sun gives but a feeble light."" LW

—oblivious: "We sing an exquisite passage out of tune and innocently repeat it for the greater pleasure of our hearers. Who can be aware of what his foreign accent is in the ears of a native? And how can a man be conscious of that dull perception which causes him to mistake altogether what will make him agreeable to a particular woman, and to persevere eagerly in a behaviour which she is privately recording against him?" TS 1

—obtuseness: "It was his characteristic bias to shrink from the moral stupidity of valuing lightly what had come close to him, and of missing blindly in his own life of to-day the crises which he recognised as momentous and sacred in the historic life of men." DD 41

—others' envy: "An imaginary envy, the idea that others feel their comparative deficiency, is the ordinary *cortège* of egoism . . . . " DD 25

—pathos: "He was at present too ill acquainted with disaster to enter into the pathos of a lot where everything is below the

level of tragedy except the passionate egoism of the sufferer." MM 42

—perspective: "If a squint or other ocular defect disturbs my vision, I can get instructed in the fact, be made aware that my condition is abnormal, and either through spectacles or diligent imagination I can learn the average appearance of things: is there no remedy or corrective for that inward squint which consists in a dissatisfied egoism or other want of mental balance?" TS 1

—pier-glass metaphor: "An eminent philosopher among my friends, who can dignify even your ugly furniture by lifting it into the serene light of science, has shown me this pregnant little fact. Your pier-glass or extensive surface of polished steel made to be rubbed by a housemaid, will be minutely and multitudinously scratched in all directions; but place now against it a lighted candle as a centre of illumination, and lo! the scratches will seem to arrange themselves in a fine series of concentric circles round that little sun. It is demonstrable that the scratches are going everywhere impartially, and it is only your candle which produces the flattering illusion of a concentric arrangement, its light falling with an exclusive optical selection. These things are a parable. The scratches are events, and the candle is the egoism of any person now absent—of Miss Vincy for example." MM 27

—point of view: " . . . to shift one's point of view beyond certain limits is impossible to the most liberal and expansive mind: we are none of us aware of the impression we produce on Brazilian monkeys of feeble understanding—it is possible they see hardly anything in us." AB 18

"So many things were more distinctly visible to him, and touched him more acutely, than the effect of his acts or words on Mrs Transome's feelings! In fact—he asked, with a touch of something that makes us all akin—was it not preposterous, this excess of feeling on points which he himself did not find powerfully moving?" FH 42

"The standing-ground worth striving after seemed to be some Delectable Mountain, whence I could see things in proportions as little as possible determined by that self-partiality which certainly plays a necessary part in our bodily sustenance, but has a starving effect on the mind." TS 1

—prejudged: "To persons possessing a great deal of that facile psychology which prejudges individuals by means of formulae, and casts them, without further trouble, into duly lettered pigeon-holes, the Evangelical curate might seem to be doing simply what all other men like to do—carrying out objects which were identified not only with his theory, which is but a kind of secondary egoism, but also with the primary egoism of his feelings. Opposition may become sweet to a man when he has christened it persecution: a self-obtrusive, over-hasty reformer complacently disclaiming all merit, while his friends call him a martyr, has not in reality a career the most arduous to the fleshly mind." JR 8

—renunciation: "It is not the fact that what duty calls on us to renounce, will invariably prove 'not worth the keeping;' and if it were the fact, renunciation would cease to be moral heroism, and would be simply a calculation of prudence . . . it is this very perception that the thing we renounce is precious, is something never to be compensated to us, which constitutes the beauty and heroism of renunciation." BL 1 295

—retrospect: "We try to believe that the egoism within us would have easily been melted, and that it was only the narrowness of our knowledge which hemmed in our generosity, our awe, our human piety, and hindered them from submerging our hard indifference to the sensations and emotions of our fellow. Our tenderness and self-renunciation seem strong when our egoism has had its day—when after our mean striving for a triumph that is to be another's loss, the triumph comes suddenly, and we shudder at it, because it is held out by the chill hand of death." LV 1

—self in the way: "Will not a tiny speck very close to our vision blot out the glory of the world, and leave only a margin by which we see the blot? I know no speck so troublesome as self." MM 42

—self-love: "It is possible to have a strong self-love without any self-satisfaction, rather with a self-discontent which is the more intense because one's own little core of egoistic sensibility is a supreme care . . . . " DD 2

—wisdom: "They must be rather old and wise persons who are not apt to see their own anxiety or elation about themselves reflected in other minds . . . . " DD 44

And see Self and Selfishness

Emotions

"Our good depends on the quality and breadth of our emotion . . . . " MM 47

—agony revealed: see FL:Life—*artificial*

—amiability: "But milk and mildness are not the best things for keeping, and when they turn only a little sour they may disagree with young stomachs seriously." MF I 2

—anomie: " . . . our moments of temptation to a mean opinion of things in general being usually dependent on some susceptibility about ourselves and some dulness to subjects which every one else would consider more important." DD 24

—*bad temper:* "A man out of temper does not wait for proofs before feeling towards all things animate and inanimate as if they were in a conspiracy against him, but at once thrashes his horse or kicks his dog in consequence." DD 54

—*breaking out:* "There are moments when by some strange impulse we contradict our past selves—fatal moments, when a fit of passion, like a lava stream, lays low the work of half our lives." JR 14

—*changing a life direction:* "The strong emotions from which the life of a human being receives a new bias, win their victory as the sea wins his: though their advance may be sure, they will often, after a mightier wave than usual, seem to roll back so far as to lose all the ground they had made." JR 25

—*disappointment:* "Some discouragement, some faintness of heart at the new real future which replaces the imaginary, is not unusual, and we do not expect people to be deeply moved by what is not unusual." MM 20

—*encouragement:* " . . . it is a little trying to human flesh to be conscious of expressing one's self better than others and never to have it noticed, and in the general dearth of admiration for the right thing, even a chance bray of applause falling exactly in time is rather fortifying." MM 46

—*excitement:* "The excitement had not passed away: it had only reached that stage when the keenness of the susceptibility makes external stimulus intolerable—when there is no sense of weariness, but rather an intensity of inward life, under which sleep is an impossibility. Any one who has watched such moments in other men remembers the brightness of the eyes and the strange definiteness that comes over coarse features from that transient influence. It is as if a new fineness of ear for all spiritual voices had sent wonder-working vibrations through the heavy mortal frame—as if 'beauty born of murmuring sound' had passed into the face of the listener." SM 19

—*exultation:* "Obstacles, incongruities, all melted into the sense of completion with which his soul was flooded by this outward satisfaction of his longing. His exultation was not widely different from that of the experimenter, bending over the first stirrings of change that correspond to what in the fervour of concentrated prevision his thought has foreshadowed." DD 40

—*humiliation:* "We are all humiliated by the sudden discovery of a fact which has existed very comfortably and perhaps been staring at us in private while we have been making up our world entirely without it." MM 35

—*influenced by speech:* "It is so with emotional natures, whose thoughts are no more than the fleeting shadows cast by feeling: to them words are facts, and even when known to be false, have a mastery over their smiles and tears." GL 7

—*ill-temper:* "People who seem to enjoy their ill-temper have a way of keeping it in fine condition by inflicting privations on themselves." MF I 12

—*irrational:* "Doubtless a complacency resting on that basis [of statistics] is highly rational; but emotion, I fear, is obstinately irrational: it insists on caring for individuals; it absolutely refuses to adopt the quantitative view of human anguish, and to admit that thirteen happy lives are a set-off against twelve miserable lives, which leaves a clear balance on the side of satisfaction. This is the inherent imbecility of feeling, and one must be a great philosopher to have got quite clear of all that, and to have emerged into the serene air of pure intellect, in which it is evident that individuals really exist for no other purpose than that abstractions may be drawn from them—abstractions that may rise from heaps of ruined lives like the sweet savour of a sacrifice in the nostrils of philosophers, and of a philosophic Deity.

"And so it comes to pass that for the man who knows sympathy because he has known sorrow, that old, old saying about the joy of angels over the repentant sinner outweighing their joy over the ninety-nine just, has a meaning which does not jar with the language of his own heart. It only tells him, that for angels too there is a transcendent value in human pain, which refuses to be settled by equations; that the eyes of angels too are turned away from the serene happiness of the righteous to bend with yearning pity on the poor erring soul wandering in the desert where no water is; that for angels too the misery of one casts so tremendous a shadow as to eclipse the bliss of ninety-nine." ¶JR 22

—*moral:* " . . . in proportion as morality is emotional, it will exhibit itself in direct sympathetic feeling and action, and not as the recognition of a rule. Love does not say, 'I ought to love'—it loves. Pity does not say, 'It is right to be pitiful'—it pities. Justice does not say, 'I am bound to be just'—it feels justly. It is only where moral emotion is comparatively weak that the contemplation of a rule or theory habitually mingles with its action; and in accordance with this, we think experience, both in literature and life, has shown that the minds which are predominantly didactic, are deficient in sympathetic emotion." PY 40

—*passion missing:* "But a good deal of life goes on without strong passion: myriads of cravats are carefully tied, dinners attended, even speeches made proposing the health of august personages, without the zest arising from a strong desire. And a man may make a good appearance in high social positions—may be supposed to know the classics, to have his reserves on science, a strong though repressed opinion on politics, and all the sentiments of the English gentleman, at a small expense of vital energy.

"Also, he may be obstinate or persistent at the same low rate, and may even show sudden impulses which have a false air of daemonic strength because they seem inexplicable, though perhaps their secret lies merely in the want of regulated channels for the soul to move in—good and sufficient ducts of habit without which our nature easily turns to mere ooze and mud, and at any pressure yields nothing but a spurt or a puddle." ¶DD 15

—*remembering:* "The secret of our emotions never lies in the bare object, but in its subtle relations to our own past: no wonder the secret escapes the unsympathising observer, who might as well put on his spectacles to discern odours." AB 18

—*revulsion of feeling:* "The commonest things seemed to touch the spring of love within her, just as, when we are suddenly released from an acute absorbing bodily pain, our heart and senses leap out in new freedom; we think even the noise of streets harmonious, and are ready to hug the tradesman who is wrapping up our change." JR 21

—*surprise:* "On reflection I discovered that there was not the least ground for surprise, unless I had beforehand believed that nobody could be anybody's cousin without my knowing it. This sort of surprise, I take it, depends on a liveliness of the spine, with a more or less constant nullity of brain." DD 52

—*uncontrollable:* " . . . there are moments when our passions speak and decide for us, and we seem to stand by and wonder. They carry in them an inspiration of crime, that in once instant does the work of long premeditation." R 22

—*vexation:* "But the disappointments of life can never, any more than its pleasures, be estimated singly; and the healthiest and most agreeable of men is exposed to that coincidence of various vexations, each heightening the effect of the other, which may produce in him something corresponding to the spontaneous and externally unaccountable moodiness of the morbid and disagreeable." FH 34

—*violent:* "The exhaustion consequent on violent emotion is apt to bring a dreamy disbelief in the reality of its cause . . . . " R 36

—*in a voice:* "We do not argue the existence of the anger or the scorn that thrills through us in a voice; we simply feel it, and it admits of no disproof." DD 65

And see Happiness

Empathy

—*its danger:* "That element of tragedy which lies in the very fact of frequency, has not yet wrought itself into the coarse emotion of mankind; and perhaps our frames could hardly bear much of it. If we had a keen vision and feeling of all ordinary human life, it would be like hearing the grass grow and the squirrel's heart beat, and we should die of that roar which lies on the other side of silence. As it is, the quickest of us walk about well wadded with stupidity." MM 20

Enthusiasm

—*absent danger:* "But the fervour of sympathy with which we contemplate a grandiose martyrdom is feeble compared with the enthusiasm that keeps unslacked where there is no danger, no challenge—nothing but impartial midday falling on commonplace, perhaps half-repulsive, objects which are really the beloved ideas made flesh." DD 33

—*at ease:* "Enthusiasm, we know, dwells at ease among ideas, tolerates garlic breathed in the middle ages, and sees no shabbiness in the official trappings of classic processions: it gets squeamish when ideals press upon it as something warmly incarnate, and can hardly face them without fainting." DD 33

—*fact and folly:* "The kinship of human passion, the sameness of mortal scenery, inevitably fill fact with burlesque and paradox. Error and folly have had their hecatombs of martyrs. Reduce the grandest type of man hitherto known to an abstract statement of his qualities and efforts, and he appears in dangerous company: say that, like **Copernicus** and **Galileo**, he was immovably convinced in the face of hissing incredulity; but so is the contriver of perpetual motion. We cannot fairly try the spirits by this sort of test. If we want to avoid giving the dose of hemlock or the sentence of banishment in the wrong case, nothing will do but a capacity to understand the subject-matter on which the immovable man is convinced, and fellowship with human travail, both near and afar, to hinder us from scanning any deep experience lightly. Shall we say, 'Let the ages try the spirits, and see what they are worth?' Why, we are the beginning of the ages, which can only be just by virtue of just judgments in separate human breasts—separate yet combined. Even steam-engines could not have got made without that condition, but must have stayed in the mind of **James Watt**." DD 41

—fanaticism: "While Mordecai was waiting on the bridge for the fulfilment of his visions, another man was convinced that he had the mathematical key of the universe which would supersede **Newton**, and regarded all known physicists as conspiring to stifle his discovery and keep the universe locked; another, that he had the metaphysical key, with just that hair's-breadth of difference from the old wards which would make it fit exactly. Scattered here and there in every direction you might find a terrible person, with more or less power of speech, and with an eye either glittering or preternaturally dull, on the look-out for the man who must hear him, and in most cases he had volumes which it was difficult to get printed, or if printed to get read." DD 41

" 'I call a man fanatical when his enthusiasm is narrow and hoodwinked, so that he has no sense of proportions, and becomes unjust and unsympathetic to men who are out of his own track.' " DD 46

—and indifference: "For an enthusiastic spirit to meet continually the fixed indifference of men familiar with the object of his enthusiasm is the acceptance of a slow martyrdom, beside which the fate of a missionary tomahawked without any considerate rejection of his doctrines seems hardly worthy of compassion." DD 42

—isolated: " . . . he for the first time saw in a complete picture and felt as a reality the lives that burn themselves out in solitary enthusiasm: martyrs of obscure circumstance, exiled in the rarity of their own minds, whose deliverances in other ears are no more than a long passionate soliloquy—unless perhaps at last, when they are nearing the invisible shores, signs of recognition and fulfilment may penetrate the cloud of loneliness . . . . " DD 43

—passionate belief: " . . . perhaps his might be one of the natures where a wise estimate of consequences is fused in the fires of that passionate belief which determined the consequences it believes in. The inspirations of the world have come in that way too: even strictly-measuring science could hardly have got on without that forecasting ardour which feels the agitations of discovery beforehand, and has a faith in its preconception that surmounts many failures of experiment. And in relation to human motives and actions, passionate belief has a fuller efficacy. Here enthusiasm may have the validity of proof, and, happening in one soul, give the type of what will one day be general." DD 41

—resisted: "There is a sort of human paste that when it comes near the fire of enthusiasm is only baked into harder shape." DD 42

Evil

—good effect: " 'For the evil will of man makes not a people's good except by stirring the righteous will of man . . . . ' " DD 63

—in the heart: " 'Within ourselves our evil will is momentous, and sooner or later it works its way outside us—it may be in the vitiation that breeds evil acts, but also it may be in the self-abhorrence that stings us into better striving . . . .

" 'No evil dooms us hopelessly except the evil we love, and desire to continue in, and make no effort to escape from.' " DD 57

—restless: "Was she beautiful or not beautiful? and what was the secret of form or expression which gave the dynamic quality to her glance? Was the good or the evil dominant in those beams? Probably the evil; else why was the effect that of unrest rather than of undisturbed charm? Why was the wish to look again felt as coercion and not as a longing in which the whole being consents?" DD 1

—sociopath: "Having once begun to explain away Baldassarre's claim, Tito's thought showed itself as active as a virulent acid, eating its rapid way through all the tissues of sentiment. His mind was destitute of the dread which has been erroneously decried as if it were nothing higher than a man's animal care for his own skin: that awe of the *Divine Nemesis* which was felt by religious pagans, and, though it took a more positive form under Christianity, is still felt by the mass of mankind simply as a vague fear at anything which is called wrong-doing. Such terror of the unseen is so far above mere sensual cowardice that it will annihilate that cowardice: it is the initial recognition of a moral law restraining desire, and checks the hard bold scrutiny of imperfect thought into obligations which can never be proved to have any sanctity in the absence of feeling. 'It is good,' sing the old *Eumenides*, in **Æschylus**, 'that fear should sit as the guardian of the soul, forcing it into wisdom—good that men should carry a threatening shadow in their hearts under the full sunshine; else, how should they learn to revere the right?' That guardianship may become needless, but only when all outward law has become needless—only when duty and love have united in one stream and made a common force." R 11

—a terror: "Godfrey felt a great throb: there was one terror in his mind at that moment: it was, that the woman might *not* be dead.

That was an evil terror—an ugly inmate to have found a nestling-place in Godfrey's kindly disposition; but no disposition is a security from evil wishes to a man whose happiness hangs on duplicity." SM 13

—*wrong-doing:* "For there is seldom any wrong-doing which does not carry along with it some downfall of blindly-climbing hopes, some hard entail of suffering, some quickly-satiated desire that survives, with the life in death of old paralytic vice, to see itself cursed by its woeful progeny—some tragic mark of kinship in the one brief life to the far-stretching life that went before, and to the life that is to come after, such as has raised the pity and terror of men ever since they began to discern between will and destiny." FH *I*

Fraud

—*martyr?* "The pitiable lot is that of the man who could not call himself a martyr even though he were to persuade himself that the men who stoned him were but ugly passions incarnate—who knows that he is stoned, not for professing the Right, but for not being the man he professed to be." MM 85

The Good and Goodness

—*absent:* " . . . he had been nurtured in contempt for the tales of priests whose impudent lives were a proverb, and in erudite familiarity with disputes concerning the Chief Good, which had after all, he considered, left it a matter of taste." R 11

—*in action:* "Some one highly susceptible to the contemplation of a fine act has said, that it produces a sort of regenerating shudder through the frame, and makes one feel ready to begin a new life." MM 66

—*battered:* " . . . I must observe that goodness is of a modest nature, easily discouraged, and when much elbowed in early life by unabashed vices, is apt to retire into extreme privacy, so that it is more easily believed in by those who construct a selfish old gentleman theoretically, than by those who form the narrower judgments based on his personal acquaintance." MM 34

—*and beauty: see* B:Beauty—*and goodness*

—*blight:* "Goodness is a large, often a prospective word; like harvest, which at one stage when we talk of it lies all underground, with an indeterminate future: is the germ prospering in the darkness? at another, it has put forth delicate green blades, and by-and-by the trembling blossoms are ready to be dashed off by an hour of rough wind or rain. Each stage has its peculiar blight, and may have the healthy life choked out of it by a particular action of the foul land which rears or neighbours it, or by damage brought from foulness afar." DD 7

—*duality:* " 'Pray define your Good
Beyond rejection by majority;
Next, how it may subsist without the Ill
Which seems its only outline.' " CB 378-81

See CB:Rosencranz— *human good*

—*and evil:* "If the subtle mixture of good and evil prepared suffering for human truth and purity, there is also suffering prepared for the wrong-doer by the same mingled conditions." R 12

—*invisible:* "In many of our neighbours' lives, there is much not only of error and lapse, but of a certain exquisite goodness which can never be written or even spoken—only divined by each of us, according to the inward instruction of our own privacy." DD 16

—*mortality:* "Nay, it is conceivable that in some minds the deep pathos lying in the thought of human mortality—that we are here for a little while and then vanish away, that this earthly life is all that is given to our loved ones and to our many suffering fellow-men—lies nearer the fountains of moral emotion than the conception of extended existence.

"And surely it ought to be a welcome fact, if the thought of *mortality,* as well as of immortality, be favorable to virtue. We can imagine that the proprietors of a patent water-supply may have a dread of common springs; but for those who only share the general need there cannot be too great a security against a lack of fresh water—or of pure morality. It should be matter of unmixed rejoicing if this latter necessary of healthful life has its evolution insured in the interaction of human souls as certainly as the evolution of science or of art, with which, indeed, it is but a twin ray, melting into them with undefinable limits." ¶PY 37

—*noticed in oneself:* "We are not obliged to identify our own acts according to a strict classification, any more than the materials of our grocery and clothes." MM 65

—*overlooked:* " . . . we never find [**Young**] dwelling on virtue or religion as it really exists—in the emotions of a man dressed in an ordinary coat, and seated by his fireside of an evening, with his hand resting on the head of his little daughter; in courageous effort for unselfish ends, in the internal triumph of justice and pity over personal resentment, in all the sublime self-renunciation and sweet charities which are found in the details of ordinary life." PY 34

—*spontaneous:* "[He] was in one of his best humours . . . the greater part of it was doubtless due to those stirrings of the more kindly, healthy sap of human feeling, by which goodness tries to get the upper hand in us whenever it seems to have the slightest chance—on Sunday mornings, perhaps, when we are set free from the grinding hurry of the week, and take the little three-year-old on our knee at breakfast to share our egg and muffin; in moments of trouble, when death visits our roof or illness makes us dependent on the tending hand of a slighted wife; in quiet talks with an aged mother, of the days when we stood at her knee with our first picture-book, or wrote her loving letters from school. In the man whose childhood has known caresses there is always a fibre of memory that can be touched to gentle issues . . . :" JR 7

—*a town view:* "Assuredly Milby had that salt of goodness which keeps the world together, in greater abundance than was visible on the surface: innocent babes were born there, sweetening their parents' hearts with simple joys; men and women withering in disappointed worldliness, or bloated with sensual ease, had better moments in which they pressed the hand of suffering with sympathy, and were moved to deeds of neighbourly kindness. In church and in chapel there were honest-hearted worshippers who strove to keep a conscience void of offence; and even up the dimmest alleys you might have found here and there a Wesleyan to whom Methodism was the vehicle of peace on earth and goodwill to men." JR 2

—*and the true:* "The spirit which doubts the ultimately beneficial tendency of inquiry, which thinks that morality and religion will not bear the broadest daylight our intellect can throw on them, though it may clothe itself in robes of sanctity and use pious phrases, is the worst form of atheism; while he who believes, whatever else he may deny, that the true and the good are synonymous, bears in his soul the essential element of religion." PI 365

Gratitude

—*of others:* "I have known persons who have been suspected of undervaluing gratitude, and excluding it from the list of virtues; but on closer observation it has been seen that, if they have never felt grateful, it has been for want of an opportunity; and that, far from despising gratitude, they regard it as the virtue most of all incumbent—on others toward them." FH 17

—*reasonable:* " . . . when gratitude has become a matter of reasoning there are many ways of escaping from its bonds." R 37

Grief and Suffering

—*in bereavement:* " . . . it was all of a piece with the sad confusion of her mind—that confusion which belongs to the first hours of a sudden sorrow, when the poor human soul is like one who has been deposited sleeping among the ruins of a vast city; and wakes up in dreary amazement, not knowing whether it is the growing or the dying day—not knowing why and whence came this illimitable scene of desolation, or why he too finds himself desolate in the midst of it." AB 10

" . . . grief in its freshness feels the need of associating its loss and its lament with every change of scene and incident . . . " AB 10

—*endured:* "But we get accustomed to mental as well as bodily pain, without, for all that, losing our sensibility to it: it becomes a habit of our lives, and we cease to imagine a condition of perfect ease as possible for us. Desire is chastened into submission; and we are contented with our day when we have been able to bear our grief in silence, and act as if we were not suffering. For it is at such periods that the sense of our lives having visible and invisible relations beyond any of which either our present or prospective self is the centre, grows like a muscle that we are obliged to lean on and exert." AB 50

" ' . . . there are many thoughts and habits that may help us to bear inevitable sorrow. Multitudes have to bear it.' " DD 36

—*escape?* "At the entrance of the chill dark cavern, we turn with unworn courage from the warm light: but how, when we have trodden far in the damp darkness, and have begun to be faint and weary—how, if there is a sudden opening above us, and we are invited back again to the life-nourishing day? The leap of natural longing from under the pressure of pain is so strong that all less immediate motives are likely to be forgotten—till the pain has been escaped from." MF VII 5

—*false ideas:* "If there is an angel who records the sorrows of men as well as their sins, he knows how many and deep are the sorrows that spring from false ideas for which no man is culpable." SM 1

—*grief:* "Her withered look of grief, such as the sun often shines on when the blinds are drawn up after the burial of life's joy . . . . " DD 69

—*its lesson:* "It was the first sign within the poor child of that new sense which is the gift of sorrow—that susceptibility to the bare offices of humanity which raises them into a bond of loving fellowship, as to haggard men among the icebergs the mere presence of an ordinary comrade stirs the deep fountains of affection." MF II 7

—*in old age:* "Oh, it is piteous—that sorrow of aged women! In early youth, perhaps, they said to themselves, 'I shall be happy when I have a husband to love me best of all'; then, when the husband was too careless, 'My child will comfort me'; then, through the mother's watching and toil, 'My child will repay me all when it grows up.' And at last, after the long journey of years has been wearily travelled through, the mother's heart is weighed down by a heavier burden, and no hope remains but the grave." JR 7

" 'It cuts one sadly to see the grief of old people; they've no way of working it off; and the new spring brings no new shoots out on the withered tree.' " AB 16

—once: "It is but once that we can know our worst sorrows, and Romola had known them while life was new." R *E*

—silent: " . . . there is much pain that is quite noiseless; and vibrations that make human agonies are often a mere whisper in the roar of hurrying existence. There are glances of hatred that stab and raise no cry of murder; robberies that leave man or woman for ever beggared of peace and joy, yet kept secret by the sufferer—committed to no sound except that of low moans in the night, seen in no writing except that made on the face by the slow months of suppressed anguish and early morning tears. Many an inherited sorrow that has marred a life has been breathed into no human ear." FH *I*

—transformative: "It would be a poor result of all our anguish and our wrestling, if we won nothing but our old selves at the end of it—if we could return to the same blind loves, the same self-confident blame, the same light thoughts of human suffering, the same frivolous gossip over blighted human lives, the same feeble sense of that Unknown towards which we have sent forth irrepressible cries in our loneliness. Let us rather be thankful that our sorrow lives in us as an indestructible force, only changing its form, as forces do, and passing from pain into sympathy—the one poor word which includes all our best insight and our best love." AB 50

—transcended: "After a great excitement, the ebbing strength of impulse is apt to leave us in this aloofness from our active self." DD 42

—wounding: "And indeed the Mr Gilfil of those late Shepperton days had more of the knots and ruggedness of poor human nature than there lay any clear hint of in the open-eyed loving Maynard. But it is with men as with trees: if you lop off their finest branches, into which they were pouring their young life-juice, the wounds will be healed over with some rough boss, some odd excrescence; and what might have been a grand tree expanding into liberal shade, is but a whimsical misshapen trunk. Many an irritating fault, many an unlovely oddity, has come of a hard sorrow, which has crushed and maimed the nature just when it was expanding into plenteous beauty; and the trivial erring life which we visit with our harsh blame, may be but as the unsteady motion of a man whose best limb is withered." GL epilogue

Guilt and Shame

—apportioned: " 'It is not for us men to apportion the shares of moral guilt and retribution. We find it impossible to avoid mistakes even in determining who has committed a single criminal act, and the problem how far a man is to be held responsible for the unforeseen consequences of his own deed, is one that might well make us tremble to look into it. The evil consequences that may lie folded in a single act of selfish indulgence, is a thought so awful that it ought surely to awaken some feeling less presumptuous than a rash desire to punish.' " AB 41

—infectious: " 'There is no sort of wrong deed of which a man can bear the punishment alone: you can't isolate yourself, and say that the evil which is in you shall not spread. Men's lives are as thoroughly blended with each other as the air they breathe: evil spreads as necessarily as disease.' " AB 41

—secret: "Under every guilty secret there is hidden a brood of guilty wishes, whose unwholesome infecting life is cherished by the darkness. The contaminating effect of deeds often lies less in the commission than in the consequent adjustment of our desires—the enlistment of our self-interest on the side of falsity; as, on the other hand, the purifying influence of public confession springs from the fact, that by it the hope in lies is for ever swept away, and the soul recovers the noble attitude of simplicity." R 9

—shame: "But the inward shame, the reflex of that outward law which the great heart of mankind makes for every individual man, a reflex which will exist even in the absence of the sympathetic impulses that need no law, but rush to the deed of fidelity and pity as inevitably as the brute mother shields her young from the attack of the hereditary enemy—that inward shame was showing its blushes in Tito's determined assertion to himself that his father was dead, or that at least search was hopeless." R 9

—vengeance: " ' . . . you could not bear the punishment alone; you would entail the worst sorrows on every one who loves you. You would have committed an act of blind fury, that would leave all the present evils just as they were, and add worse evils to them. You may tell me that you meditate no fatal act of vengeance: but the feeling in

your mind is what gives birth to such actions, and as long as you indulge it, as long as you do not see that to fix your mind on Arthur's punishment is revenge, and not justice, you are in danger of being led on to the commission of some great wrong.' " AB 41

Happiness

—*active gladness:* "[He was] brimful of pleasure, and not trying to conceal it. The gladness in his face was of that active kind which seems to have energy enough not only to flash outwardly, but to light up busy vision within: one seemed to see thoughts, as well as delight, in his glances." MM 52

—*a definition:* " 'You are a happy woman, Denner; you have loved somebody for forty years who is old and weak now, and can't do without you.' " FH 39

—*late in life?* "No man believes that many-textured knowledge and skill—as a just idea of the solar system, or the power of painting flesh, or of reading written harmonies—can come late and of a sudden; yet many will not stick at believing that happiness can come at any day and hour solely by a new disposition of events; though there is nought less capable of a magical production than a mortal's happiness, which is mainly a complex of habitual relations and dispositions not to be wrought by news from foreign parts, or any whirling of fortune's wheel for one on whose brow time has written legibly." FH 39

—*a lover's:* " . . . the beloved lover is always called happy, and happiness is considered as a well-fleshed indifference to sorrow outside it." DD 69

—*seen by the jealous:* "It is to such as you that the good of this world falls: dulness, healthy selfishness, good-tempered conceit—these are the keys to happiness." LV 2

—*in simplicity:* "Does one who has been all but lost in a pit of darkness complain of the sweet air and the daylight? There is a way of looking at our life daily as an escape, and taking the quiet return of morn and evening—still more the starlike out-glowing of some pure fellow-feeling, some generous impulse breaking our inward darkness—as a salvation that reconciles us to hardship. Those who have a self-knowledge prompting such self-accusation as *Hamlet*'s, can understand this habitual feeling of rescue." DD 69

Hatred

—*anticipation:* "The prevision of an enemy's triumphant ease is in any case sufficiently irritating to hatred . . . . " FH 42

—*feared:* "And he passed.
The Gypsies made wide pathway, shrank aloof
As those who fear to touch the thing they hate;
Lest hate triumphant, mastering all the limbs,
Should tear, bite, crush, in spite of hindering will." SG IV iii

—*intensification:* "In the irritable, fluctuating stages of despair, gleams of hope came in the form of some possible accident. To dwell on the benignity of accident was a refuge from worse temptation.

"The embitterment of hatred is often as unaccountable to onlookers as the growth of devoted love, and it not only seems but is really out of direct relation with any outward causes to be alleged. Passion is of the nature of seed, and finds nourishment within, tending to a predominance which determines all currents towards itself, and makes the whole life its tributary. And the intensest form of hatred is that rooted in fear, which compels to silence and drives vehemence from a constructive vindictiveness, an imaginary annihilation of the detested object, something like the hidden rites of vengeance with which the persecuted have made a dark vent for their rage, and soothed their suffering into dumbness." DD 54

—*retaliaion:* "But most of us are apt to settle within ourselves that the man who blocks our way is odious, and not to mind causing him a little of the disgust which his personality excites in ourselves." MM 47

—*stolen goods:* "It is one thing to hate stolen goods, and another thing to hate them the more because their being stolen hinders us from making use of them." DD 21

—*time required:* "But a passionate hate, as well as a passionate love, demands some leisure and mental freedom. Persecution and revenge, like courtship and toadyism, will not prosper without a considerable expenditure of time and ingenuity . . . .." JR 10

Hypocrisy

—*obvious:* "The air of society is poisoned by transparent hypocrisies, which every one sees through and laughs at in his fellow men, yet strangely enough believes to be impenetrable in his own case." BL 3 297

—*pervasive:* "One could not fairly describe the generality of one's neighbours as too lucidly aware of manifesting in their own persons the weaknesses which they observe in the rest of her Majesty's subjects; on the contrary, a hasty conclusion as to schemes of Providence might lead to the supposition that one man was intended to correct another by being most intolerant of the ugly quality or trick which he himself possesses. Doubtless philosophers will be able to explain how it must necessarily be so, but pending the full extension of the *à priori* method, which will show that only blockheads could expect anything to be otherwise, it does seem surprising . . . . " TS 13

—protestation: "To be unaware of our own little tricks of manner or our own mental blemishes and excesses is a comprehensible unconsciousness; the puzzling fact is that people should apparently take no account of their deliberate actions, and should expect them to be equally ignored by others. It is an inversion of the accepted order: *there* it is the phrases that are official and the conduct or privately manifested sentiment that is taken to be real; *here* it seems that the practice is taken to be official and entirely nullified by the verbal representation which contradicts it." TS 13

"The thief making a vow to heaven of full restitution and whispering some reservations, expecting to cheat Omniscience by an 'aside,' is hardly more ludicrous than the many ladies and gentlemen who have more belief, and expect others to have it, in their own statement about their habitual doings than in the contradictory fact which is patent in the daylight. One reason [for] the absurdity is that we are led by a tradition about ourselves, so that long after a man has practically departed from a rule or principle, he continues innocently to state it as a true description of his practice—just as he has a long tradition that he is not an old gentleman, and is startled when he is seventy at overhearing himself called by an epithet which he has only applied to others." TS 13

—subtle: "There may be coarse hypocrites, who consciously affect beliefs and emotions for the sake of gulling the world, but Bulstrode was not one of them. He was simply a man whose desires had been stronger than his theoretic beliefs, and who had gradually explained the gratification of his desires into satisfactory agreement with those beliefs. If this be hypocrisy, it is a process which shows itself occasionally in us all, to whatever confession we belong, and whether we believe in the future perfection of our race or in the nearest date fixed for the end of the world; whether we regard the earth as a putrefying nidus for a saved remnant, including ourselves, or have a passionate belief in the solidarity of mankind.

"The service he could do to the cause of religion had been through life the ground he alleged to himself for his choice of action: it had been the motive which he had poured out in his prayers. Who would use money and position better than he meant to use them? Who could surpass him in self-abhorrence and exaltation of God's cause? And to Mr Bulstrode God's cause was something distinct from his own rectitude of conduct: it enforced a discrimination of God's enemies, who were to be used merely as instruments, and whom it would be as well if possible to keep out of money and consequent influence. Also, profitable investments in trades where the power of the prince of the world showed its most active devices, became sanctified by a right application of the profits in the hands of God's servant.

"The implicit reasoning is essentially no more peculiar to evangelical belief than the use of wide phrases for narrow motives is peculiar to Englishmen. There is no general doctrine which is not capable of eating out our morality if unchecked by the deep-seated habit of direct fellow-feeling with individual fellow-men." MM 61

Ideal and Idealism

—benign illusion: "But I check myself. Perhaps this England of my affections is half visionary—a dream in which things are connected according to my well-fed, lazy mood, and not at all by the multitudinous links of graver, sadder fact, such as belong everywhere to the story of human labour. Well, well, the illusions that began for us when we were less acquainted with evil have not lost their value when we discern them to be illusions. They feed the idea better, and in loving them still, we strengthen the precious habit of loving something not visibly, tangibly existent, but a spiritual product of our visible tangible selves." TS 2

—feminine: "Many **Theresa**s have been born who found for themselves no epic life wherein there was a constant unfolding of far-resonant action; perhaps only a life of mistakes, the offspring of a certain spiritual grandeur ill-matched with the meanness of opportunity; perhaps a tragic failure which found no sacred poet and sank unwept into oblivion. With dim light and tangled circumstance they tried to shape their thought and deed in noble agreement; but after all, to common eyes their struggle seemed mere inconsistency and formlessness; for these later-born Theresas were helped by no coherent social faith and order which could perform the function of knowledge for the ardently willing soul. Their ardour alternated between a vague ideal and the common yearning of womanhood; so that the one was disapproved as extravagance, and the other condemned as a lapse." MM P

"Here and there a cygnet is reared uneasily among the ducklings in the brown pond, and never finds the living stream in fellowship; with its own oary-footed kind. Here and there is born a **Saint Theresa**, foundress of nothing, whose loving heart-beats and sobs after an unattained goodness tremble off and are dispersed among hindrances, instead of centering in some long-recognisable deed." MM *P*

—the future: "In transactions between fellow-men it is well to consider a little, in the first place, what is fair and kind towards the person immediately concerned, before we spit and roast him on behalf of the next century but one. Wide-reaching motives, blessed and glorious as they are, and of the highest sacramental virtue, have their dangers, like all else that touches the mixed life of the earth. They are archangels with awful brow and flaming sword, summoning and encouraging us to do the right and the divinely heroic, and we feel a beneficent tremor in their presence; but to learn what it is they thus summon us to do, we have to consider the mortals we are elbowing, who are of our own stature and our own appetites.

"I cannot feel sure how my voting will affect the condition of Central Asia in the coming ages, but I have good reason to believe that the future populations there will be none the worse off because I abstain from conjectural vilification of my opponents during the present parliamentary session, and I am very sure that I shall be less injurious to my contemporaries. On the whole, and in the vast majority of instances, the action by which we can do the best for future ages is of the sort which has a certain beneficence and grace for contemporaries." ¶TS 8

—and joy: " 'For you will grant
The Ideal has discoveries which ask
No test, no faith, save that we joy in them:
A new-found continent with spreading lands
Where pleasure charters all, where virtue, rank,
Use, right, and truth have but one name, Delight.' " CB 858-63

—political improvement: "I never smiled at Mr Lyon's trustful energy without falling to penitence and veneration immediately after. For what we call illusions are often, in truth, a wider vision of past and present realities—a willing movement of a man's soul with the larger sweep of the world's forces—a movement towards a more assured end than the chances of a single life. We see human heroism broken into units and say, this unit did little—might as well not have been. But in this way we might break up a great army into units; in this way we might break the sunlight into fragments, and think that this and the other might be cheaply parted with. Let us rather raise a monument to the soldiers whose brave hearts only kept the ranks unbroken, and met death—a monument to the faithful who were not famous, and who are precious as the continuity of the sunbeams is precious, though some of them fall unseen and on barrenness." FH 16

Integrity and Ethics

—absent: "The prevarication and white lies which a mind that keeps itself ambitiously pure is as uneasy under as a great artist under the false touches that no eye detects but his own, are worn as lightly as mere trimmings when once the actions have become a lie." SM 13

"Under the stimulus of small many-mixed motives like these, a great deal of business has been done in the world by well-clad and, in 1833, clean-shaven men, whose names are on charity-lists, and who do not know that they are base. Mr Johnson's character was not much more exceptional than his double chin.

"No system, religious or political, I believe, has laid it down as a principle that all men are alike virtuous, or even that all the people rated for £80 houses are an honour to their species." FH 37

"Unscrupulousness gets rid of much, but not of toothache, or wounded vanity, or the sense of loneliness, against which, as the world at present stands, there is no security but a thoroughly healthy jaw, and a just, loving soul." R 31

"Unprincipled men were useful, enabling those who had more scruples to keep their hands tolerably clean in a world where there was much dirty work to be done. Indeed, it was not clear . . . how life was to be carried on in any department without human instruments whom it would not be unbecoming to kick or to spit upon in the act of handing them their wages." R 57

—backsliding: " . . . to the end of men's struggles a penalty will remain for those who sink from the ranks of the heroes into the crowd for whom the heroes fight and die." FH 6

—farm labour: "The conventional countryman of the stage, who picks up pocket-books and never looks into them, and who is too simple even to know that honesty has its opposite, represents the still lingering mistake, that an unintelligible dialect is a guaranty for ingenuousness, and that slouching shoulders indicate an upright disposition. It is quite true that a thresher is likely to be innocent of any adroit arithmetical cheating, but he is not the less likely to carry home his master's corn in his shoes and pocket; a reaper is not given to writing begging-letters, but he is quite capable of cajoling the dairymaid into filling his small-beer bottle

with ale. The selfish instincts are not subdued by the sight of buttercups, nor is integrity in the least established by that classic rural occupation, sheep-washing. To make men moral, something more is requisite than to turn them out to grass." NH 124

—moral conflict: "The conduct that issues from a moral conflict has often so close a resemblance to vice, that the distinction escapes all outward judgments, founded on a mere comparison of actions. It is clear to you, I hope, that Stephen was not a hypocrite—capable of deliberate doubleness for a selfish end; and yet his fluctuations between the indulgence of a feeling and the systematic concealment of it might have made a good case in support of Philip's accusation." MF VI 9

—promise made: "A man vows, and yet will not cast away the means of breaking his vow. Is it that he distinctly means to break it? Not at all; but the desires which tend to break it are at work in him dimly, and make their way into his imagination, and relax his muscles in the very moments when he is telling himself over again the reasons for his vow." MM 70

—rationalization: "If we only look far enough off for the consequences of our actions, we can always find some point in the combination of results by which those actions can be justified: by adopting the point of view of a Providence who arranges results or of a philosopher who traces them, we shall find it possible to obtain perfect complacency in choosing to do what is most agreeable to us in the present moment." MF V 3

—rigid yet tender: " . . . it is as possible to be rigid in principle and tender in blame, as it is to suffer from the sight of things hung awry, and yet to be patient with the hanger who sees amiss." DD 59

—standard of virtue: "But what to one man is the virtue which he has sunk below the possibility of aspiring to, is to another the backsliding by which he forfeits his spiritual crown." FH 6

—weakening: "It is the moment when our resolution seems about to become irrevocable—when the fatal iron gates are about to close upon us—that tests our strength. Then, after hours of clear reasoning and firm conviction, we snatch at any sophistry that will nullify our long struggles and bring us the defeat that we love better than victory." MF V 3

—at work: " . . . when a man whose business hours, the solid part of every day, are spent in an unscrupulous course of public or private action which has every calculable chance of causing widespread injury and misery, can be called moral because he comes home to dine with his wife and children and cherishes the happiness of his own hearth, the augury is not good for the use of high ethical and theological disputation." TS 16

Jealousy

—in the diffident: " . . . that jealousy and distrust which in diffident natures is almost inevitably linked with a strong feeling . . . . " MF VI 7

—ingenious: "Jealousy of all sorts—whether for our fortune or our love—is ready at combinations, and likely even to outstrip the fact." FH 43

—nearest thing: "This was his state of mind—not jealousy; still, his behaviour in some respects was as like jealousy as yellow is to yellow, which colour we know may be the effect of very different causes." DD 48

—obsessive: "Jealousy is never satisfied with anything short of an omniscience that would detect the subtlest fold of the heart." MF VI 10

—passionless: "There is a sort of jealousy which needs very little fire: it is hardly a passion, but a blight bred in the cloudy, damp despondency of uneasy egoism." MM 21

—tormenting: "One of the tortures of jealousy is, that it can never turn away its eyes from the thing that pains it." GL 5

Jesus Christ

—comfort: " 'You are weary and heavy-laden; well, it is you Christ invites to come to him and find rest. He asks you to cling to him, to lean on him; he does not command you to walk alone without stumbling. He does not tell you, as your fellow men do, that you must first merit his love; he neither condemns nor reproaches you for the past, he only bids you come to him that you may have life: he bids you stretch out your hands, and take of the fullness of his love. You have only to rest on him as a child rests on its mother's arms, and you will be upborne by his divine strength. That is what is meant by faith. Your evil habits, you feel, are too strong for you; you are unable to wrestle with them; you know beforehand you shall fall. But when once we feel our helplessness in that way, and go to the Saviour, desiring to be freed from the power as well as the punishment of sin, we are no longer left to our own strength. As long as we live in rebellion against God, desiring to have our own will, seeking happiness in the things of this world, it is as if we shut ourselves up in a crowded stifling room, where we breathe only poisoned air; but we have only to walk out under the infinite heavens,

and we breathe the pure free air that gives us health, and strength, and gladness. It is just so with God's spirit: as soon as we submit ourselves to his will, as soon as we desire to be united to him, and made pure and holy, it is as if the walls had fallen down that shut us out from God, and we are fed with his spirit, which gives us new strength.' " JR 18

—and the Jews: "The Jews, it is said, resisted the expansion of their own religion into Christianity; they were in the habit of spitting on the cross; they have held the name of Christ to be *Anathema.* Who taught them that? The men who made Christianity a curse to them: the men who made the name of Christ a symbol for the spirit of vengeance, and, what was worse, made the execution of the vengeance a pretext for satisfying their own savageness, greed, and envy: the men who sanctioned with the name of Christ a barbaric and blundering copy of pagan fatalism in taking the words 'His blood be upon us and on our children' as a divinely appointed verbal warrant for wreaking cruelty from generation to generation on the people from whose sacred writings Christ drew his teaching. Strange retrogression in the professor of an expanded religion, boasting an illumination beyond the spiritual doctrine of Hebrew prophets!

"For Hebrew prophets proclaimed a God who demanded mercy rather than sacrifices. The Christians also believed that God delighted not in the blood of rams and of bulls, but they apparently conceived Him as requiring for His satisfaction the sighs and groans, the blood and roasted flesh of men whose forefathers had misunderstood the metaphorical character of prophecies which spoke of spiritual pre-eminence under the figure of a material kingdom.

"Was this the method by which Christ desired His title to the Messiahship to be commended to the hearts and understandings of the nation in which He was born? . . . And did the words 'Father, forgive them, they know not what they do,' refer only to the centurion and his band, a tacit exception being made of every Hebrew there present from the mercy of the Father and the compassion of the Son?—nay, more, of every Hebrew yet to come who remained unconverted after hearing of His claim to the Messiahship, not from His own lips or those of His native apostles, but from the lips of alien men whom cross, creed, and baptism had left cruel, rapacious, and debauched?

"It is more reverent to Christ to believe that He must have approved the Jewish martyrs who deliberately chose to be burned or massacred rather than be guilty of a blaspheming lie, more than He approved the rabble of crusaders who robbed and murdered them in His name." ¶TS 18

Joy and Sorrow

—alien: "That sudden clang, that leaping light, fell on Romola like sharp wounds . . . the general joy seemed cruel to her: she stood aloof from that common life—that Florence which was flinging out its loud exultation to stun the ears of sorrow and loneliness. She could never join hands with gladness again, but only with those whom it was in the hard nature of gladness to forget. And in her bitterness she felt that all rejoicing was mockery. Men shouted pæans with their souls full of heaviness, and then looked in their neighbours' faces to see if there was really such a thing as joy. Romola had lost her belief in the happiness she had once thirsted for: it was a hateful, smiling, soft-handed thing, with a narrow, selfish heart." R 36

—at another's happiness: "We should be churlish creatures if we could have no joy in our fellow-mortals' joy, unless it were in agreement with our theory of righteous distribution and our highest ideal of human good: what sour corners our mouths would get—our eyes, what frozen glances! and all the while our own possessions and desires would not exactly adjust themselves to our ideal. We must have some comradeship with imperfection, and it is, happily, possible to feel gratitude even where we discern a mistake that may have been injurious, the vehicle of the mistake being an affectionate intention prosecuted through a lifetime of kindly offices." DD 59

—expectations realised: "But it is not in human nature—only in human pretence—that a young man like Arthur, with a fine constitution and fine spirits, thinking well of himself, believing that others think well of him, and having a very ardent intention to give them more and more reason for that good opinion—it is not possible for such a young man, just coming into a splendid estate through the death of a very old man whom he was not fond of, to feel anything very different from exultant joy." AB 44

—little deaths: "It is in these acts called trivialities that the seeds of joy are for ever wasted, until men and women look round with haggard faces at the devastation their own waste has made, and say, the earth bears no harvest of sweetness—calling their denial knowledge." MM 42

—and Sorrow: "Sorrow and joy have each their peculiar narrowness; and a religious enthusiasm like **Savonarola**'s which ultimately blesses mankind by giving the soul a strong propulsion towards sympathy with

pain, indignation against wrong, and the subjugation of sensual desire, must always incur the reproach of a great negation." R 49

—*statistics:* "It was probably a hard saying to the Pharisees, that 'there is more joy in heaven over one sinner that repenteth, than over ninety and nine just persons that need no repentance'. And certain ingenious philosophers of our own day must surely take offence at a joy so entirely out of correspondence with arithmetical proportion. But a heart that has been taught by its own sore struggles to bleed for the woes of another—that has 'learned pity through suffering'—is likely to find very imperfect satisfaction in the 'balance of happiness', 'doctrine of compensations', and other short and easy methods of obtaining through complacency in the presence of pain; and for such a heart that saying will not be altogether dark.

"The emotions, I have observed, are but slightly influenced by arithmetical considerations: the mother, when her sweet lisping little ones have all been taken from her one after another, and she is hanging over her last dead babe, finds small consolation in the fact that the tiny dimpled corpse is but one of a necessary average, and that a thousand other babes brought into the world at the same time are doing well, and are likely to live; and if you stood beside that mother—if you knew her pang and shared it—it is probable you would be equally unable to see a ground of complacency in statistics." ¶JR 22

—*wrong sort:* "That is a base and selfish, even a blasphemous, spirit, which rejoices and is thankful over the past evil that has blighted or crushed another, because it has been made a source of unforeseen good to ourselves." AB 54

—*but:* "But it is not ignoble to feel that the fuller life which a sad experience has brought us is worth our own personal share of pain: surely it is not possible to feel otherwise, any more than it would be possible for a man with cataracts to regret the painful process by which his dim blurred sight of men as trees walking had been exchanged for clear outline and effulgent day. The growth of higher feeling within us is like the growth of faculty, bringing with it a sense of added strength: we can no more wish to return to a narrower sympathy, than a painter or a musician can wish to return to his cruder manner, or a philosopher to his less complete formula." AB 54

Justice

—*the downtrodden:* " 'Does the man who has the ear of the public use his advantage tenderly towards poor fellows who may be hindered of their due if he treats their pretensions with scorn? That is my test of his justice and benevolence.' " TS 8

—*location:* "Who shall put his finger on the work of justice, and say, 'It is there'? Justice is like the Kingdom of God—it is not without us as a fact, it is within us as a great yearning." R 67

—*personal interest:* "What could be more contemptible than the mood of mind which makes a man measure the justice of divine or human law by the agreeableness of his own shadow and the ample satisfaction of his own desires?" TS 1

Laughter

—*appropriate and not:* "The world seems to me well supplied with what is genuinely ridiculous: wit and humour may play as harmlessly or beneficently round the changing facets of egoism, absurdity, and vice, as the sunshine over the rippling sea or the dewy meadows. Why should we make our delicious sense of the ludicrous, with its invigorating shocks of laughter and its irrepressible smiles which are the outglow of an inward radiation as gentle and cheering as the warmth of morning, flourish like a brigand on the robbery of our mental wealth?" TS 10

—*in large people:* " . . . that comfortable slow enjoyment of a laugh which one only sees in stout people." AB 20

—*ostentatious:* "[Spini] and his companions, also young men dressed expensively and wearing arms, were exchanging jokes with that sort of ostentatious laughter which implies a desire to prove that the laughter is not mortified though some people might suspect it." R 45

—*superiority:* "That a gratified sense of superiority is at the root of barbarous laughter may be at least half the truth. But there is a loving laughter in which the only recognised superiority is that of the ideal self, the God within, holding the mirror and the scourge for our own pettiness as well as our neighbours'." TS 1

Misery and Despair

—*aftershock:* "There is something sustaining in the very agitation that accompanies the first shocks of trouble, just as an acute pain is often a stimulus, and produces an excitement which is transient strength. It is in the slow, changed life that follows—in the time when sorrow has become stale and has no longer an emotive intensity that counteracts its pain, in the time when day follows day in dull unexpectant sameness and trial is a dreary routine—it is then that despair threatens: it is then that the peremptory hunger of the soul is felt, and eye and ear are strained after some unlearned secret of our existence which shall give to endurance the nature of satisfaction." MF IV 2

—cause perceived: "It is seldom that the miserable can help regarding their misery as a wrong inflicted by those who are less miserable." SM 12

—cultured and uncultured: "The subtle and varied pains springing from the higher sensibility that accompanies higher culture, are perhaps less pitiable than that dreary absence of impersonal enjoyment and consolation which leaves ruder minds to the perpetual urgent companionship of their own griefs and discontents. The lives of those rural forefathers, whom we are apt to think very prosaic figures—men whose only work was to ride round their land, getting heavier and heavier in their saddles, and who passed the rest of their days in the half-listless gratification of senses dulled by monotony—had a certain pathos in them nevertheless." SM 3

—denial: "A man falling into dark waters seeks a momentary footing even on sliding stones; and Silas, by acting as if he believed in false hopes, warded off the moment of despair." SM 5

—despair: "There is a strength of self-possession which is the sign that the last hope has departed. Despair no more leans on others than perfect contentment, and in despair pride ceases to be counteracted by the sense of dependence." AB 37

—first time: "For there is no despair so absolute as that which comes with the first moments of our first great sorrow, when we have not yet known what it is to have suffered and be healed, to have despaired and to have recovered hope." AB 31

—hidden: "While we are discussing a man's career, sneering at his mistakes, blaming his rashness, and labelling his opinions—'Evangelical and narrow', or 'Latitudinarian and Pantheistic', or 'Anglican and supercilious'—that man, in his solitude, is perhaps shedding hot tears because his sacrifice is a hard one, because strength and patience are failing him to speak the difficult word, and do the difficult deed." JR 8

—misery: "But Maggie, gifted with that superior power of misery which distinguishes the human being and places him at a proud distance from the most melancholy chimpanzee, sat still on her bough, and gave herself up to the keen sense of unmerited reproach." MF I 6

—morning: "She had no tears this morning. She had wept them all away last night, and now she felt that dry-eyed morning misery, which is worse than the first shock, because it has the future in it as well as the present." AB 31

—nagging pain: "Under protracted ill every living creature will find something that makes a comparative ease, and even when life seems woven of pain, will convert the fainter pang into a desire." FH 1

—quiet: "So the night wore on in agitation, till the chill dawn and the growing light brought the tremulous quiet that comes on the brink of despair." AB 46

—repulsion: "Energetic natures, strong for all strenuous deeds, will often rush away from a hopeless sufferer, as if they were hard-hearted. It is the overmastering sense of pain that drives them. They shrink by an ungovernable instinct, as they would shrink from laceration." AB 42

—resisted: "Even to the man who presents the most elastic resistance to whatever is unpleasant, there will come moments when the pressure from without is too strong for him, and he must feel the smart and the bruise in spite of himself. Such a moment had come to Tito. There was no possible attitude of mind, no scheme of action by which the uprooting of all his newly-planted hopes could be made otherwise than painful." R 14

—respite: "When our life is a continuous trial, the moments of respite seem only to substitute the heaviness of dread for the heaviness of actual suffering: the curtain of cloud seems parted an instant only that we may measure all its horror as it hangs low, black, and imminent, in contrast with the transient brightness; the water-drops that visit the parched lips in the desert bear with them only the keen imagination of thirst." JR 5

—unaccustomed: "Those who have been indulged by fortune and have always thought of calamity as what happens to others, feel a blind incredulous rage at the reversal of their lot, and half believe that their wild cries will alter the course of the storm. Mirah felt no such surprise when familiar Sorrow came back from brief absence, and sat down with her according to the old use and wont." DD 61

—to the uncultured: "When uncultured minds, confined to a narrow range of personal experience, are under the pressure of continued misfortune, their inward life is apt to become a perpetually repeated round of sad and bitter thoughts: the same words, the same scenes are revolved over and over again, the same mood accompanies them—the end of the year finds them as much what they were at the beginning as if they were machines set to a recurrent series of movements." MF IV 2

Notable individuals

—Girolamo Savonarola: see R *at* Romola di Bardi *and at* Girolamo Savonarola

—Saint Theresa of Avila: "Theresa's passionate, ideal nature demanded an epic life: what were many-volumed romances of chivalry and the social conquests of a brilliant girl to her? Her flame quickly burned up that light fuel; and, fed from within, soared after some illimitable satisfaction, some object which would never justify weariness, which would reconcile self-despair with the rapturous consciousness of life beyond self. She found her epos in the reform of a religious order." MM P

—Thomas à Kempis: " 'Beauties of the Spectator,' 'Rasselas,' Economy of Human Life,' 'Gregory's Letters'—she knew the sort of matter that was inside all these: the 'Chrstian Year'—that seemed to be a hymn-book, and she laid it down again; but *Thomas à Kempis?*—the name had come across her in her reading, and she felt the satisfaction, which every one knows, of getting some ideas to attach to a name that strays solitary in the memory.

"She took up the little, old, clumsy book with some curiosity: it had the corners turned down in many places, and some hand, now for ever quiet, had made at certain passages strong pen and ink marks, long since browned by time. Maggie turned from leaf to leaf and read where the quiet hand pointed . . . .

" 'Know that the love of thyself doth hurt thee more than anything in the world . . . . If thou seekest this or that, and wouldst be here or there, to enjoy thy own will and pleasure thou shalt never be quiet nor free from care: for in everything somewhat will be wanting, and in every place there will be some that will cross thee . . . . Both above and below, which way soever thou dost turn thee, everywhere thou shalt find the Cross: and everywhere of necessity thou must have patience, if thou wilt have inward peace, and enjoy an everlasting crown . . . .

" 'If thou desire to mount unto this height, thou must set out courageously, and lay the axe to the root; that thou mayst pluck up and destroy that hidden inordinate inclination to thyself, and unto all private and earthly good. On this sin, that a man inordinately loveth himself, almost all dependeth, whatsoever is thoroughly to be overcome; which evil being once overcome and subdued, there will presently ensue great peace and tranquillity . . . .

" 'It is but little thou sufferest in comparison of them that have suffered so much, were so strongly tempted, so grievously afflicted, so many ways tried and exercised. Thou oughtest therefore to call to mind the more heavy sufferings of others, that thou mayst the easier bear thy little adversities. And if they seem not little unto thee, beware lest thy impatience be the cause thereof . . . . Blessed are those ears that receive the whispers of the divine voice, and listen not to the whisperings of the world. Blessed are those ears which hearken not unto the voice which soundeth outwardly, but unto the Truth which teacheth inwardly . . . . ' " ¶MF IV 3 [*GE's ellipses*] *See* MF Maggie Tulliver,—*new inspiration,* I: 144

Prayer

—intercessory: "There are unseen elements which often frustrate our wisest calculations—which raise up the sufferer from the edge of the grave, contradicting the prophecies of the clear-sighted physician, and fulfilling the blind clinging hopes of affection; such unseen elements Mr Tryan called the Divine Will, and filled up the margin of ignorance which surrounds all our knowledge with the feelings of trust and resignation. Perhaps the profoundest philosophy could hardly fill it up better." JR 22

—nonintercessory: "The most powerful movement of feeling with a liturgy is the prayer which seeks for nothing special, but is a yearning to escape from the limitations of our own weakness and an invocation of all Good to enter and abide with us: or else a self-oblivious lifting up of gladness, a *Gloria in excelsis* that such Good exists; both the yearning and the exultation gathering their utmost force from the sense of communion in a form which has expressed them both, for long generations of struggling fellow-men." DD 32

—private: "Does any one suppose that private prayer is necessarily candid—necessarily goes to the roots of action? Private prayer is inaudible speech, and speech is representative: who can represent himself just as he is, even in his own reflections?" MM 70

—sure to succeed: "He was striving to purify his feeling in this matter from selfish or worldly dross—a striving which is that prayer without ceasing, sure to wrest an answer by its sublime importunity." FH 38

—with another: " . . . she could now believe the message of mercy; the water-floods that had threatened to overwhelm her rolled back again, and life once more spread its heaven-covered space before her. She had been unable to pray alone; but now his prayer bore her own soul along with it, as the broad tongue of flame carries upwards in its vigorous leap the little flickering fire that could hardly keep alight by itself." JR 25

—*with the condemned:*

" 'Jesus, thou present Saviour! Thou hast known the depths of all sorrow: thou hast entered that black darkness where God is not, and hast uttered the cry of the forsaken. Come, Lord, and gather of the fruits of thy travail and thy pleading: stretch forth thy hand, thou who art mighty to save to the uttermost, and rescue this lost one. She is clothed round with thick darkness: the fetters of her sin are upon her, and she cannot stir to come to thee: she can only feel her heart is hard, and she is helpless. She cried to me, thy weak creature . . . . Saviour! it is a blind cry to thee. Hear it! Pierce the darkness! Look upon her with thy face of love and sorrow, that thou didst turn on him who denied thee; and melt her hard heart.

" 'See, Lord—I bring her, as they of old brought the sick and helpless, and thou didst heal them: I bear her on my arms and carry her before thee. Fear and trembling have taken hold on her; but she trembles only at the pain and death of the body: breathe upon her thy life-giving Spirit, and put a new fear within her—the fear of her sin. Make her dread to keep the accursed thing within her soul: make her feel the presence of the living God, who beholds all the past, to whom the darkness is as noonday; who is waiting now, at the eleventh hour, for her to turn to him, and confess her sin, and cry for mercy—now, before the night of death comes, and the moment of pardon is for ever fled, like yesterday that returneth not.

" 'Saviour! it is yet time—time to snatch this poor soul from everlasting darkness. I believe—I believe in thy infinite love. What is *my* love or *my* pleading? It is quenched in thine. I can only clasp her in my weak arms, and urge her with my weak pity. Thou—thou wilt breathe on the dead soul, and it shall arise from the unanswering sleep of death.

" 'Yea, Lord, I see thee, coming through the darkness, coming, like the morning, with healing on thy wings. The marks of thy agony are upon thee—I see, I see thou art able and willing to save—thou wilt not let her perish for ever.

" 'Come, mighty Saviour! let the dead hear thy voice; let the eyes of the blind be opened: let her see that God encompasses her; let her tremble at nothing but at the sin that cuts her off from him. Melt the hard heart; unseal the closed lips: make her cry with her whole soul, "Father, I have sinned." . . . . ' "

—*Dinah Morris's prayer for Hetty Sorrel* AB 45

Pride

—*attribute:* " . . . pride only helps us to be generous; it never makes us so, any more than vanity makes us witty." MM 8

—*in denial:* "It is precisely the proudest and most obstinate men who are the most liable to shift their position and contradict themselves in this sudden manner: everything is easier to them than to face the simple fact, that they have been thoroughly defeated and must begin life anew. And Mr Tulliver, you perceive, though nothing more than a superior miller and maltster, was as proud and obstinate as if he had been a very lofty personage, in whom such dispositions might be a source of that conspicuous, far-echoing tragedy which sweeps the stage in regal robes, and makes the dullest chronicler sublime.

"The pride and obstinacy of millers and other insignificant people, whom you pass unnoticingly on the road every day, have their tragedy too, but it is of that unwept, hidden sort, that goes on from generation to generation and leaves no record—such tragedy, perhaps, as lies in the conflicts of young souls, hungry for joy, under a lot made suddenly hard to them, under the dreariness of a home where the morning brings no promise with it, and where the unexpectant discontent of worn and disappointed parents weighs on the children like a damp, thick air in which all the functions of life are depressed; or such tragedy as lies in the slow or sudden death that follows on a bruised passion, though it may be a death that finds only a parish funeral.

"There are certain animals to which tenacity of position is a law of life—they can never flourish again after a single wrench: and there are certain human beings to whom predominance is a law of life and who can only sustain humiliation so long as they can refuse to believe in it, and, in their own conception, predominate still." ¶MF III 1

—*fearing pity:* "Every proud mind knows something of this experience, and perhaps it is only to be overcome by a sense of fellowship deep enough to make all efforts at isolation seem mean and petty instead of exalting." MM 42

—*lack:* "If you are not proud of your cellar, there is no thrill of satisfaction in seeing your guest hold up his wine-glass to the light and look judicial. Such joys are reserved for conscious merit." MM 13

—*womanly:* "A proud woman who has learned to submit, carries all her pride to the reinforcement of her submission, and looks down with severe superiority on all feminine assumption as 'unbecoming.' " GL 10

Purpose

—*and art:* "We should all be painting our picture, whether it be a home scene after **Wilkie**, a **Paul** preaching at Athens, or a **Brutus** passing sentence on his son. We should all have a purpose in life as perfectly recognized and definite as the painter's idea of his subject . . . . Who would not have some purpose in life as independent in its value as art is to the artist?" NE 2

—*ideal:* "It is to live, not for our friends, not for those hostages to fortune, wives and children; not for any individual, any specific form; but for something which, while it dwells in these, has an existence beyond them. It is to live for the good, the true, the beautiful, which outlive every generation and are all-pervading as the light which vibrates from the remotest nebula to our own sun. The spirit which has ascertained its true relation to these can never be an orphan: it has its home in the eternal mind, from which neither things present nor to come can separate it." NE 2

Religion

—*burden of the past:* "Our civilization, and, yet more, our religion, are an anomalous blending of lifeless barbarisms, which have descended to us like so many petrifactions from distant ages, with living ideas, the offspring of a true process of development. We are in bondage to terms and conceptions which, having had their root in conditions of thought no longer existing, have ceased to possess any vitality, and are for us as spells which have lost their virtue." PI 353

—*the Cabbala:* " 'In the doctrine of the Cabbala, souls are born again and again in new bodies till they are perfected and purified, and a soul liberated from a worn-out body may join the fellow-soul that needs it, that they may be perfected together, and their earthly work accomplished. Then they will depart from the mortal region, and leave place for new souls to be born out of the store in the eternal bosom. It is the lingering imperfection of the souls already born into the mortal region that hinders the birth of new souls and the preparation of the Messianic time—thus the mind has given shape to what is hidden as the shadow of what is known, and has spoken truth, though it were only in parable.' " DD 43

—*"the" Church:* "The question where the duty of obedience ends, and the duty of resistance begins, could in no case be an easy one; but it was made overwhelmingly difficult by the belief that the Church was—not a compromise of parties to secure a more or less approximate justice in the appropriation of funds, but—a living organism, instinct with Divine power to bless and to curse.

"To most of the pious Florentines, who had hitherto felt no doubt in their adherence to the Frate, that belief in the Divine potency of the Church was not an embraced opinion, it was an inalienable impression, like the concavity of the blue firmament; and the boldness of **Savonarola**'s written arguments that the Excommunication was unjust, and that, being unjust, it was not valid, only made them tremble the more, as a defiance cast at a mystic image, against whose subtle immeasurable power there was neither weapon nor defence." ¶R 55

—*contradiction?* "What thought could reconcile that worn anguish in her brother's face—that straining after something invisible—with this satisfied strength and beauty, and make it intelligible that they belonged to the same world? Or was there never any reconciling of them, but only a blind worship of clashing deities, first in mad joy and then in wailing? Romola for the first time felt this questioning need like a sudden uneasy dizziness and want of something to grasp, it was an experience hardly longer than a sigh, for the eager theorising of ages is compressed, as in a seed, in the momentary want of a single mind. But there was no answer to meet the need, and it vanished before the returning rush of young sympathy with the glad loving beauty that beamed upon her in new radiance, like the dawn after we have looked away from it to the grey west." R 17

—*conversion:* "It is one of the secrets in that change of mental poise which has been fitly named conversion, that to many among us neither heaven nor earth has any revelation till some personality touches theirs with a peculiar influence, subduing them into receptiveness." DD 35

—*Dissent:* " . . . Trebian Dissent gradually altered its character. Formerly it had been of a quiescent, well-to-do kind, represented architecturally by a small, venerable, dark-pewed chapel, built by Presbyterians, but long occupied by a sparse congregation of Independents, who were as little moved by doctrinal zeal as their church-going neighbours, and did not feel themselves deficient in religious liberty, inasmuch as they were not hindered from occasionally slumbering in their pews, and were not obliged to go regularly to the weekly prayer-meeting. But when stone-pits and coal-pits made new hamlets that threatened to spread up to the very town, when the tape-weavers came with their news-reading inspectors and book-keepers, the Independent chapel began to be filled with eager men and women to whom the exceptional possession of religious truth was the condition which reconciled them to a meagre existence, and made them feel in secure alliance with the unseen but supreme rule of a world in which their own visible part was small.

"There were Dissenters in Treby now who could not be regarded by the Church people in the light of old neighbours to whom the habit of going to chapel was an innocent, unenviable inheritance along with a particular house and garden, a tan-yard, or a grocery business—Dissenters who, in their turn, without meaning to be in the least abusive, spoke of the high-bred Rector as a blind leader of the blind." ¶FH 3

" ' . . . that awful creed, which makes this world a vestibule with double doors to hell, and a narrow stair on one side whereby the thinner sort may mount to heaven . . . . ' " FH 5

—divisive: "We are inclined to think that it is less frequently devotion which alienates men, than something infused in the devotion—a certain amount of silliness, or temper, or *exigeance,* for example, which, though given in small doses, will, if persevered in, have a strongly alterative effect." BL 1 296

—dogma irrelevant: "No wonder the sick-room and the lazaretto have so often been a refuge from the tossings of intellectual doubt—a place of repose for the worn and wounded spirit. Here is a duty about which all creeds and all philosophies are at one: here, at least, the conscience will not be dogged by doubt, the benign impulse will not be checked by adverse theory: here you may begin to act without settling one preliminary question. To moisten the sufferer's parched lips through the long night-watches, to bear up the drooping head, to lift the helpless limbs, to divine the want that can find no utterance beyond the feeble motion of the hand or beseeching glance of the eye—these are offices that demand no self-questionings, no casuistry, no assent to propositions, no weighing of consequences.

"Within the four walls where the stir and glare of the world are shut out, and every voice is subdued—where a human being lies prostrate, thrown on the tender mercies of his fellow, the moral relation of man to man is reduced to its utmost clearness and simplicity; bigotry cannot confuse it, theory cannot pervert it, passion, awed into quiescence, can neither pollute nor perturb it. As we bend over the sick-bed, all the forces of our nature rush towards the channels of pity, of patience, and of love, and sweep down the miserable choking drift of our quarrels, our debates, our would-be wisdom, and our clamorous selfish desires. This blessing of serene freedom from the importunities of opinion lies in all simple direct acts of mercy, and is one source of that sweet calm which is often felt by the watcher in the sick-room, even when the duties there are of a hard and terrible kind." JR 24

" 'But,' said Adam [Bede], 'I've seen pretty clear, ever since I was a young un, as religion's something else besides notions. It isn't notions sets people doing the right thing—It's feelings. It's the same with the notions in religion as it is with math'matics—a man may be able to work problems straight off in's head as he sits by the fire and smokes his pipe; but if he has to make a machine or a building, he must have a will and a resolution, and love something else better than his own ease.' " AB 17 *See —elemental* and *—spiritual side*

—elemental: " ' . . . and it all come pouring in—if *I* felt i' my inside what was the right and just thing by you, and them as prayed and drawed the lots, all but that wicked un, if *they'd* ha' done the right thing by you if they could, isn't there Them as was at the making on us, and knows better and has a better will? And that's all as ever I can be sure on, and everything else is a big puzzle to me when I think on it. For there was the fever come and took off them as were full-growed, and left the helpless children; and there's the breaking o' limbs, and them as 'ud do right and be sober have to suffer by them as are contrairy—eh, there's trouble i' this world, and there's things as we can niver make out the rights on. And all as we've got to do is to trusten, Master Marner —to do the right thing as fur as we know, and to trusten. For if us as knows so little can see a bit o' good and rights, we may be sure as there's a good and a rights bigger nor what we can know—I feel it i' my own inside as it must be so.' " SM 16

—energetic belief: "It was inevitable that [Romola] should judge the Frate unfairly on a question of individual suffering, at which *she* looked with the eyes of personal tenderness, and *he* with the eyes of theoretic conviction. In that declaration of his, that the cause of his party was the cause of God's kingdom, she heard only the ring of egoism. Perhaps such words have rarely been uttered without that meaner ring in them; yet they are the implicit formula of all energetic belief. And if such energetic belief, pursuing a grand and remote end, is often in danger of becoming a demon-worship, in which the votary lets his son and daughter pass

through the fire with a readiness that hardly looks like sacrifice; tender fellow-feeling for the nearest has its danger too, and is apt to be timid and sceptical towards the larger aims without which life cannot rise into religion. In this way poor Romola was being blinded by her tears." R 61

—*errand of mercy:* "Dinah began to doubt whether Hetty was conscious who it was that sat beside her. She thought suffering and fear might have driven the poor sinner out of her mind. But it was borne in upon her, as she afterwards said, that she must not hurry God's work: we are over-hasty to speak—as if God did not manifest himself by our silent feeling, and make his love felt through ours." AB 45

—*Evangelicalism* "had brought into palpable existence and operation in Milby society that idea of duty, that recognition of something to be lived for beyond the mere satisfaction of self, which is to the moral life what the addition of a great central ganglion is to animal life. No man can begin to mould himself on a faith or an idea without rising to a higher order of experience: a principle of subordination, of self-mastery, has been introduced into his nature; he is no longer a mere bundle of impressions, desires, and impulses. Whatever might be the weaknesses of the ladies who pruned the luxuriance of their lace and ribbons, cut out garments for the poor, distributed tracts, quoted Scripture, and defined the true Gospel, they had learned this—that there was a divine work to be done in life, a rule of goodness higher than the opinion of their neighbours; and if the notion of a heaven in reserve for themselves was a little too prominent, yet the theory of fitness for that heaven consisted in purity of heart, in Christ-like compassion, in the subduing of selfish desires. They might give the name of piety to much that was only puritanic egoism; they might call many things sin that were not sin; but they had at least the feeling that sin was to be avoided and resisted, and colour-blindness, which may mistake drab for scarlet, is better than total blindness, which sees no distinction of colour at all . . . . The first condition of human goodness is something to love; the second, something to reverence. And this latter precious gift was brought to Milby by Mr Tryan and Evangelicalism." JR 10

"The real drama of Evangelicalism—and it has abundance of fine drama for any one who has genius enough to discern and reproduce it—lies among the middle and lower classes; and are not Evangelical opinions understood to give an especial interest to the weak things of the earth, rather than in the mighty?" SN 457

—*experience:* "The first religious experience of her life—the first self-questioning, the first voluntary subjection, the first longing to acquire the strength of greater motives and obey the more strenuous rule . . . . " FH 27

—*faith annihilated:* "For continual suffering had annihilated religious faith within me: to the utterly miserable—the unloving and the unloved—there is no religion possible, no worship but a worship of devils." LV 2

—*faith prophetic:* "But faith, the stronger for extremity,
Becomes prophetic, hears the far-off tread
Of western chivalry, sees downward sweep
The archangel *Michael* with the gleaming sword,
And listens for the shriek of hurrying fiends
Chased from their revels in God's sanctuary.
So trusts the monk, and lifts appealing eyes
To the high dome, the Church's firmament,
Where the blue light-pierced curtain, rolled away,
Reveals the throne and Him who sits thereon.
So trust the men whose best hope for the world
Is ever that the world is near its end:
Impatient of the stars that keep their course
And make no pathway for the coming Judge." SG I i

—*of fear:* "The divine tribunal had changed its aspect for him: self-prostration was no longer enough, and he must bring restitution in his hand. It was really before his God that Bulstrode was about to attempt such restitution as seemed possible: a great dread had seized his susceptible frame, and the scorching approach of shame wrought in him a new spiritual need. Night and day, while the resurgent threatening past was making a conscience within him, he was thinking by what means he could recover peace and trust—by what sacrifice he could stay the rod. His belief in these moments of dread was, that if he spontaneously did something right, God would save him from the consequences of wrong-doing. For religion can only change when the emotions which fill it are changed; and the religion of personal fear remains nearly at the level of the savage." MM 61

—*the God within: see* Laughter—*superiority*

—*Inquisition:* " 'Their theory,
Abstracting inconvenience of racks,
Whip-lashes, dragonnades and all things coarse

Inherent in the fact or concrete mass,
Presents the pure idea—utmost good
Secured by Order only to be found
In strict subordination, hierarchy
Of forces where, by nature's law, the strong
Has rightful empire, rule of weaker proved
Mere dissolution. What can you object?
The Inquisition—if you turn away
From narrow notice how the scent of gold
Has guided sense of damning heresy—
The Inquisition is sublime, is love
Hindering the spread of poison in men's souls:
The flames are nothing: only smaller pain
To hinder greater, or the pain of one
To save the many, such as throbs at heart
Of every system born into the world.' " CB 258-77

—*literary influence:* "On two points we wish [**Keightly**] had been more full and particular: namely, on the degree in which the story of the Fall, both of the angels and of man, was created by **Milton**, and on the influence of his creations in determining popular theological notions. It helps us to understand how the poets of primitive ages give fixity to national religions, when we find that in quite modern times an Epic gets itself accepted as a sort of gloss on the Scriptures, and that perhaps to the majority of English minds at this moment, it would be difficult to say how much of their belief about Satan, about the temptation of our 'first parents,' and the consequences of the Fall, is gathered from the Bible, and how much from Paradise Lost." BL 2 604

—*love:* "The more there was said about her husband, the more there was done for him, surely the safer he would be. It was poor Lisbeth's blind way of feeling that human love and pity are a ground of faith in some other love. " AB 18

—*martyrdom:* "When **Savonarola** felt himself dragged and pushed along in the midst of that hooting multitude; when lanterns were lifted to show him deriding faces; when he felt himself spit upon, smitten and kicked with grossest words of insult, it seemed to him that the worst bitterness of life was past. If men judged him guilty, and were bent on having his blood, it was only death that awaited him. But the worst drop of bitterness can never be wrung on to our lips from without: the lowest depth of resignation is not to be found in martyrdom; it is only to be found when we have covered our heads in silence and felt, 'I am not worthy to be a martyr; the Truth shall prosper, but not by me.' " R 66

—*the Messiah:* "There is a legend told of the Emperor **Domitian** that having heard of a Jewish family, of the house of **David**, whence the ruler of the world was to spring, he sent for its members in alarm, but quickly released them on observing that they had the hands of work-people—being of just the opposite opinion with that Rabbi who stood waiting at the gate of Rome in confidence that the Messiah would be found among the destitute who entered there. Both Emperor and Rabbi were wrong in their trust of outwards signs: poverty and poor clothes are no sign of inspiration . . . but they have gone with it in some remarkable cases. And to regard discipleship as out of the question because of them, would be mere dulness of imagination." DD 41

—*Methodism:* " . . . the picture we are apt to make of Methodism in our imagination is not an amphitheatre of green hills, or the deep shade of broad-leaved sycamores, where a crowd of rough men and weary-hearted women drank in a faith which was a rudimentary culture, which linked their thoughts with the past, lifted their imagination above the sordid details of their own narrow lives, and suffused their souls with the sense of a pitying, loving infinite Presence, sweet as summer to the houseless needy. It is too possible that to some of my readers Methodism may mean nothing more than low-pitched gables up dingy streets, sleek grocers, sponging preachers and hypocritical jargon—elements which are regarded as an exhaustive analysis of Methodism in many fashionable quarters.

"This would be a pity; for I cannot pretend that Seth and Dinah were anything else than Methodists—not indeed of that modern type which reads quarterly reviews and attends in chapels with pillared porticoes; but of a very old-fashioned kind. They believed in present miracles, in instantaneous conversions, in revelations by dreams and visions; they drew lots, and sought for Divine guidance by opening the Bible at hazard; having a literal way of interpreting the Scriptures, which is not at all sanctioned by approved commentators; and it is impossible for me to represent their diction as correct, or their instructions as liberal. Still—if I have read religious history aright—faith, hope, and charity have not always been found in a direct ratio with a sensibility to the three concords; and it is possible, thank Heaven! to have very erroneous theories and very sublime feelings. The raw bacon which clumsy Molly spares from her own scanty store, that she may carry it to her neighbour's child to 'stop the fits,' may be a piteously inefficacious remedy; but the generous stirring of neighbourly kindness that prompted the deed, has a beneficent radiation that is not lost." AB 3

—and veracity: "And it is commonly seen that, in proportion as religious sects believe themselves to be guided by direct inspiration rather than by a spontaneous exertion of their faculties, their sense of truthfulness is misty and confused. No one can have talked to the more enthusiastic Methodists and listened to their stories of miracles without perceiving that they require no other passport to a statement than that it accords with their wishes and their general conception of God's dealings; nay, they regard as a symptom of sinful scepticism an inquiry into the evidence for a story which they think unquestionably tends to the glory of God, and in retailing such stories, new particulars, further tending to His glory, are 'borne in' upon their minds." TE 85

—mystery: "The Church
Takes mystery as her empire, brings its wealth
Of possibility to fill the void
'Twixt contradictions—warrants so a faith
Defying sense and all its ruthless train
Of arrogant 'Therefores' . . . .
The Church explains not, governs—feeds resolve
By vision fraught with heart-experience
And human yearning.' " CB 228-33, 237-9

—new ideas: "Religious ideas have the fate of melodies, which, once set afloat in the world, are taken up by all sorts of instruments, some of them woefully coarse, feeble, or out of tune, until people are in danger of crying out that the melody itself is detestable. It may be that some of Mr Tryan's hearers had gained a religious vocabulary rather than religious experience; that here and there a weaver's wife, who, a few months before, had been simply a silly slattern, was converted into that more complex nuisance, a silly and sanctimonious slattern; that the old Adam, with the pertinacity of middle age, continued to tell fibs behind the counter, notwithstanding the new Adam's addiction to Bible-reading and family prayer; that the children in the Paddiford Sunday school had their memories crammed with phrases about the blood of cleansing, imputed righteousness, and justification by faith alone, which an experience lying principally in chuck-farthing, hopscotch, parental slappings, and longings after unattainable lollipop, served rather to darken than to illustrate; and that at Milby, in those distant days, as in all other times and places where the mental atmosphere is changing, and men are inhaling the stimulus of new ideas, folly often mistook itself for wisdom, ignorance gave itself airs of knowledge, and selfishness, turning its eyes upward, called itself religion." JR 10

—perfection not required: "The blessed work of helping the world forward, happily does not wait to be done by perfect men; and I should imagine that neither Luther nor John Bunyan, for example, would have satisfied the modern demand for an ideal hero, who believes nothing but what is true, feels nothing but what is exalted, and does nothing but what is graceful. The real heroes, of God's making, are quite different: they have their natural heritage of love and conscience which they drew in with their mother's milk; he'll know one or two of those deep spiritual truths which are only to be won by long wrestling with their own sins and their own sorrows; they have earned faith and strength so far as they have done genuine work; but the rest is dry barren theory, blank prejudice, vague hearsay. Their insight is blended with mere opinion; their sympathy is perhaps confined in narrow conduits of doctrine, instead of flowing forth with the freedom of a stream that blesses every weed in its course; obstinacy or self-assertion will often interfuse itself with their grandest impulses; and their very deeds of self-sacrifice are sometimes only the rebound of a passionate egoism." JR 10

—and philosophy: " . . . religion and philosophy are not merely conciliated, they are identical; or rather, religion is the crown and consummation of philosophy—the delicate corolla, which can only spread out its petals in all their symmetry and brilliance to the sun, when root and branch exhibit the conditions of a healthy and vigorous life." PI 355-6

—poverty: see —the Messiah

—prophet: " 'If a prophet is to keep his power [said **Macchiavelli**], he must be a prophet like **Mahomet**, with an army at his back, that when the people's faith is fainting it may be frightened into life again.' " R 45

—spiritual side: " ' . . . I know there's a deal in a man's inward life as you can't measure by the square, and say, "do this and that'll follow," and, "do that and this'll follow." There's things go on in the soul, and times when feelings come into you like a rushing mighty wind, as the Scripture says, and part your life in two a'most, so as you look back on yourself as if you was somebody else. Those are things as you can't bottle up in a "do this" and "do that;" and I'll go so far with the strongest Methodist ever you'll find. That shows me there's deep, speritial things in religion. You can't make much out wi' talking about it, but you feel it.' " AB 17

—vision: " 'For in the painful linking together of our waking thoughts we can never be sure that we have not mingled our own error with the light we have prayed for; but

in visions and dreams we are passive, and our souls are as an instrument in the Divine hand.' " R 15

And see M:Belief

Religious observance

—bells: "But the bells
Pealing on high from two quaint convent towers,
Still ring the Catholic signals, summoning
To grave remembrance of the larger life
That bears our own, like perishable fruit
Upon its heaven-wide branches." AG 38-43

—community: " 'Your prompting to go to your nearest friends . . . is a true prompting, to which the Church in its original constitution and discipline responds—opening its arms to the penitent—watching over its children to the last—never abandoning them until they are hopelessly reprobate. And the Church ought to represent the feeling of the community, so that every parish should be a family knit together by Christian brotherhood under a spiritual father. But the ideas of discipline and Christian fraternity are entirely relaxed—they can hardly be said to exist in the public mind: they hardly survive except in the partial, contradictory form they have taken in the narrow communities of schismatics; and if I were not supported by the firm faith that the Church must ultimately recover the full force of that constitution which is alone fitted to human needs, I should often lose heart at observing the want of fellowship and sense of mutual responsibility among my own flock. At present everything seems tending towards the relaxation of ties—towards the substitution of wayward choice for the adherence to obligation which has its roots in the past.' " MF VII 2

—confirmation: " . . . the Confirmation that day was a pretty sight, at least when those slight girlish forms and fair young faces moved in a white rivulet along the aisles, and flowed into kneeling semicircles under the light of the great chancel window, softened by patches of dark old painted glass; and one would think that to look on while a pair of venerable hands pressed such young heads, and a venerable face looked upward for a blessing on them, would be very likely to make the heart swell gently, and to moisten the eyes. Yet I remember the eyes seemed very dry in Milby Church that day, notwithstanding that the Bishop was an old man, and probably venerable (for though he was not an eminent Grecian, he was the brother of a Whig lord); and I think the eyes must have remained dry, because he had small delicate womanish hands adorned with ruffles, and, instead of laying them on the girls' heads, just let them hover over each in quick succession, as if it were not etiquette to touch them, and as if the laying on of hands were like the theatrical embrace—part of the play, and not to be really believed in. To be sure there were a great many heads, and the Bishop's time was limited. Moreover, a wig can, under no circumstances, be affecting, except in rare cases of illusion; and copious lawn-sleeves cannot be expected to go directly to any heart except a washerwoman's." JR 6

—feast-day procession: " . . . the very saints, surrounded with their almond-shaped glory, and floating on clouds with their joyous companionship of winged cherubs . . . seemed, on the eve of San Giovanni, to have brought their piece of the heavens down into the narrow streets, and to pass slowly through them; and, more wonderful still, saints of gigantic size, with attendant angels, might be seen, not seated, but moving in a slow mysterious manner along the streets, like a procession of colossal figures come down from the high domes and tribunes of the churches.

"The clouds were made of good woven stuff, the saints and cherubs were unglorified mortals supported by firm bars, and those mysterious giants were really men of very steady brain, balancing themselves on stilts, and enlarged, like Greek tragedians, by huge masks and stuffed shoulders; but he was a miserably unimaginative Florentine who thought only of that—nay, somewhat impious, for in the images of sacred things was there not some of the virtue of sacred things themselves?

"And if, after that, there came a company of merry black demons well armed with claws and thongs, and other implements of sport, ready to perform impromptu farces of bastinadoing and clothes-tearing, why, that was the demons' way of keeping a vigil, and they, too, might have descended from the domes and the tribunes. The Tuscan mind slipped from the devout to the burlesque, as readily as water round an angle; and the saints had already had their turn, had gone their way, and made their due pause before the gates of San Giovanni, to do him honour on the eve of his *festa*." ¶R 8

—historically speaking: "The days were gone when people could be greatly wrought upon by their faith, still less change it: the Catholics were formidable because they would lay hold of government and property, and burn men alive; not because any sane and honest parishioner of St Ogg's could be brought to believe in the Pope. One aged person remembered how a rude multitude had been swayed when **John Wesley** preached in the cattle-market, but for a long while it had not been expected of preachers

that they should shake the souls of men. An occasional burst of fervour in dissenting pulpits on the subject of infant baptism was the only symptom of a zeal unsuited to sober times when men had done with change. Protestantism sat at ease, unmindful of schisms, careless of proselytism: dissent was an inheritance along with a superior pew and a business connection, and Churchmanship only wondered contemptuously at Dissent as a foolish habit that clung greatly to families in the grocery and chandlering lines, though not incompatible with prosperous wholesale dealing. But with the Catholic question had come a slight wind of controversy to break the calm . . . . " MF I 12

—hymn-singing: "And the singing was no mechanical affair of official routine; it had a drama. As the moment of psalmody approached, by some process to me as mysterious and untraceable as the opening of the flowers or the breaking-out of the stars, a slate appeared in front of the gallery, advertising in bold characters the psalm about to be sung, lest the sonorous announcement of the clerk should still leave the bucolic mind in doubt on that head. Then followed the migration of the clerk to the gallery, where, in company with a bassoon, two key-bugles, a carpenter understood to have an amazing power of singing 'counter', and two lesser musical stars, he formed the complement of a choir regarded in Shepperton as one of distinguished attraction, occasionally known to draw hearers from the next parish. The innovation of hymn-books was as yet undreamed of; even the New Version was regarded with a sort of melancholy tolerance, as part of the common degeneracy in a time when prices had dwindled, and a cotton gown was no longer stout enough to last a lifetime; for the lyrical taste of the best heads in Shepperton had been formed on **Sternhold** and **Hopkins**. But the greatest triumphs of the Shepperton choir were reserved for the Sundays when the slate announced an ANTHEM, with a dignified abstinence from particularisation, both words and music lying far beyond the reach of the most ambitious amateur in the congregation —an anthem in which the key-bugles always ran away at a great pace, while the bassoon every now and then boomed a flying shot after them." SF 1

—Jewish: "The Hebrew liturgy, like others, has its transitions of litany, lyric, proclamation, dry statement and blessing; but this evening all were one for Deronda: the chant of the *Chazan's* or Reader's grand wide-ranging voice with its passage from monotony to sudden cries, the outburst of sweet boys' voices from the little quire, the devotional swaying of men's bodies backwards and forwards, the very commonness of the building and shabbiness of the scene where a national faith, which had penetrated the thinking of half the world, and moulded the splendid forms of the world's religion, was finding a remote, obscure echo—all were blent for him as one expression of a binding history, tragic and yet glorious. He wondered at the strength of his own feeling; it seemed beyond the occasion—what one might imagine to be a divine influx in the darkness, before there was any vision to interpret. The whole scene was a coherent strain, its burthen a passionate regret, which, if he had known the liturgy for the Day of Reconciliation, he might have clad in its antithetic burthen: 'Happy the eye which saw all these things, but verily to hear only of them afflicts our soul. Happy the eye that saw our temple and the joy of our congregation; but verily to hear only of them afflicts our soul. Happy the eye that saw the fingers when tuning every kind of song; but verily to hear only of them afflicts our soul.' " DD 32

—labouring class: " . . . there are many among its myriads of souls who have absolutely needed an emphatic belief, life in this unpleasurable shape demanding some solution even to unspeculative minds; just as you inquire into the stuffing of your couch when anything galls you there, whereas eider-down and perfect French springs excite no question. Some have an emphatic belief in alcohol, and seek their *ekstasis* or outside standing-ground in gin, but the rest require something that good society calls enthusiasm, something that will present motives in an entire absence of high prizes, something that will give patience and feed human love when the limbs ache with weariness and human looks are hard upon us—something, clearly, that lies outside personal desires, that includes resignation for ourselves and active love for what is not ourselves." MF IV 3

—moderate: "The inhabitants of Raveloe were not severely regular in their church-going, and perhaps there was hardly a person in the parish who would not have held that to go to church every Sunday in the calendar would have shown a greedy desire to stand well with Heaven, and get an undue advantage over their neighbours—a wish to be better than the 'common run,' that would have implied a reflection on those who had had godfathers and godmothers as well as themselves, and had an equal right to the burying-service. At the same time, it was understood to be requisite for all who were not household servants, or young men, to take the sacrament at one of the great festivals. Squire Cass himself took it on Christ-

mas-day; while those who were held to be 'good livers' went to church with greater, though still with moderate, frequency." SM 10

—*mysticism:* "All the instruction, all the main influences of her life had gone to fortify her scorn of that sickly superstition which led men and women, with eyes too weak for the daylight, to sit in dark swamps and try to read human destiny by the chance flame of wandering vapours." R 36

—*Protestantism*

—*rural:* "If [a hamlet's] face was to be seen, it was most likely dirty; but the dirt was Protestant dirt, and the big, bold, gin-breathing tramps were Protestant tramps. There was no sign of superstition near, no crucifix or image to indicate a misguided reverence: the inhabitants were probably so free from superstition that they were in much less awe of the parson than of the overseer. Yet they were saved from the excesses of Protestantism by not knowing how to read, and by the absence of handlooms and mines to be the pioneers of Dissent: they were kept safely in the *via media* of indifference, and could have registered themselves in the census by a big black mark as members of the Church of England." FH *I*

—*way of life:* "Certainly, the religious and moral ideas of the Dodsons and Tullivers were of too specific a kind to be arrived at deductively, from the statement that they were part of the Protestant population of Great Britain. Their theory of life had its core of soundness, as all theories must have on which decent and prosperous families have been reared and have flourished; but it had the very slightest tincture of theology. If, in the maiden days of the Dodson sisters, their bibles opened more easily at some parts than others, it was because of dried tulip petals, which had been distributed quite impartially, without preference for the historical, devotional, or doctrinal. Their religion was of a simple, semi-pagan kind, but there was no heresy in it, if heresy properly means choice, for they didn't know there was any other religion, except that of chapel-goers, which appeared to run in families, like asthma." MF IV 1

—*Puritans:* "Again, the Scotch Puritans, during the comparatively short period of their ascendency, surpassed all Christians before them in the elaborate ingenuity of the tortures they applied for the discovery of witchcraft and sorcery, and did their utmost to prove that if Scotch Calvinism was the true religion, the chief 'note' of the true religion was cruelty. It is hardly an endurable task to read the story of their doings; thoroughly to imagine them as a past reality is already a sort of torture. One detail is enough, and it is a comparatively mild one. It was the regular profession of men called 'prickers' to thrust long pins into the body of a suspected witch in order to detect the insensible spot which was the infallible sign of her guilt." IR 112

—*Quakers:* "It was impossible to leave the question of church-rates without noting the grounds of their injustice . . . Mr Lyon, for his own part, would not present that passive resistance to a legal imposition which had been adopted by the Friends (whose heroism in this regard was nevertheless worthy of all honour)." FH 16

—*Roman Catholicism: See* RW:Rome

—*sabbath:* " 'And this is my way o'looking at it [said Adam Bede]: there's the sperrit o' God in all things and all times—weekday as well as Sunday—and i' the great works and inventions, and i' the figuring and the mechanics. And God helps us with our headpieces and our hands as well as with our souls; and if a man does bits o' jobs out o' working hours—builds a oven for's wife to save her from going to the bakehouse, or scratch at his bit o' garden and makes two potatoes grow istead o' one, he's doing more good, and he's just as near to God, as if he was running after some preacher and a-praying and a-groaning.' " AB 1

—*sect*

—*offense:* "Any resort to legal measures for ascertaining the culprit was contrary to the principles of the church in Lantern Yard, according to which prosecution was forbidden to Christians, even had the case held less scandal to the community. But the members were bound to take other measures for finding out the truth, and they resolved on praying and drawing lots. This resolution can be a ground of surprise only to those who are unacquainted with that obscure religious life which has gone on in the alleys of our towns." SM 1

—*simplicity:* "To people accustomed to reason about the forms in which their religious feeling has incorporated itself, it is difficult to enter into that simple, untaught state of mind in which the form and the feeling have never been severed by an act of reflection." SM 1

—*tangibles:* "The whitewashed walls; the little pews where well-known figures entered with a subdued rustling, and where first one well-known voice and then another, pitched in a peculiar key of petition. Uttered phrases at once occult and familiar, like the amulet worn on the heart; the pulpit where the minister delivered unquestioned doctrine, and swayed to and fro, and handled the book in a long-accustomed manner; the very pauses between the couplets of the hymn, as it was given out, and the recurrent swell of voices in song: these things had been the channel of divine influences to Marner—they were the fostering home of his religious emotions— they were Christianity and God's kingdom upon earth." SM 2

—*sermon:* " . . . all with that brisk and cheerful air which a sermon is often observed to produce when it is quite finished." GL 11

Remorse and Regret

—*amends:* " . . . as the true penitent, hating his self-besotted error, asks from all coming life duty instead of joy, and service instead of ease, so Rufus was perpetually on the watch lest he should ever again postpone to some private affection a great public opportunity which to him was equivalent to a command." FH 15

—*character development:* " 'I meant that those who would be comparatively uninteresting beforehand may become worthier of sympathy when they do something that awakens in them a keen remorse. Lives are enlarged in different ways. I daresay some would never get their eyes opened if it were not for a violent shock from the consequences of their own actions. And when they are suffering in that way one must care for them more than for the comfortably self-satisfied. " DD 36

—*inaccessible:* "There is heroism even in the circles of hell for fellow-sinners who cling to each other in the fiery whirlwind and never recriminate. But these things, which are easy to discern when they are painted for us on the large canvass of poetic story, become confused and obscure even for well-read gentlemen when their affection for themselves is alarmed by pressing details of actual experience. If their comparison of instances is active at such times, it is chiefly in showing them that their own case has subtle distinctions from all other cases, which should free them from unmitigated condemnation." FH 42

—*new start:* "Very slight words and deeds may have a sacramental efficacy, if we can cast our self-love behind us, in order to say or do them. And it has been well believed through many ages that the beginning of compunction is the beginning of a new life; that the mind which sees it self blameless may be called dead in trespasses—in trespasses on the love of others, in trespasses on their weakness, in trespasses on all those great claims which are the image of our own need." FH 13

—*noble mind:* "In a mind of any nobleness, a lapse into transgression against an object still regarded as supreme, issues in a new and purer devotedness, chastised by humility and watched over by a passionate regret." FH 15

—*punishment:* "Men do not become penitent and learn to abhor themselves by having their backs cut open with the lash; rather, they learn to abhor the ash." FH 42

—*reformation:* " . . . a landed proprietor with a mixture of noble blood in his veins was not to be an object of suspicious inquiry like a reformed character who offers himself as your butler or footman. Reformation, where a man can afford to do without it, can hardly be other than genuine." DD 9

—*spurious:* "A man who had stolen the pyx, and got frightened when justice was at his heels, might feel the sort of penitence which would induce him to run back in the dark and lay the pyx where the sexton might find it; but if in doing so he whispered to the Blessed Virgin that he was moved by considering the sacredness of all property, and the peculiar sacredness of the pyx, it is not to be believed that she would like him the better for it. Indeed, one often seems to see why the saints should prefer candles to words, especially from penitents whose skin is in danger." FH 42

Self and Selfishness

—*awareness:* "The character of the publican and sinner is not always practically incompatible with that of the modern Pharisee, for the majority of us scarcely see more distinctly the faultiness of our own conduct than the faultiness of our own arguments, or the dulness of our own jokes." MM 18

—*centered:* "Mr Casaubon, too, was the center of his own world; if he was liable to think that others were providentially made for him, and especially to consider them in the light of their fitness for the author of a 'Key to all Mythologies,' this trait is not quite alien to us, and, like the other mendicant hopes of mortals, claims some of our pity." MM 1

—*confidence:* "But self-confidence is apt to address itself to an imaginary dulness in others; as people who are well off speak in a cajoling tone to the poor, and those who are in the prime of life raise their voice and talk artificially to seniors, hastily conceiving them to be deaf and rather imbecile." DD 5

—*cornered:* "A doomed animal, with every issue earthed up except that where its enemy stands, must, if it has teeth and fierceness, try its one chance without delay. And a man may reach a point in his life in which his impulses are not distinguished from those of a hunted brute by any capability of scruples. Our selfishness is so robust and many-clutching, that, well encouraged, it easily devours all sustenance away from our poor little scruples." FH 47

—discontent: "But his endurance was mingled with a self-discontent which, if we know how to be candid, we shall confess to make more than half our bitterness under grievances, wife or husband included. It always remains true that if we had been greater, circumstance would have been less strong against us." MM 58

—and sunlight: "There are few of us that are not rather ashamed of our sins and follies as we look out on the blessed morning sunlight, which comes to us like a bright-winged angel beckoning us to quit the old path of vanity that stretches its dreary length behind us; and Tina, little as she knew about doctrines and theories, seemed to herself to have been both foolish and wicked yesterday. Today she would try to be good . . . . " GL 6

—esteem: "Indeed, what mortal is there of us, who would find his satisfaction enhanced by an opportunity of comparing the picture he presents to himself of his own doings, with the picture they make on the mental retina of his neighbours? We are poor plants buoyed up by the air-vessels of our own conceit: alas for us, if we get a few pinches that empty us of that windy self-subsistence! The very capacity for good would go out of us. For, tell the most impassioned orator, suddenly, that his wig is awry, or his shirt-lap hanging out, and that he is tickling people by the oddity of his person, instead of thrilling them by the energy of his periods, and you would infallibly dry up the spring of his eloquence. That is a deep and wide saying, that no miracle can be wrought without faith—without the worker's faith in himself, as well as the recipient's faith in him. And the greater part of the worker's faith in himself is made up of the faith that others believe in him.

"Let me be persuaded that my neighbour Jenkins considers me a blockhead, and I shall never shine in conversation with him any more. Let me discover that the lovely Phoebe thinks my squint intolerable, and I shall never be able to fix her blandly with my disengaged eye again.

"Thank heaven, then, that a little illusion is left to us, to enable us to be useful and agreeable—that the world is not made of looking-glass, to show us just the figure we are making, and just what is going on behind our backs! By the help of dear friendly illusion, we are able to dream that we are charming—and our faces wear a becoming air of self-possession; we are able to dream that other men admire our talents—and our benignity is undisturbed; we are able to dream that we are doing much good—and we do a little." SF 2

—indulgent: " . . . her new scorn of that thing called pleasure which made men base —that dexterous contrivance for selfish ease, that shrinking from endurance and strain, when others were bowing beneath burdens too heavy for them, which now made one image with her husband." R 36

—insidious: "The *Hazaels* of our world who are pushed on quickly against their preconceived confidence in themselves to do dog-like actions by the sudden suggestion of a wicked ambition, are much fewer than those who are led on through the years by the gradual demands of a selfishness which has spread its fibres far and wide through the intricate vanities and sordid cares of an everyday existence." FH 42

—knowledge: "For though Amos thought himself strong, he did not *feel* himself strong. Nature had given him the opinion, but not the sensation. Without that opinion he would probably never have worn cambric bands, but would have been an excellent cabinetmaker and deacon of an Independent church, as his father was before him. . . . " SF 2

—magnified self-importance: " . . . an uneasy vanity that happened to have been directed towards authorship. Its importance was that of a polypus, tumour, fungus, or other erratic outgrowth, noxious and disfiguring in its effect on the individual organism which nourishes it . . . which makes the Self disagreeably larger . . . . " TS 15

—past views: "We have all of us considerable regard for our past self, and are not fond of casting reflections on that respected individual by a total negation of his opinions." JR 12

—perception of another: "Fred fancied that he saw to the bottom of his uncle's . . . soul, though in reality half what he saw there was no more than the reflex of his own inclinations. The difficult task of knowing another soul is not for young gentlemen whose consciousness is chiefly made up of their own wishes." MM 12

—reproof: "Just and self-reproving thoughts do not come to us too thickly, even in the purest air and with the best lessons of heaven and earth; how should those white-winged delicate messengers make their way to Molly's poisoned chamber . . . ?" SM 12

—result: "Among the things we may gamble away in a lazy selfish life is the capacity for ruth, compunction, or any unselfish regret—which we may come to long for as one in slow death longs to feel laceration, rather than be conscious of a widening margin where consciousness once was." DD 62

—self-consciousness: "My self-consciousness was heightened to that pitch of intensity in which our own emotions take the form of a drama which urges itself imperatively on our contemplation, and we begin to weep, less under the sense of our suffering than at the thought of it." LV 2

And see Egoism and Egotism

Sincerity

—inconsistency: "It is but a shallow haste which concludeth insincerity from what outsiders call inconsistency—putting a dead mechanism of 'ifs' and 'therefores' for the loving myriad of hidden suckers whereby the belief and the conduct are wrought into mutual sustainment." MM 53 ep *And see* M:Consistency

Soul

—bargain: "It is an old story, that men sell themselves to the tempter, and sign a bond with their blood, because it is only to take effect at a distant day; then rush on to snatch the cup their souls thirst after with an impulse not the less savage because there is a dark shadow beside them for evermore. There is no short cut, no patent train-road, to wisdom: after all the centuries of invention, the soul's path lies through the thorny wilderness which must be still trodden in solitude, with bleeding feet, with sobs for help, as it was trodden by them of old time." LV 1

—change: "Since, as we know, men change their skies and see new constellations without changing their souls, it will follow sometimes that they don't change their business under those novel circumstances." BJ 3

—higher nature: "It is our habit to say that while the lower nature can never understand the higher, the higher nature commands a complete view of the lower. But I think the higher nature has to learn this comprehension, as we learn the art of vision, by a good deal of hard experience, often with bruises and gashes incurred in taking things up by the wrong end, and fancying our space wider than it is." AB 15

—hospitable: "For the human soul is hospitable, and will entertain conflicting sentiments and contradictory opinions with much impartiality." R *P*

—need for trust: "No soul is desolate as long as there is a human being for whom it can feel trust and reverence." R 44

—sick: "Inwardly he was in a state of rebellion, but he had no arguments to meet his father's; and while he was feeling in spite of anything that might be said, that he should like to go off to 'the colonies' to-morrow, it lay in a deep fold of his consciousness that he ought to feel—if he had been a better fellow he would have felt—more about his old ties. This is the sort of faith we live by in our soul-sicknesses." DD 8

—vibration: ". . . we must learn to accommodate ourselves to the discovery that some of those cunningly-fashioned instruments called human souls have only a very limited range of music, and will not vibrate in the least under a touch that fills others with tremulous rapture or quivering agony." AB 9

Suicide

—impossible: "The clear waves seemed to invite her: she wished she could lie down to sleep on them and pass from sleep into death. But Romola could not directly seek death; the fulness of young life in her forbade that. She could only wish that death would come." R 61

—thoughts: "Only those who have known what hardest inward conflict is can know what Maggie felt as she sat in her loneliness the evening after hearing that news from Mrs Glegg [that her dear cousin Lucy was going away]—only those who have known what it is to dread their own selfish desires as the watching mother would dread the sleeping-potion that was to still her own pain." MF VII 4

". . . no image of rest coming across her mind, except of that far, far off rest, from which there would be no more waking for her into this struggling earthly life." MF VII 5

Temptation

—a story: "A German poet was intrusted with a particularly fine sausage, which he was to convey to the donor's friend at Paris. In the course of a long journey he smelt the sausage; he got hungry, and desired to taste it; he pared a morsel off, then another, and another, in successive moments of temptation, till at last the sausage was, humanly speaking, at an end. The offence had not been premeditated. The poet had never loved meanness, but he loved sausage; and the result was undeniably awkward.

"As it was with Matthew Jermyn. He was far from liking that ugly abstraction rascality, but he had liked other things which had suggested nibbling. He had had to do many things in law and in daily life which, in the abstract, he would have condemned; and indeed he had never been tempted by them in the abstract. Here, in fact, was the inconvenience; he had sinned for the sake of particular concrete things, and particular concrete consequences were likely to follow." FH 9

—*another story:* " 'I want to tell you what it was that came over me in that boat. I was full of rage at being obliged to go—full of rage—and I could do nothing but sit there like a galley-slave. And then we got away—out of the port—into the deep—and everything was still— and we never looked at each other, only he spoke to order me—and the very light about me seemed to hold me a prisoner and force me to sit as I did. It came over me that when I was a child I used to fancy sailing away into a world where people were not forced to live with any one they did not like—I did not like my father-in-law to come home. And now, I thought, just the opposite had come to me. I had stept into a boat, and my life was a sailing and sailing away—gliding on and no help—always into solitude with *him,* away from deliverance. And because I felt more helpless than ever, my thoughts went out over worse things—I longed for worse things—I had cruel wishes—I fancied impossible ways of—I did not want to die myself, I was afraid of our being drowned together. If it had been any use I should have prayed—I should have prayed that something might befall him. I should have prayed that he might sink out of my sight and leave me alone. I knew no way of killing him there, but I did, I did kill him in my thoughts.'

"She sank into silence for a minute, submerged by the weight of memory which no words could represent.

" 'But yet all the while I felt I was getting more wicked. And what had been with me so much, came to me just then—what you once said—about dreading to increase my wrong-doing and my remorse—I should hope for nothing then. It was all like a writing of fire within me. Getting wicked was misery—being shut out for ever from knowing what you—what better lives were. That had always been coming back to me in the midst of bad thoughts—it came back to me then—but yet with a despair—a feeling that it was no use—evil wishes were too strong. I remember then letting to the tiller and saying "God help me!" But then I was forced to take it again and go on; and the evil longings, the evil prayers came again and blotted everything else dim, till, in the midst of them—I don't know how it was—he was turning the sail—there was a gust—he was struck—I knew nothing—I only know that I saw my wish outside me.'

"She began to speak more hurriedly, and in more of a whisper.

" 'I saw him sink, and my heart gave a leap as if it were going out of me. I think I did not move. I kept my hands tight. It was long enough for me to be glad, and yet to think it was no use—he would come up again. And he *was* come—farther off—the boat had moved. It was all like lightning. "The rope!" he called out in a voice—not his own—I hear it now—and I stooped for the rope—I felt I must—I felt sure he could swim, and he would come back whether or not, and I dreaded him. That was in my mind—he would come back. But he was gone down again, and I had the rope in my hand—no, there he was again—his face above the water—and he cried again—and I held my hand, and my heart said, "Die!"—and he sank; and I felt "It is done—I am wicked, I am lost!"—and I had the rope in my hand—I don't know what I thought—I was leaping from my crime, and there it was—close to me as I fell—there was the dead face—dead, dead. It can never be altered. That was what happened. That was what I did. You know it all. It can never be altered.' " DD 56

Trust and Loyalty

—*faith:* " 'Great heaven: what relation has proved itself more potent in the world than faith even when mistaken—than expectation even when perpetually disappointed?' " DD 40

—*in a mentor:* "Without the aid of sacred ceremony or costume, her feelings had turned this man, only a few years older than herself, into a priest, a sort of trust less rare than the fidelity that guards it. Young reverence for one who is also young is the most coercive of all: there is the same level of temptation, and the higher motive is believed in as a fuller force—not suspected to be a mere residue from weary experience." DD 35

—*mutual, of Gypsies:* "Oh, it is a faith
Taught by no priest, but by their beating
hearts:
Faith to each other: the fidelity
Of fellow-wanderers in a desert place
Who share the same dire thirst, and therefore share
The scanty water: the fidelity
Of men whose pulses leap with kindred
fire,
Who in the flash of eyes, the clasp of hands,
The speech that even in lying tells the
truth
Of heritage inevitable as birth,
Nay, in the silent bodily presence feel
The mystic stirring of a common life
Which makes the many one: fidelity
To the consecrating oath our sponsor Fate

Made through our infant breath when we were born
The fellow-heirs of that small island, Life . . . " SG I vi

—the reciprocal: "Those who trust us educate us." DD 335

—in a subordinate: "Matthew Jermyn was under no misgivings as to the fealty of Johnson. He had 'been the making of Johnson'; and this seems to many men a reason for expecting devotion, in spite of the fact that they themselves, though very fond of their own persons and lives, are not at all devoted to the Maker they believe in." FH 29

—in a teacher: "No one who has ever known what it is thus to lose faith in a fellow-man whom he has profoundly loved and reverenced, will lightly say that the shock can leave the faith in the Invisible Goodness unshaken. With the sinking of high human trust, the dignity of life sinks too; we cease to believe in our own better self, since that also is part of the common nature which is degraded in our thought; and all the finer impulses of the soul are dulled." R 61

Truth and Falsehood

—analysis: " 'I myself, from my youth up, have been given to question too curiously concerning the truth—to examine and sift the medicine of the soul rather than to apply it.' " FH 5

—and beauty: " 'If people have thought what is the most beautiful and the best thing, it must be true. It is always there.' " DD 37

—evidence: "A distinct appreciation of the value of evidence—in other words, the intellectual perception of truth—is more closely allied to truthfulness of statement, or the moral quality of veracity, than is generally admitted. That highest moral habit, the constant preference of truth, both theoretically and practically, pre-eminently demands the co-operation of the intellect with the impulses—as is indicated by the fact that it is only found in anything like completeness in the highest class of minds." TE 84-5

—fact: "[He] could not, more than the rest of us, continuously escape suffering from the pressure of that hard unaccommodating Actual, which has never consulted our taste and is entirely unselect." DD 33

—falseness: "It is possible to pass a great many bad halfpennies and bad half-crowns, but I believe there has no instance been known of passing a halfpenny or a half-crown as a sovereign. A sharper can drive a brisk trade in this world: it is undeniable that there may be a fine career for him, if he will dare consequences . . . . " BJ 3

—in journalism: "We cannot command veracity at will: the power of seeing and reporting truly is a form of health that has to be delicately guarded . . . . " TS 14

—occasion for lying: "Tito had never had occasion to fabricate an ingenious lie before: the occasion was come now—the occasion which circumstance never fails to beget on tacit falsity . . . . " R 11

—simple: "Thy simple truth is but a false opinion:

The simple truth of asses who believe
Their thistle is the very best of food." SG I i

—a tangled web: " . . . he had borrowed from the terrible usurer Falsehood, and the loan had mounted and mounted with the years, till he belonged to the usurer, body and soul." R 39

—and torture (verbal): "The serene and beneficent goddess Truth, like other deities whose disposition has been too hastily inferred from that of the men who have invoked them, can hardly be well pleased with much of the worship paid to her even in this milder age, when the stake and the rack have ceased to form part of her ritual.

"Some cruelties still pass for service done in her honour: no thumb-screw is used, no iron boot, no scorching of flesh; but plenty of controversial bruising, laceration, and even lifelong maiming. Less than formerly; but so long as this sort of truth-worship has the sanction of a public that can often understand nothing in a controversy except personal sarcasm or slanderous ridicule, it is likely to continue. The sufferings of its victims are often as little regarded as those of the sacrificial pig offered in old time, with what we now regard as a sad miscalculation of effects." ¶TS 3

—veracity: " 'But veracity is a plant of paradise [said **Macchiavelli**], and the seeds have never flourished beyond the walls. You . . . tell poetical lies only; partly compelled by the poet's fervour, partly to please your audience; but you object to lies in prose. Well, the Frate differs from you as to the boundary of poetry, that's all. When he gets into the pulpit of the Duomo, he has the fervour within him, and without him he has the audience to please. Ecco!' " R 45

—vow: "Deronda had made a vow to himself that—since the truths which disgrace mortals are not all of their own making—the truth should never be made a disgrace to another by his act. He was not without terror lest he should break this vow, and fall into the apologetic philosophy which explains the world into containing nothing better than one's own conduct." DD 19

—*with two parents:* "For Truth to us is like
a living child
Born of two parents: if the parents part
And divide the child, how shall it live?
Or, I will rather say: Two angels guide
The path of man, both aged and yet young,
As angels are, ripening through endless
years.
On one he leans: some call her Memory,
And some, Tradition; and her voice is
sweet,
With deep mysterious accords: the other,
Floating above, holds down a lamp which
streams
A light divine and searching on the earth,
Compelling eyes and footsteps. Memory
yields,
Yet clings with loving cheek, and shines
anew
Reflecting all the rays of that bright lamp
Our angel Reason holds. We had not
walked
But for Tradition; we walk evermore
To higher paths, by brightening Reason's
lamp." SG II ii

Vanity and Conceit

—*controllable:* "Will any one be so hardy as to maintain that an otherwise worthy man cannot be vain and arrogant? I think most of us have some interest in arguing the contrary. And it is of the nature of vanity and arrogance, if unchecked, to become cruel and self-justifying. There are fierce beasts within: chain them, chain them, and let them learn to cower before the creature with wider reason. This is what one wishes for Mordax—that his heart and brain should restrain the outleap of roar and talons." TS 8

—*depreciated:* "The general conviction that we are admirable does not easily give way before a single negative; rather when any of Vanity's large family, male or female, find their performance received coldly, they are apt to believe that a little more of it will win over the unaccountable dissident." DD 1

—*male:* " . . . it would be a great mistake to estimate passionate effort by the effect it produces on our perception or understanding. It is conceivable that a man may have concentrated no less will and expectation on his wristbands, gaiters, and the shape of his hatbrim, or an appearance which impresses you as that of the modern 'swell,' than the Ojibbeway on an ornamentation which seems to us much more elaborate." TS 15

"Merely to maintain an attitude and gait which I notice in certain club men, and especially an inflation of the chest accompanying very small remarks, there goes, I am convinced, an expenditure of psychical energy little appreciated by the multitude—a mental vision of Self and deeply impressed beholders . . . . " TS 15

—*sour grapes:* "Thus I finally gave up any attempt to make out that I preferred cutting a bad figure, and that I liked to be despised, because in this way I was getting more virtuous than my successful rivals; and I have long looked with suspicion on all views which are recommended as peculiarly consolatory to wounded vanity or other personal disappointment." TS 1

—*startling:* "[He] was vain, but not more so than many contemporaries of heavy aspect, whose vanity leaps out and startles one like a spear out of a walking-stick . . . . " DD 39

—*trans-gender:* "Depend upon it, vanity is human, native alike to men and women; only in the male it is of denser texture, less volatile, so that it less immediately informs you of its presence, but is more massive and capable of knocking you down if you come into collision with it; while in women vanity lays by its small revenges as in a needle-case always at hand. The difference is in muscle and finger-tips, in traditional habits and mental perspective, rather than in the original appetite of vanity." TS 15

"No! there is no need to admit that women would carry away the prize of vanity in a competition where differences of custom were fairly considered. A man cannot show his vanity in a tight skirt which forces him to walk sideways down the staircase; but let the match be between the respective vanities of largest beard and tightest skirt, and here too the battle would be to the strong." TS 15

—*uneasy:* " . . . vanity is as ill at ease under indifference as tenderness is under a love which it cannot return . . . . " DD 10

—*vicarious:* "Esther recognized the pair too well, and felt very uncomfortable. We are so pitiably in subjection to all sorts of vanity—even the very vanities we are practically renouncing! And in spite of the almost solemn memories connected with Mrs Holt, Esther's first shudder was raised by the idea of what things this woman would say, and by the mortification of having Felix in any way represented by his mother." FH 43

—*woman's:* "Still, vanity, with a woman's whole mind and day to work in, can construct abundantly on slight hints, especially on such a hint as the possibility of indefinite conquests. How delightful to make captives from the throne of marriage with a husband as crown-prince by your side—himself in fact a subject—while the captives look up for ever hopeless, losing their rest probably, and if their appetite too, so much the better!" MM 43

Vengeance

—*convenient:* "Still, among the various excesses to which human nature is subject, moralists have never numbered that of being too fond of the people who openly revile us. The successful Yellow candidate for the borough of Old Topping perhaps feels no pursuant meditative hatred toward the Blue editor who consoles his subscribers with vituperative rhetoric against Yellow men who sell their country and are the demons of private life: but he might not be sorry, if law and opportunity favoured, to kick that Blue editor to a deeper shade of his favourite colour.

"Prosperous men take a little vengeance now and then, as they take a diversion, when it comes easily in their way and is no hindrance to business; and such small unimpassioned revenges have an enormous effect in life, running through all degrees of pleasant infliction, blocking the fit men out of places, and blackening characters in unpremeditated talk. Still more, to see people who have been only insignificantly offensive to us, reduced in life and humiliated without any special efforts of ours is apt to have a soothing, flattering influence: Providence, or some other prince of this world, it appears, has undertaken the task of retribution for us; and really, by an agreeable constitution of things, our enemies, somehow, *don't* prosper." ¶MF III 7

—*sweet:* "To see an enemy humiliated gives a certain contentment, but this is jejune compared with the highly blent satisfaction of seeing him humiliated by your benevolent action of concession on his behalf. That is a sort of revenge which falls into the scale of virtue . . . . Such things give a completeness to prosperity, and contribute elements of agreeable consciousness that are not dreamed of by that short-sighted overheated vindictiveness, which goes out of its way to wreak itself in direct injury." MF III 7

Will

—*and motive:* "And whatever reverence could be shown to woman, he was bent on showing to this girl. Why? He gave himself several good reasons; but whatever one does with a strong unhesitating outflow of will, has a store of motive that it would be hard to put into words. Some deeds seem little more than interjections which give vent to the long passion of a life." DD 20

—*our own way:* "And certainly, the mistakes that we male and female mortals make when we have our own way might fairly raise some wonder that we are so fond of it." MM 9

—*prophecy:* "Among the heirs of Art, as at the division of the promised land, each has to win his portion by hard fighting: the bestowal is after the manner of prophecy, and is a title without possession. To carry the map of an ungotten estate in your pocket is a poor sort of copyhold. And in fancy to cast his shoe over Edom is little warrant that a man shall ever set the sole of his foot on an acre of his own there." DD 23 ep

—*when stung:* "Every other feeling on the subject, however, was quickly merged in a resistant belief to the contrary of hers, accompanied with a new determination to prove that he was right. This sort of certainty had just enough kinship to doubt and uneasiness to hurry on a confession which an untouched security might have delayed." DD 7

—*yielding:* "All yielding is attended with a less vivid consciousness than resistance— it is the partial sleep of thought—it is the submergence of our own personality by another." MF VI 13

Fellow Man, in Relation

"Yet surely, surely the only true knowledge of our fellow man is that which enables us to feel with him—which gives us a fine ear for the heart-pulses that are beating under the mere clothes of circumstance and opinion. Our subtlest analysis of schools and sects must miss the essential truth, unless it be lit up by the love that sees in all forms of human thought and work, the life and death struggles of separate human beings." JR 10

Arabs

—new life: " 'A sentiment may seem to be dying and yet revive into strong life,' said Deronda. 'Nations have revived. We may live to see a great outburst of force in the Arabs, who are being inspired with a new zeal.' " DD 42

Behaviour

—goal: "Few lives are shaped, few characters formed, by the contemplation of definite consequences seen from a distance and made the goal of continuous effort or the beacon of a constantly avoided danger: such control by foresight, such vivid picturing and practical logic are the distinction of exceptionally strong natures . . . . " TS 5

—motive: "[People] are misled by the common mistake of supposing that men's behaviour, whether habitual or occasional, is chiefly determined by a distinctly conceived motive, a definite object to be gained or a definite evil to be avoided. The truth is, that, the primitive wants of nature once tolerably satisfied, the majority of mankind, even in a civilised life full of solicitations, are with difficulty aroused to the distinct conception of an object towards which they will direct their actions with careful adaptation, and it is yet rare to find one who can persist in the systematic pursuit of such an end." TS 5

—routine: " . . . society is chiefly made up of human beings whose daily acts are all performed either in unreflecting obedience to custom and routine or from immediate promptings of thought or feeling to execute an immediate purpose. They pay their poor-rates, give their vote in affairs political or parochial, wear a certain amount of starch, hinder boys from tormenting the helpless, and spend money on tedious observances called pleasures, without mentally adjusting these practices to their own well-understood interest or to the general, ultimate welfare of the human race. . . . " TS 5

Blacks

"There is understood to be a peculiar odour from the negro body, and we know that some persons, too rationalistic to feel bound by the curse on **Ham**, used to hint very strongly that this odour determined the question on the side of negro slavery." TS 18

Censure and Judgment

—against evidence: "Even on the supposition that required the utmost stretch of belief—namely, that none of the things said about Miss Tulliver were true; still, since they *had* been said about her, they had cast an odour around her which must cause her to be shrunk from by every woman who had to take care of her own reputation—and of society." MF VII 4

—denigration: "We imagine the *Philister* [Philistine] is the personification of the spirit which judges everything from a lower

point of view than the subject demands—which judges the affairs of the parish from the egotistic or purely personal point of view—which judges the affairs of the nation from the parochial point of view, and does not hesitate to measure the merits of the universe from the human point of view." NH 150

—ideal of conduct: "To have taken Maggie by the hand and said, 'I will not believe unproved evil of you: my lips shall not utter it; my ears shall be closed against it. I, too, am an erring mortal, liable to stumble, apt to come short of my most earnest efforts. Your lot has been harder than mine, your temptation greater. Let us help each other to stand and walk without more falling'—to have done this would have demanded courage, deep pity, self-knowledge, generous trust—would have demanded a mind that tasted no piquancy in evil-speaking, that felt no self-exaltation in condemning, that cheated itself with no large words into the belief that life can have any moral end, any high religion, which excludes the striving after perfect truth, justice, and love towards the individual men and women who come across our own path." MF VII 4

—judging: "The casuists have become a byword of reproach; but their perverted spirit of minute discrimination was the shadow of a truth to which eyes and hearts are too often fatally sealed: the truth, that moral judgments must remain false and hollow, unless they are checked and enlightened by a perpetual reference to the special circumstances that mark the individual lot." MF VII 2

—of the mild: "We are often startled by the severity of mild people on exceptional occasions; the reason is, that mild people are most liable to be under the yoke of traditional impressions." AB 39

—the mob: "The baser part of the multitude delight in degradations, apart from any hatred; it is the satire they best understand." R 72

—precipitate: " 'The mind that is too ready at contempt and reprobation is . . . as a clenched fist that can give blows, but is shut up from receiving and holding ought that is precious—though it were heaven-sent manna.' " FH 5

—punishment: "The Roman emperor in the legend put to death ten learned Israelites to avenge the sale of **Joseph** by his brethren. And there have always been enough of his kidney, whose piety lies in punishing, who can see the justice of grudges but not of gratitude. For you shall never convince the stronger feeling that it hath not the stronger reason, or incline him who hath no love to believe that there is good ground for loving." DD 60

—results: " 'We judge others according to results; how else?—not knowing the process by which results are arrived at . . . . Public opinion, in these cases, is always of the feminine gender—not the world, but the world's wife . . . . " MF VII 2

—retribution: "Retribution may come from any voice—the hardest, cruelest, most imbruted urchin at the street-corner can inflict it: surely help and pity are rarer things—more needful for the righteous to bestow." MF VII 2

—rules by rote: "All people of broad, strong sense have an instinctive repugnance to the men of maxims; because such people early discern that the mysterious complexity of our life is not to be embraced by maxims, and that to lace ourselves up in formulas of that sort is to repress all the divine promptings and inspirations that spring from growing insight and sympathy. And the man of maxims is the popular representative of the minds that are guided in their moral judgment solely by general rules, thinking that these will lead them to justice by a ready-made patent method, without the trouble of exerting patience, discrimination, impartiality, without any care to assure themselves whether they have the insight that comes from a hardly-earned estimate of temptation, or from a life vivid and intense enough to have created a wide fellow-feeling with all that is human." MF VII 2

Charity

"One must be poor to know the luxury of giving." MM 17

—glance: "there is a power in the direct glance of a sincere and loving human soul, which will do more to dissipate prejudice and kindle charity than the most elaborate arguments. The fullest exposition of Mr Tryan's doctrine might not have sufficed to convince Janet that he had not an odious self-complacency in believing himself a peculiar child of God; but one direct, pathetic look of his had dissociated him with [*sic; from?*] that conception for ever." JR 12

Charm

—in humankind: "A human being in this aged nation of ours is a very wonderful whole, the slow creation of long interchanging influences; and charm is a result of two such wholes, the one loving and the one loved." MM 40

Connection

—fated: "But anyone watching keenly the stealthy convergence of human lots, sees a slow preparation of effects from one life on another, which tells like a calculated irony

on the indifference or the frozen stare with which we look at our unintroduced neighbour. Destiny stands by sarcastic with our *dramatis personæ* folded in her hand." MM 11

—lens: "The beings closest to us, whether in love or hate, are often virtually our interpreters of the world, and some feather-headed gentleman or lady whom in passing we regret to take as legal tender for a human being may be acting as a melancholy theory of life in the minds of those who live with them—like a piece of yellow and wavy glass that distorts form and makes colour an affliction. Their trivial sentences, their petty standards, their low suspicions, their loveless *ennui,* may be making somebody else's life no better than a promenade through a pantheon of ugly idols." DD 54

—relation: " . . . was it that the sense of his being divided from her in her feeling about her god-father roused the slumbering sources of alienation, and marred her own vision? . . . Our relations with our fellow-men are most often determined by coincident currents of that sort; the inexcusable word or deed seldom comes until after affection or reverence has been already enfeebled by the strain of repeated excuses." R 59

—of strangers: "It was one of those moments of implicit revelation which will sometimes happen even between people who meet quite transiently—on a mile's journey, perhaps, or when resting by the wayside. There is always this possibility of a word or look from a stranger to keep alive the sense of human brotherhood." MF VI 9

Crime and Criminal

—the nurture excuse: " . . . it would be easy for any felon to say that his ancestors ought to have been hanged instead of him. If those who had bad fathers and mothers were bad themselves, they were hanged for that. There was no need to go back on what you couldn't see.

" 'My mother is like old **George the Third**,' said the Vicar, 'she objects to metaphysics.' " MM 17

—robbery: "Besides, it is not robbery to take property belonging to your mother: she doesn't prosecute you." BJ 1

"David had made up his mind not to steal any more, even from people who were fond of him: it was an unpleasant way of making your fortune in a world where you were likely to be surprised in the act by brothers." BJ 1

Demeanour

—generous purpose: " . . . we are all of us made more graceful by the inward presence of what we believe to be a generous purpose; our actions move to a hidden music—a melody that's sweetly pitched in tune.' " FH 46

—under stress: "We are so made, almost all of us, that the false seeming which we have thought of with painful shrinking when beforehand in our solitude it has urged itself on us as a necessity, will possess our muscles and move our lips as if nothing but that were easy when once we have come under the stimulus of expectant eyes and ears." R 65

—unusual circumstances: "Unwonted circumstances may make us all rather unlike ourselves: there are conditions under which the most majestic person is obliged to sneeze, and our emotions are liable to be acted on in the same incongruous manner." MM 62

Friend and Friendship

—aptitude: "He looked around him with the quiet air of respect habitual to him among equals, ordered whisky and water, and offered the contents of his cigar-case, which, characteristically enough, he always carried and hardly ever used for his own behoof, having reasons for not smoking himself, but liking to indulge others. Perhaps it was his weakness to be afraid of seeming strait-laced, and turning himself into a sort of diagram instead of a growth which can exercise the guiding attraction of fellowship." DD 42

—constraint: " . . . she found to her surprise that an old friend is not always the person whom it is easiest to make a confidant of: there was the barrier of remembered communication under other circumstances—there was the dislike of being pitied and informed by one who had been long wont to allow her the superiority." MM 74

—disputation: "Perhaps the most delightful friendships are those in which there is much agreement, much disputation, and yet more personal liking; and the advent of the public-spirited, contradictory, yet affectionate Felix, into Treby life, had made a welcome epoch to the minister." FH 10

—early stages: "Perhaps one had need to be nineteen again to be quite convinced of the feelings that were crowded for Maggie into those twelve days—of the length to which they were stretched for her by the novelty of her experience in them and the varying attitudes of her mind. The early days of an acquaintance almost always have this importance for us, and fill up a larger space in our memory than longer subsequent periods which have been less filled with discovery and new impressions." MF VI 6

—egoistic: "He wanted no confidence in return, but seemed to take Deronda as an Olympian who needed nothing—an egotism

in friendship which is common enough with mercurial, expansive natures." DD 16

" . . . what outpourer of his own affairs is not tempted to think any hint of his friend's affairs as an egoistic irrelevance?" DD 69

—influence lost: " . . . much of our lives is spent in marring our own influence and turning others' belief in us into a widely concluding unbelief which they call knowledge of the world, while it is really disappointment in you or me." DD 64

—influential: "It is hard to say how much we could forgive ourselves if we were secure from judgment by another whose opinion is the breathing-medium of all our joy—who brings to us with close pressure and immediate sequence that judgment of the Invisible and Universal which self-flattery and the world's tolerance would easily melt and disperse. In this way our brother may be in the stead of God to us, and his opinion which has pierced even to the joints and marrow, may be our virtue in the making." DD 64

—maintained: "The friendship of the two had been kept up warmly since the memorable Cambridge time, not only by correspondence but by little episodes of companionship abroad and in England, and the original relation of confidence on one side and indulgence on the other had been developed in practice, as is wont to be the case where such spiritual borrowing and lending has been well begun." DD 37

—patronized: " . . . our treatment of acquaintances and friends from whom we are expecting gratitude because we are so very kind in thinking of them, inviting them, and even listening to what they say—considering how insignificant they must feel themselves to be. We are often fallaciously confident in supposing that our friend's state of mind is appropriate to our moderate estimate of his importance: almost as if we imagined the humble mollusc (so useful as an illustration) to have a sense of his own exceeding softness and low place in the scale of being. Your mollusc, on the contrary, is inwardly objecting to every other grade of solid rather than to himself." TS 4

—rival: " 'Friendliness is much such a steed as **Ser Benghi**'s [not traced]: it will hardly show much alacrity unless it has got the thistle of hatred under its tail.' " R 3

—a strain: "A difference of taste in jokes is a great strain on the affections." DD 15

—surprising: "Moreover, it is always at their peril that our friends turn out to be something more than we were aware of." DD 69

Gypsies

— destiny: "My vagabonds are a seed more generous,
Quick as the serpent, loving as the hound,
And beautiful as disinherited gods.
They have a promised land beyond the sea:
There I may lead them, raise my standard, call
The wandering Zincali to that new home,
And make a nation—bring light, order, law
Instead of chaos . . . . " SG I vi

—fidelity: "Our people's faith
Is faithfulness; not the rote-learned belief
That we are heaven's highest favorites,
But the resolve that being most forsaken
Among the sons of men, we will be true
Each to the other, and our common lot."
SG III *And see* S:Trust and Loyalty—*mutual*

—in prison: "What if the Gypsies are but savage beasts
And must be hunted?—let them be set free,
Have benefit of chase, or stand at bay
And fight for life and offspring. Prisoners!
Oh! they have made their fires beside the streams,
Their walls have been the rocks, the pillared pines,
Their roof the living sky that breathes with light:
They may well hate a cage, like strong-winged birds . . . . " SG I iii

—rootless: "ZARCA: Yes: wanderers whom no God took knowledge of
To give them laws, to fight for them, or blight
Another race to make them ampler room;
Who have no Whence or Whither in their souls,
No dimmest lore of glorious ancestors
To make a common hearth for piety.
FEDALMA: A race that lives on prey as foxes do
With stealthy, petty rapine: so despised,
It is not persecuted, only spurned,
Crushed underfoot, warred on by chance like rats,
Or swarming flies, or reptiles of the sea.
Dragged in the net unsought, and flung far off,
To perish as they may?" SG I vi

Impression

—*convincing:* "Looked into closely, the conclusion from a man's profile, voice, and fluency to his certainty in multiplication beyond the twelves, seems to show a confused notion of the way in which very common things are connected; but it is on such false correlations that men found half their inferences about each other, and high places of trust may sometimes be held on no better foundation." TS 11

—*deceptive:* "If there were anything that was not thoroughly genuine about Mr Stelling, it lay quite beyond Tom's power to detect it: it is only by a wide comparison of facts that the wisest full-grown man can distinguish well-rolled barrels from more supernal thunder." MF II 1

—*display:* "We mortals sometimes cut a pitiable figure in our attempts at display. We may be sure of our own merits, yet fatally ignorant of the point of view from which we are regarded by our neighbours. Our fine patterns in tattooing may be far from throwing him into a swoon of admiration, though we turn ourselves all round to show them." FH 11

—*introduction:* "The beginning of an acquaintance whether with persons or things is to get a definite outline for our ignorance." DD 11 ep

—*the name:* "It is a commonplace that words, writings, measures, and performances in general, have qualities assigned them not by a direct judgment on the performances themselves, but by a presumption of what they are likely to be, considering who is the performer. We all notice in our neighbours this reference to names as guides in criticism, and all furnish illustrations of it in our own practice; for, check ourselves as we will, the first impression from any sort of work must depend on a previous attitude of mind, and this will constantly be determined by the influences of a name.

"But that our prior confidence or want of confidence in given names is made up of judgments just as hollow as the consequent praise or blame they are taken to warrant, is less commonly perceived, though there is a conspicuous indication of it in the surprise or disappointment often manifested in the disclosure of an authorship about which everybody has been making wrong guesses." ¶TS 11

—*persona:* "Doubtless some ancient Greek has observed that behind the big mask and the speaking-trumpet, there must always be our poor little eyes peeping as usual and our timorous lips more or less under anxious control." MM 29

—*prepossession:* "It is this foolish trust in prepossessions, founded on spurious evidence, which makes a medium of encouragement for those who, happening to have the ear of the public, give other people's ideas the advantage of appearing under their own well-received name, while any remonstrance from the real producer becomes an unwelcome disturbance of complacency with each person who has paid complimentary tributes in the wrong place." TS 11

—*varied:* "The same substance, we know, will exhibit different qualities under different tests; and, after all, imperfect reports of individual impressions, whether immediate or traditional, are a very frail basis on which to build our opinion of a man. One character may be very indifferently mirrored in the mind of the most intimate neighbor; it all depends on the quality of that gentleman's reflecting surface." PY 21

Jews

"The sons of Judah have to choose that God may again choose them." DD 42

—*abandoned:* "The strongly marked type of race in their features, and their peculiar garb, made her conjecture that they were Spanish or Portuguese Jews, who had perhaps been put ashore and abandoned there by rapacious sailors, to whom their property remained as a prey. Such things were happening continually to Jews compelled to abandon their homes by the Inquisition: the cruelty of greed thrust them from the sea, and the cruelty of superstition thrust them back to it." R 68

—*appearance:* "No question had ever been raised as to Mr Nolan's extraction on the strength of his hooked nose, or of his name being Baruch. Hebrew names 'ran' in the best Saxon families; the Bible accounted for them; and no one among the uplands and hedgerows of that district was suspected of having an Oriental origin unless he carried a pedlar's jewel-box. Certainly, whatever genealogical research might have discovered, the worthy Baruch Nolan was so free from any distinctive marks of religious persuasion—he went to church with so ordinary an irregularity, and so often grumbled at the sermon—that there was no ground for classing him otherwise than with good Trebian Churchmen. He was generally regarded as a good-looking old gentleman, and a certain thin eagerness in his aspect was attributed to the life of the metropolis, where narrow space had the same sort of effect on men as on thickly-planted trees." FH 20

—*choice:* " . . . one of two issues was possible: either from being of feebler nature than their persecutors, and caring more for ease than for the sentiments and ideas which constituted their distinctive character, they would everywhere give way to pressure and get rapidly merged in the populations around them; or, being endowed with uncommon tenacity, physical and mental, feeling peculiarly the ties of inheritance both in blood and faith, remembering national glories, trusting in their recovery, abhorring apostasy, able to bear all things and hope all things with the consciousness of being steadfast to spiritual obligations, the kernel of their number would harden into an inflexibility more and more insured by motive and habit. They would cherish all differences that marked them off from their hated oppressors, all memories that consoled them with a sense of virtual though unrecognised superiority; and the separateness which was made their badge of ignominy would be their inward pride, their source of fortifying defiance." TS 18

—cursed: " . . . edicts issued to protect 'the King's Jews' equally with the King's game from being harassed and hunted by the commonalty were only slight mitigations to the deplorable lot of a race held to be under the divine curse, and had little force after the Crusades began." TS 18 [*GE nowhere attempts to explain this "divine curse" except for a hint: see —persecuted.*]

—dispersion: "More exceptional . . . has been their dispersion and their subsistence as a separate people through ages in which for the most part they were regarded and treated very much as beasts hunted for the sake of their skins, or of a valuable secretion peculiar to their species." TS 18

—education: "But all that need be noticed here is the continuity of that national education (by outward and inward circumstance) which created in the Jews a feeling of race, a sense of corporate existence, unique in its intensity." TS 18

"At any rate, seeing that the Jews were more specifically than any other nation educated into a sense of their supreme moral value, the chief matter of surprise is that any other nation is found to rival them in this form of self-confidence." TS 18

—excepted: "The European world has long been used to consider the Jews as altogether exceptional, and it has followed naturally enough that they have been excepted from the rules of justice and mercy, which are based on human likeness. But to consider a people whose ideas have determined the religion of half the world, and that the more cultivated half, and who made the most eminent struggle against the power of Rome, as a purely exceptional race, is a demoralising offence against rational knowledge, a stultifying inconsistency in historical interpretation. Every nation of forcible character—*i.e.,* of strongly marked characteristics, is so far exceptional. The distinctive note of each bird-species is in this sense exceptional, but the necessary ground of such distinction is a deeper likeness. The superlative peculiarity in the Jews admitted, our affinity with them is only the more apparent when the elements of their peculiarity are discerned." TS 18

—feared: " 'The Jews,' it is felt, 'have a dangerous tendency to get the uppermost places not only in commerce but in political life. Their monetary hold on governments is tending to perpetuate in leading Jews a spirit of universal alienism (euphemistically called cosmopolitanism), even where the West has given them a full share in civil and political rights. A people with oriental sunlight in their blood, yet capable of being everywhere acclimatised, they have a force and toughness which enables them to carry off the best prizes; and their wealth is likely to put half the seats in Parliament at their disposal.' " TS 18

—financial acumen: "The Jews showed a talent for accumulating what was an object of more immediate desire to Christians than animal oils or well-furred skins, and their cupidity and avarice were found at once particularly hateful and particularly useful: hateful when seen as a reason for punishing them by mulcting or robbery, useful when this retributive process could be successfully carried forward." TS 18

—a Gentile's view: "Spite of his strong tendency to side with the objects of prejudice, and in general with those who got the worst of it, his interest had never been practically drawn towards existing Jews, and the facts he knew about them, whether they walked conspicuous in fine apparel or lurked in bystreets, were chiefly of the sort most repugnant to him. Of learned and accomplished Jews he took it for granted that they had dropped their religion, and wished to be merged in the people of their native lands. Scorn flung at a Jew as such would have roused all his sympathy in griefs of inheritance; but the indiscriminate scorn of a race will often strike a specimen who has well earned it on his own account, and might fairly be gibbeted as a rascally son of Adam. . . . Deronda could not escape (who can?) knowing ugly stories of Jewish characteristics and occupations; and though one of his favourite protests was against the severance of past and present history, he was like others who shared his protest, in never having cared to reach any more special conclusions about actual Jews than that they retained the virtues and vices of a long-oppressed race." DD 19

—*in Germany:* " 'Our youth fell on evil days; but this we have won: we increase our wealth in safety, and the learning of all Germany is fed and fattened by Jewish brains . . . .' " DD 60

—*hardship:* " . . . among the thoughts that most filled his mind . . . was that of the multitudinous Spanish Jews centuries ago driven destitute from their Spanish homes, suffered to land from the crowded ships only for brief rest on this grand quay of Genoa, overspreading it with a pall of famine and plague—dying mothers with dying children at their breasts—fathers and sons agaze at each other's haggardness, like groups from a hundred Hunger-towers turned out beneath the mid-day sun." DD 50

—*historic suffering:* " 'If there are ranks in suffering, Israel takes precedence of all the nations—if the duration of sorrows and the patience with which they are borne ennoble, the Jews are among the aristocracy of every land—if a literature is called rich in the possession of a few classic tragedies, what shall we say to a National Tragedy lasting for fifteen hundred years, in which the poets and the actors were also the heroes?' " DD 42 (*GE's translation of a passage from historian Theodor Zunz*)

—*leadership:* " . . . memories wakened among the sparse *talithim* and keen dark faces of worshippers whose way of taking awful prayers and invocations with the easy familiarity which might be called Hebrew dyed Italian, made him reflect that his grandfather . . . must have been almost as exceptional a Jew as Mordecai. But were not men of ardent zeal and far-reaching hope everywhere exceptional?—the men who had the visions which, as Mordecai said, were the creators and feeders of the world—moulding and feeding the more passive life which without them would dwindle and shrivel into the narrow tenacity of insects, unshaken by thoughts beyond the reaches of their antennae." DD 55

—*liturgy in diaspora:* " . . . his mind went to the synagogue and saw faces there probably little different from those of his grandfather's time, and heard the Spanish-Hebrew liturgy which had lasted through the seasons of wandering generations like a plant with wandering seed, that gives the far-off lands a kinship to the exile's home . . . . " DD 55

—*the Messianic time:* " 'The Messianic time is the time when Israel shall will the planting of the national ensign. The Nile overflowed and rushed onward: the Egyptian could not choose the overflow, but he chose to work and make channels for the fructifying waters, and Egypt became the land of corn. Shall man, whose soul is set in the royalty of discernment and resolve, deny his rank and say, I am an onlooker, ask no choice or purpose of me? That is the blasphemy of this time. The divine principle of our race is action, choice, resolved memory. Let us contradict the blasphemy, and help to will our own better future and the better future of the world—not renounce our higher gift and say, "Let us be as if we were not among the populations"; but choose our full heritage, claim the brotherhood of our nations, and carry into it a new brotherhood with the nations of the Gentiles. The vision is there; it will be fulfilled.' " DD 42

—*mysterious:* " . . . extraordinary Jewish friends . . . astonished questioning from minds to which the idea of live Jews, out of a book, suggested a difference deep enough to be almost zoological, as of a strange race in **Pliny**'s Natural History that might sleep under the shade of its own ears. Bertha could not imagine what Jews believed now; and had a dim idea that they rejected the Old Testament since it proved the New; Miss Merry thought that Mirah and her brother could 'never have been properly argued with,' and the amiable Alice did not mind what the Jews believed, she was sure she 'couldn't bear them.' Mrs Davilow corrected her by saying that the great Jewish families who were in society were quite what they ought to be both in London and Paris, but admitted that the commoner unconverted Jews were objectionable; and Isabel asked whether Mirah talked just as they did, or whether you might be with her and not find out that she was a Jewess." DD 58

—*his nation defended:* "Where else is there a nation of whom it may be as truly said that their religion and law and moral life mingled as the stream of blood in the heart and made one growth—where else a people who kept and enlarged their spiritual store at the very time when they were hunted with a hatred as fierce as the forest fires that chase the wild beast from his covert?

"There is a fable of the Roman, that swimming to save his life he held the roll of his writings between his teeth and saved them from the waters. But how much more than that is true of our race? They struggled to keep their place among the nations like heroes—yea, when the hand was hacked off, they clung with the teeth; but when the plough and the harrow had passed over the last visible signs of their national covenant, and the fruitfulness of their land was stifled with the blood of the sowers and planters, they said, 'The spirit is alive, let us make it a lasting habitation —lasting because movable—so that it may be carried from generation to generation, and our sons unborn may be rich in the things that have been, and possess a hope built on an unchangeable foundation.'

"They said it and they wrought it, though often breathing with scant life, as in a coffin, or as lying wounded amid a heap of slain. Hooted and scared like the unknown dog, the Hebrew made himself envied for his wealth and wisdom, and was bled of them to fill the bath of Gentile luxury; he absorbed knowledge, he diffused it; his dispersed race was a new Phoenicia working the mines of Greece and carrying their products to the world. The native spirit of our tradition was not to stand still, but to use records as a seed, and draw out the compressed virtues of law and pro'hecy; and while the Gentile, who had said, 'What is yours is ours, and no longer yours,' was reading the letter of our law as a dark inscription, or was turning its parchments into shoe-soles for an army rabid with lust and cruelty, our Masters were still enlarging and illuminating with fresh-fed interpretation.

"But the dispersion was wide, the yoke of oppression was a spiked torture as well as a load; the exile was forced afar among brutish people, where the consciousness of his race was no clearer to him than the light of the sun to our fathers in the Roman persecution, who had their hiding-place in a cave, and knew not that it was day save by the dimmer burning of their candles. What wonder that multitudes of our people are ignorant, narrow, superstitions? What wonder?' " ¶DD 42

" 'What wonder? The night is unto them, that they have no vision; in their darkness they are unable to divine; the sun is gone down over the prophets, and the day is dark above them; their observances are as nameless relics. But which among the chief of the Gentile nations has not an ignorant multitude? They scorn our people's ignorant observance; but the most accursed ignorance is that which has no observance—sunk to the cunning greed of the fox, to which all law is no more than a trap or the cry of the worrying hound.

" 'There is a degradation deep down below the memory that has withered into superstition. In the multitudes of the ignorant on three continents who observe our rites and make the confession of the divine Unity, the soul of Judaism is not dead. Revive the organic centre: let the unity of Israel which has made the growth and form of its religion be an outward reality. Looking towards a land and a polity, our dispersed people in all the ends of the earth may share the dignity of a national life which has a voice among the peoples of the East and the West—which will plant the wisdom and skill of our race so that it may be, as of old, a medium of transmission and understanding. Let that come to pass, and the living warmth will spread to the weak extremities of Israel, and superstition will vanish, not in the lawlessness of the renegade, but in the illumination of great facts which widen feeling, and make all knowledge alive as the young offspring of beloved memories.' " ¶DD 42

—*a national home: see* DD *Editor's epilogue*

—*nationality:* " 'I say that the effect of our separateness will not be completed and have its highest transformation unless our race takes on again the character of a nationality. That is the fulfilment of the religious trust that moulded them into a people, whose life has made half the inspiration of the world. What is it to me that the ten tribes are lost untraceably, or that multitudes of the children of Judah have mixed themselves with the Gentile populations as a river with rivers?

" 'Behold our people still! Their skirts spread afar; they are torn and soiled and trodden on; but there is a jewelled breastplate. Let the wealthy men, the monarchs of commerce, the learned in all knowledge, the skilful in all arts, the speakers, the political counsellors, who carry in their veins the Hebrew blood which has maintained its vigour in all climates, and the pliancy of the Hebrew genius for which difficulty means new device—let them say, "we will lift up a standard, we will unite in a labour hard but glorious like that of **Moses** and **Ezra**, a labour which shall be a worthy fruit of the long anguish whereby our fathers maintained their separateness, refusing the ease of falsehood."

" 'They have wealth enough to redeem the soil from debauched and paupered conquerors; they have the skill of the statesman to devise, the tongue of the orator to persuade. And is there no prophet or poet among us to make the ears of Christian Europe tingle with shame at the hideous obloquy of Christian strife which the Turk gazes at as at the fighting of beasts to which he has lent an arena? There is more of wisdom among us to found a new Jewish polity, grand, simple, just, like the old—a republic where there is equality of protection, an equality which shone like a star on the forehead of our ancient community, and gave it more than the brightness of Western freedom amid the despotisms of the East.

" 'Then our race shall have an organic centre, a heart and brain to watch and guide and execute; the outraged Jew shall have a defence in the court of nations, as the outraged Englishman or American. And the world will gain as Israel gains. For there will be a community in the van of the East which carries the culture and the sympathies of every great nation in its bosom; there will be a land set for a halting-place of enmities, a neutral ground for the East as Belgium is for the West. Difficulties? I know there are difficulties. But let the spirit of sublime achievement move in the great among our people, and the work will begin.' " ¶DD 42

—*negatives:* "An oppressive government and a persecuting religion, while breeding vices in those who hold power, are well known to breed answering vices in those who are powerless and suffering. What more direct plan than the course presented by European history could have been pursued in order to give the Jews a spirit of bitter isolation, of scorn for the wolfish hypocrisy that made victims of them, of triumph in prospering at the expense of the blunderers who stoned them away from the open paths of industry?—or, on the other hand, to encourage in the less defiant a lying conformity, a pretence of conversion for the sake of the social advantages attached to baptism, an outward renunciation of their hereditary ties with the lack of real love towards the society and creed which exacted this galling tribute?" TS 18

—*predators:* "—or again, in the most unhappy specimens of the race, to rear transcendent examples of odious vice, reckless instruments of rich men with bad propensities, unscrupulous grinders of the alien people who wanted to grind *them?*" TS 18

—*persecuted:* "As the slave-holders in the United States counted the curse on **Ham** a justification of negro slavery, so the curse on the Jews was counted a justification for hindering them from pursuing agriculture and handicrafts; for marking them out as execrable figures by a peculiar dress; for torturing them to make them part with their gains, or for more gratuitously spitting at them and pelting them; for taking it as certain that they killed and ate babies, poisoned the wells, and took pains to spread the plague; for putting it to them whether they would be baptised or burned, and not failing to burn and massacre them when they were obstinate; but also for suspecting them of disliking the baptism when they had got it, and then burning them in punishment of their insincerity; finally, for hounding them by tens on tens of thousands from the homes where they had found shelter for centuries, and inflicting on them the horrors of a new exile and a new dispersion. All this to avenge the Saviour of mankind, or else to compel these stiff-necked people to acknowledge a Master whose servants showed such beneficent effects of His teaching." TS 18 *And see* S:Jesus Christ

—*separateness:* " . . . we find [in the canonical Hebrew books] a people educated from an earlier or later period to a sense of separateness unique in its intensity, a people taught by many concurrent influences to identify faithfulness to its national traditions with the highest social and religious blessings." TS 18

—*criticism:* " . . . philosophic thinkers and discriminating critics . . . condemning the Jews on the ground that they are obstinate adherents of an outworn creed, maintain themselves in moral alienation from the peoples with whom they share citizenship, and are destitute of real interest in the welfare of the community and state with which they are thus identified." TS 18

—*shopping quarter:* "In fact, Deronda saw various queer-looking Israelites not altogether without guile, and just distinguishable from queer-looking Christians of the same mixed *morale.* In his anxiety about Mirah's relatives, he had lately been thinking of vulgar Jews with a sort of personal alarm. But a little comparison will often diminish our surprise and disgust at the aberrations of Jews and other dissidents whose lives do not offer a consistent or lovely pattern of their creed; and this evening Deronda, becoming more conscious that he was falling into unfairness and ridiculous exaggeration, began to use that corrective comparison . . . . " DD 32

—*in Spain (15th c.):* "For men who make
obeisance with degrees
Of good-will shading towards servility,
Where good-will ends and secret fear begins
And curses, too, low-muttered through the teeth,
Explanatory to the God of **Shem.**" SG I i

—*subject for study:* "Not only the Meyricks, whose various knowledge had been acquired by the irregular foraging to which clever girls have usually been reduced, but Deronda himself, with all his masculine instruction, had been roused by this apparition of Mirah to the consciousness of knowing hardly anything about modern Judaism or the inner Jewish history. The Chosen People have been commonly treated as a people chosen for the sake of somebody else; and their thinking as something (no matter exactly what) that ought to have been entirely otherwise; and Deronda, like his neighbours, had regarded Judaism as a sort of eccentric fossilised form which an accomplished man might dispense with studying, and leave to specialists. But Mirah, with her terrified flight from one parent, and her yearning after the other, had flashed on him the hitherto neglected reality that Judaism was something still throbbing in human lives, still making for them the only conceivable vesture of the world. . . . " DD 32

—valuable: "On the whole, one of the most remarkable phenomena in the history of this scattered people, made for ages 'a scorn and a hissing' is . . . they have come out of it (in any estimate which allows for numerical proportion) rivalling the nations of all European countries in healthiness and beauty of *physique,* in practical ability, in scientific and artistic aptitude, and in some forms of ethical value." TS 18

And see Kindness

—woman: see LM:Woman—*suppressed*

Kindness

—ignorant: "Ignorant kindness may have the effect of cruelty; but to be angry with it as if it were direct cruelty would be an ignorant *un*kindness . . . . " DD 59

—ineffective: "He had a sense that the old man meant to be good-natured and neighbourly; but the kindness fell on him as sunshine falls on the wretched—he had no heart to taste it, and felt that it was very far off him." SM 10

—the Jews: "And again, a varied, impartial observation of the Jews in different countries tends to the impression that they have a predominant kindliness which must have been deeply ingrained in the constitution of their race to have outlasted the ages of persecution and oppression. The concentration of their joys in domestic life has kept up in them the capacity of tenderness: the pity for the fatherless and the widow, the care for the women and the little ones, blent intimately with their religion, is a well of mercy that cannot long or widely be pent up by exclusiveness. And the kindliness of the Jew overflows the line of division between him and the Gentile." TS 18

Neighbour

—community: see S:Religious observance—*community*

—crowd in a courtroom: " . . . the knock which told that the jury had come to their decision, fell as a signal for silence on every ear. It is sublime—that sudden pause of a great multitude, which tells that one soul moves in them all. Deeper and deeper the silence seemed to become, like the deepening night, while the jurymen's names were called over . . . . " AB 43

—his paradise: "But how little we know what would make paradise for our neighbours. We judge from our own desires, and our neighbours themselves are not always open enough even to throw out a hint of theirs." MM 53

—a party: "This was the occasion when all the society of Raveloe and Tarley, whether old acquaintances separated by long rutty distances, or cooled acquaintances separated by misunderstandings concerning runaway calves, or acquaintances founded on intermittent condescension, counted on meeting and on comporting themselves with mutual appropriateness." SM 10

—standing around: " . . . any human figure standing at ease under the archway in the early afternoon was as certain to attract companionship as a pigeon which has found something worth pecking at. In this case there was no material object to feed on, but the eye of reason saw a probability of mental sustenance in the shape of gossip." MM 71

—unhappy for her own good: " . . . when a woman with her thoughts much at leisure got them suddenly employed on something grievously disadvantageous to her neighbours, various moral impulses were called into play which tended to stimulate utterance. Candour was one. To be candid . . . meant, to use an early opportunity of letting your friends know that you did not take a cheerful view of their capacity, their conduct, or their position; and a robust candour never waited to be asked for its opinion. Then again, there was the love of truth—a wide phrase, but meaning in this relation, a lively objection to seeing a wife look happier than her husband's character warranted, or manifest too much satisfaction in her lot: the poor thing should have some hint given her that if she knew the truth she would have less complacency in her bonnet, and in light dishes for a supper-party. Stronger than all, there was the regard for a friend's moral improvement, sometimes called her soul, which was likely to be benefited by remarks tending to gloom, uttered with the accompaniment of pensive staring at the furniture and a manner implying that the speaker would not tell what was on her mind, from regard to the feelings of her hearer. On the whole, one might say that an ardent charity was at work setting the virtuous mind to make a neighbour unhappy for her good." MM 74

—visited: " . . . heaven knows what would become of our sociality if we never visited people we speak ill of: we should live, like Egyptian hermits, in crowded solitude." JR 25

The Poor

—poorhouse: " 'The parish!' You can perhaps hardly understand the effect of that word on a mind like Hetty's, brought up among people who were somewhat hard in their feelings even towards poverty; who lived among the fields, and had little pity for want and rags as a hard inevitable fate such as they sometimes seem in cities, but held

them a mark of idleness and vice—and it was idleness and vice that brought burthens on the parish." AB 37

—*rural slum:* "Basset had a poor soil, poor roads, a poor non-resident landlord, a poor non-resident vicar, and rather less than half a curate, also poor. If any one strongly impressed with the power of the human mind to triumph over circumstances, will contend that the parishioners of Basset might nevertheless have been a very superior class of people, I have nothing to urge against that abstract proposition: I only know that in point of fact the Basset mind was in strict keeping with its circumstances. The muddy lanes, green or clayey, that seemed to the unaccustomed eye to lead nowhere but into each other, did really lead, with patience, to a distant high-road . . . . " MF I 8

Recognition and Acclaim

—*difficult:* "It is easier to make our conduct seem justifiable to ourselves than to make our ability strike others." DD 29

—*fame:* "For what is fame/but the benignant strength of One, transformed/To joy of Many?" AR I

—*a party:* " . . . there was to be a family party at Garum to discuss and celebrate a change in the fortunes of the Tullivers, which was likely finally to carry away the shadow of their demerits like the last limb of an eclipse, and cause their hitherto obscured virtues to shine forth in full-rounded splendour. It is pleasant to know that a new ministry just come into office are not the only fellow-men who enjoy a period of high appreciation and full-blown eulogy: in many respectable families throughout this realm relatives becoming creditable meet with a similar cordiality of recognition, which in its fine freedom from the coercion of any antecedents, suggests the hopeful possibility that we may some day without any notice find ourselves in full millennium, with cockatrices who have ceased to bite and wolves that no longer show their teeth with any but the blandest intentions." MF VI 12

—*pre-eminence:* "Pre-eminence is sweet to those who love it, even under mediocre circumstances: perhaps it is not quite mythical that a slave has been proud to be bought first; and probably a barn-door fowl on sale, though he may not have understood himself to be called the best of a bad lot, may have a self-informed consciousness of his relative importance, and strut consoled. But for complete enjoyment the outward and the inward must concur. And that concurrence was happening to Gwendolen." DD 10

Stranger

—*observant:* " . . . the stranger's eye detects what the familiar unsuspecting eye leaves unnoticed." AB 36

—*rescue:* "The moment of finding a fellow-creature is often as full of mingled doubt and exultation as the moment of finding an idea." DD 17

Humankind, in Activity

"The same society has had a gibbet for the murderer and a gibbet for the martyr, an execrating hiss for a dastardly act, and as loud a hiss for many a word of generous truthfulness or just insight: a mixed condition of things which is the sign, not of hopeless confusion, but of struggling order." R 57

" . . . beating the weeds, according to the foible of our common humanity when it has a stick in its hand." FH 27

Architecture

—incompetent: "Like an incompetent architect with too much interest at his back, he obtrudes his ill-considered work where place ought to have been left to better men." TS 14

—public hall: "In the bare squareness of a public hall, where there was not one jutting angle to hang a guess or a thought upon, not an image or a bit of colour to stir the fancy, and where the only objects of speculation, of admiration, or of any interest whatever, were human beings . . . . " FH 46

Art and Artists

—aesthetic meaning: " . . . [in both] a good and a bad picture of the Last Judgment . . . the subject is a combination never actually witnessed, and in the good picture the general combination may be of surpassing boldness; but on examination it is seen that the separate elements have been closely studied from real objects. And even where we find the charm of ideal elevation with wrong drawing and fantastic colour, the charm is dependent on the selective sensibility of the painter to certain real delicacies of form which confer the expression he longed to render; for apart from this basis of an effect perceived in common, there could be no conveyance of aesthetic meaning by the painter to the beholder. In this sense it is as true to say of **Fra Angelico**'s Coronation of the Virgin, that it has a strain of reality, as to say so of a portrait by **Rembrandt**, which also has its strain of ideal elevation due to Rembrandt's virile selective sensibility." TS 13

—centrality: "Art is the nearest thing to life; it is a mode of amplifying experience and extending our contact with our fellow-men beyond the bounds of our personal lot." NH 125

—conditions required: " 'Higher arts
Subsist on freedom—eccentricity—
Uncounted inspirations—influence
That comes with drinking, gambling, talk turned wild,
Then moody misery and lack of food—
With every dithyrambic fine excess:
These make at last a storm which flashes out
In lightning revelations. Steady work
Turns genius to a loom; the soul must lie
Like grapes beneath the sun till ripeness comes
And mellow vintage.' " S 117-27

—essence: " 'The life of Art,
The sweet perennial youth of Poesy,
Which asks no logic but its sensuous growth,
No right but loveliness; which fearless strolls
Betwixt the burning mountain and the sea,
Reckless of earthquake and the lava stream,
Fillings its hours with beauty. It knows nought
Of bitter strife, denial, grim resolve,
Sour resignation, busy emphasis
Of fresh illusions named the new-born True,
Old Error's latest child; but as a lake
Images all things, yet within its depths
Dreams them all lovelier—thrills with sound
And makes a harp of plenteous liquid chords—
So Art or Poesy . . . . " CB 731-45

—festa painting: "But the latter half of the century was getting rather ashamed of the towers with their circular or spiral paintings, which had delighted the eyes and the hearts of the other half, so that they had become a contemptuous proverb, and any ill-painted figure looking, as will sometimes happen to figures in the best ages of art, as if it had been boned for a pie, was called a *fantoccio de cero,* a tower-puppet . . . " R 8

—gallery: "Besides, one get tired of a 'manner' . . . in painting, when one theme after another is treated with the same lines and touches. I begin with a liking for an estimable master, but by the time he has stretched his interpretation of the world unbrokenly along a palatial gallery, I have had what the cautious Scotch mind calls 'enough' of him." TS 14

—Leonardo da Vinci: see BL 3

—misleading: "All the more sacred is the task of the artist when he undertakes to paint the life of the People. Falsification here is far more pernicious than in the more artificial aspects of life. It is not so very serious that we should have false ideas about evanescent fashions—about the manners and conversation of beaux and duchesses; but it *is* serious that our sympathy with the perennial joys and struggles, the toil, the tragedy, and the humor in the life of our more heavily laden fellow-men, should be perverted, and tuned towards a false object instead of the true one." NH 125

—peasant scenes: "What English artist even attempts to rival in truthfulness such studies of popular life as the pictures of Teniers or the ragged boys of Murillo? Even one of the greatest painters of the pre-eminently realistic school [**Wm. Holman Hunt**], while, in his picture of 'The Hireling Shepherd,' he gave us a landscape of marvellous truthfulness, placed a pair of peasants in the foreground who were not much more real than the idyllic swains and damsels of our chim-

ney ornaments. Only a total absence of acquaintance and sympathy with our peasantry could give a moment's popularity to such a picture as 'Cross Purposes,' where we have a peasant girl who looks as if she knew L.E.L.'s poems by heart, and English rustics, whose costume seems to indicate that they are meant for ploughmen, with exotic features that remind us of a handsome *primo tenore.*" NH 123

—physiognomy: "Sensitive to physical characteristics, he had, both abroad and in England, looked at pictures as well as men, and in a vacant hour he had sometimes lingered in the National Gallery in search of paintings which might feed his hopefulness with grave and noble types of the human form, such as might well belong to men of his own race. But he returned in disappointment. The instances are scattered but thinly over the galleries of Europe, in which the fortune or selection even of the chief masters has given to Art a face at once young, grand, and beautiful, where, if there is any melancholy, it is no feeble passivity, but enters into the foreshadowed capability of heroism." DD 38

—portrait: "**Sir Joshua** would have been glad to take her portrait; and he would have had an easier task than the historian at least in this, that he would not have had to represent the truth of change—only to give stability to one beautiful moment." DD 11

"We may be satisfied that we know at least the form of **Schiller**'s features, for in this particular his busts and portraits are in striking accordance; unlike the busts and portraits of **Goethe**, which are a proof, if any were wanted, how inevitably subjective art is, even when it professes to be purely imitative—how the most active perception gives us rather a reflex of what we think and feel, than the real sum of objects before us." 3M 159

Cause and Effect

—astonishment: "For in general mortals have a great power of being astonished at the presence of an effect towards which they have done everything, and at the absence of an effect towards which they have done nothing but desire it. Parents are astonished at the ignorance of their sons, though they have used the most time-honoured and expensive means of securing it; husbands and wives are mutually astonished at the loss of affection which they have taken no pains to keep; and all of us in our turn are apt to be astonished that our neighbours do not admire us. In this way it happens that the truth seems highly improbable. The truth is something different from the habitual lazy combinations begotten by our wishes." DD 22

—fable: "Such guesses [about an origination] remind one of a fabulist's imaginary council of animals assembled to consider what sort of creature had constructed a honeycomb found and much tasted by Bruin and other epicures. The speakers all started from the probability that the maker was a bird, because this was the quarter from which a wondrous nest might be expected; for the animals at that time, knowing little of their own history, would have rejected as inconceivable the notion that a nest could be made by a fish; and as to the insects, they were not willingly received in society and their ways were little known.

"Several complimentary presumptions were expressed that the honeycomb was due to one or the other admired and popular bird, and there was much fluttering on the part of the Nightingale and Swallow, neither of whom gave a positive denial, their confusion perhaps extending to their sense of identity; but the Owl hissed at this folly, arguing from his particular knowledge that the animal which produced honey must be the Musk-rat, the wondrous nature of whose secretions required no proof; and, in the powerful logical procedure of the Owl, from musk to honey was but a step.

"Some disturbance arose hereupon, for the Musk-rat began to make himself obtrusive, believing in the Owl's opinion of his powers, and feeling that he could have produced the honey if he had thought of it; until an experimental Butcher-bird proposed to anatomise him as a help to decision. The hubbub increased, the opponents of the Musk-rat inquiring who his ancestors were; until a diversion was created by an able discourse of the Macaw on structures generally, which he classified so as to include the honeycomb, entering into so much admirable exposition that there was a prevalent sense of the honeycomb having probably been produced by one who understood it so well. But Bruin, who had probably eaten too much to listen with edification, grumbled in his low kind of language, that 'Fine words butter no parsnips,' by which he meant to say that there was no new honey forthcoming.

"Perhaps the audience generally was beginning to tire, when the Fox entered with his snout dreadfully swollen, and reported that the beneficent originator in question was the Wasp, which he had found much smeared with undoubted honey, having applied his nose to it—whence indeed the able insect, perhaps justifiably irritated at what might seem a sign of scepticism, had stung him with some severity, an infliction Reynard could hardly regret, since the swelling of a snout normally so delicate would corroborate his statement and satisfy the assembly that he had really found the honey-creating genius.

"The Fox's admitted acuteness, combined with the visible swelling, were taken as undeniable evidence, and the revelation undoubtedly met a general desire for information on a point of interest. Nevertheless, there was a murmur the reverse of delighted, and the feelings of some eminent animals were too strong for them: the Orang-outang's jaw dropped so as seriously to impair the vigour of his expression, the edifying Pelican screamed and flapped her wings, the Owl hissed again, the Macaw became loudly incoherent, and the Gibbon gave his hysterical laugh; while the Hyena, after indulging in a more splenetic guffaw, agitated the question whether it would not be better to hush up the whole affair, instead of giving public recognition to an insect whose produce, it was now plain, had been much overestimated.

"But this narrow-spirited motion was negatived by the sweet-toothed majority. A complimentary deputation to the Wasp was resolved on, and there was a confident hope that this diplomatic measure would tell on the production of honey." TS 11

Chance

—apprehensions: " 'I am afraid of ever expecting anything good again.'

" 'That's weakness, madam. Things don't happen because they're bad or good, else all eggs would be addled or none at all, and at the most it is but six to the dozen. There's good chances and bad chances, and nobody's luck is pulled only by one string.' " FH 1

—likelihood: " . . . a great deal of what passes for likelihood in the world is simply the reflex of a wish." DD 9

—propitious: "And when events turn out so much better for a man than he has had reason to dread, is it not a proof that his conduct has been less foolish and blameworthy than it might otherwise have appeared? When we are treated well, we naturally begin to think that we are not altogether unmeritorious, and that it is only just we should treat ourselves well, and not mar our own good fortune." SM 13

—trusting it: "In this point of trusting to some throw of fortune's dice, Godfrey can hardly be called old-fashioned. Favourable Chance is the god of all men who follow their own devices instead of obeying a law they believe in. Let even a polished man of these days get into a position he is ashamed to avow, and his mind will be bent on all the possible issues that may deliver him from the calculable results of that position. Let him live outside his income, or shirk the resolute honest work that brings wages, and he will presently find himself dreaming of a possible benefactor, a possible simpleton who may be cajoled into using his interest, a possible state of mind in some possible person not yet forthcoming.

"Let him neglect the responsibilities of his office, and he will inevitably anchor himself on the chance, that the thing left undone may turn out not to be of the supposed importance. Let him betray his friend's confidence, and he will adore that same cunning complexity called Chance, which gives him the hope that his friend will never know. Let him forsake a decent craft that he may pursue the gentilities of a profession to which nature never called him, and his religion will infallibly be the worship of blessed Chance, which he will believe in as the mighty creator of success. The evil principle deprecated in that religion, is the orderly sequence by which the seed brings forth a crop after its kind." ¶SM 9

Commerce and Industry

—corrupt: "Until we have altered our dictionaries and have found some other word than *morality* to stand in popular use for the duties of man to man, let us refuse to accept as moral the contractor who enriches himself by using large machinery to make pasteboard soles pass as leather for the feet of unhappy conscripts fighting at miserable odds against invaders: let us rather call him a miscreant, though he were the tenderest, most faithful of husbands, and contend that his own experience of home happiness makes his reckless infliction of suffering on others all the more atrocious." TS 16

—incompetent: "There were many men of business, however, in Rome in no respect inferior in the art of mismanagement to the most adroit of our railway boards." BL 3 311

—robotics: "When, in the Bank of England, I see a wondrously delicate machine for testing sovereigns, a shrewd implacable little steel *Rhadamanthus* that, once the coins are delivered up to it, lifts and balances each in turn for the fraction of an instant, finds it wanting or sufficient, and dismisses it to right or left with rigorous justice; when I am told of micrometers and thermopiles and tasimeters which deal physically with the invisible, the impalpable, and the unimaginable, of cunning wires and wheels and

pointing needles which will register your and my quickness so as to exclude flattering opinion; of a machine for drawing the right conclusion, which will doubtless by-and-by be improved into an automaton for finding true premises; of a microphone which detects the cadence of the fly's foot on the ceiling, and may be expected presently to discriminate the noises of our various follies as they soliloquise or converse in our brains—my mind seeming too small for these things, I get a little out of it, like an unfortunate savage too suddenly brought face to face with civilisation, and I exclaim—

" 'Am I already in the shadow of the Coming Race? and will the creatures who are to transcend and finally supersede us be steely organisms, giving out the effluvia of the laboratory, and performing with infallible exactness more than everything that we have performed with a slovenly approximativeness and self-defeating inaccuracy?' " TS 17

And see Work

Crowds and Mobs

—*destructive:* "The destructive spirit tends towards completeness; and any object once maimed or otherwise injured, is as readily doomed by unreasoning men as by unreasoning boys." FH 33

—*impulsive:* ". . . where there is no strong counter-movement, any proposition to do something unspecified stimulates stupid curiosity." FH 33

—*led:* "A man with a definite will and an energetic personality acts as a sort of flag to draw and bind together the foolish units of a mob. It was on this sort of influence over men whose mental state was a mere medley of appetites and confused impressions, that Felix had dared to count. He hurried them along with words of invitation . . . and those behind followed him, with a growing belief that he had some design worth knowing, while those in front were urged along partly by the same notion, partly by the sense that there was a motive in those behind them, not knowing what the motive was." FH 33

—*out of control:* " . . . his very movements seemed to him only an image of the day's fatalities, in which the multitudinous small wickednesses of small selfish ends, really undirected towards any larger result, had issued in widely-shared mischief that might yet be hideous." FH 33

—*pushing:* "It was that mixture of pushing forward and being pushed forward, which is a brief history of most human things." FH 33

Dance and Dancing

—*country dance:* " . . . and now the music struck up, and the glorious country dance, best of all dances, began.

"Pity it was not a boarded floor! Then the rhythmic stamping of the thick shoes would have been better than any drums. That merry stamping, that gracious nodding of the head, that waving bestowal of the hand—where can we see them now? That simple dancing of well-covered matrons, laying aside for an hour the cares of house and dairy, remembering but not affecting youth, not jealous but proud of the young maidens by their side—that holiday sprightliness of portly husbands paying little compliments to their wives, as if their courting days were come again—those lads and lasses a little confused and awkward with their partners, having nothing to say—it would be a pleasant variety to see all that sometimes, instead of low dresses and large skirts, and scanning glances exploring costumes, and languid men in lackered boots smiling with double meaning." AB 26

—*dance procession:* "A quaint procession! Old Solomon, in his seedy clothes and long white locks, seemed to be luring that decent company by the magic scream of his fiddle—luring discreet matrons in turban-shaped caps . . . luring fair lasses complacently conscious of very short waists and skirts blameless of front-folds—luring burly fathers in large variegated waistcoats, and ruddy sons, for the most part shy and sheepish, in short nether garments and very long coat-tails." SM 11

—*spontaneous:* "But she, sole swayed by
impulse passionate,
Feeling all life was music and all eyes
The warming quickening light that music
makes,
Moved as, in dance religious, **Miriam**,
When on the Red Sea shore she raised her
voice
And led the chorus of the people's joy;
Or as the Trojan maids that reverent sang
Watching the sorrow-crownéd *Hecuba:*
Moved in slow curves voluminous, gradual,
Feeling and action flowing into one,
In Eden's natural taintless marriage-bond;
Ardently modest, sensuously pure,
With young delight that wonders at itself
And throbs as innocent as opening flowers,
Knowing not comment—soilless, beautiful.
The spirit in her gravely glowing face
With sweet community informs her limbs,
Filling their fine gradation with the breath
Of virgin majesty; as full vowelled words
Are new impregnate with the master's
thought." SG I ii

Deed(s)

—consequences: "Our deeds determine us as much as we determine our deeds." AB 29

—mixed: "The same society has had a gibbet for the murderer and a gibbet for the martyr, an execrating hiss for a dastardly act, and as loud a hiss for many a word of generous truthfulness or just insight: a mixed condition of things which is the sign, not of hopeless confusion, but of struggling order." R 57

—enthusiasm: "Felix knew he was incurring great risks; but 'his blood was up': we hardly allow enough in common life for the results of that enkindled passionate enthusiasm which, under other conditions, makes world-famous deeds." FH 33

—irrevocable: "But our deeds are like children that are born to us; they live and act apart from our own will. Nay, children may be strangled, but deeds never: they have an indestructible life both in and out of our consciousness, and the dreadful vitality of deeds was pressing hard . . . ." R 16

Fashion

—current interest: "For that optical law by which an insignificant object, if near, excludes very great and glorious things that lie in the distance, has its moral parallel in the judgments of the public: men's speech is too apt to be exclusively determined by the unsuccessful deed or book of to-day, the successful doings and writings of past years being for the moment lost sight of." BL 2 597

Games and Pastimes

—archery: "Who can deny that bows and arrows are among the prettiest weapons in the world for feminine forms to play with? They prompt attitudes full of grace and power, where that fine concentration of energy seen in all marksmanship, is freed from associations of bloodshed. The time-honoured British resource of 'killing something' is no longer carried on with bow and quiver; bands defending their passes against an invading nation fight under another sort of shade than a cloud of arrows; and poisoned darts are harmless survivals either in rhetoric or in regions comfortably remote. Archery has no ugly smell of brimstone; breaks nobody's shins, breeds no athletic monsters; its only danger is that of failing, which for generous blood is enough to mould skilful action." DD 10

—chess: "The Rev. Amos was very fond of chess, as most people are who can continue through many years to create interesting vicissitudes in the game, by taking long-meditated moves with their knights, and subsequently discovering that they have thereby exposed their queen." SF 3

—with the Devil: "Most of us remember Retzsch's drawing of destiny in the shape of *Mephistopheles* playing at chess with man for his soul, a game in which we may imagine the clever adversary making a feint of unintended moves so as to set the beguiled mortal on carrying his defensive pieces away from the true point of attack." DD 37

—in the world: "Fancy what a game at chess would be if all the chessmen had passions and intellects, more or less small and cunning: if you were not only uncertain about your adversary's men, but a little uncertain also about your own; if your knight could shuffle himself on to a new square by the sly; if your bishop, in disgust at your castling, could wheedle your pawns out of their places; and if your pawns, hating you because they are pawns, could make away from their appointed posts that you might get checkmate on a sudden. You might be the longest-headed of deductive reasoners, and yet you might be beaten by your own pawns. You would be especially likely to be beaten, if you depended arrogantly on your mathematical imagination, and regarded your passionate pieces with contempt.

"Yet this imaginary chess is easy compared with the game a man has to play against his fellow-men with other fellow-men for his instruments. He thinks himself sagacious, perhaps, because he trusts no bond except that of self-interest; but the only self-interest he can safely rely on is what seems to be such to the mind he would use or govern. Can he ever be sure of knowing this?" FH 29

—embroidery: "A little daily embroidery had been a constant element in Mrs Transome's life; that soothing occupation of taking stitches to produce what neither she nor any one else wanted, was then the resource of many a well-born and unhappy woman." FH 7

—watering-places: " . . . chiefly stocked with men whose whiskers might be dyed, and whose incomes were still more problematic. . . . " SF 4

—yachting: "Moreover, he was himself very fond of yachting: its dreamy do-nothing absolutism, unmolested by social demands, suited his disposition . . . . " DD 54

—young women: "[Her] slight regard for domestic music and feminine fine art must be forgiven her, considering the small tinkling and smearing in which they chiefly consisted at that dark period [1830]." MM 7

Horseback riding

—for the disposition: "Nothing like 'taking' a few bushes and ditches for exorcising a demon; and it is really astonishing that the Centaurs, with their immense advantages in

this way, have left so bad a reputation in history." AB 12

Host and Guest

—guest

—for archery: "What could make a better background for the flower-groups of ladies, moving and bowing and turning their necks as it would become the leisurely lilies to do if they took to locomotion?" DD 10

—cossetted: "Mr Riley, meanwhile, was not impatient. Why should he be? Even *Hotspur,* one would think, must have been patient in his slippers on a warm hearth, taking copious snuff, and sipping gratuitous brandy and water." MF I 3

—tolerated: " . . . even those ladies who did not quite like her, felt a comfort in having a new, striking girl to invite; for hostesses who entertain much must make up their parties as ministers make up their cabinets, on grounds other than personal liking." DD 5

The Hunt

—seductive: "The colour, the stir of the field had taken possession of Gwendolen with a strength which was not due to habitual association, for she had never yet ridden after the hounds—only said she should like to do it. . . .

"Some of the most unexceptionable women in the neighbourhood occasionally went to see the hounds throw off; but it happened that none of them were present this morning to abstain from following, while Mrs Gadsby, with her doubtful antecedents grammatical and otherwise, was not visible to make following seem unbecoming. Thus Gwendolen felt no check on the animal stimulus that came from the stir and tongue of the hounds, the pawing of the horses, the varying voices of men, the movement hither and thither of vivid colour on the background of green and grey stillness—that utmost excitement of the coming chase which consists in feeling something like a combination of dog and horse, with the superadded thrill of social vanities and consciousness of centaur-power which belong to humankind." DD 7

Labour

—farm: " . . . no one who is well acquainted with the English peasantry can pronounce them merry. The slow gaze, in which no sense of beauty beams, no humor twinkles —the slow utterance, and the heavy slouching walk, remind one rather of that melancholy animal the camel, than of the sturdy countryman, with striped stockings, red waistcoat, and hat aside, who represents the traditional English peasant [in genre painting]. Observe a company of haymakers. When you see them at a distance, tossing up the forkfuls of hay in the golden light, while the wagon creeps slowly with its increasing burden over the meadow, and the bright green space which tells of work done gets larger and larger, you pronounce the scene 'smiling,' and you think these companions in labor must be as bright and cheerful as the picture to which they give animation. Approach nearer, and you will certainly find that haymaking-time is a time for joking, especially if there are women among the laborers; but the coarse laugh that bursts out every now and then, and expresses the triumphant taunt, is as far as possible from your conception of idyllic merriment. That delicious effervescence of the mind which we call fun has no equivalent for the northern peasant, except tipsy revelry; the only realm of fancy and imagination for the English clown exists at the bottom of the third quart-pot." NH 124

—outstanding example: "Yet such men as [Adam Bede] are reared here and there in every generation of our peasant artisans —with an inheritance of affections nurtured by a simple family life of common need and common industry, and an inheritance of faculties trained in skilful courageous labour: they make their way upward, rarely as geniuses, most commonly as painstaking honest men, with the skill and conscience to do well the tasks that lie before them. Their lives have no discernible echo beyond the neighbourhood where they dwelt, but you are almost sure to find there some good piece of road, some building, some application of mineral produce, some improvement in farming practice, some reform of parish abuses, with which their names are associated by one or two generations after them.

"Their employers were the richer for them, the work of their hands has worn well, and the work of their brains has guided well the hands of other men. They went about in their youth in flannel or paper caps, in coats black with coal-dust or streaked with lime and red paint; in old age their white hairs are seen in a place of honour at church and at market, and they tell their well-dressed sons and daughters, seated round the bright hearth on winter evenings, how pleased they were when they first earned their twopence a-day. Others there are who die poor, and never put off the workman's coat on weekdays: they have not had the art of getting rich; but they are men of trust, and when they die before the work is all out of them, it is as if some main screw had got loose in a machine; the master who employed them says, 'Where shall I find their like?' " ¶AB 19

—persuasive effort: "Caleb was in a difficulty known to any person attempting in

dark times and unassisted by miracle to reason with rustics who are in possession of an undeniable truth which they know through a hard process of feeling, and can let it fall like a giant's club on your neatly-carved argument for a social benefit which they *not* feel." MM 56

" 'The cattle may have a heavy load, but it won't help 'em to throw it over into the road-side pit, when it's partly their own fodder.' " AB 56

—servant class: " . . . this class of men and women are but slightly determined in their estimate of others by general considerations, or even experience, of character. They judge of persons as they judge of coins, and value those who pass current at a high rate." LV 2

—speaking out: " 'But the railroad's a good thing.'

" 'Aw! good for the big folks to make money out on . . . . I'n seen lots o'things turn up sin' I war a young un—the war an' the peace, and the canells, an' the oald King George, an' the Regen', an' the new King George, an' the new un as has got a new ne-ame—an' it's been all aloike to the poor mon. What's the canells been t'him? They'n brought him nether me-at nor be-acon, nor wage to lay by, if he didn't save it wi' clem-min' [starving] his own inside. Times ha' got wusser for him sin' I war a young un. An' so it'll be wi' the railroads. They'll on'y leave the poor mon furder behind. But them are fools as meddle, and so I told the chaps here. This is the big folks's world, this is.' " MM 56

Leadership

—in obscurity: "Most of us, indeed, know little of the great originators until they have been lifted up among the constellations and already rule our fates . . . . Each of those Shining Ones had to walk on the earth among neighbours who perhaps thought much more of his gait and his garments than of anything which was to give him a title to everlasting fame: each of them had his little local personal history sprinkled with small temptations and sordid cares, which made the retarding friction of his course towards final companionship with the immortals." MM 15

Leisure

—in former times: "Surely all other leisure is hurry compared with a sunny walk through the fields from 'afternoon church,'—as such walks used to be in those old lei-surely times, when the boat, gliding sleepily along the canal, was the newest locomotive wonder; when Sunday books had most of them old brown-leather covers, and opened with remarkable precision always in one place. Leisure is gone—gone where the spinning-wheels are gone, and the pack-horses, and the slow waggons, and the ped-lars who brought bargains to the door on sunny afternoons. Ingenious philosophers tell you, perhaps, that the great work of the steam-engine is to create leisure for man-kind. Do not believe them: it only creates a vacuum for eager thought to rush in. Even idleness is eager now—eager for amuse-ment: prone to excursion-trains, art-museums, periodical literature, and exciting novels: prone even to scientific theorising, and cursory peeps through microscopes.

"Old Leisure was quite a different person-age: he only read one newspaper, innocent of leaders, and was free from that periodicity of sensations which we call post-time. He was a contemplative, rather stout gentle-man, of excellent digestion—of quiet percep-tions, undiseased by hypothesis: happy in his inability to know the causes of things, preferring the things themselves. He lived chiefly in the country, among pleasant seats and homesteads, and was fond of sauntering by the fruit-tree wall, and scenting the apri-cots when they were warmed by the morn-ing sunshine, or of sheltering himself under the orchard boughs at noon, when the sum-mer pears were falling.

"He knew nothing of weekday services, and thought none the worse of the Sunday sermon, if it allowed him to sleep from the text to the blessing—liking the afternoon service best, because the prayers were the shortest, and not ashamed to say so; for he had an easy, jolly conscience, broad-backed like himself, and able to carry a great deal of beer or port-wine—not being made squeam-ish by doubts and qualms and lofty aspira-tions. Life was not a task to him, but a sine-cure: he fingered the guineas in his pocket, and ate his dinners, and slept the sleep of the irresponsible; for had he not kept up his character by going to church on the Sunday afternoons?

"Fine old Leisure! Do not be severe upon him, and judge him by our modern standard: he never went to Exeter Hall, or heard a popular preacher, or read *Tracts for the Times* or *Sartor Researtus*." ¶AB 52

Mankind

—conventional: " . . . this old-fashioned fam-ily life on the banks of the Floss, which even sorrow hardly suffices to lift above the level of the tragi-comic. It is a sordid life, you say, this of the Tullivers and Dodsons—ir-radiated by no sublime principles, no ro-mantic visions, no active, self-renouncing faith— moved by none of those wild, uncon-trollable passions which create the dark shadows of misery and crime—without that primitive rough simplicity of wants, that hard submissive ill-paid toil, that child-like

spelling-out of what nature has written, which gives its poetry to peasant life. Here, one has conventional worldly notions, and habits without instruction and without polish—surely the most prosaic form of human life: proud respectability in a gig of unfashionable build: worldliness without side-dishes." MF IV 1

—imperfect: "These fellow-mortals, every one, must be accepted as they are: you can neither straighten their noses, nor brighten their wit, nor rectify their dispositions; and it is these people—amongst whom your life is passed—that it is needful you should tolerate, pity, and love: it is these more or less ugly, stupid, inconsistent people, whose movements of goodness you should be able to admire—for whom you should cherish all possible hopes, all possible patience." AB 17

"No doubt there are abject specimens of the visionary, as there is a minim mammal which you might imprison in the finger of your glove. That small relative of the elephant has no harm in him; but what great mental or social type is free from specimens whose insignificance is both ugly and noxious? One is afraid to think of all that the genus 'patriot' embraces; or of the elbowing there might be at the day of judgment for those who ranked as authors, and brought volumes either in their hands or on trucks." DD 38

—insignificant: "At least eighty out of a hundred of your adult male fellow Britons returned in the last census are neither extraordinarily silly, nor extraordinarily wicked, nor extraordinarily wise; their eyes are neither deep and liquid with sentiment, nor sparkling with suppressed witticisms; they have probably had no hairbreadth escapes or thrilling adventures; their brains are certainly not pregnant with genius, and their passions have not manifested themselves at all after the fashion of a volcano. They are simply men of complexions more or less muddy, whose conversation is more or less bald and disjointed. Yet these commonplace people—many of them—bear a conscience, and have felt the sublime prompting to do the painful right; they have their unspoken sorrows, and their sacred joys; their hearts have perhaps gone out towards their first-born, and they have mourned over the irreclaimable dead. Nay, is there not a pathos in their very insignificance—in our comparison of their dim and narrow existence with the glorious possibilities of that human nature which they share?" SF 4

"Nevertheless, to speak paradoxically, the existence of insignificant people has very important consequences in the world. It can be shown to affect the price of bread and the rate of wages, to call forth many evil tempers from the selfish, and many heroisms from the sympathetic, and, in other ways, to play no small part in the tragedy of life." AB 5

—lovable: " . . . the way in which I have come to the conclusion that human nature is lovable—the way I have learnt something of its deep pathos, its sublime mysteries—has been by living a great deal among people more or less commonplace and vulgar, of whom you would perhaps hear nothing very surprising if you were to inquire about them in the neighbourhoods where they dwelt." AB 17

—starting out: " . . . pulling his bell violently and bringing down the small bell-rope.

". . . Tom, with masculine philosophy, flung the bell-rope to the farther end of the room—not very far either: a touch of human experience which I flatter myself will come home to the bosoms of not a few substantial or distinguished men who were once at an early stage of their rise in the world and were cherishing very large hopes in very small lodgings." MV VI 4

Manners

—evolving: "Even the patriarch *Job,* if he had been a gentleman of the modern West, would have avoided picturesque disorder and poetical laments; and the friends who called on him, though not less disposed than *Bildad the Shuhite* to hint that their unfortunate friend was in the wrong, would have sat on chairs and held their hats in their hands. The harder problems of our life have changed less than our manners; we wrestle with the old sorrows, but more decorously." FH 40

—stage and reality: "It is to be believed that attendance at the *opéra bouffe* in the present day would not leave men's minds entirely without shock, if the manners observed there with some applause were suddenly to start up in their own families." DD 14

Music and Music-making

—absent: "There was no music for her any more—no piano, no harmonised voices, no delicious stringed instruments with their passionate cries of imprisoned spirits sending a strange vibration through her frame." MF IV 3

—amateur: " We should have a poor life of it if we were reduced for all our pleasure to our own performances. A little private imitation of what is good is a sort of private devotion to it, and most of us ought to practise art only in the light of private study —preparation to understand and enjoy what the few can do for us.' " DD 36

—*anarchy avoided:* " 'I apprehend that there is a law in music, disobedience whereunto would bring us in our singing to the level of shrieking maniacs or howling beasts: so that herein we are well instructed how true liberty can be nought but the transfer of obedience from the will of one or of a few men to that will which is the norm or rule for all men.' " FH 13

—*church hymn:* " . . . while good old **Bishop Ken**'s evening hymn was being sung to one of those lively psalm-tunes which died out with the last generation of rectors and choral parish-clerks. Melodies die out, like the pipe of *Pan,* with the ears that love them and listen for them." AB 18

—*composer's lament:* "Peace, now, peace!
I hate my phrases to be smothered o'er
With sauce of paraphrase, my sober tune
Made bass to rambling trebles, showering down
In endless demi-semi-quavers." AR I

—*craved:* " 'I think I should have no other mortal wants, if I could always have plenty of music. It seems to infuse strength into my limbs and ideas into my brain. Life seems to go on without effort, when I am filled with music. At other times one is conscious of carrying a weight.' " MF VI 3

—*excellence:* " 'For my part' said Deronda, 'people who do anything finely always inspirit me to try. I don't mean that they make me believe I can do it as well. But they make the thing, whatever it may be, seem worthy to be done. I can bear to think my own music not good for much, but the world would be more dismal if I thought music itself not good for much. Excellence encourages one about life generally; it shows the spiritual wealth of the world.' " DD 36

—*expressing feelings:* " . . . there is no feeling, perhaps, except the extremes of fear and grief, that does not find relief in music —that does not make a man sing or play the better . . . . " MF VI 7

—*independence:* " . . . the important opening of that work which was to secure her independence, as we rather arbitrarily call one of the more arduous and dignified forms of our dependence." DD 46

—*inspiration:* "So the highest degree of musical inspiration must overmaster all other conceptions in the mind of the musical genius; and music will be great and ultimately triumphant over men's ears and souls in proportion as it is less a studied than an involuntary symbol." LW

—*lute and song:* " . . . while at the door
Gazed the lank boys and lazy-shouldered men.
'Tis likely too the rats and insects peeped,
Being southern Spanish ready for a lounge.
The singer smiled, as doubtless *Orpheus* smiled,
To see the animals both great and small,
The mountainous elephant and scampering mouse,
Held by the ears in decent audience . . . . "
SG I i

—*melody:* "As to melody—who knows? It is just possible that melody, as we conceive it, is only a transitory phase of music, and that the musicians of the future may read the airs of **Mozart** and **Beethoven** and **Rossini** as scholars read the *Stabreim* and assonance of early poetry. We are but in 'the morning of the times,' and must learn to think of ourselves as tadpoles unprescient of the future frog. Still the tadpole is limited to tadpole pleasures; and so, in our state of development, we are swayed by melody. When, a little while after hearing *Lohengrin,* we happened to come on a party of musicians who were playing exquisitely a quartette of Beethoven's, it was like returning to the pregnant speech of men after a sojourn among glums and gowries." LW

—*multiplier effect:* " 'O yes,' he said, seating himself at the piano, 'it is a way of eking out one's imperfect life and being three people at once—to sing and make the piano sing, and hear them both all the while . . .' " MF VI 7

—*performed despite misery:* "In her happiest moments she could never have played it so well; for now all the passion that made her misery was hurled by a convulsive effort into her music, just as pain gives new force to the clutch of the sinking wrestler, and as terror gives far-sounding intensity to the shriek of the feeble." GL 13

—*preparation:* " 'The desire and the training should have begun seven years ago—or a good deal earlier. A mounte-bank's child who helps her father to earn shillings when she is six years old—a child that inherits a singing throat from a long line of choristers and learns to sing as it learns to talk, has a likelier beginning. Any great achievement in acting or in music grows with the growth. Whenever an artist has been able to say, "I came, I saw, I conquered," it has been at the end of patient practice. Genius at first is little more than a great capacity for receiving discipline. Singing and acting, like the fine dexterity of the juggler with his cups and balls, require a shaping of the organs towards a finer and finer certainty of effect. Your muscles—your whole frame—must go like a watch, true, true, true, to a hair. That is the work of spring-time, before habits have been determined.' " DD 23

—*singing gift:* "But that is Nature's way: she will allow a gentleman of splendid physiognomy and poetic aspirations to sing woefully out of tune, and not give him the slightest hint of it; and takes care that some narrow-browed fellow, trolling a ballad in the corner of a pot-house, shall be as true to his intervals as a bird." AB 18

—some knowledge: " 'I know the notes of many birds, and I know many melodies by ear; but the music that I don't know at all, and have no notion about, delights me— affects me. How stupid the world is that it does not make more use of such a pleasure within its reach!' " MM 16

—soul: "A hidden soul seemed to be flowing forth from Rosamond's fingers; and so indeed it was, since souls live on in perpetual echoes and to all fine expression there goes somewhere an originating activity, if it be only that of an interpreter." MM 16

—tone-deaf: "All's one to me. I note no
change of tune,
Not I, save in the ring of horses' hoofs,
Or in the drums and trumpets when they call
To action or retreat. I ne'er could see
The good of singing." SG I i

Nobility

—disadvantaged: "A chief misfortune of high birth is that it usually shuts a man out from the large sympathetic knowledge of human experience which comes from contact with various classes on their own level, and in my father's time that entail of social ignorance had not been disturbed as we see it now. To look always from overhead at the crowd of one's fellow-men must be in many ways incapacitating, even with the best will and intelligence. The serious blunders it must lead to in the effort to manage them for their good, one may see clearly by the mistaken ways people take of flattering and enticing those whose associations are unlike their own." TS 2

Occupations

—ambition undermined: "For in the multitude of middle-aged men who go about their vocations in a daily course determined for them much in the same way as the tie of their cravats, there is always a good number who once meant to shape their own deeds and alter the world a little. The story of their coming to be shapen after the average and fit to be packed by the gross, is hardly ever told even in their consciousness, for perhaps their ardour in generous unpaid toil cooled as imperceptibly as the ardour of other youthful loves, till one day their earlier self walked like a ghost in its old home and made the new furniture ghastly. Nothing in the world more subtle than the process of their gradual change! In the beginning they inhaled it unknowingly; you and I may have sent some of our breath towards infecting them, when we uttered our conforming falsities or drew our silly conclusions or perhaps it came with the vibrations from a woman's glance." MM 15

"We are on a perilous margin when we begin to look passively at our future selves, and see our own figures led with dull consent into insipid misdoing and shabby achievement. Poor Lydgate was inwardly groaning on that margin, and Will was arriving at it . . . he dreaded his own distaste for his spoiled life, which would leave him in motiveless levity." MM 79

—artist: " 'I am not decrying the life of a true artist. I am exalting it. I say, it is out of the reach of any but choice organisations—natures framed to love perfection and to labour for it; ready, like all true lovers, to endure, to wait, to say, I am not yet worthy, but she—Art, my mistress—is worthy, and I will live to merit her. An honourable life? Yes. But the honour comes from the inward vocation and the hard-won achievement: there is no honour in donning the life as a livery.' " DD 23

—auctioneer: "And surely among all men whose vocation requires them to exhibit their powers of speech, the happiest is a prosperous provincial auctioneer keenly alive to his own jokes and sensible of his encyclopaedic knowledge." MM 60

—authorship: " . . . Deronda set himself against authorship—a vocation which is understood to turn foolish thinking into funds." DD 17

—barber: " 'See now, how by diligent shaving, the nether region of your face may preserve its human outline, instead of presenting no distinction from the physiognomy of a bearded owl or a Barbary ape. I have seen men whose beards have so invaded their cheeks, that one might have pitied them as the victims of a sad, brutalising chastisement befitting our **Dante**'s Inferno, if they had not seemed to strut with a strange triumph in their extravagant hairiness.' " R 3

" 'You have an adroit way of inserting your comb, which flatters the skin, and stirs the animal spirits agreeably in that region; and a little of your most delicate orange-scent would not be amiss . . . . ' " R 13

—beauty: "Then there was the pleasure of producing an effect by her appearance in society: what did celebrated beauties do in town when their husbands could afford display? All men were fascinated by them: they had a perfect equipage and toilet, walked into public places, and bowed, and made the usual answers, and walked out again: perhaps they bought china, and practised accomplishments." DD 35

—butler: "He returned with the lanterns and the coat-tail and a most uncomfortable consciousness in that great seat of a butler's emotion, the stomach." FH 12

—calling: "Most of us who turn to any subject with love remember some morning or evening hour when we got on a high stool to reach down an untried volume, or sat with parted lips listening to a new talker, or for very lack of books began to listen to the voices within, as the first traceable beginning of our love." MM 15

—coachman: "The coachman was an excellent travelling companion and commentator on the landscape: he could tell the names of sites and persons, and explain the meaning of groups, as well as the shade of *Virgil* in a more memorable journey; he had as many stories about parishes, and the men and women in them, as the Wanderer in the 'Excursion' only his style was different. His view of life had originally been genial, and such as became a man who was well warmed within and without, and held a position of easy, undisputed authority; but the recent initiation of Railways had embittered him: he now, as in a perpetual vision, saw the ruined country strewn with shattered limbs . . . . 'Why, every inn on the road would be shut up!' and at that word the coachman looked before him with the blank gaze of one who had driven his coach to the outermost edge of the universe, and saw his leaders plunging into the abyss.

"Still he would soon relapse from the high prophetic strain to the familiar one of narrative. He knew whose the land was wherever he drove; what noblemen had half-ruined themselves by gambling; who made handsome returns of rent; and who was at daggers-drawn with his eldest son. He perhaps remembered the fathers of actual baronets, and knew stories of their extravagant or stingy housekeeping; whom they had married, whom they had horsewhipped, whether they were particular about preserving their game, and whether they had had much to do with canal companies.

"About any actual landed proprietor he could also tell whether he was a Reformer or an Anti-Reformer. That was a distinction which had 'turned up' in latter times, and along with it the paradox, very puzzling to the coachman's mind, that there were men of old family and large estate who voted for the Bill. He did not grapple with the paradox; he let it pass, with all the discreetness of an experienced theologian or learned scholiast, preferring to point his whip at some object which could raise no questions." ¶FH *I*

—confectioner: "Among the many fatalities attending the bloom of young desire, that of blindly taking to the confectionery line has not, perhaps, been sufficiently considered. How is the son of a British yeoman, who has been fed principally on salt pork and yeast dumplings, to know that there is satiety for the human stomach even in a paradise of glass jars full of sugared almonds and pink lozenges, and that the tedium of life can reach a pitch where plum-buns at discretion cease to offer the slightest enticement? Or how, at the tender age when a confectioner seems to him a very prince whom all the world must envy—who breakfasts on macaroons, dines on marengs, sups on twelfth-cake, and fills up the intermediate hours with sugar-candy or peppermint—how is he to foresee the day of sad wisdom, when he will discern that the confectioner's calling is not socially influential, or favorable to a soaring ambition?" BJ 1

—dancing-master: "I have known a man who turned out to have a metaphysical genius, incautiously, in the period of youthful buoyancy, commence his career as a dancing-master; and you may imagine the use that was made of this initial mistake by opponents who felt themselves bound to warn the public against his doctrine of the Inconceivable. He could not give up his dancing-lessons, because he made his bread by them, and metaphysics would not have found him in so much as salt to his bread." BJ 1

—Don: " 'But talking of Dons, I have seen a Don make a capital figure in society; and occasionally he can shoot you down a cart-load of learning in the right place, which will tell in politics. Such men are wanted; and if you have any turn for being a Don, I say nothing against it.' " DD 16

—election agent: "To have the pleasure and the praise of electioneering ingenuity, and also to get paid for it, without too much anxiety whether the ingenuity will achieve its ultimate end, perhaps gives to some select persons a sort of satisfaction in their superiority to their more agitated fellow-men that is worthy to be classed with those generous enjoyments of having the truth chiefly to yourself, and of seeing others in danger of drowning while you are high and dry, which seems to have been regarded as unmixed privileges by **Lucretius** and **Lord Bacon**." FH 30

—farm labour: "The bucolic character at Hayslope, you perceive, was not of that entirely genial, merry, broad-grinning sort, apparently observed in most districts visited by artists. The mild radiance of a smile was a rare sight on a field-labourer's face, and

there was seldom any gradation between bovine gravity and a laugh." AB 53

—governess: "As to the sweetness of labour and fulfilled claims, the interest of inward and outward activity; the impersonal delights of life as a perpetual discovery; the dues of courage, fortitude, industry, which it is mere baseness not to pay towards the common burthen; the supreme worth of the teacher's vocation;—these, even if they had been eloquently preached to her, could have been no more than faintly apprehended doctrines: the fact which wrought upon her was her invariable observation that for a lady to become a governess—to 'take a situation'—was to descend in life and to be treated at best with a compassionate patronage." DD 24

—idealistic: see S:Idealism

—linen-weaver: "In the days when the spinning-wheels hummed busily in the farmhouses . . . there might be seen in districts far away among the lanes, or deep in the bosom of the hills, certain pallid undersized men, who, by the side of the brawny country-folk, looked like the remnants of a disinherited race . . . those scattered linen-weavers—emigrants from the town into the country—were to the last regarded as aliens by their rustic neighbours, and usually contracted the eccentric habits which belong to a state of loneliness." SM 1

—miller

—mill: "The resolute din, the unresting motion of the great stones giving her a dim delicious awe as at the presence of an uncontrollable force, the meal for ever pouring, pouring, the fine white powder softening all surfaces and making the very spider-nets look like faery lace-work, the sweet pure scent of the meal—all helped Maggie feel that the mill was a little world apart from her outside everyday life." MF I 4

—mistaken: "A tallow dip, of the long-eight description, is an excellent thing in the kitchen candlestick, and Betty's nose and eye are not sensitive to the difference between it and the finest wax; it is only when you stick it in the silver candlestick, and introduce it into the drawing-room, that it seems plebeian, dim, and ineffectual. Alas for the worthy man who, like that candle, gets himself into the wrong place! It is only the very largest souls who will be able to appreciate and pity him—who will discern and love sincerity of purpose amid all the bungling feebleness of achievement." SF 2

—pawn-broker: " "I wouldn't exchange my business with any in the world. There's none more honourable, nor more charitable, nor more necessary for all classes, from the good lady who wants a little of the ready for the banker, to a gentleman like yourself, sir, who may want it for amusement. I like my business, I like my street, and I like my shop. I wouldn't have it a door further down. And I wouldn't be without a pawn-shop, sir, to be the Lord Mayor. It puts you in connection with the world at large. I say it's like the Government revenue—it embraces the brass as well as the gold of the country. And a man who doesn't get money, sir, can't accommodate.' " DD 33

—second-hand books: " . . . he took [the book] from its place, and entered the shop to pay for [it], expecting to see behind the counter a grimy personage showing that *nonchalance* about sales which seems to belong universally to the second-hand book-business. In most other trades you find generous men who are anxious to sell you their wares for your own welfare, but even a Jew will not urge **Simson**'s Euclid on you with an affectionate assurance that you will have pleasure in reading it, and that he wishes he had twenty more of the article, so much is it in request. One is led to fear that a second-hand bookseller may belong to that unhappy class of men who have no belief in the good of what they get their living by, yet keep conscience enough to be morose rather than unctuous in their vocation." DD 33

—shepherd, "head-servant of the farm . . . with a slow and slouching walk, timed by the walk of grazing beasts, moved aside, as if unwillingly, throwing out a monosyllabic hint to his cattle; his glance, accustomed to rest on things very near the earth, seemed to lift itself with difficulty to the coachman. Mail or stage coach for him belonged to that mysterious distant system of things called 'Gover'ment', which, whatever it might be, was no business of his, any more than the most outlying nebula or the coal-sacks of the southern hemisphere: his solar system was the parish; the master's temper and the casualties of lambing-time were his region of storms. He cut his bread and bacon with his pocket-knife, and felt no bitterness except in the matter of pauper labourers and the bad-luck that sent contrarious seasons and the sheep-rot." FH *I*

Pleasures

—appetite, at least: "Many courses are actually pursued—follies and sins both convenient and inconvenient—without pleasure or hope of pleasure; but to solace ourselves with imagining any course beforehand, there must be some foretaste of pleasure in the shape of appetite . . . . " DD 35

—older people: " ' . . . there's a good deal of pleasure in life for you yet.'

" 'Nonsense! there's no pleasure for old women, unless they get it out of tormenting other people. What are your pleasures, Denner, besides being a slave to me?'

" 'Oh, there's pleasure in knowing one's not a fool, like half the people one sees about. And managing one's husband is some pleasure; and doing all one's business well. Why, if I've only got some orange flowers to candy, I shouldn't like to die till I see them all right. Then there's the sunshine now and then; I like that, as the cats do. I look upon it, life is like our game at whist, when Banks and his wife come to the still-room of an evening. I don't enjoy the game much, but I like to play my cards well, and see what will be the end of it . . . . ' " FH 1

—*vulgar humour:* " 'Oh, sir, 'twas that mixture of spite and over-fed merriment which passes for humour with the vulgar. In their fun they have much resemblance to a turkey-cock. It has a cruel beak, and a silly iteration of ugly sounds; it spreads its tail in self-glorification, but shows you the wrong side of that ornament—liking admiration, but knowing not what is admirable.' " FH 12 ep

Social class

—*acceptability:* " . . . to most mortals there is a stupidity which is unendurable and a stupidity which is altogether acceptable—else, indeed, what would become of social bonds? Captain Lydgate's stupidity was delicately scented, carried itself with 'style,' talked with a good accent, and was closely related to Sir Godwin. Rosamond found it quite agreeable and caught many of its phrases." MM 58

—*advancement declined:* " 'Why should I want to get into the middle class because I have some learning? The most of the middle class are as ignorant as the working people about everything that doesn't belong to their own Brummagem life. That's how the working men are left to foolish devices and keep worsening themselves: the best heads among them forsake their born comrades, and go in for a house with a high door-step and a brass knocker.' " FH 5

" 'If there's anything our people want convincing of, it is, that there's some dignity and happiness for a man other than changing his station.' " FH 45

—*affectation:* "The affectation that decks trivial things in fine language, belongs essentially to a class which sees another above it, and is uneasy in the sense of its inferiority; and this affectation is precisely the opposite of the original *genre précieux.*" WF 454

—*animosity:* "Pray excuse Deronda that in this moment he felt a transient renewal of his first repulsion from Gwendolen, as if she and her beauty and her failings were to blame for the undervaluing of Mirah as a woman—a feeling something like class animosity, which affection for what is not fully recognised by others, whether in persons or in poetry, rarely allows us to escape." DD 45

—*awareness:* "She knew quite well that, to Harold Transome, Felix Holt was one of the common people who could come into question in no other than a public light. She had a native capability for discerning that the sense of ranks and degrees has its repulsions corresponding to the repulsions dependent on difference of race and colour, and she remembered her own impressions too well . . . . " FH 43

—*awe:* "For in those days the keenest of bucolic minds felt a whispering awe at the sight of the gentry, such as of old men felt when they stood on tip-toe to watch the gods passing by in tall human shape." AB 6

—*"betters":* " . . . tall, powerful, florid men, seen chiefly on horse-back . . . . " SM 19

—*country gentry:* "The country gentry of old time [the late 1820s] lived in a rarefied social air: dotted apart on their stations up the mountain they looked down with imperfect discrimination on the belts of thicker life below. And Dorothea was not at ease in the perspective and chilliness of that height." MM 34

—*cheer:* "Already Mr Macey and a few other privileged villagers, who were allowed to be spectators on these great occasions, were seated on benches placed for them near the door; and great was the admiration and satisfaction in that quarter when the couples had formed themselves for the dance, and the Squire led off with Mrs Crackenthorp, joining hands with the Rector and Mrs Osgood. That was as it should be—that was what everybody had been used to—and the charter of Raveloe seemed to be renewed by the ceremony. It was not thought of as an unbecoming levity for the old and middle-aged people to dance a little before sitting down to cards, but rather as part of their social duties. For what were these if not to be merry at appropriate times, interchanging visits and poultry with due frequency, paying each other old-established compliments in sound traditional phrases, passing well-tried personal jokes, urging your guests to eat and drink too much out of hospitality, and eating and drinking too much in your neighbour's house to show that you liked your cheer?" SM 11

—*ignorant:* "But a man of Sir Maximus's rank is like those antediluvian animals whom the system of things condemned to carry such a huge bulk that they really could not inspect their bodily appurtenance, and had no conception of their own tails:

their parasites doubtless had a merry time of it, and often did extremely well when the high-bred saurian himself was ill at ease." FH 7

—distinction in a narration: "And here I am naturally led to reflect on the means of elevating a low subject. Historical parallels are remarkably efficient in this way. The chief objection to them is, that the diligent narrator may lack space, or (what is often the same thing) may not be able to think of them with any degree of particularity, though he may have a philosophical confidence that if known they would be illustrative. It seems an easier and shorter way to dignity, to observe that—since there never was a true story which could not be told in parables where you might put a monkey for a margrave, and *vice versa*—whatever has been or is to be narrated by me about low people, may be ennobled by being considered a parable; so that if any bad habits and ugly consequences are brought into view, the reader may have the relief of regarding them as not more than figuratively ungenteel, and may feel himself virtually in company with persons of some style. Thus while I tell the truth about loobies [clumsy louts], my reader's imagination need not be entirely excluded from an occupation with lords; and the petty sums which any bankrupt of high standing would be sorry to retire upon, may be lifted to the level of high commercial transactions by the inexpensive addition of proportional ciphers." MM 35

—fallen: " . . . there is a chill air surrounding those who are down in the world and people are glad to get away from them, as from a cold room: human beings, mere men and women, without furniture, without anything to offer you, who have ceased to count as anybody, present an embarrassing negation of reasons for wishing to see them, or of subjects on which to converse with them. At that distant day, there was a dreary isolation in the civilised Christian society of these realms for families that had dropped below their original level, unless they belonged to a sectarian church, which gets some warmth of brotherhood by walling in the sacred fire." MF IV 2

—farming people: " . . . she was most afraid of spending her money, and becoming so destitute that she would have to ask people's charity; for Hetty had the pride not only of a proud nature but of a proud class —the class that pays the most poor-rates, and most shudders at the idea of profiting by a poor-rate." AB 36

—fine-lady: " 'A real fine-lady does not wear clothes that flare in people's eyes, or use importunate scents, or make a noise as she moves: she is something refined, and graceful, and charming, and never obtrusive.'

" 'O yes,' said Felix, contemptuously. 'And she reads **Byron** also, and admires Childe Harold—gentlemen of unspeakable woes, who employ a hairdresser, and look seriously at themselves in the glass.

" . . . 'A fine lady is a squirrel-headed thing, with small airs and small notions, about as applicable to the business of life as a pair of tweezers to the clearing of a forest.' " FH 5

—gentrified ideas: " . . . a life of middling delights, overhung with the languorous haziness of motiveless ease, where poetry was only literature, and the fine ideas had to be taken down from the shelves of the library when her husband's back was turned." FH 44

—good society: " . . . where principles and beliefs are not only of an extremely moderate kind, but are always presupposed, no subjects being eligible but such as can be touched with a light and graceful irony. But then, good society has its claret and its velvet carpets, its dinner-engagements six weeks deep, its opera and its faëry ballrooms; rides off its ennui on thoroughbred horses, lounges at the club, has to keep clear of crinoline vortices, gets its science done by **Faraday**, and its religion by the superior clergy who are to be met in the best houses. . . . " MF IV 3

—its support: "But good society, floated on gossamer wings of light irony, is of very expensive production; requiring nothing less than a wide and arduous national life condensed in unfragrant deafening factories, cramping itself in mines, sweating at furnaces, grinding, hammering, weaving under more or less oppression of carbonic acid—or else, spread over sheepwalks, and scattered in lonely houses and huts on the clayey or chalky corn-lands, where the rainy days look dreary. This wide national life is based entirely on emphasis—the emphasis of want, which urges it into all the activities necessary for the maintenance of good society and light irony: it spends its heavy years oft en in a chill, uncarpeted fashion amidst family discord unsoftened by long corridors. Under such circumstances there are many among its myriads of souls who have absolutely needed an emphatic belief . . . . " MF IV 3

See S:Religious observance—*labouring class*

—gradations: " . . . there were distinctions of rank in Middlemarch; and though old manufacturers could not any more than dukes be connected with none but equals, they were conscious of an inherent social superiority which was defined with great nicety in practice, though hardly expressible theoretically." MM 23

—mixture: "Hence I have always thought that the most fortunate Britons are those whose experience has given them a practical share in many aspects of the national lot, who have lived long among the mixed commonalty, roughing it with them under difficulties, knowing how their food tastes to them, and getting acquainted with their notions and motives not by inference from traditional types in literature or from philosophical theories, but from daily fellowship and observation." TS 2

—open market vendors: " . . . and, better than all, there were young, softly-rounded cheeks and bright eyes, freshened by the start from the far-off castello at daybreak, not to speak of older faces with the unfading charm of honest goodwill in them, such as are never quite wanting in scenes of human industry." R 1

—prejudices: "Prejudices about rank and status . . . like odorous bodies, have a double existence both solid and subtle— solid as the pyramids, subtle as the twentieth echo of an echo, or as the memory of hyacinths which once scented the darkness." MM 43

—uncultured classes: "The tendency created by the splendid conquests of modern generalization, to believe that all social questions are merged in economical science, and that the relations of men to their neighbors may be settled by algebraic equations—the dream that the uncultured classes are prepared for a condition which appeals principally to their moral sensibilities—the aristocratic dilettantism which attempts to restore the 'good old times' by a sort of idyllic masquerading, and to grow feudal fidelity and veneration as we grow prize turnips, by an artificial system of culture—none of these diverging mistakes can coexist with a real knowledge of the People, with a thorough study of their habits, their ideas, their motives.

"The land-holder, the clergyman, the mill-owner, the mining-agent, have each an opportunity for making precious observations on different sections of the working classes; but unfortunately their experience is too often not registered at all, or its results are too scattered to be available as a source of information and stimulus to the public mind generally.

"If any man of sufficient moral and intellectual breadth, whose observations would not be vitiated by a foregone conclusion, or by a professional point of view, would devote himself to studying the natural history of our social classes, especially of the small shopkeepers, artisans, and peasantry—the degree in which they are influenced by local conditions, their maxims and habit, the points of view from which they regard their religious teachers, and the degree in which they are influenced by religious doctrines, the interaction of the various classes on each other, and what are the tendencies in their position towards disintegration or towards development—and if, after all this study, he would give us the result of his observations in a book well nourished with specific facts, his work would be a valuable aid to the social and political reformer." ¶NH 126-7

—visiting: " . . . in no part of the world is genteel visiting founded on esteem, in the absence of suitable furniture and complete dinner-service." MM 23

—well-bred young man: "We use round, general, gentlemanly epithets about a young man of birth and fortune; and ladies, with that fine intuition which is the distinguishing attribute of their sex, see at once that he is 'nice.' The chances are that he will go through life without scandalising any one; a sea-worthy vessel that no one would refuse to insure. Ships, certainly, are liable to casualties, which sometimes make terribly evident some flaw in their construction, that would never have been discoverable in smooth water; and many a 'good fellow,' through a disastrous combination of circumstances, has undergone a like betrayal." AB 12

Society

—culpable: "Society is a very culpable entity, and has to answer for the manufacture of many unwholesome commodities, from bad pickles to bad poetry. But society, like 'matter,' and Her Majesty's Government, and other lofty abstractions, has its share of excessive blame as well as excessive praise." SN 461

—entertained: "It will be understood that the food and champagne were of the best—the talk and laughter too, in the sense of belonging to the best society, where no one makes an invidious display of anything in particular, and the advantages of the world are taken with that high-bed depreciation which follows from being accustomed to them." DD 14

—in flux: "Old provincial society had its share of this subtle movement: had not only its striking downfalls, its brilliant young professional dandies who ended by living up an entry with a drab and six children for their establishment, but also those less marked vicissitudes which are constantly shifting the boundaries of social intercourse, and begetting new consciousness of interdependence. Some slipped a little downward, some got higher footing; people denied aspirates, gained wealth, and fastidious gentlemen stood for boroughs; some were caught in political currents, some in ecclesiastical,

and perhaps found themselves surprisingly grouped in consequence; while a few personages or families that stood with rocky firmness amid all this fluctuation, were slowly presenting new aspects in spite of solidity, and altering with the double change of self and beholder." MM 11

—great: "The greatest people, even kings and queens, must visit with somebody, and the equals of the great are scarce." BJ 2

Success and Failure

—on failure: " 'The only failure a man ought to fear is failure in cleaving to the purpose he sees to be best. As to just the amount of result he may see from his particular work —that's a tremendous uncertainty: the universe has not been arranged for the gratification of his feelings. As long as a man sees and believes in some great good, he'll prefer working towards that in the way he's best fit for, come what may. I put effects at their minimum, but I'd rather have the minimum of effect, if it's of the sort I care for, than the maximum of effect I don't care for—a lot of fine things that are not to my taste—and if they were, the conditions of holding them while the world is what it is, are such as would jar on me like grating metal.' " FH 45

War and Conflict

—army on a visit: "Tall and tough Scotch archers, Swiss halberdiers fierce and ponderous, nimble Gascons ready to wheel and climb, cavalry in which each man looked like a knight-errant with his indomitable spear and charger—it was satisfactory to be assured that they would injure nobody but the enemies of God! With that confidence at heart it was a less dubious pleasure to look at the array of strength and splendour in nobles and knights, and youthful pages of choice lineage—at the bossed and jewelled sword-hilt, at the satin scarfs embroidered with strange symbolical devices of pious or gallant meaning, at the gold chains and jewelled aigretts, at the gorgeous horse-trappings and brocaded mantles, and at the transcendent canopy carried by select youths above the head of the Most Christian King." R 26

—disrupting lives: "There comes a terrible moment to many souls when the great movements of the world, the larger destinies of mankind, which have lain aloof in newspapers and other neglected reading, enter like an earthquake into their own lives—when the slow urgency of growing generations turns into the tread of an invading army or the dire clash of civil war, and grey fathers know nothing to seek for but the corpses of their blooming sons, and girls forget all vanity to make lint and bandages which may serve for the shattered limbs of their betrothed husbands.

"Then it is as if the Invisible Power that has been the object of lip-worship and lip-resignation became visible, according to the imagery of the Hebrew poet [e.g. *Psalms* 97 and 104], making the flames his chariot, and riding on the wings of the wind, till the mountains smoke and the plains shudder under the rolling fiery visitation.

"Often the good cause seems to lie prostrate under the thunder of unrelenting force, the martyrs live reviled, they die, and an angel is seen holding forth the crown and the palm branch. Then it is that the submission of the soul to the Highest is tested, and even in the eyes of frivolity life looks out from the scene of human struggle with the awful face of duty, and a religion shows itself which is something else than a private consolation." ¶DD 69

—make-believe: "If you think a lad of thirteen would not have been so childish, you must be an exceptionally wise man, who, although you are devoted to a civil calling, requiring you to look bland rather than formidable, yet never, since you had a beard, threw yourself into a martial attitude and frowned before the looking-glass. It is doubtful whether our soldiers would be maintained if there were not pacific people at home who like to fancy themselves soldiers. War, like other dramatic spectacles, might possibly cease for want of a 'public.' " MF II 4

Work

—healing effect: " 'There's nothing but what's bearable as long as a man can work,' he said to himself: 'the natur o' things doesn't change, though it seems as if one's own life was nothing but change. The square o' four is sixteen, and you must lengthen your lever in proportion to your weight, is as true when a man's miserable as when he's happy; and the best o' working is, it gives you a grip hold o' things outside your own lot.' " AB 11

—initial effort: "We assume a load with confident readiness, and up to a certain point the growing irksomeness of pressure is tolerable, but at last the desire for relief can no longer be resisted." R 26

—lax: " . . . lax, makeshift work, from the high conspicuous kind to the average and obscure, is allowed to pass unstamped with the disgrace of immorality, though there is not a member of society who is not daily suffering from it materially and spiritually, and though it is the fatal cause that must degrade our national rank and our commerce in spite of all open markets and discovery of available coal-seams." TS 16

—necessary: " 'And I perceive with gladness that you do not shrink from labour, without which, the poet has wisely said, life has given nothing to mortals. It is too often the "palma sine pulvere," the prize of glory without the dust of the race, that attracts young ambition.' " R 12

—pride in: "To 'make a good job' of anything, however small, was always a pleasure to Adam; and he sat on a block, with his book resting on a planing-table, whistling low every now and then, and turning his head on one side with a just perceptible smile of gratification—or pride, too, for if Adam loved a bit of good work, he loved also to think, 'I did it!' And I believe the only people who are free from that weakness are those who have no work to call their own." AB 27

—scanted: "But the sort of public spirit that scamps its bread-winning work, whether with the trowel, the pen, or the overseeing brain, that it may hurry to scenes of political or social agitation, would be as baleful a gift to our people as any malignant demon could devise." TS 16

"I have known
A man so versatile, he tried all arts,
But when in each by turns he had achieved
Just so much mastery as made men say,
'He could be king here if he would,' he threw
The lauded skill aside . . . .
He used to say himself he was too sane
To give his life away for excellence
Which yet must stand, an ivory statuette
Wrought to perfection through long lonely years,
Huddled in the mart of mediocrities.
He said, the very finest doing wins
The admiring only; but to leave undone,
Promise and not fulfil, like buried youth,
Wins all the envious, makes them sigh your name
As that fair Absent, blameless Possible,
Which could alone impassion them; and thus,
Serene negation has free gift of all,
Panting achievement struggles, is denied,
Or wins to lose again. What say you, Armgart?
Truth has rough flavors if we bite it through;
I think this sarcasm came from out its core
Of bitter irony." AR II

—standards: "One best part of educational training is that which comes through special knowledge and manipulative or other skill, with its usual accompaniment of delight, in relation to work which is the daily bread-winning occupation—which is a man's contribution to the effective wealth of society in return for what he takes as his own share. But his duty of doing one's proper work well, and taking care that every product of one's labour shall be genuinely what it pretends to be, is not only left out of morals in popular speech, it is very little insisted on by public teachers, at least in the only effective way—by tracing the continuous effects of ill-done work." TS 16

—unsuccessful: " . . . the emptiness of all things, from politics to pastimes, is never so striking to us as when we fail in them." DD 16

Dorothea Casaubon has a Gentleman Caller

Love, Marriage, and the Sexes

"They looked straight into each other's eyes, as angels do when they tell some truth." FH 45

" 'Affection is the broadest basis of good in life.' " DD 35

Courtship

—*after first avowal:* "They were both contented to be silent and separate, for that first blissful experience of mutual consciousness was all the more exquisite for being unperturbed by immediate sensation." R 12

—*appraisal:* "There is no point on which young women are more easily piqued than this of their sufficiency to judge the men who make love to them." FH 41

—*an arm offered:* " 'Do take my arm,' he said, in a low tone, as if it were a secret.

"There is something strangely winning to most women in that offer of the firm arm: the help is not wanted physically at that moment, but the sense of help—the presence of strength that is outside them and yet theirs, meets a continual want of the imagination." MF VI 6

—*astonishment:* "To astonish a woman by turning into her lover when she has been thinking of you merely as a Lord Chancellor is what a man naturally shrinks from: he is anxious to create an easier transition." DD 63

—*awe:* " . . . to an ardent reverential love, the loved woman has always a kind of wealth and rank which makes a man keenly susceptible about the aspect of his addresses." DD 63

"Even a man who has practised himself in love-making till his own glibness has rendered him sceptical, may at last be overtaken by the lover's awe—may tremble, stammer, and show other signs of recovered sensibility no more in the range of his acquired talents than pins and needles after numbness: how much more may that energetic timidity possess a man whose inward history has cherished his susceptibilities instead of dulling them, and has kept all the language of passion fresh and rooted as the lovely leafage about the hillside spring!" DD 63

—*betrothal kiss:* "Now put the seal
Of your lips to that.
FEDALMA: A solemn kiss?—
Such as I gave you when you came that day
From Córdoba, when first we said we loved?
When you had left the ladies of the Court
For thirst to see me; and you told me so,
And then I seemed to know why I had lived.
I never knew before. A kiss like that?
DON SILVA: Yes, yes, you face divine! When was our kiss/Like any other?
FEDALMA: Nay, I cannot tell
What other kisses are. But that one kiss
Remains upon my lips. The angels, spirits,
Creatures with finer sense, may see it there.
And now another kiss that will not die,
Saying, To-morrow I shall be your wife!" SG I iii

—*damage to a dress:* "One's thoughts may be much occupied with love-struggles, but hardly so as to be insensible to a disorder in the general framework of things." SM 11

—*delicious:* "Little Lucy felt very proud and happy. She and Stephen were in that stage of courtship which makes the most exquisite moment of youth, the freshest blossom-time of passion—when each is sure of the other's love, but no formal declaration has been made and all is mutual divination, exalting the most trivial word, the lightest gesture, into thrills delicate and delicious as wafted jasmine scent. The explicitness of an engagement wears off this finest edge of susceptibility: it is jasmine gathered and presented in a large bouquet." MF VI 1

—*the dynamic:* " . . . when a man has seen the woman whom he would have chosen if he had intended to marry speedily, his remaining a bachelor will usually depend on her resolution rather than on his." MM 11

—*early progress:* "It was to Adam the time that a man can least forget in after-life—the time when he believes that the first woman he has ever loved betrays by a slight something, a word, a tone, a glance, the quivering of a lip or an eyelid, that she is at least beginning to love him in return. The sign is so slight, it is scarcely perceptible to the ear or eye—he could describe it to no one—it is a mere feather-touch, yet it seems to have changed his whole being, to have merged an uneasy yearning into a delicious unconsciousness of everything but the present moment . . . . But the first glad moment in our first love is a vision which returns to us to the last, and brings with it a thrill of feeling intense and special as the recurrent sensation of a sweet odour breathed in a far-off hour of happiness. It is a memory that gives a more exquisite touch to tenderness, that feeds the madness of jealousy, and adds the last keenness to the agony of despair." AB 20

—*engagement:* All young ladies think lightly of gentlemen to whom they are not engaged. BJ 2

—*expected:* "Let every wooer make himself strongly expected; he may succeed by dint of being absent, but hardly in the first instance." FH 40

—*halcyon moment:* "She was laughing at his equipment, for he was the reverse of a dandy, and he was enjoying her laughter: the freshness of the morning mingled with the freshness of their youth; and every sound that came from their clear throats, every glance they gave each other, was the bubbling outflow from a spring of joy. It was all morning to them, within and without." DD 7

—*hesitancy:* "He had never admitted to himself that Gwendolen might refuse him, but—heaven help us all!—we are often unable to act on our certainties; our objection to a contrary issue (were it possible) is so strong that it rises like a spectral illusion between us and our certainty: we are rationally sure that the blind-worm cannot bite us mortally, but it would be so intolerable to be bitten, and the creature has a biting look—we decline to handle it." DD 13

—*hope:* "How could the rose help it when several bees in succession took its sweet odour as a sign of personal attachment?" DD 39

—*idyll:* " . . . all their vision, all their thoughts of each other, had been as in a world apart, where the sunshine fell on tall white lilies, where no evil lurked, and no other soul entered." MM 82

—*imagination:* "She filled up all the blanks with unmanifested perfections, interpreting him as she interpreted the works of Providence, and accounting for seeming discords by her own deafness to the higher harmonies. And there are many blanks left in the weeks of courtship, which a loving faith fills with happy assurance." MM 9

—*mutual discovery:* " 'There must be treble the interest to you anywhere else. I have never thought of your consenting to come here as anything else than a sacrifice.'

" 'Why should I make the sacrifice?' said Klesmer, going to seat himself at the piano, and touching the keys so as to give with the delicacy of an echo in the far distance a melody which he had set to **Heine**'s 'Ich hab' dich geliebet und liebe dich noch.'

" 'That is the mystery,' said Catherine, not wanting to affect anything, but from mere agitation. From the same cause she was tearing a piece of paper into minute morsels, as if at a task of utmost multiplication imposed by a cruel fairy.

" 'You can conceive no motive?' said Klesmer folding his arms.

" 'None that seems in the least probable.'

" 'Then I shall tell you. It is because you are to me the chief woman in the world—the throned lady whose colour I carry between my heart and my armour.'

"Catherine's hands trembled so much that she could no longer tear the paper: still less could her lips utter a word. Klesmer went on—

" 'This would be the last impertinence in me, if I meant to found anything upon it. That is out of the question. I mean no such thing. But you once said it was your doom to suspect every man who courted you of being an adventurer, and what made you angriest was men's imputing to you the folly of believing that they courted you for your own sake. Did you not say so?'

" 'Very likely,' was the answer, in a low murmur.

" 'It was a bitter word. Well, at least one man who has seen women as plenty as flowers in May has lingered about you for your own sake. And since he is one whom you can never marry, you will believe him. That is an argument in favour of some other man . . . . I shall go now and pack. I shall make my excuses to Mrs Arrowpoint.' Klesmer rose as he ended, and walked quickly towards the door.

" 'You must take this heap of manuscript, then,' said Catherine, suddenly making a desperate effort. She had risen to fetch the heap from another table. Klesmer came back, and they had the length of the folio sheets between them.

" 'Why should I not marry the man who loves me, if I love him?' said Catherine. To her the effort was something like the leap of a woman from the deck into the lifeboat.

" 'It would be too hard—impossible—you could not carry it through. I am not worth what you would have to encounter. I will not accept the sacrifice. It would be thought a *mésalliance* for you, and I should be liable to the worst accusations.'

" 'Is it the accusations you are afraid of? I am afraid of nothing but that we should miss the passing of our lives together.' " DD 22

—peremptory: " 'Ah, but mayhap Miss Nancy hung off like, and your lass didn't,' said Ben.

" 'I should say she didn't' said Mr Macey, significantly. 'Before I said "sniff," I took care to know as she'd say "snaff," and pretty quick too. I wasn't a-going to open my mouth, like a dog at a fly, and snap it to again, wi' nothing to swaller.' " SM 11

—preconceptions: "Dorothea's inferences may seem large; but really, life could never have gone on at any period but for this liberal allowance of conclusions, which has facilitated marriage under the difficulties of civilisation.

"Has any one ever pinched into its pilulous smallness the cobweb of pre-matrimonial acquaintanceship?" ¶MM 2

—proposal of marriage: "My dear Miss Brooke,—I have your guardian's permission to address you on a subject than which I have none more at heart. I am not, I trust, mistaken in the recognition of some deeper correspondence than that of date in the fact that a consciousness of need in my own life had arisen contemporaneously with the possibility of my becoming acquainted with you. For in the first hour of meeting you, I had an impression of your eminent and perhaps exclusive fitness to supply that need (connected, I may say, with such activity of the affections as even the preoccupations of a work too special to be abdicated could not uninterruptedly dissimulate); and each succeeding opportunity for observation has given the impression of an added depth by convincing me more emphatically of that fitness which I had preconceived, and thus evoking more decisively those affections to which I have but now referred. Our conversations have, I think, made sufficiently clear to you the tenor of my life and purposes: a tenor unsuited, I am aware, to the commoner order of minds. But I have discerned in you an elevation of thought and a capability of devotedness, which I had hitherto not conceived to be compatible either with the early bloom of youth or with those graces of sex that may be said at once to win and to confer distinction when combined, as they notably are in you, with the mental qualities above indicated. It was, I confess, beyond my hope to meet with this rare combination of elements both solid and attractive, adapted to supply aid in graver labours and to cast a charm over vacant hours; and but for the event of my introduction to you (which, let me again say, I trust not to be superficially coincident with foreshadowing needs, but providentially related thereto as stages towards the completion of a life's plan), I should presumably have gone on to the last without any attempt to lighten my solitariness by a matrimonial union.

"Such, my dear Miss Brooke, is the accurate statement of my feelings; and I rely on your kind indulgence in venturing now to ask you how far your own are of a nature to confirm my happy presentiment. To be accepted by you as your husband and the earthly guardian of your welfare, I should regard as the highest of providential gifts. In return I can at least offer you an affection hitherto unwasted, and the faithful consecration of a life which, however short in the sequel, has no backward pages whereon, if you choose to turn them, you will find records such as might justly cause you either bitterness or shame. I await the expression of your sentiments with an anxiety which it would be the part of wisdom (were it possible) to divert by a more arduous labour than usual. But in this order of experience I am still young, and in looking forward to an unfavourable possibility I cannot but feel that resignation to solitude will be more difficult after the temporary illumination of hope. In any case, I shall remain, yours with sincere devotion,

"Edward Casaubon" MM 5

—and rain: "The next morning was very wet—the sort of morning on which male neighbours who have no imperative occupation at home are likely to pay their fair friends an illimitable visit. The rain, which has been endurable enough for the walk or ride one way, is sure to become so heavy and at the same time so certain to clear up by and by, that nothing but an open quarrel can abbreviate the visit: latent detestation will not do at all. And if people happen to be lovers, what can be so delightful—in England—as a rainy morning? English sunshine is dubious: bonnets are never quite secure; and if you sit down on the grass, it may lead to catarrhs. But the rain is to be depended on. You gallop through it in a mackintosh and presently find yourself in the seat you like best—a little above or a little below the one on which your goddess sits—(it is the same thing to the metaphysic mind, and that is the reason why women are at once worshipped and looked down upon)—with a satisfactory confidence that there will be no lady-callers." MF VI 7

—rejection: "We mortals, men and women, devour many a disappointment between breakfast and dinner-time; keep back the tears and look a little pale about the lips, and in answer to inquiries say, 'Oh, nothing!' Pride helps us; and pride is not a bad thing when it only urges us to hide our own hurts—not to hurt others." MM 6

—*seamstress power:* "When a man is happy enough to win the affections of a sweet girl, who can soothe his cares with crochet, and respond to all his most cherished ideas with beaded urn-rugs and chair-covers in German wool, he has, at least, a guarantee of domestic comfort, whatever trials may await him out of doors. What a resource it is under fatigue and irritation to have your drawing-room well supplied with small mats, which would always be ready if you ever wanted to set anything on them! And what styptic for a bleeding heart can equal copious squares of crochet, which are useful for slipping down the moment you touch them? How our father managed without crochet is the wonder; but I believe some small and feeble substitute existed in their time under the name of 'tatting.' " JR 3

—*singing together:* "Surely the only courtship unshaken by doubts and fears must be that in which the lovers can sing together. The sense of mutual fitness that springs from the two deep notes fulfilling expectation just at the right moment between the notes of the silvery soprano, from the perfect accord of descending thirds and fifths, from the preconcerted loving chase of a fugue, is likely enough to supersede any immediate demand for less impassioned forms of agreement. The contralto will not care to catechise the bass; the tenor will foresee no embarrassing dearth of remark in evenings spent with the lovely soprano. In the provinces, too, where music was so scarce in that remote time, how could the musical people avoid falling in love with each other? Even political principle must have been in danger of relaxation under such circumstances; and a violin faithful to rotten boroughs must have been tempted to fraternise in a demoralising way with a reforming violoncello. In this case, the linnet-throated soprano, and the full-toned bass, singing,

'With thee delight is ever new,
With thee is life incessant bliss,'

believed what they sang all the more *because* they sang it." MF VI 1

—*specifications:* "The betrothed bride must see her future home, and dictate any changes that she would like to have made there. A woman dictates before marriage in order that she may have an appetite for submission afterwards." MM 9

—*suitors:* "Suitors must often be judged as words are, by their standing and the figure they make in polite society: it is difficult to know much else of them." DD 28

—*suspense:* " . . . being just now bound to tell a story of life at a stage when the blissful beauty of earth and sky entered only by narrow and oblique inlets into the consciousness, which was busy with a small social drama almost as little penetrated by a feeling of wider relations as if it had been a puppet-show." DD 14

—*tender moment:* " 'They're going to waltz again,' said Stephen, bending to speak to her, with that glance and tone of subdued tenderness which young dreams create to themselves in the summer woods when low cooing voices fill the air. Such glances and tones bring the breath of poetry with them into a room that is half-stifling with glaring gas and hard flirtation." MF VI 10

—*unconscious:* "That is a simple scene, reader. But it is almost certain that you, too, have been in love—perhaps, even, more than once, though you may not choose to say so to all your lady friends. If so, you will no more think the slight words, the timid looks, the tremulous touches, by which two human souls approach each other gradually, like two little quivering rain-streams, before they mingle into one—you will no more think these things trivial, than you will think the first-detected signs of coming spring trivial, though they be but a faint, indescribable something in the air and in the song of the birds, and the tiniest perceptible budding on the hedgerow branches.

"Those slight words and looks and touches are part of the soul's language; and the finest language, I believe, is chiefly made up of unimposing words, such as 'light,' 'sound,' 'stars,' 'music'—words really not worth looking at, or hearing in themselves, any more than 'chips' or 'sawdust:' it is only that they happen to be the signs of something unspeakably great and beautiful. I am of opinion that love is a great and beautiful thing too; and if you agree with me, the smallest signs of it will not be chips and sawdust to you: they will rather be like those little words, 'light' and 'music,' stirring the long-winding fibres of your memory, and enriching your present with your most precious past." ¶AB 50

—*universal—not:* "Care has been taken not only that the trees should not sweep the stars down, but also that every man who admires a fair girl should not be enamoured of her, and even that every man who is enamoured should not necessarily declare himself. There are various refined shapes in which the price of corn, known to be a potent cause in this relation, might, if inquired into, show why a young lady, perfect in person, accomplishments, and costume, has not the trouble of rejecting many offers; and nature's order is certainly benignant in not obliging us one and all to be desperately in love with the most admirable mortal we have ever seen." DD 9

Love

—affection: "He was very fond of these round-cheeked, wide-eyed human things that clung about him and knew no evil of him. And wherever affection can spring, it is like the green leaf and the blossom—pure, and breathing purity, whatever soil it may grow in." R 50

—almost: "In the wonderful mixtures of our nature there is a feeling distinct from that exclusive passionate love of which some men and women (by no means all) are capable, which yet is not the same with friendship, nor with a merely benevolent regard, whether admiring or compassionate: a man . . . hardly represents to himself this shade of feeling towards a woman more nearly than in the words, 'I should have loved her, if—'; the 'if' covering some prior growth in the inclinations, or else some circumstances which have made an inward prohibitory law as a stay against the emotions ready to quiver out of balance." DD 50

—anguish: " 'Tis a great and mysterious gift, this clinging of the heart, my Esther, whereby it hath often seemed to me that even in the very moment of suffering our souls have the keenest foretaste of heaven. I speak not lightly, but as one who hath endured. And 'tis a strange truth that only in the agony of parting we look into the depths of love.' " FH 44

—at first: "Let a woman say what she will after she has once told a man that she loves him, he is a little too flushed and exalted with that first draught she offers him to care much about the taste of the second: he treads the earth with a very elastic step as he walks away from her, and makes light of all difficulties. But that sort of glow dies out: memory gets sadly diluted with time, and is not strong enough to revive us." AB 54

—avowal and response: " 'Dinah,' he said suddenly, taking both her hands between his, 'I love you with my whole heart and soul. I love you next to God who made me.'

"Dinah's lips became pale, like her cheeks, and she trembled violently under the shock of painful joy. Her hands were cold as death between Adam's. She could not draw them away, because he held them fast.

" 'Don't tell me you can't love me, Dinah. Don't tell me we must part, and pass our lives away from one another.'

"The tears were trembling in Dinah's eyes, and they fell before she could answer. But she spoke in a quiet low voice.

" 'Yes, dear Adam, we must submit to another Will. We must part.'

" 'Not if you love me, Dinah—not if you love me,' Adam said, passionately. 'Tell me—tell me if you can love me better than a brother.'

"Dinah was too entirely reliant on the Divine will to attempt to achieve any end by a deceptive concealment. She was recovering now from the first shock of emotion, and she looked at Adam with simple sincere eyes as she said,

" 'Yes, Adam, my heart is drawn strongly towards you; and of my own will, if I had no clear showing to the contrary, I could find my happiness in being near you, and ministering to you continually. I fear I should forget to rejoice and weep with others; nay, I fear I should forget the Divine presence, and seek no love but yours.'

"Adam did not speak immediately. They sat looking at each other in delicious silence —for the first sense of mutual love excludes other feelings, it will have the soul all to itself." AB 52

—and awe: " . . . he felt for the first time, without defining it to himself, that loving awe in the presence of noble womanhood, which is perhaps something like the worship paid of old to a great nature-goddess, who was not all-knowing, but whose life and power were something deeper and more primordial than knowledge." R 9

—in bereavement: "He stood a few minutes reading over and over again the words on the tombstone, as if to assure himself that all the happy and unhappy past was a reality. For love is frightened at the intervals of insensibility and callousness that encroach by little and little on the dominion of grief, and it makes efforts to recall the keenness of the first anguish." SF 10

—betrayed by tears: "In all failures, the beginning is certainly the half of the whole. After sitting two long moments while he moved his whip and could say nothing, Lydgate rose to go, and Rosamond, made nervous by her struggle between mortification and the wish not to betray it, dropped her chain as if startled, and rose too, mechanically. Lydgate instantaneously stopped to pick up the chain. When he rose he was very near to a lovely little face set on a fair long neck which he had been used to see turning about under the most perfect management of self-contented grace. But as he raised his eyes now he saw a certain helpless quivering which touched him quite newly, and made him look at Rosamond with a questioning flash. At this moment she was as natural as she had ever been when she was five years old: she felt that her tears had risen, and it was no use to try to do anything else than let them stay like water on a blue flower or let them fall over her cheeks, even as they would.

"That moment of naturalness was the crystallising feather-touch: it shook flirtation into love. Remember that the ambitious man who was looking at those Forget-me-nots under the water was very warm-hearted and rash. He did not know where the chain went; an idea had thrilled through the recesses within him, which had a miraculous effect in raising the power of passionate love lying buried there in no sealed sepulchre, but under the lightest, easily pierced mould. His words were quite abrupt and awkward; but the tone made them sound like an ardent, speaking avowal.

" 'What is the matter? you are distressed. Tell me—pray.'

"Rosamond had never been spoken to in such tones before. I am not sure that she knew what the words were; but she looked at Lydgate and tears fell over her cheeks. There could have been no more complete answer than that silence, and Lydgate, forgetting everything else, completely mastered by the outrush of tenderness at the sudden belief that this sweet young creature depended on him for her joy, actually put his arms around her, folding her gently and protectingly—he who was used to being gentle with the weak and suffering—and kissed each of the two large tears. This was a strange way of arriving at an understanding, but it was a short way. Rosamond was not angry, but she moved backward a little in timid happiness, and Lydgate could now sit near her and speak less incompletely. Rosamond had to make her little confession, and he poured out words of gratitude and tenderness with impulsive lavishment. In half an hour he left the house an engaged man, whose soul was not his own, but the woman's to whom he had bound himself." MM 31

—its blessings: "Among the blessings of love there is hardly one more exquisite than the sense that in uniting the beloved life to ours we can watch over its happiness, bring comfort where hardship was, and over memories of privation and suffering open the sweetest fountains of joy." DD 70

—blind: " . . . the long lustrous eyes told nothing of the many wishes that would have brought about [her brother's] death long ago if there had been such potency in mere wishes. Romola only read her own pure thoughts in their dark depths, as we read letters in happy dreams." R 17

—bliss: " . . . the unspeakable content in his soul of feeling that he was in the presence of a creature worthy to be perfectly loved. I think his own feelings at that moment were perfect, for we mortals have our divine moments, when love is satisfied in the completeness of the beloved object." AB 37

—conscience: "But every strong feeling makes to itself a conscience of its own—has its own piety; just as much as the feeling of the son towards the mother, which will sometimes survive amid the worst fumes of depravation [*sic;* depravity]; and Tito could not yet be easy in committing a secret offence against his wedded love: R 34

—constancy: "Mr Gilfil felt as if in the long hours of that night the bond that united his love for ever and alone to Caterina had acquired fresh strength and sanctity. It is so with the human relations that rest on the deep emotional sympathy of affection: every new day and night of joy or sorrow is a new ground, a new consecration, for the love that is nourished by memories as well as hopes —the love to which perpetual repetition is not a weariness but a want, and to which a separated joy is the beginning of pain." GL 19

—a definition: "For what is love itself, for the one we love best?—an unfolding of immeasurable cares which yet are better than any joys outside our love." DD 69

—distance: "However slight the terrestrial intercourse between **Dante** and **Beatrice** or **Petrarch** and **Laura**, time changes the proportion of things, and in later days it is preferable to have fewer sonnets and more conversation." MM 37

—distraction: "Young souls, in such pleasant delirium as hers, are as unsympathetic as butterflies sipping nectar; they are isolated from all appeals by a barrier of dreams—by invisible looks and impalpable arms." AB 9

—embracing: " . . . our love is inwrought in our enthusiasm as electricity is inwrought in the air, exalting its power by a subtle presence." AB 33

—expressed: " 'You *are* a poem—and that is to be the best part of a poet—what makes up the poet's consciousness in his best moods,' said Will, showing such originality as we all share with the morning and the spring-time and other endless renewals." MM

—faithlessness: "An early deep-seated love to which we become faithless has its unfailing *Nemesis,* if only in that division of soul which narrows all newer joys by the intrusion of regret and the established presentiment of change . . . . And faithlessness here means not a gradual conversion dependent on enlarged knowledge, but a yielding to seductive circumstance; not a conviction that the original choice was a mistake, but a subjection to incidents that flatter a growing desire. In this sort of love it is the forsaker who has the melancholy lot; for an abandoned belief may be more effectively vengeful than *Dido.*" TS 9

—first: "Among all the many kinds of first love, that which begins in childish companionship is the strongest and most enduring: when passion comes to unite its force to long affection, love is at its spring tide." GL 4

—first kiss: " . . . his lips are meeting those pouting child-lips, and for a long moment time has vanished. He may be a shepherd in Arcadia for aught he knows, he may be the first youth kissing the first maiden, he may be *Eros* himself, sipping the lips of *Psyche*—it is all one." AB 13

"Since she and Felix had kissed each other in the prison, she felt as if she had vowed herself away, as if memory lay on her lips like a seal of possession." FH 49

—first mutual awareness: "Neither of them spoke; they stood looking at each other's faces with that sweet wonder which belongs to young love—she with her long white hands on the dark-brown curls, and he with his dark fingers bathed in the streaming gold. Each was so beautiful to the other; each was experiencing that undisturbed mutual consciousness for the first time." R 17

—forbearing: " . . . that wondrous patience which love gives to the quickest temperament . . . . " AB 14

—from afar: "There are characters which are continually creating collisions and nodes for themselves in dramas which nobody is prepared to act with them. Their susceptibilities will clash against objects that remain innocently quiet." MM 19

—a girl's: "There is often something maternal even in a girlish love . . . . " MM 25

—the hard and the easy: "It comes in so many forms in this life of ours—the knowledge that there is something sweetest and noblest of which we despair, and the sense of something present that solicits us with an immediate and easy indulgence. And there is a pernicious falsity in the pretence that a woman's love lies above the range of such temptations." FH 43

—hard-won: "There was something which she now felt profoundly to be the best thing that life could give her. But—if it was to be had at all—it was not to be had without paying a heavy price for it, such as we must pay for all that is greatly good. A supreme love, a motive that gives a sublime rhythm to a woman's life, and exalts habit into partnership with the soul's highest needs, is not to be had where and how she wills: to know that high initiation, she must often tread where it is hard to tread, and feel the chill air, and watch through darkness. It is not true that love makes all things easy: it makes us choose what is difficult." FH 49

—idealistic: "Will, we know, could not bear the thought of any flaw appearing in his crystal: he was at once exasperated and delighted by the calm freedom with which Dorothea looked at him and spoke to him, and there was something so exquisite in thinking of her just as she was, that he could not long for a change which must somehow change her.

"Do we not shun the street version of a fine melody?—or shrink from the news that the rarity—some bit of chiselling or engraving perhaps—which we have dwelt on even with exultation in the trouble it has cost us to snatch glimpses of it, is really not an uncommon thing, and may be obtained as an everyday posses-sion? Our good depends on the quality and breadth of our emotion; and to Will, a creature who cared little for what are called the solid things of life and greatly for its subtler influences, to have within him such a feeling as he had towards Dorothea, was like the inheritance of a fortune." MM 47

—illusion: "Men and women make sad mistakes about their own symptoms, taking their vague uneasy longings, sometimes for genius, sometimes for religion, and oftener still for a mighty love." MM 75

—incompatibility: "If boys and men are to be welded together in the glow of transient feeling, they must be made of metal that will mix: else they inevitably fall asunder when the heat dies out." MF II 6

—infatuation: "[He] went to finish his evening at the theatre of the Porte Saint Martin, where there was a melodrama which he had already seen several times; attracted, not by the ingenious work of the collaborating authors, but by an actress whose part it was to stab her lover, mistaking him for the evil-designing duke of the piece. Lydgate was in love with this actress, as a man is in love with a woman whom he never expects to speak to. She was a Provençale, with dark eyes, a Greek profile, and rounded majestic form, having that sort of beauty which carries a sweet matronliness even in youth, and her voice was a soft cooing. She had but lately come to Paris, and bore a virtuous reputation, her husband acting with her as the unfortunate lover. It was her acting which was 'no better than it should be,' but the public was satisfied. Lydgate's only relaxation now was to go and look at this woman, just as he might have thrown himself under the breath of the sweet south [wind] on a bank of violets for a while, without prejudice to his galvanism, to which he would presently return.

"But this evening the old drama had a new catastrophe. At the moment when the heroine was to act the stabbing of her lover, and he was to fall gracefully, the wife veritably stabbed her husband, who fell as death willed. A wild shriek pierced the house, and the Provençale fell swooning: a shriek and a swoon were demanded by the play, but the swooning too was real this time. Lydgate leaped and climbed, he hardly knew how, on to the stage, and was active in help, making the acquaintance of his heroine by finding a contusion on her head and lifting her gently in his arms.

"Paris rang with the story of this death:—was it a murder? Some of the actress's warmest admirers were inclined to believe in her guilt, and liked her the better for it (such was the taste of those times); but Lydgate was not one of these. He vehemently contended for her innocence, and the remote impersonal passion for her beauty which he had felt before, had passed now into personal devotion, and tender thought of her lot. The notion of murder was absurd; no motive was discoverable, the young couple being understood to dote on each other; and it was not unprecedented that an accidental slip of the foot should have brought these grave consequences.

"The legal investigation ended in Madame Laure's release. Lydgate by this time had had many interviews with her, and found her more and more adorable. She talked little; but that was an additional charm. She was melancholy, and seemed grateful; her presence was enough, like that of the evening light. Lydgate was madly anxious about her affection, and jealous lest any other man than himself should win it and ask her to marry him. But instead of re-opening her engagement at the Porte Saint Martin, where she would have been all the more popular for the fatal episode, she left Paris without warning, forsaking her little court of admirers.

"Perhaps no one carried inquiry far except Lydgate, who felt that all science had come to a stand-still while he imagined the unhappy Laure, stricken by ever-wandering sorrow, herself wandering, and finding no faithful comforter. Hidden actresses, however, are not so difficult to find as some other hidden facts, and it was not long before Lydgate gathered indications that Laure had taken the route to Lyons. He found her at last acting with great success at Avignon under the same name, looking more majestic than ever as a forsaken wife carrying her child in her arms. He spoke to her after the play, was received with the usual quietude which seemed to him beautiful as clear depths of water, and obtained leave to visit her the next day; when he was bent on telling her that he adored her, and on asking her to marry him. He knew that this was like the sudden impulse of a madman—incongruous even with his habitual foibles. No matter! It was the one thing which he was resolved to do. He had two selves within him apparently, and they must learn to accommodate each other and bear reciprocal impediments. Strange, that some of us, with quick alternate vision, see beyond our infatuations, and even while we rave on the heights, behold the wide plain where our persistent self pauses and awaits us.

"To have approached Laure with any suit that was not reverentially tender would have been simply a contradiction of his whole feeling towards her.

" 'You have come all the way from Paris to find me?' she said to him the next day, sitting before him with folded arms, and looking at him with eyes that seemed to wonder as an untamed ruminating animal wonders. 'Are all Englishmen like that?'

" 'I came because I could not live without trying to see you. You are lonely; I love you; I want you to consent to be my wife: I will wait, but I want you to promise that you will marry me—no one else.'

"Laure looked at him in silence with a melancholy radiance from under her grand eyelids, until he was full of rapturous certainty, and knelt close to her knees.

" 'I will tell you something,' she said, in her cooing way, keeping her arms folded. 'My foot really slipped.'

" 'I know, I know,' said Lydgate, deprecatingly. 'It was a fatal accident—a dreadful stroke of calamity that bound me to you the more.'

"Again Laure paused a little and then said, slowly, *'I meant to do it.'*

"Lydgate, strong man as he was, turned pale and trembled: moments seemed to pass before he rose and stood at a distance from her.

" 'There was a secret, then,' he said at last, even vehemently. 'He was brutal to you: you hated him.'

" 'No! he wearied me; he was too fond: he would live in Paris, and not in my country; that was not agreeable to me.'

" 'Great God!' said Lydgate, in a groan of horror. 'And you planned to murder him?'

" 'I did not plan: it came to me in the play—*I meant to do it.'*

"Lydgate stood mute, and unconsciously pressed his hat on while he looked at her. He saw this woman—the first to whom he had given his young adoration—amid the throng of stupid criminals.

" 'You are a good young man,' she said. 'But I do not like husbands. I will never have another.' " ¶MM 15

"There is no tyranny more complete than that which a self-centred negative nature exercises over a morbidly sensitive nature perpetually craving sympathy and support. The most independent people feel the effect of a man's silence in heightening their value for his opinion—feel an additional triumph in conquering the reverence of a critic habitually captious and satirical: no wonder, then, that an enthusiastic self-distrusting youth should watch and wait before the closed secret of a sarcastic woman's face, as if it were the shrine of the doubtfully benignant deity who ruled his destiny." LV 1

—infiltrating: " . . . she reflected that her walking alone with Felix might be a subject of remark . . . . Esther was a little amazed herself at what she had come to. So our lives glide on: the river ends we don't know where, and the sea begins, and then there is no more jumping ashore." FH 27

—inspiring in purity: "There are natures in which, if they love us, we are conscious of having a sort of baptism and consecration: they bind us ever to rectitude and purity by their pure belief about us; and our sins become that worst kind of sacrilege which tears down the invisible altar of trust. 'If you are not good, none is good'—those little words may give a terrific meaning to responsibility, may hold a vitriolic intensity for remorse." MM 77

—long nurtured: "When a tender affection has been storing itself in us through many of our years, the idea that we could accept any exchange for it seems to be a cheapening of our lives. And we can set a watch over our affections and our constancy as we can over other treasures." MM 57

—looking: "We look at the one little woman's face we love, as we look at the face of our mother earth, and see all sorts of answers to our own yearnings." AB 19

—lost: "Calamities came to [our rural forefathers] too, and their early errors carried hard consequences: perhaps the love of some sweet maiden, the image of purity, order, and calm, had opened their eyes to the vision of a life in which the days would not seem too long, even without rioting, but the maiden was lost, and the vision passed away, and then what was left to them, especially when they had become too heavy for the hunt, or for carrying a gun over the furrows, but to drink and get merry, or to drink and get angry, so that they might be independent of variety, and say over again with eager emphasis the things they had said already any time that twelve-month?" SM 3

—magic: "For effective magic is transcendent nature; and who shall measure the subtlety of those touches which convey the quality of mind as well as body, and make a man's passion for one woman differ from his passion for another as joy in the morning light over valley and river and white mountain-top differs from joy among Chinese lanterns and glass pannels?" MM 30

—in marriage: " . . . the certainty, 'She will never love me much,' is easier to bear than the fear, 'I shall love her no more.' " MM 64

—and the mind: "In all ages it hath been a favourite text that a potent love hath the nature of an isolated fatality, whereto the mind's opinions and wonted resolves are altogether alien; as, for example, *Daphnis* his frenzy, wherein it had little availed him to have been convinced of **Heraclitus** his doctrine; or the philtre-bred passion of *Tristan,* who, thought he had been as deep as **Duns Scotus**, would have had his reasoning marred by that cup too much; or *Romeo* in his sudden taking for *Juliet*, wherein any objection he might have held against **Ptolemy** had made little difference to his discourse under the balcony. Yet all love is not such, even though potent; nay, this passion hath as large scope as any for allying itself with every operation of the soul: so that it shall acknowledge an effect from the imagined light of unproven firmaments, and have its scale set to the grander orbits of what hath been and shall be." DD 32 ep

—mother's: "But the mother yearning, that completest type of the life in another life which is the essence of real human love, feels the presence of the cherished child even in the debased, degraded man . . . . " AB 43

—mystery: " 'It's a strange thing to think of a man as can lift a chair with his teeth, and walk fifty mile on end, trembling and turning hot and cold at only a look from one woman out of all the rest i' the world. It's a mystery we can give no account of; but no more we can of the sprouting o' the seed, for that matter.' " AB 11

—need to be perfect: "The sense of defect in her devotedness to [her father] made her cling with all the force of compunction as well as affection to the duties of memory. Love does not aim simply at the conscious good of the beloved object: it is not satisfied

without perfect loyalty of heart; it aims at its own completeness." R 28

—*needed* "It is a wonderful subduer, this need of love, this hunger of the heart: as peremptory as that other hunger by which Nature forces us to submit to the yoke, and change the face of the world." MF I 5

—*passion:* "We object less to be taxed with the enslaving excess of our passions than with our deficiency in wider passion; but if the truth were known, our reputed intensity is often the dulness of not knowing what else to do with ourselves. *Tannhäuser*, one suspects, was a knight of ill-furnished imagination, hardly of larger discourse than a heavy Guardsman; *Merlin* had certainly seen his best days, and was merely repeating himself, when he fell into that hopeless captivity; and we know that *Ulysses* felt so manifest an *ennui* under similar circumstances that *Calypso* herself furthered his departure. There is indeed a report that he afterwards left *Penelope;* but since she was habitually absorbed in worsted work, and it was probably from her that *Telemachus* got his mean, pettifogging disposition, always anxious about the property and the daily consumption of meat, no inference can be drawn from this already dubious scandal as to the relation between companionship and constancy." DD 22

—*passions mixed:* "If you think it incredible that to imagine Lydgate as a man of family could cause thrills of satisfaction which had anything to do with the sense that she was in love with him, I will ask you to use your power of comparison a little more effectively, and consider whether red cloth and epaulets have never had an influence of that sort. Our passions do not live apart in locked chambers, but, dressed in their small wardrobe of notions, bring their provisions to a common table and mess together, feeding out of the common store according to their appetite." MM 16

—*perfect:* "Perfect love has a breath of poetry which can exalt the relations of the least-instructed human beings; and this breath of poetry had surrounded Eppie from the time when she had followed the bright gleam that beckoned her to Silas's hearth, so that it is not surprising if, in other things besides her delicate prettiness, she was not quite a common village maiden, but had a touch of refinement and fervour which came from no other teaching than that of tenderly-nurtured unvitiated feeling." SM 16

—*pervasive:* "Rex's love had been of that sudden, penetrating, clinging sort which the ancients knew and sung, and in singing made a fashion of talk for many moderns whose experience has been by no means of a fiery, daemonic character. To have the consciousness suddenly steeped with another's personality, to have the strongest inclinations possessed by an image which retains its dominance in spite of change and apart from worthiness—nay, to feel a passion which clings the faster for the tragic pangs inflicted by a cruel, recognised unworthiness—is a phase of love which in the feeble and common-minded has a repulsive likeness to a blind animalism insensible to the higher sway of moral affinity or heaven-lit admiration. But when this attaching force is present in a nature not of brutish unmodifiableness, but of a human dignity that can risk itself safely, it may even result in a devotedness not unfit to be called divine in a higher sense than the ancient. Phlegmatic rationality stares and shakes its head at these unaccountable prepossessions, but they exist as undeniably as the winds and waves, determining here a wreck and there a triumphant voyage." DD 58

—*poet's:* ". . . but the poor poet
Worships without reward, nor hopes to find
A heaven save in his worship. He adores
The sweetest woman for her sweetness' sake,
Joys in the love that was not born for him,
Because 'tis lovingness, as beggars joy,
Warming their naked limbs on wayside walls,
To hear a tale of princes and their glory,
There's a poor poet (poor, I mean, in coin)
Worships Fedalma with so true a love
That if her silken robe were changed for rags,
And she were driven out to stony wilds
Barefoot, a scornéd wanderer, he would kiss
Her ragged garment's edge, and only ask
For leave to be her slave." SG I i

—*purgatory endured:* "She was surprised and annoyed to find that her heart was palpitating violently, and that it was quite useless to try after a recovery of her former animation. Alarmed at herself—fearing some further betrayal of a change so marked in its occasion, she rose and said in a low voice with undisguised anxiety, 'I must go; I have overtired myself . . . .

Dorothea comes upon Will and Rosamond

"The limit of resistance was reached, and she had sunk back helpless within the clutch of inescapable anguish . . . she locked her door, and turning away from it towards the vacant room she pressed her hands on the top of her head, and moaned out—

" 'Oh, I did love him!'

"Then came the hour in which the waves of suffering shook her too thoroughly to leave any power of thought. She could only cry in loud whispers, between her sobs, after her lost belief which she had planted and kept alive from a very little seed since the days in Rome—after her lost joy of clinging with silent love and faith to one who, misprized by others, was worthy in her thought—after her lost woman's pride of reigning in his memory—after her sweet dim perspective of hope, that along some pathway they should meet with unchanged recognition and take up the backward years as a yesterday.

"In that hour she repeated what the merciful eyes of solitude have looked on for ages in the spiritual struggles of man—she besought hardness and coldness and aching weariness to bring her relief from the mysterious incorporeal might of her anguish: she lay on the bare floor and let the night grow cold around her; while her grand woman's frame was shaken by sobs as if she had been a despairing child.

"There were two images—two living forms that tore her heart in two, as if it had been the heart of a mother who seems to see her child divided by the sword, and presses one bleeding half to her breast while her gaze goes forth in agony towards the half which is carried away by the lying woman that has never known the mother's pang.

"Here, with the nearness of an answering smile, here within the vibrating bond of mutual speech, was the bright creature whom she had trusted—who had come to her like the spirit of morning visiting the dim vault where she sat as the bride of a worn-out life; and now, with a full consciousness which had never awakened before, she stretched out her arms towards him and cried with bitter cries that their nearness was a parting vision: she discovered her passion to herself in the unshrinking utterance of despair.

"And there, aloof, yet persistently with her, moving wherever she moved, was the **Will Ladislaw** who was a changed belief exhausted of hope, a detected illusion—no, a living man towards whom there could not yet struggle any wail of regretful pity, from the midst of scorn and indignation and jealous offended pride. The fire of **Dorothea**'s anger was not easily spent, and it flamed out in fitful returns of spurning reproach. Why had he come obtruding his life into hers, hers that might have been whole enough without him? Why had he brought his cheap regard and his lip-born words to her who had nothing paltry to give in exchange? He knew that he was deluding her—wished, in the very moment of farewell, to make her believe that he gave her the whole price of her heart, and knew that he had spent it half before. Why had he not stayed among the crowd of whom she asked nothing—but only prayed that they might be less contemptible?

"But she lost energy at last even for her loud-whispered cries and moans: she subsided into helpless sobs, and on the cold floor she sobbed herself to sleep.

"In the chill hours of the morning twilight, when all was dim around her, she awoke—not with any amazed wondering where she was or what had happened, but with the clearest consciousness that she was looking into the eyes of sorrow. She rose, and wrapped warm things around her, and seated herself in a great chair where she had often watched before. She was vigorous enough to have borne that hard night without feeling ill in body, beyond some aching and fatigue; but she had waked to a new condition: she felt as if her soul had been liberated from its terrible conflict; she was no longer wrestling with her grief, but could sit down with it as a lasting companion and make it a sharer in her thoughts. For now the thoughts came thickly. It was not in Dorothea's nature, for longer than the duration of a paroxysm, to sit in the narrow cell of her calamity, in the besotted misery of a consciousness that only sees another's lot as an accident of its own.

"She began now to live through that yesterday morning deliberately again, forcing herself to dwell on every detail and its possible meaning. Was she alone in that scene? Was it her event only? She forced herself to think of it as bound up with another woman's life—a woman towards whom she had set out with a longing to carry some clearness and comfort into her beclouded youth. In her first outleap of jealous indignation and disgust, when quitting the hateful room, she had flung away all the mercy with which she had undertaken that visit. She had enveloped both Will and **Rosamond** in her burning scorn, and it seemed to her as if Rosamond were burned out of her sight for ever. But that base prompting which makes a woman more cruel to a rival than to a faithless lover, could have no strength of recurrence in Dorothea when the dominant spirit of justice within her had once overcome the tumult and had once shown her the truer measure of things. All the active thought with which she had before been representing to herself the trials of **Lydgate**'s lot, and this young marriage union which, like her own, seemed to have its hidden as well as evident troubles—all this vivid sympathetic experience returned to her now as a power: it asserted itself as acquired knowledge asserts itself and will not let us see as we saw in the day of our ignorance. She said to her own irremediable grief, that it should make her more helpful, instead of driving her back from effort.

"And what sort of crisis might not this be in three lives whose contact with hers laid an obligation on her as if they had been suppliants bearing the sacred branch? The objects of her rescue were not to be sought out by her fancy: they were chosen for her. She yearned towards the perfect Right, that it might make a throne within her, and rule her errant will. 'What should I do—how should I act now, this very day, if I could clutch my own pain, and compel it to silence, and think of those three?'

"It had taken long for her to come to that question, and there was light piercing into the room. She opened her curtains, and looked out towards the bit of road that lay in view, with fields beyond, outside the entrance-gates. On the road there was a man with a bundle on his back and a woman carrying her baby; in the field she could see figures moving—perhaps the shepherd with his dog. Far off in the bending sky was the pearly light; and she felt the largeness of the world and the manifold wakings of men to labour and endurance. She was a part of that involuntary, palpitating life, and could neither look out on it from her luxurious shelter as a mere spectator, nor hide her eyes in selfish complaining." MM 80

—recognised in retrospect: "If a princess in the days of enchantment had seen a four-footed creature from among those which live in herds come to her once and again with a human gaze which rested upon her with choice and beseeching, what would she think of in her journeying, what would she look for when the herds passed her? Surely for the gaze which had found her, and which she would know again. Life would be no better than candle-light tinsel and daylight rubbish if our spirits were not touched by what has been, to issues of longing and constancy." MM 54

—second: "Again and again his vision was interrupted by wonder at the strength of his own feeling, at the strength and sweetness of this new love—almost like the wonder a man feels at the added power he finds in himself for an art which he had laid aside for a space. How is it that the poets have said so many fine things about our first love, so few about our later love? Are their first poems their best? Or are not those the best which come from their fuller thought, their larger experience, their deeper-rooted affections? The boy's flute-like voice has its own spring charm; but the man should yield a richer, deeper music." AB 51

—self-deceiving: "Love has a way of cheating itself consciously, like a child who plays at solitary hide-and-seek; it is pleased with assurances that it all the while disbelieves." AB 11

—sensible: "Of course, I know that, as a rule, sensible men fall in love with the most sensible women of their acquaintance, see through all the pretty deceits of coquettish beauty, never imagine themselves loved when they are not loved, cease loving on all proper occasions, and marry the woman most fitted for them in every respect—indeed, so as to compel the approbation of all the maiden ladies in their neighbourhood. But even to this rule an exception will occur now and then in the lapse of centuries and my friend Adam was one." AB 33

—sex: "Doubtless there was another sort of fascination at work—that subtle physical attraction which delights in cheating our psychological predictions, and in compelling the men who paint sylphs, to fall in love with some *bonne et brave femme,* heavy-heeled and freckled." LV 1

—silent understanding: "Their words were charged with a meaning dependent entirely on the secret consciousness of each. Nothing had been said which was necessarily personal. They walked a few yards along the road by which they had come, without further speech, till Felix said gently, 'take my arm.' She took it, and they walked home so, entirely without conversation. Felix was struggling as a firm man struggles with a temptation, seeing beyond it and disbelieving its lying promise. Esther was struggling as a woman struggles with the yearning for some expression of love, and with vexation under that subjection to a yearning which is not likely to be satisfied. Each was conscious of a silence which each was unable to break . . . . " FH 27

—time in suspense: "Any one who imagines ten days too short a time—not for falling into leanness, lightness, or other measurable effects of passion, but—for the whole spiritual circuit of alarmed conjecture and disappointment, is ignorant of what can go on in the elegant leisure of a young lady's mind." MM 31

—trusting: " . . . Romola was carried, by a sudden wave of memory, back again into the

time of perfect trust, and felt again the presence of the husband whose love made the world as fresh and wonderful to her as to a little child that sits in stillness among the sunny flowers: heard the gentle tones and saw the soft eyes without any lie in them, and breathed again that large freedom of the soul which comes from the faith that the being who is nearest to us is greater than ourselves. And in those brief moments the tears always rose: the woman's lovingness felt something akin to what the bereaved mother feels when the tiny fingers seem to lie warm on her bosom, and yet are marble to her lips as she bends over the silent bed." R 36

—*ungovernable:* "But I believe there have been men since his day who have ridden a long way to avoid a rencontre, and then galloped hastily back lest they should miss it. It is the favourite stratagem of our passions to sham a retreat, and to turn sharp round upon us at the moment we have made up our minds that the day is our own." AB 12

—*unrequited:* " . . . he had been laid low by an archer who sometimes touches his arrow with a subtle, lingering poison. The disappointment of a youthful passion has effects as incalculable as those of small-pox, which may make one person plain and a genius, another less plain and more foolish, another plain without detriment to his folly, and leave perhaps the majority without obvious change. Everything depends—not on the mere fact of disappointment, but—on the nature affected and the force that stirs it." DD 58

—*varied ingredients:* "There are many wonderful mixtures in the world which are all alike called love, and claim the privilege of a sublime rage which is an apology for everything (in literature and in the drama)." MM 31

—*veneration:* "He was but three-and-twenty, and had only just learned what it is to love —to love with that adoration which a young man gives to a woman whom he feels to be greater and better than himself. Love of this sort is hardly distinguishable from religious feeling. What deep and worthy love is so? whether of woman or child, or art or music.

"Our caresses, our tender words, our still rapture under the influence of autumn sunsets, or pillared vistas, or calm majestic statues, or Beethoven symphonies, all bring with them the consciousness that they are mere waves and ripples in an unfathomable ocean of love and beauty: our emotion in its keenest moment passes from expression into silence; our love at its highest flood rushes beyond its object, and loses itself in the sense of divine mystery.

"And this blessed gift of venerating love has been given to too many humble craftsmen since the world began, for us to feel any surprise that it should have existed in the soul of a Methodist carpenter half a century ago, while there was yet a lingering afterglow from the time when **Wesley** and his fellow-labourer fed on the hips and haws of the Cornwall hedges, after exhausting limbs and lungs in carrying a divine message to the poor." ¶AB 3

" . . . reverent love has a politeness of its own which it teaches to men otherwise of small schooling." SM 11

—*wrong:* "They had begun the morning with an indifferent salutation and both had rejoiced in being aloof from each other, like a patient who has actually done without his opium, in spite of former failures in resolution." MF VI 9

—*young:* "Love is such a simple thing when we have only one-and-twenty summers and a sweet girl of seventeen trembles under our glance; as if she were a bud first opening her heart with wondering rapture to the morning. Such young unfurrowed souls roll to meet each other like two velvet peaches that touch softly and are at rest; they mingle as easily as two brooklets that ask for nothing but to entwine themselves and ripple with ever-interlacing curves in the leafiest hiding-places." AB 12

"Young love-making—that gossamer web! Even the points it clings to—the things whence its subtle interlacings are swung—are scarcely perceptible: momentary touches of finger-tips, meetings of rays from blue and dark orbs, unfinished phrases, lightest changes of cheek and lip, faintest tremors. The web itself is made of spontaneous beliefs and indefinable joys, yearnings of one life towards another, visions of completeness, infinite trust." MM 36

—*in youth: see* A:Youth—*and love*

Lovers

—*alone together:* "They were alone together for the first time. What an overpowering presence that first privacy is!" AB 12

—*boating:* " . . . the sweet solitude of a twofold consciousness that was mingled into one by that grave untiring gaze which need not be averted—what else could there be in their minds for the first hour? Some low, subdued, languid exclamation of love came from Stephen from time to time, as he went on rowing idly, half automatically: otherwise, they spoke no word; for what could words have been, but an inlet to thought? and thought did not belong to that enchanted haze in which they were enveloped—it belonged to the past and the future that lay outside the haze." MF VI 13

—*look:* "They looked straight into each other's eyes, as angels do when they tell some truth." FH 45

—*triangle:* "It is not sublime, but it is common, for a man to see the beloved object unhappy because his rival loves another, with more fortitude and a milder jealousy than if he saw her entirely happy in his rival." DD 61

Man

—*admiring at a distance:* "The remote worship of a woman throned out of their reach plays a great part in men's lives, but in most cases the worshipper longs for some queenly recognition, some approving sign by which his soul's sovereign may cheer him without descending from her high place." MM 22

—*appetite:* " ' I don't eat such things myself, for a bit o' bread's what I like from one year's end to the other; but men's stomichs are made so comical, they want a change—they do, know, God help 'em.' " SM 10

—*arousing impatience:* " 'It drives me past patience . . . that way o' the men—always wanting and wanting, and never easy with what they've got: they can't sit comfortable in their chairs when they've neither ache nor pain, but either they must stick a pipe in their mouths, to make 'em better than well, or else they must be swallowing something strong, though they're forced to make haste before the next meal comes in.' " SM 17

—*and baby:* " '. . . the strong, skilful men are often the gentlest to the women and children; and it's pretty to see 'em carrying the little babies as if they were no heavier than little birds. And the babies always seem to like the strong arm best.' " AB 14

" 'I've seen men as are wonderful handy wi' children. The men are awk'ard and contrary mostly, God help 'em—but when the drink's out of 'em, they aren't unsensible, though they're bad for leeching and bandaging—so fiery and unpatient.' " SM 14

—*barbershop camaraderie:* "It was the busiest time of the day . . . and in this warm season and at an hour when clients were numerous, most men preferred being shaved under the pretty red and white awning in front of the shop rather than within narrow walls. It is not a sublime attitude for a man, to sit with lathered chin thrown backward, and have his nose made a handle of; but to be shaved was a fashion of Florentine respectability, and it is astonishing how gravely men look at each other when they are all in the fashion. It was the hour of the day, too, when yesterday's crop of gossip was freshest, and the barber's tongue was always in its glory when his razor was busy; the deft activity of those two instruments seemed to be set going by a common spring." R 16

—*calm:* "The image of Mirah had never yet had that penetrating radiation which would have been given to it by the idea of her loving him. When this sort of effluence is absent from the fancy (whether from the fact or not) a man may go far in devotedness without perturbation." DD 32

—*chilled:* "A man is seldom ashamed of feeling that he cannot love a woman so well when he sees a certain greatness in her: nature having intended greatness for men." MM 39

—*commanding:* "A man who seems to have been able to command the best, has a sovereign power of depreciation." DD 29

—*different:* " . . . she took her husband's jokes and joviality as patiently as everything else, considering that 'men would be so,' and viewing the stronger sex in the light of animals whom it had pleased Heaven to make naturally troublesome, like bulls and turkey-cocks." SM 10

—*envying:* "It was too intolerable that Dorothea should be worshipping this husband: such weakness in a woman is pleasant to no man but the husband in question. Mortals are easily tempted to pinch the life out of their neighbour's buzzing glory, and think that such killing is no murder." MM 21

—*fatuous: see* B:Beauty—*misleading*

—*his love:* "In the love of a brave and faithful man there is always a strain of maternal tenderness; he gives out again those beams of protecting fondness which were shed on him as he lay on his mother's knee." GL 19

—*mind:* "A man's mind—what there is of it—has always the advantage of being masculine—as the smallest birch-tree is of a higher kind than the most soaring palm—and even his ignorance is of a sounder quality." MM 2

—*misogynist:* " 'Would you have had me wait for a consumptive lackadaisical Englishwoman, who would have hung all her relations round my neck? I hate English wives; they want to give their opinion about everything. They interfere with a man's life. I shall not marry again.' " FH 1

—*not admired:* " 'And I shouldn't like to be a man—to cough so loud, and stand straddling about on a wet day, and be so wasteful with meat and drink. They're a coarse lot, I think.' " FH 39

—*obtuse:* "One thought in the mind of Felix was, that Esther was sure to marry Harold Transome. Men readily believe these things of the women who love them." FH 45

—opinions: "When a man is inclined to marry a particular woman, and has made any committal of himself, this woman's opinions, however different from his own, are readily regarded as part of her pretty ways, especially if they are merely negative; as, for example, that she does not insist on the Trinity or on the rightfulness or expediency of church rates, but simply regards her lover's troubling himself in disputation on these heads as stuff and nonsense. The man feels his own superior strength, and is sure that marriage will make no difference to him on the subjects about which he is in earnest. And to laugh at men's affairs is a woman's privilege, tending to enliven the domestic hearth." TS 9

—prospect: "For surely all must admit that a man may be puffed and belauded, envied, ridiculed, counted upon as a tool and fallen in love with, or at least selected as a future husband, and yet remain virtually unknown—known merely as a cluster of signs for his neighbours' false suppositions." MM 15

—prowess: "A man is bound to know something of his own weight and muscular dexterity, and the puny athlete is called foolish before he is seen to be thrown." TS 5

—seen at home: "The Vicar himself seemed to wear rather a changed aspect, as most men do when acquaintances made elsewhere see them for the first time in their own homes; some indeed showing like an actor of genial parts disadvantageously cast for the curmudgeon in a new piece." AB 17

—self-deceiving: " . . . a man never lies with more delicious languor under the influence of a passion, than when he has persuaded himself that he shall subdue it to-morrow." AB 26

—unusual: "[He] found himself . . . in the rather ludicrous position of sitting up severely holding a Hebrew grammar in his hands . . . with the consciousness that he had been in that attitude nearly an hour, and had thought of nothing but Gwendolen and her husband. To be an unusual young man means for the most part to get a difficult mastery over the usual, which is often like the sprite of ill-luck you pack up your goods to escape from, and see grinning at you from the top of your luggage-van." DD 35

Marriage and Matrimony

"Marriage must be a relation either of sympathy or of conquest." R 48

—adorable bride: see A:Beauty*—misleading*

—ambivalence: "To be very much sued or hopelessly sighed for as a bride was indeed an indispensable and agreeable guarantee of womanly power; but to become a wife and wear all the domestic fetters of that condition, was on the whole a vexatious necessity. Her observation of matrimony had inclined her to think it rather a dreary state, in which a woman could not do what she liked, had more children than were desirable, was consequently dull, and became irrevocably immersed in humdrum. Of course marriage was social promotion; she could not look forward to a single life; but promotions have sometimes to be taken with bitter herbs—a peerage will not quite do instead of leadership to the man who meant to lead . . . . " DD 4

—at first: "A bride and bridegroom, surrounded by all the appliances of wealth, hurried through the day by the whirl of society, filling their solitary moments with hastily-snatched caresses, are prepared for their future life together as the novice is prepared for the cloister—by experiencing its utmost contrast." LV 2

—broken pledge: "There may come a moment when even an excellent husband who has dropt smoking under more or less of a pledge during courtship, for the first time will introduce his cigar-smoke between himself and his wife, with the tacit understanding that she will have to put up with it. Mr Lush was, so to speak, a very large cigar.

"If these are the sort of lovers' vows at which *Jove* laughs, he must have a merry time of it." DD 45

—civility: "Tito and Romola never jarred, never remonstrated with each other. They were too hopelessly alienated in their inner life ever to have that contest which is an effort towards agreement." R 46

—contrast: "While Gwendolen, throned on her cushions at evening, and beholding the glory of sea and sky softening as if with boundless love around her, was hoping that Grandcourt in his march up and down was not going to pause near her, not going to look at her or speak to her, some woman under a smoky sky, obliged to consider the price of eggs in arranging her dinner, was listening for the music of a footstep that would remove all risk from her foretaste of joy; some couple, bending, cheek by cheek, over a bit of work done by the one and delighted in by the other, were reckoning the earnings that would make them rich enough for a holiday among the furze and heather." DD 54

—disaffection: "The seeds of things are very small: the hours that lie between sunrise and the gloom of midnight are travelled through by tiniest markings of the clock: and Janet, looking back along the fifteen years of her married life, hardly knew how or where this total misery began; hardly

knew when the sweet wedded love and hope that had set for ever had ceased to make a twilight of memory and relenting, before the oncoming of the utter dark." JR 13

—*disillusion:* " . . . whatever else remained the same, the light had changed, and you cannot find the pearly dawn at noonday. The fact is unalterable, that a fellow-mortal with whose nature you are acquainted solely through the brief entrances and exits of a few imaginative weeks called courtship, may, when seen in the continuity of married companionship, be disclosed as something better or worse than what you have preconceived, but will certainly not appear altogether the same. And it would be astonishing to find how soon the change is felt if we had no kindred changes to compare with it. To share lodgings with a brilliant dinner-companion, or to see your favourite politician in the Ministry, may bring about changes quite as rapid: in these cases too we begin by knowing little and believing much, and we sometimes end by inverting the quantities." MM 20

"I suppose it was that in courtship everything is regarded as provisional and preliminary, and the smallest sample of virtue or accomplishment is taken to guarantee delightful stores which the broad leisure of marriage will reveal. But the door-sill of marriage once crossed, expectation is concentrated on the present. Having once embarked on your marital voyage, it is impossible not to be aware that you make no way and that the sea is not within sight—that, in fact, you are exploring an enclosed basin." MM 20

—*dissolution:* "There is no compensation for the woman who feels that the chief relation of her life has been no more than a mistake. She has lost her crown. The deepest secret of human blessedness has half whispered itself to her, and then for ever passed her by." R 61

—*divorce:* "She had drunk in deeply the spirit of that teaching by which **Savonarola** had urged her to return to her place. She felt that the sanctity attached to all close relations, and, therefore, preeminently to the closest, was but the expression in outward law of that result towards which all human goodness and nobleness must spontaneously tend; that the light abandonment of ties, whether inherited or voluntary, because they had ceased to be pleasant, was the uprooting of social and personal virtue." R 56

—*effective:* "But it is undeniable, that unions formed in the maturity of thought and feeling, and grounded only on inherent attraction, tended to bring women into more intelligent sympathy with men, and to heighten and complicate their share in the political drama. The quiescence and security of the conjugal relation, are doubtless favourable to the manifestation of the highest qualities by persons who have already attained a high standard of culture, but rarely foster a passion sufficient to rouse all the faculties to aid in winning or retaining its beloved object—to convert indolence into activity, indifference into ardent partisanship, dulness into perspicuity. Gallantry and intrigue are sorry enough things in themselves, but they certainly serve better to arouse the dormant faculties of woman than embroidery and domestic drudgery . . . . " WF 451

—*end and beginning:* "Marriage, which has been the bourne of so many narratives, is still a great beginning as it was to *Adam* and *Eve,* who kept their honeymoon in Eden, but had their first little one among the thorns and thistles of the wilderness. It is still the beginning of the home epic—the gradual conquest or irremediable loss of that complete union which makes the advancing years a climax, and age the harvest of sweet memories in common.

"Some set out, like Crusaders of old, with a glorious equipment of hope and enthusiasm, and get broken by the way, wanting patience with each other and the world." MM 87

—*the greatest thing:* "What greater thing is there for two human souls, than to feel that they are joined for life—to strengthen each other in all labour, to rest on each other in all sorrow, to minister to each other in all pain, to be one with each other in silent unspeakable memories at the moment of the last parting?" AB 54

—*honeymoon*

—*disturbed:* "To have changed your longitude extensively, and placed yourselves in a moral solitude in order to have small explosions, to find conversation difficult and to hand a glass of water without looking, can hardly be regarded as satisfactory fulfillment even to the toughest minds." MM 20

—*husband thwarted:* "Romola had an energy of her own which thwarted his, and no man, who is not exceptionally feeble, will endure being thwarted by his wife." R 48

—*husband's hobby:* "The economising of a gardener's wages might perhaps have induced Mrs Glegg to wink at this folly, if it were possible for a healthy female mind even to simulate respect for a husband's hobby. But it is well known that this conjugal complacency belongs only to the weaker portion of the sex, who are scarcely alive to the responsibilities of a wife as a constituted check on her husband's pleasures— which are hardly ever of a rational or commendable kind." MF I 12

—ignorance: "Gwendolen had about as accurate a conception of marriage—that is to say, of the mutual influences, demands, duties of man and woman in the state of matrimony—as she had of magnetic currents and the law of storms." DD 27

—impulsive: "It is a common enough case, that of a man being suddenly captivated by a woman nearly the opposite of his ideal; or if not wholly captivated, at least effectively captured by a combination of circumstances along with an unwarily manifested inclination which might otherwise have been transient." TS 9

—inauspicious: see M:Consciousness*—vision of portent*

—mutual trust: "That quiet mutual gaze of a trusting husband and wife is like the first moment of rest or refuge from a great weariness or a great danger—not to be interfered with by speech or action which would distract the sensations from the fresh enjoyment of repose." SM 20

—observed: "In general, one may be sure that whenever a marriage of any mark takes place, male acquaintances are likely to pity the bride, female acquaintances the bridegroom: each, it is thought, might have done better; and especially where the bride is charming, young gentlemen on the scene are apt to conclude that she can have no real attachment to a fellow so uninteresting to themselves as her husband, but has married him on other grounds. Who under such circumstances pities the husband? Even his female friends are apt to think his position retributive: he should have chosen someone else." DD 35

—suitability: "Whether Providence had taken equal care of Miss Brooke in presenting her with Mr Casaubon was an idea which could hardly occur to him. Society never made the preposterous demand that a man should think as much about his own qualifications for making a charming girl happy as he thinks of hers for making himself happy. As if a man could choose not only his wife but his wife's husband! Or as if he were bound to provide charms for his posterity in his own person!" MM 29

—symbol: "But that force of outward symbols by which our active life is knit together so as to make an inexorable external identity for us, not to be shaken by our wavering consciousness, gave a strange effect to this simple movement towards taking off her ring—a movement which was but a small sequence of her energetic resolution. It brought a vague but arresting sense that she was somehow violently rending her life in two: a presentiment that the strong impulse which had seemed to exclude doubt and make her path clear might after all be blindness, and that there was something in human bonds which must prevent them from being broken with the breaking of illusions." R 36

Romance

—absorbing memory: "Fedalma came,
And with her visionary presence brought
What seemed a waking in the warm spring morn.
He still was pacing on the stony earth
Under the deepening night; the fresh-lit fires
Were flickering on dark forms and eyes that met
His forward and his backward tread; but she,
She was within him, making his whole self
Mere correspondence with her image: sense,
In all its deep recesses where it keeps
The mystic stores of ecstasy, was turned
To memory that killed the hour, like wine.
Then Silva said, 'She, by herself, is life.
What was my joy before I loved her—what
Shall heaven lure us with, love being lost?'—
For he was young." SG III

—dreams: "Poor little Penny! the days were so very long among the daisies on a grazing farm, and thought is so active—how was it possible that the inward drama should not get the start of the outward? I have known young ladies, much better educated, and with an outward world diversified by instructive lectures, to say nothing of literature and highly-developed fancy-work, who have spun a cocoon of visionary joys and sorrows for themselves, just as Penny did." BJ 2

—a stranger: "Strangers, whether wrecked and clinging to a raft, or duly escorted and accompanied by portmanteaus, have always had a circumstantial fascination for the virgin mind, against which native merit has urged itself in vain." MM 12

—superficiality: "We are not afraid of telling over and over again how a man comes to fall in love with a woman and be wedded to her, or else be fatally parted from her. Is it due to excess of poetry or of stupidity that we are never weary of describing what **King James** called a woman's 'makdom and her fairnesse,' never weary of listening to the twanging of the old Troubadour strings, and are comparatively uninterested in that other kind of 'makdom and fairnesse' which must be wooed with industrious thought and patient renunciation of small desires. In the story of this passion, too, the development varies: sometimes it is the glorious marriage, sometimes frustration and final parting. And not seldom the catastrophe is

bound up with the other passion, sung by the Troubadours." MM 15

—*teacher and pupil:* "When there is a passion between an heiress and a proud independent-spirited man, it is difficult for them to come to an understanding; but the difficulties are likely to be overcome unless the proud man secures himself by a constant *alibi.* Brief meetings after studied absence are potent in disclosure: but more potent still in frequent companionship, with full sympathy in taste, and admirable qualities on both sides; especially where the one is in the position of teacher, and the other is delightedly conscious of receptive ability which also gives the teacher delight. The situation is famous in history, and has no less charm now than it had in the days of **Abelard**." DD 22

The Sexes

—*ascendancy:* "Every man who is not a monster, a mathematician, or a mad philosopher, is the slave of some woman or other." SF 4

—*assumptions:* "The man who awakes the wondering tremulous passion of a young girl always thinks her affectionate; and if he chances to look forward to future years, probably imagines himself being virtuously tender to her, because the poor thing is so clingingly fond of him. God made these dear women so—and it is a convenient arrangement in case of sickness." AB 15

—*babies:* " 'Well, mayhap that'll do, as it's a little gell, for they're easier persuaded to sit i' one place nor the lads. I know what the lads are; for I've had four—four I've had, God knows—and if you was to take and tie 'em up, they'd made a fighting and a crying as if you was ringing the pigs.' " SM 14

—*bachelor:* "Still, a bachelor's heart is an outlying fortress that some fair enemy may any day take either by storm or stratagem. . . ." SF 4

—*boys:* " 'My dear child, the boys are such a trouble—we could never put up with them, if we didn't make believe they were worth more,' said Mrs Meyrick, just as her boy entered." DD 39

—*bravery:* "Not that St Ogg's was empty of women with some tenderness of heart and conscience . . . . But until every good man is brave, we must expect to find many good women timid: too timid even to believe in the correctness of their own best promptings, when these would place them in a minority. And the men of St Ogg's were not all brave . . . . It was the general feeling of the masculine mind at St Ogg's that women were not to be interfered with in their treatment of each other." MF VII 4

—*companionable:* " . . . he was gradually discovering the delight there is in frank kindness and companionship between a man and a woman who have no passion to hide or confess." MM 8

—*disparate intellects:* "Some men's kindness and love-making are more exasperating, more humiliating than others' derision; but the pitiable woman who has once made herself secretly dependent on a man who is beneath her in feeling, must bear that humiliation for fear of worse. Coarse kindness is at least better than coarse anger; and in all private quarrels the duller nature is triumphant by reason of its dulness." FH 9

—*lessons to learn:* " . . . one of the lessons a woman most rarely learns, is never to talk to an angry or a drunken man." AB 4

—*in literature:* "Now, we think it an immense mistake to maintain that there is no sex in literature. Science has no sex: the mere knowing and reasoning faculties, if they act correctly, must go through the same process, and arrive at the same result. But in art and literature, which imply the action of the entire being, in which every fibre of the nature is engaged, in which every peculiar modification of the individual makes itself felt, woman has something specific to contribute. Under every imaginable social condition, she will necessarily have a class of sensations and emotions—the maternal ones—which must remain unknown to man; and the fact of her comparative physical weakness, which, however it may have been exaggerated by a vicious civilization, can never be cancelled, introduces a distinctively feminine condition into the wondrous chemistry of the affections and sentiments, which inevitably gives rise to distinctive forms and combinations. A certain amount of psychological difference between man and woman necessarily arises out of the difference of sex, and instead of being destined to vanish before a complete development of woman's intellectual and moral nature, will be a permanent source of variety and beauty, as long as the tender light and dewy freshness of morning affect us differently from the strength and brilliancy of the midday sun." WF 449

—*looks deceiving:* "After all, I believe, the wisest of us must be beguiled in this way sometimes, and must think both better and worse of people than they deserve. Nature has her language, and she is not unveracious; but we don't know all the intricacies of her syntax just yet, and in a hasty reading we may happen to extract the very opposite of her real meaning." AB 15

—*loving:* " 'Twere hard of Love to make us
women fear

And leave you bold. Yet Love is not quite even.
For feeble creatures, little birds and fawns,
Are shaken more by fear, while large strong things
Can bear it stoutly. So we women still
Are not well dealt with." SG I iii

—*mind: see* M:Mind—*the sexes*

—*preoccupations:* "While Maggie's life-struggles had lain almost entirely within her own soul, one shadowy army fighting another, and the slain shadows for ever rising again, Tom was engaged in a dustier, noisier war-fare, grappling with more substantial obstacles, and gaining more definite conquests. So it has been since the days of **Hecuba**, and of **Hector**, Tamer of horses: inside the gates, the women with streaming hair and uplifted hands offering prayers, watching the world's combat from afar, filling their long, empty days with memories and fears: outside, the men in fierce struggle with things divine and human, quenching memory in the stronger light of purpose, losing the sense of dread and even of wounds in the hurrying ardour of action." MF V 2

—*toddlers:* " 'You have a mamma?' said Romola, as they set out, looking down at the boy with a certain yearning. But he was mute. A girl under those circumstances might perhaps have chirped abundantly: not so this square-shouldered little man with the big cloud of curls." R 56

—*tolerance of emotion:* "Tom was almost ready to rush away, with that impatience of painful emotion which makes one of the differences between youth and maiden, man and woman." MF III 8

"Of these two young hearts Tom's suffered the most unmixed pain, for Maggie, with all her keen susceptibility, yet felt as if the sorrow made larger room for her love to flow in, and gave breathing space to her passionate nature. No true boy feels that: he would rather go and slay the Nemean lion, or perform any round of heroic labours, than endure perpetual appeals to his pity for evils over which he can make no conquest." MF III 8

—*vanity: see* S:Vanity and Conceit—*trans-gender*

—*verbal combat* " 'What!' said Bartle, with an air of disgust. 'Was there a woman concerned? Then I give you up, Adam.'

" 'But it's a woman you'n spoke well on, Bartle,' said Mr Poyser. 'Come, now, you canna draw back; you said once as women wouldna ha' been a bad invention if they'd all been like Dinah.'

" 'I meant her voice, man—I meant her voice, that was all,' said Bartle. 'I can bear to hear her speak without wanting to put wool in my ears. As for other things, I daresay she's like the rest o' the women—thinks two and two'll come to make five, if she cries and bothers enough about it.'

" 'Ay, ay!' said Mrs Poyser; 'one 'ud think, an' hear some folks talk, as the men war 'cute enough to count the corns in a bag o' wheat wi' only smelling at it. They can see through a barn-door, *they* can. Perhaps that's the reason they can see so little o' this side on't.'

"Martin Poyser shook with delighted laughter, and winked at Adam, as much as to say, the schoolmaster was in for it now.

" 'Ah!' said Bartle, sneeringly, 'the women are quick enough—they're quick enough. They know the rights of a story before they hear it, and can tell a man what his thoughts are before he knows 'em himself.'

" 'Like enough,' said Mrs Poyser ; 'for the men are mostly so slow, their thoughts overrun 'em, an' they can only catch 'em by the tail. I can count [knit] a stocking-top while a man's get's tongue ready; an' when he outs wi' his speech at last, there's little broth to be made on't. It's your dead chicks take the longest hatchin'. Howiver, I'm not denyin' the women are foolish: God Almighty made 'em to match the men.'

" 'Match!' said Bartle; 'ay, as vinegar matches one's teeth. If a man says a word, his wife'll match it with a contradiction; if he's a mind for hot meat, his wife'll match it with cold bacon; if he laughs, she'll match him with whimpering. She's such a match as the horse-fly is to th' horse: she's got the right venom to sting him with—the right venom to sting him with.'

" 'Yes,' said Mrs Poyser, 'I know what the men like—a poor soft, as 'ud simper at 'em like the pictur o' the sun, whether they did right or wrong, an' say thank you for a kick, an' pretend she didna know which end she stood uppermost, till her husband told her. That's what a man wants in a wife, mostly: he wants to make sure o' one fool as 'll tell him he's wise. But there's some men can do wi'out that—they think so much o' themselves a'ready; an' that's how it is there's old bachelors.'

" 'Come, Craig,' said Mr Poyser, jocosely, 'you mun get married pretty quick, else you'll be set down for an old bachelor; an' you see what the women 'ull think on you.'

" 'Well,' said Mr Craig, willing to conciliate Mrs Poyser, and setting a high value on his own compliments, 'I like a cleverish woman—a woman o' sperrit—a managing woman.'

" 'You're out there, Craig,' said Bartle, dryly; 'you're out there. You judge o' your garden-stuff on a better plan than that: you pick the things for what they can excel in—for what they can excel in. You don't value your peas for their roots, or your carrots for their flowers. Now that's the way you should choose women: their cleverness'll never come to much—never come to much; but they make excellent simpletons, ripe and strong-flavoured.'

" 'What dost say to that?' said Mr Poyser, throwing himself back and looking merrily at his wife.

" 'Say!' answered Mrs Poyser, with dangerous fire kindling in her eye; 'why, I say as some folks' tongues are like the clocks as run on strikin', not to tell you the time o' the day, but because there's summat wrong i' their own inside.'

"Mrs Poyser would probably have brought her rejoinder to a further climax, if every one's attention had not at this moment been called to the other end of the table . . . . " AB 53

Wife

—bad tempered: "A pretty woman may fan the flame of distant adorers by harassing them, but if she lets one of them make her his wife, the point of view from which he will look at her poutings and tossings and mysterious inability to be pleased will be seriously altered . . . slavery to a pretty woman, which seems among the least conditional forms of abject service, will not bear too great a strain from her bad temper even though her beauty remain the same . . . ." TS 6

—blind suffering: "The future took shape after shape of misery before her, always ending in her being dragged back again to her old life of terror, and stupor, and fevered despair. Her husband had so long overshadowed her life that her imagination could not keep hold of a condition in which that great dread was absent; and even his absence—what was it? only a dreary vacant flat, where there was nothing to strive after, nothing to long for." JR 15

—making allowances: "The vindication of the loved object is the best balm affection can find for its wounds:—'A man must have so much on his mind,' is the belief by which a wife often supports a cheerful face under rough answers and unfeeling words." SM 17

—privacy: "There was one thing that would have made the pang of disappointment in her husband harder to bear; it was, that any one should know he gave her cause for disappointment. This might be a woman's weakness, but it is closely allied to a woman's nobleness. She who willingly lifts up the veil of her married life has profaned it from a sanctuary into a vulgar place." R 31

—second: "[Her husband] had married a woman much older than himself—a Dissenter, and in other ways probably of that disadvantageous quality usually perceptible in a first wife if inquired into with the dispassionate judgment of a second . . . . " MM 61

—stupid: "The possession of a wife conspicuously one's inferior in intellect, is, like other high privileges, attended with a few inconveniences . . . . " MF III 1

—subordinate: "The new sensibilities and questions . . . were quieted again by that subjection to her husband's mind which is felt by every wife who loves her husband with passionate devotedness and full reliance." R 27

Woman

" 'We don't ask what a woman does—we ask whom she belongs to.' " MF VI 8

—acute: " 'Too 'cute for a woman, I'm afraid . . . . It's no mischief much while she's a little un, but an over 'cute woman's no better nor a long-tailed sheep—she'll fetch none the bigger price for that.' " MF I 2

—alike: "For if a country beauty in clumsy shoes be only shallow-hearted enough, it is astonishing how closely her mental processes may resemble those of a lady in society and crinoline, who applies her refined intellect to the problem of committing indiscretions without compromising herself." AB 30

—bitter appraisal: " 'A woman's love is always freezing into fear. She wants everything, she is secure of nothing. This girl has a fine spirit—plenty of fire and pride and wit. Men like such captives, as they like horses that champ the bit and paw the ground: they feel more triumph in their mastery. What is the use of a woman's will?—if she tries, she doesn't get it, and she ceases to be loved. God was cruel when he made women.' " FH 39

—and business: "The fact that she had been active in the management of the estate—had ridden about it continually, had busied herself with accounts, had been head-bailiff

of the vacant farms, and had yet allowed things to go wrong—was set down by [her son] simply to the general futility of women's attempts to transact men's business . . . .

"It was the way of women, and all weak minds, to think that what they had been used to was inalterable." FH 8

—childless: "This excessive rumination and self-questioning is perhaps a morbid habit inevitable to a mind of much moral sensibility when shut out from its due share of outward activity and of practical claims on its affections—inevitable to a noble-hearted, childless woman, when her lot is narrow. 'I can do so little—have I done it all well?' is the perpetually recurring thought; and there are no voices calling her away from that soliloquy, no peremptory demands to divert energy from vain regret or superfluous scruple." SM 17

—complacent: " . . . the fair blonde dame seemed to look down on her with that benignant unconcern, that mild wonder, with which happy self-possessed women are apt to look down on their agitated and weaker sisters." GL 11

—complaining: "Women who are never bitter and resentful are often the most querulous; and if **Solomon** was as wise as he is reputed to be, I feel sure that when he compared a contentious woman to a continual dropping on a very rainy day, he had not a vixen in his eye—a fury with long nails, acrid and selfish. Depend upon it, he meant a good creature, who had no joy but in the happiness of the loved ones whom she contributed to make uncomfortable, putting by all the tid-bits for them, and spending nothing on herself." AB 4

—a conventional view: " 'But there is a lightness about the feminine mind—a touch and go—music, the fine arts, that kind of thing—they should study those up to a certain point, women should; but in a light way, you know. A woman should be able to sit down and play you or sing you a good old English tune.' " MM 7

—cultured: "A really cultured woman, like a really cultured man, is all the simpler and the less obtrusive for her knowledge; it has made her see herself and her opinions in something like just proportions; she does not make it a pedestal from which she flatters herself that she commands a complete view of men and things, but makes it a point of observation from which to form a right estimate of herself. She neither spouts poetry nor quotes **Cicero** on slight provocation; not because she thinks that a sacrifice must be made to the prejudices of men, but because that mode of exhibiting her memory and Latinity does not present itself to her as edifying or graceful. She does not write books to confound philosophers, perhaps because she is able to write books that delight them. In conversation she is the least formidable of women, because she understands you, without wanting to make you aware that you *can't* understand her. She does not give you information, which is the raw material of culture—she gives you sympathy, which is its subtlest essence." SN 45

—criticizing: "In this way poor women, whose power lies solely in their influence, make themselves like music out of tune, and only move men to run away." FH 34

—debased: "And I confess that sometimes when I see a certain style of young lady, who checks our tender admiration with rouge and henna and all the blazonry of an extravagant expenditure, with slang and bold *brusquerie* intended to signify her emancipated view of things, and with cynical mockery which she mistakes for penetration, I am sorely tempted to hiss out *'Pétroleuse!'** It is a small matter to have our palaces set aflame compared with the misery of having our sense of a noble womanhood, which is the inspiration of a purifying shame, the promise of life-penetrating affection, stained and blotted out by images of repulsiveness." **arsonist* TS 10

—destiny: " . . . it is too painful to think that she is a woman, with a woman's destiny before her—a woman spinning in young ignorance a light web of folly and vain hopes which may one day close round her and press upon her, a rancorous poisoned garment, changing all at once her fluttering, trivial butterfly sensations into a life of deep human anguish." AB 22

—in France: "What were the causes of this earlier development and more abundant manifestation of womanly intellect in France? The primary one, perhaps, lies in the physiological characteristics of the Gallic race:—the small brain and vivacious temperament which permit the fragile system of woman to sustain the superlative activity requisite for intellectual creativeness; while, on the other hand, the larger brain and slower temperament of the English and Germans are, in the womanly organization, generally dreamy and passive . . . . And thus the *physique* of a woman may suffice as the substratum for a superior Gallic mind, but is too thin a soil for a superior Teutonic one. Our theory is borne out by the fact, that among our own country-women, those who distinguish themselves by literary production, more frequently approach the Gallic than the Teutonic type; they are intense and rapid rather than comprehensive. The woman of large capacity can seldom rise be-

yond the absorption of ideas; her physical conditions refuse to support the energy required for spontaneous activity; the voltaic-pile is not strong enough to produce crystallizations; phantasms of great ideas float through her mind, but she has not the spell which will arrest them, and give them fixity. This, more than unfavourable external circumstances, is, we think, the reason why woman has not yet contributed any new form to art, any discovery in science, any deep-searching inquiry in philosophy. The necessary physiological conditions are not present in her." WF 450-1

"No wise person . . . considers the ideal programme of woman's life to be a *mariage de convenance* at fifteen, a career of gallantry from twenty to eight-and-thirty, and peni-tence and piety for the rest of her days." WF 452

"Women became superior in France by being admitted to a common fund of ideas, to common subjects of interest with men; and this must ever be the essential condition at once of true womanly culture and of true social well-being. We have no faith in feminine *conversazioni,* where ladies are eloquent on **Apollo** and **Mars**; though we sympathize with the yearning activity of faculties which, deprived of their proper material, waste themselves in weaving fabrics out of cobwebs. Let the whole field of reality be laid upon to woman as well as to man, and then that which is peculiar in her mental modification, instead of being, as it is now, a source of discord and repulsion between the sexes, will be found to be a necessary complement to the truth and beauty of life. Then we shall have that marriage of minds which alone can blend all the hues of thought and feeling in one lovely rainbow of promise for the harvest of human happiness." WF 472-3

—heiress: "Heiresses vary, and persons interested in one of them beforehand are prepared to find that she is too yellow or too red, tall and toppling or short and square, violent and capricious or moony and insipid; but in every case it is taken for granted that she will consider herself an appendage to her fortune, and marry where others think her fortune ought to go. Nature, however, not only accommodates herself ill to our favourite practices by making 'only children' daughters, but also now and then endows the misplaced daughter with a clear head and a strong will." DD 22

—her hopes: "A woman's hopes are woven of sunbeams; a shadow annihilates them." FH 1

—her lot: "After all, she was a woman, and could not make her own lot. As she had once said to Felix, 'A woman must choose meaner things, because only meaner things are offered to her.' Her lot is made for her by the love she accepts." FH 43

—her love: "The best part of a woman's love is worship; but it is hard to her to be sent away with her precious spikenard rejected, and her long tresses too, that were let fall ready to soothe the wearied feet." FH 37

—husband-hunting: "Now, she had ascertained, by tentative residences, that the kind of bite she was angling for was difficult to be met with at watering-places, which were already preoccupied with abundance of angling beauties, and were chiefly stocked with men whose whiskers might be dyed, and whose incomes were still more problematic . . . . " SF 4

—hypocritical: " . . . a woman who was loving and thoughtful for other women, not giving them Judas-kisses with eyes askance on their welcome defects . . . . " MF VI 1

—intuition: "We use round, general, gentlemanly epithets about a young man of birth and fortune; and ladies, with that fine intuition which is the distinguishing attribute of their sex, see at once that he is 'nice.' " AB 12

—lightweight: " 'It is true [said father to daughter], I have been careful to keep thee aloof from the debasing influence of thy own sex, with their sparrow-like frivolity and their enslaving superstition, except, indeed, from that of our cousin Brigida, who may well serve as a scarecrow and warning.' " R 5

—opinions: " 'Women, very properly, don't change their views, but keep to the notions in which they have been brought up. It doesn't signify what they think—they are not called upon to judge or to act.' " FH 2

"Women were expected to have weak opinions; but the great safeguard of society and of domestic life was, that opinions were not acted on. Sane people did what their neighbours did, so that if any lunatics were at large, one might know and avoid them." MM 1

—passion: " . . . a passionate woman's love is always overshadowed by fear." GL 4

—power of eloquence: "When a woman feels purely and nobly, that ardour of hers which breaks through formulas too rigorously urged on men by daily practical needs, makes one of her most precious influences: she is the added impulse that shatters the stiffening crust of cautious experience. Her inspired ignorance gives a sublimity to actions so incongruously simple, that otherwise they would make men smile." FH 46

—problem: "In short, woman was a problem which, since Mr Brooke's mind felt blank before it, could be hardly less compli-

cated than the revolutions of an irregular solid." MM 4

—*a Radical view:* " 'I can't bear to see you going the way of the foolish women who spoil men's lives. Men can't help loving them, and so they make themselves slaves to the petty desires of petty creatures. That's the way those who might do better spend their lives for nought—get checked in every great effort—toil with brain and limb for things that have no more to do with a manly life than tarts and confectionery. That's what makes women a curse; all life is stunted to suit their littleness. That's why I'll never love, if I can help it; and if I love, I'll bear it, and never marry.' " FH 10

—*scholarship:* " 'For the sustained zeal and unconquerable patience demanded from those who would tread the unbeaten paths of knowledge are still less reconcilable with the wandering, vagrant propensity of the feminine mind than with the feeble powers of the feminine body.' " R 5

—*sentiment and passion:* "Women are peculiarly fitted to further such a combination [exaltation of sentiment and simplicity of language]—first, from their greater tendency to mingle affection and imagination with passion, and thus subtilize it into sentiment; and next, from that dread of what over-taxes their intellectual energies, either by difficulty or monotony, which gives them an instinctive fondness for lightness of treatment and airiness of expression, thus making them cut short all prolixity and reject all heaviness." WF 453

—*speech:* "She, poor woman, knew quite well that she had been unwise, and that she had been making herself disagreeable to Harold to no purpose. But half the sorrows of women would be averted if they could repress the speech they know to be useless; nay, the speech they have resolved not to utter." FH 2

—*suppressed:* " 'You are not a woman. You may try—but you can never imagine what it is to have a man's force of genius in you, and yet to suffer the slavery of being a girl. To have a pattern cut out—"this is the Jewish woman; this is what you must be; this is what you are wanted for; a woman's heart must be of such a size and no larger, else it must be pressed small, like Chinese feet; her happiness is to be made as cakes are, by a fixed receipt." ' " DD 51

—*vain:* "Do not . . . say that Hetty, being very pretty, must have known that it did not signify whether she had on any ornaments or not; and that, moreover, to look at earrings which she could not possibly wear out of her bedroom could hardly be a satisfaction, the essence of vanity being a reference to the impressions produced on others: you will never understand women's natures if you are so excessively rational." AB 22

—*vulnerable:* "It is such vague undefinable states of susceptibility as this—states of excitement or depression, half mental, half physical—that determine many a tragedy in women's lives." JR 25

—*West and East:* "Western women were not to his taste: they showed a transition from the feeble animal to the thinking being, which was simply troublesome. Harold preferred a shallow-witted large-eyed woman, silent and affectionate, with a load of black hair weighing much more heavily than her brain. He had seen no such woman in England, except one whom he had brought with him from the East." FH 36

Letters and Communication

"... conversation consists a good deal in the denial of what is true." FH 29

"Nathless, I love words: they are the quoits, the bows, the staves that furnish the gymnasium of the mind. Without them in our present condition our intellectual strength would have no implements." (1841; an epigraph in a 1919 reprinting of NE)

Advice

—casual: "If you blame Mr Riley very severely for giving a recommendation on such slight grounds, I must say you are rather hard upon him. Why should an auctioneer and appraiser thirty years ago, who had as good as forgotten his free-school Latin, be expected to manifest a delicate scrupulosity which is not always exhibited by gentlemen of the learned professions even in our present advanced stage of morality?

"Besides, a man with the milk of human kindness in him can scarcely abstain from doing a good-natured action, and one can't be good-natured all round. Nature herself occasionally quarters an inconvenient parasite on an animal towards whom she has otherwise no ill-will. What then? We admire her care for the parasite. If Mr Riley had shrunk from giving a recommendation that was not based on valid evidence, he would not have helped Mr Snelling to a paying pupil, and that would not have been so well for the reverend gentleman. Consider, too, that all the pleasant little dim ideas and complacencies—of standing well with Timpson, of dispensing advice when he was asked for it, of impressing his friend Tulliver with additional respect, of saying something and saying it emphatically, with other inappreciably minute ingredients that went along with the warm hearth and the brandy and water to make up Mr Riley's consciousness on this occasion, would have been a mere blank." MF 3

—*opinion requested:* "His friend Tulliver had asked him for an opinion: it is always chilling in friendly intercourse to say you have no opinion to give. And if you deliver an opinion at all, it is mere stupidity not to do it with an air of conviction and well-founded knowledge. You make it your own in uttering it, and naturally get fond of it." MF I 3

—*sinless?* "Our guides, we pretend, must be sinless: as if those were not often the best teachers who only yesterday got corrected for their mistakes." DD 37

Authorship

—*appraisal:* "In endeavouring to estimate a remarkable writer who aimed at more than temporary influence, we have first to consider what was his individual contribution to the spiritual wealth of mankind? Had he a new conception? Did he animate long-known but neglected truths with new vigour, and cast fresh light on their relation to other admitted truths? Did he impregnate any ideas with a fresh store of emotion, and in this way enlarge the area of moral sentiment? Did he by a wise emphasis here, and a wise disregard there, give a more useful or beautiful proportion to aims or motives? And even where his thinking was most mixed with the sort of mistake which is obvious to the majority, as well as that which can only be discerned by the instructed, or made manifest by the progress of things, has it that salt of a noble enthusiasm which should rebuke our critical discrimination if its correctness is inspired with a less admirable habit of feeling?" LNB 2

—*audience:* "An author, keenly conscious of having written, can hardly help imagining his condition of lively interest to be shared by others, just as we are all apt to suppose that the chill or heat we are conscious of must be general, or even to think that our sons and daughters, our pet schemes, and our quarrelling correspondence, are themes to which intelligent persons will listen long without weariness. But if the ardent author happens to be alive to practical teaching he will soon learn to divide the larger part of the enlightened public into those who have not read him and think it necessary to tell him so when they meet him in polite society, and those who have equally abstained from reading him, but wish to conceal this negation and speak of his 'incomparable works' with that trust in testimony which always has its cheering side." TS 11

—*autobiography:* "Is it then possible to describe oneself at once faithfully and fully? In all autobiography there is, nay, ought to be, an incompleteness which may have the effect of falsity. We are each of us bound to reticence by the piety we owe to those who have been nearest to us and have had a mingled influence over our lives; by the fellow-feeling which should restrain us from turning our volunteered and picked confessions into an act of accusation against others, who have no chance of vindicating themselves; and most of all by that reverence for the higher efforts of our common nature, which commands us to bury its lowest fatalities, its invincible remnants of the brute, its most agonising struggles with temptation, in unbroken silence." TS 1

—*biography* "But the conditions required for the perfection of life writing—personal intimacy, a loving and poetic nature which sees the beauty and the depth of familiar things, and the artistic power which seizes characteristic points and renders them with life-like effect—are seldom found in combination."" JS 249

—*book:* "Books are but persons in a transmigrated form." BL 7 306

—*brevity:* "Brevity is justified at once to those who readily understand, and to those who will never understand." LV 2

—*cause and effect:* "In watching effects, if only of an electric battery, it is often necessary to change our place and examine a particular mixture or group at some distance from the point where the movement we are interested in was set up." MM 40

—*commentaries:* "Is it out of the question that we should entertain some scruple about mixing our own flavour, as of the too cheap and insistent nutmeg, with that of every great writer and every great subject?—especially, when our flavour is all we have to give, the matter of knowledge having been already given by somebody else. What if we were only like the Spanish wine-skins which impress the innocent stranger with the notion that the Spanish grape has naturally a taste of leather' " TS 14

—*compendium:* "In the present day, the busy retailer of other people's knowledge which he has spoiled in the handling, the restless guesser and commentator, the importunate hawker of undesirable superfluities, the everlasting word-compeller who rises early in the morning to praise what the world has already glorified, or makes himself haggard at night in writing out his dissent from what nobody ever believed, is not simply 'gratis anhelans, multa agendo nihil agens'*—he is an obstruction. Like an incompetent architect with too much interest at his back, he obtrudes his ill-considered work where place ought to have been left to better men." TS 14 **"out of breath about nothing, with much ado doing nothing"* (Phaedrus)

—diseases: "Authors are so miscellaneous a class that their personified diseases, physical and moral, might include the whole procession of human disorders, led by dyspepsia and ending in madness—the awful Dumb Show of a world-historic tragedy. Take a large enough area of human life and all comedy melts into tragedy, like the *Fool's* part by the side of *Lear*. The chief scenes get filled with erring heroes, guileful usurpers, persecuted discoverers, dying deliverers: everywhere the protagonist has a part pregnant with doom. The comedy sinks to an accessory, and if there are loud laughs they seem a convulsive transition from sobs; or if the comedy is touched with a gentle lovingness, the panoramic scene is one where

Sadness is a kind of mirth
So mingled as if mirth did make us sad
And sadness merry.

TS 15

—easy: "No position could be suited to Mr David Faux that was not in the highest degree easy to the flesh and flattering to the spirit. If he had fallen on the present times, and enjoyed the advantages of a Mechanics' Institute, he would certainly have taken to literature and have written reviews . . . . " BJ 1

—economy: "One could wish that even the greatest minds should leave some themes unhandled, or at least leave us no more than a paragraph or two on them to show how well they did in not being more lengthy." TS 14

—German language: see RW:Germany

—ineffective: " . . . the production of feeble literature being found compatible with the most diverse forms of *physique,* masculine as well as feminine." DD 5

—maimed hero: "Life has sadness and bitterness enough for a disappointed philanthropist like Romney Leigh, short of maiming or blindness; and the outflow of love and compassion towards physical ills is less rare in woman than complete sympathy with mental sorrows. Hence we think the lavish mutilation of heroes' bodies, which has become the habit of novelists, while it happily does not represent probabilities in the present state of things, weakens instead of strengthening tragic effect; and, as we said, we regret that Mrs Browning has given this habit her strong sanction." BL 7 306-7

—motivation: "Men, like planets, have both a visible and an invisible history. The astronomer threads the darkness with strict deduction, accounting so for every visible arc in the wanderer's orbit; and the narrator of human actions, if he did his work with the same completeness, would have to thread the hidden pathways of feeling and thought which lead up to every moment of action, and to those moments of intense suffering which take the quality of action—like the cry of *Prometheus,* whose chained anguish seems a greater energy than the sea and sky he invokes and the deity he defies." DD 16 ep

—narration of travail: "That course of our life which I have indicated in a few sentences filled the space of years. So much misery—so slow and hideous a growth of hatred and sin, may be compressed into a sentence! And men judge of each other's lives through this summary medium. They epitomise the experience of their fellow-mortal, and pronounce judgment on him in neat syntax, and feel themselves wise and virtuous—conquerors over the temptations they define in well-selected predicates. Seven years of wretchedness glide glibly over the lips of the man who has never counted them out in moments of chill disappointment, of head and heart throbbings, of dread and vain wrestling, of remorse and despair." LV 2

—obscurity in prose: "All effort to understand mere expression is an expenditure of strength, which must enfeeble instead of aiding our apprehension of ideas. We can imagine, indeed, that to a German a lucid style must be a serious obstacle to comprehension; he has been too much used to the twilight of sentences, where the writer never sees the end from the beginning, to find his way readily in the broad daylight of clear writing; and we should think that to him **Macaulay** would be the toughest of all writers. But for the plain English intellect, we cannot agree . . . that its perception will be at all aided by obscurity." BL 2 602

—plagiarism: "To lay false claim to an invention or discovery which has an immediate market value; to vamp up a professedly new book of reference by stealing from the pages of one already produced at the cost of much labour and material; to copy somebody else's poem and send the manuscript to a magazine, or hand it about among friends as an original 'effusion;' to deliver an elegant

extract from a known writer as a piece of improvised eloquence:—these are the limits within which the dishonest pretence of originality is likely to get hissed or hooted and bring more or less shame on the culprit." TS 11 *And see* M:Idea—*appropriated*

—*egoistic:* " . . . to cite an author whose ideas may pass as higher currency under our own signature can have no object except the contradictory one of throwing the illumination over his figure when it is important to be seen oneself." TS 11

—*excusable:* " . . . one cannot give a genealogical introduction to every long-stored item of fact or conjecture that may happen to be a revelation for the large class of persons who are understood to judge soundly on a small basis of knowledge." TS 11

—*proof:* " . . . hardly any accusation is more difficult to prove, and more liable to be false, than that of a plagiarism which is the conscious theft of ideas and deliberate reproduction of them as original. The arguments on the side of acquittal are obvious and strong:—the inevitable coincidences of contemporary thinking; and our continual experience of finding notions turning up in our minds without any label on them to tell us whence they came . . . . Then, in relation to the elder authors, there is the difficulty first of learning and then of remembering exactly what has been wrought into the backward tapestry of the world's history, together with the fact that ideas acquired long ago reappear as the sequence of an awakened interest or a line of inquiry which is really new in us . . . . " TS 11

—*preface:* "Prefaces are privileged places; they are the antechambers in which the author, not having yet donned wig and gown, talks familiarly of any personal matter he thinks proper to acquaint you with." BL 7 323

—*reference works:* "Works of this convenient stamp, easily obtained and well nourished with matter, are felt to be like rich but unfashionable relations who are visited and received in privacy, and whose capital is used or inherited without any ostentatious insistence on their names and places of abode." TS 11

—*satire:* "**Young** is not a satirist of a high order. His satire has neither the terrible vigor, the lacerating energy of genuine indignation, nor the humor which owns loving fellowship with the poor human nature it laughs at; nor yet the personal bitterness which, as in **Pope**'s characters of *Sporus* and *Atticus*, insures those living touches by virtue of which the individual and particular in Art becomes the universal and immortal." PY 25

—*small:* "Males of more than one nation recur to my memory who produced from their pocket on the slightest encouragement a small pink or buff duodecimo pamphlet, wrapped in silver paper, as a present held ready for an intelligent reader. 'A mode of propagandism,' you remark in excuse; 'they wished to spread some useful corrective doctrine.' Not necessarily: the indoctrination aimed at was perhaps to convince you of their own talents by the sample of an 'Ode on **Shakspere**'s Birthday,' or a translation from **Horace**." TS 15

—*supernatural:* "Nothing is easier to write than a story the machinery of which is supernatural; nothing, perhaps, more difficult than to achieve complete success with such machinery. When all men believed in ghosts it was easy to make them sup full of horrors; now that few men believe in ghosts the task becomes difficult. The supernatural requires a strange union of imagination with reason. Probabilities have to be kept up amid all improbabilities. **Edgar Poe** is a master in this. **Wilkie Collins** promises to rival him . . . . " LWG

—*uneven quality:* "One is afraid to think of . . . the elbowing there might be at the day of judgment for those who ranked as authors, and brought volumes either in their hands or on trucks." DD 38

—*wit:* "Indeed it may be said that there is no really fine writing in which wit has not an implicit, if not an explicit action. The wit may never rise to the surface, it may never flame out into a witticism; but it helps to give brightness and transparency, it warns off from flights and exaggerations which verge on the ridiculous . . . . And it is eminently needed for this office in humorous writing; for, as humor has no limits imposed on it by its material, no law but its own exuberance, it is apt to become preposterous and wearisome unless checked by wit, which is the enemy of all monotony, of all lengthiness, of all exaggeration." HH 48-9

Communication

—*after an avowal of love:* "It was one of those dangerous moments when speech is at once sincere and deceptive—when feeling, rising high above its average depth, leaves flood-marks which are never reached again." MF V 4

—*angry:* "Human beings in moments of passionate reproach and denunciation, especially when their anger is on their own account, are never so wholly in the right that the person who has to wince cannot possibly protest against some unreasonableness or unfairness in their outburst." FH 42

—*animal:* " 'Poor dog!' said Dinah, patting the rough grey coat, 'I've a strange feeling about the dumb things as if they wanted to speak, and it was a trouble to 'em because they couldn't. I can't help being sorry for the dogs always, though perhaps there's no need. But they may well have more in them than they know how to make us understand, for we can't say half what we feel, with all our words.' " AB 11

—*at a meal:* "The progress of civilisation has made a breakfast or a dinner an easy and cheerful substitute for more troublesome and disagreeable ceremonies. We take a less gloomy view of our errors now our father confessor listens to us over his egg and coffee. We are more distinctly conscious that rude penances are out of the question for gentlemen in an enlightened age, and that mortal sin is not incompatible with an appetite for muffins; an assault on our pockets, which in more barbarous times would have been made in the brusque form of a pistol-shot, is quite a well-bred and smiling procedure now it has become a request for a loan thrown in as an easy parenthesis between the second and third glasses of claret." AB 16

—*between the generations:* "Age does not easily distinguish between what it needs to express and what youth needs to know—distance seeming to level the objects of memory . . . . " DD 60

—*confession of love:* "Express confessions give definiteness to memories that might more easily melt away without them . . . . " FH 32

—*contradictory:* " . . . perhaps he was not distinctly conscious that he was impelled to [sing] by a secret longing, running counter to all his self-confessed resolves, to deepen the hold he had on her. Watch your own speech, and notice how it is guided by your less conscious purposes, and you will understand that contradiction in Stephen." MF VI 13

—*irony:* "Perhaps some of the most terrible irony of the human lot is this of a deep truth coming to be uttered by lips that have no right to it." FH 42

—*learning by speaking* "It happened to Deronda at that moment, as it has often happened to others, that the need for speech made an epoch in resolve. His respect for the questioner would not let him decline to answer, and by the necessity to answer he found out the truth for himself." DD 60

—*news event:* "Imagine how some of us feel and behave when an event, not disagreeable, seems to be confirming and carrying out our private constructions. We say, 'What do you think?' in a pregnant tone to some innocent person who has not embarked his wisdom in the same boat with ours, and finds our information flat." DD 61

—*painful:* " . . . in all momentous communication likely to give pain we feel dependent on some preparatory turn of words or associations, some agreement of the other's mood with the probable effect of what we have to impart." DD 69

—*persuasive:* "Perhaps if he had been strong enough to persist in his determination to be the more because she was less, that evening might have had a better issue. If his energy could have borne down that check, he might still have wrought on Rosamond's vision and will. We cannot be sure that any natures, however inflexible or peculiar, will resist this effect from a more massive being than their own. They may be taken by storm and for the moment converted, becoming part of the soul which enwraps them in the ardour of its movement." MM 75

—*plaint:* " . . . he could not help being irritated by this plaint. It was not possible for poor Lisbeth to know how it affected Adam, any more than it is possible for a wounded dog to know how his moans affect the nerves of his master. Like all complaining women, she complained in the expectation of being soothed, and when Adam said nothing, she was only prompted to complain more bitterly." AB 10

—*preaching:* " . . . there is this sort of fascination in all sincere unpremeditated eloquence, which opens to one the inward drama of the speaker's emotions . . . . " AB 2

—*speaking truth to power:* " 'If I'm called upon to speak, sir,' said Mrs Poyser, after glancing at her husband with pity at his softness, 'you know better than me; but I don't see what the Chase Farm is t' us—we've cumber enough wi' our own farm. Not but what I'm glad to hear o' anybody respectable coming into the parish: there's some as ha' been brought in as hasn't been looked on i' that character.'

" 'You're likely to find Mr Thurle an excellent neighbour, I assure you: such a one as you will feel glad to have accommodated by the little plan I'm going to mention; especially as I hope you will find it as much to your own advantage as his.'

" 'Indeed, sir, if it's anything t' our advantage, it'll be the first offer o' the sort I've heared on. It's them as take advantage that get advantage i' this world, I think: folks have to wait long enough afore it's brought to 'em.'

" 'The fact is, Poyser,' said the Squire, ignoring Mrs Poyser's theory of worldly prosperity, 'there is too much dairy land, and too little plough land, on the Chase Farm, to suit

Thurle's purpose—indeed, he will only take the farm on condition of some change in it: his wife, it appears, is not a clever dairy-woman, like yours. Now, the plan I'm thinking of is to effect a little exchange. If you were to have the Hollow Pastures, you might increase your dairy, which must be so profitable under your wife's management; and I should request you, Mrs Poyser, to supply my house with milk, cream, and butter at the market prices. On the other hand, Poyser, you might let Thurle have the Lower and Upper Ridges, which really, with our wet seasons, would be a good riddance for you. There is much less risk in dairy land than corn land.'

"Mr Poyser was leaning forward, with his elbows on his knees, his head on one side, and his mouth screwed up—apparently absorbed in making the tips of his fingers meet so as to represent with perfect accuracy the ribs of a ship. He was much too acute a man not to see through the whole business, and to foresee perfectly what would be his wife's view of the subject; but he disliked giving unpleasant answers: unless it was on a point of farming practice, he would rather give up than have a quarrel, any day; and after all, it mattered more to his wife than to him. So after a few moments' silence, he looked up at her and said mildly, 'What dost say?'

"Mrs Poyser had had her eyes fixed on her husband with cold severity during his silence, but now she turned away her head with a toss, looked icily at the opposite roof of the cow-shed, and spearing her knitting together with the loose pin, held it firmly between her clasped hands.

" 'Say? Why, I say you may do as you like about giving up any o' your corn land, afore your lease is up, which it won't be for a year come next Michaelmas Lady Day, but I'll not consent to take more dairy work into my hands, either for love or money; and there's nayther love nor money here, as I can see, on'y other folks's love o' their selves, and the money as is to go into other folks's pockets. I know there's them as is born t' own the land, and them as is born to sweat on't,'—here Mrs Poyser paused to gasp a little—'and I know it's christened folks's duty to submit to their betters as far as flesh and blood 'ull bear it; but I'll not make a martyr o' myself, and wear myself to skin and bone, and worret myself as if I was a churn wi' butter a-coming in't, for no landlord in England, not if he was **King George** himself.'

" 'No, no, my dear Mrs Poyser, certainly not,' said the Squire, still confident in his own powers of persuasion, you must not overwork yourself; but don't you think your work will rather be lessened than increased in this way? There is so much milk required at the Abbey, that you will have little increase of cheese and butter making from the addition to your dairy; and I believe selling the milk is the most profitable way of disposing of dairy produce, is it not?'

" 'Ay, that's true,' said Mr Poyser, unable to repress an opinion on a question of farming profits, and forgetting that it was not in this case a purely abstract question.

" 'I daresay,' said Mrs Poyser bitterly, turning her head half-way towards her husband, and looking at the vacant arm-chair—'I daresay it's true for men as sit i' th' chimney-corner and make believe as everything's cut wi' ins an' outs to fit int' everything else. If you could make a pudding wi' thinking o' the batter, it' ud be easy getting dinner. How do I know whether the milk 'll be wanted constant? What's to make me sure as the house won't be put o' board-wage afore we're many months older, and then I may have to lie awake o' nights wi' twenty gallons o' milk on my mind—and Dingall 'ull take no more butter, let alone paying for it; and we must fat pigs till we're obliged to beg the butcher on our knees to buy 'em, and lose half of 'em wi' the measles. And there's the fetching and carrying, as 'ud be welly half a day's work for a man an' hoss—*that's* to be took out o' the profits, I reckon? But there's folks 'ud hold a sieve under the pump and expect to carry away the water.'

" 'That difficulty—about fetching and carrying—you will not have, Mrs Poyser,' said the Squire, who thought that this entrance into particulars indicated a distant inclination to compromise on Mrs Poyser's part—'Bethell will do that regularly with the cart and pony.'

" 'O, sir, begging your pardon, I've never been used t' having gentlefolks's servants coming about my back places, a-making love to both the gells at once, and keeping 'em with their hands on their hips listening to all manner o' gossip when they should be down on their knees a-scouring If we're to go to ruin, it shanna be wi' having our back kitchen turned into a public.'

" 'Well, Poyser,' said the Squire, shifting his tactics, and looking as if he thought Mrs Poyser had suddenly withdrawn from the proceedings and left the room, 'you can turn the Hollows into feeding-land. I can easily make another arrangement about supplying my house. And I shall not forget your readiness to accommodate your landlord as well as a neighbour. I know you will be glad to have your lease renewed for three years, when the present one expires; otherwise, I daresay Thurle, who is a man of some capital, would be glad to take both the farms, as they could be worked so well together. But I don't want to part with an old tenant like you.'

"To be thrust out of the discussion in this way would have been enough to complete Mrs Poyser's exasperation, even without the final threat. Her husband, really alarmed at the possibility of their leaving the old place where he had been bred and born—for he believed the old Squire had small spite enough for anything—was beginning a mild remonstrance explanatory of the inconvenience he should find in having to buy and sell more stock, with—

" 'Well, sir, I think as it's rether hard' . . . when Mrs Poyser burst in with the desperate determination to have her say out this once, though it were to rain notices to quit, and the only shelter were the workhouse.

" 'Then, sir, if I may speak—as, for all I'm a woman, and there's folks as thinks a woman's fool enough to stan' by an' look on while the men sign her soul away—I've a right to speak, for I make one quarter o' the rent, an' save th' other quarter—I say, if Mr Thurle's so ready to take farms under you, it's a pity but what he should take this, and see if he likes to live in a house wi' all the plagues o' Egypt in't—wi' the cellar full o' water, and frogs and toads hoppin' up the steps by dozens—and the floors rotten, and the rats and mice gnawing every bit o' cheese, and runnin' over our heads as we lie i' bed till we expect em to eat us up alive—as it's a mercy they hanna eat the children long ago. I should like to see if there's another tenant besides Poyser as 'ud put up wi' never having a bit o' repairs done till a place tumbles down—and not then on'y wi' begging and praying, and having to pay half—and being strung up wi' the rent as it's much if he gets enough out o' the land to pay, for all he's put his own money into the ground beforehand. See if you'll get a stranger to lead such a life here as that: a maggot must be born i' the rotten cheese to like it, I reckon. You may run away from my words, sir,' continued Mrs Poyser, following the old Squire beyond the door—for after the first moments of stunned surprise he had got up, and waving his hand towards her with a smile, had walked out towards his pony. But it was impossible for him to get away immediately for John was walking the pony up and down the yard, and was some distance from the causeway when his master beckoned.

" 'You may run away from my words, sir, and you may go spinnin' underhand ways o' doing us a mischief, for you've got old Harry to your friend, though nobody else is, but I tell you for once as we're not dumb creaturs to be abused and made money on by them as ha' got the lash i' their hands, for want o' knowing how t' undo the tackle. An' if I'm th' only one as speaks my mind, there's plenty o' the same way o' thinking i' this parish and the next to't, for your name's no better than a brimstone match in everybody's nose—if it isna two-three old folks as you think o' saving your soul by giving 'em a bit o' flannel and a drop o' porridge. An' you may be right i' thinking it'll take but little to save your soul, for it'll be the smallest savin' y' iver made, wi' all your scrapin'.'

"There are occasions on which two servant-girls and a waggoner may be a formidable audience, and as the Squire rode away on his black pony, even the gift of short-sightedness did not prevent him from being aware that Molly, and Nancy, and Tim were grinning not far from him. Perhaps he suspected that sour old John was grinning behind him—which was also the fact. Meanwhile the bull-dog, the black-and-tan terrier, Alick's sheep-dog, and the gander hissing at a safe distance from the pony's heels, carried out the idea of Mrs Poyser's solo in an impressive quartet.

"Mrs Poyser, however, had no sooner seen the pony move off than she turned round, gave the two hilarious damsels a look which drove them into the back kitchen, and unspearing her knitting, began to knit again with her usual rapidity, as she re-entered the house.

" 'Thee'st done it now,' said Mr Poyser, a little alarmed and uneasy, but not without some triumphant amusement at his wife's outbreak.

" 'Yis, I know I've done it,' said Mrs Poyser; 'but I've had my say out, and I shall be th' easier for't all my life. There's no pleasure i' living, if you're to be corked up for iver, and only dribble your mind out by the sly, like a leaky barrel. I shan't repent saying what I think, if I live to be as old as th' old Squire; and there's little likelihoods—for it seems as if them as aren't wanted here are th' only folks as aren't wanted i' th' other world.' " AB 32

—telegraph: "In fact, the evident tendency of things to contract personal communication within the narrowest limits makes us tremble lest some further development of the electric telegraph should reduce us to a society of mutes, or to a sort of insects, communicating by ingenious antennae of our own invention." WF 455

—in writing: "In reading unwelcome news, instead of hearing it, there is the advantage that one avoids a hasty expression of impatience which may afterwards be repented of. Deronda dreaded that verbal collision which makes otherwise pardonable feeling lastingly offensive." DD 69

Conversation

—about oneself: "But how can a man avoid himself as a subject in conversation? And he must make some sort of decent toilet in words, as in cloth and linen. Lush's listener was not severe: a member of Parliament could allow for the necessities of verbal toilet; and the dialogue went on without any change of mutual estimate." DD 25

—accusation: "And now she felt a tingling shame at the words of ignominy she had cast at Tito—'Have you robbed some one else who is *not* dead?' To have had such words wrung from her—to have uttered them to her husband seemed a degradation of her whole life. Hard speech between those who have loved is hideous in the memory, like the sight of greatness and beauty sunk into vice and rags." R 36

—admonition: " . . . a full-fed fountain will be generous with its waters even in the rain, when they are worse than useless, and a fine fount of admonition is apt to be equally irrepressible." MM 13

—argument: "There are answers which, in turning away wrath, only send it to the other end of the room, and to have a discussion coolly waived when you feel that justice is all on your own side is even more exasperating in marriage than in philosophy." MM 29

—aspect of success: " 'But pardon me . . . said **Macchiavelli**, sticking his thumbs into his belt, and speaking with that cool enjoyment of exposition which surmounts every other force in discussion . . . . " R 45

—automatic: " . . . much of human speech is mere purposeless impulse or habit . . . . " AB 5

—awkward: "When a conversation has taken a wrong turn for us, we only get farther and farther into the swamp of awk wardness." MM 14

—bore: " . . . I have usually found that it is the rather dull person who appears to be disgusted with his contemporaries because they are not always strikingly original, and to satisfy whom the party at a country house should have included the prophet **Isaiah**, **Plato**, **Francis Bacon**, and **Voltaire**. It is always your heaviest bore who is astonished at the tameness of modern celebrities: naturally; for a little of his company has reduced them to a state of flaccid fatigue." TS 5

—change of subject: "Besides, the introduction of a new subject after very momentous words have passed, and are still dwelling on the mind, is necessarily a sort of concussion, shaking us into a new adjustment of ourselves." FH 49

—conventionalities: "Still, it must happen to her as to every one else to speak of many subjects on which the best things were said long ago, and in conversation with a person who has been newly introduced those well-worn themes naturally recur as a further development of salutations and preliminary media of understanding, such as pipes, chocolate, or mastic-chewing, which serve to confirm the impression that our new acquaintance is on a civilised footing and has enough regard for formulas to save us from shocking outbursts of individualism, to which we are always exposed with the tamest bear or baboon." TS 5

—criticism: "Thin ladies, who take little exercise, and whose livers are not strong enough to bear stimulants, are so extremely critical about one's personal habits!" SF 4

"In London drums and clubs he was spoken of abundantly as one who had written ridiculously . . . the leaders of conversation, whether Christians, Jews, infidels, or of any other confession except the confession of ignorance, pronouncing him shallow and indiscreet if not presumptuous and absurd." TS 3

—an effort: " . . . the talk seemed more of an effort to her: that might have come from the gradual companionship, in which repetition is not felt to be as desirable as novelty." FH 45

—explanation: "But let the wise be warned against too great readiness at explanation: it multiplies the sources of mistake, lengthening the sum for reckoners sure to go wrong." MM 45

—farewell: "It is certainly trying to a man's dignity to reappear when he is not expected to do so: a first farewell has pathos in it, but to come back for a second lends an opening to comedy . . . . " MM 62

—frustration: " 'Tito, it would not be useless for us to speak openly,' said Romola, with the sort of exasperation that comes from using living muscle against some lifeless insurmountable resistance." R 48

"Romola was mute. To speak was only like rushing with bare breast against a shield." R 48

—*on horseback:* "That is the great advantage of dialogue on horseback; it can be merged any minute into a trot or a canter, and one might have escaped from **Socrates** himself in the saddle." AB 9

—*intimates:* "When people are well known to each other, they talk rather of what befalls them externally, leaving their feelings and sentiments to be inferred." LV 2

—*misguided:* "Few friendly remarks are more annoying than the information that we are always seeming to do what we never mean to do." DD 32

—*permissible insincerity:* "A little unpremeditated insincerity must be indulged under the stress of social intercourse. The talk even of an honest man must often represent merely his wish to be inoffensive or agreeable rather than his genuine opinion or feeling on the matter in hand. His thought, if uttered, might be wounding; or he has not the ability to utter it with exactness and snatches at a loose paraphrase; or he has really no genuine thought on the question and is driven to fill up the vacancy by borrowing the remarks in vogue. These are the winds and currents we have all to steer amongst, and they are often too strong for our truthfulness or our wit. Let us not bear too hardly on each other for this common incidental frailty, or think that we rise superior to it by dropping all considerateness and deference." TS 5

—*politeness:* "[She] still made her morning greetings with that finished easy politeness and consideration of tone which to rougher people seems like affection." FH 45

—*restful:* "We mortals should chiefly like to talk to each other out of goodwill and fellowship, not for the sake of hearing revelations or being stimulated by witticisms . . . . It is right and meet that there should be an abundant utterance of good sound commonplaces. Part of an agreeable talker's charm is that he lets them fall continually with no more than their due emphasis. Giving a pleasant voice to what we are all well assured of, makes a sort of wholesome air for more special and dubious remark to move in." TS 5

—*reticence:* "Comprehensive talkers are apt to be tiresome when we are not athirst for information, but, to be quite fair, we must admit that superior reticence is a good deal due to the lack of matter. Speech is often barren; but silence also does not necessarily brood over a full nest. Your still fowl, blinking at you without remark, may all the while be sitting on one addled nest-egg; and when it takes to cackling, will have nothing to announce but that addled delusion." FH 16

"If you have any reason for not indulging a wish to speak to a fair woman, it is a bad plan to look long at her back: the wish to see what it screens becomes the stronger. There may be a very sweet smile on the other side." DD 35

—*revealing:* "Will was not without his intentions to be always generous, but our tongues are little triggers which have usually been pulled before general intentions can be brought to bear." MM 37

—*rustic:* "The jocose talk of hay-makers is best at a distance; like those clumsy bells round the cows' necks, it has rather a coarse sound when it comes close, and may even grate on your ears painfully; but heard from far off, it mingles very prettily with the other joyous sounds of nature. Men's muscles move better when their souls are making merry music, though their merriment is of a poor blundering sort, not at all like the merriment of birds." AB 19

—*talker:* "One who talks too much, hindering the rest of the company from taking their turn, and apparently seeing no reason why they should not rather desire to know his opinion or experience in relation to all subjects, or at least to renounce the discussion of any topic where he can make no figure, has never been praised for this industrious monopoly of work which others would willingly have shared in. However various and brilliant his talk may be, we suspect him of impoverishing us by excluding the contributions of other minds, which attract our curiosity the more because he has shut them up in silence . . . . " TS 14

—*trivia overemphasized:* "Considered purely as a matter of information, it cannot any longer be important for us to learn that a British subject included in the last census holds **Shakspere** to be supreme in the presentation of character; still, it is as admissible for any one to make this statement about himself as to rub his hands and tell you that the air is brisk, if only he will let it fall as a matter of course, with a parenthetic lightness, and not announce his adhesion to a commonplace with an emphatic insistence, as if it were a proof of singular insight." TS 5

—*uneven quality:* " . . . 'he does not talk equally well on all subjects.'

" 'I should think none but disagreeable people do,' said Celia, in her usual purring way. 'They must be very dreadful to live with. Only think! at breakfast and always.' " MM 4

—*useless question:* "That idea . . . prompted the sort of question which often comes without any other apparent reason than the faculty of speech and the not knowing what to do with it." DD 9

—*villagers:* "The men were chiefly gathered in the neighbourhood of the blacksmith's shop. But do not imagine them gathered in a knot. Villagers never swarm: a whisper is unknown among them, and they seem almost as incapable of an undertone as a cow or a stag. Your true rustic turns his back on his interlocutor, throwing a question over his shoulder as if he meant to run away from the answer, and walking a step or two farther off when the interest of the dialogue culminates." AB 2

—*wallflower:* "Was it in the least true that I was wiser than several of my friends who made an excellent figure, and were perhaps praised a little beyond their merit? Is the ugly unready man in the corner, outside the current of conversation, really likely to have a fairer view of things than the agreeable talker, whose success strikes the unsuccessful as a repulsive example of forwardness and conceit?" TS 1

Correspondence

—*delayed:* "The bias of human nature to be slow in correspondence triumphs even over the present quickening in the general pace of things: what wonder then that in 1832 old Sir Godwin Lydgate was slow to write a letter which was of consequence to others rather than to himself?" MM 65

—*handwriting:* "At that time the opinion existed that it was beneath a gentleman to write legibly, or with a hand in the least suitable to a clerk. Fred wrote the lines demanded in a hand as gentlemanly as that of any viscount or bishop of the day: the vowels were all alike and the consonants only distinguishable as turning up or down, the strokes had a blotted solidity and the letters disdained to keep the line—in short, it was a manuscript of that venerable kind easy to interpret when you know beforehand what the writer means." MM 56

—*irksome:* "But Grandcourt hated writing: even writing a note was a bore to him, and he had long been accustomed to have all his writing done by Lush. We know that there are persons who will forego their own obvious interest rather than do anything so disagreeable as to write letters; and it is not probable that these imperfect utilitarians would rush into manuscript and syntax on a difficult subject in order to save another's feelings." DD 48

—*lost and found:* "Who shall tell what may be the effect of writing? If it happens to have been cut in stone, though it lie face downmost for ages on a forsaken beach, or 'rest quietly under the drums and tramplings of many conquests,' it may end by letting us into the secret of usurpations and other scandals gossiped about long empires ago:—this world being apparently a huge whispering-gallery. Such conditions are often minutely represented in our petty lifetimes. As the stone which has been kicked by generations of clowns may come by curious little links of effect under the eyes of a scholar, through whose labours it may at last fix the date of invasions and unlock religions, so a bit of ink and paper which has long been an innocent wrapping or stop-gap may at last be laid open under the one pair of eyes which have knowledge enough to turn it into the opening of a catastrophe. To *Uriel* watching the progress of planetary history from the Sun, the one result would be just as much of a coincidence as the other." MM 41

Fiction

—*anti-hero:* " . . . perhaps I am doing a bold thing to bespeak your sympathy on behalf of a man who was so very far from remarkable—a man whose virtues were not heroic, and who had no undetected crime within his breast; who had not the slightest mystery hanging about him, but was palpably and unmistakably commonplace; who was not even in love, but had had that complaint favourably many years ago." SF 4

—*an art:* "Fiction is art, and like all other art ought not to be undertaken in the absence of an artistic impulse. What should we say to a man who became a painter simply that he might familiarize the public with mediæval costumes?" BL 7 323.

—*the ideal:* "Mrs Farthingale, for example, who prefers the ideal in fiction; to whom tragedy means ermine tippets, adultery, and murder; and comedy, the adventures of some personage who is quite a 'character.' " SF 4

—*short stories:* " 'We no longer travel, we *arrive at places,*' says **Thackeray**, regretting the incident and variety of the old-fashioned journey; and perhaps there is the same sort of disadvantage in short tales, which are always bringing one to the shock or the terminus of a *dénouement.*" BL 1 307

Notable individuals

—*George Gordon, Lord Byron:* "Who that has a spark of generous feeling, that rejoices in the presence of good in a fellow-being, has not dwelt with pleasure on the thought that Lord Byron's unhappy career was ennobled and purified towards its close by a high and sympathetic purpose, by honest and energetic efforts for his fellow-men? Who has not read with deep emotion those last pathetic lines, beautiful as the after-glow of sunset, in which love and resignation are mingled with something of a melancholy heroism. Who has not lingered with compassion over the dying scene at Missolonghi—the sufferer's inability to make his farewell messages of love intelligible, and the last long hour of silent pain?" TE 87

—*Geoffrey Chaucer:* ". . . with [Chaucer], as with all true poets, the minutest details of language are as essential to his creation as the skin to the beauty of the human form." BL 1 300

—*William Cowper:* "On some grounds, we might have anticipated a more morbid view of things from Cowper than from [**Edward**] **Young**. Cowper's religion was dogmatically the more gloomy, for he was a Calvinist. . . . There was deep and unusual sadness involved in Cowper's personal lot . . . .

"Yet see how a lovely, sympathetic nature manifests itself in spite of creed and circumstance! Where is the poem that surpasses the 'Task' in the genuine love it breathes, at once towards inanimate and animate existence—in truthfulness of perception and sincerity of presentation—in the calm gladness that springs from a delight in objects for their own sake, without self-reference —in divine sympathy with the lowliest pleasures, with the most short-lived capacity for pain?

"Here is no railing at the earth's 'melancholy map,' but the happiest lingering over her simplest scenes with all the fond minuteness of attention that belongs to love; no pompous rhetoric about the inferiority of the 'brutes,' but a warm plea on their behalf against man's inconsiderateness and cruelty, and a sense of enlarged happiness from their companionship in enjoyment: no vague rant about human misery and human virtue, but that close and vivid presentation of particular sorrows and privations, or particular deeds and misdeeds, which is the direct road to the emotions.

"How Cowper's exquisite mind falls with the mild warmth of morning sunlight on the commonest objects, at once disclosing every detail and investing every detail with beauty! No object is too small to prompt his song—not the sooty film on the bars, or the spoutless teapot holding a bit of mignonette that serves to cheer the dingy town-lodging with a 'hint that Nature lives'; and yet his song is never trivial, for he is alive to small objects, not because his mind is narrow, but because his glance is clear and his heart is large.

"Instead of trying to edify us by supercilious allusions to the 'brutes' and the 'stalls,' he interests us in that tragedy of the henroost when the thief has wrenched the door—

> When Chanticleer amidst his harem sleeps
> *In unsuspecting pomp* . . . .

in the patient cattle, that on the winter's morning

> Mourn in corners where the fence
> Screens them, and seem half petrified to sleep
> *In unrecumbent sadness* . . . .

in the little squirrel, that, surprised by him in his woodland walk,

> At once, swift as a bird,
> Ascends the neighboring beech; there whisks his brush,
> And perks his ears, and stamps, and cries aloud,
> With all the prettiness of feigned alarm
> And anger insignificantly fierce.

And then he passes into reflection, not with curt apothegm and snappish reproof, but with that melodious flow of utterance which belongs to thought when it is carried in a stream of feeling . . . . His large and tender heart embraces the most every-day forms of human life: the carter driving his team through the wintry storm; the cottager's wife who, painfully nursing the embers on her hearth, while her infants 'sit cowering o'er the sparks,'

> Retires, content to quake, so they be warmed

or the villager, with her little ones, going out to pick

> A cheap but wholesome salad from the brook

and he compels our colder natures to follow his in its manifold sympathies, not by exhortations, not by telling us to meditate at midnight, to 'indulge' the thought of death, or to ask ourselves how we shall 'weather an eternal night,' *but by presenting to us the object of his compassion truthfully and lovingly.* And when he handles greater themes, when he takes a wider survey, and considers the men or the deeds which have a direct influence on the welfare of communities and nations, there is the same unselfish warmth of feeling, the same scrupulous truthfulness. He is never vague in his remonstrance or his satire; but puts his finger on some particular vice or folly, which excites his indignation or 'dissolves his heart in pity,' because of some specific injury it does to his fellow-man or to a sacred cause." ¶PY 42-4

—*Charles Dickens:* "We have one great novelist who is gifted with the utmost power of rendering the external traits of our town population; and if he could give us their psychological character—their conceptions of life, and their emotions—with the same truth as their idiom and manners, his books would be the greatest contribution Art has ever made to the awakening of social sympathies. But while he can copy *Mrs Plornish*'s colloquial style with the delicate accuracy of a sun-picture, while there is the same startling inspiration in his description of the gestures and phrases of 'Boots,' as in the speeches of **Shakespeare**'s mobs or numskulls, he scarcely ever passes from the humorous and external to the emotional and tragic, without becoming as transcendent in his unreality as he was a moment before in his artistic truthfulness.

"But for the precious salt of his humor, which compels him to reproduce external traits that serve, in some degree, as a corrective to his frequently false psychology, his preternaturally virtuous poor children and artisans, his melodramatic boatmen and courtesans, would be as noxious as **Eugène Sue**'s idealized proletaires in encouraging the miserable fallacy that high morality and refined sentiment can grow out of harsh social relations, ignorance, and want; or that the working classes are in a condition to enter at once into a millennial state of *altruism,* wherein every one is caring for every one else, and no one for himself." NH 125-6

—Henry Fielding: "A great historian, as he insisted on calling himself [GE slips here: he may have called himself an historian, but he did not call himself "great"], who had the happiness to be dead a hundred and twenty years ago, and so to take his place among the colossi whose huge legs our living pettiness is observed to walk under, glories in his copious remarks and digressions as the least imitable part of his work, and especially in those initial chapters to the successive books of his history, where he seems to bring his arm-chair to the proscenium and chat with us in all the lusty ease of his fine English." MM 15

—Blaise Pascal: "The manuscripts of Pascal show that many of the *Pensées,* which are commonly supposed to be raw materials for a great work on religion, were remodelled again and again, in order to bring them to the highest degree of terseness and finish, which would hardly have been the case if they had only been part of a quarry for a greater production. Thoughts which are merely collected as materials, as stones out of which a building is to be erected, are not cut into facets, and polished like amethysts or emeralds . . . .

"Many of them have an epigrammatic piquancy, which was just the thing to charm a circle of vivacious and intelligent women; they seem to come from a La Rochefoucauld, who has been dipped over again in philosophy and wit, and received a new layer." WF 467

—François de Marsillac, duc de La Rochefoucauld: " . . . at last, La Rochefoucauld began to be conscious of his pre-eminence in the circle of maxim-mongers, and thought of a wider audience. Thus grew up the famous 'Maxims,' about which little need be said. Every one is now convinced, or professes to be convinced, that, as to form, they are perfect, and that as to matter, they are at once undeniably true and miserably false; true as applied to that condition of human nature in which the selfish instincts are still dominant, false if taken as a representation of all the elements and possibilities of human nature. We think La Rochefoucauld himself wavered as to their universality, and that this wavering is indicated in the qualified form of some of the maxims; it occasionally struck him that the shadow of virtue must have a substance, but he had never grasped that substance—it had never been present to his consciousness." WF 468

—Jean-Jacques Rousseau: "But the incompleteness which comes of self-ignorance may be compensated by self-betrayal. A man who is affected to tears in dwelling on the generosity of his own sentiments makes me aware of several things not included under those terms. Who has sinned more against those duteous reticences than Jean Jacques? Yet half our impressions of his character come not from what he means to convey, but from what he unconsciously enables us to discern." TS 1

Oratory

—crescendo: "Mrs Holt, like all orators, had waxed louder and more energetic, ceasing to propel her arguments, and being propelled by them." FH 43

—delight: "The sublime delight of truthful speech to one who has the great gift of uttering it, will make itself felt even through the pangs of sorrow." FH 46

—easy part: "The least lucid and impressive of orators may be perfectly successful in showing us the weak points of his grammar." TS 1

—of a great preacher: " 'What miracle showest thou?' Slowly at first, then faster and faster, that fatal demand had been swelling in **Savonarola**'s ear, provoking a response, outwardly in the declaration that at the fitting time the miracle would come; inwardly in the faith—not unwavering, for what faith is so?—that if the need for miracle became urgent,,the work he had before him was too great for the Divine power to leave it halting. His faith wavered, but not his speech: it is the lot of every man who has to speak for the satisfaction of the crowd, that he must often speak in virtue of yesterday's faith, hoping it will come back to-morrow." R 62

—on the hustings: "But, perhaps, the moment of most diffusive pleasure from public speaking is that in which the speech ceases and the audience can turn to commenting on it. The one speech, sometimes uttered under great responsibility as to missiles and other consequences, has given a text to

twenty speakers who are under no responsibility. Even in the days of duelling a man was not challenged for being a bore, nor does this quality apparently hinder him from being much invited to dinner, which is the great index of social responsibility in a less barbarous age." FH 19

—irksome: "There is hardly any mental misery worse than that of having our own serious phrases, our own rooted beliefs, caricatured by a charlatan or a hireling." FH 11

—its secret: " 'The secret of oratory lies, not in saying new things, but in saying things with a certain power that moves the hearers—without which . . . your speaker deserves to be called, "non *o*ratorem sed *a*ratorem."* And, according to that test, Fra **Girolamo** [**Savonarola**] is a great orator.' " R 16 *"not an orator but a scolder" *GE attributes this speech to her fictional Niccolò Macchiavelli [sic]*

—under attack: "In the career of a great public orator who yields himself to the inspiration of the moment, that conflict of selfish and unselfish emotion which in most men is hidden in the chamber of the soul, is brought into terrible evidence: the language of the inner voices is written out in letters of fire." R 52.

Poet and Poetry

—bad: "The same skies that make our garden flowers flourish encourage the growth of weeds, and so a time that produces real poets has generally a large crop of versifiers, whom the Reviewer must resignedly expect as so much inevitable chickweed or dandelion which will spring up round the heliotropes and anemones. On laying down **Matthew Arnold**, for example, we had to take up Mr. **A. M. Morgan** . . . . " BL 1 300

—bliss: "But as a poet, who sweet verses saith

Within his soul, and joys in music there,
Nor seeks another heaven, nor can bear
Disturbing pleasures . . . . " HL 502-5

—condescension: "If you had questioned him closely, he would perhaps have confessed that he did think something better might be done in the way of Eclogues and Georgics, or of Odes and Epodes, and that to his mind poetry was something very different from what had hitherto been known under that name." TS 4

—fantastic: "The fantastic or the boldly imaginative poet may be as sincere as the most realistic: he is true to his own sensibilities or inward vision, and in his wildest flights he never breaks loose from his criterion—the truth of his own mental state." PY 30

—format: "Poets, of all writers, should be given to us in a portable shape; we study them less at our desk than under the branching shade of a beech or a chestnut, or when we are resting in our easy chair from the fatigues of prosaic life, or still more prosaic learning; and in such circumstances we shudder at a double-columned royal octavo, or at an edition which scatters our favourite passages in majestic type through ten or twelve cumbrous volumes." BL 1 299

—greatness: "Now, the products of poetic Art are great in proportion as they result from the immediate prompting of innate power, and not from labored obedience to a theory or rule; and the presence of genius or innate prompting is directly opposed to the perpetual consciousness of a rule. The action of faculty is imperious, and supersedes the reflection *why* it should act." PY 40

—heart: "Listen, little one.

Juan is not a living man by himself:
His life is breathed in him by other men,
And they speak out of him. He is their voice.
Juan's own life he gave once quite away.
Pepíta's lover sang that song—not Juan.
We old, old poets, if we kept our hearts,
Should hardly know them from another man's.
They shrink to make room for the many more
We keep within us." SG I iv

—iteration: " . . . that device of iteration which, under proper restraint, forms the delicately-shaded boundary where lyric poetry melts into music proper." BL 6 567

—poetry in life: "And perhaps poetry and romance are as plentiful as ever in the world except for those phlegmatic natures who I suspect would in any age have regarded them as a dull form of erroneous thinking. They exist very easily in the same room with the microscope and even in railway carriages: what banishes them is the vacuum in gentlemen and lady passengers. How should all the apparatus of heaven and earth, from the farthest firmament to the tender bosom of the mother who nourished us, make poetry for a mind that has no movements of awe and tenderness, no sense of fellowship which thrills from the near to the distant, and back again from the distant to the near?" DD 19

—poet's attributes: " 'To be a poet is to have a soul so quick to discern that no shade of quality escapes it, and so quick to feel, that discernment is but a hand playing with a finely-ordered variety on the chords of emotion—a soul in which knowledge passes instantaneously into feeling, and feeling flashes back as a new organ of knowledge. One may have that condition by fits only.' " MM 22

—rhyme: "[**Young**'s] want of mastery in rhyme is especially a drawback on the effect of his Satires; for epigrams and witticisms are peculiarly susceptible to the intrusion of a superfluous word, or to an inversion which implies constraint. Here, even more than elsewhere, the art that conceals art is an absolute requisite, and to have a witticism presented to us in limping or cumbrous rhythm is as counteractive to any electrifying effect as to see the tentative grimaces by which a comedian prepares a grotesque countenance. We discern the process, instead of being startled by the result." PY 25

—sensibility: see M:Sensibility*—poet's*

And see V, page 229 in Volume I

The Press

—critic: "Pepin made for himself a necessity of writing (and getting printed) before he had considered whether he had the knowledge or belief that would furnish eligible matter. At first perhaps the necessity galled him a little, but it is now as easily borne, nay, is as irrepressible a habit as the outpouring of inconsiderate talk. He is gradually being condemned to have no genuine impressions, no direct consciousness of enjoyment or the reverse from the quality of what is before him: his perceptions are continually arranging themselves in forms suitable to a printed judgment, and hence they will often turn out to be as much to the purpose if they are written without any direct contemplation of the object, and are guided by a few external conditions which serve to classify it for him. In this way he is irrevocably losing the faculty of accurate mental vision: having bound himself to express judgments which will satisfy some other demands than that of veracity, he has blunted his perceptions by continual preoccupation." TS 14

"It is apparently too often a congenial task to write severe words about the transgressions committed by men of genius, especially when the censor has the advantage of being himself a man of no genius, so that those transgressions seem to him quite gratuitous; he, forsooth, never lacerated any one by his wit, or gave irresistible piquancy to a coarse allusion, and his indignation is not mitigated by any knowledge of the temptation that lies in transcendent power. We are also apt to measure what a gifted man has done by our arbitrary conception of what he might have done, rather than by a comparison of his actual doings with our own or those of other ordinary men. We make ourselves over-zealous agents of heaven, and demand that our brother should bring usurious interest for his five Talents, forgetting that it is less easy to manage five Talents than two." HH 52

—handbill: "Already handbills were in circulation; some presenting, in large print, the alternative of justice on the conspirators or ruin to the Republic; others in equally large print urging the observance of the law and the granting of the Appeal. Round these jutting islets of black capitals there were lakes of smaller characters setting forth arguments less necessary to be read: for it was an opinion entertained at that time (in the first flush of triumph at the discovery of printing), that there was no argument more widely convincing than question-begging phrases in large type." R 59

—irresponsible: "And though we were to find among that class of journalists who live by recklessly reporting injurious rumours, insinuating the blackest motives in opponents, descanting at large and with an air of infallibility on dreams which they both find and interpret, and stimulating bad feeling between nations by abusive writing which is as empty of real conviction as the rage of a pantomime king, and would be ludicrous if its effects did not make it appear diabolical—though we were to find among these a man who was benignancy itself in his own circle, a healer of private differences, a soother in private calamities, let us pronounce him nevertheless flagrantly immoral, a root of hideous cancer in the commonwealth, turning the channels of instruction into feeders of social and political disease." TS 16

—new journalism: "As the old coach-roads have sunk into disuse through the creation of railways, so journalism tends more and more to divert information from the channel of conversation into the channel of the Press; no one is satisfied with a more circumscribed audience than that very indeterminate abstraction 'the public,' and men find a vent for their opinions not in talk, but in 'copy.' " WF 455

—provincial town: " . . . which had its own newspaper press, with the usual divisions of political partisanship and the usual varieties of literary criticism—the florid and allusive, the *staccato* and peremptory, the clairvoyant and prophetic, the safe and pattern-phrased, or what one might call 'the many-a-long-day style.' " TS 15

Rumour and Report

—broad brush: "The enthusiasms of the world are not to be stimulated by a commentary in small and subtle characters which alone can tell the whole truth . . . . " FH 37

—characterized: "That talkative maiden, Rumour, though in the interest of art she is figured as a youthful winged beauty with

flowing garments, soaring above the heads of men, and breathing world-thrilling news through a gracefully-curved trumpet, is in fact a very old maid, who puckers her silly face by the fireside, and really does no more than chirp a wrong guess or a lame story into the ear of a fellow-gossip; all the rest of the work attributed to her is done by the ordinary working of those passions against which men pray in the Litany, with the help of a plentiful stupidity against which we have never yet had any authorized form of prayer." FH 8

—conjecture: "Everybody liked better to conjecture how the thing was, than simply to know it; for conjecture soon became more confident than knowledge, and had a more liberal allowance for the incompatible. Even the more definite scandal concerning Bulstrode's earlier life was, for some minds, melted into the mass of mystery, as so much lively metal to be poured out in dialogue, and to take such fantastic shapes as heaven pleased." MM 71

—gossip: "Gossip is a sort of smoke that comes from the dirty tobacco-pipes of those who diffuse it: it proves nothing but the bad taste of the smoker." DD 13

—new development: "Naturally, people did not tell each other all they felt and thought about young Grandcourt's advent: on no subject is this openness found prudentially practicable—not even on the generation of acids, or the destination of the fixed stars; for either your contemporary with a mind turned towards the same subjects may find your ideas ingenious and forestall you in applying them, or he may have other views on acids and fixed stars, and think ill of you in consequence." DD 9

—news passed on: "News is often dispersed as thoughtlessly and effectively as that pollen which the bees carry off (having no idea how powdery they are) when they are buzzing in search of their particular nectar." MM 59

—nuance: "Nice distinctions are troublesome. It is much easier to say that a thing is black, than to discriminate the particular shade of brown, blue, or green, to which it really belongs. It is so much easier to make up your mind that your neighbour is good for nothing, than to enter into all the circumstances that would oblige you to modify that opinion." SF 4

—scandal: " 'People say what they like to say, not what they have chapter and verse for,' said Brooke, becoming acute about the truths that lay on the side of his own wishes." MM 49

Secret

—guilty: see S:Guilt and Shame*—secret*

—impossible to keep: "I never had the virtue to hide aught [says the poet],
Save what a man is whipped for publishing.
I'm no more reticent than the voluble air—
Dote on disclosure—never could contain
The latter half of all my sentences,
But for the need to utter the beginning.
My lust to tell is so importunate
That it abridges every other vice,
And makes me temperate for want of time." SG III

—mode of discovery: "Secrets are rarely betrayed or discovered according to any programme our fear has sketched out. Fear is almost always haunted by terrible dramatic scenes, which recur in spite of the best argued probabilities against them; and during a year that Maggie had had the burthen of concealment on her mind, the possibility of discovery had continually presented itself under the form of a sudden meeting with her father or Tom when she was walking with Philip in the Red Deeps. She was aware that this was not one of the most likely events; but it was the scene that most completely symbolised her inward dread. Those slight indirect suggestions which are dependent on apparently trivial coincidences and incalculable states of mind are the favourite machinery of Fact, but are not the stuff in which imagination is apt to work." MF V 5

—pairing off: "Since we cannot tell a man his own secrets, the restraint of being in his company often breeds a desire to pair off in conversation with some more ignorant person . . . . " DD 36

Smile

—the Duke's:

"A true hidalgo's smile,
That gives much favor, but beseeches none.
His smile is sweetened by his gravity:
It comes like dawn upon Sierra snows,
Seeming more generous for the coldness gone;
Breaks from the calm—a sudden opening flower
On dark deep water: now a chalice shut,
A mystic shrine, the next a full-rayed star,
Thrilling, pulse-quickening as a living word." SG I i

Theatre

—distance: "Perspective, as its inventor remarked, is a beautiful thing. What horrors of damp huts, where human beings languish, may not become picturesque through aerial distance! What hymning of cancerous vices may we not languish over as sublimest art in the safe remoteness of a strange lan-

guage and artificial phrase! Yet we keep a repugnance to rheumatism and other painful effects when presented in our personal experience." DD 14

And see H:Manners—*stage and reality*

Wit and Humour

—*in ancient times:* "Many a witty man will remember how, in his school-days, a practical joke, more or less **Rabelais**ian, was for him the *ne plus ultra* of the ludicrous. It seems to have been the same with the boyhood of mankind. The fun of early races was, we fancy, of the after-dinner kind—loud-throated laughter over the wine-cup, taken too little account of in sober moments to enter as an element into their Art, and differing as much from the laughter of a **Chamfort** or a **Sheridan** as the gastronomic enjoyment of an ancient Briton, whose dinner had no other 'removes' than from acorns to beechmast and back again to acorns, differed from the subtle pleasures of the palate experienced by his turtle-eating descendant. It was their lot to live seriously through stages which to later generations were to become comedy . . . . " HH 46

—*class distinction:* "The last thing in which the cultivated man can have community with the vulgar is their jocularity; and we can hardly exhibit more strikingly the wide gulf which separates him from them than by comparing the object which shakes the diaphragm of a coal-heaver with the highly complex pleasure derived from a real witticism." HH 46

—*essential: see* Authorship—*wit*

—*medieval:* "A great deal of humor may coexist with a great deal of barbarism, as we see in the middle ages; but the strongest flavor of the humor in such cases will come, not from sympathy, but more probably from triumphant egoism or intolerance; at best it will be the love of the ludicrous exhibiting itself in illustrations of successful cunning and of the *lex talionis* . . . . " HH 47

—*origination of humor:* "Strange as the genealogy may seem, the original parentage of that wonderful and delicious mixture of *fun, fancy, philosophy, and feeling* which constitutes modern humor, was probably the cruel mockery of a savage at the writhings of a suffering enemy . . . . " HH 47-8 [*emphasis added; note this exceedingly rare example of prose alliteration in GE.*]

—*practical joke:* "Again, it is impossible to deny a high degree of humor to many practical jokes, but no sympathetic nature can enjoy them." HH 47

—*in youth:* "That any high order of wit is exceedingly complex, and demands a ripe and strong mental development, has one evidence in the fact that we do not find it in boys at all in proportion to their manifestation of other powers. Clever boys generally aspire to the heroic and poetic rather than the comic, and the crudest of all their efforts are their jokes." HH 46

Words

"We learn *words* by rote, but not their meaning; *that* must be paid for with our lifeblood, and printed in the subtle fibres of our nerves." LV 2

—*abstractions:* "It is an interesting branch of psychological observation to note the images that are habitually associated with abstract or collective terms—what may be called the picture-writing of the mind, which it carries on concurrently with the more subtle symbolism of language. Perhaps the fixity or variety of these associated images would furnish a tolerably fair test of the amount of concrete knowledge and experience which a given word represents, in the minds of two persons who use it with equal familiarity." NH 122

—*burning:* "Every word that Klesmer had said seemed to have been branded into her memory, as most words are which bring with them a new set of impressions and make an epoch for us." DD 23

—*epithet:* "Ganymede had been first introduced into the writing world as remarkably young, and it was no exceptional consequence that the first deposit of information about him held its ground against facts which, however open to observation, were not necessarily thought of. It is not so easy, with our rates and taxes and need for economy in all directions, to cast away an epithet or remark that turns up cheaply, and to go in expensive search after more genuine substitutes. There is high Homeric precedent for keeping fast hold of an epithet under all changes of circumstance; and so the precocious author . . . heard the echoes repeating 'Young Ganymede' when an illiterate beholder at a railway station would have given him forty years at least." TS 12

—*euphemism:* " 'O, your niceties—I know what they are . . . . They all go on your system of makebelieve. "Rottenness" may suggest what is unpleasant, so you'd better say "sugar-plums", or something else such a long way off the fact that nobody is obliged to think of it. Those are your roundabout euphusms [*sic*] that dress up swindling till it looks as well as honesty, and shoot with boiled peas instead of bullets. I hate your gentlemanly speakers.' " FH 5

—*grandiloquence:* "The source of all grandiloquence is the want of taking for a criterion the true qualities of the object described, or the emotion expressed. The grandiloquent man is never bent on saying what he feels or what he sees, but on producing a certain effect on his audience; hence he may float away into utter inanity without meeting any criterion to arrest him. Here lies the distinction between grandiloquence and genuine fancy or bold imaginativeness." PY 30

—*inadequate:* "FEDALMA: These gems have life in them: their colors speak,
Say what words fail of. So do many things—
The scent of jasmine, and the fountain's plash,
The moving shadows on the far-off hills,
The slanting moonlight, and our clasping hands.
O Silva, there's an ocean round our words
That overflows and drowns them. Do you know
Sometimes when we sit silent, and the air
Breathes gently on us from the orange-trees,
It seems that with the whisper of a word
Our souls must shrink, get poorer, more apart.
Is it not true?
DON SILVA: Yes, dearest, it is true.
Speech is but broken light upon the depth
Of the unspoken: even your loved words
Float in the larger meaning of your voice
As something dimmer." SG I iii

—*niceties:* " 'My daughter is a critic of words, Mr Holt,' said the minister, smiling complacently, 'and often corrects mine on the ground of niceties, which I profess are as dark to me as if they were the reports of a sixth sense which I possess not. I am an eager seeker for precision, and would fain find language subtle enough to follow the utmost intricacies of the soul's pathways, but I see not why a round word that means some object, made and blessed by the Creator, should be branded and banished as a malefactor.' " FH 5

—*powerful:* "The right word is always a power, and communicates its definiteness to our action. Considered as a demise, old Featherstone's death assumed a merely legal aspect, so that Mr Vincy could tap his snuff-box over it and be jovial, without even an intermittent affectation of solemnity . . . . Who was ever awe-struck about a testator, or sang a hymn on the title to real property?" MM 31

Words and Phrases

—*conceit:* "A complacent self-estimate, unwarranted by performance." TS 4

—*morality* and *morals:* " . . there seems a deeper and more melancholy irony in the shrunken meaning that popular or polite speech assigns to 'morality' and 'morals.' The poor part these words are made to play recalls the fate of those pagan divinities who, after being understood to rule the powers of the air and the destinies of men, came down to the level of insignificant demons, or were even made a farcical show for the amusement of the multitude." TS 16

" . . . among the influences that must retard a right public judgment, the degradation of words which involve praise and blame will be reckoned worth protesting against by every mature observer. To rob words of half their meaning, while they retain their dignity as qualifications, is like allowing to men who have lost half their faculties the same high and perilous command which they won in their time of vigour; or like selling food and seeds after fraudulently abstracting their best virtues: in each case what ought to be beneficently strong is fatally enfeebled, if not empoisoned." TS 16

—*temper:* "What is temper? Its primary meaning, the proportion and mode in which qualities are mingled, is much neglected in popular speech, yet even here the word often carries a reference to an habitual state or general tendency of the organism in distinction from what are held to be specific virtues and vices." TS 6

—*what a man is worth:* "It is a familiar example of irony in the degradation of words that [the phrase] has come to mean how much money he possesses . . . ." TS 16

—*what can I do?* " 'What can *I* do?' . . . . That little speech of four words, like so many others in all languages, is capable by varied vocal inflexions of expressing all states of mind from helpless dimness to exhaustive argumentative perception, from the completed self-devoting fellowship to the most neutral aloofness." MM 58

Government and Politics

"Public spirit can never be wholly immoral, since its essence is care for a common good." R *P*

" 'An election is coming. Universal peace is declared, and the foxes have a sincere interest in prolonging the lives of the poultry.' " FH 5

Committee

—close question: "How could a man be satisfied with a decision between such alternatives and under such circumstances? No more than he can be satisfied with his hat, which he has chosen from among such shapes as the resources of the age offer him, wearing it at best with a resignation which is chiefly supported by comparison." MM 18

Deviousness and Diplomacy

—duplicitous: "To act with doubleness towards a man whose own conduct was double, was so near an approach to virtue that it deserved to be called by no meaner name than Diplomacy." FH 29

—in grand affairs: "When greed and unscrupulousness exhibit themselves on a grand historical scale, and there is a question of peace or war or amicable partition, it often occurs that gentlemen of high diplomatic talents have their minds bent on the same object from different points of view. Each, perhaps, is thinking of a certain duchy or province, with a view to arranging the ownership in such a way as shall best serve the purposes of the gentleman with high diplomatic talents in whom each is more especially interested. But these select minds in high office can never miss their aims from ignorance of each other's existence or whereabouts. Their high titles may be learned even by common people from every pocket almanac." FH 29

—indirection: "The man who has failed in the use of some indirectness, is helped very little by the fact that his rivals are men to whom that indirectness is a something human, very far from being alien. There remains this grant distinction, that he has failed, and the jet of light is thrown entirely on his misdoings." FH 34

Election

—advocates: "Trueblue. These men have no votes. Why should I court them?

Greyfox. No votes, but power.

Trueblue. What! over charities?

Greyfox. No, over brains; which disturbs the canvass. In a natural state of things the average price of a vote at Paddlebrook is nine-and-sixpence, throwing the fifty-pound tenants, who cost nothing, into the divisor. But these talking men cause an artificial rise of prices." FH 16 ep

—amorality: "What men do in elections, is not to be classed either among sins or marks of grace: it would be profane to include business in religion, and conscience refers to failure, not to success." FH 29

—canvassing: "What would conciliate the personal regard of old Mr Lyon became a curious problem to Harold, now the little man made his appearance. But canvassing makes a gentleman acquainted with many strange animals, together with the ways of catching and taming them; and thus the knowledge of natural history advances amongst the aristocracy and the wealthy commoners of our land." FH 16

—foreseen: " 'Politics of course,' said Felix. 'He's on some committee. An election is coming. Universal peace is declared, and the foxes have a sincere interest in prolonging the lives of the poultry.' " FH 5

—practicalities: "A practical man must seek a good end by the only possible means; that is to say, if he is to get into Parliament he must not be too particular." FH 17

—property: "It was observed by a sound thinker in these parts that property was ballast; and when once the aptness of that metaphor had been perceived, it followed that a man was not fit to navigate the sea of politics without a great deal of such ballast; and that, rightly understood, whatever increased the expense of election, inasmuch as it virtually raised the property qualification, was an unspeakable boon to the country." FH 8

—unruly crowd: "There was only evidence that the majority of the crowd were excited with drink, and that their action could hardly be calculated on more than those of oxen and pigs congregated amidst hootings and pushings. The confused deafening shouts, the incidental fighting, the knocking over, pulling and scuffling, seemed to increase every moment. Such of the constables as were mixed with the crowd were quite helpless, and if an official staff was seen above the heads, it moved about fitfully, showing as little sign of a guiding hand as the summit of a buoy on the waves." FH 33

Government

—authority attacked: " 'I hold it blasphemy to say that a man ought not to fight against authority: there is no great religion and no great freedom that has not done it, in the beginning." FH 46

—choice: " . . . was Florence to have a Great Council after the Venetian mode, where all the officers of government might be elected, and all laws voted by a wide number of citizens of a certain age and of ascertained qualifications, without question of rank or party? or, was it to be governed on a narrower and less popular scheme, in which the hereditary influence of good families would be less adulterated with the votes of shopkeepers. Doctors of law disputed day after day, and far on into the night. Messer **Pagolantonio Soderini** alleged excellent reasons on the side of the popular scheme;

Messer **Guidantonio Vespucci** alleged reasons equally excellent on the side of a more aristocratic form. It was a question of boiled or roast, which had been prejudged by the palates of the disputants, and the excellent arguing might have been protracted a long while without any other result than that of deferring the cooking. The majority of the men inside the palace, having power already in their hands, agreed with Vespucci, and thought change should be moderate; the majority outside the palace, conscious of little power and many grievances, were less afraid of change." R 35

—*monarch:* "The king repents too late of his cruel precipitation, as is proverbially the case with wrong-headed fathers of all nations." BL 7 317

—*refuge:* ". . . incompetent gentlemen must live, and without private fortune, it is difficult to see how they could all live genteelly if they had nothing to do with education or government." MF II 1

—*two sorts:* " 'After all the talk of scholars, there are but two sorts of government: one where men show their teeth at each other, and one where men show their tongues and lick the feet of the strongest.' " R 39

History and Biography

—*biography:* "History is becoming more and more biographical, while biography aspires more and more to historical fulness. In many cases biographers bestow greater pains on what they mean for a 'picture of the times,' than on the life of their hero; just as theatrical managers bestow enormous labour and expense in scenery and costume, leaving the play to be performed by a very sorry company of actors." HB 295

—*foreshadowed:* "What elegant historian would neglect a striking opportunity for pointing out that his heroes did not foresee the history of the world, or even their own actions?—For example, that **Henry of Navarre**, when a Protestant baby, little thought of being a Catholic monarch; or that **Alfred the Great**, when he measured his laborious nights with burning candles, had no idea of future gentlemen measuring their idle days with watches. Here is a mine of truth, which, however vigorously it may be worked, is likely to outlast our coal." MM 7

—*past remembered:* "No impassioned personage wishes he had been born in the age of **Pitt**, that his ardent youth might have eaten the dearest bread, dressed itself with the longest coat-tails and the shortest waist, or heard the loudest grumbling at the heaviest war-taxes; and it would be really something original in polished verse if one of our young writers declared he would gladly be turned eighty-five that he might have known the joy and pride of being an Englishman when there were fewer reforms and plenty of highwaymen, fewer discoveries and more faces pitted with the small-pox, when laws were made to keep up the price of corn, and the troublesome Irish were more miserable. Three-quarters of a century ago is not a distance that lends much enchantment to the view. We are familiar with the average men of that period, and are still consciously encumbered with its bad contrivances and mistaken acts." TS 2 *And see* A:Ancestor

—*pre-Reform:* "Certainly that elder England with its frankly saleable boroughs, so cheap compared with the seats obtained under the reformed method, and its boroughs kindly presented by noblemen desirous to encourage gratitude; its prisons with a miscellaneous company of felons and maniacs and without any supply of water; its bloated, idle charities; its non-resident, jovial clergy; its militia-balloting; and above all, its blank ignorance of what we, its posterity, should be thinking of it—has great differences from the England of to-day." TS 2

Nationhood

It is notable that patriotism and nationhood are totally absent from GE's fiction until her very last piece (which is not fiction anyway though it is part of a fictional work).

—*centre:* "Affection, intelligence, duty, radiate from a centre, and nature has decided that for us English folk that centre can be neither China nor Peru. Most of us feel this unreflectingly; for the affectation of undervaluing everything native, and being too fine for one's own country, belongs only to a few minds of no dangerous leverage. What is wanting is, that we should recognise a corresponding attachment to nationality as legitimate in every other people, and understand that its absence is a privation of the greatest good." TS 18

—*consciousness:* "It is this living force of sentiment in common which makes a national consciousness. Nations so moved will resist conquest with the very breasts of their women, will pay their millions and their blood to abolish slavery, will share privation in famine and all calamity, will produce poets to sing 'some great story of a man,' and thinkers whose theories will bear the test of action." TS 18

—*the individual:* "An individual man, to be harmoniously great, must belong to a nation of this order [*see preceding*], if not in actual existence yet existing in the past, in memory as a departed, invisible, beloved ideal, once a reality, and perhaps to be restored. A common humanity is not yet enough to feed the rich blood of various activity which makes a complete man." TS 18

" . . . not only the nobleness of a nation depends on the presence of this national consciousness, but also the nobleness of each individual citizen. Our dignity and rectitude are proportioned to our sense of relationship with something great, admirable, pregnant with high possibilities, worthy of sacrifice, a continual inspiration to self-repression and discipline by the presentation of aims larger and more attractive to our generous part than the securing of personal ease or prosperity." TS 18

—*race:* "The tendency of things is towards the quicker or slower fusion of races. It is impossible to arrest this tendency: all we can do is to moderate its course so as to hinder it from degrading the moral status of societies by a too rapid effacement of those national traditions and customs which are the language of the national genius—the deep suckers of healthy sentiment. Such moderating and guidance of inevitable movement is worthy of all effort." TS 18

Notable Individuals

—*Christopher Columbus:*

"Columbus watches, or he sails in dreams
Between the setting stars, and finds new day;
Then wakes again to the old weary days,
Girds on the cord and frock of pale **St Francis**,
And like him zealous pleads with foolish men.
'I ask but for a million maravedis:
Give me three caravels to find a world,
New shores, new realms, new soldiers for the Cross.
Son cosas grandes! Thus he pleads in vain;
Yet faints not utterly, but pleads anew,
Thinking, 'God means it, and has chosen me.'
For this man is the pulse of all mankind
Feeding an embryo future, offspring strange
Of the fond Present . . . . " SG I i

—*Giuseppe Mazzini:* " 'Look into Mazzini's account of his first yearning, when he was a boy, after a restored greatness and a new freedom to Italy, and of his first efforts as a young man to rouse the same feelings in other young men, and get them to work towards a united nationality. Almost everything seemed against him: his countrymen were ignorant or indifferent, governments hostile, Europe incredulous. Of course the scorners often seemed wise. Yet you see the prophecy lay with him. As long as there is a remnant of national consciousness, I suppose nobody will deny that there may be a new stirring of memories and hopes which may inspire arduous action.' " DD 42

" . . . the pathos of his country's lot pierced the youthful soul of Mazzini, because, like **Dante**'s, his blood was fraught with the kinship of Italian greatness, his imagination filled with a majestic past that wrought itself into a majestic future." TS 18

Politics and Politicians

—*enlightened:* "Let us refuse to accept as moral any political leader who should allow his conduct in relation to great issues to be determined by egoistic passion, and boldly say that he would be less immoral even though he were as lax in his personal habits as **Sir Robert Walpole**, if at the same time his sense of the public welfare were supreme in his mind, quelling all pettier impulses beneath a magnanimous impartiality." TS 16

—*and food:* "Good dishes and good wine were at that time [1494] believed to heighten the consciousness of political preferences, and in the inspired ease of after-supper talk it was supposed that people ascertained their own opinions with a clearness quite inaccessible to uninvited stomachs." R 39

—*a game:* "And the game that might be played in Florence [in 1494] promised to be rapid and exciting; it was a game of revolutionary and party struggle, sure to include plenty of that unavowed action in which brilliant ingenuity, able to get rid of all inconvenient beliefs except that 'ginger is hot in the mouth,' is apt to see the path of superior wisdom." R 35

—*humbug:* " 'I'll tell you what, Dan,' said Sir Hugo, 'a man who sets his face against every sort of humbug is simply a three-cornered, impracticable fellow. There's a bad style of humbug, but there is also a good style—one that oils the wheels and makes progress possible. If you are to rule men, you must rule them through their own ideas; and I agree with the Archbishop at Naples who had a St Januarius procession against the plague. It's no use having an Order in Council against popular shallowness. There is no action possible without a little acting.' " DD 33

—*leadership:* "And there was a force outside the palace which was gradually tending to give the vague desires of that majority the character of a determinate will. That force was the preaching of Savonarola. Impelled partly by the spiritual necessity that was laid upon him to guide the people, and partly by the prompting of public men who could get no measures carried without his aid, he was rapidly passing in his daily sermons from the general to the special— from telling his hearers that they must postpone their private passions and interests to the public good, to telling them precisely what sort of government they must have in order to promote that good . . . . " R 35

—party: " 'But as long as parties are in question, I am a Medicean, and will be a Medicean till I die. I am of the same mind as **Farinata degli Uberti**: if any man asks me what is meant by siding with a party, I say, as he did, "To wish ill or well, for the sake of past wrongs or kindnesses." ' " R 6

—Radical: "Mr Chubb's notion of a Radical was that he was a new and agreeable kind of lickspittle who fawned on the poor instead of on the rich . . . . " FH 11

Power and Strength

—achieved gradually: "His private minor loans were numerous, but he would inquire strictly into the circumstances both before and after. In this way a man gathers a domain in his neighbours' hope and fear as well as gratitude; and power, when once it has got into that subtle region, propagates itself, spreading out of all proportion to its external means." MM 16

—acting a part: "Perhaps no man has ever had a mighty influence over his fellows with-out having the innate need to dominate, and this need usually becomes the more imperious in proportion as the complications of life make Self inseparable from a purpose which is not selfish. In this way it came to pass that on the day of the Trial by Fire, the doubleness which is the pressing temptation in every public career, whether of priest, orator, or statesman, was more strongly defined in **Savonarola**'s consciousness as the acting of a part, than at any other period in his life. He was struggling not against impending martyrdom, but against impending ruin." R 65

—ambition for it: "It was weakness only that was despised; power of any sort carried its immunity; and no man, unless by very rare good fortune, could mount high in the world without incurring a few unpleasant necessities which laid him open to enmity, and perhaps to a little hissing, when enmity wanted a pretext." R 57

—in primitive thinking: " . . . the rude mind with difficulty associates the ideas of power and benignity. A shadowy conception of power that by much persuasion can be induced to refrain from inflicting harm, is the shape most easily taken by the sense of the Invisible in the minds of men who have always been pressed close by primitive wants, and to whom a life of hard toil has never been illuminated by any enthusiastic religious faith. To them pain and mishap present a far wider range of possibilities than gladness and enjoyment: their imagination is almost barren of the images that feed desire and hope, but is all overgrown by recollections that are a perpetual pasture to fear." SM 1

—strength: "The stronger will always rule, say some, with an air of confidence which is like a lawyer's flourish, forbidding exceptions or additions. But what is strength? Is it blind wilfulness that sees no terrors, no many-linked consequences, no bruises and wounds of those whose cords it tightens? Is it the narrowness of a brain that conceives no needs differing from its own, and looks to no results beyond the bargains of today; that tugs with emphasis for every small purpose, and thinks it weakness to exercise the sublime power of resolved renunciation? There is a sort of subjection which is the peculiar heritage of largeness and of love; and strength is often only another name for willing bondage to irremediable weakness." FH 6

—two types: " 'In my opinion . . . that was a true word spoken by your friend when he said the great question was how to give every man a man's share in life. But I think he expects voting to do more towards it than I do. I want the working men to have power. I'm a working man myself, and I don't want to be anything else. But there are two sorts of power. There's a power to do mischief—to undo what has been done with great expense and labour, to waste and destroy, to be cruel to the weak, to lie and quarrel, and to talk poisonous nonsense. That's the sort of power that ignorant numbers have. It never made a joint stool or planted a potato. Do you think it's likely to do much towards governing a great country, and making wise laws, and giving shelter, food, and clothes to millions of men? Ignorant power comes in the end to the same thing as wicked power; it makes misery.

" 'It's another sort of power that I want us working men to have, and I can see plainly enough that our all having votes will do little towards it at present. I hope we, or the children that come after us, will get plenty of political power some time. I tell everybody plainly, I hope there will be great changes, and that some time, whether we live to see it or not, men will have come to be ashamed of things they're proud of now. But I should like to convince you that votes would never give you political power worth having while things are as they are now, and that if you go the right way to work you may get power sooner without votes. Perhaps all you who hear me are sober men, who try to learn as much of the nature of things as you can, and to be as little like fools as possible. A fool or idiot is one who expects things to happen that never can happen; he pours milk into a can without a bottom, and expects the milk to stay there. The more of such vain expectations a man has, the more he is of a fool or idiot. And if any working man expects a vote to do for him what it never can do, he's foolish to that amount, if no more. I think that's clear enough, eh? . . .

" 'The way to get rid of folly is to get rid of vain expectations, and of thoughts that don't agree with the nature of things. The men who have had true thoughts about water, and what it will do when it is turned into steam and under all sorts of circumstances, have made themselves a great power in the world: they are turning the wheels of engines that will help to change most things. But no engines would have done, if there had been false notions about the way water would act. Now, all the schemes about voting, and districts, and annual Parliaments, and the rest, are engines, and the water or steam—the force that is to work them—must come out of human nature—out of men's passions, feelings, desires. Whether the engines will do good work or bad depends on these feelings; and if we have false expectations about men's characters, we are very much like the idiot who thinks he'll carry milk in a can without a bottom. In my opinion, the notions about what mere voting will do are very much of that sort . . . .

" 'I'll tell you what's the greatest power under heaven,' said Felix, 'and that is public opinion—the ruling belief in society about what is right and what is wrong, what is honourable and what is shameful. That's the steam that is to work the engines. How can political freedom make us better, any more than a religion we don't believe in, if people laugh and wink when they see men abuse and defile it? And while public opinion is what it is—while men have no better beliefs about public duty—while corruption is not felt to be a damning disgrace—while men are not ashamed in Parliament and out of it to make public questions which concern the welfare of millions a mere screen for their own petty private ends—I say, no fresh scheme of voting will much mend our condition.

" 'For, take us working men of all sorts. Suppose out of every hundred who had a vote there were thirty who had some soberness, some sense to choose with, some good feeling to make them wish the right thing for all. And suppose there were seventy out of the hundred who were, half of them, not sober, who had no sense to choose one thing in politics more than another, and who had so little good feeling in them that they wasted on their own drinking the money that should have helped to feed and clothe their wives and children; and another half of them who, if they didn't drink, were too ignorant or mean or stupid to see any good for themselves better than pocketing a five-shilling piece when it was offered them. Where would be the political power of the thirty sober men? The power would lie with the seventy drunken and stupid votes; and I'll tell you what sort of men would get the power —what sort of men would end by returning whom they pleased to Parliament." FH 30

—political agent: "They would be men who would undertake to do the business for a candidate, and return him: men who have no real opinions, but who pilfer the words of every opinion, and turn them into a cant which will serve their purpose at the moment; men who look out for dirty work to make their fortunes by, because dirty work wants little talent and no conscience; men who know all the ins and outs of bribery, because there is not a cranny in their own souls where a bribe can't enter. Such men as these will be the masters wherever there's a majority of voters who care more for money, more for drink, more for some mean little end which is their own and nobody else's, than for anything that has ever been called Right in the world." FH 30

Public life

—bad temper: "For it is among the repulsive effects of this bad temper . . . that it is apt to determine a man's sudden adhesion to an opinion . . . without leaving him time to consider his grounds . . . . This determination of partisanship by temper has its worst effects in the career of the public man, who is always in danger of getting so enthralled by his own words that he looks into facts and questions not to get rectifying knowledge, but to get evidence that will justify his actual attitude which was assumed under an impulse dependent on something else than knowledge. There has been plenty of insistence on the evil of swearing by the words of a master, and having the judgment uniformly controlled by a 'He said it;' but a much worse woe to befall a man is to have every judgment controlled by an 'I said it'—to make a divinity of his own shortsightedness or passion-led aberration and explain the world in its honour. There is hardly a more pitiable degradation than this for a man of high gifts." TS 6

Felix Holt is Wounded in the Election Day Riot

—and private: " . . . there is no private life which has not been determined by a wider public life, from the time when the primeval milk-maid had to wander with the wanderings of her clan, because the cow she milked was one of a herd which had made the pastures bare. Even in the conservatory existence where the fair Camelia is sighed for by the noble young Pine-apple, neither of them needing to care about the frost or rain outside, there is a nether apparatus of hot-water pipes liable to cool down on a strike of the gardeners or a scarcity of coal." FH 3

Reform

—the ballot: "Now on the question of the ballot the minister strongly took the negative side . . . . 'I engage to show to any impartial mind, duly furnished with the principles of public and private rectitude, that the ballot would be pernicious, and that if it were not pernicious it would still be futile. I will show, first, that it would be futile as a preservative from bribery and illegitimate influence; and, secondly, that it would be in the worst kind pernicious, as shutting the door against those influences whereby the soul of a man and the character of a citizen are duly educated for their great functions.' " FH 16

—compromise: " ' . . . at this epoch, when the mind of the nation has been strained on the passing of one measure. Where a great weight has to be moved, we require not so much selected instruments as abundant horse-power. But it is an unavoidable evil of these massive achievements that they encourage a coarse undiscriminatingness obstructive of more nicely-wrought results, and an exaggerated expectation inconsistent with the intricacies of our fallen and struggling condition. I say not that compromise is unnecessary, but it is an evil attendant on our imperfection; and I would pray every one to mark that, where compromise broadens, intellect and conscience are thrust into narrower room. Wherefore it has been my object to show our people that there are many who have helped to draw the car of Reform, whose ends are but partial, and who forsake not the ungodly principle of selfish alliances, but would only substitute Syria for Egypt—thinking chiefly of their own share in peacocks, gold and ivory.' " FH 16

—exhilaration: "At that time, when faith in the efficacy of political change was at fever-heat in ardent Reformers, many measures which men are still discussing with little confidence on either side, were then talked about and disposed of like property in near reversion. Crying abuses—'bloated paupers', 'bloated pluralists', and other corruptions hindering men from being wise and happy—had to be fought against and slain. Such a time is a time of hope. Afterwards, when the corpses of those monsters have been held up to the public wonder and abhorrence, and yet wisdom and happiness do not follow, but rather a more abundant breeding of the foolish and unhappy, comes a time of doubt and despondency. But in the great Reform-year Hope was mighty: the prospect of Reform had even served the voters instead of drink; and in one place, at least, there had been a 'dry election'. And now the speakers at Reform banquets were exuberant in congratulation and promise. Liberal clergymen of the Establishment toasted Liberal Catholic clergymen without any allusion to scarlet, and Catholic clergymen replied with a like tender reserve. Some dwelt on the abolition of all abuses, and on millennial blessedness generally; others, whose imaginations were less suffused with exhalations of the dawn, insisted chiefly on the ballot-box." FH 16

—in rural England: " . . . till the agitation about the Catholics in '29, rural Englishmen had hardly known more of Catholics than of the fossil mammals, and . . . their notion of Reform was a confused combination of rick-burners, trades-unions, Nottingham riots, and in general whatever required the calling-out of the yeomanry." FH *I*

—success: "The Reformers had triumphed: it was clear that the wheels were going whither they were pulling, and they were in fine spirits for exertion. But if they were pulling towards the country's ruin, there was the more need for others to hang on behind and get the wheels to stick if possible. In Treby, as elsewhere, people were told they must 'rally' at the coming election; but there was now a large number of waverers —men of flexible, practical minds, who were not such bigots as to cling to any views when a good tangible reason could be urged against them; while some regarded it as the most neighbourly thing to hold a little with both sides, and were not sure that they should rally or vote at all. It seemed an invidious thing to vote for one gentleman rather than another." FH 3

Three Professions

Clergyman

—*bishop:* " 'And what's a bishop? A bishop's a parson dressed up, who sits in the House of Lords to help and throw out Reform Bills. And because it's hard to get anything in the shape of a man to dress himself up like that, and do such work, they give him a palace for it, and plenty of thousands year.' " FH 30

—*confessor:* "There are men whose presence infuses trust and reverence; there are others to whom we have need to carry our trust and reverence ready-made . . . . " R 41

—*country parson:* "And the parson naturally set an example in these social duties. For it would not have been possible for the Raveloe mind, without a peculiar revelation, to know that a clergyman should be a pale-faced memento of solemnities, instead of a reasonably faulty man whose exclusive authority to read prayers and preach, to christen, marry, and bury you, necessarily coexisted with the right to sell you the ground to be buried in and to take tithe in kind, on which last point, of course, there was a little grumbling, but not to the extent of irreligion—not of deeper significance than the grumbling at the rain, which was by no means accompanied with a spirit of impious defiance, but with a desire that the prayer for fine weather might be read forthwith." SM 11

—parishioners: "[My father] knew very well what could be wisely expected from the miners, the weavers, the field-labourers, and farmers of his own time—yes, and from the aristocracy, for he had been brought up in close contact with them and had been companion to a young nobleman who was deaf and dumb. 'A clergyman, lad,' he used to say to me, 'should feel in himself a bit of every class;' and this theory had a felicitous agreement with his inclination and practice, which certainly answered in making him beloved by his parishioners." TS 2

—sermons: "[My father] was a pithy talker, and his sermons bore marks of his own composition. It is true, they must have been already old when I began to listen to them, and they were no more than a year's supply, so that they recurred as regularly as the Collects. But though this system has been much ridiculed, I am prepared to defend it as equally sound with that of a liturgy; and even if my researches had shown me that some of my father's yearly sermons had been copied out from the works of elder divines, this would only have been another proof of his good judgment. One may prefer fresh eggs though laid by a fowl of the meanest understanding, but why fresh sermons?" TS 2

—tithe: " . . . I am contented that my father was a country parson, born much about the same time as **Scott** and **Wordsworth**, notwithstanding certain qualms I have felt at the fact that the property on which I am living was saved out of tithe before the period of commutation, and without the provisional transfiguration into a modus. It has sometimes occurred to me when I have been taking a slice of excellent ham that, from a too tenable point of view, I was breakfasting on a small squealing black pig which, more than half a century ago, was the unwilling representative of spiritual advantages not otherwise acknowledged by the grudging farmer or dairyman who parted with him." TS 2

—curate

—income: "And now, pray, can you solve me the following problem? Given a man with a wife and six children: let him be obliged always to exhibit himself when outside his own door in a suit of black broadcloth, such as will not undermine the foundations of the Establishment by a paltry plebeian glossiness or an unseemly whiteness at the edges; in a snowy cravat, which is a serious investment of labour in the hemming, starching, and ironing departments; and in a hat which shows no symptom of taking to the hideous doctrine of expediency, and shaping itself according to circumstances; let him have a parish large enough to create an external necessity for abundant shoe-leather, and an internal necessity for abundant beef and mutton, as well as poor enough to require frequent priestly consolation in the shape of shillings and sixpences; and, last, let him be compelled, by his own pride and other people's, to dress his wife and children with gentility from bonnet-strings to shoe-strings. By what process of division can the sum of eighty pounds per annum be made to yield a quotient which will cover that man's weekly expenses?" SF 1

—object of interest: "Poor women's hearts! Heaven forbid that I should laugh at you, and make cheap jests on your susceptibility towards the clerical sex, as if it had nothing deeper or more lovely in it than the mere vulgar angling for a husband. Even in these enlightened days, many a curate who, considered abstractedly, is nothing more than a sleek bimanous animal in a white neckcloth, with views more or less Anglican, and furtively addicted to the flute; is adored by a girl who has coarse brothers, or by a solitary woman who would like to be a helpmate in good works beyond her own means, simply because he seems to them the model of refinement and of public usefulness." JR 3

—disappointment: "It was naturally disappointing to Dr Kenn, after two years of superfluous incense from his feminine parishioners, to find them suddenly maintaining their views in opposition to his; but then, they maintained them in opposition to a higher authority, which they had venerated longer. That authority had furnished a very explicit answer to persons who might inquire where their social duties began, and might be inclined to take wide views as to the starting-point. The answer had not turned on the ultimate good of society, but on 'a certain man' who was found in trouble by the wayside." MF VII 4

—established church: "The Rector was always of the Debarry family, associated only with county people, and was much respected for his affability; a clergyman who would have taken tea with the townspeople would have given a dangerous shock to the mind of a Treby Churchman." FH 2

—exasperating: "What was more exasperating to a zealous preacher, with whom copious speech was not a difficulty but a relief—who never lacked argument, but only combatants and listeners—than to reflect

that there were thousands on thousands of pulpits in this kingdom, supplied with handsome sounding-boards, and occupying an advantageous position in buildings far larger than the chapel in Malthouse Yard—buildings sure to be places of resort, even as the markets were, if only from habit and interest; and that these pulpits were filled, or rather made vacuous, by men whose privileged education in the ancient centres of instruction issued in twenty minutes' formal reading of tepid exhortation or probably infirm deductions from premises based on rotten scaffolding?" FH 15

—*evangelical:* "Given, a man with moderate intellect, a moral standard not higher than the average, some rhetorical affluence and great glibness of speech, what is the career in which, without the aid of birth or money, he may most easily attain power and reputation in English society? Where is that Goshen of mediocrity in which a smattering of science and learning will pass for profound instruction, where platitudes will be accepted as wisdom, bigoted narrowness as holy zeal, unctuous egoism as God-given piety? Let such a man become an evangelical preacher; he will then find it possible to reconcile small ability with great ambition, superficial knowledge with the prestige of erudition, a middling morale with a high reputation for sanctity.

"Let him shun practical extremes and be ultra only in what is purely theoretic: let him be stringent on predestination, but latitudinarian on fasting; unflinching in insisting on the eternity of punishment, but diffident of curtailing the substantial comforts of time; ardent and imaginative on the premillennial advent of **Christ**, but cold and cautious towards every other infringement of the *status quo*. Let him fish for souls not with the bait of inconvenient singularity, but with the drag-net of comfortable conformity. Let him be hard and literal in his interpretation only when he wants to hurl texts at the heads of unbelievers and adversaries, but when the letter of the Scriptures presses too closely on the genteel Christianity of the nineteenth century, let him use his spiritualizing alembic and disperse it into impalpable ether.

"Let him preach less of Christ than of Antichrist; let him be less definite in showing what sin is than in showing who is the Man of Sin, less expansive on the blessedness of faith than on the accursedness of infidelity. Above all, let him set up as an interpreter of prophecy, and rival **Moore**'s Almanack in the prediction of political events, tickling the interests of hearers who are but moderately spiritual by showing how the Holy Spirit has dictated problems and charades for their benefit, and how, if they are ingenious enough to solve these they may have their Christian graces nourished by learning precisely to whom they may point as the 'horn that had eyes,' 'the lying prophet,' and the 'unclean spirits.'

"In this way he will draw men to him by the strong cords of their passions, made reason-proof by being baptized with the name of piety. In this way he may gain a metropolitan pulpit; the avenues to his church will be as crowded as the passages to the opera; he has but to print his prophetic sermons and bind them in lilac and gold, and they will adorn the drawing-room table of all evangelical ladies, who will regard as a sort of pious 'light reading' the demonstration that the prophecy of the locusts whose sting is in their tail, is fulfilled in the fact of the Turkish commander's having taken a horse's tail for his standard, and that the French are the very frogs predicted in the Revelation." ¶ET 79-80

—*good type:* Rev. Martin Cleves, "a man about forty—middle-sized, broad-shouldered, with a negligently tied cravat, large irregular features, and a large head, thickly covered with lanky brown hair. To a superficial glance, Mr Cleves is the plainest and least clerical-looking of the party; yet, strange to say, *there* is the true parish priest, the pastor beloved, consulted, relied on by his flock; a clergyman who is not associated with the undertaker, but thought of as the surest helper under a difficulty, as a monitor who is encouraging rather than severe. Mr Cleves has the wonderful art of preaching sermons which the wheelwright and the blacksmith can understand; not because he talks condescending twaddle, but because he can call a spade a spade, and knows how to disencumber ideas of their wordy frippery.

"Look at him more attentively, and you will see that his face is a very interesting one—that there is a great deal of humour and feeling playing in his grey eyes, and about the corners of his roughly cut mouth: a man, you observe, who has most likely sprung from the harder-working section of the middle class, and has hereditary sympathies with the chequered life of the people. He gets together the working men in his parish on a Monday evening, and gives them a sort of conversational lecture on useful practical matters, telling them stories, or reading some select passages from an agreeable book, and commenting on them; and if you were to ask the first labourer or artisan in Tripplegate what sort of man the parson was, he would say—'a uncommon knowin', sensable, free-spoken gentleman; very kind an' good-natur'd too'. Yet for all this, he is perhaps the best Grecian of the party . . . . " ¶ SF 6

—*high vocation:* " . . . for many years he had walked through life with the sense of having for a space been unfaithful to what he esteemed the highest trust ever committed to man—the ministerial vocation." FH 15

—*moral ailments:* " . . . the poor curate, equally with the rector, is liable to clergyman's sore throat, but he would probably be found free from the chronic moral ailments encouraged by the possession of glebe and those higher chances of preferment which follow on having a good position already. On the other hand, the poor curate might have severe attacks of calculating expectancy concerning parishioners' turkeys, cheeses, and fat geese, or of uneasy rivalry for the donations of clerical charities." TS 15

—*mutual affection:* "The affection of the clergy for each other, we have observed, is, like that of the fair sex, not at all of a blind and infatuated kind; and we may therefore the rather believe them when they give each other any extra-official praise." PY 20

—*parson:* " 'If I want to believe in **Jesus Christ**, I must shut my eyes for fear I should see a parson.' " FH 30

—*pastoral glance:* "The source of the impression his glance produced on Romola was the sense it conveyed to her of interest in her and care for her apart from any personal feeling. It was the first time she had encountered a gaze in which simple human fellowship expressed itself as a strongly-felt bond. Such a glance is half the vocation of the priest or spiritual guide of men . . . . " R 40

—*poor facility:* "Alas! a natural incapacity for teaching, finished by keeping 'terms' at Cambridge, where there are able mathematicians, and butter is sold by the yard, is not apparently the medium through which Christian doctrine will distil as welcome dew on withered souls." SF 2

—*preacher:* "He has an immense advantage over all other public speakers. The platform orator is subject to the criticism of hisses and groans. Council [*sic*] for the plaintiff expects the retort of council for the defendant. The honorable gentleman on one side of the House is liable to have his facts and figures shown up by his honorable friend on the opposite side. Even the scientific or literary lecturer, if he is dull or incompetent, may see the best part of his audience slip quietly out one by one. But the preacher is completely master of the situation: no one may hiss, no one may depart.

"Like the writer of imaginary conversations, he may put what imbecilities he pleases into the mouths of his antagonists, and swell with triumph when he has refuted them. He may riot in gratuitous assertions, confident that no man will contradict him; he may exercise perfect free-will in logic, and invent illustrative experience; he may give an evangelical edition of history with the inconvenient facts omitted;—all this he may do with impunity, certain that those of his hearers who are not sympathizing are not listening." ¶TE 80

—*and the press:* "For the Press has no band of critics who go the round of the churches and chapels, and are on the watch for a slip or defect in the preacher, to make a 'feature' in their article: the clergy are, practically, the most irresponsible of all talkers." TE 80

—*priorities:* " 'Nay, child, I trust that while I would willingly depart from my evil habit of a somewhat slovenly forgetfulness in my attire, I shall never arrive at the opposite extreme . . . the brevity of our life, and the hurry and crush of the great battle with error and sin, often oblige us to an advised neglect of what is less momentous.' " FH 18

—*taking orders:* ". . . that friend of **Arnold**'s who recommended a curacy as the best means of clearing up Trinitarian difficulties, that 'orders' are a sort of spiritual backboard, which, by dint of obliging a man to look as if he were strait, end by making him so." JS 250

—*workhouse duty:* " . . . I think you will admit that the university-taught clergyman, whose office it is to bring home the gospel to a handful of such souls, has a sufficiently hard task. For, to have any chance of success, short of miraculous intervention, he must bring his geographical, chronological, exegetical mind pretty nearly to the pauper point of view, or of no view; he must have some approximate conception of the mode in which the doctrines that have so much vitality in the plenum of his own brain will support themselves *in vacuo*—that is to say, in a brain that is neither geographical, chronological, nor exegetical. It is a flexible imagination that can take such a leap as that, and an adroit tongue that can adapt its speech to so unfamiliar a position." SF 2

Judge

—*the charge:* "The counsel's duty of restoring all unfavourable facts to due prominence in the minds of the jurors, had its effect altogether reinforced by the summing-up of the judge. Even the bare discernment of facts, much more their arrangement with a view to inferences, must carry a bias: human impartiality, whether judicial or not, can hardly escape being more or less loaded. It was not that the judge had severe intentions; it was only that he saw with severity. The conduct of Felix was not such as inclined him to indulgent consideration, and, in his directions to the jury, that mental attitude necessarily told on the light in which he placed the homicide." FH 46

The Law

—*bankruptcy wind-up:* ". . . the taxing-masters had done their work like any respectable gunsmith conscientiously preparing the musket that, duly pointed by a brave arm, will spoil a life or two. Allocaturs, filing of bills in Chancery, decrees of sale, are legal chain-shot or bomb-shells that can never hit a solitary mark but must fall with widespread shattering. So deeply inherent is it in this life of ours that men have to suffer for each other's sins, so inevitably diffusive is human suffering, that even justice makes its victims, and we can conceive no retribution that does not spread beyond its mark in pulsations of unmerited pain." MF III 7

—*disreputable:* "In a profession where much that is noxious may be done without disgrace, is a conscience likely to be without balm when circumstances have urged a man to overstep the line where his good technical information makes him aware that (with discovery) disgrace is likely to begin?" FH 21

" '[Felix Holt] would not accept . . . a defence wherein the truth was screened or avoided—not from a vainglorious spirit of self-exhibition . . . but from an averseness to a profession wherein a man may without shame seek to justify the wicked for reward, and take away the righteousness of the righteous from him.' " FH 38

—*reading:* " 'I don't see that law-rubbish is worse than any other sort. It is not so bad as the rubbishy literature that people choke their minds with. It doesn't make one so dull. Our wittiest men have often been lawyers. Any orderly way of looking at things as cases and evidence seems to me better than a perpetual wash of odds and ends bearing on nothing in particular. And then, from a higher point of view, the foundations and the growth of law make the most interesting aspects of philosophy and history.' " DD 58

—*to the uninitiated:* " . . . to the non-legal mind there are dim possibilities in law and heirship which prevent any issue from seeming too miraculous." FH 25

Lawyer

—*esteemed (or not):* " 'I wouldn't make a downright lawyer o' the lad—I should be sorry for him to be a raskill . . . . ' " MF 2

" 'These lawyers are the fellows for getting on in the world with the least expense of civility. With this cursed conjuring secret of theirs called Law, they think everybody's frightened at them. My Lord Jermyn seems to have his insolence as ready as his soft sawder. He's as sleek as a rat, and has as vicious a tooth. I know the sort of vermin well enough. I've helped to fatten one or two.' " FH 21

—*game bird:* "Mr Tulliver was a strictly honest man, and proud of being honest, but he considered that in law the ends of justice could only be achieved by employing a stronger knave to frustrate a weaker. Law was a sort of cock-fight in which it was the business of injured honesty to get a game bid with the best pluck and the strongest spurs." MF II 2

Medical Man

—*beneficence:* "Many of us looking back through life would say that the kindest man we have ever known has been a medical man, or perhaps that surgeon whose fine tact, directed by deeply-informed perception, has come to us in our need with a more sublime beneficence than that of miracle-workers." MM 66

—*family doctor:* "For everybody's family doctor was remarkably clever, and was understood to have immeasurable skill in the management and training of the most skittish or vicious diseases. The evidence of his cleverness was of the higher intuitive order, lying in his lady-patients' immovable conviction, and was unassailable by any objection except that their intuitions were opposed by others equally strong; each lady who saw medical truth in Wrench and 'the strengthening treatment' regarding Toller and 'the lowering system' as medical perdition . . . . The strengtheners and the lowerers were all 'clever' men in somebody's opinion, which is really as much as can be said for any living talents." MM 15

—*fever research:* "Whereas Fever had obscure conditions, and gave him that delightful labour of the imagination which is not mere arbitrariness, but the exercise of disciplined power—combining and constructing with the clearest eye for probabilities and the fullest obedience to knowledge; and then, in yet more energetic alliance with impartial Nature, standing aloof to invent tests by which to try its own work." MM 16

—*general principle:* " . . . this advice [to smoke a pipe daily] was sanctioned by Dr Kimble, on the ground that it was as well to try what could do no harm—a principle which was made to answer for a great deal of work in that gentleman's medical practice." SM 16

—*primitive milieu:* "For it must be remembered that this [the 1820s] was a dark period; and in spite of venerable colleges which used great efforts to secure purity of knowledge by making it scarce, and to exclude error by a rigid exclusiveness in relation to fees and appointments, it happened that very ignorant young gentlemen were promoted in town, and many more got a legal right to practise over large areas in the country. Also, the high standard held up to the public mind by the College of Physicians, which gave its peculiar sanction to the expensive and highly-ratified medical instruction obtained by graduates of Oxford and Cambridge, did not hinder quackery from having an excellent time of it; for since professional practice chiefly consisted in giving a great many drugs, the public inferred that it might be better off with more drugs still, if they could only be got cheaply, and hence swallowed large cubic measures of physic prescribed by unscrupulous ignorance which had taken no degrees." MM 15

—psychology: "A medical man likes to make psychological observations, and sometimes in the pursuit of such studies is too easily tempted into momentous prophecy which life and death easily set at nought." MM 30

—reflections: " 'I should never have been happy in any profession that did not call forth the highest intellectual strain, and yet keep me in good warm contact with my neighbours. There is nothing like the medical profession for that: one can have the exclusive scientific life that touches the distance and befriend the old fogies in the parish too.' " MM 16

—religion: "At all events, it is certain that if any medical man had come to Middlemarch with the reputation of having very definite religious views, of being given to prayer, and of otherwise showing an active piety, there would have been a general presumption against his medical skill." MM 18

—surgery: " 'It is but fitting that a great medicus like you,' said Nello, adjusting the cloth, 'should be shaved by the same razor that has shaved the illustrious **Antonio Benevieni**, the greatest master of the chirurgic art.'

" 'The chirurgic art!' interrupted the doctor, with an air of contemptuous disgust, 'Is it your Florentine fashion to put the masters of the science of medicine on a level with men who do carpentry on broken limbs, and sew up wounds like tailors, and carve away excrescences as a butcher trims meat? *Via!* A manual art, such as any artificer might learn, and which has been practised by simple barbers like yourself—on a level with the noble science of **Hippocrates**, **Galen**, and **Avicenna**, which penetrates into the occult influences of the stars and plants and gems! —a science locked up from the vulgar!' " R 16

Notable Individuals

—Marie François Xavier Bichat: "That great Frenchman first carried out the conception that living bodies, fundamentally considered, are not associations of organs which can be understood by studying them first apart, and then as it were federally; but must be regarded as consisting of certain primary webs or tissues, out of which the various organs—brain, heart, lungs, and so on—are compacted, as the various accommodations of a house are built up in various proportions of wood, iron, stone, brick, zinc, and the rest, each material having its peculiar composition and proportions. No man, one sees, can understand and estimate the entire structure or its parts—what are its frailties and what its repairs, without knowing the nature of the materials. And the conception wrought out by Bichat, with his detailed study of the different tissues, acted necessarily on medical questions as the turning on of gas-light would act on a dim, oil-lit street, showing new connections and hitherto hidden facts of structure which must be taken into account in considering the symptoms of maladies and the action of medicaments." MM 15

Will and Testament

—expectant heirs: "When the animals entered the Ark in pairs, one may imagine that allied species made such private remark on each other, and were tempted to think that so many forms feeding on the same store of fodder were eminently superfluous, as tending to diminish the rations. I fear the part played by the vultures on that occasion would be too painful for art to represent, those birds being disadvantageously naked about the gullet, and apparently without rites and ceremonies." MM 35

—spite: " 'Even a wise man generally lets some folly ooze out of him in his will—my father did, I know; and if a fellow has any spite or tyranny in him, he's likely to bottle off a good deal for keeping in that sort of document.' " DD 59

Witness

—unreliable: "Man cannot be defined as an evidence-giving animal; and in the difficulty of getting up evidence on any subject, there is room for much unrecognized action of diligent persons who have the extra stimulus of some private motive." FH 46

Great Britain

Agriculture

—depressed: "The farms actually tenanted were held by men who had begged hard to succeed their fathers in getting a little poorer every year, on land which was also getting poorer, where the highest rate of increase was in the arrears of rent, and where the master, in crushed hat and corduroys, looked pitiably lean and care-worn by the side of pauper labourers, who showed that superior assimilating power often observed to attend nourishment by the public money." FH 8.

—prosperous: "It was still that glorious war-time which was felt to be a peculiar favour of Providence towards the landed interest, and the fall of prices had not yet come to carry the race of small squires and yeomen down that road to ruin for which extravagant habits and bad husbandry were plentifully anointing their wheels. I am speaking now in relation to Raveloe and the parishes that resembled it; for our old-fashioned country life had many different aspects, as all life must have when it is spread over a various surface, and breathed on variously by multitudinous currents, from the winds of heaven to the thoughts of men, which are for ever moving and crossing each other with incalculable results.

"Raveloe lay low among the bushy trees and the rutted lanes, aloof from the currents of industrial energy and Puritan earnestness: the rich ate and drank freely, accepting gout and apoplexy as things that ran mysteriously in respectable families, and the poor thought that the rich were entirely in the right of it to lead a jolly life; besides, their feasting caused a multiplication of orts [scraps], which were the heirlooms of the poor." ¶SM 3

Bridges

—*Blackfriars:* "Leaning on the parapet of Blackfriars Bridge, and gazing meditatively, the breadth and calm of the river, with its long vista half hazy, half luminous, the grand dim masses or tall forms of buildings which were the signs of world-commerce, the oncoming of boats and barges from the still distance into sound and colour, entered into his mood and blent themselves indistinguishably with his thinking, as a fine symphony to which we can hardly be said to listen makes a medium that bears up our spiritual wings." DD 38 (*GE dangles a participle every so often.*)

The English

—*advice:* " 'I want to be an Englishman, but I want to understand other points of view. And I want to get rid of a merely English attitude in studies.'

" 'I see; you don't want to be turned out in the same mould as every other youngster. And I have nothing to say against your doffing some of our national prejudices. I feel the better myself for having spent a good deal of my time abroad. But, for God's sake, keep an English cut, and don't become indifferent to bad tobacco.' " DD 16

—*blood:* "In fact, pure English blood (if leech or lancet can furnish us with the precise product) did not declare itself predominantly in the party at present assembled." DD 42

—*colonisers:* " . . . we have been fortunate enough to keep the island-home [our forebears] won for us, and have been on the whole a prosperous people, rather continuing the plan of invading and spoiling other lands than being forced to beg for shelter in them . . . . The Red Indians, not liking us when we settled among them . . . were too ignorant, and besides their opinions did not signify, because we were able, if we liked, to exterminate them. The Hindoos also have doubtless had their rancours against us and still entertain enough ill-will to make unfavourable remarks on our character, especially as to our historic rapacity and arrogant notions of our own superiority; they perhaps do not admire the usual English profile, and they are not converted to our way of feeding: but though we are a small number of an alien race profiting by the territory and produce of these prejudiced people, they are unable to turn us out; at least, when they tried we showed them their mistake. We do not call ourselves a dispersed and a punished people: we are a colonising people, and it is we who have punished others." TS 18

—*diverse:* "We English are a miscellaneous people, and any chance fifty of us will present many varieties of animal architecture or facial ornament; but it must be admitted that our prevailing expression is not that of a lively, impassioned race, preoccupied with the ideal and carrying the real as a mere make-weight. The strong point of the English gentleman pure is the easy style of his figure and clothing; he objects to marked ins and outs in his costume, and he also objects to looking inspired." DD 10

—*forebears:* " 'Let us' [our historian] virtually says, 'let us know who were our forefathers, who it was that won the soil for us, and brought the good seed of those institutions through which we should not arrogantly but gratefully feel ourselves distinguished among the nations as possessors of long-inherited freedom; let us not keep up an ignorant kind of naming which disguises our true affinities of blood and language but let us see thoroughly what sort of notions and traditions our forefathers had, and what sort of song inspired them. Let the poetic fragments which breathe forth their fierce bravery in battle and their trust in fierce gods who helped them, be treasured with affectionate reverence. These seafaring, invading, self-asserting men were the English of old time, and were our fathers who did rough work by which we are profiting. They had virtues which incorporated themselves in wholesome usages to which we trace our own political blessings. Let us know and acknowledge our common relationship to them, and be thankful that over and above the affections and duties which spring from our manhood, we have the closer and more constantly guiding duties which belong to us as Englishmen.' " TS 18

—*free and independent:* "The only point in this connection [concerning oppressed peoples] on which Englishmen are agreed is, that England itself shall not be subject to foreign rule. The fiery resolve to resist invasion, though with an improvised array of pitchforks, is felt to be virtuous, and to be worthy of a historic people. Why? Because there is a national life in our veins. Because there is something specifically English which we feel to be supremely worth striving for, worth dying for, rather than living to renounce it. Because we too have our share—perhaps a principal share—in that spirit of separateness which has not yet done its work in the education of mankind, which has created the varying genius of nations, and, like the Muses, is the offspring of memory." TS 18

—heirship: "It would have been matter of congratulation if one who had the luck to inherit two old family estates had had more hair, a fresher colour, and a look of greater animation; but that fine families dwindled off into females, and estates ran together into the single heirship of a mealy-complexioned male, was a tendency in things which seemed to be accounted for by a citation of other instances. It was agreed that Mr Grandcourt could never be taken for anything but what he was—a born gentleman and that, in fact, he looked like an heir." DD 36

—and the Jews: "There is more likeness than contrast between the way we English got our island and the way the Israelites got Canaan. We have not been noted for forming a low estimate of ourselves in comparison with foreigners, or for admitting that our institutions are equalled by those of any other people under the sun. Many of us have thought that our sea-wall is a specially divine arrangement to make and keep us a nation of sea-kings after the manner of our forefathers, secure against invasion and able to invade other lands when we need them, though they may lie on the other side of the ocean.

"Again, it has been held that we have a peculiar destiny as a Protestant people, not only able to bruise the head of an idolatrous Christianity in the midst of us, but fitted as possessors of the most truth and the most tonnage to carry our purer religion over the world and convert mankind to our way of thinking.

"The Puritans, asserting their liberty to restrain tyrants, found the Hebrew history closely symbolical of their feelings and purpose; and it can hardly be correct to cast the blame of their less laudable doings on the writings they invoked, since their opponents made use of the same writings for different ends, finding there a strong warrant for the divine right of kings and the denunciation of those who, like **Korah**, **Dathan**, and **Abiram**, took on themselves the office of the priesthood which belonged of right solely to **Aaron** and his sons, or, in other words, to men ordained by the English bishops.

"We must rather refer the passionate use of the Hebrew writings to affinities of disposition between our own race and the Jewish. Is it true that the arrogance of a Jew was so immeasurably beyond that of a Calvinist? And the just sympathy and admiration which we give to the ancestors who resisted the oppressive acts of our native kings, and by resisting rescued or won for us the best part of our civil and religious liberties—is it justly to be withheld from those brave and steadfast men of Jewish race who fought and died, or strove by wise administration to resist, the oppression and corrupting influences of foreign tyrants, and by resisting rescued the nationality which was the very heart of our own religion?" ¶TS 18

—language: "To one who loves his native language, who would delight to keep our rich and harmonious English undefiled by foreign accent, foreign intonation, and those foreign tinctures of verbal meaning which tend to confuse all writing and discourse, it is an affliction as harassing as the climate, that on our stage, in our studios, at our public and private gatherings, in our offices, warehouses, and workshops, we must expect to hear our beloved English with its words clipped, its vowels stretched and twisted, its phrases of acquiescence and politeness, of cordiality, dissidence or argument, delivered always in the wrong tones, like ill-rendered melodies, marred beyond recognition . . . a modern Englishman is invited from his after-dinner repose to hear **Shakspere** delivered under circumstances which offer no other novelty than some novelty of false intonation, some new distribution of strong emphasis on prepositions, some new misconception of a familiar idiom.

"Well! it is our inertness that is in fault, our carelessness of excellence, our willing ignorance of the treasures that lie in our national heritage, while we are agape after what is foreign, though it may be only a vile imitation of what is native." ¶TS 18

—recreation abroad: "And when they came down again at five o'clock, equipped for their boating, the scene was as good as a theatrical representation for all beholders. This handsome, fair-skinned English couple manifesting the usual eccentricity of their nation, both of them proud, pale, and calm, without a smile on their faces, moving like creatures who were fulfilling a supernatural destiny—it was a thing to go out and see, a thing to paint. The husband's chest, back, and arms, showed very well in his close-fitting dress, and the wife was declared to be like a statue." DD 54

—reserve: "It was the first time Deronda had seen them speak to each other since their arrival, and he thought their exchange of looks as cold and official as if it had been a ceremony to keep up a charter.

Still, the English fondness for reserve will account for much negation; and Grandcourt's manners with an extra veil of reserve over them might be expected to present the extreme type of the national taste." DD 35

—*suppressed:* "The correct Englishman, drawing himself up from his bow into rigidity, assenting severely, and seemed to be in a state of internal drill, suggests a suppressed vivacity, and may be suspected of letting go with some violence when he is released from parade . . . . " DD 11

The Irish

"As for the Irish, it is felt in high quarters that we have always been too lenient towards them;—at least if they had been harried a little more there might not have been so many of them on the English press, of which they divide the power with the Scotch, thus driving many Englishmen to honest and ineloquent labour." TS 18

Public-house

—*Cross-Keys:* "The Cross-Keys was a very old-fashioned 'public': its bar was a big rambling kitchen, with an undulating brick floor; the small-paned windows threw an interesting obscurity over the far-off dresser, garnished with pewter and tin, and with large dishes that seemed to speak of better times; the two settles were half pushed under the wide-mouthed chimney; and the grate, with its brick hobs, massive iron crane, and various pothooks, suggested a generous plenty possibly existent in all moods and tenses except the indicative present.

"One way of getting an idea of our fellow-countrymen's miseries is to go and look at their pleasures. The Cross-Keys had a fungous-featured landlord and a yellow sickly landlady, with a large white kerchief bound round her cap, as if her head had recently required surgery; it had doctored ale, an odour of bad tobacco, and remarkably strong cheese. It was not what *Astræa*, when come back, might be expected to approve as the scene of ecstatic enjoyment for the beings whose special prerogative it is to lift their sublime faces towards heaven. Still, there was ample space on the hearth—accommodation for narrative bagmen or boxmen —room for a man to stretch his legs; his brain was not pressed upon by a white wall within a yard of him, and the light did not stare in mercilessly on bare ugliness, turning the fire to ashes. Compared with some beer-houses of this more advanced period, the Cross-Keys of that day presented a high standard of pleasure." ¶FH 28

Regions

—*agricultural midlands:* "But there were trim cheerful villages too, with a neat or handsome parsonage and grey church set in the midst; there was the pleasant tinkle of the blacksmith's anvil, the patient cart-horses waiting at his door; the basket-maker peeling his willow wands in the sunshine; the wheelwright putting the last touch to a blue cart with red wheels; here and there a cottage with bright transparent windows showing pots full of blooming balsams or geraniums, and little gardens in front all double daisies or dark wall-flowers; at the well, clean and comely women carrying yoked buckets, and towards the free school small Britons dawdling on, and handling their marbles in the pockets of unpatched corduroys adorned with brass buttons.

"The land around was rich and marly, great corn-stacks stood in the rick-yards—for the rick-burners had not found their way hither; the homesteads were those of rich farmers who paid no rent, or had the rare advantage of a lease, and could afford to keep their corn till prices had risen. The coach would be sure to overtake some of them on their way to their outlying fields, or to the market-town, sitting heavily on their well-groomed horses, or weighing down one side of an olive-green gig. They probably thought of the coach with some contempt, as an accommodation for people who had not their own gigs, or who, wanting to travel to London and such distant places, belonged to the trading and less solid part of the nation.

"The passenger on the box could see that this was the district of protuberant optimists, sure that old England was the best of all possible countries, and that if there were any facts which had not fallen under their own observation, they were facts not worth observing: the district of clean little market–towns without manu-factures, of fat livings, an aristocratic clergy, and low poor-rates." ¶FH *I*

—*inertia:* "It was still easier to see that, for the most part, they resisted the rotation of crops and stood by their fallows: and the coachman would perhaps tell how in one parish an innovating farmer, who talked of **Sir Humphry Davy**, had been fairly driven out by popular dislike, as if he had been a confounded Radical; and how, the parson having one Sunday preached from the words, 'Break up your fallow-ground,' the people thought he had made the text out of his own head, otherwise it would never have come 'so pat' on a matter of business; but when they found it in the Bible at home, some said it was an argument for fallows (else why should the Bible mention fallows?), but a few of the weaker sort were shaken, and thought it was an argument that fallows should be done away with, else the Bible would have said, 'Let your fallows be'; and the next morning the parson had a stroke of apoplexy, which, as coincident with a dispute about fallows, so set the parish against the innovating farmer and the rotation of crops, that he could stand his ground no longer, and transferred his lease." FH *I*

—*manufacturing north:* "But as the day wore on the scene would change: the land would begin to be blackened with coal-pits, the rattle of handlooms to be heard in hamlets and villages. Here were powerful men walking queerly with knees bent outward from squatting in the mine, going home to throw themselves down in their blackened flannel and sleep through the daylight, then rise and spend much of their high wages at the alehouse with their fellows of the Benefit Club: here the pale eager faces of handloom-weavers, men and women, haggard from sitting up late at night to finish the week's work, hardly begun till the Wednesday.

"Everywhere the cottages and the small children were dirty, for the languid mothers gave their strength to the loom; pious Dissenting women, perhaps, who took life patiently, and thought that salvation depended chiefly on predestination, and not at all on cleanliness . . . . The breath of the manufacturing town, which made a cloudy day and a red gloom by night on the horizon, diffused itself over all the surrounding country, filling the air with eager unrest. Here was a population not convinced that old England was as good as possible; here were multitudinous men and women aware that their religion was not exactly the religion of their rulers, who might therefore be better than they were, and who, if better, might alter many things which now made the world perhaps more painful than it need be, and certainly more sinful.

"Yet there were the grey steeples too, and the churchyards, with their grassy mounds and venerable headstones, sleeping in the sunlight; there were broad fields and homesteads, and the old woods covering a rising ground, or stretching far by the roadside, allowing only peeps at the park and mansion which they shut in from the working-day world. In these midland districts the traveller passed rapidly from one phase of English life to another: after looking down on a village dingy with coal-dust, noisy with the shaking of looms, he might skirt a parish all of fields, high hedges, and deep-rutted lanes, after the coach had rattled over the pavement of a manufacturing town, the scene of riots and trades-union meetings, it would take him in another ten minutes into a rural region, where the neighbourhood of the town was only felt in the advantages of a near market for corn, cheese, and hay, and where men with a considerable banking account were accustomed to say that 'they never meddled with politics themselves.'

"The busy scenes of the shuttle and the wheel, of the roaring furnace, of the shaft and the pulley, seemed to make but crowded nests in the midst of the large-spaced, slow-moving life of homesteads and far-away cottages and oak-sheltered parks. Looking at the dwellings scattered amongst the woody flats and the ploughed uplands, under the low grey sky which overhung them with an unchanging stillness as if Time itself were pausing, it was easy for the traveller to conceive that town and country had no pulse in common, except where the handlooms made a far-reaching straggling fringe about the great centres of manufacture . . . . " FH *I*

—*mining country:* "Outside the gate the country, once entirely rural and lovely, now black with coal-mines, was chiefly peopled by men and brethren with candles stuck in their hats, and with a diabolic complexion which laid them peculiarly open to suspicion in the eyes of the children at Gadsmere . . . . " DD 30

—*rural tracts:* "Our rural tracts—where no Babel-chimney scales the heavens—are without mighty objects to fill the soul with the sense of an outer world unconquerably aloof from our efforts. The wastes are playgrounds (and let us try to keep them such for the children's children who will inherit no other sort of demesne); the grasses and reeds nod to each other over the river, but we have cut a canal close by; the very heights laugh with corn in August or lift the plough-team against the sky in September. Then comes a crowd of burly navvies with pickaxes and barrows, and while hardly a wrinkle is made in the fading mother's face or a new curve of health in the blooming girl's, the hills are cut through or the breaches between them spanned, we choose our level and the white steam-pennon flies along it." TS 2

—*under improvement:* "But because our land shows this readiness to be changed, all signs of permanence upon it raise a tender attachment instead of awe: some of us, at least, love the scanty relics of our forests, and are thankful if a bush is left of the old hedgerow. A crumbling bit of wall where the delicate ivy-leaved toad-flax hangs its light branches, or a bit of grey thatch with patches of dark moss on its shoulder and a troop of grass-stems on its ridge, is a thing to visit. And then the tiled roof of cottage and homestead, of the long cow-shed where generations of the milky mothers have stood patiently, of the broad-shouldered barns where the old-fashioned flail once made resonant music, while the watch-dog barked at the timidly venturesome fowls making pecking raids on the outflying grain—the roofs that have looked out from among the elms and walnut-trees, or beside the yearly group of hay and corn stacks, or below the square stone steeple, gathering their grey or ochre-tinted lichens and their olive-green mosses under all ministries—let us praise the sober harmonies they give to our landscape, helping to unite us pleasantly with the elder generations who tilled the soil for us before we were born, and paid heavier and heavier taxes, with much grumbling, but without that deepest root of corruption—the self-indulgent despair which cuts down and consumes and never plants." TS 2

The Scotch

"Some judges think that the Scotch are more numerous and prosperous here in the South than is quite for the good of us Southerners; and the early inconvenience felt under the **Stuarts** of being quartered on by a hungry, hard-working people with a distinctive accent and form of religion, and higher cheekbones than English taste requires, has not yet been quite neutralised." TS 18

Stately home

—Brackenshaw Park

—archery ground: "The archery-ground was a carefully-kept enclosure on a bit of table-land at the farthest end of the park, protected towards the south-west by tall elms and a thick screen of hollies, which kept the gravel walk and the bit of newly-mown turf where the targets were placed in agreeable afternoon shade. The Archery Hall with an arcade in front showed like a white temple against the greenery on the northern side." DD 10

—situation: "Brackenshaw Park, where the Archery Meeting was held, looked out from its gentle heights far over the neighbouring valley to the outlying eastern downs and the broad slow rise of cultivated country hanging like a vast curtain towards the west. The castle, which stood on the highest platform of the clustered hills, was built of rough-hewn limestone, full of lights and shadows made by the dark dust of lichens and the washings of the rain. Masses of beech and fir sheltered it on the north, and spread down here and there along the green slopes like flocks seeking the water which gleamed below." DD 10

—Cheverel Manor: "And a charming picture Cheverel Manor would have made that evening, if some English **Watteau** had been there to paint it: the castellated house of grey-tinted stone, with the flickering sunbeams sending dashes of golden light across the many-shaped panes in the mullioned windows, and a great beech leaning athwart one of the flanking towers, and breaking, with its dark flattened boughs, the too formal symmetry of the front; the broad gravel-walk winding on the right, by a row of tall pines, alongside the pool—on the left branching out among swelling grassy mounds, surmounted by clumps of trees, where the red trunk of the Scotch fir glows in the descending sunlight against the bright green of limes and acacias; the great pool, where a pair of swans are swimming lazily with one leg tucked under a wing, and where the open water lilies lie calmly accepting the kisses of the fluttering light-sparkles; the lawn, with its smooth emerald greenness, sloping down to the rougher and browner herbage of the park, from which it is invisibly fenced by a little stream that winds away from the pool, and disappears under a wooden bridge in the distant pleasure-ground. . . ." GL 2

—dining-room: " . . . anyone entering that dining-room for the first time, would perhaps have had his attention . . . strongly arrested by the room itself, which was so bare of furniture that it impressed one with its architectural beauty like a cathedral. A piece of matting stretched from door to door, a bit of worn carpet under the dining-table, and a sideboard in a deep recess, did not detain the eye for a moment from the lofty groined ceiling, with its richly carved pendants, all of creamy white, relieved here and there by touches of gold. On one side, this lofty ceiling was supported by pillars and arches, beyond which a lower ceiling, a miniature copy of the higher one, covered the square projection which, with its three large pointed windows, formed the central feature of the building. The room looked less like a place to dine in than a piece of space enclosed simply for the sake of

beautiful outline; and the small dining-table, with the party round it, seemed an odd and insignificant accident, rather than anything connected with the original purpose of the apartment." GL 2

—*Gadsmere:* "Imagine a rambling, patchy house, the best part built of grey stone, and red-tiled, a round tower jutting at one of the corners, the mellow darkness of its conical roof surmounted by a weather-cock making an agreeable object either amidst the gleams and greenth of summer or the low-hanging clouds and snowy branches of winter: the ground shady with spreading trees: a great cedar flourishing on one side, backward some Scotch firs on a broken bank where the roots hung naked, and beyond, a rookery: on the other side a pool overhung with bushes, where the water-fowl fluttered and screamed: all around, a vast meadow which might be called a park, bordered by an old plantation and guarded by stone lodges which looked like little prisons." DD 30

—*Lowick manor house:* "It had a small park, with a fine old oak here and there, and an avenue of limes towards the south-west front, with a sunk fence between park and pleasure-ground, so that from the drawing-room windows the glance swept uninterruptedly along a slope of greensward till the limes ended in a level of corn and pastures, which often seemed to melt into a lake under the setting sun. This was the happy side of the house, for the south and east looked rather melancholy even under the brightest morning. The grounds here were more confined, the flower-beds showed no very careful tendance, and large clumps of trees, chiefly of sombre yews, had risen high, not ten yards from the windows. The building, of greenish stone, was in the old English style, not ugly, but small windowed and melancholy-looking: the sort of house that must have children, many flowers, open windows, and little vistas of bright things, to make it seem a joyous home. In this latter end of autumn, with a sparse remnant of yellow leaves falling slowly athwart the dark evergreens in a stillness without sunshine, the house too had an air of autumnal decline, and Mr Casaubon, when he presented himself, had no bloom that could be thrown into relief by that background." MM 9

—*Transome Court:* "For, though Transome Court was a large mansion, built in the fashion of **Queen Anne**'s time, with a park and grounds as fine as any to be seen in Loamshire, there were very few servants about it. Especially, it seemed, there must be a lack of gardeners; for, except on the terrace surrounded with a stone parapet in front of the house, where there was a parterre kept with some neatness, grass had spread itself over the gravel walks, and over all the low mounds once carefully cut as black beds for the shrubs and larger plants. Many of the windows had the shutters closed, and under the grand Scotch fir that stooped towards one corner, the brown fir-needles of many years lay in a small stone balcony in front of two such darkened windows.

"All round, both near and far, there were grand trees, motionless in the still sunshine, and, like all large motionless things, seeming to add to the stillness. Here and there a leaf fluttered down; petals fell in a silent shower; a heavy moth floated by; and, when it settled, seemed to fall wearily; the tiny birds alighted on the walks, and hopped about in perfect tranquillity . . . . No sound was to be heard louder than a sleepy hum, and the soft monotony of running water hurrying on to the river that divided the park. Standing on the south or east side of the house, you would never have guessed that an arrival was expected.

"But on the west side, where the carriage entrance was, the gates under the stone archway were thrown open; and so was the double door of the entrance-hall, letting in the warm light on the scagliola pillars, the marble statues, and the broad stone staircase, with its matting worn into large holes." FH 1

—*Treby Manor:* " . . . measured from the front saloon to the remotest shed, was as large as a moderate-sized village, and there were certainly more lights burning in it every evening, more wine, spirits, and ale drunk, more waste and more folly, than could be found in some large villages. There was fast revelry in the steward's room, and slow revelry in the Scotch bailiff's room; short whist, costume, and flirtation in the housekeeper's room, and the same at a lower price in the servants' hall; a select Olympian feast in the private apartment of the cook, who was a much grander person than her ladyship, and wore gold and jewellery to a vast amount of suet; a gambling group in the stables, and the coachman, perhaps the most innocent member of the establishment, tippling in majestic solitude by a fire in the harness room." FH 7

Towns and Villages

—*Raveloe:* "And Raveloe was a village where many of the old echoes lingered, undrowned by new voices. Not that it was one of those barren parishes lying on the outskirts of civilisation—inhabited by meagre sheep and thinly-scattered shepherds: on the contrary, it lay in the rich central plain of what we are pleased to call Merry England, and held farms which, speaking from a spiritual point of view, paid highly-desirable tithes.

"But it was nestled in a snug well-wooded hollow, quite an hour's journey on horseback from any turnpike, where it was never reached by the vibrations of the coach-horn, or of public opinion. It was an important-looking village, with a fine old church and large churchyard in the heart of it, and two or three large brick-and-stone homesteads, with well-walled orchards and ornamental weather-cocks, standing close upon the road, and lifting more imposing fronts than the rectory, which peeped from among the trees on the other side of the church-yard—a village which showed at once the summits of its social life, and told the practised eye that there was no great park and manor-house in the vicinity, but that there were several chiefs in Raveloe who could farm badly quite at their ease, drawing enough money from their bad farming, in those war times, to live in a rollicking fashion, and keep a jolly Christ-mas, Whitsun, and Easter tide." SM 1

—a contrast: "Nothing could be more unlike his native town, set within sight of the widespread hillsides, than this low, wooded region, where he felt hidden even from the heavens by the screening trees and hedgerows. There was nothing here, when he rose in the deep morning quiet and looked out on the dewy brambles and rank tufted grass, that seemed to have any relation with that life centering in Lantern Yard . . . .

"And what could be more unlike that Lantern Yard world than the world in Raveloe?—orchards looking lazy with neglected plenty; the large church in the wide churchyard, which men gazed at lounging at their own doors in service-time; the purple-faced farmers jogging along the lanes or turning in at the Rainbow; homesteads, where men supped heavily and slept in the light of the evening hearth, and where women seemed to be laying up a stock of linen for the life to come." SM 2

—Treby Magna, "on which the Reform Bill had thrust the new honour of being a polling-place, had been, at the beginning of the century, quite a typical old market-town, lying in pleasant sleepiness among green pastures, with a rush-fringed river meandering through them. Its principal street had various handsome and tall-windowed brick houses with walled gardens behind them; and at the end, where it widened into the marketplace, there was the cheerful rough-stuccoed front of that excellent inn, the Marquis of Granby, where the farmers put up their gigs, not only on fair and market days, but on exceptional Sundays when they came to church.

"And the church was one of those fine old English structures worth travelling to see, standing in a broad churchyard with a line of solemn yew-trees beside it, and lifting a majestic tower and spire far above the red-and-purple roofs of the town. It was not large enough to hold all the parishioners of a parish which stretched over distant villages and hamlets; but then they were never so unreasonable as to wish to be all in at once, and had never complained that the space of a large side-chapel was taken up by the tombs of the Debarrys, and shut in by a handsome iron screen.

"For when the black Benedictines ceased to pray and chant in this church, when the Blessed Virgin and **St Gregory** were expelled, the Debarrys, as lords of the manor, naturally came next to Providence and took the place of the saints. Long before that time, indeed, there had been a Sir Maximus Debarry who had been at the fortifying of the old castle, which now stood in ruins in the midst of the green pastures, and with its sheltering wall towards the north made an excellent strawyard for the pigs of Wace & Co., brewers of the celebrated Treby beer.

"Wace & Co. did not stand alone in the town as prosperous traders on a large scale, to say nothing of those who had retired from business; and in no country town of the same small size as Treby was there a larger proportion of families who had handsome sets of china without handles, hereditary punch-bowls, and large silver ladles with a Queen Anne's guinea in the centre." ¶FH 2

Germany and the Rest of the World

America

—founding: " 'How long is it?—only two centuries since a vessel carried over the ocean the beginning of the great North American nation. The people grew like meeting waters—they were various in habit and sect—there came a time, a century ago, when they needed a polity, and there were heroes of peace among them. What had they to form a polity with but memories of Europe, corrected by the vision of a better?' " DD 42

Cities and Towns

—Genoa in July: "In Genoa, the noons were getting hotter, the converging outer roads getting deeper with white dust, the oleanders in the tubs along the wayside gardens looking more and more like fatigued holiday-makers, and the sweet evening changing her office—scattering abroad those whom the mid-day had sent under shelter, and sowing all paths with happy social sounds, little tinklings of mule-bells and whirrings of thrumbed strings, light footsteps and voices, if not leisurely, then with the hurry of pleasure in them; while the encircling heights, crowned with forts, skirted with fine dwellings and gardens, seemed also to come forth and gaze in fulness of beauty after their long siesta, till all strong colour melted in the stream of moonlight which made the streets a new spectacle with shadows, both still and moving, on cathedral steps and against the façades of massive palaces; and then slowly with the descending moon all sank in deep night and silence, and nothing shone but the port lights of the great Lanterna in the blackness below, and the glimmering stars in the blackness above." DD 50

—Prague (in a vision): " . . . a city under the broad sunshine, that seemed to me as if it were the summer sunshine of a long-past century arrested in its course—unrefreshed for ages by the dews of night, or the rushing rain-cloud; scorching the dusty, weary, time-eaten grandeur of a people doomed to live on in the stale repetition of memories, like deposed and superannuated kings in their regal gold-inwoven tatters. The city looks so thirsty that the broad river seemed to me a sheet of metal; and the blackened statues, as I passed under their blank gaze, along the unending bridge, with their ancient gar-

ments and their saintly crowns, seemed to me the real inhabitants and owners of this place, while the busy, trivial men and women, hurrying to and fro, were a swarm of ephemeral visitants infesting it for a day. It is such grim, stony beings as these, I thought, who are the fathers of ancient faded children, in those tanned time-fretted dwellings that crowd the steep before me; who pay their court in the worn and crumbling pomp of the palace which stretches its monotonous length on the height; who worship wearily in the stifling air of the churches, urged by no fear or hope, but compelled by their doom to be ever old and undying, to live on in the rigidity of habit, as they live on in perpetual mid-day, without the repose of night or the new birth of morning." LV 1

—Rome

—art and architecture: "Ruins and basilicas, palaces and colossi, set in the midst of a sordid present, where all that was living and warm-blooded seemed sunk in the deep degeneracy of a superstition divorced from reverence: the dimmer but yet eager Titanic life gazing and struggling on walls and ceilings; the long vistas of white forms whose marble eyes seemed to hold the monotonous light of an alien world: all this vast wreck of ambitious ideals, sensuous and spiritual, mixed confusedly with the signs of breathing forgetfulness and degradation . . . . " MM 20

—city of history: "Rome, The city of visible history, where the past of a whole hemisphere seems moving in a funeral procession with strange ancestral images and trophies gathered from afar." MM 20

—recalled: " . . . in certain states of dull forlornness Dorothea all her life continued to see the vastness of St Peter's, the huge bronze canopy, the excited intention in the attitudes and garments of the prophets and evangelists in the mosaics above, and the red drapery which was being hung for Christmas spreading itself everywhere like a disease of the retina." MM 20

—retrospect: "[His] romance was to present the splendours of the Roman Empire at the culmination of its grandeur, when decadence was spiritually but not visibly imminent: it was to show the workings of human passion in the most pregnant and exalted of human circumstances, the designs of statesmen, the interfusion of philosophies, the rural relaxation and converse of immortal poets, the majestic triumphs of warriors, the mingling of the quaint and sublime in religious cere-mony, the gorgeous delirium of gladiatorial shows, and under all the secretly working leaven of Christianity." TS 14

—spiritual centre: "To those who have looked at Rome with the quickening power of a knowledge which breathes a growing soul into all historic shapes, and traces out the suppressed transitions which unite all contrasts, Rome may still be the spiritual centre and interpreter of the world." MM 20

Germany and the Germans

—climate: "In the northern plains the atmosphere is damp and heavy; in the southern mountain region it is dry and rare, and there are abrupt changes of temperature, sharp contrasts between the seasons, and devastating storms; but in both these zones men are hardened by conflict with the roughnesses of the climate. In Middle Germany, on the contrary, there is little of this struggle; the seasons are more equable, and the mild, soft air of the valleys tends to make the inhabitants luxurious and sensitive to hardships. It is only in exceptional mountain districts that one is here reminded of the rough, bracing air on the heights of Southern Germany. It is a curious fact that, as the air becomes gradually lighter and rarer from the North German coast towards Upper Germany, the average of suicides regularly decreases. Mecklenburg has the highest number, then Prussia, while the fewest suicides occur in Bavaria and Austria." NH 145-6

—divided into three parts: "[**Riehl**] shows that the ordinary antithesis of North and South Germany represents no real ethnographical distinction, and that the natural divisions of Germany, founded on its physical geography, are threefold—namely, the low plains, the middle mountain region, and the high mountain region, or Lower, Middle, and Upper Germany; and on this primary natural division all the other broad ethnographical distinctions of Germany will be found to rest.

"The plains of North or Lower Germany include all the seaboard the nation possesses; and this, together with the fact that they are traversed to the depth of 600 miles by navigable rivers, makes them the natural seat of a trading race.

"Quite different is the geographical character of Middle Germany. While the northern plains are marked off into great divisions, by such rivers as the Lower Rhine, the Weser, and the Oder, running almost in parallel lines, this central region is cut up like a mosaic by the capricious lines of valleys and rivers. Here is the region in which you find those famous roofs from which the rain-water runs towards two different seas, and the mountain-tops from which you may look into eight or ten German States. The abundance of water-power and the presence of extensive coal-mines allow of a very diversified industrial development in Middle Germany.

"In Upper Germany, or the high mountain region, we find the same symmetry in the lines of the rivers as in the north; almost all the great Alpine streams flow parallel with the Danube. But the majority of these rivers are neither navigable nor available for industrial objects, and instead of serving for communication, they shut off one great tract from another. The slow development, the simple peasant-life of many districts, is here determined by the mountain and the river." ¶NH 145

—food: "A very fair dinner is to be had at several *tables d'hôte* in Weimar . . . . the Germans certainly excel us in their *Melspeise,* or farinaceous puddings, and in their mode of cooking vegetables; they are bolder and more imaginative in their combination of sauces, fruits, and vegetables with animal food, and they are faithful to at least one principle of dietetics—variety. The only thing at table we have any pretext for being supercilious about is the quality and dressing of animal food . . . . The basis of the national food seems to be raw ham and sausage, with a copious superstratum of *Blaukraut, Sauerkraut,* and black bread. Sausage seems to be to the German what potatoes were to the Irish—the *sine quâ non* of bodily sustenance." 3M 162-3

—greatness: "All honor to her for the still greater [than comedy] things she has done for us! She has fought the hardest fight for freedom of thought, has produced the grandest inventions, has made magnificent contributions to science, has given us some of the divinest poetry, and quite the divinest music, in the world. We revere and treasure the products of the German mind. To say that that mind is not fertile in wit, is only like saying that excellent wheat-land is not rich pasture; to say that we do not enjoy German facetiousness, is no more than to say, that though the horse is the finest of quadrupeds, we do not like him to lay his hoof playfully on our shoulder." HH 51

—lacking fine-tuning: "To the typical German . . . it is indifferent whether his door-lock will catch; whether his teacup be more or less than an inch thick; whether or not his book have every other leaf unstitched; whether his neighbor's conversation be more or less of a shout; whether he pronounce *b* or *p, t* or *d;* whether or not his adored one's teeth be few and far between. He has the same sort of insensibility to gradations in time. A German comedy is like a German sentence: you see no reason in its structure why it should ever come to an end, and you accept the conclusion as an arrangement of Providence rather than of the author.

"We have heard Germans use the word *Langeweile,* the equivalent for *ennui,* and we have secretly wondered what it can be that produces *ennui* in a German. Not the longest of long tragedies, for we have known him to pronounce that *höchst fesselnd*; not the heaviest of heavy books, for he delights in that as *gründlich;* not the slowest of journeys in a *Post-wagen,* for the slower the horses the more cigars he can smoke before he reaches his journey's end. German *ennui* must be something as superlative as **Barclay**'s treble X, which, we suppose, implies an extremely unknown quantity of stupefaction." ¶HH 50

—language: "The German language easily lends itself to all the purposes of poetry; like the ladies of the Middle Ages, it is gracious and compliant to the Troubadours. But as these same ladies were often crusty and repulsive to their unmusical mates, so the German language generally appears awkward and unmanageable in the hands of prose writers. Indeed the number of really fine German prosaists before Heine would hardly have exceeded the numerating powers of a New Hollander, who can count three and no more. Persons the most familiar with German prose testify that there is an extra fatigue in reading it, just as we feel an extra fatigue from our walk when it takes us over a ploughed clay." HH 75

—theatre: "It is charming to see how real an amusement the theatre is to the Weimar people. The greater number of places are occupied by subscribers, and there is no fuss about toilet or escort. The ladies come alone, and slip quietly into their places without need of 'protection'—a proof of civilization perhaps more than equivalent to our pre-eminence in patent locks and carriage springs . . . . " 3M 164

Greece

—tradition: "That there is a free modern Greece is due—through all infiltration of other than Greek blood—to the presence of ancient Greece in the consciousness of European men; and every speaker would feel his point safe if he were to praise **Byron**'s devotion to a cause made glorious by ideal identification with the past; hardly so, if he were to insist that the Greeks were not to be helped further because their history shows that they were anciently unsurpassed in treachery and lying, and that many modern Greeks are highly disreputable characters, while others are disposed to grasp too large a share of our commerce." TS 18

Italy

—Renaissance: "Altogether this world, with its partitioned empire and its roomy universal Church, seemed to be a handsome establishment for the few who were lucky or wise enough to reap the advantages of human folly: a world in which lust and obscenity, lying and treachery, oppression and murder, were pleasant, useful, and when properly managed, not dangerous. And as sort of fringe or adornment to the substantial delights of tyranny, avarice, and lasciviousness, there was the patronage of polite learning and the fine arts, so that flattery could always be had in the choicest Latin to be commanded at that time, and sublime artists were at hand to paint the holy and the unclean with impartial skill.

"The Church, it was said, had never been so disgraced in its head, had never shown so few signs of renovating, vital belief in its lower members; nevertheless it was much more prosperous than in some past days. The heavens were fair and smiling above; and below there were no signs of earthquake." ¶R 21

—then and now: "Half a century ago, what was Italy? An idling-place of dilettantism or of itinerant motiveless wealth, a territory parcelled out for papal sustenance, dynastic convenience, and the profit of an alien Government. What were the Italians? No people, no voice in European counsels, no massive power in European affairs: a race thought of in English and French society as chiefly adapted to the operatic stage, or to serve as models for painters; disposed to smile gratefully at the reception of halfpence; and by the more historical remembered to be rather polite than truthful, in all probably a combination of **Machiavelli**, **Rubini**, and **Masaniello**. Thanks chiefly to the divine gift of a memory which inspires the moments with a past, a present, and a future, and gives the sense of corporate existence that raises man above the otherwise more respectable and innocent brute, all that, or most of it, is changed." TS 18

Rivers

—the Rhône and the Rhine: "Journeying down the Rhône on a summer's day, you have perhaps felt the sunshine made dreary by those ruined villages which stud the banks in certain parts of its course, telling how the swift river once rose, like an angry, destroying god sweeping down the feeble generations whose breath is in their nostrils and making their dwellings a desolation.

"Strange contrast, you may have thought, between the effect produced on us by these dismal remnants of commonplace houses, which in their best days were but the sign of a sordid life, belonging in all its details to our own vulgar era—and the effect produced by those ruins on the castled Rhine which have crumbled and mellowed into such harmony with the green and rocky steeps, that they seem to have a natural fitness, like the mountain pine: nay, even in the day when they were built they must have had this fitness, as if they had been raised by an earth-born race who had inherited from their mighty parent a sublime instinct of form.

"And that was a day of Romance! If those robber barons were somewhat grim and drunken ogres, they had a certain grandeur of the wild beast in them—they were forest boars with tusks tearing and rending, not the ordinary domestic grunter: they represented the demon forces for ever in collision with beauty, virtue, and the gentle uses of life: they made a fine contrast in the picture with the wandering minstrel, the soft-lipped princess, the pious recluse and the timid Israelite.

"That was a time of colour when the sunlight fell on glancing steel and floating banners: a time of adventure and fierce struggle—nay, of living, religious art and religious enthusiasm; for were not cathedrals built in those days and did not great emperors leave their western palaces to die before the infidel strongholds in the sacred east? Therefore it is that these Rhine castles thrill me with a sense of poetry: they belong to the grand historic life of humanity, and raise up for me the vision of an epoch.

"But these dead-tinted, hollow-eyed, angular skeletons of villages on the Rhône, oppress me with the feeling that human life—very much of it—is a narrow, ugly, grovelling existence, which even calamity does not elevate, but rather tends to exhibit in all its bare vulgarity of conception; and I have a cruel conviction that the lives these ruins are the traces of were part of a gross sum of obscure vitality, that will be swept into the same oblivion with the generations of ants and beavers." ¶MF IV 1

Transportation and Travel

"Tis grievous, that with all amplification of travel both by sea and land, a man can never separate himself from his past history." FH 21 ep

Canal-boat

—on a Sunday: "Felix retained something of his boyish impression that the days in a canal-boat were all like Sundays; but the horse, if it had been put to him, would probably have preferred a more Judaic or Scotch rigour with regard to canal-boats, or at least that the Sunday towing should be done by asses, as a lower order." FH 11

Coaches and Inns

—innkeeper: "It is in the nature of innkeepers, and all men who have no pressing business of their own, to ask as many questions as possible before giving any information." AB 36

—Marquis of Granby, Treby Magna: "The market dinner at 'the Marquis' was in high repute in Treby and its neighbourhood. The frequenters of this three-and-sixpenny ordinary liked to allude to it, as men allude to anything which implies that they move in good society, and habitually converse with those who are in the secret of the highest affairs. The guests were not only such rural residents as had driven to market, but some of the most substantial townsmen, who had always assured their wives that business required this weekly sacrifice of domestic pleasure." FH 20

—the old days: "Five-and-thirty years ago [before 1832] the glory had not yet departed from the old coach-roads: the great roadside inns were still brilliant with well-polished tankards, the smiling glances of pretty barmaids, and the repartees of jocose ostlers; the mail still announced itself by the merry notes of the horn; the hedge-cutter or the rick-thatcher might still know the exact hour by the unfailing yet otherwise meteoric apparition of the pea-green Tally-ho or the yellow Independent; and elderly gentlemen in pony-chaises, quartering nervously to make way for the rolling swinging swiftness, had not ceased to remark that times were finely changed since they used to see the pack-horses and hear the tinkling of their bells on this very highway." FH *I*

—passenger: " . . . the happy outside passenger seated on the box from the dawn to the gloaming gathered enough stories of English life, enough of English labours in town and country, enough aspects of earth and sky, to make episodes for a modern Odyssey. Suppose only that his journey took him through that central plain, watered at one extremity by the Avon, at the other by the Trent. As the morning silvered the meadows, with their long lines

or bur-nished the golden corn-ricks clustered near the long roofs of some mid-land homestead, he saw the full-uddered cows driven from their pasture to the early milking." FH *I*

—*The Red Lion, Houndsley:* " . . . to get down at the Red Lion in a street shaded with coal-dust, and dine in a room furnished with a dirt-enamelled map of the county, a bad portrait of an anonymous horse in a stable, His Majesty **George the Fourth** with legs and cravat, and various leaden spittoons, might have seemed bad business, but for the sustaining power of nomenclature which determined that the pursuit of these things was 'gay.' " MM 23

Journey

—*lonely:* "A long, lonely journey, with sadness in the heart, away from the familiar to the strange: that is a hard and dreary thing even to the rich, the strong, the instructed: a hard thing, even when we are called by duty, not urged by dread." AB 36

—*rail:* "No tipsiness can be more dead to all appeals than that which comes from fitful draughts of sleep on a railway journey by night. To the disgust of your wakeful companions, you are totally insensible to the existence of your umbrella, and to the fact that your carpet-bag is stowed under your seat, or that you have borrowed books and tucked them behind the cushion. 'What's the odds, so long as one can sleep?' is your philo-sophic formula, and it is not until you have begun to shiver on the platform in the early morning air that you become alive to pro-perty and its duties—i.e., to the necessity of keeping a fast grip upon it." 3M 153

Sight-seeing

—*entrapment:* "You arrive some sunshiny morning at a cathedral town, and think you will spend the half hour between the arrival and departure of the trains, in looking at the cathedral. But not being satisfied with a glance at the outside only, you peep through the half-open door, which perhaps has a chain or a locked gate before it, and you are immediately pounced upon by a fat sexton or a thin crone, who regards you as a prospec-tive shilling, and offers to 'show' you the cathedral. This is one of the opprobriums of Protestantism." BL 5 273

Transportation

—*future and past:* "Posterity may be shot, like a bullet through a tube, by atmospheric pressure from Winchester to Newcastle: that is a fine result to have among our hopes; but the slow old-fashioned way of getting from one end of our country to the other is the better thing to have in the memory. The tube-journey can never lend much to picture and narrative; it is as barren as an exclamatory O!" FH *I*

Nature

"I looked up at the departing glow leaving one mountain-top after the other, as if the prophet's chariot of fire were passing over them on its way to the home of light." LV 1

Bird

—*crane:* "The serious cranes, unstung by ridicule . . . . " MP 123

—*farmyard:* "Still the sight of the peacock opportunely spreading his tail on the stock-yard wall . . . was only the beginning of beautiful sights at Garum Firs. All the farmyard life was wonderful there—bantams, speckled and topknotted—Friesland hens, with their feathers all turned the wrong way; Guinea-fowls that flew and screamed and dropped their pretty-spotted feathers—pouter pigeons and a tame magpie . . . . " MF I 9

—*goose:* " . . . the weak-brained geese/Hissing fallaciously at sound of wheels . . . . " MP 126-7

—*hen laying:* " . . . as a hen, when advertising her accouchement, passes at irregular intervals from pianissimo semiquavers to fortissimo crotchets." SF 1

—*male:* "It is the uneven allotment of nature that the male bird alone has the tuft. . . . " DD 9

Countryside

—*abandoned quarry:* " . . . it had the charm for her which any broken ground, any mimic rock and ravine have for the eyes that rest habitually on the level, especially in summer, when she could sit on a grassy hollow under the shadow of a branching ash, stooping aslant from the steep above her, and listen to the hum of insects, like tiniest bells on the garment of Silence, or see the sunlight piercing the distant boughs, as if to chase and drive home the truant heavenly blue of the wild hyacinths . . . the dogroses were in their glory . . . . " MF V 1

—*approaching home:* "She saw the grey shoulders of the downs, the cattle-specked fields, the shadowy plantations with rutted lanes where the barked timber lay for a wayside seat, the neatly-clipped hedges on the road from the parsonage to Offendene. . . . " DD 64

—*a bank:* " . . . an insignificant rise of ground crowned by trees, lying along the side of the road . . . . Insignificant, I call it, because in height it was hardly more than a bank;—but there may come moments when Nature makes a mere bank a means towards a fateful result . . . . " MF V 1

—*beauty and apprehension:* "She continued to stand, however, looking at the placid churchyard with the long shadows of the gravestones across the bright green hillocks, and at the glowing autumn colours of the Rectory trees beyond. Before such calm external beauty the presence of a vague fear is more distinctly felt—like a raven flapping its slow wing across the sunny air." SM 17

—*hedgerows:* "For the hedgerows in those days shut out one's view, even on the better-managed farms; and this afternoon, the dog-roses were tossing out their pink wreaths, the nightshade was in its yellow and purple glory, the pale honeysuckle grew out of reach, peeping high up out of a holly bush, and over all, an ash or a sycamore every now and then threw its shadow across the path." AB 18

"But everywhere the bushy hedgerows wasted the land with their straggling beauty, shrouded the grassy borders of the pastures with cat-kinned hazels, and tossed their long blackberry branches on the corn-fields. Perhaps they were white with May, or starred with pale pink dogroses; perhaps the urchins were already nutting amongst them, or gathering the plenteous crabs. It was worth the journey only to see those hedgerows, the liberal homes of unmarketable beauty—of the purple-blossomed ruby-berried nightshade, of the wild convolvulus climbing and spreading in tendrilled strength till it made a great curtain of pale-green hearts and white trumpets, of the many-tubed honeysuckle which, in its most delicate fragrance, hid a charm more subtle and penetrating than beauty. Even if it were winter the hedgerows showed their coral, the scarlet haws, the deep-crimson hips, with lingering brown leaves to make a resting-place for the jewels of the hoar-frost. Such hedgerows were often as tall as the labourers' cottages dotted along the lanes. . . . " FH *I*

—*the ride to Stone Court*: "[It] lay through a pretty bit of midland landscape, almost all meadows and pastures, with hedgerows still allowed to grow in busy beauty and to spread out coral fruit for the birds. Little details gave each field a particular physiognomy, dear to the eyes that have looked on them from childhood: the pool in the corner where the grasses were dank and trees leaned whisperingly; the great oak shadowing a bare place in mid-pasture; the high bank where the ash-trees grew; the sudden slope of the old marl-pit making a red background for the burdock; the huddled roofs and ricks of the homestead without a traceable way of approach; the grey gate and fences against the depths of the bordering wood; and the stray hovel, its old, old thatch full of mossy hills and valleys with wondrous modulations of light and shadow such as we travel far to see in later life, and see larger, but not more beautiful. These are the things that make the gamut of joy in landscape to midland-bred souls—the things they toddled among, or perhaps learned by heart standing between their father's knees while he drove leisurely." MM 12

Fauna

"Animals are such agreeable friends—they ask no questions, they pass no criticisms." GL 7

—ass: "Some listeners incautious in their epithets would have called Hinze an 'ass.' For my part I would never insult that intelligent and unpretending animal who no doubt brays with perfect simplicity and substantial meaning to those acquainted with his idiom, and if he feigns more submission than he feels, has weighty reasons for doing so—I would never, I say, insult that historic and ill-appreciated animal, the ass, by giving his name to a man whose continuous pretence is so shallow in its motive, so unexcused by any sharp appetite as this of Hinze's." TS 5

—cat: ". . . the lady-mother of the kitten sat sunning her white bosom in the window, and looked round with a sleepy air of expecting caresses, though she was not going to take any trouble for them." SM 16

—crocodile: "Even the slow, slime-loving crocodile,/The last of animals to take a hint,/Will then retire for ever from a scene/Where public feeling strongly sets against him." MP 81-4

—dog: "He showed the white object under his arm, which was a tiny Maltese puppy, one of nature's most naive toys." MM 3

"We are apt to be kinder to the brutes that love us than to the women that love us. Is it because the brutes are dumb?" AB 4

—domestic scene: "[His] hand was playing along Juno's brown curly back; and close to Juno's tail, which was wagging with calm matronly pleasure, the two brown pups were rolling over each other in an ecstatic duet of worrying noises. On a cushion a little removed sat Pug, with the air of a maiden lady who looked on these familiarities as animal weaknesses, which she made as little show as possible of observing." AB 16

—officious: ". . . the bull-dog lay stretched on the straw outside his kennel, with the black-and-tan terrier by his side, when the falling-to of the gate disturbed them, and set them barking, like good officials, before they had any distinct knowledge of the reason." AB 14

—puppies: " 'They *will* worry and gnaw—worry and gnaw they will, if it was one's Sunday cap as hung anywhere so as they could drag it. They know no difference, God help 'em: it's the pushing o' the teeth as sets 'em on, that's what it is.' " SM 14

—sheep-dog: ". . . following with a heedless unofficial air as of a beadle in undress." FH *I*

—showing off: "The sharp bark was the sign of an excited welcome that was awaiting them from a knowing brown terrier, who, after dancing at their legs in a hysterical manner, rushed with a worrying noise at a tortoise-shell kitten under the loom, and then rushed back with a sharp bark again, as much as to say, 'I have done my duty by this feeble creature, you perceive' . . . . " SM 16

—vegetarian future: "Boys will be boys, but dogs will all be moral,/With longer alimentary canals/Suited to diet vegetarian./The uglier breeds will fade from memory,/Or, being palæontological,/Live but as portraits in large learnèd books,/Distasteful to the feelings of an age/Nourished on purest beauty." MP 109-16

—donkey: "But the strength of the donkey mind lies in adopting a course inversely as the arguments urged, which, well considered, requires as great a mental force as the direct sequence; and the present donkey proved the first-rate order of his intelligence by coming to a dead stand-still just when the blows were thickest. Great was the shouting of the crowd, radiant the grinning of Bill Downes the stone-sawyer and the fortunate rider of this superior beast, which stood calm and stiff-legged in the midst of its triumph." AB 25

" . . . a friendly donkey, browsing with a log fastened to his foot—a meek donkey, not scornfully critical of human trivialities, but thankful to share in them, if possible, by getting his nose scratched . . . . " SM 16

—farm: " . . . a farm homestead, with its little cluster of beehive ricks, and placid groups of cows . . . . Contented speckled hens, industriously scratching for the rarely found corn, may sometimes do more for a

sick heart than a grove of nightingales; there is something irresistibly calming in the unsentimental cheeriness of topknotted pullets, unpetted sheep-dogs, and patient cart-horses enjoying a drink of muddy water." GL 20

—horses: " . . . the strong, submissive, meek-eyed beasts, who, I fancy, are looking mild reproach at [the waggoner] from between their blinkers, that he should crack his whip at them in that awful manner, as if they needed that hint! See how they stretch their shoulders, up the slope towards the bridge, with all the more energy because they are so near home. Look at their grand shaggy feet that seem to grasp the firm earth, at the patient strength of their necks bowed under the heavy collar, at the mighty muscles of their struggling haunches! I should like well to hear them neigh over their hardly-earned feed of corn, and see them, with their moist necks freed from the harness, dipping their eager nostrils into the muddy pond." MF I 1

—pets: "She was fond of feeding dependent creatures, and knew the private tastes of all the animals about the house, delighting in the little rippling sounds of her canaries when their beaks were busy with fresh seed, and in the small nibbling pleasures of certain animals which, lest she should appear too trivial, I will here call the more familiar rodents." MF VI 1

—rabbit: " . . . even a stray rabbit sat nibbling a leaf that was to its liking, in the middle of a grassy space, with an air that seemed quite impudent in so timid a creature." FH 1

—walrus: "But it is well known that the walrus, though not in the least a malignant animal, if allowed to display its remarkably plain person and blundering performances at ease in any element it chooses, becomes desperately savage and musters alarming auxiliaries when attacked or hurt." TS 3

—wart-pig: " . . . with tender and parental grunts . . . . " MP 119

—wombat: "Wombats much flattened as to their contour,/Perhaps from too much crushing in the ark,/But taking meekly that fatality . . . . " MP 120-22

Flora

—in Europe: " . . . When Europe fed afresh
from eastern story,
Was like a garden tangled with the glory
Of flowers hand-planted and of flowers air-
sown,
Climbing and trailing, budding and full-
blown,
Where purple bells are tossed amid pink
stars,
And springing blades, green troops in inno-
cent wars,
Crowd every shady spot of teeming earth,
Making invisible motion visible birth . . . . "
HL 3-10

—garden: " . . . the garden and orchards were Mr Jerome's glory, as well they might be; and there was nothing in which he had a more innocent pride . . . than in conducting a hitherto uninitiated visitor over his grounds, and making him in some degree aware of the incomparable advantages possessed by the inhabitants of the White House in the matter of red-streaked apples, russets, northern greens (excellent for baking), swan-egg pears, and early vegetables, to say nothing of flowering 'srubs', pink hawthorns, lavender bushes more than ever Mrs Jerome could use . . . . The garden was one of those old-fashioned paradises which hardly exist any longer except as memories of our childhood: no finical separation between flower- and kitchen-garden there; no monotony of enjoyment for one sense to the exclusion of another; but a charming paradisiacal mingling of all that was pleasant to the eyes and good for food. The rich flower-border running along every walk, with its endless succession of spring flowers, anemones, auriculas, wallflowers, sweet-williams, campanulas, snapdragons, and tiger-lilies, had its taller beauties, such as moss- and Provence roses, varied with espalier apple trees; the crimson of a carnation was carried out in the lurking crimson of the neighbouring strawberry-beds; you gathered a moss-rose one moment and a bunch of currants the next; you were in a delicious fluctuation between the scent of jasmine and the juice of gooseberries." JR 8

—silver birch: " . . . the delicious labyrinthine wood . . . called Fir-tree Grove, not because the firs were many, but because they were few. It was a wood of beeches and limes, with here and there a light-silver-stemmed birch—just the sort of wood most haunted by the nymphs; you see their white sun-lit limbs gleaming athwart the boughs, or peeping from behind the smooth-sweeping outline of a tall lime; you hear their soft liquid laughter—but if you look with a too curious sacrilegious eye, they vanish behind the silvery beeches [*sic*], they make you believe that their voice was only a running brooklet, perhaps they metamorphose themselves into a tawny squirrel that scampers away and mocks you from the topmost bough. Not a grove with measured grass or rolled gravel for you to tread upon, but with narrow, hollow-shaped, earthy paths, edged with faint dashes of delicate moss—paths which look as if they were made by the freewill of the trees and under-

wood, moving reverently aside to look at the tall queen of the white-footed nymphs." AB 12

—*trees in a park:* "All round, both near and far, there were grand trees, motionless in the still sunshine, and, like all large motionless things, seeming to add to the stillness." FH 1

Insect

—*spider:* "The spiders were especially a subject of speculation with her: she wondered if they had any relations outside the mill, for in that case there must be a painful difficulty in their family intercourse: a fat and floury spider, accustomed to take his fly well dusted with meal, must suffer a little at a cousin's table where the fly was *au naturel*, and the lady spiders must be mutually shocked at each other's appearance." MF I 4

—*wisdom:* "But for point of wisdom, I would choose
To know the mind that stirs between the wings
Of bees and building wasps, or fills the woods
With myriad murmurs of responsive sense
And true-aimed impulse, rather than to know
The thoughts of warriors." SG II ii

Lake

—*in Switzerland:* "My least solitary moments were those in which I pushed off in my boat, at evening, towards the centre of the lake; it seemed to me that the sky, and the glowing mountain-tops, and the wide blue water, surrounded me with a cherishing love such as no human face had shed on me since my mother's love had vanished out of my life. I used to do as **Jean Jacques** [**Rousseau**] did—lie down in my boat and let it glide where it would, while I looked up at the departing glow leaving one mountain-top after the other, as if the prophet's chariot of fire were passing over them on its way to the home of light. Then, when the white summits were all sad and corpse-like, I had to push homeward . . . . " LV 1

Landscape

—*Italy's Mediterranean shore:* "Her boat was lying still in a little creek; on her right hand lay the speckless sapphire-blue of the Mediterranean; on her left one of those scenes which were and still are repeated again and again like a sweet rhythm, on the shores of that loveliest sea.

"In a deep curve of the mountains lay a breadth of green land, curtained by gentle tree-shadowed slopes leaning towards the rocky heights. Up these slopes might be seen here and there, gleaming between the tree-tops, a pathway leading to a little irregular mass of building that seemed to have clambered in a hasty way up the mountain-side, and taken a difficult stand there for the sake of showing the tall belfry as a sight of beauty to the scattered and clustered houses of the village below. The rays of the newly-risen sun fell obliquely on the westward horn of this crescent-shaped nook: all else lay in dewy shadow. No sound came across the stillness; the very waters seemed to have curved themselves there for rest." R 68

—*north midlands:* "High up against the horizon were the huge conical masses of hill, like giant mounds intended to fortify this region of corn and grass against the keen and hungry winds of the north; not distant enough to be clothed in purple mystery, but with sombre greenish sides visibly specked with sheep, whose motion was only revealed by memory, not detected by sight; wooed from day to day by the changing hours, but responding with no change in themselves—left for ever grim and sullen after the flush of morning, the winged gleams of the April noonday, the parting crimson glory of the ripening summer sun. And directly below them the eye rested on a more advanced line of hanging woods, divided by bright patches of pasture or furrowed crops, and not yet deepened into the uniform leafy curtain of high summer, but still showing the warm tints of the young oak and the tender green of the ash and lime.

"Then came the valley, where the woods grew thicker, as if they had rolled down and hurried together from the patches left smooth on the slope, that they might take the better care of the tall mansion which lifted its parapets and sent its faint blue summer smoke among them. Doubtless there was a large sweep of park and a broad glassy pool in front of that mansion, but the swelling slope of meadow would not let our traveller see them from the village green. He saw instead a foreground which was just as lovely—the level sunlight lying like transparent gold among the gently-curving stems of the feathered grass and the tall red sorrel, and the white umbels of the hemlocks lining the bushy hedgerows. It was that moment in summer when the sound of the scythe being whetted makes us cast more lingering looks at the flower-sprinkled tresses of the meadows." ¶AB 2

—*panorama:* "More than three centuries and a half ago, in the mid spring-time of 1492, we are sure that the angel of the dawn, as he travelled with broad slow wing from the Levant to the Pillars of Hercules, and from the summits of the Caucasus across all the snowy Alpine ridges to the dark nakedness of the Western isles, saw nearly the same outline of firm land and unstable sea—saw the same great mountain shadows on the same valleys as he has seen to-day—saw olive mounts, and pine forests, and the broad plains green with young corn or rain-freshened grass—saw the domes and spires of cities rising by the river-sides or mingled with the sedge-like masts on the many-curved sea-coast, in the same spots where they rise to-day.

"And as the faint light of his course pierced into the dwellings of men, it fell, as now, on the rosy warmth of nestling children; on the haggard waking of sorrow and sickness; on the hasty uprising of the hard-handed labourer; and on the late sleep of the night-student, who had been questioning the stars or the sages, or his own soul, for that hidden knowledge which would break through the barrier of man's brief life, and show its dark path, that seemed to bend no whither, to be an arc in an immeasurable circle of light and glory. The great river-courses which have shaped the lives of men have hardly changed; and those other streams, the life-currents that ebb and flow in human hearts, pulsate to the same great needs, the same great loves and terrors. As our thought follows close in the slow wake of the dawn, we are impressed with the broad sameness of the human lot, which never alters in the main headings of its history—hunger and labour, seed-time and harvest, love and death." ¶R *P*

—valley near Weimar: "It would be difficult to imagine a more peace-inspiring scene than this little valley. The hanging woods—the soft coloring and graceful outline of the uplands—the village, with its roofs and spire of a reddish-violet hue, muffled in luxuriant trees—the white Kurhaus glittering on a grassy slope—the avenue of poplars contrasting its pretty primness with the wild bushy outline of the wood-covered hill, which rises abruptly from the smooth, green meadows—the clear winding stream, now sparkling in the sun, now hiding itself under soft gray willows—all this makes an enchanting picture." 3M 167-8

Nature

—beauty and apprehension: "She continued to stand, however, looking at the placid churchyard with the long shadows of the gravestones across the bright green hillocks, and at the glowing autumn colours of the Rectory trees beyond. Before such calm external beauty the presence of a vague fear is more distinctly felt—like a raven flapping its slow wing across the sunny air." SM 17

—benign: "She tried to have hope and trust, though it was hard to believe that the future would be anything else than the harvest of the seed that was being sown before her eyes. But always there is seed being sown silently and unseen, and everywhere there come sweet flowers without our foresight or labour. We reap what we sow, but nature has love over and above that justice, and gives us shadow and blossom and fruit that spring from no planting of ours." JR 5

—deceptive: "It was a still afternoon—the golden light was lingering languidly among the upper boughs, only glancing down here and here on the purple pathway and its edge of faintly-sprinkled moss: an afternoon in which destiny disguises her cold awful face behind a hazy radiant veil, encloses us in warm downy wings, and poisons us with violet-scented breath." AB 12

—heat: "Heat is a great agent and a useful word, but considered as a means of explaining the universe it requires an extensive knowledge of differences; and as a means of explaining character 'sensitiveness' is in much the same predicament." DD 6

—indifferent: "A merry day for the children . . . and the grown-up people, too, were in good spirits . . . .

"And yet a day on which a blighting sorrow may fall upon a man. For if it be true that Nature at certain moments seems charged with a presentiment of one individual lot, must it not also be true that she seems unmindful, unconscious of another? For there is no hour that has not its births of gladness and despair, no morning brightness that does not bring new sickness to desolation as well as new forces to genius and love. There are so many of us, and our lots are so different: what wonder that Nature's mood is often in harsh contrast with the great crisis of our lives? We are children of a large family, and must learn, as such children do, not to expect that our hurts will be made much of—to be content with little nurture and caressing, and help each other the more." AB 27

—inexorable: "While this poor little heart was being bruised with a weight too heavy for it, nature was holding on her calm inexorable way, in unmoved and terrible beauty. The stars were rushing in their eternal courses; the tides swelled to the level of the last expectant weed; the sun was making brilliant day to busy nations on the other side of the swift earth. The stream of human thought and deed was hurrying and broadening onward. The astronomer was at his telescope; the great ships were labouring over the waves; the toiling eagerness of commerce, the fierce spirit of revolution [it is 1788], were only ebbing in brief rest; and sleepless statesmen were dreading the possible crisis of the morrow. What were our

little Tina and her trouble in this mighty torrent, rushing from one awful unknown to another? Lighter than the smallest centre of quivering life in the water-drop, hidden and uncared for as the pulse of anguish in the breast of the tiniest bird that has fluttered down to its nest with the long-sought food, and has found the nest torn and empty." GL 5

—vision of joy: " . . . and now in the warm sunlight she saw that rich dark beauty which seemed to gather round it all images of joy—purple vines festooned between the elms, the strong corn perfecting itself under the vibrating heat, bright winged creatures hurrying and resting among the flowers, round limbs beating the earth in gladness with cymbals held aloft, light melodies chanted to the thrilling rhythm of strings—all objects and all sounds that tell of Nature revelling in her force." R 17

See A:Family—*resemblance*

River

—boating: "They glided rapidly along . . . helped by the backward-flowing tide . . . on between the silent, sunny fields and pastures which seemed filled with a natural joy that had no reproach for theirs. The breath of the young, unwearied day, the delicious rhythmic dip of the oars, the fragmentary song of a passing bird heard now and then as if it were only the overflowing of brim-full gladness, the sweet solitude of a twofold consciousness that was mingled into one by that grave untiring gaze which need not be averted—what else could there be in their minds for the first hour?" MF VI 13

—flood aftermath: "Nature repairs her ravages—repairs them with her sunshine, and with human labour. The desolation wrought by that flood, had left little visible trace on the face of the earth, five years after. The fifth autumn was rich in golden corn-stacks, rising in thick clusters among the distant hedgerows; the wharves and warehouses on the Floss were busy again, with echoes of eager voices, with hopeful lading and unlading . . . .

"Nature repairs her ravages—but not all. The uptorn trees are not rooted again—the parted hills are left scarred: if there is a new growth, the trees are not the same as the old, and the hills underneath their green vesture bear the marks of the past rending. To the eyes that have dwelt on the past, there is no thorough repair." MF VII 6

—flood and rescue: " 'The water's rising so fast,' said Bob, 'I doubt it'll be in at the chambers before long—th' house is so low. I've more mind to get Prissy and the child and the mother into the boat, if I could and trusten to the water—for th' old house is none so safe. And if I let go the boat—but *you,*' he exclaimed, suddenly lifting the light of his lanthorn on Maggie, as she stood in the rain with the oar in her hand and her black hair streaming.

"Maggie had no time to answer, for a new tidal current swept along the line of the houses, and drove both the boats out on to the wide water, with a force that carried them far past the meeting current of the river . . . .

"The whole thing had been so rapid—so dreamlike—that the threads of ordinary association were broken: she sank down on the seat clutching the oar mechanically, and for a long while had no distinct conception of her position. The first thing that waked her to fuller consciousness, was the cessation of the rain, and a perception that the darkness was divided by the faintest light, which parted the overhanging gloom from the immeasurable watery level below. She was driven out upon the flood:—that awful visitation of God which her father used to talk of—which had made the nightmare of her childish dreams. And with that thought there rushed in the vision of the old home—and Tom—and her mother—they had all listened together.

" 'O God, where am I? Which is the way home?' she cried out, in the dim loneliness.

"What was happening to them at the Mill? The flood had once nearly destroyed it. They might be in danger—in distress: her mother and her brother, alone there, beyond reach of help! Her whole soul was strained now on that thought; and she saw the long-loved faces looking for help into the darkness, and finding none.

"She was floating in smooth water now—perhaps far on the over-flooded fields. There was no sense of present danger to check the outgoing of her mind to the old home; and she strained her eyes against the curtain of gloom that she might seize the first sight of her whereabouts—that she might catch some faint suggestion of the spot towards which all her anxieties tended.

"O how welcome, the widening of that dismal watery level—the gradual uplifting of the cloudy firmament—the slowly defining blackness of objects above the glassy dark! Yes—she must be out on the fields—those were the tops of hedgerow trees. Which way did the river lie? Looking behind her, she saw the lines of black trees: looking before her there were none: then, the river lay before her. She seized an oar and began to paddle the boat forward with the energy of wakening hope: the dawning seemed to advance more swiftly, now she was in action; and she could soon see the poor dumb beasts crowding piteously on a mound where they had taken refuge. Onward she paddled and rowed by turns in the growing twilight: her wet clothes clung round her, and her streaming hair was dashed about by the wind, but she was hardly conscioius of any bodily sensations—except a sensation of strength, inspired by mighty emotion . . . .

"But now there was a large dark mass in the distance, and near to her Maggie could discern the current of the river. The dark mass must be—yes, it was—St Ogg's. Ah, now she knew which way to look for the first glimpse of the well-known trees—the grey willows, the now yellowing chestnuts—and above them the old roof; but there was no colour, no shape yet: all was faint and dim . . . .

"She must get her boat into the current of the Floss—else she would never be able to pass the Ripple, and approach the house: this was the thought that occurred to her, as she imagined with more and more vividness the state of things round the old home. But then she might be carried very far down, and be unable to guide her boat out of the current again. For the first time distinct ideas of danger began to press upon her; but there was no choice of courses, no room for hesitation, and she floated into the current. Swiftly she went now, without effort; more and more clearly in the lessening distance and the growing light, she began to discern the objects that she knew must be the well-known trees and roofs: nay, she was not far off a rushing muddy current that must be the strangely altered Ripple.

"Great God! there were floating masses in it, that might dash against her boat as she passed, and cause her to perish too soon [*sic*]. What were those masses?—

"For the first time Maggie's heart began to beat in an agony of dread. She sat helpless —dimly conscious that she was being floated along—more intensely conscious of the anticipated clash. But the horror was transient: it passed away before the oncoming warehouses of St Ogg's: she had passed the mouth of the Ripple, then: *now,* she must use all her skill and power to manage the boat and get it if possible, out of the current. She could see now that the bridge was broken down: she could see the masts of a stranded vessel far out over the watery field. But no boats were to be seen moving on the river—such as had been laid hands on must be employed in the flooded streets.

"With new resolution, Maggie seized her oar, and stood up again to paddle: but the now ebbing tide added to the swiftness of the river, and she was carried along beyond the bridge. She could hear shouts from the windows overlooking the river, as if the people there were calling to her. It was not till she had passed on nearly to Tofton that she could get the boat clear of the current. Then with one yearning look towards her uncle Deane's house that lay farther down the river, she took to both her oars and rowed with all her might across the watery fields, back towards the Mill. Colour was beginning to awake now, and as she approached the Dorlcote fields, she could discern the tints of the trees—could see the old Scotch firs far to the right, and the home chestnuts—Oh! how deep they lay in the water: deeper than the trees on this side the hill. And the roof of the Mill—where was it? Those heavy fragments hurrying down the Ripple—what had they meant? But it was not the house—the house stood firm: drowned up to the first story, but still firm—or was it broken in at the end towards the Mill?

"With panting joy that she was there at last—joy that overcame all distress, Maggie neared the front of the house. At first she heard no sound: she saw no object moving. Her boat was on a level with the upstairs windows. She called out in a loud piercing voice,

" 'Tom, where are you? Mother, where are you? Here is Maggie!'

"Soon, from the window of the attic in the central gable, she heard Tom's voice:

" 'Who is it? Have you brought a boat?'

" 'It is I, Tom—Maggie . . . . '

" 'Alone, Maggie?' said Tom, in a voice of deep astonishment, as he opened the middle window on a level with the boat.

" 'Yes, Tom: God has taken care of me, to bring me to you. Get in quickly. Is there no one else?'

" 'No,' said Tom, stepping into the boat, 'I fear the man is drowned—he was carried down the Ripple, I think, when part of the mill fell with the crash of trees and stones against it: I've shouted again and again, and there has been no answer. Give me the oars, Maggie' . . . .

"Tom rowed with untired vigour, and with a different speed from poor Maggie's. The boat was soon in the current of the river again, and soon they would be at Tofton . . . .

"Nothing else was said; a new danger was being carried towards them by the river. Some wooden machinery had just given way on one of the wharves, and huge fragments were being floated along. The sun was rising now, and the wide area of watery desolation was spread out in the dreadful clearness around them—in dreadful clearness floated onwards the hurrying, threatening masses. A large company in a boat that was working its way along under the Tofton houses, observed their danger, and shouted, 'Get out of the current!'

"But that could not be done at once, and Tom, looking before him, saw Death rushing on them. Huge fragments, clinging together in fatal fellowship, made one wide mass across the stream." MV VII 5

—panorama: "A wide plain, where the broadening Floss hurries on between its green banks to the sea, and the loving tide, rushing to meet it, checks its passage with an impetuous embrace. On this mighty tide the black ships—laden with the fresh-scented fir-planks, with rounded sacks of oil-bearing seed, or with the dark glitter of coal—are borne along to the town of St Ogg's, which shows its aged, fluted red roofs and the broad gables of its wharves between the low wooded hill and the river brink, tinging the water with a soft purple hue under the transient glance of this February sun. Far away on each hand stretch the rich pastures and the patches of dark earth, made ready for the seed of broad-leaved green crops, or touched already with the tint of the tender-bladed autumn-sown corn. There is a remnant still of the last year's golden clusters of bee-hive ricks rising at intervals beyond the hedgerows; and everywhere the hedgerows are studded with trees: the distant ships seem to be lifting their masts and stretching their red-brown sails close among the branches of the spreading ash. Just by the red-roofed town the tributary Ripple flows with a lively current into the Floss. How lovely the little river is with its dark, changing wavelets! It seems to me like a living companion while I wander along the bank and listen to its low placid voice, as to the voice of one who is deaf and loving. I remember those large dipping willows . . . I remember the stone bridge . . . " MF I 1

—tributary: "The stream is brim full now, and lies high in this little withy plantation, and half drowns the grassy fringe of the croft in front of the house. As I look at the full stream, the vivid grass, the delicate bright-green powder softening the outline of the great trunks and branches that gleam from under the bare purple boughs, I am in love with moistness, and envy the white ducks that are dipping their heads far into the water here among the withes—unmindful of the awkward appearance they make in the drier world above." MF I 1

Seasons

—autumn: "The inexorable ticking of the clock is like the throb of pain to sensations made keen by a sickening fear. And so it is with the great clockwork of nature. Daisies and buttercups give way to the brown waving grasses, tinged with the warm red sorrel; the waving grasses are swept away, and the meadows lie like emeralds set in the bushy hedgerows; the tawny-tipped corn begins to bow with the weight of the full ear; the reapers are bending amongst it, and it soon stands on sheaves; then, presently, the patches of yellow stubble lie side by side with streaks of dark-red earth, which the plough is turning up in preparation for the new-thrashed seed. And this passage from beauty to beauty, which to the happy is like the flow of a melody, measures for many a human heart the approach of foreseen anguish—seems hurrying on the moment when the shadow of dread will be followed up by the reality of despair." GL 5

—sunshine: "The sunshine was on [the fields]: that early autumn sunshine which we should know was not summer's, even if there were not the touches of yellow on the lime and chestnut: the Sunday sunshine, too which has more than autumnal calmness for the working man: the morning sun-shine, which still leaves the dew-crystals on the fine gossamer webs in the shadow of the bushy hedgerows." AB 51

And see A:Old Maid

—February: "Bright February days have a stronger charm of hope about them than any other days in the year. One likes to pause in the mild rays of the sun, and look over the gates at the patient plough-horses turning at the end of the furrow, and think that the beautiful year is all before one. The birds seem to feel just the same: their notes are as clear as the clear air. There are no leaves on the trees and hedgerows, but how green all the grassy fields are! and the dark purplish brown of the ploughed earth and the bare branches, is beautiful too. What a glad world this looks like, as one drives or rides along the valleys and over the hills!" AB 35

"One fine February day, when already the golden and purple crocuses were out on the terrace—one of those flattering days which sometimes precede the north-east winds of March, and make believe that the coming spring will be enjoyable . . . . " FH 43

—early summer: "There was one time of the year which was held in Raveloe to be especially suitable for a wedding. It was when the great lilacs and laburnums in the old-fashioned gardens showed their golden and purple wealth above the lichen-tinted walls, and when there were calves still young enough to want bucketfuls of fragrant milk. People were not so busy then as they must become when the full cheese-making and the mowing had set in; and besides, it was a time when a light bridal dress could be worn with comfort and seen to advantage." SM concl

—harvest-time: "It was a fine mid-harvest time, not too warm for a noonday ride of five miles to be delightful: the poppies glowed on the borders of the fields, there was enough breeze to move gently like a social spirit among the ears of uncut corn, and to wing the shadow of a cloud across the soft grey downs; here the sheaves were standing, there the horses were straining their muscles under the last load from a wide space of stubble, but everywhere the green pastures made a broader setting for the corn-fields, and the cattle took their rest under wide branches. The road lay through a bit of country where the dairy-farms looked much as they did in the days of our forefathers—where peace and permanence seemed to find a home away from the busy change that sent the railway train flying in the distance." DD 13

—January: "It was an exquisite January morning in which there was no threat of rain, but a grey sky making the calmest background for the charms of a mild winter scene—the grassy borders of the lanes, the hedgerows sprinkled with red berries and haunted with low twitterings, the purple bareness of the elms, the rich brown of the furrows." DD 7

—midsummer: "The thirtieth of July was come; and it was one of those half-dozen warm days which sometimes occur in the middle of a rainy English summer. No rain had fallen for the last three or four days, and the weather was perfect for that time of the year: there was less dust than usual on the dark green hedgerows, and on the wild camomile that starred the roadside, yet the grass was dry enough for the little children to roll on it, and there was no cloud but a long dash of light, downy ripple, high, high up in the far-off blue sky. Perfect weather for an outdoor July merrymaking, yet surely not the best time of year to be born in.

"Nature seems to make a hot pause just then—all the loveliest flowers are gone; the sweet time of early growth and vague hopes is past; and yet the time of harvest and ingathering is not come, and we tremble at the possible storms that may ruin the precious fruit in the moment of its ripeness. The woods are all one dark monotonous green; the waggon-loads of hay no longer creep along the lanes, scattering their sweet-smelling fragments on the blackberry branches; the pastures are often a little tanned, yet the corn has not got its last splendour of red and gold; the lambs and calves have lost all traces of their innocent frisky prettiness, and have become stupid young sheep and cows. But it is a time of leisure on the farm—that pause between hay and corn-harvest . . . . " AB 22

"It is easy to northern people to rise early on Midsummer morning, to see the dew on the grassy edge of the dusty pathway, to notice the fresh shoots among the darker green of the oak and fir in the coppice, and to look over the gate at the shorn meadow, without recollecting that it is the Nativity of St John the Baptist." R 8

—spring: "But the sweet spring came to Milby notwithstanding: the elm-tops were red with buds; the churchyard was starred with daisies; the lark showered his love-music on the flat fields; the rainbows hung over the dingy town, clothing the very roofs and chimneys in a strange transfiguring beauty." JR 2

—winter: "The wintry days passed for Romola as the white ships pass one who is standing lonely on the shore—passing in silence and sameness, yet each bearing a hidden burden of coming change." R 49

Sun

—a burden: "The eye of day,
The insistent summer sun, seems pitiless,
Shining in all the barren crevices
Of weary life, leaving no shade, no dark,
Where I may dream that hidden waters lie;
As pitiless as to some shipwrecked man,
Who gazing from his narrow shoal of sand
On the wide unspecked round of blue and blue
Sees that full light is errorless despair." SG III

—light of day: "The rain had ceased, and the light from the breaking clouds fell on **Savonarola** . . . . But there seemed no glory in the light that fell on him now, no smile of heaven: it was only that light which shines on, patiently and impartially, justifying or condemning by simply showing all

things in the slow history of their ripening." R 65

—*sudden:* "It seemed that the sun was going to chase away the greyness. The light is perhaps never felt more strongly as a divine presence stirring all those inarticulate sensibilities which are our deepest life, than in these moments when it instantaneously awakens the shadows. A certain awe which inevitably accompanied this most momentous act of her life became a more conscious element in Romola's feeling as she found herself in the sudden presence of the impalpable golden glory and the long shadow of herself that was not to be escaped." R 37

Time of Day

—*before dawn:* "But by degrees
Stealthily faint, disturbing with slow loss
That showed not yet full promise of a gain,
The light was changing, and the watch intense
Of moon and stars seemed weary, shivering:
The sharp white brightness passed from off the rocks
Carrying the shadows: beauteous Night lay dead
Under the pall of twilight, and the love-star
Sickened and shrank." SG II i

—*dawn* " . . . where the new-bathed Day
With oriflamme uplifted o'er the peaks
Saddens the breasts of northward-looking snows
That loved the night . . . . " SG I i

—*daylight:* "The daylight changes the aspect of misery to us, as of everything else. In the night it presses on our imagination—the forms it takes are false, fitful, exaggerated; in broad day, it sickens our sense with the dreary existence of definite measurable reality. The man who looks with ghastly horror on all his property aflame in the dead of night, has not half the sense of destitution he will have in the morning, when he walks over the ruins lying blackened in the pitiless sunshine." JR 16

—*dusk:* "It was a cloudy day, and nearing dusk. Arno ran dark and shivering; the hills were mournful; and Florence with its girdling stone towers had that silent, tomb-like look, which unbroken shadow gives to a city seen from above." R 36

"Soon the gold was shrinking and getting duskier in sea and sky, and there was no living thing in sight, no sound but the lulling monotony of the lapping waves . . . . Then she loosed the boat from its moorings, and tried to urge it with an oar, till she was far out from the land, till the sea was dark even to the west, and the stars were disclosing themselves like a palpitating life over the wide heavens." R 61

—*late afternoon:* " . . . it was half-past four, and the grey day was dying gloriously, its western clouds all broken into narrowing purple strata before a wide-spreading saffron clearness, which in the sky had a monumental calm, but on the river, with its changing objects, was reflected as a luminous movement, the alternate flash of ripples or currents, the sudden glow of the brown sail, the passage of laden barges from blackness into colour, making an active response to that brooding glory." DD 40

—*morning:* "It was one of those grey mornings after light rains, which become delicious about twelve o'clock, when the clouds part a little, and the scent of the earth is sweet along the lanes and by the hedgerows." MM 56

—*Sunday:* "You might have known it was Sunday if you had only waked up in the farmyard. The cocks and hens seemed to know it, and made only crooning subdued noises; the very bull-dog looked less savage, as if he would have been satisfied with a smaller bite than usual. The sunshine seemed to call all things to rest and not to labour: it was asleep itself on the moss-grown cow-shed; on the group of white ducks nestling together with their bills tucked under their wings; on the old black sow stretched languidly on the straw, while her largest young one found an excellent spring bed on his mother's fat ribs . . . . " AB 18

—*noon:* "One day—it was just about noon, when bad news always seems most sickening . . . . " JR 24

—*sunset:* "The sun was on the point of setting, and was sending level crimson rays among the great trunks of the old oaks, and touching every bare patch of ground with a transient glory, that made it look like a jewel dropt upon the grass." AB 27

"There was to be no rain, after all; the clouds rolled off to the horizon again, making the great purple rampart, and long purple isles of that wondrous land which reveals itself to us when the sun goes down—the land that the evening star watches over." MF VI 13

—*on the river:* "He used his oars little, satisfied to go with the tide and be taken back by it. It was his habit to indulge himself in that solemn passivity which easily comes with the lengthening shadows and mellowing light, when thinking and desiring melt together imperceptibly, and what in other hours may have seemed argument takes the quality of passionate vision . . . the sun was near setting, and the approach of his favourite hour—with its deepening stillness, and darkening masses of tree and building between the double glow of the sky and the river—disposed him to linger as if they had been an unfinished strain of music. He looked out for a perfectly solitary spot where he . . . could watch out the light of sunset and the opening of that bead-roll which some oriental poet describes as God's call to the little stars, who each answer, 'Here am I.' " DD 17

—in Weimar: "Here, too, was the place for seeing a lovely sunset—such a sunset as September sometimes gives us—when the western horizon is like a rippled sea of gold, sending over the whole hemisphere golden vapors, which, as they near the east, are subdued to a deep rose-color." 3M 157

—twilight: "But what scene was ever commonplace in the descending sunlight, when colour has awakened from its noonday sleep, and the long shadows awe us like a disclosed presence?" JR 26

" . . . the evening light that lay gently in the grassy alleys between the fern, and made the beauty of their living green more visible than it had been in the overpowering flood of noon . . . . " AB 13

"The lamps were already lit, though the sun had not long set, and there was that calm light out of doors in which we seem to see all objects more distinctly than in the broad day." AB 26

" . . . that golden sky which was the doubly blessed symbol of advancing day and of approaching rest." DD 38

Weather

—benign: "He is glad to see the promise of settled weather now, for getting in the hay, about which the farmers have been fearful; and there is something so healthful in the sharing of a joy that is general and not merely personal, that this thought about the hay-harvest reacts on his state of mind, and makes his resolution seem an easier matter. A man about town might perhaps consider that these influences were not to be felt out of a child's story-book; but when you are among the fields and hedgerows, it is impossible to maintain a consistent superiority to simple natural pleasures." AB 16

—climate: " . . . it was like the influence of climate, which no resistance can overcome." AB 10

—partly cloudy: "Driving was pleasant, for rain in the night had laid the dust, and the blue sky looked far off, away from the region of the great clouds that sailed in masses. The earth looked like a happy lace under the vast heavens . . . ." MM 62

—rain—for lovers: see LM:Courtship*—and rain*

—sun and rain: " . . . there is always a stronger sense of life when the sun is brilliant after rain . . . . " AB 6

—wind: "All earthly things have their lull: even on nights when the most unappeasable wind is raging, there will be a moment of stillness before it crashes among the boughs again, and storms against the windows, and howls like a thousand lost demons through the keyholes." GL 10

—and sun: "Grand masses of cloud were hurried across the blue, and the great round hills . . . seemed alive with their flying shadows; the sun was hidden for a moment, and then shone out warm again like a recovered joy; the leaves, still green, were tossed off the hedgerow trees by the wind; around the farmhouses there was a sound of clapping doors, the apples fell in the orchards, and the stray horses on the green sides of the lanes and on the common had their manes blown about their faces. And yet the wind seemed only part of the general gladness, because the sun was shining." AB 27

First and Last Things

"She felt that intensity of life which seems to transcend both grief and joy—in which the mind seems to itself akin to elder forces that wrought out existence before the birth of pleasure and pain." R 60

Angels

—*good:* "When the earth was thrown on Mamsey's coffin, and the son, in crape scarf and hatband, turned away homeward, his good angel, lingering with outstretched wing on the edge of the grave, cast one despairing look after him, and took flight forever." JR 13

—*hand extended:* "In old days there were angels who came and took men by the hand and led them away from the city of destruction. We see no white-winged angels now. But yet men are led away from threatening destruction: a hand is put into theirs, which leads them forth gently towards a calm and bright land, so that they look no more backward; and the hand may be a little child's." SM 14

—*missing:* "No radiant angel came across the gloom with a clear message for her. In those times, as now, there were human beings who never saw angels or heard perfectly clear messages. Such truth as came to them was brought confusedly in the voices and deeds of men not at all like the seraphs of unfailing wing and piercing vision—men who believed falsities as well as truths, and did the wrong as well as the right. The helping hands stretched out to them were the hands of men who stumbled and often saw dimly, so that these beings unvisited by angels had no other choice than to grasp that stumbling guidance along the path of reliance and action which is the path of life, or else to pause in loneliness and disbelief, which is no path, but the arrest of inaction and death." R 36

Death

"This was God's last gift to Moses, this the hour when soul must part from self and be but soul." DM 14-6

—*corpse:* "In the corpse we love, it is the *likeness* we see—it is the likeness, which makes itself felt the more keenly because something else *was,* and *is not.*" AB 43

—*the dead:* "Our dead are never dead to us until we have forgotten them; they can be injured by us, they can be wounded; they know all our penitence, all our aching sense that their place is empty; all the kisses we bestow on the smallest relic of their presence. And the aged peasant-woman most of all believes that her dead are conscious." AB 10

—*evidences:* "The heart will by-and-by be still—*ubi sæva indignatio ulterius cor lacerare nequit** the eye will cease to entreat, the ear will be deaf; the brain will have ceased from all wants as well as from all work." LV 1

*"Where savage indignation can no longer tear the heart"—Swift, drawing on Juvenal *Satire* I 79

—*the fact:* "Darkness—darkness—no pain—nothing but darkness: but I am passing on and on through the darkness: my thought stays in the darkness, but always with a sense of moving onward." LV 1

—*funeral:* " . . . worldly faces never look so worldly as at a funeral. They have the same effect of grating incongruity as the sound of a coarse voice breaking the solemn silence of night." JR 25

—*sermon:* "It spoke briefly and simply of the words, 'In the midst of life we are in death'—how the present moment is all we can call our own for works of mercy, of righteous dealing, and of family tenderness. All very old truths—but what we thought the oldest truth becomes the most startling to us in the week when we have looked on the dead face of one who has made a part of our own lives. For when men want to impress us with the effect of a new and wonderfully vivid light, do they not let it fall on the most familiar objects, that we may measure its intensity by remembering the former dimness?" AB 18

—*of grace:* "Upon the death-dewed lips
A kiss descended, pure, unspeakable—
The bodiless Love without embracing Love
That lingered in the body, drew it forth
With heavenly strength and carried it to heaven." DM 91-5

—*imminent:* "Here was a man who now for the first time found himself looking into the eyes of death—who was passing through one of those rare moments of experience when we feel the truth of a commonplace, which is as different from what we call knowing it, as the vision of waters upon the earth is different from the delirious vision of the water which cannot be had to cool the burning tongue. When the commonplace 'We must all die' transforms itself suddenly into the acute consciousness 'I must die—and soon,' then death grapples us, and his fingers are cruel; afterwards, he may come to fold us in his arms as our mother did, and our last moment of dim earthly discerning may be like the first." MM 42

—*last moments:* "The drowning man, urged by the supreme agony, lives in an instant through all his happy and unhappy past: when the dark flood has fallen like a curtain, memory, in a single moment, sees the drama acted over again. And even in those earlier crises, which are but types of death—when we are cut off abruptly from the life we have known, when we can no longer expect tomorrow to resemble yesterday, and find ourselves by some sudden shock on the confines of the unknown—there is often the same sort of lightning-flash through the dark and unfrequented chambers of memory." JR 14

—*of a loved one:* "Can we believe that the dear dead are gone?
Love in sad weeds forgets the funeral day,
Opens the chamber door and almost smiles—
Then sees the sunbeams pierce athwart the bed
Where the pale face is not." SG II i

—*and memory:* " . . . she had forgotten his faults as we forget the sorrows of our departed childhood . . . . " AB 10

—*regret:* "Oh, the anguish of that thought that we can never atone to our dead for the stinted affection we gave them, for the light answers we returned to their plaints or their pleadings, for the little reverence we showed to their sacred human soul that lived so close to us, and was the divinest thing God had given us to know!" SF 9

"When death, the great Reconciler, has come, it is never our tenderness that we repent of, but our severity." AB 4

" . . . his thoughts ran constantly on what the old man's feelings had been in moments of humiliation, when he had held down his head before the rebukes of his son. When our indignation is borne in submissive silence, we are apt to feel twinges of doubt afterwards as to our own generosity, if not justice: how much more when the object of our anger has gone into everlasting silence, and we have seen his face for the last time in the meekness of death?" AB 18

—*romance:* "It is a sad weakness in us, after all, that the thought of a man's death hallows him anew to us; as if life were not sacred too—as if it were comparatively a light thing to fall in love and reverence to the brother who has to climb the whole toilsome steep with us, and all our tears and tenderness were due to the one who is spared that hard journey." JR 11

—*unanticipated:* " . . . it is often observable, that the older a man gets, the more difficult it is to him to retain a believing conception of his own death." SM 5

—*words to a friend:* " 'Death is coming to me as the divine kiss which is both parting and reunion—which takes me from your bodily eyes and gives me full presence in your soul.' " DD 70

The Divine

" . . . the one Unknown Presence revealed and yet hidden by the moving curtain of the earth and sky." LV 2

—*confronted:* "What are all our personal loves when we have been sharing in that supreme agony? In the first moments when we come away from the presence of death, every other relation to the living is merged, to our feeling, in the great relation of a common nature and a common destiny." LV 2

—*marriages:* " 'The Omnipresent,' said a Rabbi, 'is occupied in making marriages.' The levity of the saying lies in the ear of him who hears it; for by marriages the speaker meant all the wondrous combinations of the universe whose issue makes our good and evil." DD 62

—*miracle:* "[They] stood bare-headed in the presence of a rescue which had come from outside the limit of their own power—from that region of trust and resignation which has been in all ages called divine." R 43

Fate

—*inexorable:* "Fate was too strong for him; he had thought to master her inclination and had fled over the seas to that end; but she caught him, tied an apron round him, and snatching him from all other devices, made him devise cakes and patties in a kitchen at Kingstown. He was getting submissive to her, since she paid him with tolerable gains . . . . " BJ 3

—*Nemesis:* "Nemesis is lame, but she is of colossal stature, like the gods; and sometimes, while her sword is not yet unsheathed, she stretches out her huge left arm and grasps her victim. The mighty hand is invisible, but the victim totters under the dire clutch." JR 13

—*our common lot:* " . . . he felt the hard pressure of our common lot, the yoke of that mighty resistless destiny laid upon us by the acts of other men as well as our own." FH 49

—*present:* "And yet she was shaken, as if that destiny which men thought of as a sceptred deity had come to her, and grasped her with fingers of flesh." R 40

—*synchronicity:* " ' . . . we know not all the pathways. Has there not been a meeting among them, as of the operations in one soul, where an idea being born and breathing draws the elements towards it, and is fed and grows? For all things are bound together in that Omnipresence which is the place and habitation of the world, and events are as a glass where-through our eyes see some of the pathways.' " DD 63

Life

—*artificial:* "In this artificial life of ours, it is not often we see a human face with all a heart's agony in it, uncontrolled by self-consciousness; when we do see it, it startles us as if we had suddenly waked into the real world of which this everyday one is but a puppet-show copy." JR 18

—*the best:* " 'That must be the best life.'

" 'What life, my dear child?'

" 'Why, that where one bears and does everything because of some great and strong feeling—so that this and that in one's circumstances don't signify.' " FH 26

—*complex:* "Life was so complicated a game that the devices of skill were liable to be defeated at every turn by air-blown chances, incalculable as the descent of thistle-down." R 47

—*depressing details:* "Contemptible details these, to make part of a history; yet the turn of most lives is hardly to be accounted for without them. They are continually entering with cumulative force into a mood until it gets the mass and momentum of a theory or a motive. Even philosophy is not quite free from such determining influences; and to be dropt solitary at an ugly irrelevant-looking spot with a sense of no income on the mind, might well prompt a man to discouraging speculation on the origin of things and the reason of a world where a subtle thinker found himself so badly off." DD 21

—*diversity:* "In the chequered area of human experience the seasons are all mingled as in the golden age: fruit and blossom hang together: in the same moment the sickle is reaping and the seed is sprinkled; one tends the green cluster and another treads the winepress. Nay, in each of our lives harvest and spring-time are continually one, until Death himself gathers us and sows us anew in his invisible fields." DD 70 ep

—*how measured:* "But life is measured by the rapidity of change, the succession of influences that modify the being; and Esther had undergone something little short of an inward revolution." FH 49

—*inspired:* "Life never seems so clear and easy as when the heart is beating faster at the sight of some generous self-risking deed. We feel no doubt then what is the highest prize the soul can win; we almost believe in our own power to attain it." R 55

—*the nature of things:* " 'Ah . . . it's like the night and the morning, and the sleeping and the waking, and the rain and the harvest—one goes and the other comes, and we know nothing how nor where. We may strive and scratch and fend, but it's little we can do after all—the big things come and go wi' no striving o' our'n—they do, that they do . . . . ' " SM 14

—*the power of Now:* " . . . when Maggie became conscious that she was the person he sought, she felt in spite of all the thoughts that had gone before, a glowing gladness at heart. Her eyes and cheeks were still brightened with her child-like enthusiasm in the dance; her whole frame was set to joy and tenderness:—even the coming pain could not seem bitter—she was ready to welcome it as a part of life, for life at this moment seemed a keen vibrating consciousness poised above the pleasure or pain. This one, this last night, she might expand unrestrainedly in the warmth of the present, without those chill eating thoughts of the past and the future." MF VI 10

"He was forgetting everything else in a half-speculative, half-involuntary identification of himself with the objects he was looking at, thinking how far it might be possible habitually to shift his centre till his own personality would be no less outside him than the landscape . . . . " DD 17

—*simple:* "Within her world
The dial has not stirred since first she woke:
No changing light has made the shadows die,
And taught her trusting soul sad difference.
For her, good, right, and law are all summed up
In what is possible: life is one web
Where love, joy, kindred, and obedience
Lie fast and even, in one warp and woof
With thirst and drinking, hunger, food, and sleep.
She knows no struggles, sees no double path:
Her fate is freedom, for her will is one
With her own people's law, the only law
She ever knew." SG III

—*stimulant:* "So absolute is our soul's need of something hidden and uncertain for the maintenance of that doubt and hope and effort which are the breath of its life, that if the whole future were laid bare to us beyond to-day, the interest of all mankind would be bent on the hours that lie between; we should pant after the uncertainties of our one morning and our one afternoon; we should rush fiercely to the Exchange for our last possibility of speculation, of success, of disappointment; we should have a glut of political prophets foretelling a crisis or a no-crisis within the only twenty-four hours left open to prophecy.

"Conceive the condition of the human mind if all propositions whatsoever were self-evident except one, which was to become self-evident at the close of a summer's day, but in the meantime might be the subject of question, of hypothesis, of debate. Art and philosophy, literature and science, would fasten like bees on that one proposition which had the honey of probability in it, and be the more eager because their enjoyment would end with sunset. Our impulses, our spiritual activities, no more adjust themselves to the idea of their future nullity, than the beating of our heart, or the irritability of our muscles." LV 2

—*transcended:* "She felt that intensity of life which seems to transcend both grief and joy—in which the mind seems to itself akin to elder forces that wrought out existence before the birth of pleasure and pain." R 60

—*uncertainty:* " ' . . . the uncertainty of things is a text rather too wide and obvious for fruitful application; and to discourse of it is, as one may say, to bottle up the air, and make a present of it to those who are already standing out of doors.' " FH 41

Time

—*the future:* " ' . . . our race will have diminished with the diminishing call on their energies, and by the time that the self-repairing and reproducing machines arise, all but a few of the rare inventors, calculators, and speculators will have become pale, pulpy, and cretinous from fatty or other degeneration, and behold around them a scanty hydrocephalous offspring. As to the breed of the ingenious and intellectual, their nervous systems will at last have been overwrought in following the molecular revelations of the immensely more powerful unconscious race, and they will naturally, as the less energetic combinations of movement, subside like the flame of a candle in the sunlight." TS 17

—*its measure:* " . . . for time, like money, is measured by our needs . . . . " MM 15.

—*procrastination:* " 'I will wait till after Christmas.'

"What should we all do without the calendar, when we want to put off a disagreeable duty? The admirable arrangements of the solar system, by which our time is measured, always supply us with a term before which it is hardly worth while to set about anything we are disinclined to." DD 32

—*relative:* " . . . the time is great.
(What times are little? To the sentinel
That hour is regal when he mounts on
guard.)" SG I i

—*varying effect:* "Extension, we know, is a very imperfect measure of things, and the length of the sun's journeying can no more tell us how far life has advanced than the acreage of a field can tell us what growths may be active within it.

"A man may go south, and, stumbling over a bone, may meditate upon it till he has found a new starting-point for anatomy; or eastward, and discover a new key to language telling a new story of races; or he may head an expedition that opens new continental pathways, get himself maimed in body, and go through a whole heroic poem of resolve and endurance; and at the end of a few months he may come back to find his neighbours grumbling at the same parish grievance as before, or to see the same elderly gentleman treading the pavement in discourse with himself, shaking his head after the same percussive butcher's boy, and pausing at the same shop-window to look at the same prints.

"If the swiftest thinking has about the pace of a greyhound, the slowest must be supposed to move, like the limpet, by an apparent sticking, which after a good while is discerned to be a slight progression. Such differences are manifest in the variable intensity which we call human experience, from the revolutionary rush of change which makes a new inner and outer life, to that quiet recurrence of the familiar, which has no other epochs than those of hunger and the heavens." ¶DD 58

The farm offices at Griff, Eliot's home 1820-41

Self-Revelation

"And it was by being brought within the long lingering vibrations of such a voice [as that of **Thomas à Kempis**] that Maggie, with her girl's face and unnoted sorrows, found an effort and a hope that helped her through two years of loneliness, making out a faith for herself without the aid of established authorities and appointed guides—for they were not at hand, and her need was pressing." MF IV 3

Authorship

—blonds: " 'As soon as I came to the blond-haired young lady reading in the park, I shut it up and determined to read no further. I foresaw that that light complexioned girl would win away all the love from *Corinne* and make her miserable. I'm determined to read no more books where the blond-haired women carry away all the happiness. I should begin to have a prejudice against them.—If you could give me some story, now, where the dark woman triumphs, it would restore the balance—I want to avenge *Rebecca* and *Flora Mac-Ivor,* and *Minna* and all the rest of the dark unhappy ones' " MF V 4

—character description: "Attempts at description are stupid: who can all at once describe a human being? even when he is presented to us we only begin that knowledge of his appearance which must be completed by innumerable impressions under differing circumstances. We recognise the alphabet; we are not sure of the language." DD 11

—fantasy: " . . . Maggie could think of no comfort but to sit down by the holly or wander by the hedgerow, and fancy it was all

different, refashioning her little world into just what she should like it to be.

"Maggie's was a troublous life, and this was the form in which she took her opium." MF I 6

" . . . I imagine a far-off, hazy, multitudinous assemblage, as in a picture of Paradise, making an approving chorus to the sentences and paragraphs of which I myself particularly enjoy the writing. The haze is a necessary condition. If any physiognomy becomes distinct in the foreground, it is fatal. The countenance is sure to be one bent on discountenancing my innocent intentions: it is pale-eyed, incapable of being amused when I am amused or indignant at what makes me indignant; it stares at my presumption, pities my ignorance, or is manifestly preparing to expose the various instances in which I unconsciously disgrace myself. I shudder at this too corporeal auditor, and turn towards another point of the compass where the haze is unbroken." TS 1

—focus: "But **Fielding** lived when the days were longer . . . when summer afternoons were spacious, and the clock ticked slowly in the winter evenings. We belated historians must not linger after his example; and if we did so, it is probable that our chat would be thin and eager, as if delivered from a campstool in a parrot-house. I at least have so much to do in unravelling certain human lots, and seeing how they were woven and interwove, that all the light I can command must be concentrated on this particular web, and not dispersed over that tempting range of relevancies called the universe." MM 15

—homely life: "I turn without shrinking, from cloud-borne angels, from prophets, sibyls, and heroic warriors, to an old woman bending over her flower-pot, or eating her solitary dinner, while the noonday light, softened perhaps by a screen of leaves, falls on her mob-cap, and just touches the rim of her spinning-wheel, and her stone jug, and all those cheap common things which are the precious necessaries of life to her;—or I turn to that village wedding, kept between four brown walls, where an awkward bridegroom opens the dance with a high-shouldered, broad-faced bride, while elderly and middle-aged friends look on, with very irregular noses and lips, and probably with quart pots in their hands, but with an expression of unmistakable contentment and good-will. 'Foh!' says my idealistic friend, 'what vulgar details! What good is there in taking all these pains to give an exact likeness of old women and clowns? What a low phase of life!—what clumsy, ugly people!' " AB 17

—labouring classes: "It is more needful that I should have a fibre of sympathy connecting me with that vulgar citizen who weighs out my sugar in a vilely assorted cravat and waistcoat, than with the handsomest rascal in red scarf and green feathers—more needful that my heart should swell with loving admiration at some trait of gentle goodness in the faulty people who sit at the same hearth with me, or in the clergyman of my own parish, who is perhaps rather too corpulent, and in other respects not an **Oberlin** or a **Tillotson**, than at the deeds of heroes whom I shall never know except by hearsay, or at the sublimest abstract of all clerical graces that was ever conceived by an able novelist." AB 17

—sensation: "For not having a lofty imagination, as you perceive, and being unable to invent thrilling incidents for your amusement, my only merit must lie in the truth with which I represent to you the humble experience of ordinary fellow mortals. I wish to stir your sympathy with commonplace troubles—to win your tears for real sorrow: sorrow such as may live next door to you—such as walks neither in rags nor in velvet, but in very ordinary decent apparel." SF 7

—subtlety: " . . . the subtly-varied drama between man and woman is often such as can hardly be rendered in words put together like dominoes, according to obvious fixed marks. The word of all work Love will no more express the myriad modes of mutual attraction, than the word Thought can inform you what is passing through your neighbour's mind." DD 27

—translation: "Maggie found the Latin Grammar quite soothing after her mathematical mortification; for she delighted in new words, and quickly found that there was an English Key at the end, which would make her very wise about Latin at slight expense. She presently made up her mind to skip the rules in the Syntax—the examples became so absorbing. These mysterious sentences snatched from an unknown context—like strange horns of beasts and leaves of unknown plants, brought from some far-off region, gave boundless scope to her imagination, and were all the more fascinating because they were in a peculiar tongue of their own, which she could learn to interpret. It was really very interesting—the Latin Grammar that Tom had said no girls could learn: and she was proud because she found it interesting. The most fragmentary examples were her favourites." MF II 1

—truth: "So I am content to tell my simple story, without trying to make things seem better than they were; dreading nothing, indeed, but falsity, which, in spite of one's best efforts, there is reason to dread. False-

hood is so easy, truth so difficult. The pencil is conscious of a delightful facility in drawing a griffin—the longer the claws, and the larger the wings, the better; but that marvellous facility which we mistook for genius, is apt to forsake us when we want to draw a real unexaggerated lion. Examine your words well, and you will find that even when you have no motive to be false, it is a very hard thing to say the exact truth, even about your own immediate feelings—much harder than to say something fine about them which is *not* the exact truth." AB 17

—*what came after?* "Every limit is a beginning as well as an ending. Who can quit young lives after being long in company with them, and not desire to know what befell them in their after-years? For the fragment of a life, however typical, is not the sample of an even web: promises may not be kept, and an ardent outset may be followed by declension; latent powers may find their long-waited opportunity; a past error may urge a grand retrieval." MM 87

—*wish:* "And thinking of them in these moments one is tempted to that futile sort of wishing—if only things could have been a little otherwise then, so as to have been greatly otherwise after!—if only these two beautiful young creatures could have pledged themselves to each other then and there, and never through life have swerved from that pledge!" DD 7

—*youth:* "One morning, some weeks after her arrival at Lowick, Dorothea—but why always Dorothea? Was her point of view the only possible one with regard to this marriage? I protest against all our interest, all our effort at understanding being given to the young skins that look blooming in spite of trouble; for these too will get faded, and will know the older and more eating griefs which we are helping to neglect." MM 29

Background

—*milieu:* "Observing these people narrowly, even when the iron hand of misfortune has shaken them from their unquestioning hold on the world, one sees little trace of religion, still less of a distinctively Christian creed. Their belief in the unseen, so far as it manifests itself at all, seems to be rather of a pagan kind: their moral notions, though held with strong tenacity, seem to have no standard beyond hereditary custom. You could not live among such people; you are stifled for want of an outlet towards something beautiful, great, or noble: you are irritated with these dull men and women, as a kind of population out of keeping with the earth on which they live—with this rich plain where the great river flows for ever onward and links the small pulse of the old English town with the beatings of the world's mighty heart. A vigorous superstition that lashes its gods or lashes its own back, seems to be more congruous with the mystery of the human lot, than the mental condition of these emmet-like Dodsons and Tullivers." MF IV 1

—*moving onward:* "I share with you this sense of oppressive narrowness; but it is necessary that we should feel it, if we care to understand how it acted on the lives of Tom and Maggie—how it has acted on young natures in many generations, that in the onward tendency of human things have risen above the mental level of the generation before them, in which they have been nevertheless tied by the strongest fibres of their hearts. The suffering, whether of martyr or victim, which belongs to every historical advance of mankind, is represented in this way in every town and by hundreds of obscure hearths: and we need not shrink from this comparison of small things with great; for does not science tell us that its highest striving is after the ascertainment of a unity which shall bind the smallest things with the greatest? In natural science, I have understood, there is nothing petty in the mind that has a large vision of relations, and to which every single object suggests a vast sum of conditions. It is surely the same with the observation of human life." MF IV 1

Childhood

—*discordant note:* "And many of us know how, even in our childhood, some blank discontented face on the background of our home marred our summer mornings. Why was it, when the birds were singing, when the fields were a garden, and when we were clasping another little hand just larger than our own, there was somebody who found it hard to smile?" FH 49

—*first lessons:* "At five years old, mortals are not prepared to be citizens of the world, to be stimulated by abstract nouns, to soar above preference into impartiality; and that prejudice in favour of milk with which we blindly begin, is a type of the way body and soul must get nourished at least for a time. The best introduction to astronomy is to think of the nightly heavens as a little lot of stars belonging to one's own homestead." DD 3

—*happiness:* "So much of our early gladness vanishes utterly from our memory: we can never recall the joy with which we laid our heads on our mother's bosom or rode on our father's back in childhood; doubtless that joy is wrought up into our nature, as the sunlight of long-past mornings is wrought up in the soft mellowness of the apricot; but it is gone for ever from our imagination, and we can only *believe* in the joy of childhood." AB 20

—*walking in a wood:* "The wood I walk in on this mild May day, with the young yellow-brown foliage of the oaks between me and the blue sky, the white star-flowers and the blue-eyed speedwell and the ground ivy at my feet—what grove of tropic palms, what strange ferns or splendid broad-petalled blossoms, could ever thrill such deep and delicate fibres within me as this home-scene? These familiar flowers, these well-remembered bird-notes, this sky with its fitful brightness, these furrowed and grassy fields, each with a sort of personality given to it by the capricious hedgerows—*such things as these are the mother tongue of our imagination,* the language that is laden with all the subtle inextricable associations the fleeting hours of our childhood left behind them. Our delight in the sunshine on the deep bladed grass today, might be no more than the faint perception of wearied souls, if it were not for the sunshine and the grass in the far-off years, which still live in us and transform our perception into love." MF I 5 [emphasis added]

—*whey:* "Ah! I think I taste that whey now—with a flavour so delicate that one can hardly distinguish it from an odour, and with that soft gliding warmth that fills one's imagination with a still, happy dreaminess. And the light music of the dropping whey is in my ears, mingling with the twittering of a bird outside the wire network windows—the window overlooking the garden, and shaded by tall gueldre roses." AB 20

Clerical matters

—*bishop:* "The talk of the clergy about their bishop belongs to the esoteric part of their profession; so we will at once quit the dining-room at Milby Vicarage, lest we should happen to overhear remarks unsuited to the lay understanding, and perhaps dangerous to our repose of mind." SF 6

Home

—*fireside:* "But it was worth purchasing, even at the heavy price of the Latin Grammar—the happiness of seeing the bright light in the parlour at home as the gig passed noiselessly over the snow-covered bridge: the happiness of passing from the cold air to the warmth and the kisses and the smiles of that familiar hearth where the pattern of the rug and the grate and the fire-irons were 'first ideas' that it was no more possible to criticise than the solidity and extension of matter." MF 11

—*garden:* "One's delight in an elderberry bush overhanging the confused leafage of a hedgerow bank as a more gladdening sight than the finest cistus or fuchsia spreading itself on the softest undulating turf, is an entirely unjustifiable preference to a landscape-gardener, or to any of those severely regulated minds who are free from the weakness of any attachment that does not rest on a demonstrable superiority of qualities. And there is no better reason for preferring this elderberry bush than that it stirs an early memory—that it is no novelty in my life speaking to me merely through my present sensibilities to form and colour, but the long companion of my existence that wove itself into my joys when joys were vivid." MF II 1

—*land:* "A human life, I think, should be well rooted in some spot of a native land, where it may get the love of tender kinship for the face of earth, for the labours men go forth to, for the sounds and accents that haunt it, for whatever will give that early home a familiar unmistakable difference amidst the future widening of knowledge: a spot where the definiteness of early memories may be inwrought with affection, and kindly acquaintance with all neighbours, even to the dogs and donkeys, may spread not by sentimental effort and reflection, but as a sweet habit of the blood." DD 3

—*remembered:* "There is no sense of ease like the ease we felt in those scenes where we were born, where objects became dear to us before we had known the labour of choice, and where the outer world seemed only an extension of our own personality: we accepted and loved it as we accepted our own sense of existence and our own limbs. Very commonplace, even ugly, that furniture of our early home might look if it were put up to auction: an improved taste in upholstery scorns it; and is not the striving after something better and better in our surroundings, the grand characteristic that distinguishes man from the brute—or, to satisfy a scrupulous accuracy of definition, that distinguishes the British man from the foreign brute? But heaven knows where that striving might lead us, if our affections had not a trick of twining round those old inferior things, if the loves and sanctities of our life had no deep immovable roots in memory." MF 11

Memories

—*dying father:* "Poor child! It was very early for her to know one of those supreme moments in life when all we have hoped or delighted in, all we can dread or endure, falls away from our regard as insignificant—is lost, like a trivial memory, in that simple, primitive love which knits us to the beings who have been nearest to us, in their times of helplessness or of anguish." MF III 1 *See* MF Maggie Tulliver—*longings,* page 143

—experiences: "I cherish my childish loves—the memory of that warm little nest where my affections were fledged. Since then I have learned to care for foreign countries, for literatures foreign and ancient, for the life of Continental towns dozing round old cathedrals, for the life of London, half sleepless with eager thought and strife, with indigestion or with hunger; and now my consciousness is chiefly of the busy, anxious metropolitan sort. My system responds sensitively to the London weather-signs, political, social, literary; and my bachelor's hearth is imbedded where by much craning of head and neck I can catch sight of a sycamore in the Square garden: I belong to the 'Nation of London.' Why? There have been many voluntary exiles in the world . . . some of those who sallied forth went for the sake of a loved companionship, when they would willingly have kept sight of the familiar plains, and of the hills to which they had first lifted up their eyes." TS 2

See Home*—remembered*

Scholarship

—Shakespeare: " 'Ah, now I see how it is you know Shakespeare and everything, and have learned so much since you left school—which always seemed to me witchcraft before—part of your general uncanniness' . . . . " MF VI 3

Spiritual insight

—reading Thomas à Kempis: "It flashed through her like the suddenly apprehended solution of a problem, that all the miseries of her young life had come from fixing her heart on her own pleasure, as if that were the central necessity of the universe; and for the first time she saw the possibility of shifting the position from which she looked at the gratification of her own desires, of taking her stand out of herself, and looking at her own life as an insignificant part of a divinely guided whole . . . in the ardour of first discovery, renunciation seemed to her the entrance into that satisfaction which she had so long been craving in vain. She had not perceived—how could she until she had lived longer?—the inmost truth of the old monk's outpourings, that renunciation remains sorrow, though a sorrow borne willingly.

"Maggie was still panting for happiness, and was in ecstasy because she had found the key to it. She knew nothing of doctrines and systems—of mysticism or quietism: but this voice out of the far-off middle ages, was the direct communication of a human soul's belief and experience, and came to Maggie as an unquestioned message." ¶MF IV 3

"I suppose that is the reason why the small old-fashioned book, for which you need only pay sixpence at a book-stall, works miracles to this day, turning bitter waters into sweetness; while expensive sermons and treatises newly issued leave all things as they were before. It was written down by a hand that waited for the heart's prompting, it is the chronicle of a solitary, hidden anguish, struggle, trust and triumph—not written on velvet cushions to teach endurance to those who are treading with bleeding feet on the stones.

"And so it remains to all time, a lasting record of human needs and human consolations, the voice of a brother who, ages ago, felt and suffered and renounced—in the cloister, perhaps, with serge gown and tonsured head, with much chanting and long fasts, and with a fashion of speech different from ours—but under the same silent far-off heavens, and with the same passionate desires, the same strivings, the same failures, the same weariness." ¶MF IV 3

Griff, Eliot's home 1820-41

Indexes to the Nonfiction

(bold face indicates a title figure)

Authors Quoted

Authors Referred to

Authors Reviewed

Biblical and Other Religious Figures

Other Historical Figures

Literary and Mythological Figures

Coinages

Subjects and Selected Works

See also "Also mentioned" pages 24, 39-40, 42, 60, 74, 103, and 130; and HB p218, most entries in which, since they amount to a list without GE comment, are not reflected above.

Notable Individuals mentioned in the *Topicon*

About the Editor

Until 1988, GEORGE NEWLIN had spent his professional career combining activities in law and finance with volunteer service in the arts and serious avocational musical performance. At that time, he withdrew from most of his activities in venture capital and assets management and began developing his concept for a new kind of analytical literary anthology, beginning with the works of Charles Dickens. His *Everyone in Dickens* was published in three volumes in 1995, and a topical concordance, *Every Thing in Dickens,* appeared the following year. Subsequent works on Dickens concentrated on assembling historical documents and other materials to provide a context for the study of *A Tale of Two Cities* (1998) and *Great Expectations* (2000). His monumental four-volume work *Everyone and Everything in Trollope* was published by M.E. Sharpe in 2004. Having completed his volumes on George Eliot, he has begun work on a four-volume anthology of the prose and poetry of Thomas Hardy. Mr Newlin has phased out of most of his not-for-profit work in the arts but continues to give piano concerts. His specialty is the Beethoven piano concertos.

Printed in the United States
by Baker & Taylor Publisher Services